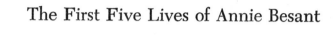

The First Five Lives of Annie Besant

THE
FIRST FIVE LIVES
of
ANNIE BESANT

By Arthur H. Nethercot

 THE UNIVERSITY OF CHICAGO PRESS

Library of Congress Catalog Number: 59-11624

THE UNIVERSITY OF CHICAGO PRESS, CHICAGO 37
Cambridge University Press, London, N.W. 1, England
The University of Toronto Press, Toronto 5, Canada

© *1960 by The University of Chicago. Published 1960*
Composed and printed by THE UNIVERSITY OF CHICAGO PRESS
Chicago, Illinois, U.S.A.

TO MARGOT

without whose wanderlust

this book about another woman

who couldn't stay home

would never have been written

Preface

The present book, dealing with what can be called the "English phase" of the strange lives of Mrs. Annie Besant, is the first volume of a projected two-volume biography of this remarkable woman. The second, to be published in another year or so, will deal with her "Indian phase."

For many years I have been the victim of a great curiosity about Dr. Besant, as she preferred to be called in her later years. This curiosity was aroused particularly through my interest in Bernard Shaw, and when my book on him—*Men and Supermen: The Shavian Portrait Gallery* —was completed, I decided that no better subject for a biography could exist than the unbelievable Annie, any one of whose nine lives would have been sufficient for a more normal person. When I made this decision, I had no idea of the chase she would lead me. Now, some eight years later, I find that she has taken me all the way around the world, bringing me—in addition to my travels in the United States—six months in England and Germany in 1954 through a generous leave of absence granted me by Northwestern University, and almost a year in the Orient, especially in India proper and Kashmir, on a Fulbright research appointment in 1956–57. I regret that my facilities in time and money did not permit me to pursue her also to Australia. For her visits there I have been compelled to rely on printed materials alone, whereas in the other places mentioned above I have been able to supplement the conventional library research with many vastly interesting and valuable interviews with people from the lowest social ranks to the highest—people who once knew her, worked with her, and were influenced by her.

Accordingly, I wish to express my gratitude for help freely given by members of the staffs of the following libraries: the Deering Library of Northwestern University; Robert Rosenthal of the Special Collections Room of the Harper Library in the University of Chicago; the library of the national American headquarters of the Theosophical Society at Wheaton, Illinois, where I enjoyed not only the extensive collection of Theosophical works but also some gratuitously proffered vegetarian lunches; the library of the British Museum in London, and especially its newspaper and magazine branch at Colindale; the Public Record Office in London; the *Hindu* newspaper in Madras, India; and, most of all, the library of the international headquarters of the Theosophical Society at Adyar, Madras. Here I spent many months with books, magazines, and newspapers available nowhere else in the world.

I wish that I could do more than merely list names to thank the following individuals who talked with me and helped me in various ways:

James S. Perkins, national president of the American Section of the Theosophical Society; Mrs. Viva J. Emmons and Ann Kerr of the Theosophical Society library—all of Wheaton, Illinois. Arthur Groves, general secretary of the Theosophical Society in Great Britain; Arthur Digby Besant; Esther Bright; and Felix Barker—all of London. Direktor Martin Boyken, of Hamburg, general secretary of the Theosophical Society in Germany; and Krister Kuylenstierna, of Västerås, Sweden.

At Adyar: N. Sri Ram, international president of the Theosophical Society; Srimati Rukmini Devi Arundale; N. Yagnesvara Sastry; Ruth Hunt; Katherine A. Beechey; Siitaa Devi Peterson; B. Sanjeeva Rao; G. V. Subba Rao; Shankara Menon; and Pm. Ramachandran.

Kanji Dwarkadas, of Bombay; B. P. Wadia and W. Dallas Ten Broek, of Bombay and Bangalore. At Benares: Rohit Mehta, general secretary of the Theosophical Society in India; and Dr. Bhagavan Das. L. S. Sambath Kumar, principal of the Agricultural College at Poona. Srimati Mangal Das, of Ahmedabad; and F. Gordon Pearce, former commissioner of the Indian Boy Scouts Association, of Rishi Valley.

J. Krishnamurti, of Madras and Ojai, California.

J. N. Bhan, secretary to the government, Ministry of Education, Srinagar, Kashmir.

At Madras: Sri Prakasa, then governor of Madras, now governor of Bombay; Sir C. P. Ramaswami Aiyar, lawyer, former dewan of Travancore, etc.

At New Delhi: B. Shiva Rao, journalist and M.P., and Srimati Shiva Rao; V. K. Krishna Menon, minister of defense; Dr. S. Radhakrishnan, vice-president; and Jawaharlal Nehru, prime minister of India.

Finally, to all my kind and helpful friends in the Theosophical Society all over the world, but especially to those at Adyar, with whom and in whose beautiful compound my wife and I lived for several weeks, I wish to express my special gratitude as well as my hope that what I have written about Mrs. Besant and the Theosophical Society will not cause them any offense or injured feelings. It is the duty of every biographer with any sense of integrity to gather all the accessible facts about his subject, to weigh and compare them, and, without partiality or personal bias, to state the conclusions he has reached. This is the goal I hope I have attained in this book on Annie Besant, one of the most extraordinary women who ever lived.

For permission to reproduce many of the photographs used as illustrations in this biography I wish to thank N. Sri Ram for those from the Adyar edition of Mrs. Besant's *Autobiography,* from *The Golden Book of the Theosophical Society,* and from *The Annie Besant Centenary Book.* For various kinds of special help in connection with this book I also wish to thank Eric Batson of London, editor of *The Shavian,* and Dan Laurence of New York, former editor of the *Shaw Bulletin.*

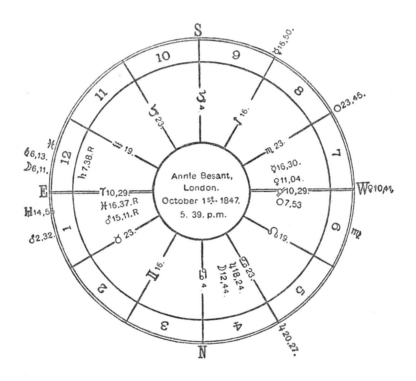

Contents

IV. *Fourth Life:* THE SOCIALIST LABOR AGITATOR

V. *Fifth Life:* THE CHELA OF THE MAHATMAS

I. *First Life:* THE CHRISTIAN WIFE

1

"Out of the Everywhere into the Here"

In 1885, before she was forty, Mrs. Annie Besant was known all over the English-speaking world, and by many people on the Continent, as one of the most remarkable women of her day. She was a Freethinker; a consorter with materialists like Charles Bradlaugh; an agitator in Radical political circles, again like Bradlaugh; a feminist; an early convert to Fabian Socialism, through the agency of Bernard Shaw; a teacher of science; an author-editor-publisher; the first prominent woman to dare fight openly for what is now called birth control; a social and educational reformer; and an orator whose power was so compelling and whose charm was so potent that Shaw was only one among thousands who extolled her as the greatest woman speaker of the century.

Shortly after 1885 she was to become still more notorious as a strike leader and union organizer—anathema to the conventional and conservative in both church and state. But by 1893 she had cut completely loose from her rebellious and sensational past and had embarked on her even more rebellious and sensational future. She was to become the successor to the fantastic Madame Helena Petrovna Blavatsky and the international president of the stormy and mystical Theosophical Society. Later, in India, she would be a conspicuous and idolized religious, educational, and political leader; onetime president of the Indian National Congress; and an admired older friend and example to Mohandas Gandhi, whose eventual break with her over the best methods for achieving Indian independence led to his fame and martyrdom and her eclipse. In 1933 the newspapers of the world, in long obituary articles, announced her return into the "everywhere," from whence she was convinced she would come back in a new reincarnation to carry on the work which she had left unfinished at the age of eighty-five. She had led many lives during those years—all of them full, many of them so different that they could have belonged to utterly different people, and some of them so incredible that it seems impossible they were lived at all.

Always a prolific writer, Mrs. Besant produced two versions of an autobiography. The first, *Autobiographical Sketches,* was published in 1885 after being serialized in her "advanced" magazine, the *National Reformer.* Here she recounted her birth brusquely and prosaically, but with a touch of her characteristic rhetoric: "On Oct. 1st, 1847, I made my appearance in this 'vale of tears.'" By 1893, when her revised *Autobiography* (in its previous serial form appealingly entitled *From Storm to Peace*) was published, the fact of her birth was no longer prosaic but bore otherworldly implications. "Out of the Everywhere into the Here," a line from the mystic poet George Macdonald's popular poem "Baby," became the title of the first chapter. The intervening years had marked a conversion which stunned the intellectual world and set the general public buzzing on both sides of the Atlantic and in India as well.[1]

Annie Wood, though born in London, was three-fourths Irish, and she never forgot the fact. As she put it: "It has always been somewhat of a grievance to me that I was born in London, 'within the sound of Bow Bells,' when three-quarters of my blood and all my heart are Irish." From this point of view she was even prouder of her mother's family than of her father's, for both her mother's parents had come to England from Ireland, whereas only her father's mother had done so. Her mother was a Morris—a spelling which, she implied, had somewhat come down in the world from its pure form "Maurice" five centuries earlier. In fact, so great was the family pride in its past (always greatest in "decayed" families in Ireland, Annie admitted) that the spinster aunt who adopted Annie's mother Emily had hanging over her mantelpiece a majestic family tree on parchment, which traced the family descent to the "seven kings of France"—or, as Annie further identified them, the "Milesian kings." Unfortunately, the spinster aunt was somewhat shaky in her prehistoric Irish history, and she took Annie in. (According to the legend the Milesians came to Ireland about 1300 B.C. not from France but from Spain, which itself had been only a way station on their migration from Scythia via Egypt and Crete.) But the fact of the error is unimportant; the important thing is that the Maurices had royal blood in their veins,

[1] Material in Part I of the present book is based largely on the *Autobiographical Sketches* (London, 1885) and the *Autobiography* (London, 1893). Additional sources for chapter 1 are: Theodore Besterman, *Mrs. Annie Besant: A Modern Prophet* (London, 1934), pp. 6–10; Arthur Digby Besant, *The Besant Pedigree* (London, 1930); and W. T. Stead, "Annie Besant: A Character Sketch," *Review of Reviews,* 1891 (reprinted by Theosophical Publishing House, Adyar, India, 1946).

however diluted. Much later in her life Annie was to discover that in most of her reincarnations she had come from royal blood.

Emily Roche Morris, a gray-eyed, raven-haired, and sweet-faced Irish colleen, had been the second daughter of a large family and had watched her father and mother, a gay, handsome, and extravagant pair, run so quickly and merrily through the patrimony which remained to them that they were glad to let their maiden sister adopt their pretty child. Annie could vividly remember her grandfather as a "bent old man, with hair like driven snow, splendidly handsome in his old age, hot-tempered to passion at the lightest provocation, loving and wrathy in quick succession." Emily's marriage to William Burton Persse Wood had unfortunately not helped matters much financially, for he came from the wrong branch of the highly respectable Wood family, most of whom, perhaps because they were English, had done very well for themselves.

William Wood, the son of Robert Wright Wood and Emily Trueman, an Irish girl, had been born in Galway and lived his early life in Ireland. He took his medical degree at Trinity College, Dublin, and "walked the hospitals as a medical student." But before he had established himself in this profession, a London relative offered him a good business appointment in the City, with excellent prospects of living up to the expectations of the other branches of the Wood family, who had prospered exceedingly in commerce. William's uncle, Matthew Wood, had been successively a chemist and druggist, a hop merchant, and a member of the Company of Fishmongers. Passing through the offices of common councilor, deputy alderman, and alderman, to an appointment as sheriff of London and Middlesex, he had twice thereafter been chosen lord mayor of London, in 1815 and 1816, and had been a Member of Parliament for the City from 1817 until his death in 1843. Always a staunch supporter of the cause of the unhappy Queen Caroline, he had paid the debts of the Duke of Kent "in order that that reputable individual might return to England with his Duchess" and the future heir to the throne—who turned out to be Victoria—might be born on English soil. For these inestimable services he had been paid off cheaply with a baronetcy. Sir Matthew's three sons had become, respectively, a clergyman, a distinguished barrister who became lord chancellor of England, and a successful businessman and Member of Parliament. Another cousin had accumulated a fortune in mining. And so it went—in the other branches.

But Robert Wood's sons were different. They all had "somewhat of a fight for life." One finally prospered and became comfortably well off, and another led a rough and wandering life for years and ultimately emigrated to South Africa. The career of the eldest son, William, fell somewhere between these two.

William was too versatile and too volatile a half-Irishman to be able to settle down very steadily to anything. Besides keeping up his interest

3

in medicine and surgery after coming to London, he was, as his daughter described him, a mathematician, a good classical scholar, and something of a paragon at modern languages—"thoroughly master of French, German, Italian, Spanish, and Portuguese, with a smattering of Hebrew and Gaelic." The treasures of ancient and modern literature were his "daily household delight," and he loved to read aloud to his wife while she worked, declaiming from *Queen Mab* or translating at sight from foreign poets. He was also a student of philosophy, and "deeply and steadily skeptical," though his mother and sister were strict Roman Catholics. Another of his very religious relatives told Annie how he often had driven her out of the room "by his light, playful mockery of the tenets of the Christian faith." This sardonic propensity also worried his wife, who could not quite bring herself to share his views, although she was unwillingly influenced by them, and who tried to reconcile her deeply rooted piety with his iconoclasm by maintaining that "Women ought to be religious" no matter what men were. Still, little by little, Mrs. Wood began to discard as errors such doctrines as eternal punishment, vicarious atonement, biblical infallibility, and the equality of the Son with the Father in the Trinity; and in her mature years she even began to enjoy reading such theological liberals as Jowett, Colenso, and Stanley, who became her "ideal Christian gentlemen." The baldness of evangelical services and the crudity of evangelical dogmas outraged her taste and her intellect, respectively. In religion she loved reverence, solemn music, and beautiful architecture, so that she was never happier than when attending a service at Westminster Abbey. As Annie put it rather harshly, considering her devoted love for her mother, "this dainty and well-bred piety seemed perilously like Laodicean lukewarmness."

To this queerly matched but affectionate couple three children were born. Annie was the middle one, between two brothers. In her *Autobiography* she described the event thus, making the first of many significant changes from the earlier version in her *Autobiographical Sketches:* "On October 1, 1847, I am credibly informed, my baby eyes opened to the light (?) of a London afternoon at 5:39. A friendly astronomer has drawn for me the following chart, showing the position of the planets at this, to me fateful, moment." But more of this horoscope later; it took Annie herself almost half her life to grow into such beliefs.

So it was within the famous sound of Bow bells, muffled somewhat by the fog and smoke of the City, the banking and commercial district of London, that Annie Wood drew her first breath. The Bank, the Royal Exchange, the Guildhall, the Stock Exchange, even St. Paul's were all within a short stroll with the perambulator. But the associations of the district, running the gamut from St. Thomas à Becket to Dick Whittington, were to mean nothing to her until later in her life, since the little family was soon to move to a more pleasant part of London. She was then about three years old.

But before she left she was to be the victim of an accident which was to leave its stamp on her till her death. A delicate and somewhat fractious infant, whose health at first gave her parents some cause for anxiety, she one day through her nurse's carelessness struck her forehead on the molded iron canopy of her cradle. The heavy cut, marked by a permanent scar, so injured the muscles on that side of her head that always afterward when Annie raised her eyebrows she had the peculiarity of being able to wrinkle up only one side of her brow. No injury to the brain, however, was discovered.

The earliest recollections of "Little Pheasantina," as Annie had been oddly nicknamed by a "giddy aunt," were of a house and garden in what was then named Grove Road, St. John's Wood, a respectable middle-class neighborhood in northwest London. She always remembered happily her mother's bright preparations for dinner for the "home-coming husband," the way in which she and her older brother, Henry Trueman, watched for "papa," the loving welcome, and the romps which always were held before the older people sat down to their dinner. She recalled particularly how on her fourth birthday she had jumped up in her little cot and shouted triumphantly: "Papa! Mamma! I am four years old!" and how Henry (called Harry in the family) at dinnertime that evening, conscious of his superior age, demanded gravely: "May not Annie have a knife today, as she is four years old?" She also remembered her own disappointment that she was not yet considered old enough to go to the Great Exhibition in that same year, but was partially consoled when the considerate Harry brought home to her a folded picture strip on which were reproduced some of the glories she now longed even more to see.

Annie was a sensitive little girl who responded acutely to all sorts of impressions, physical and emotional. When she saw a Punch and Judy show, she wept over its realistic tragedy and ran home to hide her head in a pillow so that she would not have to listen to the thwacking of the blows and the cries of the abused baby. Belief in ghosts of all kinds was general in her family, with the exception of her skeptical father. Her mother once told her of hearing the wailing of a banshee back in Ireland just before she learned that a relative had died. So, all through Annie's childhood, elves and fairies were quite real things to her. Inanimate objects became endowed with life, and she loved "making believe" and living out lovely stories with her playthings.

The house of Grandfather Morris at 8 Albert Square, Clapham, in what is now Stockwell, was a second home to all the relatives, but especially to Annie and Henry, even though they had to travel all the way across London and the Thames to get to it. After all, they were the only

5

grandchildren within reach and were therefore made much of by this very clannish family. Annie remembered the house vividly in her later years, and it is still standing, though the plaster of the imitation stone wall of the first story is peeling and the grayish brick of the two upper floors is dirty and bedraggled. Albert Square itself, with its low, dingy green iron railing, is not at all inviting. But to Annie as a child the place was heaven. It had a little strip of garden at the back, and at the far end there were little nooks where she could sit cozily out of sight with some favorite book. This was much more romantic than at home, where by the age of five she had frequently been "unswathed from a delightful curtain," in which she had rolled herself with a book, and told to go out and play.

Inside, the house was quite commonplace, except for one room, her grandfather's workshop, which was fitted up with a lathe and various tools. For Grandfather Morris was an inventor. Unfortunately, he always lost money on his inventions, which other people with more money took up and capitalized upon. Several railways used his "chair" device for fastening together the ends of rails, but he himself never profited. Still, the old man was always merry, full of Irish songs and tales of his youthful exploits in Dublin.

Only three of Annie's seven aunts and uncles lived with their parents. The two sons were married and living in India—thus India became early established in her imagination as a place of challenging mystery; one daughter lived in Constantinople, and another, the youngest, was mysteriously "much away from home." But the three other girls, all spinsters, filled up the extra rooms in the house. Annie was not very fond of Aunt Bessie, the eldest, who was a woman "of rigid honor and conscientiousness" but whose struggle to keep out of debt had soured her so that she was dreaded rather than loved. Once she had been engaged to a young clergyman, who one day had preached in her hearing a sermon plagiarized from some old divine. Bessie had recognized its source, had immediately broken off the engagement, and had remained unmarried the rest of her life. Bessie, who admired Martha in the Bible story, literally worked herself to death and died in patient and enjoyable torment. The other two aunts, however, were Annie's playfellows, and she was their pet. Minnie, whom she described as a "brilliant pianiste," eked out a precarious living by teaching music in any weather and in all sorts of places. The gayest and merriest of all Annie's friends, she gave particular vent to her exuberance when she could escape from her musical treadmill to the country for a holiday. The third "auntie," Marion, was such a soft, pretty, quiet, loving little woman that she had been nicknamed "Co" by her father, because she was "such a cosy little thing." "Co," who was Mrs. Wood's favorite sister, her "child" as she called her because of her youth and her need for protection, was the most faithful of all to Annie in her later years, clinging to her in spite of everything—denial of religion, the shattering of social codes, and all that "Co" herself held so dear.

But the smooth mirror of this almost flawless and inbred domestic life was soon to be smashed. Annie's father, though a City man, must have had some qualms of professional conscience, for he made many medical friends, and every now and then would go with them on their hospital rounds, even begging them to let him help in post mortems. One day in 1852 Dr. Wood cut his finger on the breastbone of a person who had died of a rapid consumption and was being dissected. The cut did not heal. One surgeon-friend recommended amputation, but other doctors, more optimistic but less well advised, persuaded Wood to wait. In August he caught cold while riding on the top of a bus in the rain. The "eminent" but rough doctor who was called told Mrs. Wood that her husband had galloping consumption and would be dead in six weeks. The poor wife promptly fainted, but within half an hour she was back "at her husband's side, never to leave it again for ten minutes, night or day, till he was lying with cold eyes asleep in death" in early October. Near the end his mother and sister forced a Roman Catholic priest into the room, but the dying man made such a wrathful protest, supported by his wife's "fierce resolve" that no messenger of the detested creed should disturb her beloved husband, that the priest fled. The day before her father's death, Annie, who with her elder brother had been staying at her maternal grandfather's, was brought home and lifted onto the bed to "say good-bye to dear papa." She remembered being frightened by his large eyes and changed voice as he made her promise always to be "a very good girl to darling mamma, as papa was going away." She insisted that he kiss the doll which he had had given to her on her birthday three days before. Then she was removed, crying and struggling, from the room. It was her first experience with tragedy.

When William Wood died, his wife broke down again. On her recovery, she locked herself alone in her bedroom for the night. When she opened the door the next morning, her mother, who had finally persuaded her to come out, started back with the cry, "Good God, Emily! your hair is white!" That was the way Annie always remembered her mother, her face framed "in exquisite silver bands of hair as white as the driven unsullied snow."

The family thought it best that Mrs. Wood should not attend the funeral service at Kensal Green. So Annie sat in an upstairs room with her mother and her aunts, awe-struck by her mother's pallid face and clouded, vacant eyes. But Mrs. Wood reclined on the sofa counting the minutes till the procession should reach the cemetery; then, taking her prayer book, she mechanically followed the service, stage by stage, until, to the child's "unspeakable terror," she dully uttered the words, "It is all over," and once more fell back in a faint.

Nor was this the strangest part of it all. Several weeks later Mrs.

Wood resolved to see her husband's grave. A relative who had been at the funeral volunteered to guide her, since she had never been in the Kensal Green Cemetery, but he lost his way among the wilderness of stones. Another member of the small party went off to find an official, but Mrs. Wood said to her relative, "If you will take me to the chapel where the first part of the service was read I will find the grave." To humor her he did so, whereupon she followed the obscure path where the coffin had been carried, and was standing at the grave, marked as yet only by a wooden peg with a number on it, when the official arrived to point it out. She explained later that on the day of the funeral she had in spirit followed the hearse, attended the service, and walked behind the coffin to its resting place. When Annie first described this remarkable episode, she referred to it simply as "a curious psychological problem which has often puzzled me" and attributed it to her mother's "state of abnormal nervous excitation" and "her strong strain of Celtic superstition." Eight years later, however, the explanation became simple enough to her: "With my present knowledge . . . I now know that the consciousness can leave the body, take part in events going on at a distance, and, returning, impress on the physical brain what it has experienced."

Peculiar as it was that such a proper and well-balanced churchwoman should have such visions, Mrs. Wood gave further proof of her clairvoyant powers a few months afterward. The youngest child of the family was a little boy named Alfred, born three years after Annie—a delicate, blue-eyed, pale-golden-haired infant passionately devoted to his father. Soon after Mr. Wood's death the child began to fret continually for "papa." With no marked disease (although in her first autobiographical sketches Annie speculated on his being touched by the "consumptive taint"), he wasted away steadily during the winter. Mrs. Wood held him in her arms all one night, and the next morning calmly informed her sister: "Alf is going to die." When the sister tried to assure her that the coming spring would restore his health, Mrs. Wood replied firmly, "No. He was lying asleep in my arms last night, and William came and said that he wanted Alf with him, but that I might keep the other two." She refused to listen when the normal members of the family told her she had been dreaming, and so she was not surprised when in March "a waxen form lay lifeless in the baby's cot." Annie and her brother Harry were allowed to see the body just before it was placed in its coffin. She always remembered how she had seen a black spot in the middle of her dead brother's forehead and how she was informed that it had come from a passionate kiss his mother had placed there at the moment of death. She also recalled the deadly cold which startled her when she was told to kiss her little brother herself. It was the first time she had touched death.

2

From Harrow to the Rhine

The sudden death of William Burton Persse Wood left his family almost destitute. They—and apparently also he—had believed that they would be provided for. The children never learned the details, but when the estate was settled it was discovered that nothing was left but a little ready money.

The first thing the distracted widow did to retrench was to move her little flock down to Richmond Terrace, Clapham, which was as close to the protection of her mother and father as she could get. It was not a good neighborhood—not even as good as Albert Square—but they lived there, "poorly enough," for several months. The other branch of the Woods, perhaps impelled partly by genuine compassion and partly by a feeling of family honor, then decided to intervene. Two of the cousins, Western Wood and Sir William Page Wood, sons of the former lord mayor, offered to take young Henry in hand. They would give him a good education at a City school and then start him off on a commercial life like their own. But Henry's parents long before had decided that their son must go to a "public school" and then on to a university, so that he could enter one of the learned professions—Emily wished him to take holy orders; William strongly preferred the law. Since, however, her husband had reiterated his desire on his deathbed, Emily loyally changed her mind and held out doggedly against the heated arguments of the other Woods. Harry, she announced, was to go to Harrow, because of the comparatively low fees it offered to "town boys," and then on to Oxford or Cambridge. The cousins, though half-disapproving, bowed gracefully and "lent many a helping hand to her in her first difficult struggles."

To make Harry a "town boy" it was obviously necessary to move the whole family to Harrow and to find some means of earning an income. At first, to give herself time to look for a suitable house, Mrs. Wood took lodgings over the shop of a pompous grocer and soon found a boy whose parents were glad to place him in her charge and pay her enough so that she could hire a tutor to prepare both him and Harry to enter school. A resolute and aggressive woman in her own way, Mrs. Wood had a scheme to rent a house of her own large enough to be turned into a boardinghouse for some of the Harrow boys and thus to earn enough to support her own family. She proposed her idea to Dr. Vaughan, headmaster of the school, who, with his wife, gave her enthusiastic co-operation. He stipulated only that one of the masters should also live in the house, so that a house-tutor would be present to enforce study hours and other discipline.

The house that she found soon replaced the Morrises' home in Annie's affection. It was an old, rambling structure, once the vicarage, which stood commandingly on top of Harrow Hill, and in summer it was covered with roses in front and ivy behind. An old-fashioned half-window–half-door (on the bolt of which it seemed the flying Annie was always tearing her new frocks) opened from the drawing room onto a large garden which sloped down the hill and was covered with old fruit trees as well as with currant and gooseberry bushes and fragrant strawberry beds. Annie had her private country house in a wide-spreading Portugal laurel, in the "study" of which she would sit with the birds, reading or declaiming from such loved books as *The Pilgrim's Progress* or *Paradise Lost*, in which her favorite character was Satan. In spite of her bookishness and introspection, however, she claimed to be as good a climber and cricketer as any of the boys who lived with them.

Into this delectable place they moved on Annie's eighth birthday, and she regarded it as home for eleven years—until after Henry—who, helped by his mother's wise counsel and Dr. Vaughan's guidance, proved to be a studiously clever lad—had left for Clare College, Cambridge, on a scholarship. But she herself was to live in this house only sporadically during this period, for a new turn came almost immediately into her fortunes.

Shortly after she came to live in the house on Harrow Hill, the companionable Annie dropped in to visit one of her new neighbors. In the drawing room she was introduced to a stranger—a "lame lady with a strong face," as she later described her, but a face which softened into a smile as she took Annie onto her lap and petted her. The lady was Miss Ellen Marryat, the youngest sister of the famous novelist Captain Frederick Marryat of the Royal Navy, the author of many popular stories for boys, among them *Mr. Midshipman Easy* and also the somewhat autobiographical and best-selling novel, *Peter Simple*.[1] In 1848 Captain Frederick had died on his estate at Langham. His favorite and much younger sister Ellen had assisted his daughter Augusta and his housekeeper in nursing him during his last months. Ellen, whose motherly instincts had been unsatisfied by her spinsterhood, but who was locally noted for her "genius for teaching," helped look after his daughters for a while after she returned to live with her mother on Wimbledon Common. Later, when her mother died, Ellen looked around for work of further service to the world and, since another philoprogenitive brother had a large family of girls, offered to take one, Amy, and care for her. For companionship she had also taken on little Walter Powys, the son of a clergyman with a similarly large family.

But when, in 1855, Miss Ellen saw pretty little Annie Wood, she immediately decided that her niece needed female companionship as well. The next day she asked Mrs. Wood whether she would consider letting Annie come into the Marryat family circle. Miss Marryat would take over full responsibility for the child's education but allow her to come home regularly for holidays. At first the mother would not listen, for she and Annie were inseparable. But after she had had time to reflect on the advantages of Miss Marryat's proposal, she yielded.[2]

So Annie went to live with "Auntie," as Miss Marryat wanted the children to call her, on her beautiful new estate, Fern Hill, near Charmouth, Dorsetshire, on the Devon border; and there they lived for five years, adding other protégés from time to time, all selected from poor, "but gently born and gently trained," children—sometimes a boy, sometimes a girl. Miss Marryat was a sort of Lady Bountiful to the whole neighborhood, not merely to her young brood. She visited the poor, sent the sick the best food from her own table, and found or made employment for the out-of-work so that she would not undermine their independence with gifts of money.

In her little private school she herself taught all the subjects except music, for which she hired a master. Her methods were very "progressive" for her day, as she believed in learning by doing and not by rote. She did not believe in teaching spelling or grammar directly, but had the children write short compositions or letters to one another, always based

[1] For information on the Marryat family, see Florence Marryat (Mrs. Ross Church), *The Life and Letters of Captain Marryat* (London, 1872); Cecil T. Davis, *Pedigree and Memoranda of the Family of Marryat* (London, 1909); and Oliver Warner, *Captain Marryat* (London, 1953).

[2] Gertrude Marvin Williams, in her somewhat sensationalized and often fictionalized life of Annie Besant, *The Passionate Pilgrim* (New York, 1931), p. 10, speculates on the assumed psychological conflict brought on in Annie by this move, which caused "a growing jealousy of her brother, this casual male who took her mother's every sacrifice for granted." There is actually no evidence that Annie's extravagant language in describing the love between herself and her mother had any such compensatory origin.

on their immediate lives or on some book they had just read; then she herself would explain any errors and suggest improvements. The only grammar they learned as such was Latin, and that came only after they had studied much composition. In French and German the stress was on reading, speaking, and understanding; history was taught by one member reading aloud while the others worked at sewing and other useful occupations—boys as well as girls. Vocabulary-building was made competitive. Geography was learned by painting skeleton maps and putting together cutouts; Annie got special satisfaction from putting the big empires, like Russia, in their proper places.

But advanced as Auntie was in the academic aspects of education, she was characteristically Victorian in her treatment of another sector of her training—religion, which, as with Dr. Thomas Arnold at Rugby, became the real core of the curriculum. Miss Marryat was an evangelical of the evangelicals. She started a Sunday-school class and a Bible class and later had the children also teach in them. They learned by heart many hymns and passages from the Bible, and Annie excelled in these lessons. She admitted, though, that the reputation she got for piety when she memorized the whole Epistle of James and other Old and New Testament passages should really have been attributed to her vanity and desire to distinguish herself above the rest. Moreover, the children were all called on to "speak to the Lord" extemporaneously, but this sort of prayer meeting was an agonizing ordeal to the shy Annie, in spite of her secret feeling that she did it very well. On Sundays no books but the Bible and *Sunday at Home* were permitted, but Miss Marryat introduced a little variety by sometimes giving them Bible quizzes or by telling them of the exciting adventures of such missionaries as Moffat and Livingstone, whose experiences with savages and wild animals Annie found as thrilling as any tale of Captain Mayne Reid's (yet she never mentioned reading anything by Captain Marryat himself). These tales led her far back to the early Christian martyrs, and she spent many an hour daydreaming about being tried before Roman judges or Dominican inquisitors and being flung to the lions, tortured on the rack, or burned at the stake for her faith. Once she envisioned herself preaching to a vast crowd and converting them to her new religion; and then, brought back to reality, she regretted that she had been born too late to suffer for her beliefs as the old martyrs had done. The martyr complex, indeed, took early root in little Annie Wood's soul.

After lessons on weekdays the children had much innocent fun taking long walks and drives, riding on "a lovely pony, who found small children most amusing," and going on all-day picnics in the neighborhood. But the seriousness of life began to weigh down upon Annie. As she said later, "On the whole, the somewhat Calvinistic teaching tended, I think, to make me a little morbid, especially as I always fretted silently after my mother." On one of her visits home, carrying a sort of report card from Miss Marryat, she was surprised to learn that Auntie had cited "cheerfulness" as a lack in her character; at home she was "ever the blithest of children" and the pet name "Sunshine Annie" had replaced the infant "little Pheasantina." But at Miss Marryat's she sometimes felt a vague distress and deprivation when she could not produce the "sense of sin" demanded by the more evangelical preachers or could not recall some definite hour of "conversion" which had set her on the path to being "saved." Her misty yearnings and dreamy longings for a career of self-sacrifice were not a sufficient substitute. Nevertheless, many of the religious matters that she learned at Miss Marryat's fostered the "germ of mysticism" which Annie later stressed as having been in her from the beginning, but which for many of her most active years was smothered by the materialism of the age.

In the spring of 1861 an important innovation was made in the educational routine. By that time the personnel of Miss Marryat's little class had changed considerably. Walter Powys had dropped silently from the picture. Amy Marryat had been taken back home soon after the death of her mother in childbirth and had been replaced by another girl, Emma Mann, a few months older than Annie. Emma was one of the several daughters of another lusty but impecunious clergyman, who had married the sister of the Mary Stanley who had done "such noble work in nursing in the Crimea." Not long afterward, in addition, Auntie had not only legally adopted the boy who had been the cause of his mother's death, but she had also been responsible for having him named after her idolized dead brother, whose own son Frederick had been drowned in a naval wreck in 1847.

When it was discovered that the small new Frederick had developed cataract, there was nothing for it but that Auntie must take him to Düsseldorf, where there was a famous oculist. Knowing the educative value of foreign travel from her own considerable experience, Auntie applied for, and got, Mrs. Wood's permission to take Annie along. Emma was also to go. For several months the girls worked diligently on their German, guided by Miss Marryat. In the expectation of seeing something of France also on their trip, they all three talked French conscientiously at dinner. As a result, counting on their expertness as linguists, the girls were dismayed when they reached Antwerp and were suddenly engulfed in the babel of tongues; Miss Marryat, however, triumphantly extricated them with her French.

In Bonn a sitting room on the ground floor and bedrooms above had been reserved for them at a pension, the beautiful Chateau du Rhin, overhanging the broad blue river. Frederick had apparently been sent on alone to Düsseldorf; at least, Annie tacitly and rather heartlessly dismissed him from her narrative. The whole of the drawing-room floor of the pension was occupied by the two sons of the Duke of Hamilton, the Marquis of Douglas and Lord Charles, who had come to study at the university with their private tutor. These young blades soon discovered that Auntie had a strong aversion to, if not fear of, what Annie archly referred to as the "male sect"—at least so far as her charges were concerned, even though they were only in their earliest teens. Emma, a "plump, rosy, fair-haired, typical English maiden," was full of frolic and harmless fun. Annie, a "very slight, pale, black-haired girl," with a shy charm, alternated between her extreme pensiveness and a wild sense of humor. The young noblemen promptly saw the chance for a lark, in which a mild flirtation with the young ladies could be combined with a mild exasperating of the stern-looking lady with them. So whenever the female party started out for a walk or drive, the lads would just happen to be trotting out for a ride on their horses, and would salute them with exaggerated low bows and doffed hats; or they would make their horses caracole in the gravel before the girls' window; or they would waylay the pair on their descent of the stairs with a demure "Good morning." They would even go to church and place themselves in unavoidable view of the Marryat pew, and Lord Charles would wrinkle the skin of his scalp so that the girls were soon choking with irreverent laughter.

Though the two were hugely enjoying all this attention, it soon became too much for Auntie to bear, and she removed herself from the chateau, taking refuge, much to the others' disgust, in a girls' school. But even there she was not let alone. Bonn University was just then experiencing a sort of Anglophilia, and the two young English girls gave the students an excellent opportunity to pursue it. Annie and Emma were followed around by mischievous German youths wherever they went; young men with cheeks gashed in dueling would whisper sentimental and complimentary words as the girls whisked past—words which their newly acquired vocabularies apparently proved adequate to understand.[3] It was only harmless, boyish nonsense, but it was too much for the proper English spinster to bear. Young men were all ravening wolves and young ladies were all innocent lambs. After bearing the torture for three months and fearing for their morals if she exposed them any longer, Auntie sent the pair back to England for the holidays, "somewhat in disgrace." But Annie would never forget clambering up the nearby Siebengebirge, rowing on the Rhine, wandering in the beautiful valleys; she would never

[3] Apparently, however, Annie did not keep up her spoken German as she did her written German, though she was always perfectly at home in French of both kinds. At least, Martin Boyken, general secretary of the Theosophical Society in Germany, told me in an interview at Hamburg in June, 1954, that so far as he knew Mrs. Besant never lectured in German or even tried to use it in either public or private. He recalled her once trying to recite a poem in German in the 1920's but said that she did not do it very well. Nevertheless, the power of her personality and her judicious use of an interpreter made her a very effective speaker even for those who could not understand English.

forget the stories of Drachenfels and Rolandseck and the pictures they left in her memory.

Apparently and peculiarly, however, Miss Marryat did not have the same fear of the French would-be Romeos as she had of the German. At any rate, after a two months' cooling-off period in England, she called her charges back to her in Paris, where they spent seven "happy, workful months." On Wednesdays and Saturdays they were free from lessons. They visited the Louvre and became familiar with its masterpieces. They acquainted themselves with almost every church in Paris, observing the "solemn beauty" of Notre Dame, the "somewhat gaudy magnificence" of La Sainte Chapelle, the "stateliness" of La Madeleine, and the "impressive gloom" of St. Roche—Annie's favorite was St. Germain de l'Auxerrois because of the richness of its deep and pure stained glass. They enjoyed mixing with the bright crowds on the Champs Elysées and the Bois, strolling in the Tuileries gardens, and climbing to the top of every monument from which they could get a view. They marveled at the fashionables of the Empire in its glittering heyday and especially at the imperial carriage containing the exquisite Empress, escorted by her brilliant guards in waving plumes and shining accoutrements and accompanied by the shy little boy who "was thought to be born to an imperial crown, but whose brief career was to find an ending from the spears of savages in a quarrel in which he had no concern." This was romance that Annie and Emma would never forget.[4]

The Parisian stay had another important result, the culmination of Annie's religious life so far. Except for "that little aberration in Germany," she was still a decidedly pious girl. She never ventured into a Paris theater, for theaters were "traps set by Satan for the destruction of foolish souls." She was determined never to go to a dance or ball, even if she were invited to one—which she was not. But during the spring of 1862 in Paris, Mr. Forbes, the English chaplain at the Church of the Rue d'Aguesseau, decided to take advantage of the visit of the Bishop of Ohio to Paris by arranging a confirmation class. Annie saw a God-sent opportunity to take on herself all the vows and duties pledged in her name by others at her baptism. She prepared solemnly and assiduously to renounce the world, the flesh, and the devil. Her mother left the boys at Harrow and came over for the service and the first communion on Easter Sunday. When Annie knelt at the altar rail and felt the gentle touch of the aged bishop on her bowed head, she could scarcely control herself.

The confirmation was an exciting and intense experience and it went deep. Insensibly the cold and crude evangelicalism that Miss Marryat had so carefully tried to instil began to be absorbed and conquered by the

---

[4] Mrs. Williams, in *The Passionate Pilgrim*, again reads all sorts of psychological—if not psychopathic—meanings into the relationship between the two girls which there is absolutely no evidence to warrant.

sensuous pleasure that Annie now found in the color, incense-laden fragrance, exquisite music, pomp, and ritual of the High Church Anglican and the Roman Catholic churches. Keble's *Christian Year* took the place of *Paradise Lost* in her favor. Her mother had never allowed her to read love stories, and certainly Miss Marryat had not broadened her horizon in this respect. Consequently her romantic daydreams did not take the direction of those of more normally reared young girls. She did not dream of forming closer friendships with men in the world of reality. Instead, she brooded again "over the days when girl-martyrs were blessed with visions of the King of Martyrs, when sweet St. Agnes saw her celestial Bridegroom, and angels stooped to whisper melodies in St. Cecilia's raptured ear." It was the bride of Christ she dreamed of being, not the bride of any mere mortal man.

3

Holy Orders and Disorders

On their return from the Continent, Miss Marryat took her charges to Sidmouth, Devonshire, for the summer. Now that her girls were past their middle teens, she began giving them more freedom. An essentially wise woman, she realized that a transition period from dependence to independence was necessary for the proper adjustment from the schoolroom to the world. Naturally there was no thought of a college education for a young woman at this time; if Annie were to learn more, she must learn it by herself, not in a school. Thus, little by little, the girls were trained to work alone. Once when Annie complained that Auntie was not teaching her enough, she was told that she should not expect "to have Auntie for a crutch all through life."

For the winter of 1862–63, Miss Marryat moved to London, and Annie remained with her, perfecting her French in the "admirable" classes of a M. Roche. In the spring, however, the break began, with Annie's returning to live with her mother at Harrow, but continuing to go up to London each week for her classes. When these were over, the break was made permanent. Miss Marryat told Annie she thought she had done all she could; Annie should now try her wings alone. And at this point Auntie vanished from her pupil's life. Close as their relationship had been and great as was Annie's gratitude, she never mentioned Miss Marryat again, although the bittersweet old lady lived to the age of ninety-one and must have watched her protégé's impetuous career with both pride and trepidation.[1]

So well had she laid her foundations, however, that Annie started out to turn herself into a thorough and precocious bluestocking. She was now sixteen and a half. She continued to read German at home with a master.

[1] Cecil T. Davis, *Pedigree . . . of Marryat,* p. 6.

The music which she loved so much and knew so well she also continued under the able tutelage of John Farmer, muscial director at Harrow School. Mrs. Wood had always had a passion for music, and since Beethoven and Bach were her favorite composers, there was scarcely a sonata by Beethoven or a fugue by Bach that Annie did not master on her piano. The lighter side of her repertoire was filled out by the "Songs without Words" by Mendelssohn. She and her mother spent many happy evenings playing to and with each other, and, since one of the popular amusements at Harrow consisted of musical "At Homes," Annie's "facile fingers" made her a welcome guest.

She also turned athletic, at least to the extent that a well-bred Victorian young lady could do so. The cricket and tree-climbing of her childhood now being a bit too rowdy, she practiced archery so devotedly that she won as a prize for the best score in a contest the first ring she ever owned. She also took up croquet very zealously. Dearest of all, however, she kept up her horseback-riding and remained an accomplished horsewoman until she could no longer put her foot in a stirrup.

And there were balls, too. She had quickly rid herself of the scruples against such recreation which had been inculcated by Miss Marryat. Her mother laid out each article of clothing for her, dressed her dense, curly black hair, which fell almost to her knees, placed flowers in it, and fastened up her dress before Annie ran off. She was really "Sunshine Annie" now. There were plenty of young men around by this time, even though Henry was still away at college. After all, Oxford and Cambridge were glad to send the picked graduates of their Schools to Harrow as junior masters, so that "one's partners at balls and croquet and archery could talk as well as flirt."

The talk meant as much to Annie as the fun. Although the atmosphere surrounding her was literary rather than scientific, she read a few stray scientific works. But she was most drawn to literature, philosophy, and theology. A translation of Plato delighted her, but she was much annoyed "by the insatiable questionings of Socrates." She adored Derby's translation of the *Iliad* and devoured Dante, also in translation. She disliked Wordsworth and Cowper and all the seventeenth- and eighteenth-century poets, even though her nagging conscience made her read them. Southey's fanciful oriental poetic narratives fascinated her, and Spenser's *Faerie Queene* had its place beside Milton and Dante. Her novel-reading, however, was extremely limited, if not quite nonexistent. Since her mother regarded the usual love story of the three-volume circulating library type as unhealthy reading for a young girl, Annie was given Scott and Kingsley, but not Miss Braddon or Mrs. Henry Wood (no relation, she was glad to say!). The theater was also still out of bounds. Though her mother loved to see young girls bright and gay, she had a horror of sentimentality in them and wished to keep them "above all things absolutely ignorant of all evil things and of premature love-dreams." This maternal policy, in which modesty was a virtual synonym for ignorance, was soon to have its unfortunate consequences for Annie.

But the girl's specialty in her studies at this time was theology. She almost lived with the Fathers of the early Christian church, poring over the Shepherd of Hermas; the epistles of Polycarp, Barnabas, Ignatius, and Clement; Chrysostom's commentaries; and Augustine's *Confessions*. When she became an old lady, however, it was Origen, "the great Gnostic of the early Christian Church," that she particularly remembered. It was he, she maintained with retrospective dogmatism, who had called her attention to "the Mysteries of Jesus," those secret teachings which had been communicated only orally to the disciples and which later were to contribute considerably to the heritage of modern Theosophy.[2]

The continuity of the Christian church through its apostles and martyrs from Christ to her own day also preoccupied her; but it was the halfway liberalism of Pusey, Liddon, Keble, and their followers which drew her into the modern church. If it had not been for Pusey, she might well have gone over to Rome then and there. Her devotional life revolved around her weekly communion. She went into ecstatic meditations, she fasted, she even occasionally tried a little self-flagellation (usually recognized by psychologists as a sexual outlet) to see if she could stand physical pain in case she should ever be called upon to tread the path of the sainted martyrs. She felt she could nearly draw Christ Himself down from His throne by the passion of her devotion. It was almost as if she were reliving some previous life in which she had already had these experiences. The mainspring of her life had always been the desire for self-sacrifice for a cause.

It was the custom among the Morris clan to congregate in large numbers during the religious holiday seasons at the home of Grandfather Morris in Albert Square. Christmas and Easter had particularly potent powers of attraction. Thus, Christmastide of 1865, just after Annie's eighteenth birthday, found her and her mother down from Harrow.

Close to Stockwell, in a very poor district of Clapham, a little mission church was opening, in which Aunt Minnie had become interested. The chief of the clergy working there, a Reverend Mr. Hoare, an intensely earnest and devout man, was very "High Church" whereas the vicars of all the other churches in the neighborhood were very "Low." Annie's studies, of course, had made her "High," and she immediately saw where her pleasure and her duty lay. Minnie and she promptly offered their aid to the distraught Mr. Hoare, who was only too glad to get any sort of help he could. The pair, thinking they were serving God when they were really only amusing themselves in a small place where, Annie later ad-

[2] Annie Besant, *The Theosophical Society and the Occult Hierarchy* (London, 1925), pp. 32–37.

mitted, their services were probaby overestimated and they themselves were flattered by being overpraised, pitched in zealously. They prepared Christmas ornaments with their own hands and tried to make the drab little building as pretty as possible for the season.

Among those who were laboring in the little mission vineyard was a young deacon, a recent Cambridge graduate, who was also an undermaster at the Stockwell Grammar School a few narrow streets away to the southwest of Albert Square. His name was Frank Besant. Annie did not meet him at this time; she only saw him at the altar helping with the services.

In the spring, however, came Easter, bringing Annie and Mrs. Wood again from Harrow. With them they brought armfuls of flowers from the country. Minnie was delighted. She and Annie devoted all their spare time to the little church. On the altar and throughout the choir and nave they placed spring blossoms—to the delight of the poor and the little London children, many of whom, Annie swore, had never before seen a flower. And this time she was introduced to the man who was soon to become her husband, with such unanticipated results—the Rev. Frank Besant.

Frank Besant came from an old English family, the origin of whose name he himself—when he became an amateur antiquarian many years later—traced back to at least the twelfth century.[3] It was, he thought, a craft name, probably deriving from the name of the gold coin, besant, which the Byzantine emperors awarded as a disc or medal to the Crusaders who passed through their city on the way back from a campaign. But upon the proper pronunciation of the name, the members of the family itself could not agree. A friend of Frank's brother Albert once wrote him in puzzled doggerel and even more confused punctuation:

> Tell me is it right or decent
> To refer to Walter Besant;
> Should the name be rhymed with crescent,
> Should it be Sir Walter Besant.
> Or do eager maidens pant
> After novels by Besánt.

Albert preferred the second alternative, as his friend indicated:

> To call you aught but Albert Bésant
> Would spoil the past and mar the present:
> To alter now I really can't
> But let Sir Walter be Besánt.

Brother Walter, in 1876, merely ambitious to become the popular author that he later was, had his own French preference, although he was him-

---

[3] For the most complete study of the Besant family, see Arthur Digby Besant, *Pedigree,* esp. pp. 15–27, 189–236.

self forced to reject the theory that the name was a corruption of Beau-
séant. Walter later versified more literately:

> Gladly would I split the weasand
> Of the wretch who calls me Beesant;
> Nor are things a whit more pleasant,
> When fellow-creatures call me Bésant.
> If you'd give me what I want,
> Gentle stranger, say Besánt.

Brother Frank, however, must have sided with Albert, as most of the family apparently had done, for ten years later, in the *National Reformer*,
Annie informed a correspondent that her last name rhymed with "pleasant." Certainly she could not have been thinking of her husband when
she said so.

Frank Besant came from the family of a woolen draper in Portsea,
Portsmouth. He had nine brothers and sisters, and he was seven years
older than Annie Wood. At an early age he had joined his brother Albert
at "Jerry" Andrews' school at Portsea and had made a good record as an
all-round student. Then in March, 1855, he followed his brother Walter's
example and became a boarder at the Stockwell Proprietary Grammar
School, London. Like Walter, Frank distinguished himself as a student
and became "head of the school." He was rewarded by being granted a
scholarship in mathematics at King's College, London, with which the
Stockwell Grammar School was "in union." He did so well there that
after a year he was awarded an open mathematical scholarship at Cambridge, where he entered Emmanuel College in 1860. The pace at Cambridge proved to be a bit faster than before, so that in the mathematical
tripos examinations of 1863 he came out twenty-eighth Wrangler, which
placed him well down in the first class.

Nevertheless, learning that the post of mathematics master in his old
school at Stockwell was vacant, Frank immediately applied, and was selected for the job out of twenty-six applicants. Being of a religious nature and probably realizing that advancement would come more rapidly
in a church school if he were in orders, he pursued his theological studies
along with his teaching, and in December, 1865, was admitted to the
diaconate.

Full of ambition in his cold way, Frank threw himself energetically into
his new duties. As a clergyman, however, he was never able to forget that
he had been trained as a mathematician. As his son Arthur Digby Besant
was later to analyze his father:

With his customary precision he records every service in which he took part—a
practice which he continued throughout the fifty years of his ministry. Indeed, I
think there can never have been any member of the cloth with a more orderly,
methodical and statistical mind. He recorded and numbered everything, including his sermons, which ranged from No. 1 which he preached at an afternoon

service at St. Barnabas, South Kennington, on February 11th, 1866, to No. 3,110, preached in Sibsey Church on March 18th, 1917, shortly before his death.

But the Rev. Frank was not really so prolific as these figures might imply, for he often used the same sermon more than once, though sometimes in revised form. He also kept similarly detailed accounts of his proceeds as a clergyman, gross and net.

He first served an appointment as assistant in connection with the Stockwell Chapel, next at St. Barnabas, South Kennington, and then at Clapham Parish House and Mission Hall. He eked out his income during school holidays by advertising in church papers for parochial work or by getting temporary work through private introductions. And in every case he set down minutely his fees and his expenses—if there were any fees. Sometimes, unfortunately, he failed to collect his debts from parishes that were even poorer than he was.

When the Bishop of Winchester ordained Frank Besant in 1865, he exacted a pledge that the young man would remain at his present school for at least two years. This pledge was redeemed. He was a good teacher in his way, for he was able to develop the full potential of every boy, brilliant or backward; yet he was never popular. For one thing he never went in for games, and the English schoolboy was inclined to look down on such a deficiency. Moreover, he was not only austere but painfully shy. And he was conscientious to a degree. He would never compromise or accommodate himself to the views of others. For this would be tampering with the truth, and he was sure he knew the truth. It was this young man whom the intense and dedicated Annie Wood met at Eastertide, 1866.

Annie herself had been undergoing an unsettling experience at this very time. She had realized, of course, that there were some people who doubted the absolute historical accuracy of everything in the Bible. In fact, one or two of the masters at Harrow had actually been friends of John William Colenso, "the heretic Bishop of Natal," whose views on polygamy, eternal punishment, and the traditional interpretation of the Pentateuch were already fluttering the orthodox ecclesiastical dovecotes. But Annie, fresh from her patristic studies, looked on all such heretics with horror. Her mother, too, objected to her young daughter's reading any controversial religious books, even those of her own favorite, Arthur Stanley, dean of Westminster, because Edward Pusey, canon of Christ Church, Oxford, and leader of the Oxford Movement, regarded him as "unsound." Besides, Annie herself had read and admired Pusey's book on the prophet Daniel.

During Holy Week, desiring to project herself back as fully as possible to A.D. 33 and all its tragic events, she started to make herself a harmony of the gospels, as so many had done before her. Completely innocent and fearless of what she might find, she was shocked and confounded to discover that the different accounts in the infallible gospels did not agree. Her harmony, as she phrased it, produced a discord; but she was familiar enough with the methods of medieval casuistry by now to reassure herself by saying that these apparent contradictions had been placed there only as a test of faith. She also recalled and quoted to herself Tertullian's famous formula for just such occasions: "Credo quia impossibile."[4] Thus Pusey conquered Colenso. Annie hastily smothered her first doubt and buried it. But it was not dead; it was only in a state of suspended animation.

As Annie put it in her *Sketches* (which are much more frank and detailed about this period of her life than is the *Autobiography*), "The spring ripened into summer in uneventful fashion, so far as I was concerned, the smooth current of my life flowing on untroubled, hard reading and merry play filling the happy days." She did not know until later that two or three unnamed young men had proposed themselves as suitors for her hand through her mother. But Mrs. Wood always put them off with the maternal but fact-blinking explanation, "She is too young. I will not have her troubled." Annie herself still had no love-dreams of a mundane nature, partly, she surmised, because "fiery novels" were utterly absent from her reading and partly because her "whole dream-tendencies were absorbed by religion." To prove the point of this confession she subjoined some specimens of the kind of prayers in which she found daily delight, "in order to show how an emotional girl may be attracted by these so-called devotional exercises." These prayers were torrid, however, with erotic imagery, such as "fresh ardors of love," "pant after Thee," "fairer than the sons of men," "cords of love," "heavenly Bridegroom," "a new gift of espousal and the meet consummation of Thy love," "long to be dissolved and be with Thee," "Oh, that I could embrace Thee with that most burning love of angels," "Let Him kiss me with the kisses of His mouth," "the sweet and burning power of Thy love," and "The King has brought me into His chambers." Such language was revolting to Mrs. Wood, although she had been a devoted and loving wife. Annie had had no such experience. Still she was a "child awakening into womanhood," all of whose "dawning feelings" she possessed without understanding them.

In the summer the family took their customary month's vacation at their favorite St. Leonard's on the Sussex coast. Their cottage was at the "far, unfashionable end, right away from the gay, watering-place folk," but they settled down unenviously to enjoy the ocean and the country. Minnie Morris and Annie were the tomboys of the party, made up—with one important exception—of adults. Minnie was especially happy to escape her dull teaching routine, which was so rapidly undermining her health

---

[4] Of course, Tertullian had actually written: "Certum est, quia impossibile est."

that she died before the end of the year. Not foreseeing this sad and imminent tragedy, however, the three women had "many a merry gallop" over their favorite fields, Annie on a beloved black mare, Gipsy Queen, who bore her hundred pounds as easily and gaily over the hedges and ditches as if the girl were part of herself.

Somehow or other—Annie herself never seemed quite to understand it —Frank Besant appeared at St. Leonard's to spend his own meager week's holiday. Being the only young people in the party, Frank and Annie were natural companions; they walked, drove, and rode together. Just an hour or so before he had to leave for London, he asked her—almost in the process of saying good-by—to marry him. Annie was so astounded and confused that she could not speak. Her first impulse was to refuse. She did not want to be thought to have been merely flirting with him, however, and he assumed that because she had been granting him such full companionship, she was expecting his proposal. He therefore concluded that silence meant consent and, hurrying away to catch his train, bound her over to further silence until he had time to speak to her mother.

For a fortnight Annie was miserable. For the first time she had a secret from her dear mother. Finally, as soon as the rest of the party got back to town or to Harrow, respectively, she told her suitor she could keep silence no longer. But she did not refuse him. Thus, as she described the situation, "out of sheer weakness and fear of inflicting pain I drifted into an engagement with a man I did not pretend to love." Mrs. Wood was not happy about it either and for some time refused to consent to a definite engagement. In fact—although Annie did not put it so bluntly—she apparently tried to dissolve the relationship by sending her daughter away for more traveling.

Among the friends of the Woods were the Roberts family of Manchester. William Prowting Roberts was a solicitor, with offices in Bath, Manchester, and London.[5] He was known both as "the poor man's lawyer," because of his interest in popular causes, and as "the miners' attorney general," because of his appointment as standing legal adviser to the Miners' Association of Great Britain and Ireland. He was a close friend of Ernest Charles Jones, the fiery Chartist and radical leader, an early admirer of Karl Marx, and a minor novelist and member of the eccentric Spasmodic school of poetry; and with him Roberts worked hand in hand in all his struggles, ready to fight a poor man's battle without fee and to champion any worker he thought had been unfairly treated. Except for the fact that he had made a trip to the Holy Land in 1862–63 and on his return to Manchester had been invited by the local clergy to deliver a series of lectures on the Bible, Roberts was the sort of person with whom one would expect the dead Mr. Wood, rather than Emily Wood, to have been friendly.

[5] In addition to Mrs. Besant's description, see the *Dictionary of National Biography.*

At any rate, it was with Mr. Roberts, his second wife, and his two daughters that Annie traveled to Switzerland in the late summer and early fall. They went to all the proper places. They went to Chamonix, worshiped Mont Blanc, crossed the Mer de Glace and the Mauvais Pas, visited the Monastery of St. Bernard, took the steamer down the Lake of Thun, gazed at the Jungfrau and Staubbach Falls, visited Lausanne, Bern, and Geneva, "stood beside the wounded Lion, and shuddered in the dungeon of Chillon," walked holes in their shoes, and finally one Sunday afternoon got lost climbing a mountain but found their way in time to meet a search party going out to look for them with lanterns and ropes.

It was very thrilling and very educational, but it did not succeed in breaking up the engagement. Annie went back home and the betrothal was announced officially. It was not quite as heroic as she had hoped for, but romantic young English girls of the time were in the habit of idealizing clergymen. Annie reconciled herself to the thought of marriage in place of the ascetic religious life she had envisioned, because she would be the wife of a priest, "working ever in the Church and among the poor" and doing good for the world. This, at least, was one of the main arguments used on her by Frank. In spite of this consideration, nevertheless, she tried to break the engagement once when her imagination depicted her future with him too vividly, but this time it was her mother who balked. Mrs. Wood's pride would not let her daughter break the pledge she had made.

It was of course their mutual interest in the church that pinned Annie and Frank together, however precariously. During this same year—1866 —Annie made her first attempt at writing. She entitled it "A Paper on the Duty of Fasting," and her fiancé made a copy of it, which she annotated in her own handwriting. Soon afterward she wrote a supplementary paper on "Fasting Communion," which Frank also copied and kept, so that both manuscripts, meticulously dated, later passed into the possession of their son. The two were getting to know each other a little better, but it was scarcely a rousing courtship.

The year 1867, however, saw three major events in the life of the Woods. First, they left Harrow. The wrench of parting from the "dear Old Vicarage" on the hill was great, but Mrs. Wood's purpose in moving there in the first place had been accomplished. Her son Henry had graduated from Harrow and gone on to Cambridge. The master who had lived with them so long had married and moved to a house of his own. Mrs. Wood felt she was growing old and was feeling the burden of management too heavily. She had saved enough to pay for Henry's college career in spite of the various trips and vacations; in fact, she had enough savings over and above all this to buy a house at Warrior Square in St. Leonard's, where she could live during most of the year, renting it for a nice profit during the "season." By summer she and Annie were comfortably en-sconced there.

The date of the wedding had been set for December, but Annie could not have seen a great deal of her fiancé in the interim. At the end of the summer she and her mother went up to Pendleton, near Manchester, to pay a visit to the Robertses. As usual, she had a very pleasant time, a large part of her recreation being devoted to riding horseback over the coun-tryside. Then, suddenly, tragedy again stalked onto the stage. To the Woods, Lawyer Roberts was a "dear old man," but to the poor he was a god. Annie would often drive him to his Manchester office in the morn-ing, bask in his praise of her skill in guiding the horses through the crowded city streets, and watch the women in the coal district lift their children up to see their champion go by. He would talk to her on these and other occasions, preaching the cause of the people, giving her her first political lessons, and weaning her away from the "decorous Whig-gism" with which she had previously been surrounded. She would hang on his stories of how he had helped save women from working in the mines with their men. He had seen them there himself, naked to the waist, in short petticoats hardly reaching to their knees, brutalized and foul-tongued. He had seen little children working there, too. Babies of three and four years would be set to watch a door and then cursed and kicked when they fell asleep at their task.

"What do you think of John Bright?" he had abruptly demanded one day, looking at her "with fiery eyes from under heavy brows."

Annie carelessly answered, "I have never thought of him at all. Isn't he a rather rough sort of man, who goes about making rows?"

Roberts was shocked at her naïveté. "There, just as I thought!" he thun-dered fiercely. "I believe some of you fine ladies would not go to heaven if you had to rub shoulders with John Bright, the noblest man God ever gave to the cause of the poor." Later in her life Annie was to learn at first hand why Roberts thought so. Now it was enough that Roberts himself suddenly became her "first tutor in Radicalism," and she his apt pupil.

Then, to cap these theoretical lessons, came a realistic culmination. The cause of a free Ireland was suddenly transferred to England—in fact, to Manchester itself. Two of the Fenian leaders, Colonel Kelly and Captain Deasy, who had come secretly to England to raise funds and supporters, were arrested in Manchester and put on trial. On September 18 a police van carrying them back to the jail was waylaid by a band of Irish sym-pathizers resolved to rescue their heroes. When the constable inside re-fused to open the door, one of the rescuers, fearing the quick arrival of the police, blew off the lock with his revolver. The shot killed the con-stable as he was looking through the keyhole. Kelly and Deasy were dragged out to safety, while their retreat was protected by others with drawn revolvers. Five of these were caught, one after the other, and placed on trial; but the man who had fired the accidentally fatal shot escaped. Manchester went race-mad. No Irish workman was safe in an English crowd; no Englishman was safe in the Irish quarter. A special commission was appointed, with Mr. Justice Blackburn as its head—"the hanging judge," Roberts groaned at the news—and sent to Manchester.

The conclusion was foregone. Ernest Jones was the prisoners' counsel; Digby Seymour, Q.C., was also briefed for the defense, and Roberts was their assistant.[6] Roberts, feeling that his fellows were not vigorous enough in challenging prospective jurors, was almost committed for contempt by Justice Blackburn. But his valiant efforts were useless. All five men (one was really only a seventeen-year-old boy) were adjudged guilty and sentenced to death, though two (not including the boy) were later reprieved. On November 23 the three were hanged outside Salford Gaol. As Annie commented bitterly, if they had been fighting for freedom for Italy, England would have honored and perhaps aided them. But because they were Irish rebels, England "buried them as murderers in quicklime in the prison yard."

Annie had a special reason to be bitter. She had attended the trial on October 29 with her mother and the three Roberts women. They had driven through the thronged and barricaded streets, guarded by soldiers, and had been stopped and threatened when passing through an Irish section of the crowd. But when Annie "gently touched the nearest fist," and timidly announced, "Friends, these are Mr. Roberts's wife and daughters," the curses changed to cheers. In the courtroom the women saw the partiality of the judge and the lethal determination of the jury. From her place in a little room behind the bench Annie could see an official quietly preparing the black caps, which were the sign of "Guilty," even before the verdict was brought. She saw the seventeen-year-old's sweetheart kneel and cry to the crowd, "Save my William!" It was a harrowing and never-forgotten experience. In fact, fifty-seven years later, in faraway India, she was to write an article in which she told the Indians how "the love of Liberty first awoke in her" through the fate of the "Manchester Martyrs," as she heard the death sentence pronounced and heard the ringing cry from them: "God save Ireland!" "Then the flame of passionate love of liberty burst out in my heart, and has never flickered since," she wrote with all her vast power of indignation.[7]

Some years after the execution Annie derived some consoling pleasure from the discovery that Charles Bradlaugh, who was another reformer

[6] Strangely enough, Frederick Leary (Jones's pen name) in *The Life of Ernest Jones* (London, 1887), pp. 70–71, does not mention Roberts in his brief account of this affair. He does mention the praise Jones received from the two justices for the way he conducted the defense.

[7] See *New India*, November 5, 1924; also *Theosophy in Australia*, February, 1925. The episode is written up in considerable detail in both versions of Mrs. Besant's autobiography.

and crusader of the stamp of Bright, Jones, and Roberts and who was to play a leading role in her life for many years, had also been laboring much more practically than she to save the "Manchester Martyrs" and aid the Irish cause. Not only had he pleaded in an open-air speech on Clerkenwell Green for their lives and written in his *National Reformer* about their unjust and illegal trial, but he had previously been consulted for legal advice by Colonel Kelly and General Cluseret on the first draft of their manifesto proclaiming Irish independence. For these activities the Bradlaugh house in Tottenham was watched for several months, back and front, day and night, by the police, who also stationed two men in uniform at the Park Railway Station "to scrutinise all the passengers who alighted there." But Bradlaugh also protested in the *National Reformer* against the attempt to blow up Clerkenwell Prison to rescue the condemned men.[8]

All this was not a very suitable preparation for the third event of 1867 —Annie's marriage. It took place at St. Leonard's in December. Annie was twenty. But, she later commented wryly, she had no more idea of the actualities of the marriage relationship than if she had been four, even though she had become quite accustomed to them in the erotic symbolism of the Prayer Book and the lives of the mystical martyrs: "My dreamy life, into which no knowledge of evil had been allowed to penetrate, in which I had been guarded from all pain, shielded from all anxiety, kept innocent on all questions of sex, was no preparation for married existence, and left me defenceless to face a rude awakening." The Victorians did not believe in educating their women in such matters. It might be difficult for men, who got their knowledge at school or college or by living in the outside world, "to realise the possibility of such infantile ignorance in many girls." Perfect innocence may be very beautiful as an ideal, but it is perilous in practice. Yes, Annie concluded ruefully, "Many an unhappy marriage dates from its very beginning, from the terrible shock to a young girl's sensitive modesty and pride, her helpless bewilderment and fear."

It was a very unfortunate beginning. Nevertheless, one cannot help feeling at least a shadow of sympathy for young Frank Besant. Perhaps, because he was a clergyman, he was as uninstructed as his girl-wife. At any rate, he did not understand the character and emotions of the young woman he had vowed to love and cherish until death did them part.

[8] See Hypatia Bradlaugh Bonner, *Charles Bradlaugh: A Record of His Life and Work . . . with an Account of His Parliamentary Struggle, Politics, and Teachings by John M. Robertson* (London, 1902; first printing, 1894), I, 252–62. Also see Mrs. Besant's own account.

4

Black-Letter Days

To the romantic imagination of Annie Wood there could be no more propitious plan for a honeymoon than to spend it in Paris, the scene of so many happy weeks of her girlhood. But to Mrs. Annie Besant, bride of the Rev. Frank Besant, now a fully ordained clergyman, there was no honey left in Paris. The glamour was gone, even for the few days they could afford to spend there. Nor was there any to be recaptured in Southsea, Portsmouth, one of her favorite seaside resorts; there they had to make a duty call on Frank's family nearby. And then Frank had to appear promptly at Cheltenham, where he had just received an appointment as assistant master at Cheltenham College, a recently established boys' school, probably in the preparatory department.[1]

Cheltenham was a small, beautifully located resort town in Gloucestershire in the Cotswold hills, a hundred miles northwest of London. Its mineral springs supplied handsome eighteenth-century pump rooms in the public gardens. In fact, so many retired Anglo-Indians came there to take the waters that it was known among them as "Asia Minor." The hunting set also found it a profitable base for operations. The parish church of St. Mary dated from the fourteenth century, but had undergone some restorations. The College, however, was almost new, having been established in 1842.

The young Besants perforce took rather cramped and unattractive lodgings in town. They knew almost nobody, least of all the social set, and Frank had to spend most of his days in classes. Annie pined for her

---

[1] Arthur Digby Besant, *Pedigree,* pp. 198 ff. Edward Scott Skirving, *Cheltenham College Register, 1841–1927* (Cheltenham, 1927), p. xxxviii, gives only the following brief notice: "1867–72. Rev. Frank Besant. Scholar of Emmanuel College, Cambridge. Vicar of Sibsey, Lincs., 1872–1917. Died 1917."

mother, but hardly dared mention her name for fear of rousing her husband's jealousy. When a scattering of neighbor women and wives of the other masters began to drop in, she was bored by their conversation and personalities. All they could talk of was the dull, dismal routine of domestic life, and Annie as yet knew nothing of the problems of babies and servants and cared less. There was no zest in anatomizing the housemaid's latest young man or condemning the cook's extravagance in using "butter, when dripping would have done perfectly, my dear." These drab, gossiping housewives had no interest at all in Annie's intellectual concerns. Annie granted that she would have been much better off if she had had some training in household management and the handling of money. She had never had to stay within an allowance or even buy herself a pair of gloves. She had enough of a conscience to want to perform her new duties creditably, but she hated domestic details. Consequently, she slighted the more humdrum tasks; she wanted to get back to her "beloved books" and bury herself in them.

Even the parish work to which she had thought she could dedicate her philanthropic and humanitarian impulses was denied her, for her husband was still a schoolteacher and had no parish. As her famous editor-friend W. T. Stead was to sum it up many years later: "She could not be the bride of Heaven, and therefore became the bride of Mr. Frank Besant. He was hardly an adequate substitute."

Frank was inadequate in other ways, too—psychologically and spiritually, rather than physically. The fact that he was surprisingly like Samuel Butler's Theobald Pontifex suggests that there was a common Victorian type of Anglican clergyman. Victorian society as a whole was a paternal society, centered on the authority of the man as husband and father and holding a relatively low opinion of the status of woman. It idealized her in poetry and romances, without recognizing her existence as an individual in reality. When problems arose—domestic as well as social and political—it solved them by conventional and traditional rather than progressive standards. Thus, as Annie analyzed Frank, he had "very high ideas of a husband's authority and a wife's submission." He was very precise, methodical, easily angered, and slow to be appeased. She, on the other hand, was impulsive, proud, hot-tempered, undomestic, and shy. She was even afraid to rebuke her servant for careless work. And she was inordinately modest. Whereas in medieval times society, encouraged by the church, had feared and denounced woman for her supposed concupiscence and sexuality, in the nineteenth century she was supposed to be cold and sexless, with no physical desires, and was so brought up.[2]

Moreover, Annie had never been treated with even a touch of harshness, had never been reprimanded, and had never been ordered about.

[2] For a valuable treatment of these matters, see G. Rattray Taylor, *Sex in History* (London and New York, 1954).

Thus, quarrels, fits of hysterical weeping, and defiant resistance to hus-
bandly "authority" quickly marred the new marriage. An utter transformation occurred in her almost before she knew it. Although she
realized what an "unsatisfactory wife" she must have been from the beginning, she could not help herself. As she frankly confessed, it all
stemmed from the "ignorance before alluded to." She had been "so scared
and outraged at heart" from the first night of her marriage that she could
never rub out its indelible impression. For she had never guessed where
babies actually came from. Perhaps she really thought that George Macdonald had told the whole story: "Out of the everywhere into the here."
She felt now that she should never have married—anyone.

Precipitately she sought her only known refuge—her books and her
writing. And this time the latter was not only sacred, as when she had
written so ascetically on fasting communion; it was also profane. In spite
of her mother's previous prohibition, she wanted to write fiction. She
wanted to tell the world about what her life might have been, or at least
about what other more fortunate girls' lives had been.

But she started firmly with the kind of narrative to which theology
lent respectability. According to the calendar of the Church of England
there are two kinds of saints—red and black. The red are those who are
important enough to have special services appointed for them and
whose names are therefore printed in red letters; the black are those
also-rans who are remembered by few of the clergy and even fewer of
the laity and whose names are preserved chiefly in black letters on church
calendars. It struck the pious and ingenious Annie that it might be interesting to take each of these black-letter days, do some ecclesiastical
research, and write the life of the particular saint belonging to it. So,
building on her earlier patristic studies, she collected all the volumes of
church history and legend she could find and concocted an ambitious
work entitled *The Lives of the Black Letter Saints*. This she submitted
to "Macmillans," who passed it on to a person who was preparing a
series of church books for children. But no offer of publication came
forth. Later, however, she had an offer from a "Church brotherhood"
to print the book if she would donate it as an "act of piety" to their
order. That was all she could remember of the fate of the book. It was
never published, and apparently the brothers even failed to return the
manuscript to its owner.

But Annie was luckier with her secular fiction. *The Family Herald: A
Domestic Magazine of Useful Information and Amusement* described
itself further on its cover: "Select Reading for Leisure Moments. Interesting to All—Offensive to None. Facts and Philosophy for Gentlemen.
Hints and Entertainments for Ladies. Questions and Diversions for
Youth. Recreation and Harmless Pastime for All." Price: 1*d*. It was the
perfect medium for Annie's green genius. She fashioned a story called

"Sunshine and Shade. A Tale Founded on Fact," and sent it off with a prayer. She apparently knew the taste of the editor, for some weeks later she received a letter of acceptance and a check for thirty shillings. Never from any of her voluminous, almost uncountable, and quite profitable later writings did she get so much pleasure as from that tiny check. Almost automatically she fell on her knees and thanked God for sending it. In the back of her mind was a vision of "earning heaps of golden guineas and becoming quite a support of the household." Her altruistic enthusiasm, however, was promptly crushed when her husband, not waiting to hear her intentions, calmly appropriated the check, informing her that by English law any money earned by a wife belonged to her husband (she herself preferred to call him her "owner"). That was perhaps why, when the story was printed on May 2, 1868, five months after her marriage, she signed it "A. W." rather than "A. B." She still wanted to think of herself as "Annie Wood."

Her title, "Sunshine and Shade," had perhaps been suggested by an earlier story, "The Shadows and the Sunshine," which had appeared in the magazine on July 6, 1867. But Annie's title, like much of her story, was also autobiographical. The shade had fallen on "Sunshine Annie's" life, but she still hoped that the clouds might somehow dissolve. In her story Herbert and Evelyn Merton experienced an idyllic courtship and a perfect wedding. The first two months of their marriage passed like a "dream of joy." There was no flaw in their bliss; Herbert idolized Evelyn, and she not only loved but reverenced him. Herbert and Evelyn were not like Frank and Annie. (One suspects that Annie may have begun her story in the days of her engagement, before her illusions were shattered.)

But the sun cannot always shine. Evelyn, like Annie, was a devoted horsewoman. One day as she and her husband were out riding, she was seriously injured in a fall. When the young bride learned that she could never walk again, she did not wish to go on living. But from an old friend of her husband she gained the courage and wisdom she needed to bear and profit by her misfortune. She began to think of those who were less fortunate than herself and filled her house with other incurables. For thirty years, in her wheel chair, Evelyn Merton ministered to the suffering poor, and when she "was called to her rest, she could look back at a life spent in the blessing of others, and could see that from an accident, which, as she despairingly thought, made her useless and a burden, dated her real life of faithful work, and living service to her fellow-creatures." Insipid and platitudinous as the story was, it was strangely prophetic of its author's coming career.

Unfortunately, no magazine other than the *Family Herald* saw any talent in the new author. According to her statement, she received several more pounds for her contributions (which were paid for on acceptance, so that she did not have to wait for their appearance to bring a little income into the family exchequer), but none of them seems recoverable, at least under any recognizable initials or pseudonyms. Perhaps traces of her appear, however, on the weekly "To Correspondents" page, to which contributors as well as readers were accustomed to write. During the middle of 1869, for instance, the editor answered at least three questions that would fit Annie's situation all too well. On March 8 came the following piece of advice: "ANNIE W. appears to be so good a wife that we are sorry that we cannot help her to 'copying.' She must try something else. Copying requires a legal, not a lady's hand; it is very precarious, can only be done in offices, and is now seldom wanted to such an extent as to call in any extra aid. Could not ANNIE set up a sewing machine, and help neighbors with it?" Annie was balked again on June 1: "ANNIE (not up to publication standard; we wish all our correspondents were of your opinion; not bad, but you may improve it with practice)." Finally, on August 1 a notice came, perhaps in reference to her black-letter saints, since a previous answer had identified a Roman Catholic saint for an Annie: "A. W. (no such work has been published, nor do we consider it necessary)."

This rebuff ended the correspondence, which told nothing of the novel that Annie had written, encouraged by her little success. This novel, also lost, must have sprung from the other side of her character—the one stimulated by her friendship with the radical Roberts—for the editor of the *Family Herald* returned it to her with the kindly suggestion that it was "too political" for his pages but with the further suggestion that if she would write another of "purely domestic interest," it would probably be accepted. By this time, however, matters of "purely domestic interest" were the last things Annie wanted to think of. She never wrote the novel.

In 1870 Frank Besant relented sufficiently to publish his wife's four-year-old article, "Notes on Fasting, by a Layman," but on the outside of his copy of her supplementary paper on "Fasting Communion" he noted: "I would not publish this, thinking that she ought to be satisfied with publishing of the preceding pamphlet."[3] Of this evidence of paternal blindness and egotism Frank Besant's son later exclaimed: "Satisfied indeed! As if any author could feel satisfied with the publication of his first immature production."

[3] A. D. Besant, *Pedigree,* pp. 198–99.

5

Chloroform and Crisis

On January 16, 1869, a little over a year after his marriage, the Rev. Frank Besant made the following entry in his diary: "2 a.m. went for Dr. W. 9:10 a.m. child born. 10 a.m. Dr. W. left." After the appropriate interval, according to Anglican usage, he recorded in his "Register of Services" for February 28: "St. Philip & St. James, Chelt. During afternoon service Baptism of Arthur Digby Besant and 2 other infants. No fee."[1]

Frank's generosity in performing this community baptism gratis hardly betokened any new tenderness to his wife. In fact, she found much more understanding and sympathy in her physician, Dr. Lauriston Winterbotham, who was "as good as he was clever, and . . . had the merits of discretion and silence." Later, when she needed his evidence, he was at hand to give it.

Annie's pregnancy had not been a happy or comfortable one. She had been ill for some months before her confinement and had therefore almost given up her studying and writing. On the other hand, the birth of "his small majesty," as she archly referred to the young Digby (so the family preferred to call him), brought a new interest and pleasure into her life. Indeed, the child almost healed for her the pain of the temporary loss of her mother's presence. Since her husband could not afford a nurse, she had to look after the child herself and found that her "energy in reading became less feverish when it was done by the side of the baby's cradle." Apparently, too, she now was able to look more tolerantly on the preoccupation of her female associates with their own maternal responsibilities.

Annie had only a year and a half to adjust herself to this new relation-

[1] A. D. Besant, *Pedigree*, p. 202.

ship. She had not recovered her own health before, on August 28, 1870, her daughter Mabel was born, "somewhat prematurely in consequence of a shock." This "shock," it came out later, was presumably from a blow which her husband, who had refused to listen to her pleas on the necessity of limiting their family, had struck her on the shoulder, while simultaneously suggesting that she leave him and go back home.[2] As a matter of fact, however, since this incident had actually occurred in February or March—as Annie herself was to allege in an official court document—its effects would seem to have been considerably delayed so far as Mabel was concerned.

Whereas Digby was "a bright, healthy little fellow," Mabel was "delicate from birth, suffering from her mother's unhappiness." Not only was Annie's recovery from her accouchement slow and tedious, but in the spring of 1871 both infants came down with whooping cough. Mabel's developed into bronchitis, followed by congestion of the lungs, and for weeks she lay "in hourly peril of death." A screen was arranged like a tent around the fireplace and kept full of steam to aid the baby's struggling breathing, and inside this tent Annie sat, "day and night, all through those weary weeks, the tortured baby on my knees." So critical was the situation that Dr. Winterbotham finally declared that recovery was impossible. The administration of even a drop or two of milk would bring about a paroxysm of coughing. One morning the baby's body suddenly swelled up as a result of the perforation of one of her lungs, and Annie hysterically summoned the doctor. Mabel's wracking coughs convinced him she could not live through the day, so he put a drop of chloroform on his handkerchief and held it near her face to ease her suffering. Her convulsions gradually quieted, but he went away saying he feared he would never see her alive again.

He was wrong. His accidental inspiration proved a means of cure, for he left the bottle of chloroform, and Annie continued to use it whenever a new paroxysm started. After a long period of hopeless despair on the mother's part, the lung healed and Mabel recovered, though she had to be tended with the greatest care for years; in fact, Annie believed that the epileptic fits which developed some time later were the result of this early weakening of her daughter's physique.

Then it was Annie's turn. She collapsed and lay unmoving in her bed for a week. The physical strain and the anguish of her thoughts had been too great for her. All through the baby's illness she had been undergoing a spiritual crisis of far-reaching consequences. Both these overtaxations, moreover, had been intensified by some totally unexpected and depressing news from her mother.

[2] For this and similar succeeding events, see documents in the Public Record Office, High Court of Justice, Chancery Division, Master of the Rolls, August–October, 1878; also reprinted in the *National Reformer*, April 6, 1879.

Mrs. Wood was suddenly found to be bankrupt. Her lawyer, in which she had had the utmost confidence and with whom for years she had placed all her money for the payment of her large accounts, was discovered by his partners to have been systematically appropriating his clients' money for his own use. None of her liabilities had been paid, and she was seriously involved in debt. Of course, she immediately sold all she had, including the property at St. Leonard's, and used the proceeds, so far as they would go, to pay the debts she thought had been discharged long ago. But the "competence" she had counted on for her old age had vanished.

Fortunately, by this time Henry had graduated from Clare College, Cambridge, in 1868, with a second class in the Classical Tripos. In the same year, cousin William Page Wood, whose legal and governmental career had been spectacular, had been made lord chancellor of England and simultaneously created Baron Hatherley of Hatherley. On leaving the university, Harry, through the influence of this useful relative, had obtained a minor job at the Patent Office, but it brought in little pay. Shortly afterward the Lord Chancellor had got for the young man the additional post of undersecretary to the Society of Arts, which was to lead later to the editorship of the *Society of Arts Journal* and other similar offices.

It was obvious that the penniless Mrs. Wood must move in with her son. This sense of dependence, however, was intolerable to her, though she tried to conceal it from everyone but Annie. She did not want to be a drain on her son while he was just getting his start; nor could she forget that she was still in debt and could probably never pay it off. So, all day long, while Harry was at his office, Mrs. Wood would sit through the bitter winter weather without a fire, lighting it just before his return. Often she would leave the house at noon, saying she was going out to lunch, but instead of eating would walk about London until late in the afternoon to save the expense of a meal. The winter of 1870–71 was soon to lead to her death.

Only once was Annie able to help her proud mother. On a short visit to London, finding Mrs. Wood looking ill, she coaxed from her the confession that she never had a moment free from the pain of an aching back. Luckily, Annie had just received a letter with a draft for two guineas from her generous *Family Herald* editor. Knowing that her mother would take no money directly and disregarding the question of her husband's legal right to the check, she marched out and spent one pound fifteen shillings for a cushion chair. Silencing Mrs. Wood's protests by informing her that she had earned the money herself, Annie basked warmly in her mother's pleasure and her repeated exclamation during the evening: "Oh, the rest!"

All the preceding worries and agonies culminated now in a new and profound crisis in Annie's life. As she had sat day after day in the improvised steam tent caring for her baby, her mind had become more and more active. What kind of world could this really be, she wondered, in which a presumably benevolent and merciful God could allow her "helpless, sinless babe" to be "tortured for weeks and left frail and suffering"? She had also been visiting the poor and had marked the patient misery in their lives. She was dazed and stunned by the apparently purposeless cruelty and injustice of it all. She remembered her previous but quickly dismissed qualms growing from her "disharmony" of the gospels. She began to resent, to rebel. Her earlier faith in Christ's personal interest in her and in all mankind intensified her new bitterness. Her unhappiness with her clergyman-husband did not help matters. So, as she summed it up, "All the hitherto dormant and unsuspected strength of my nature rose up in rebellion; I did not yet dream of denial, but I would no longer kneel."

On April 20, 1871, while Mabel was at the height of her illness, Frank Besant, apparently recognizing his own inadequacy to deal with the situation, brought home a friend—another clergyman, whom Annie identified only as "Mr. W—— D——." Since he held wider and more liberal views of Christianity than most of his colleagues, she thought it best to suppress his full name for fear she would injure him.[3] W—— D—— said little that first day. But the next day Annie received a kind letter from him, beginning, "I am painfully conscious that I gave you but little help in your trouble yesterday," and going on to try to reconcile her to her sufferings. His arguments concerning the "mystery of pain" and the inscrutability of God's purposes were completely orthodox, but his sympathy was manifest and she needed sympathy. He seemed to have looked inside her heart and read her questioning doubts. But even his nobility of character could not still the fierce storm that was gathering inside her.

During the summer Annie became a friend of Mr. D——'s wife. They too had a child—a boy only a few months old—who was dangerously ill. Since Annie's skill and devotion as a nurse had been sung all over Cheltenham by Dr. Winterbotham, Mrs. D—— often felt that she could trust her child to her new friend while she herself "snatched a night's sorely needed rest." It was the kindness of people like these which kept some of Annie's faith in humanity alive.

[3] "Mr. W—— D——" is not identifiable. Although he might well have been the vicar or curate of the parish or neighboring church, his name does not appear in *The Parish Church of St. Mary Cheltenham with a Short Account of the Church of St. Matthew* (Gloucester, *ca.* 1950), and the present rector, the Rev. Canon J. B. Goodliffe, can add no information. Mr. H. G. Fletcher, curator of the Cheltenham Public Library, told me that the Rev. W. Dobson was second headmaster of Cheltenham College from 1845 to 1859 and after his retirement was active on the Board of Directors for some time. Such a man, however, would seem to have been far too old to be the Besants' friend. Nor does the Cheltenham College Register list anyone with his initials during a later period.

Nevertheless, it was during July or August of this same summer that she reached the emotional nadir of her life. Her quarrels with her husband had increased in violence, and his retaliation had several times taken physical form. Once, she later alleged, as they were walking through a field he seized her by the arm, dragged her along, and almost threw her over a stile. Again, about the same time, the conjugal recriminations and Annie's insubordination reached such a height that Frank, in a fit of quite uncanonical anger, pushed his young wife "violently out of bed so as she fell upon the floor and was much bruised."

One summer night after one of these fierce quarrels Frank was away and Annie was alone, "outraged, desperate." Was there no door of escape? She was standing by the drawing-room window, staring hopelessly into the evening sky. Suddenly she recalled the bottle of the baby's chloroform that she had locked away upstairs. Immediately she ran up to her room, brought the bottle downstairs, uncorked it, and was raising it to her lips when she heard a voice speaking clearly and softly: "O coward, coward, who used to dream of martyrdom, and cannot bear a few short years of pain." Overcome with shame, she flung the bottle far among the shrubs in the garden below and then fainted. Only once again during her long and turbulent career did she ever think of suicide as a way out, but that time also she put the thought aside as unworthy of a "strong soul."[4]

This rejection of the "easy way out" did not mean the end of Annie's spiritual struggles. She raised all her skeptical questions and problems with Mr. D——, who encouraged her confidences and gave his own answers without being horrified or "sanctimoniously rebukeful" as her husband would have been. In the early autumn, however, he and his family left Cheltenham, for reasons undisclosed, but Mrs. Besant continued to correspond with him and preserved some of his letters. In November, for instance, after she had been reading John M'Leod Campbell's "On the Atonement," he wrote her a long, closely reasoned argument about the goodness and perfection of God. He referred with admiration to the works of humanistic liberals and Broad Churchmen such as John Stuart Mill and J. F. D. Maurice in controverting the narrower theology of Dean Henry L. Mansel of St. Paul's on the nature of revelation and of God's goodness and justice.

But Mr. D——'s kind of casuistry did not persuade Annie out of her depression. Finally her mental anguish broke her health completely, and once more she "lay for weeks helpless and prostrate, in raging and

---

[4] It is interesting to note that it was only when Mrs. Besant revised her *Autobiographical Sketches* and turned it into her *Autobiography* that she remembered this oral admonition. Many years later, C. Jinarajadasa, in *The Annie Besant Centenary Book* (Adyar, India, 1947), p. 11, explained this mysterious voice as that of her Master, who was already watching over her to prepare her for her great task.

unceasing head-pain, unable to bear the light, . . . indifferent to everything." Dr. Winterbotham tried everything to assuage the pain—from ice to opium (which only drove her "mad"); but the attack had to wear itself out. Then, as soon as he dared do so, he tried to divert her mentally by bringing her books on anatomy, physiology, and science and taking as much time from his busy practice as he could to discuss them with her. Gradually, by these intelligent methods he brought her back to comparative health, while her uncomprehending husband stood on the side lines, fretting and fuming, unable to understand how any true woman could let such concerns interfere with her duty of looking after the comfort of her husband and children.

When this physical crisis was over, Annie determined on her future course of action. It was not calculated to mollify her husband. She decided to take every Christian dogma as taught in the churches and analyze and examine it for its demonstrable truth. Never again would she get up in church and say "I believe" what she had not proved first. The four main problems she started with were the eternity of punishment after death, the meaning of goodness and love as applied to a God who had created this world with all its sin and misery, the nature of the atonement of Christ and his vicarious suffering for man, and the meaning of "inspiration" as applied to the Bible. She was not yet ready, as she recognized later, to attack the more profound and basic problems of religion, such as the deity of Christ, the very existence of God, and the immortality of the soul. These others were enough to begin with, and they gave her plenty of occupation for some time.

As she plunged deeper and deeper into these studies, comparing the works of the orthodox theologians on the one side with those of the Broad Church and even "heretical" writers on the other, the domestic situation remained temporarily in a sort of armed truce. The despondent couple seemed caught in a mesh from which nothing provided escape. Their material circumstances had not improved, and there were two children to feed and dress. Probably, too, the social circle in the little town had started gossiping. Perhaps, thought Annie, a change of scene and in the nature of Frank's work would help.

Whenever any of the Woods were in trouble they turned naturally, almost unconsciously, to the other and more successful branch of the family, and Annie Wood Besant was in trouble. In the early autumn of 1871 she resolved to appeal once more to the great and pious Lord Hatherley, who was widely known as "the Christian statesman."[5] He

[5] For the life and character of Baron Hatherley, see Rev. Charles Bullock, "Lord Hatherley: The Christian Statesman," in *The Crown of the Road: Leaves from Consecrated Lives* (London, 1885), pp. 191–224; Rev. Prebendary Stephens, *Memoir of Lord Hatherley;* Edward Foss, *Judges of England* (London, 1848–64); and *Biographia Juridica* (London, 1871).

might give her husband one of the crown-livings within his control, where Mr. Besant could devote himself entirely to parish work. But it seems extremely unlikely that she was as candid with the Lord Chancellor as the highest principles would demand.

Less than a year before his retirement in 1872 Lord Hatherley offered the Besants their choice between two livings—one in Northumberland near Alnwick Castle, the other in the village of Sibsey in southern Lincolnshire. They weighed the advantages of the two and chose Sibsey, which had an income of about £410 per annum as well as various agricultural assets. The Besants consequently owed the Baron much; but Frank's constant recollection that he was indebted to his wife for this good fortune rankled. In February, 1872, she swore later, he once clenched his fist, shook it in her face, and swore that if she ever mentioned that she had obtained the living for him, he would kill her. This seems to be rather strong language from a vicar, but Annie's memory was always remarkably tenacious. As for Lord Hatherley, he must have been somewhat upset when, not long after his benefaction, all England began to hear his young cousin's new views on religion and the Bible. By the time of his death in 1881 he undoubtedly wished she had never been born.

The vicar-designate assumed his parochial duties at St. Margaret's, Sibsey, in October, 1871, though his appointment was not fully ratified till the end of December.[6] There were many formalities to be complied with in the induction of a new vicar, and Frank loved such ceremonies. On Sunday, December 31, he "read himself in" at morning service by reciting the Articles of Religion and afterward "rang himself in" by tolling the church bell. Early in January he officially "went into residence" in the vicarage, then returned to Cheltenham for a couple of months, and finally brought his family back with him to Sibsey at the end of March. His statistical record of his first year's work in his new parish listed twenty-eight funerals, twenty-nine baptisms, twenty-two churchings of women, ten marriages, eighty-three sermons, one hundred readings of prayers—and only ten Holy Communions.

The new surroundings proved a delight to the children, who had no inkling of their parents' squabbles. Young Arthur Digby, now a little over three, was old enough so that he later had vivid recollections of the place. The village itself was scattered over a considerable amount of ground, but this spread only provided more opportunity for fascinating rambles. The vicarage was set among large and beautiful gardens, a paddock, and green outlying fields. The main sitting rooms faced south, and their French windows opened on a broad stone terrace edged with a brilliant, narrow flower bed. The stately lawn was fringed with trees,

[6] A. D. Besant, *Pedigree,* pp. 205 ff.; *Sketches,* pp. 55–60; and *Autobiography,* p. 198.

bushes, and flowers, set in formal beds and cut with winding paths. There were ivy shelters at two of the corners and even a "plantation" or vista of carefully arranged trees. The fruit garden was thick with strawberries, raspberries, gooseberries, currants, nectarines, apricots, peaches, pears, and apples. In the great kitchen garden there were potatoes, asparagus, and the other necessary vegetables. Besides these attractions there were stables and a carriage house, a chicken-run, pigsties, and a woodshed. Annie must have felt she was back in Harrow again in her girlhood. Digby reflected later that the maintenance of this imposing estate must have been a constant nightmare to any vicar. He could recoup some of his outlay by selling the produce of his gardens, but his main stipend was derived from the rent of his glebe farm, which, even when agricultural rents were at their highest, was quite modest.

The church itself was one of the most beautiful in the celebrated Fen Country. Reputedly built first in 1087, much of it was Norman work, supplemented later in perpendicular. It had a splendid peal of bells, and the ringers were famous all around the countryside. The children loved to climb up the dark spiral staircase to the massive tower, to play among the bells in the ringing chamber, and to examine all the ancient registers and churchwardens' accounts.

Frank Besant's work was not very onerous. The village itself had perhaps eight hundred inhabitants, mostly farmers and laborers, with a sprinkling of shopkeepers. Not much in the way of services was required of the vicar, since weekday services were practically unknown and parochial activities were kept as light as possible. The new rector quickly fitted into his routine. He soon found a mass of documents and registers, going back to 1568, in the old parish chest in the vestry. He translated the old Latin, indexed and docketed the records, and learned paleography. He was as meticulous and methodical as ever, and this work occupied his leisure time for the rest of his life. He was happy, so long as he did not have to think about his wife.

Annie, of course, was not so happy. The Sibsey people were even less interesting than those at Cheltenham. As she described them, the "only 'society' was that of the neighboring clergy, Tory and prim to an appalling degree." She derived some solace from W—— D——'s continuing letters, she did some practical parish work, and she learned some of the problems of agriculture. But these were not enough for her feverishly restless mind. Naturally, then, she turned once more to her theological studies, for she now had more time than ever for them. She found new stimulation, through agreement and disagreement, in all the advanced thinkers of her agitated century. She read Matthew Arnold; Frederick William Robertson, who had officiated in Cheltenham in the forties and who had reacted even more violently than Annie against its deadening evangelicalism; Stopford Brooke, the literary cleric who had already published the life and letters of Robertson and who was to become a brilliant independent Unitarian preacher; Arthur P. Stanley, Oxford teacher, dean of Westminster, and probably the leading liberal theologian of the day; William R. Greg, businessman turned theological, political, and economic polemicist; Henry P. Liddon, canon of St. Paul's, whose Bampton Lectures on the divinity of Christ had furnished a rallying point for many against the growing skepticism of the day; and many others mentioned to her by Mr. D——. She found herself almost as little satisfied with the Broad Church and latitudinarian arguments as with the orthodox dogmas. The former were very skilful in their compromises and shadings of meanings, but they nevertheless evaded the true issues of God's role in a world of misery and sin. She found greater affinity with theists like Grey and agnostics like Arnold. All, however, made her attendance at church services more difficult, in fact "a weekly torture," but still she kept her doubts bottled up, feeling she had no right to shake the faith of others while she was yet hoping to have her own difficulties resolved.

Seeking relief from her mental torments through another channel, Annie turned to the problems of the agricultural laborer. A new movement, led by Joseph Arch, the self-educated son of a Warwickshire workman, had been started that year and was beginning to be discussed in the Fens.[7] But the farmers themselves were bitterly opposed to Arch's new National Agricultural Laborers' Union and refused to hire any Union man. Annie, while visiting a pitiful one-room cottage on one of her philanthropic tours, had witnessed a horrible scene resulting from the stiff-necked harshness of the farmers toward an "agitator." The occupant of the cottage, a young married man with two small children, had been "sinful" enough to go to a Union meeting and brave enough to talk about it when he came home. Consequently, no farmer in the neighborhood would give him work. He tramped about vainly for some time, finally gave up hope, and took to drink. Annie found his wife starving and ill, a fever-stricken child in her arms, and the second child lying dead on the only bed. Since there was no other place to put the body till the coffin came, that night the driven husband, his sick wife and child, and the dead child all lay in the same bed.

Annie wondered why these tenant farmers could not see that their resentment should have been turned against their absentee landlords rather than against their hired men. The farmers were too shortsighted to realize that they should pay less rent to the landlord who victimized them and higher wages to the men who tilled their fields and brought

[7] For Arch's own stirring and vivid story of the beginning of his political career, see Joseph Arch, *The Story of His Life Told by Himself and Edited with a Preface by the Countess of Warwick* (London, 1898), pp. 65 ff.

in their harvests. Thus Annie's political and economic education proceeded along with her theological re-education.

Whenever she could no longer endure her husband's treatment, Annie took the train down to London to seek her mother's comfort. In June, during a new altercation, Frank took her by the shoulders and "shook her violently, striking her with his knee with violence several times and thus causing her to leave his house and to return to her mother's house." Moreover, she asserted, he kept a loaded gun in his study and several times threatened to shoot her. Whether she returned to Sibsey before the end of the summer is not clear, but it was in early autumn that a chance meeting she attended in London brought new hope into her life.

II. *Second Life:* THE ATHEIST MOTHER

1

The Path to Atheism

One Sunday morning in the late summer or early autumn of 1872 Annie, being in London with her mother and searching for some new influence to help calm the chaos in her mind, wandered into St. George's Hall, Langham Place. One of the newest Dissenters in the Established Church, the Rev. Charles Voysey, had recently installed himself there.[1]

On July 31, 1871, Voysey had delivered his farewell address to his parishioners in the little Yorkshire village of Healaugh, only fifty or so miles from Sibsey; for he had been tried for heresy and deprived of his living because of his unorthodox views, freely expressed in both his sermons and his writings.[2] For several years Voysey had been in the process of discovering that he was really a theist rather than an Anglican Christian in his beliefs; that is, he believed in the existence and unity of a God who is both immanent and transcendent in the world and with whom there is the possibility of a personal relationship, but he no longer believed in many of the doctrines and dogmas of the modern church. In fact, he had boldly asserted that he would rather be a righteous atheist than a person concerned mainly with his orthodoxy or lack of it. On the other hand, he had refused to resign from his living, even though many people, both Churchmen and Dissenters, felt that no one whose opinions differed so widely from those held by the church had any right to remain within the church. So Mr. Voysey, found guilty by an

[1] Unless otherwise specified, the present chapter is based on the *Autobiography* and the *Sketches.*

[2] For Voysey, see Mrs. Besant's *Autobiography*, pp. 203–6; Gertrude Marvin Williams, *The Passionate Pilgrim*, pp. 34–35; Mary Elizabeth Burtis, *Moncure Conway* (New Brunswick, N.J., 1952), pp. 142–43; list of Voysey's works in British Museum Catalogue; *Dictionary of National Biography.*

ecclesiastical court and denied his appeal to the Privy Council, had been expelled from his vicarage. With a wife, eight children, and an aged mother to support, Voysey had set up an independent theistic meeting-house in London. Since he was an eloquent speaker and had an attractive personality, the liberals, the halfway skeptics, the anchorless, and the curiosity seekers flocked to St. George's Hall and generally found what they wanted there. For some, Voysey's struggle provoked more discussion than the just concluded Franco-Prussian War.

That first Sunday Annie listened to the sermon with delight and bought some tracts in the anteroom afterward. She discovered that there were others who had faced problems like hers and had not been beaten by them. The next Sunday, after the service, she joined the stream of listeners who were filing past Mr. and Mrs. Voysey in the vestibule and thanking him for the help his words had given them. Annie did the same, for her mind was consoled by Voysey's public assurances that God is "loving unto every man" and that His "tender mercy" prevails "over *all* His works." Her reappearance on the third Sunday in a row and her lengthy conversation with the Voyseys brought her a cordial invitation from Mrs. Voysey to visit them in their new home in Dulwich. Here their discussions were continued, and Mrs. Besant found their compromising brand of religion much to her liking. They gave her some new suggestions for her reading, including the *Discourse on Religion* by Theodore Parker, whose views had proved too advanced even for most of his American Unitarian brethren; the works of Francis Newman, younger brother of Cardinal John Henry Newman, who had passed from an early Calvinism into theism; and the writings of Miss Frances Power Cobbe, English editor of Parker's works, occasional Unitarian preacher, social reformer, and advocate of woman's suffrage. Under these agencies the anguish of Annie's tension temporarily relaxed, and "the nightmare of an Almighty Evil" taking the place of an Almighty Good disappeared.

It was probably about this time that she wrote one of her few extant poems, which did not appear in print until a great many years later.[3] Expressing her skepticism about God's direct revelation of Himself to man, she commenced:

> Never yet has been broken
> The silence eternal;
> Never yet has been spoken
> In accents supernal
> God's thought of Himself.

[3] See the *Theosophist,* XXXIX (November, 1917), 124, in which Mrs. Besant writes: "Mr. Jinarajadasa has unearthed the following old poem of mine. . . . It must have been written in 1873." But 1872 seems more likely. In October, 1932, however, this poem, together with an inferior one entitled "Prayer," was reprinted and given the still more improbable date of 1875.

Nevertheless, the following four stanzas pointed out, from the search of the "truth-seekers" through the ages has ever evolved "Fresh truth about God." And she could still assert, in the final stanza:

Human speech has not broken
The stillness supernal,
Yet there ever is spoken,
Through silence eternal,
With growing distinctness
God's thought of Himself.

Thus her central belief in the existence of God had not as yet been touched, and "all the dark spots that had sullied it" had been wiped away. But an assumption of only slightly less importance had been challenged—the doctrine of the divinity of Christ. She had read Ernest Renan's *La vie de Jésus* without caring much for it; David Strauss's *Leben Jesu* was to come later. She was already thoroughly familiar with the emphasis put by the Broad Churchmen on "the humanity of Christ at the expense of His Deity." And in her studies of oriental creeds, particularly Mohammedanism, Buddhism, and Hinduism, she had met over and over again the idea of "Avatâras," which showed her that the belief in a god's incarnating himself in man was common in all ancient religions. But she hesitated to break with the beauty and meaning of the old conception; she feared the results of such a rejection on the great traditions of music, painting, and literature. Most of all, however, she realized that if she denied the divinity of Christ, she must abandon Christianity itself as a creed. She was still a clergyman's wife, but she could not bear to be a hypocrite. If she gave up the basic doctrine, she must give up the church which was built on it.

The decision did not take long: "The struggle was keen but short." After she had thoroughly reviewed the evidence for and against the deity of Christ, she realized that she must throw that doctrine away with the others.

She knew she was no longer a Christian in heart and mind, but she remembered she was still a Christian on the church roll and it would be a difficult and unhappy task to have her name removed. So, before facing her husband and her bishop, she resolved to give the church one final chance. She had already had a brief correspondence on some of her problems with the great Dr. Pusey at Oxford, the most influential member of the Church of England for over a quarter of a century. But she had got only the old, worn-out answers along the lines of Liddon's Bampton Lectures. These three or four letters were later stolen from her desk—by whom, she does not say, except by domestic implication.[4]

In one of these letters Dr. Pusey had rather perfunctorily invited her

[4] This remark occurs only in the *Sketches*, p. 67.

47

to come to Oxford to see him. She accepted his invitation. Except for Lord Hatherley, he was the greatest man she had yet met. But Annie Besant was never one to be overawed by the presence of greatness. On being ushered into Pusey's study, she found him to be "a short, stout gentleman, dressed in a cassock, looking like a comfortable monk." His keen eyes, however, looked straight into hers, and his fine, impressive head announced the force and subtlety of his character.

Dr. Pusey was a "learned doctor," but he was not a good psychologist. He immediately took the wrong line of treatment. Although he perceived she was anxious, shy, and nervous, he did not perceive her inquisitive mind and iron determination. Thus he treated her "as a penitent going to confession and seeking the advice of a director." He absolutely refused to discuss the question of the divinity of Jesus. To him there was no question. "You are speaking of your Judge," he reminded her sternly when she pressed her problem. "You are blaspheming. The very thought is a terrible sin." When she asked if he would recommend some books to throw light on the subject, his only answer was, "No, no; you have read too much already. You must pray; you must pray." To her plea that she could not believe without proof, he quoted to her, "Blessed are they that have not seen and yet have believed." He reproached her with impatience and lack of discipline and urged only her submission to the authority of the Church. "It is not your duty to ascertain the truth," he reiterated. "It is your duty to accept and believe the truth as laid down by the Church. At your peril you reject it." When, in order to prove to him the sincerity of her search, she reminded him that she had everything to gain by following his directions and everything to lose by going her own way, he informed her that she would indeed be lost for eternity. And when she persisted in maintaining that she must find out for herself what was true, without accepting the authority of others, he accused her of intellectual pride and ended by telling her, "You have no right to make terms with God."

It was not pride that Annie felt at that moment, but only despair because of his incomprehension and his dogmatism. She sighed, rose, thanked him for his time and courtesy, and said she must go home to face her difficulties, leave the church openly, and take the consequences. For the first time in the interview, Dr. Pusey's serenity was ruffled. "I forbid you to speak of your disbelief," he cried. "I forbid you to lead into your own lost state the souls for whom Christ died."

With this command ringing in her ears, Mrs. Besant made her way back to the railway station. She recognized that she had been facing the essence of the "spirit of priestcraft, that could be tender and pitiful to the sinner, repentant, humble, submissive; but that was iron to the doubter, the heretic." Here was the reincarnation of the Inquisitors of the Middle Ages, perfectly conscientious according to their own light, perfectly rigid—and perfectly merciless.

Mrs. Besant's description and interpretation of her interview with Dr. Pusey were probably true, factually speaking. But the question may be properly raised[5] whether she had not really acted in favor of her own preconceived decision by choosing to consult the acknowledged leader of the High Church party, whose views could have been predicted with absolute certainty, instead of going to one of the equally well-known liberals. If she had told the whole truth in her *Autobiography*, she would probably have had to confess to a secret feeling of happy relief as she rode back to London and thought over her situation. At any rate, she can certainly be believed when she asseverated that she "went out into the darkness alone"—not because Protestant religion was too good for her, but because it was not good enough. It was too meager, too earthly, "too calculating in its accommodations to social conventionalities." As she summed up the situation: "The Roman Catholic Church, had it captured me, as it nearly did, would have sent me on some mission of danger and sacrifice and utilised me as a martyr; the Church established by law transformed me into an unbeliever and an antagonist."

Annie now turned with a lighter conscience to her more stimulating circle of new friends. During this same autumn the Voyseys introduced her to the Thomas Scotts, who at their beautiful home in Upper Norwood, a suburb just south of London, had maintained for years "a veritable heretical salon," shunned and denounced by the godly. Thomas Scott by this time was an old man, but his enfeebled frame still revealed the magnificent physique he had once had. Annie was immediately impressed by his "splendid lion-like head," his beautiful white hair, and his hawk-like eyes "gleaming from under shaggy eyebrows."[6] Well-born and wealthy, he had spent a varied and adventurous youth. Brought up in France as a Roman Catholic and having served briefly as a page in the court of Charles X, he had later lived and hunted for a time with Indians in North America. Finally, he traveled over most of the world and as a result completely readjusted his religious views. He married a "sweet, strong, gentle, noble woman, worthy of her husband," but young enough to have been his daughter, and at the age of about fifty settled down in Upper Norwood to propagate his views as a freethinker. For many years before Mrs. Besant met him he had issued a series of monthly pamphlets at his own expense—all of a skeptical nature, though varying in their shades of thought, since he believed in giving many viewpoints a hear-

[5] It is brought up by Williams in *The Passionate Pilgrim*, pp. 36–37.

[6] For another description of Scott, see Williams, *The Passionate Pilgrim*, p. 35; Geoffrey West, *Annie Besant* (London and New York, 1928), p. 27; Theodore Besterman, *Mrs. Annie Besant*, p. 48; Burtis, p. 143; *Dictionary of National Biography;* and British Museum Catalogue.

ing. As Annie put it, ". . . his writers might say what they liked, but they must have something to say, and must say it in good English," for Scott ruled that his pamphlets must be well written, polished, and cultured.

All the liberal thinkers of England knew Scott and he knew them. He conducted an enormous correspondence—from prime ministers downward. People of all shades of opinion congregated at his house—from the controversial Bishop Colenso to the mystical and Hermetic humanitarian Edward Maitland, from the Christian Socialist and Co-operativist E. Vansittart Neale to George Eliot's friends, Charles Bray and Sara Hennell. Literally hundreds of others—lapsing clerics and laymen, doubting scholars and thinkers—all came to this one headquarters, where the only requirement for entree was the desire to pursue truth and freedom wherever they might lead. The Christian Evidence Society was one of their main objects of pursuit—or rather of attack.

The twenty-five-year-old Mrs. Besant, whose rapidly developing physical beauty helped to gain an audience for her ideas, and the sixty-four-year-old Thomas Scott quickly contracted a strong, platonic affection for one another. Mr. Scott, in fact, was so impressed by Annie's views and her previous contributions to literature that he suggested she write a pamphlet for his series. She naturally agreed. The unavoidable subject was "On the Deity of Jesus of Nazareth." It was agreed also that this and any later essays were to be signed simply as "By the Wife of a Beneficed Clergyman," since delicacy decreed that she not use her husband's name in such a connection. On the other hand, it seems equally obvious that even this vague identification could have been omitted without affecting the validity of the ideas involved; thus her enemies might charge her with using it largely for sensational publicity purposes.

But first Mrs. Besant must go back to Sibsey to face her husband. At the beginning she effected a compromise with him. She agreed to attend the services which were "directed to God Himself," but not to participate in the Holy Communion, which posited the atoning sacrifice of Jesus as Deity. When the next "Sacrament Sunday" arrived (almost no churches celebrated the Eucharist more than once a month at this time), she rose as quietly as possible just before the Communion began and left the church. Every eye in the congregation sought her out and followed her progress. She trembled all over and felt deadly sick, but managed to make her exit. Since she had done nothing so far to draw public attention to her, however, the parishioners concluded that she had suddenly been taken ill and immediately afterward overwhelmed her with solicitous calls and inquiries. Her honest and open answer that she was "unable to take part in the profession of faith required by an honest communicant" was so far beyond the reach of "the ordinary bucolic mind" that no one suspected heresy in the vicar's wife. Moreover, the villagers were growing fond of her and were grateful for her help in her favorite role of nurse when a severe epidemic of typhoid, caused by the very primitive drainage, broke out at Christmas time. She apparently enjoyed the nursing experience and frankly admitted that death always fascinated her.

To Annie's great delight, her article for Thomas Scott was printed in the spring of 1873 as one of the "Scott Series." The thesis of this twelve-page essay on Jesus was that, "however great as a man, he is not the All-Righteous, the All-Seeing, the All-Knowing God," as he has been claimed to be by others than himself. It had the subtitle, "An Enquiry into the Nature of Jesus by an Examination of the Synoptic Gospels," and carried the further explanation, "Edited and Prefaced by Rev. Charles Voysey." But the author herself remained tantalizingly anonymous.

Her pride of authorship, however, was so overwhelming that she made a tactical error.[7] As she explained it:

But unfortunately a copy sent to a relative of Mr. Besant's brought about a storm. That gentleman did not disagree with it—indeed he admitted that all educated persons must hold the views put forward—but what would Society say? What would "the county families" think if one of the clerical party was known to be a heretic? This dreadful little paper bore the inscription "By the wife of a beneficed clergyman"; what would happen if the "wife of a beneficed clergyman" were identified with Mrs. Besant of Sibsey?

Annie carefully refrained from any exact identification of this hypocritical relative of her husband's, but it could have been none other than her literary brother-in-law, Walter Besant. Five or six years before, he had returned to London from his professorship at the Royal College, Mauritius, and was now beginning to produce the critical works on the French humorists and early French poetry which later would help to establish him as one of the English Parnassians. Many years later, after he had been knighted for his mediocre achievements as poet, novelist, critic, editor, antiquarian, historian, traveler, chronicler of London, etc., Sir Walter Besant published an autobiography in which he only vaguely recognized the existence of his older but unimportant brother Frank and gave not even the slightest hint that he had ever had a sister-in-law named Annie.

Yet Annie had every reason to think that, if anyone in the family could, Walter would understand her position. In his *Autobiography* he relates how, after winning prizes in classics, mathematics, and divinity in his three short terms at King's College, London, it was his purpose to take holy orders, even though he had made no preparation therefor. But, he goes on:

Had I done so; had I realised the terrible weight of the fetters with which the average clergyman of the time went about laden—the chain of literal inspiration

[7] This episode is described only in the *Sketches*, pp. 71–72.

and verbal accuracy, the blind opposition to science, the dreary Evangelisations of the religious literature, the wrangles over points long since consigned to the limbos of old controversies, the intolerant spirit, the artificial life, the affected piety—I should have given up the thought of taking holy orders long before the decision was forced upon me.

Nevertheless, after passing his preliminary theological examinations, he was preparing to perjure himself—he was not "sound on the Atonement" —with the bishop at his ordination. He was saved by being offered the opportunity to teach on the veld of South Africa.[8]

By 1873 Walter was back in England and in hot pursuit of respectability. He had good impulses and a good heart, as shown by his later generous treatment of young Digby Besant, but he was not strong enough to back the kind of open rebellion in his sister-in-law which in his own mind he must have approved. He thus helped to crystallize his brother Frank's position.

Annie now agreed to another compromise. She told her husband that, even though she would not alter or hide her beliefs, she would give up her correspondence with the Voyseys, which, Frank felt, would be noticed in the village and cause mischievous gossip. The Voyseys themselves, apprised of the situation, co-operated sympathetically, assuring her of their cordial friendship while their mutual letters were temporarily suspended.

This arrangement, however, did not last long. Annie followed up the success of her first pamphlet with a sequel entitled "According to St. John. On the Deity of Jesus of Nazareth. Part II. A Comparison between the Fourth Gospel and the Three Synoptics." And again she signed it "By the Wife of a Beneficed Clergyman. Edited and Prefaced by Rev. Charles Voysey." In it she rejected as unauthentic "the theological and philosophical treatise which bears the name of John," charging it with being "fatally destructive of all true faith towards God," "an outrage on the sacred memory of Jesus of Nazareth," and "an insult to the Justice, the Supremacy, and the Unity of Almighty God."

Soon she went still further. Voysey's congregation at St. George's Hall needed a hymnbook which would be theistic but non-Christian. Such a collection Annie had already made, but now her manuscript was perforce lying idle. So she compromised again in the cause of the greatest good for the greatest number. When Scott suggested that she should resume her correspondence with the Voyseys in this matter, she was glad to comply. Frank could only fume privately.

In the spring of 1873 another highly significant event occurred in Annie's life. She got her first taste of speechmaking, and she continued to relish the occupation to the end of her life. She had no audience for her

---

[8] Sir Walter Besant, *Autobiography* (London and New York, 1902), pp. 74–75, 109.

first oratorical exercise, but that did not matter. The thrill that pierced her heart was enough to prove to her that she had a genius which was only latent and would soon reveal itself to the world. When she was over eighty she recalled in an interview that Walter Besant had once accused her of having a "fatal facility for speaking."[9]

One day, after she had been practicing some organ exercises all alone in the ancient Sibsey church, a whim seized her that, after hearing so many sermons by others, she herself would like to know how it felt to preach. So she shut the organ, locked the church doors, and ascended the pulpit. Peopling the rows of empty pews with imaginary upturned faces and eager eyes, she sent her voice ringing down the aisles in balanced, rhythmical sentences. Although she was a tiny woman, almost hidden behind the pulpit rail, she had a deep, rich, vibrant voice which intoxicated even herself. As she spoke with extemporaneous eloquence on the inspiration (or lack of it) of the Bible, a delightful sense of power came over her. Her voice echoed back from the stone pillars and walls, and she knew that if ever the occasion arose, the great gift of speech was hers to use in any worthy cause.

Slightly ashamed of her foolishness, however, she kept her secret to herself for many months. Meantime, she was involved in a much greater crisis, which came in the middle of the summer. Her continued absence from Communion began to occasion some puzzled gossip, and the anonymous "relative of Mr. Besant" pressed upon Frank some "highly colored views of the social and professional dangers" which would arise if his wife's heresy became public. The question of how much her husband knew of her offensive articles in advance is a moot one. In legal affidavits five years later Annie swore that she had shown him the manuscripts and that he had agreed to their appearance so long as they were unsigned. But her husband denied flatly that he had ever seen them and swore, moreover, that he had forbidden her writing them and had supposed the matter was ended, until, horrified, he had suddenly found them in print. Somebody was obviously tampering with the truth.

Once more, Annie's health broke down under the strain. Her husband's quarreling and alleged violence combined with her illness to put her into an almost hysterical condition. At last, in the middle of the summer, Annie went to London to consult her physician, Dr. Sibson, who treated her with the same sympathy and understanding that Dr. Winterbotham had displayed. She was suffering, he told her, from a general nervous exhaustion, accompanied by much disturbance of the general functions of the heart. There was as yet no organic disease, he assured her, but one might easily develop unless she changed her whole manner of life. Such a complete change was not possible, and she grew rapidly worse. To add to her misery, "the same bad adviser," the unnamed relative of her hus-

[9] Annie Besant, in *Theosophist*, LII (March, 1931), 484.

band, again interfered and urged that pressure be put on her at least to conform to the outward ceremonies of the church and attend Holy Communion—a surrender of principle which she was determined not to make.

So she fled briefly to Southsea with her children to see if her beloved ocean air would restore her health. On her return, still under the doctor's care, she went to stay with her mother at her brother Henry's house at 65 Finborough Road, Brompton. Both her brother and her mother were struck with consternation at her predicament, but both were loyal to the family ties, Mrs. Wood from maternal love, Henry from his sense of duty.

One day in September, Frank Besant stormed suddenly into the house, carried away by his brother's advice. He stamped about the room, used violent language, and generally caused the household such alarm that Annie feared for their safety. Then he delivered his ultimatum: his wife must conform and take Communion or else she could not return to Sibsey. Faced with these Draconian alternatives, she chose the latter. Not even when her beloved mother dramatically threw herself on her knees and implored her to yield would Annie change her decision. Realizing that his sister would never acquiesce, Henry, though scarcely reconciled, persuaded Frank to go to a lawyer and draw up a deed of separation.

There were apparently legal facts which compelled him to make this concession. Divorce was of course out of the question; neither church nor state, let alone Frank himself, would consider it. So the vicar agreed to assign £110 a year, or about a quarter of his small stipend, in monthly instalments for the maintenance of his wife and baby daughter. Mabel was to remain with Annie, except for a one-month visit each year with her father. Digby was to stay with his father, except for a similar yearly visit with his mother. Mrs. Besant would be allowed to take away only her personal property and gifts; all the household goods would remain with her husband. By the latter part of the month the separation was complete.[10]

Faced with "respectable starvation" on her tiny income, the now independent Mrs. Besant began to look about her for work, at first wasting a few precious shillings in employment agencies. Her previous experience at getting copying work deterred her from trying that occupation again. She could do nothing that anyone seemed to want. She tried her hand at fancy needlework at home, offered to "ladies in reduced circumstances," and earned less than five shillings after some five weeks of stitching. A Birmingham firm advertised a vague but attractive-sounding opportunity to add easily to one's income; but when Annie naïvely sent the small fee demanded, she received by return mail a cheap pencil-case, with the suggestion that she sell similar articles to her friends.

Annie also needed a place to live. Henry would have made room for

[10] A summary of the indenture made October 25, 1873, is in the Public Record Office, High Court of Justice, Chancery Division, Master of the Rolls, August 3, 1878.

her in his small house, if she would consent to give up her heretical friends; but she was always an obstinate woman. Since she wanted to have her mother with her wherever she went, she arranged for the rental of a little house at 26 Colby Road, Gipsy Hill, Upper Norwood. There she would be near her friends the Scotts, and the Voyseys lived not far away. But the house would not be available until the following spring.

In this emergency an invitation to go to Folkestone, where her grand-mother and two aunts were living, was a godsend (Annie would have avoided such a word for it). Accompanied by her mother, she happily left London and received a warm welcome by her relatives, whose love for her overcame any religious scruples they might have had. Here in Folkestone, too, they were soon joined by the forlorn and terrified Mabel, who at the age of three had been sent all the way from Sibsey via London in the sole charge of the railway guard. For weeks afterward Mabel clung tightly to her mother wherever she went and screamed if she lost sight of her.

After they had all settled down and Mabel's essential "winsomeness" had had a chance to establish itself, Mrs. Besant again started to look for work. She thought of instructing pupils, but soon found—as she might have expected—that Victorian mothers were not easily persuaded to in-trust their offspring to a teacher suspected of heresy, separated from her husband, and encumbered with a small child. Luckily, however, the vicar of Folkestone, the Rev. M. Woodward, just then found himself with a wife in delicate health, and no governess for his several young children. One of Annie's aunts, a steady churchwoman, suggested her niece for the job, and Annie and Mabel moved into the Woodwards' house. Annie was to teach the children a few hours each day in exchange for board and room until a regular governess could be found or she was ready to return to Upper Norwood.

The Woodwards were very kind to her, in spite of the fact that the vicar was a very religious and unworldly man. He was "a 'priest' to the tips of his finger-nails," but one who was convinced that his office put him at the service of any needy person. Although he deeply lamented his new governess's "perversion," he was sure that her unbelief could be only a dimming cloud which would soon blow away. Later, to Annie's great amusement, she learned that the vicar's elder daughters, "trained in strict-est observance of all Church ceremonies," had much discussed her failure to attend the Sacrament and had decided that she must have committed some deadly sin, for which her humble work of cooking, nursing, and teaching was the appointed penance.

The Woodwards' new household factotum found for the first time that she could cook, and that it was even pleasant to make pie crust and con-coct a stew; but she also found that saucepans and kettles blistered her hands and that sweeping tired her. In the midst of this new kind of menial experience, the little Woodward girl fell ill with diphtheria, and Mrs. Besant, after dispatching Mabel safely to her grandmother's, had another opportunity to demonstrate her penchant for nursing. Hardly had she come out victorious in this bout when the youngest boy came down with scarlet fever. So Annie intrepidly isolated herself with him on the top floor, cleared away the carpets and curtains, hung sheets soaked in chloride of lime over the doorways, had her meals left on the landing, and finally handed back her charge without anyone else's having been infected.

Soon it was the spring of 1874, and Annie could have her home in Gipsy Hill. She planned to bring her mother down from London, educate little Mabel, and live there idyllically. It was a tiny house, among other small, middle-class, detached houses, but it had a pleasant view over a small valley, and the Crystal Palace park was only a mile or so to the east. In order to afford the rent and to put a little absolutely utilitarian furniture into the place, it was necessary for her to save as much of her monthly allowance as possible. The Scotts gave her an introduction to a manufacturer who agreed to let her have enough articles for a bedroom and a sitting room, to be paid for on the instalment plan. When she was ready to move in, however, she found that her own bedroom had been "neatly and prettily" furnished by her "good fairy," Mrs. Scott, who had determined that her protégée would not be as uncomfortable as she had expected to be.

Mrs. Wood, apparently in good health, had gone up to Brompton to spend a few days with Henry. Then suddenly Annie received a telegram from the doctor, saying that her mother was dying and could not live more than three days. Annie hurried to her and nursed her faithfully. Mrs. Wood lived through two crises, which ended in dropsy.

But even in her desperate straits, she clung to her passionate hope of saving her child's soul. She longed intensely to take the last sacrament, but she refused to do so unless Annie would communicate with her. "If it be necessary to salvation," she persisted doggedly, "I will not take it if darling Annie is to be shut out. I would rather be lost with her than saved without her."

Annie had not been to Communion for eighteen months. She must have realized that her mother was using a sort of spiritual blackmail against her. Yet she loved her mother devotedly. So, bottling up her former resolves, she went to two clergymen and laid the case before them. As she expected, both refused to let her communicate. Then she remembered her mother's own favorite, Dean Stanley. Saying nothing to anyone, she went to the Deanery in Westminster and timidly asked for the Dean. She followed the servant upstairs with a sinking heart.

But she felt relieved when the Dean came in and she saw his "clear, grave, piercing eyes, gazing questioningly" into hers. Falteringly she told him everything. He understood perfectly. "Of course I will go and see your mother," he said, "and I have little doubt that, if you will not mind talking over your position with me, we may see our way clear to doing as your mother wishes." He went on to suggest that he first come and chat privately with Mrs. Wood that very afternoon and then administer the sacrament the following day. And so he did, spending half an hour with Mrs. Wood and much longer with Annie herself. He told her that to him conduct was far more important than theory and that he regarded as "Christians" all those who tried to follow the moral law of Christ. The question of the absolute divinity of Jesus made little difference to him. "The Holy Communion," he concluded in his soft, musical voice, "was never meant to divide from each other hearts that are searching after the one true God." The next day he celebrated communion at Mrs. Wood's bedside, and both women were happy.

Dean Stanley made one more visit to the house, and after talking with Mrs. Wood he had another long and intimate conversation with her daughter. He answered frankly all her questions about his liberal theology, told her of himself and his career, and revealed his pride in the Abbey and its mission. His honesty, sympathy, and intelligence made such a friend of Annie that in later years she never allowed a word to be uttered against him in her presence.

The hope of this last Communion together was apparently all that had kept Mrs. Wood alive. The doctor had given permission for her to be driven down to Annie's house in Norwood in an invalid carriage, but the evening after her arrival she was suddenly taken worse. The doctor came but could do nothing; Mrs. Wood died two days later, sighing to the last about her sorrow at leaving her daughter alone. Once she murmured, "My little one, you have never made me sad or sorry except for your own sake; you have always been too religious. . . . Yes, it has been darling Annie's only fault; she has always been too religious." That was Mrs. Wood's summary of their life together, and it lost nothing of its Victorian sentimentality in Annie's retelling. She was buried near her husband and little son in the Kensal Green Cemetery.

The next two months were, in Annie's later estimation, the dreariest in her whole life. She sold her small amount of jewelry and all but her most necessary clothes, in order to keep Mabel well fed and ignorant of her real circumstances. Often she would go and study all day, without eating, at the British Museum so that she could tell the Scotts that she was having "dinner in town." Fortunately the Scotts' home was always open to her when she could resist hunger no longer, and Thomas Scott's genial greeting, "Well, little lady," helped to relieve the loneliness of her life.

English ladies always had servants around them. And through it all, Annie insisted on putting up enough of a front to maintain a little servant-maid, Mary, who had been found for her by Mrs. Scott. Mary was "the most thoughtful and generous of comrades," "a wonderful contriver," and made the little place "so bright and fresh-looking that it was always a pleasure to go into it." Annie bragged that she had always been fortunate in her servants and that as a result of these experiences she was always able better to understand the sufferings of others.

Fortunately a way was open to her by which she could forget her troubles and at the same time help to alleviate them. Her hours of study at the British Museum were being devoted to the preparation of a new series of pamphlets for Thomas Scott, from which she was to earn a few valuable guineas. She turned out half a dozen of these tracts with some speed in 1874, signing all but one, which was inexplicably anonymous, with variants of her name: first, Mrs. A. Besant; then, Annie Besant; and finally, A. Besant. There was no reason to keep the secret of her identity any longer; in fact, she probably took a sort of repressed vindictive pleasure in revealing it, though she quickly dropped her married title.

Much of the material and many of the ideas in these essays she got from scientific writers, such as Darwin, whom she credited with doing much toward freeing her from her old bonds; philosophical economists like John Stuart Mill, whom she had long been reading; pantheistic philosophers like Spinoza; and metaphysical theologians like Mansel.[11] The resulting essays were pointed, cogent, and often highly personalized attacks on churchly dogmas; she used such titles as "On the Atonement," "On Eternal Torture," "On the Mediation and Salvation of Ecclesiastical Christianity," and "On Inspiration" (perhaps inspired by her own extemporizing speech on biblical inspiration in the Sibsey church). She also wrote simple but trenchant discussions of more general topics, including "On the Religious Education of Children" and "Natural Religion vs. Revealed Religion." In all these she moved more and more firmly into the theistic position, concluding that revelation is quite superfluous, since natural religion gives man all he needs. About this time she also wrote an article, "The Ethics of Punishment," which was published in the *Inquirer* and which, in its tendency toward more purely atheistic thought, so impressed a lady who was totally unknown to Mrs. Besant that this lady republished it in separate form.[12] Annie was well started on her career as a pamphleteer.

The difference between a theist and an atheist lies only in the addition of a prefix. By the early summer of 1874 Mrs. Besant had nothing of her old faith left except her lingering belief in "a God." She had given up prayer as a "blasphemous absurdity." She re-examined the theistic axiom, "If there be a God at all, He must be at least as good as His highest creature." She turned her attention to that "if." Was it possible that those

[11] For Mrs. Besant's own summary of her intellectual development through her reading, see her Preface to *My Path to Atheism* (London, 1877).

[12] *National Reformer,* November 21, 1880.

cynics were right who asked whether God was not "only man's own image reflected in the mirror of man's mind"? She read further in Scott's valuable library as well as in the British Museum. She added Auguste Comte's *Philosophie positive* and reread Mill's examination of Sir William Hamilton; but it was the rereading of Dean Mansel's Bampton Lectures, "The Limits of Religious Thought," that did most toward turning her in the direction of atheism.

At last she said to Scott, "Mr. Scott, may I write a tract on the nature and existence of God?"

He glanced at her keenly. "Ah, little lady, you are facing, then, that problem at last? I thought it must come. Write away."

And so Mrs. Besant entered on the final stretch of her path to atheism. She began to write the essay. She had finally cut the last spiritual link of the tie which bound her to the husband she detested. Who can say how much this hate had influenced her course all along?

In the meantime she had made another friend in the widening circle of London speakers and writers who were considered so dangerous by the right-thinking. At the South Place Chapel in Finsbury an American named Moncure D. Conway had occupied the pulpit since 1864. Conway —first a Methodist, then a Unitarian, and now a theist and rationalist— had been born in Virginia and educated at Harvard. As a young and fiery Unitarian minister he had embraced the cause of the abolitionists before the Civil War and had come to England in 1863 to further that cause. To his surprise he found that many of his new English friends did not share his antislavery views, but that many more were interested in his powers as a liberal Unitarian preacher. At this juncture the discussion society of Dissenters which had been meeting in the South Place Chapel since the end of the eighteenth century under a succession of names—the Philadelphians, the Universalists, the South Place Society, and later the Free Religion Society and the South Place Ethical Society—faced the crisis of possible dissolution unless it could find a new leader. The position was offered to the surprised young Conway, who accepted with pleasure and built up his congregation to considerable numbers. He preached on emancipation, evolution, social and industrial reform, church disestablishment, oriental religions, and the whole gamut of intellectual problems of the day. And when Charles Voysey was cited for heresy, Conway prompty advised him to throw the burden of proof on the church and make her prove her charges. In February, 1871, he had supported Voysey publicly by preaching a sermon on the crime of expelling a man whose only fault was that he sought the truth.[13]

Mrs. Besant was introduced to this widely admired liberal leader by their mutual friends. She attended many of his meetings and soon began to discuss her personal problems with him. His views contributed

[13] Burtis, pp. 108–47, *passim.*

considerably to the expansion of her own attitude toward religious questions.

But it was not Conway, the first American with whom she had ever been on familiar terms, so much as his wife—"one of the sweetest and steadiest natures whom it has been my lot to meet, and to whom, as to her husband, I owe much for kindness generously shown when I was poor and had but few friends"—who first called Annie's attention seriously to the man who was to play such a central role in her life for the next two decades. He was the leading Freethinker in England, the bête noire of the churches, the terror of the Conservatives in politics—Charles Bradlaugh.

2

Ajax and the Iconoclast

One day in the late spring of 1874, while Mrs. Besant was still working on her new and most "advanced" article for Scott, Mrs. Conway casually asked her if she had ever gone to any of the lectures in the Hall of Science in Old Street. Annie replied, "with the stupid, ignorant reflexion of other people's prejudices which is but too common," as she said in her *Autobiography*, "No, I have never been. Mr. Bradlaugh is rather a rough sort of speaker, is he not?"

Mrs. Conway corrected her firmly. "He is the finest speaker of Saxon English I have ever heard, except, perhaps, John Bright, and his power over a crowd is something marvellous. Whether you agree with him or not, you should hear him."

Although the mere comparison with John Bright, whom her friend William Roberts had also set up as a sort of idol and model, should have fixed her attention, Mrs. Besant answered rather casually that she didn't really know what Bradlaugh's views were, beyond having a rather vague notion that he was "an atheist of a rather pronounced type," but that she would go to hear him when she had an opportunity.

It took another nudge to her memory, however, before she went. In July, in consequence of her having seen the name of Edward Truelove, publisher, at 256 High Holborn, on some of the works she had been reading at the British Museum, and having become interested in Positivism, she dropped in at his shop to look for some Comtist publications. On the counter she noticed a periodical with the striking title, *The National Reformer,* and bought it for twopence. In the omnibus on her way to the Victoria Station she began to read it placidly, finding its contents much to her taste, when she happened to glance up. Opposite her she saw an old gentleman gazing at her with horror. The sight of an apparently respectable young woman, dressed in crape, and reading a notorious atheistic journal, was too much for him, and he glared so hard and sternly at the paper that Annie, convulsed with inward mirth, was tempted to offer it to him. But she nobly restrained herself.

This copy of the *National Reformer*, subtitled "Secular Advocate & Freethought Journal," was dated July 19, 1874. The articles which most interested her were two long letters from a Rev. Thomas Arnold of Northampton swearing that he would never support Bradlaugh's candidacy for Parliament from that constituency; Bradlaugh's own brief and "singularly self-contained" reply; and an article by Charles Watts on the purposes and organization of the National Secular Society. There were also stories on "A Visit to the Tomb of Mill" and "The Crisis in France," as well as a rather humorously sarcastic one entitled "A National Reformer in the Dog-Days," by a "B. V."—whom she was soon to meet as the bitter, melancholy poet, James Thomson, whose famous poem of despair, *The City of Dreadful Night,* had just been serialized in the magazine by his friend and discoverer, Bradlaugh. There were also various departments of correspondence, news notes, reviews, announcements of lectures, and so on which interested her.

As soon as she had finished the little magazine, she knew she must belong to the Society which produced it. She promptly sat down and wrote a short note to the editor asking if it was necessary to be an atheist to be a member and signing herself, mysteriously, "S.E." The answer, in the issue for August 2, informed her that anyone who could accept the four basic principles outlined in an earlier number might join without avowing himself an atheist. But, continued the editor, "Candidly, we can see no logical resting-place between the entire acceptance of authority, as in the Roman Catholic Church, and the most extreme Rationalism. If, on again looking to the Principles of the Society, you can accept them, we repeat to you our invitation."

Mrs. Besant's conscience having long ago ceased to reproach her in such matters, she sent in her real name for active membership and saw it in print on August 9, along with the names of twenty-five others to whom certificates were being issued. The announcement continued, "Mr. Bradlaugh will deliver London certificates at the Hall of Science on Sunday evening, to save folding." Naturally, Annie Besant decided to save folding and be there in person. This was the first time, she pointed out, that she had set foot in a Freethought hall.[1]

The hall was crowded to suffocation. As a tall figure walked swiftly up the aisle and onto the platform at exactly the moment announced, the audience burst into a roar of cheers. Bradlaugh bowed slightly in acknowl-

---

[1] In her *Autobiography,* p. 232, she says this event took place on August 2, but this seems impossible since her name was not printed in the *National Reformer* until August 9.

edgment. Annie examined him with interest and surprise. Here was no "blatant agitator," no "ignorant demagogue." She was impressed by the "grave, quiet, stern, strong face, the massive head, the keen eyes, the magnificent breadth and height of forehead." She did not mention his great tallness and broad shoulders, his straight, chiseled nose, his slightly pouting overlip, his graying hair which streamed away from his somewhat balding forehead into a sort of comet's tail behind, or his black bow tie casually tied against a dark suit. These must have impressed her later, as did his manners and his courtesy, which—no matter to whom he was speaking—were so courtly as to seem utterly non-English. Bradlaugh was a figure to draw all eyes. He might easily have been a prime minister—or a bishop.

Beginning quietly and simply, and by a prophetic coincidence choosing Indian religions as his subject, Bradlaugh traced the resemblances between the Krishna and the Christ myths. He gradually turned all his eloquence, fire, sarcasm, and passion against Christian superstition, while the audience hung breathless on every word until "a magnificent peroration broke the spell, and a hurricane of cheers relieved the tension."

At the end he came down into the hall to deliver certificates to the new members present. He glanced around, came to Annie, and handed her hers with a questioning "Mrs. Besant?" His recognition of her impressed Annie greatly, and later she saw an occult significance in it, as of a relationship in some previous life. There was really nothing remarkable in his tentative recognition; most of the new members were not present, being from out of town, and only three women were in the group—the other two being Mrs. Watts and Mrs. Bradlaugh herself. Annie could easily have betrayed herself by some gesture or by her very expressive face. Her beauty and manners must also have set her apart from the rest of the crowd, few of whom had any claims on aristocracy.

Impressed by his new convert, Bradlaugh paused a moment to welcome her. He invited her to make an appointment with him to talk over the whole matter of her profession of atheism and offered to lend her a book he had been using in his lecture. Having accepted both offers, she went, a day or two later, to his tiny suite of two rooms at 29 Turner Street, Commercial Road, in a rather unsavory section of the East End, not far from the dock district. He ushered her into his little study, so crammed with books that there was barely room for the two of them, and they sat down to talk.

Charles Bradlaugh was at this time forty years old; Annie was twenty-six.[2] Unlike hers, his parents had had no claims to gentility; his mother had been a nursemaid and his father a law stationer and confidential

[2] For this biographical sketch, see Mrs. Besant's own descriptions; and John M. Robertson's "Account of [Bradlaugh's] Parliamentary Struggle, Politics, and Teachings," in Hypatia Bradlaugh Bonner, *Charles Bradlaugh*, II.

clerk to a firm of solicitors. When the boy was sent to the National School at the age of seven, "the teacher had striking ideas upon the value of corporal punishment, and enforced his instructions with the ruler so heavily that the scar so resulting from a wound so inflicted was deemed of sufficient importance some nine or ten years later to be marked in the enlistment description when Mr. Bradlaugh joined the army."

After Bradlaugh's parents had next tried their boy's luck at two poor, small private schools, they ended his formal education at the age of eleven; and he went to work on various odd jobs, including a position as office boy in his father's firm. He soon discovered, however, that he had a violent urge as well as a precocious ability to express himself orally. At the age of fourteen he was a Church of England Sunday-school teacher, but at the age of sixteen or seventeen he became well known as the "Baby," speaking of his two favorite subjects, Freethought and temperance, in such public forums as Bonner's Fields, Victoria Park, and the temperance halls. Consequently he soon met Austin Holyoake, who introduced him to his elder and then more widely known brother, George Jacob Holyoake, the leading Freethought advocate of the day and editor of the *Reasoner.* As a further result of these activities the young Bradlaugh quickly became acquainted with the opposition of the police to the actual application of the vaunted English principle of free speech: several times arrested, he lost his job as a wharf clerk. Then, perhaps to see how it felt to be himself on the side of law and order, he enlisted in the army, but after three years of home service decided that the military life was not for him and bought his way out with some of his mother's money.

He was now twenty-one, with no prospects. So, knowing a little of the life in a law office through his father, he took a job as a law clerk and began his self-education in the law which was eventually to make him one of the most skilful and feared advocates of "people's" causes in the English courts. Like William Roberts and Ernest Jones, he was always ready to see that the poor man and the working man got the hearing and the justice their cases deserved. With the small income from this new job in his pocket he felt safe in asking the daughter of another Radical and Freethinker to marry him. He courted her partly with verses, for he was fond of and familiar with the poets all the way from Marlowe and Spenser to Shelley, Burns, and Byron. Even more important for his future career, he began to write antitheological tracts, which he signed with the threatening pen name "Iconoclast"—the image-breaker.

The young Iconoclast's marriage did not turn out very well, for mysterious reasons which were none of his fault but which gave rise to scandalous rumors. In 1870 the family was broken up; their home, Sunderland Villa, Northumberland Park, Tottenham, had to be given up and most of their furniture sold to pay their debts. Mrs. Bradlaugh and her two daughters went to live with her father in a Sussex hamlet, and her eleven-year-old son drifted about England with the Grenadier Guards, where he soon died.

Bradlaugh's rise in Freethought circles was meteoric. He soon widened his speaking range to include Hyde Park and Trafalgar Square. He engaged in debates on the Bible and religion. He became a regular contributor to Robert Cooper's *Investigator* and in 1858 took over as its editor. In the same year, aged twenty-five, he was elected president of the London Secular Society in the place of George Jacob Holyoake himself. Soon afterward he and some Sheffield associates founded the *National Reformer* to replace the *Investigator*. Announced originally as an organ for the expression of "advanced Liberal opinions, on Social, Political, Theological, and Scientific Questions," it quickly moved under Iconoclast's leadership to such an openly atheistic and Radical position that his coeditor resigned and even Holyoake broke with him. For three or four years during the sixties John Watts took over the editorship because Bradlaugh was too busy giving his popular lectures both at home and abroad—never charging a fee, but merely pocketing what might be left after expenses were paid. However, when Watts died in 1866, Bradlaugh resumed the editorship, to hold it—not undivided—till his death. But he did appoint John Watts's brother Charles as subeditor.

Charles Watts was then thirty-one, born into a pious Methodist family in Bristol, but like Bradlaugh an adolescent convert to skepticism. A printer by trade, he was also an effective polemicist by tongue and pen, a thorough Republican and humanitarian. He was a man of distinguished presence, with a handsome, genial face and a commanding figure.[3] His appointment was to become of considerable importance to Annie Besant.

Bradlaugh's reputation continued to spread. He traveled to France and Italy and actively supported the cause of Mazzini and Garibaldi; indeed, he always had a framed portrait of Mazzini in his room. He encouraged Charles Voysey to fight the Established Church. He became a vice-president of the National Reform League, as well as orator of the Grand Lodge of Freemasons, "Des Philadelphes." He got into trouble because of his support of the Fenian Brotherhood in Ireland. When, in May, 1868, the Commissioners of Her Majesty's Inland Revenue commenced proceedings to suppress the troublesome *National Reformer,* he continued to publish his paper with the following impudent streamer above his editorials: "Published in Defiance of Her Majesty's Government, and of 60 Geo. III. cap. 9." The proceedings were finally dropped, and the great John Stuart Mill himself moved for repeal of some of the restrictive press laws, with ultimate success.

So great was the publicity from these activities that Bradlaugh decided to run for Parliament from Northampton on the Radical ticket in 1868.

[3] D. M. Bennett, *The World's Sages, Thinkers, and Reformers* (New York, *ca.* 1878), pp. 1003–4.

He hauled down the name "Iconoclast" from the editorial masthead of the *National Reformer* and replaced it boldly with his own. But he did not win. His gains were many new friends and many new debts. In the next election he ran again; he got more votes and more debts, but again he did not win.

His advocacy of the causes of freedom everywhere—almost preferably by revolution—took him to France in 1871, where he was one of the candidates nominated by the city of Paris in the general elections. Arrested at Calais both before and after the fall of the Commune, he had a difficult time because he had condemned the Franco-Prussian War, but had been bitter against both the French emperor and Bismarck. Two years later he was in Spain, supporting the republicans against the Carlists.

In the same year he took his first trip to America. It was a triumph. At the famous Lotos Club in New York he met authors like Bret Harte and Lincoln's favorite humorist, "Petroleum V. Nasby"; editors and journalists like Whitelaw Reid of the *Tribune* and Theodore Tilton of the *Independent;* and statesmen like John Hay. In Boston the great orator and reformer Wendell Phillips presided at his meetings, and on the platform were Senator Charles Sumner and Abolitionist leader William Lloyd Garrison, "who cheered him repeatedly." At dinner at the Massachusetts Club he met Henry Wilson, vice-president of the United States under Grant, who was so impressed by this Englishman who, like himself, had fought his way up from the ranks of the poor, that he invited him to Washington for a visit. From Boston, Bradlaugh swung west to Buffalo, Cincinnati, St. Louis, Kansas City, and Chicago; and everywhere he was feted and cheered—probably more for his freedom of thought in political matters than for his free thought in religion. As the culmination of his tour, Bradlaugh headed toward Washington to lecture and pay his promised visit to the Vice-President, but on the way he received a telegram from Austin Holyoake telling him that Gladstone had just dissolved Parliament. This of course meant a new campaign for the seat in Northampton, and Charles Bradlaugh must be there to fight for it. He took the first possible ship from New York.

This, then, was the remarkable man who was sitting in his minuscule study across from Annie Besant in August, 1874. He was debt-ridden, he was exhausted, he was persecuted in England—but he was intrepid. He never gave up. He had confidence in himself, for he knew he was right. And he sat and talked to Annie like any ordinary man.

She had brought along her manuscript of "On the Nature and Existence of God," to serve "as the basis for our conversation." Bradlaugh read it attentively and pleased her with his verdict that there was really little difference in their views. "You have thought yourself into Atheism without knowing it," he informed her. He might have been less surprised if he had known, as Mrs. Besant later admitted, that she had just been reading his pamphlets, "A Plea for Atheism" and "Is There a God?"[4] At any rate, the only thing she changed in her essay as a result of his suggestion was her "vulgar error" to the effect that the atheist says, "There is no God." This she corrected to the truer philosophic position that the atheist says he can find no acceptable evidence that there is a God.

At the end of the meeting Mrs. Besant invited her new friend to come down to see her at Norwood. At first he refused, reminding her of the danger in becoming associated with a man of his reputation in England. Later, when she wrote him a letter repeating her invitation, he accepted. It was the beginning of a friendship which brought them both many problems and many troubles, but which neither of them ever regretted or repudiated. To Annie, Bradlaugh was "the noblest friend that woman ever had."

Their intimacy grew rapidly. They visited freely back and forth, for they were free spirits, above the conventions of Victorian society. Mrs. Besant learned to know every article in his cramped lodgings. When his own household had broken up, Bradlaugh had taken little with him but his books. Instead of appropriating the comfortable bed which was necessary to accommodate his large frame, he had contented himself with the little bedstead on which his two small daughters, Hypatia and Alice, had slept. He had also taken the girls' nursery washstand, a chest of drawers, a writing table, and half a dozen chairs. That was all—except one picture, which hung over the head of his bed in the only wall space unoccupied by his books.

This picture, a large canvas in oils, had been painted for him by a French artist-friend. It depicted a tired hurdy-gurdy boy sleeping in a dark doorway, with a monkey anxiously watching over its little master. Whatever its intrinsic value, to Bradlaugh—as his daughter Hypatia later wrote—this painting was "beyond all price." It apparently had some symbolic significance or association which made him cling tenaciously to it, so that even in his last illness some years later, he talked about it, longed for it, and wondered where it was, though by that time it had gone out of his hands.

It did not take Bradlaugh long to recognize the value of his new convert. Only a few days after their meeting he offered Mrs. Besant a staff job on the *National Reformer* at one guinea a week. She did not feel insulted ("for national reformers are always poor," she remarked); in fact, the money was a welcome supplement to her tiny income from her husband and from Scott. In return she was to write reviews, articles, and a regular section of personal comments, which she decided to entitle "Daybreak," as most appropriate to the purpose of the paper. The use of a pen name was almost a necessity because she did not wish to hurt Scott, who

[4] See Mrs. Besant's Preface to *My Path to Atheism.*

had already paid for several articles which she had still to write, by publicly associating her name as yet with views even more extreme than his own. The pseudonym she came up with was "Ajax," suggested not so much by the Greek hero himself as by the statue, "Ajax Crying for Light," a cast of which stood in the Crystal Palace in nearby Sydenham. According to the myth, Ajax, after Achilles had been slain, cried for light in the darkness so that he could rescue the body of his friend from the Trojans. Athena granted his prayer.

On August 30, three weeks after her admission into the National Secular Society, Ajax published her first column. It began:

There is a strange interest in standing on a mountain-top, watching for the first faint signs of the coming day. Here and there a tiny white cloud warms into soft yellow, or flushes rosy red; here and there a gleam flashes across the sky. . . . But a deeper, keener interest swells the heart of those who are watching for the rising sun of Liberty; each ray, be it ever so feeble, each tiny gem of colour in the dull grey sky, brings to the foremost soldiers of the army of Freedom a message of hope. . . . The series of papers, of which this is the first, will weekly point out these signs of the coming day; whether they betoken freedom of thought or freedom of action, they are dear to us as signals of that coming reign of Liberty, when men shall dare to think for themselves in theology, and to act for themselves in politics.

The first sign of the coming light to Ajax was Dr. Christopher Wordsworth, nephew of William Wordsworth. Christopher Wordsworth was bishop of Lincoln, and it happened that Frank Besant's parish lay in his diocese. Naturally the bishop had been on his vicar's side in the late unpleasantness. Just as naturally, then, Ajax taunted the poor fellow as an "invaluable man. Few help forward as he does the cause of Freethought; few allies, such as he, have we in the enemy's ranks. This inestimable prelate must be a thorn in the side of Mother Church; he will not be quiet." Then Annie proceeded to produce a few specimens of the ecclesiastical absurdities from Wordsworth's recent churchly pronouncements and actions. In fact, she jeered a few weeks later, whenever the bishop had a chance to put his foot into anything, he was not satisfied till he also committed his entire episcopal gaiters.

She then went on in her first column to make remarks on such miscellaneous matters as secular education, cremation, international news, and table-tapping. "The Spiritualists are hard at work," she reminded her readers, for she knew that Spiritualism was one of Bradlaugh's favorite antipathies. Less than two years before, in fact, he had engaged in a set discussion of the subject with J. Burns, the editor of two of the leading Spiritualist journals, *Human Nature* and *The Medium and Daybreak.* Here he had learned nothing to make him alter his former conclusions, based on his own attendance at seances and his investigations of popular

Annie Wood at sixteen

Annie Wood and her mother

Annie Besant at Cheltenham

Rev. Frank Besant in middle age

Annie Besant and her young son Digby

Annie Besant and her young daughter Mabel

Thomas Scott

Dean Charles Vaughan

Dean Arthur Stanley

Dr. Edward Pusey

Rev. Moncure Conway

Walter Besant

South Place Chapel, Finsbury

Charles Bradlaugh and Henry D. Labouchère

Eleanor Marx

William T. Stead

Bernard Shaw in 1885   Henry M. Hyndman

Norwich branch of the Socialist League, with William Morris in the center

Annie Besant in 1885

and famous mediums, about the fakery involved and the insignificance of the results produced. Annie's own position was equally skeptical.

In the ensuing weeks she continued to demonstrate her mastery of the contemporary scene. No province of knowledge was beyond the tip of her pen. She made a careful condensation and analysis of Professor John Tyndall's address to the British Association for the Advancement of Science at Belfast. She wrote reviews of books ranging from economics and practical politics to Milton. She commented on the prospects of the ruin of Joseph Arch's Agricultural Labourers' Union and warned: "The Land Laws need a touch, but it is a touch of a bigger hand than that of Joseph Arch." She wrote on "Landlords, Tenant Farmers, and Labourers" and prepared to take over all the provincial news during the coming return trip of Bradlaugh to America.

By the end of September, Ajax was fully launched on her new career as a National Reformer. Ajax and Iconoclast were marching shoulder to shoulder.

3

Politics and the Public Platform

It is still debatable whether Annie Besant made more converts to her various causes by her pen or her tongue. Certainly it was her pen which started her on her career. Yet she had never forgotten the intoxication of her maiden speech to the empty pews of Sibsey church. She yearned to use her oratorical powers to "move hearts and brains all over the English land."[1]

Her first opportunity to try her wings came at a garden party soon after she had joined the Secularists. This extemporaneous fledgling flight in a brief, informal debate proved such a success that she next joined in a discussion at the Liberal Social Union. Here she spoke on a topic which continued to interest her for many years—the question of the "Sunday laws," that is, of the opening of museums, art galleries, and similar places of cultural entertainment to the public on Sundays. Mrs. Besant was properly unconvinced that such a breach in the Victorian blue laws would undermine the morality of the nation. However, her membership in this "liberal" society did not last very long. One night, during a discussion on the admissibility of atheists as members, a Dr. Zerffi declared he would not remain in the group if they were admitted. Mrs. Besant, in the interests of liberty, avowed that she was one. This was too shocking for the other members, whose liberalism stopped just after theism. Their cold response soon persuaded Annie to look for a warmer (they would have called it a hotter) climate for her opinions.

---

[1] So she phrased it in her autobiographies, which contain a general outline of activities described in this chapter, supplemented by references in the *National Reformer* and other papers.

Her first formal lecture to a public audience came on August 25. An officer of the Co-operative Institute in Castle Street had invited her to read a paper on any subject she chose. Being deeply involved in demonstrating in her own person the equality of women and the new feminism, she resolved that her first speech should be in behalf of her own sex and announced as her topic "The Political Status of Women." As she approached the platform, she felt like a child going to the dentist, but as soon as she pronounced her first word, all her fear gave way to an intense feeling of power and pleasure. So it was to be all her life—the same preliminary stage of nervousness and even illness, yielding quickly to assurance and command. She perceived at once how audiences responded to her petite brunette beauty; her tightly fitted dark silk dresses, edged in white; her full, rich, well-articulated voice; her ladylike deportment; and her strangely compelling personality—to say nothing of the iconoclastic ideas she was uttering.

Of course, Charles Bradlaugh and many others of her new Secularist friends were in the hall to hear and encourage her. Hypatia Bradlaugh recalled how her father described Mrs. Besant's address as "probably the best speech by a woman" he had ever listened to—and the Secularists and feminists had already developed several spellbinding woman speakers.[2] In fact, he announced triumphantly in "Rough Notes," his personal section in the *National Reformer,* for September 20:

On Sunday evening, Sept. 27th, at seven precisely, Mrs. Annie Besant, whose recent lecture at the Co-operative Institute gave so much pleasure to our friends, will lecture at Mr. Moncure Conway's Chapel, St. Paul's Road, Camden Town, on the "True Basis of Morality."

Thereafter he listed her lectures in his regular "Guide to the Lecture Platform," which informed the London intelligentsia where to go and what to hear. So well adapted was this talk to its special audience that she was asked to repeat it a few weeks later at the Rev. Peter Dean's Unitarian chapel. Soon printed in the *Reformer* and reprinted separately as a pamphlet, it had a wide circulation. By December it had even attracted the attention of the *Secular Review,* one of the many rival Freethought publications, whose reviewer, Francis Neale, spoke long and approvingly of this "admirable little pamphlet written by an intelligent lady in advocation of women's rights."

The excitement of these new outlets for her bounding vitality was soon to be interrupted by a new and even more exciting phase of journalistic activity. She became the *National Reformer's* political reporter.

The election for which Bradlaugh had broken short his American tour had actually been held before his return in February. His name had been put up again at Northampton by a friend, but, despite the fact that he

---

[2] Hypatia Bradlaugh Bonner, *Charles Bradlaugh,* II, 15–16.

had increased his votes by over 50 per cent, he had been defeated. His supporters, however, were much encouraged to discover that over two-thirds of his votes came from "plumpers"—that is, from those hard-core admirers who threw the whole power of their proportional representation strength to him only. These were the voters who by their devotion and enthusiasm finally won election after election for their hero and by so doing precipitated one of the most bitter and crucial Parliamentary fights in English history.

In the late summer the incumbent of the borough died, and it all had to be done over again. A by-election was called. Bradlaugh this time was there to contest it himself, and he suggested that Mrs. Besant accompany his party to write up the affair for the paper. She soon found herself in the midst of some extremely corrupt and disillusioning party politics. The Northampton Whigs were even more rancorous against Bradlaugh than were the Tories and were willing to lose the seat to their main rivals rather than let a Radical atheist capture it. They therefore intrigued to persuade a Liberal candidate to stand, knowing they could split the progressive vote in this way. A local banker finally agreed to run after a dozen others had refused, and this turned the trick. A "very reputable Tory lawyer" won the seat, even though Bradlaugh added a hundred voters to his support.

This sort of political maneuvering was commonplace and fair enough by universal political standards. But Bradlaugh's enemies were lured to adopt even worse devices and to descend to personal slander. He was vulnerable because he was a gentleman—by his actions if not by birth—and his opponents were not. Only his closest friends knew what had happened to his wife, because he was too chivalrous toward women to talk about her. The rest of the world knew only that she and his children had suddenly disappeared from his side. To the vulgar, an atheist naturally did not believe in the sanctity of marriage. So the story was rapidly spread round Northampton that Bradlaugh had deserted his family. As a matter of fact, as Annie knew by this time, Mrs. Bradlaugh had become an incurable dipsomaniac, and her husband was supporting her as best he could, while refusing to publicize the truth.

Most of Bradlaugh's constituents were pretty rough customers—laborers from the foundries, tanneries, brick kilns, and so on. Knowing no more of the truth than did the conservatives, they nevertheless trusted their champion and resented any slurs against him. Even during the election, stray fights had broken out; but after the results had been announced, the wilder spirits among the Radicals, attributing Bradlaugh's defeat to these sordid methods, could not contain themselves. As he, Annie, and his friends sat exhausted in the drawing room of their cheap hotel, their landlord rushed in, crying that unless Bradlaugh intervened to stop his people, there would be murder done at the rival hotel-headquarters of the victor. Bradlaugh rushed out, to find that the windows of the other hotel had already been broken by stones and the door battered in. Flinging himself before the gaping doorway, he knocked down one or two of the most violent before the crowd would listen to his admonitions and pleas for reason. They at last dispersed sullenly, and everyone thought the tumult had been quelled. By nine o'clock he thought it safe to leave Northampton alone to catch the mail steamer for America at Queenstown.

As soon as the word passed around that Bradlaugh had gone, the rioting broke out once more. The hotel and the printing office of the Whig paper were attacked. Heads, as well as doors and windows, were broken. Finally the soldiers were called out, the Riot Act was read, and the mob thereupon gave up before any further damage was done. The next morning an agitated and somewhat terrified Annie took the train back to London and hurried to the little publication office of the *National Reformer,* in a cul-de-sac just off the bustle of Fleet Street. Her excited, detailed story of the campaign and its results filled most of the issue of October 11. When she had recovered from the "severe attack of congestion of the lungs" brought on by this experience, she prepared her copy for the next week's "Daybreak," which was devoted largely to reviewing the accounts of the election in the various north-country journals. Her own inside story differed from theirs in many particulars. It was obvious that one of the many national reforms needed was in the field of politics.

So that she would not waste so much time in commuting from Norwood to the office, Annie decided to move nearer to headquarters. She and two "lady friends" arranged to divide the rent and the premises of a solid tan plaster row house at 19 Westbourne Park Terrace, in very respectable Bayswater. The house, set smugly back from the main thoroughfare by a parkway and separate road, was only a couple of minutes' walk from Hyde Park.

During Bradlaugh's absence Annie plunged deeply into her new job. As Ajax the author of "Daybreak" she wrote about fundamentalists, woman's suffrage, Bishop Wordsworth, and Spiritualism. She was especially scathing about such Spiritualist works as *The Two Discoveries; or, Key to Pine's Spiritual Telegraph.* As Ajax the book reviewer she was not satisfied merely to comment on current books and periodicals in English, but branched out into analyses of Karl Blind's *Zur Geschichte der Republikanischer Partei in England* and Odysse-Barot's *Histoire de la littérature contemporaine en Angleterre.* Her linguistic training under Miss Marryat was proving useful.

Now she had a chance to pay off debts of gratitude to some of those who had inadvertently helped her along her path to atheism. She found that "Dean Stanley often gives us a sign of Daybreak in his church; his courtesy towards his opponents, his growing liberality of sentiment, as well as his broad culture and deep learning, entitle the Broad Church

Dean to a respectful hearing at our hands"—no matter how widely the Secularists might differ from him in opinions. When Moncure Conway presided at an early December meeting of the Dialectical Society, perhaps the most distinguished of the legion of debating forums of the day, he was able to call on Mrs. Annie Besant by name to lead the discussion of the Rev. Dr. Maurice Davies's "The Poles of Religious Opinion." He listened noncommitally when the next speaker made some rather personal remarks about the lady's youth and short experience of skepticism, ending with the hope that she would follow his example and return to theism by similarly exercising her Freethought, but when another speaker tried to introduce the currently engrossing subject of Spiritualism into the discussion, Conway ruled him out of order. The next week in "Daybreak" she praised Conway for standing "alone among the London rationalistic preachers, in the cordial kindness he shows to the Secular party and its chief."

By the beginning of the new year Mrs. Besant had decided to devote herself completely to her propagandist work as freethinker and social reformer, in spite of her realization of the fact that as an atheist she was "outside the law, obnoxious to its penalties, but deprived of its protection." Much of this work was to be accomplished through her new love, the lecture platform.

Even though Charles Watts, acting editor of the *National Reformer,* had failed to mention his new assistant in his praise of the "more prominent workers in our movement" when he wrote his "New Year's Address to Our Readers," two weeks later he could no longer hold back. Annie was now sure enough of herself to determine to throw off her *nom de guerre,* and Watts co-operated in his "Notes":

> We invite special attention to a lecture announced in our advertisement column, to be given next Tuesday evening, January 19th, by Mrs. Annie Besant ("Ajax"), at South Place Chapel, Finsbury, on "Civil and Religious Liberty." Mr. Moncure D. Conway will preside. We trust our friends will make an effort to be present, as the ability of Mrs. Besant as a writer is only equalled by her elocutionary accomplishments as a lecturer.

This handsome puff paid off. Conway went so far as to send a kindly notice all the way back home to the *Cincinnati Commercial;* Watts wrote a flattering account of her tumultuous ovation in the *National Reformer;* and even Dr. Davies, her Dialectical opponent, published a very favorable article about her in the London *Sun,* which unfortunately did her no service so far as publicizing her name was concerned, because her unrelenting brother-in-law Walter Besant, getting wind of the matter, persuaded Davies to suppress the real name of the lecturer. Watts's revelation of the true identity of "Ajax" resulted in the Dialectical Society's later being locked out of its regular meeting place in Adam Street because, when Mrs. Besant was invited to read a paper on "The Existence of God," the Social Science Association would not allow its sacred precincts to be profaned by an atheist.

The newspaper suppression of her name by Walter Besant led in September to a further action by Frank. Upon learning that Dr. Davies and his publishers were thinking of reprinting the report of her lecture in a series of works dealing with religious beliefs in London, he persuaded them to omit her name. Annie thereupon charged her husband with interfering with her practice of her profession, which was the means of her livelihood.[3]

Convinced now that her friends adored her and her enemies hated and feared her, Annie decided to venture out of town. Though the Northampton audience was a rough one, they remembered her because of her assistance to Bradlaugh in his electioneering. "Civil and Religious Liberty, with Hints Taken from the French Revolution" was a torrid enough subject, and the reports that came back were so favorable that on February 14 the list of her lecturing engagements was published along with those of the veterans of the Secularist platforms like Watts, G. W. Foote, and Bradlaugh himself. In the middle of February she started off all alone on a barnstorming tour which would take her all through the north of England and well into Scotland before she returned to London to make her debut before her new comrades in the Hall of Science itself. The *National Reformer* advised all Secularists and Republicans in this section to be watching for her; the *Secular Chronicle* chimed in with the same recommendation.

Her first speech, at Birkenhead, was auspicious; the mere mention of the name of Bradlaugh produced spontaneous cheers. After this success she left for Glasgow by the night mail. Some friends put her into an unoccupied compartment, but just as the train started the porter thrust a man through the doorway. To her horror, she soon realized that he was drunk—that she was "alone at night in an express with a man not drunk enough to be helpless, but too drunk to be controlled." Never before or after was she to be so thoroughly frightened. Grasping a little penknife in her pocket and determined to sell her virtue dearly if necessary, she fenced with the leering creature verbally till the train was unexpectedly flagged down at a small station and she could call the guard for help. Arriving at Glasgow, where a room had been engaged for her at a grubby temperance hotel, she was so lonely and shaken that only her pride prevented her from breaking into tears.

Her reception by the Glasgow Eclectic and Secular Institute, however, quickly erased her unhappiness. Its secretary promptly wrote to the *Na-*

[3] See demurrer and counterclaim of Annie Besant issued in High Court of Justice, Chancery Division, Master of the Rolls (1878-B-No. 415), October 9, 1878, and affidavit of Frank Besant in Public Record Office, Chancery 5999, November 8, 1878.

tional Reformer that Mrs. Besant's two lectures, "The Gospel of Christianity" and "The Atonement," had not been equaled in eloquence and force by any of their better-known lecturers. When all the old arguments had been brought up by the heckling opposition, which could always be counted on to enliven such meetings in Victorian times, she had mercilessly knocked them all on the head with such convincing logic, combined with chaste and poetic language and a well-cultured mind, that the correspondent predicted a very prosperous future for her. Her deceptive gentleness of manner drew unwary hecklers to attack her, to their complete discomfiture.

A week later another correspondent waxed even more ecstatic about the "new star" which had just appeared in the north, which from its "extraordinary brilliancy must be . . . of the first magnitude." In fact, in an extra lecture she had even overwhelmed a famous professor from London who had spoken to the Glasgow Scientific Lecture Association on "Man Not an Automaton." Her physiological knowledge had made the audience turn to one another exclaiming, "What manner of woman can this be?" Wave after wave of "spontaneous ringing cheers" had clearly announced the verdict. Her heart warmed to these Scotchmen.

But Aberdeen at first was a harder nut to crack. Not a sound was heard as she walked to the platform. The faces before her were stern, critical, and unsmiling. These canny Scotchmen were not going to be tricked by a pretty face into applauding an unknown quantity. They listened grimly. Annie felt she would have been willing to take her head off and throw it at them if she had been sure it would produce an impression. Then after her warmest words had beaten in vain against them for twenty minutes, a lucky phrase drew a hiss from "some child of the Covenanters." This was all she needed. Her witty retort, which annihilated the enemy, brought a burst of cheering, and never again did she have need to complain of coldness in an Aberdeen audience.

The story of Annie Besant's resounding success preceded her to London. When she appeared on the platform of the Hall of Science on Sunday evening, February 28, to prove her mettle to her new friends, the wooden room was crammed to capacity with 1,200 people. As she unfolded her arguments on "The Gospel of Christianity vs. the Gospel of Freethought," the audience cheered her to the rafters. The efforts of the Rev. Mr. Turpin, a habitual and paid heckler from the Christian Evidence Society and a well-known and almost affectionately regarded figure at such gatherings, left her unscathed—in the perhaps biased view of her colleagues; and the way in which she easily turned his attacks aside earned her "golden opinions from all."

By this time any remaining doubts she had had about her future on the platform had dissolved. Remembering her weak lungs and frequent illnesses, she had even consulted a doctor on her plans. He had cautiously informed her that such work would either kill or cure her. She decided to take the chance and soon was assured that it had cured her. She realized, too, that she had reached her present pinnacle without the direct aid of her mentor, Charles Bradlaugh, who was still on the American tour which he had undertaken both to spread the doctrine of skepticism and liberalism and to accumulate funds to meet his ever pressing debts.

In the middle of March he returned, ready to deliver a lecture on "American Politics." His protégée's list of advance engagements, published in the *National Reformer* and extending all the way into June, was already twice as long as Watts's. Proud of his acumen in discovering her, and sometimes personally reprimanding groups such as that at Old Shildon, which did not work hard enough at providing an audience for her, Bradlaugh quickly resumed his intimacy with her. They were seen together everywhere—even at Moody and Sankey revival meetings.

The two of them set out to carry their own gospel to the Gentiles— sometimes singly, sometimes together. Their paths made an interlacing pattern all over the land, particularly in the north, where Bradlaugh's political support was concentrated. Sometimes he would preside at one of her lectures; sometimes she at one of his. Sometimes they would separate and then come together unexpectedly. The country must be propagandized; the appeal to reason, not faith, must be made. It did not matter whether the campaign was in a large room or meeting hall in London, its slums or its suburbs, in a provincial capital like Manchester, Newcastle, Birmingham, or Glasgow, or in a country town such as Seghill, Hillington, Longton, Stalybridge, Huddersfield, Bradford, or Oldham. Wherever two or three, or two or three hundred, could be gathered together, there were Annie Besant and Charles Bradlaugh. Annie, on her own, slept in miners' cottages and ate at miners' tables. She jounced over a ten-mile country road in a butcher's cart to give a lecture in a remote, otherwise inaccessible, village. She talked with weavers. Once she gave twelve lectures in eight days in Northumberland and Durham and came away with a deficit of eleven shillings.

But the compensations were even greater than the losses or discomforts. The corresponding secretaries of the Secularist branches vied with one another to see who could write the most fulsome reports of her appearances to the *National Reformer* and the *Secular Chronicle*. She was described as "Our New Advocate" and the "new 'Star of Freedom.'" Tributes were couched in phrases like "tremendous cheering," "beautiful peroration," "sparkling wit and sarcasm," "intelligent and appreciative audience," "took by storm," "matchless power of reasoning and eloquence," "inconceivably delighted," and "a lady of refinement, genius, and silvery eloquence." The local newspapers devoted columns to her, from the Auckland *Chronicle* to the Aberdeen *Herald, Free Press,* and *People's Journal.* "Vulcan" sent in stories about her, quoting from the Stalybridge *Reporter* and the Boston *Investigator* on her recent past, her accomplishments in language and literature, and her appearance. "She is," he wrote rhapsodically, "what may fairly be described as beautiful, being less than thirty years of age, and with the soft, clear eyes, rich brown hair, delicate oval face, and refined features, which make the best type of English beauty." Although rather under the average size, he ended, she dressed with a taste born of the combination of her education in Paris and a naturally well-endowed mind.

But life was not all honey; the churchly bulwarks did not immediately collapse. In places like Darwen and Swansea stone-throwing was "regarded as a fair argument," and sometimes the proprietor of the local hall feared violence so greatly that he demanded in advance a guarantee against damage. At times the bigoted opposition was so powerful that no local supporter dared take the chair for Mrs. Besant's lecture, and she had to introduce herself. Naturally, too, the clergy sprang to arms—sometimes trying to close all the meeting places to her, sometimes fulminating against her from the pulpit, sometimes filling the local newspapers with diatribes.

The situation in Longton, as a result of lectures by both Mrs. Besant and Bradlaugh, became so inflamed that not only the Secularist papers but also the Staffordshire *Daily Times,* the Staffordshire *Daily Sentinel,* the Middlesbrough *Exchange,* and the *Potteries Examiner* were filled with it from April to June. One local minister had the boldness to appear in person at one of Annie's lectures and expose himself to her nimble tongue by challenging some of her remarks which made the Bible look ridiculous. Another clergyman devoted his Sunday's sermon to her and was quickly joined by practically the whole local ministry, who nevertheless refused to descend from the protection of their pulpits to engage in an actual debate with their detested enemy. Francis Neale, one of Mrs. Besant's most ardent admirers among the Secularist journalists, exposed the identity of a minister who had been launching his poisoned darts from the *Potteries Examiner* disguised as "Tom Tit, Esq." Tom Tit, in reply to Mrs. Besant's earlier remark that there were some passages in the Bible which she did not consider decent enough to read aloud in a mixed audience, fumed: "Her mind seems in rather a diseased, queasy, and prurient state if she cannot read out the Bible aloud." He insulted her further in a most unchristian fashion by charging that in her obvious imitation of Bradlaugh "in voice, gesture, and substance" she was only a "very pale, weak, and watery moon to the sun of his abilities." Supporting this gentlemanly champion of the church, the Middlesbrough

Dominie called Annie "a shrewish little vixen" and Bradlaugh "the devil of Atheistic Freethought." Perhaps part of their clerical vindictiveness rose from worry, for they had heard that Mrs. Besant, at Manchester, had recently followed the practice of Bradlaugh and other Freethought leaders by herself naming an infant boy in a ceremony paralleling Christian baptism instead of sending him and the parents to church in the orthodox fashion.

At any rate, people all over England were wrangling and disputing over Mrs. Annie Besant, of whose name most of them had never heard a few months before.

4

Free Love and
Percy Bysshe Shelley

When Mrs. Besant had decided to cast her lot with the atheists, she had thought that joining the National Secular Society was the same thing. She had no way of knowing then that the Freethought "party" was almost as disunited, almost as full of sects and schisms, almost as split among rival leaders and would-be leaders, as the Christian church. She had thought that Charles Bradlaugh, being Freethought's most prominent and notorious member, as well as president of the N.S.S., would naturally be its acknowledged chief. She soon found that this was not at all the case. The Freethinkers believed in being free, at least so far as their allegiance to others was concerned, though many did not mind seeking the allegiance of others to them. The National Secular Society had succeeded in bringing together into one organization the largest number of local chapters or branches, but many other groups throughout the British Isles had their own affiliations or preferred to remain completely autonomous. Although there was a fair amount of mutual co-operation and advertising, the most famous speakers had their own patrons and circuits, with a certain amount of overlapping. The *National Reformer* itself was not so much the official organ of the N.S.S. as it was the property of its editor, Bradlaugh. The *Secular Chronicle*, similarly, was owned and published in Birmingham by a group headed by George H. Reddalls, who had his own ambitions.

In March, Bradlaugh and his friends began to lay plans for their annual convention, which was to be held at Manchester on Whitsunday—a day which the Freethinkers selected with some malicious humor. Early in April, however, Reddalls carefully pointed out to his readers that this conference would really belong to the National Secular Society, which was recognized by only a part of the whole movement, and that the independents might expect to be dominated by the others if they participated. Bradlaugh, who had long had visions of forming a strong and united body, quickly modified the original plans, and by the end of the month Reddalls felt safe in recommending that the others participate.

On May 16 the national conference was held. Mrs. Besant had been asked to act as a sort of recording secretary and to draw up a report at length for the *National Reformer*. Things started off with a slight brush between Bradlaugh and Reddalls, but matters were smoothed over and Bradlaugh read his annual presidential report. Reviewing the year's activities, he praised the platform work of such insiders as Charles Watts and, "though last in date, most certainly not least in value—Mrs. Annie Besant." Outside the ranks of the N.S.S. he saw other stars already swimming into Annie's firmament: George Jacob Holyoake, G. W. Foote, Mrs. Harriet Law, and George Reddalls himself, whose paper he complimented highly.

With the ground thus diplomatically prepared, it was only natural that Bradlaugh be unanimously re-elected president. Thereupon he proposed five vice-presidents, the first four being veteran members of the N.S.S. The fifth was Mrs. Annie Besant. All five, together with three others nominated by the meeting, were approved by acclaim. Then, to cement the feeling of good fellowship with the holdout independents, Bradlaugh suggested that Reddalls, Foote, and Mrs. Law be added to the list. Reddalls declined in the morning, but thought it over and accepted in the afternoon. The other two not being present, invitations were sent them. Various speeches were then made by several leaders, and, on Bradlaugh's request, Mrs. Besant left her secretarial duties and modestly addressed the meeting, thanking it for the honor done her, "an honor which she had as yet done nothing to win, but would strive to deserve in future."

All in all, it seemed to be a most satisfactory convention. Mrs. Besant went away from it to launch into a new series of lectures and pamphlets. A silent battle for position and length soon developed in the box devoted to lecture schedules in the *National Reformer*. Bradlaugh's list continued to lead off, but eventually Annie's took second place, pushing Watts, Foote, and Mrs. Law farther down. She presided at a meeting of the Dialectical Society addressed by Bradlaugh; she "brought down the house" at Newcastle by "the ludicrous light in which she placed several parts of the Bible"; and she enlisted large numbers of new members at Southampton, Bedlington, and North Shields. Her "powerful and brilliant" talk at Nottingham showed "with more vivid clearness the wrongs that women have had to endure, by being debarred their fair share of education." When the officials at Congelton tried to prevent the pollution of their town hall by refusing her the privilege of lecturing in it, the forces of freedom came off with a complete victory. She regularly attended meetings of the executive committee of the N.S.S. She began a long series of articles on the Positivism of Comte in the *Reformer,* and together with Bradlaugh and Watts she participated in writing a series of tracts. Photographs of her, cabinet or small size, singly or by the dozen, were put on sale at the *National Reformer* and *Secular Chronicle* offices and sold after lectures along with those of other Secularist notables.

Like St. George tilting against the dragon, she next launched unabashed into a series of attacks on Parliament itself. When one of the Radical members, Samuel Plimsoll, known as "The Sailor's Friend" because of his attempts to improve the safety of mercantile shipping—his "Plimsoll mark" still indicates how deeply a British ship may be loaded—was balked by the shipowners' influence, she opened an editorial campaign against Parliament for the shameful way it had been treating him and his reforms. Even more spectacularly, incited by popular working-class indignation against the granting of huge sums of money to members of the royal family—especially the sum of £142,000 to the Prince of Wales for a projected trip to India—she singlehandedly started and pushed a "Monster Petition" to Parliament in the matter.

It was through this crusade that she witnessed her first—but far from her last—Hyde Park "demonstration." On a Sunday in mid-July, Bradlaugh called a public outdoor meeting to support the fourteen members of Commons who had voted "against burdening the workers to provide for the amusement of a spendthrift prince."[1] Mrs. Besant, accompanied by Bradlaugh's two young daughters (since she was now practically one of the family), made her way to the park and hovered on the outskirts of the seething crowd, which Watts in his account estimated at 100,000. The London morning papers cut this number to 5,000–10,000, the *Liverpool Post* put it at 10,000–20,000, and a partisan M.P. guessed 30,000. At any rate, Mrs. Besant was much impressed by the efficient way in which her friends had organized the orderly meeting, with its system of marshals and stewards, each with their particular functions and identifying badges. She did not endeavor to press closer to the platform, thinking that unless the speakers and their party at such a gathering could make their way through the throng in a carriage, a woman was physically unfitted to push her way into the center of things. This principle, so excellent in theory, she was soon to consign to the junk heap of her memory.

In the meantime, Reddalls was not appeased by his election as vice-president. The Newcastle group, in his own paper, had officially protested his behavior at the convention. Early in August his grievances burst out again in a leading article. He had been neglected as vice-president; Bradlaugh had publicly criticized some of his remarks in the *Chron-*

[1] See *Autobiographical Sketches,* pp. 104–6, and the columns of the *National Reformer,* July, 1875–June, 1876, for a running account of this affair.

icle; his opinion had not been asked beforehand about one of Mrs. Besant's tracts, published in the *Reformer*—of course he had "the most perfect reliance on that lady's ability to pen such a document," even though this one was obviously done in a rather hasty manner and contained some errors. His hurt was scarcely concealed by his sarcasm, or healed by their replies.

Mrs. Besant was attacked from another quarter, too—and in the process made one of her staunchest, most unexpected, and most permanent friends. A totally unknown young curate of St. Matthew's Church, Bethnal Green, wrote to call her to account for inconsistency in her treatment of Christianity in a recent "Daybreak" column and in an article on "Civil and Religious Liberty." Contempt and ridicule, the Rev. Stewart D. Headlam suggested temperately, are not the best way of getting at the real truth about the Bible and Christianity. Her courteous self-defense led to an alliance between a leading Freethinker and leading liberal Anglican which was to last over a long period of years.

Involved in such multifarious matters of public concern, Mrs. Besant might well have seemed too busy to have any private life at all. But in June there began a long train of domestic events that were to make her a still more public and notorious figure. She had gone to Leicester to lecture. It was known as a highly political town, a stronghold of Radicalism, where only liberals dared contest seats in Parliament. It was also known as a Nonconformist town, the "capital of dissent."[2] There was of course a strong Secularist group there, though at first it followed George J. Holyoake rather than Reddalls, Foote, or Bradlaugh. Still, it was curious to see and hear this new female star, about whom there was so much buzzing. It invited her to speak.[3]

Annie received her usual ovation. But in the discussion period that followed there was a particularly "irate Christian opponent" who was not content with trying to refute her religious and biblical arguments but horrifiedly accused her of being responsible for a book entitled *The Elements of Social Science,* which he further identified as "The Bible of Secularists." He went on to state both that it advocated the abolition of marriage and the substitution of free love and that Bradlaugh agreed with it. She had never heard of such a book, but she felt safe in denying the truth of the Christian's statement, since she knew that her friend was very conservative on the subject of marriage and detested all such loose doctrines. He had, in fact, allied himself strongly for many years with the agitation against such conduct led by an early feminist, Mrs. Josephine Butler.

Nevertheless, as quickly as she could after returning to London, Mrs.

[2] See Malcolm Quin, *Memoirs of a Positivist* (London, 1924), pp. 26 ff.

[3] *Autobiography,* pp. 293–96, and *Sketches,* pp. 100–103.

Besant inquired about the book and its contents. She found that it had been written by an anonymous "graduate of medicine" over twenty years before and had been favorably reviewed in the *National Reformer,* as well as in Holyoake's *Reasoner,* in the *Examiner,* and in the *British Journal of Homoeopathy.* The volume, which had first appeared under the much more startling title *Physical, Sexual, and Natural Religion,* consisted of three parts: the first advocating, "from the standpoint of medical science, what is roughly known as 'Free Love' "; the second being "entirely medical" and giving certain pieces of guarded advice; and the third consisting of "a clear and able exposition of the law of population as laid down by the Rev. Mr. Malthus, and—following the lines of John Stuart Mill—insisting that it was the duty of married persons to voluntarily limit their families within their means of subsistence." These, according to the author, who turned out to be Dr. George R. Drysdale, an earlier contributor to the *National Reformer* under the initials "G.R.,"[4] were the "elements of social science."

As a matter of fact, many years before Mrs. Besant had appeared on the scene, Bradlaugh had broken with his coeditor of the *Reformer,* Joseph Barker, over the book. Now, because he had praised its sincerity and high purpose and had recommended to workingmen this explanation of the law of population, he was also charged with sharing the author's opinions concerning "the impermanence of the marriage tie." Worse, since she was already widely known as Bradlaugh's associate, Mrs. Besant now found herself also being tarred with the same brush. She was even more horrified and stunned than her mendacious Christian opponent.

All these things were too much for her husband to endure. He practically tried to kidnap little Mabel.

After the separation of the Besants in 1873, Arthur Digby, according to the arranged terms, had remained with his father at Sibsey for a year.[5] Then he was sent as a boarder to a small school in nearby Boston, kept by a Miss Louisa Everitt. There he remained not too unhappily for two more years, without ever visiting his mother. His father started to take in a long succession of resident boy pupils, whom he skilfully crammed so that they managed to scrape through their examinations. Later, Frank gave up this residence teaching and took up the reading of examination papers, first for the Cambridge University Local Examinations and then for the College Board of Preceptors; in addition, he examined for innumerable private schools. Digby remembered how thousands of papers were delivered to the vicarage in crates and how his father doggedly slaved away, day after day, marking the answers according to the time-

---

[4] For a further account of the book and its author, see James Alfred Field, *Essays on Population and Other Papers,* ed. Helen Fisher Hohman (Chicago, 1931), pp. 123, 210–12, 219, 313–14. Mrs. Besant's own summary of the book in her *Autobiography,* pp. 294–95, is quoted above.

[5] Arthur Digby Besant, *Pedigree,* pp. 210–14.

table he had drawn up, so that he could build up an annuity for his old age.

As would be expected of any such meticulous individual, the vicar had insisted on applying the provisions of the articles of separation between himself and his wife and had seen to it that Mabel came to him at Sibsey every July. On her first visit, in 1874, he had seen no change in her which caused him any worry.[6] Her baby soul as yet seemed safe, since she could still repeat the Lord's Prayer "and another simple prayer" which had been taught her jointly by her parents before her mother had been so grievously led astray by the notorious atheist Charles Bradlaugh. But in July, 1875, just before the child's fifth birthday, Besant noticed a great difference. Mabel had wholly forgotten all her prayers, and on the very first evening of her visit, when her papa had bade her good night and had automatically added, "God bless you," the little girl had innocently asked him why he said that. She further volunteered the information that her mamma had told a servant of theirs not to talk so. Even worse, the shocked father later asserted, his daughter had informed him that her mamma had forbidden her to say her prayers any more because there was no God to hear them. Faced with these charges, Mrs. Besant denied them all, maintaining that she had never forbidden Mabel to say her prayers or told her there was no God and that actually she had taken the child to Roman Catholic and other church services—though infrequently, she admitted. The truth of the matter probably was that Mabel was sharp enough even at four to see how the wind blew with her mother and to adjust herself comfortably to its breezes.

But Mr. Besant had his own ideas of what was right. Document or no document, he refused to let Mabel go back to perdition—that is, to her mother. He said he wanted to communicate with his wife's trustees, her brother Henry, and a lawyer named Cornelius Vincent Webster Neale, to insist that his child's religious training be continued and that she be removed from all association with Bradlaugh. But he discovered that Neale could not be found and that Henry Wood returned his letter unopened. He feared direct personal communication with his wife, hoping to settle the matter quietly by writing.

All his pious hopes were frustrated. On August 10 his wife and Charles Bradlaugh appeared unannounced at the Vicarage and demanded Mabel. As it seemed to Mr. Besant, Bradlaugh behaved most improperly and offensively. The big man used both threats and violence in pushing his way into the hall without explaining his business and refused to leave when ordered. Even more unbelievably, Annie stood by without interfering; in fact, she spoke only once, and that speech was to Bradlaugh when he

---

[6] For the particulars on both sides of the case, see the following documents in the previously mentioned Chancery suit in 1878: Chancery 2983, 3049, 5999, and demurrer 1878-B-No. 415. These are also printed in the *National Reformer*, May 26, 1878, *et seq.*

threatened the vicar. It was only after Besant was driven to sending for a constable that Bradlaugh was forcibly ejected.

Annie remained and demanded her daughter. When her husband answered, "She is not here," she asked, "To whom am I to apply?" After he had given her the name of his brother Albert, solicitor at Southsea, she and Bradlaugh drove away together. Besant denied that he had ever told her, in the presence of four or any other number of witnesses, "I have put her where you can't find her," and asserted that he had never refused to give information about the child's whereabouts. Nor had he ever said that Albert was his solicitor upon whom a process must be served to recover Mabel, but he admitted that, the day before, he had received a telegram from Lewis and Lewis, Bradlaugh's lawyers, about the matter, and that three letters had followed later.

After a few days' delay and the threat of court proceedings, Mabel was returned to her mother. But Bradlaugh, who had thrust himself into the role of Annie's knight and protector all along, was not content. At the head of the first page of the issue of the *Reformer* for August 22 he inserted a long "PERSONAL," in which he reviewed the pertinent circumstances of Mrs. Besant's earlier life, told his readers of the recent attempt to deprive her entirely of her child on the grounds of her atheism, and recounted the "vigorous steps," legal and otherwise, which had resulted in the return of the girl. Knowing that he was soon leaving for another American lecture trip, he ended with a warning and a threat which were prophetic of what was to come:

It was decided against Percy Bysshe Shelley that an Atheist father could not be the guardian of his own children. If this law be appealed to, and anyone dares to enforce it, we shall contest it step by step, and while we are out of England, we know that in case of any attempt to retake the child by force we may safely leave our new advocate to the protection of the stout arms of our friends. . . . So far as the law courts are concerned, we have the most complete confidence in Mr. George Henry Lewis, and we shall fight the case to the House of Lords if need be."

This allusion to the famous Shelley precedent was no idle one. To all Secularists it was a battle cry. Bradlaugh had already used it when he and Mrs. Besant had recently appeared together on the lecture platform at Southampton and, according to the report of the secretary there, had aroused public feeling to an intense state of excitement when he had "raised his terrible voice in denunciation of the wrong done Mrs. Besant herself, whom bigotry had sought to deprive of her child, as it had P. B. Shelley." But, he assured his cheering audience, Mrs. Besant, "unlike her prototype, . . . had friends who would not rest till they had seen justice done her."

It was to be a long time before they could rest, but they were to write a new chapter in English legal and social history by the time they did so.

5

The First Battle of the Atheists

Though the Secularists all prided themselves on their intellectual and rationalistic approach to life and were reproached by their enemies as being pure materialists, they nevertheless liked to indulge in most of the pleasures and recreations of ordinary middle-class human beings, realizing that even among individualists there must be a group bond and spirit to advance their cause and their reforms. Besides lectures, public meetings, and debates, they liked to get together for talks, dinners, recitations and plays, dancing, and community singing. They also had their own baptismal or "naming" ceremonies and their own burial rituals. For marriages they went to the registry.

One of Annie Besant's favorite pastimes had always been her music. She both played the piano and sang. For some time the Freethinkers had used rousing songs, some with new words and music, some with old, to stir meetings into a glow. As one of them put it, "In the 'seventies . . . people who believed in nothing else, believed in hymns." It was a sort of inverted revivalism, with an increasing hymnology; but these musical collections were desultory and local. When Annie had attended that fateful meeting at Lancaster, she had found a small printed compilation there. The Executive Committee of the N.S.S., however, now determined to issue a more official and comprehensive one; and despite her manifold other activities, Mrs. Besant was naturally chosen as editor. She was also to help prepare the *Freethinker's Text-Book*. When Reddalls heard of the plans for her *Secular Song and Hymn-Book*, he was even more upset than usual because he was already at work on a less ambitious one at Manchester. Perhaps fortunately for harmony's sake, however, he suddenly caught typhoid fever, either by Christian Providence or by atheistic chance, and died in October, thus leaving the field to Annie.[1]

Very wisely, Mrs. Besant had been advised to solicit the aid of all the members of the N.S.S. in collecting her hymns. Suggestions as well as original contributions came from many sources. In her Leicester audience had been a twenty-one-year-old man named Malcolm Quin, who had already gone through all the religious phases from Anglicanism and Evangelicalism through Spiritualism to Secularism, and was then in the midst of the study of Positivism, with which his name was eventually to be mainly associated. Quin had been carried away by the youth, attractiveness, vivacity, charm, cogency, and indignation of the speaker, though he felt that "the relieving touches of wit and humour seldom found a place in her discourses." To him, nevertheless, she was such an incomparable young prophetess that he bought her photograph at the end of the lecture and treasured it—even though its colors faded—to the end of his life.

Quin, who had already had an article in the *National Reformer,* was immediately impelled to contribute to Mrs. Besant's songbook. But he had a characteristic little quarrel with her in spite of her cordiality. Inadvertently he had used the word "divine" in one of his hymns—in the same sense, he maintained, as Tennyson had used it in "A daughter of the Gods, divinely tall." But Mrs. Besant would have none of this defense. Her book was to be avowedly "atheistic and republican," and she feared the effects of "divine" on her readers. On the other hand, she thoroughly approved Quin's apostrophe to "Mother Nature" in another of his hymns, which, she said, was "just the thing they wanted." Quin was a bit surprised because he had respect for her poetic and literary instinct, even if she was not a poet; but he deferred to her judgment. Fifty years later he had not forgotten the episode.

The songbook soon came out and ran through two editions; it would have had a third, said its editor, if she had not become dissatisfied with it. But it gave many Secularist families and group meetings a popular release for their musical emotions for some time.

The hymnal, however, was not quite enough for Mrs. Besant herself. Though she may not have been a poet, she had sufficient facility with rhymes and rhythms to compose a "Republican song" of her own, set it to the music of the "Marseillaise," and sing it herself at a Sunday evening's entertainment at the Hall of Science in mid-September. The encores and rapturous applause of the audience sent this new revolutionary marching song, known as "The English Marseillaise," off on a long career through Secularist halls. In fact, the choir of the Stalybridge branch were so ardent that when Mrs. Besant rendered her solo there, they chimed in with a chorus of their own and migrated *en masse* to Manchester to fur-

[1] Malcolm Quin, *Memoirs of a Positivist,* pp. 51 ff.; *Sketches,* pp. 107–8; *National Reformer,* August 22, 1875, *et seq.; Secular Chronicle,* August 22, October 17, 1875.

nish her with their accompaniment. No one doubted that "the fair lecturer won new laurels in unstinted abundance."[2]

This desire to foster an atmosphere of good fellowship and general coziness in the Society led Charles Watts to announce the formation of a new Hall of Science Club and Institute to take the place of an earlier one which had been dissolved because it had got into "the hands of parties whose conduct in the Club I could not approve." The two main rooms in the hall were redecorated. Dancing classes and parties as well as general social parties were to be held. Tables would be provided for games of chess or draughts. Special classes were to be formed—a debating class, an elocutionary class, a singing class, a dramatics class, even an "experience" class. Wives, sisters, and daughters were particularly invited to join. There would be a coffee room, various classrooms, and a library (to which Mrs. Besant's new friendly enemy, the Rev. Stewart Headlam, promptly contributed some volumes). The annual membership ticket was priced at a guinea, which would also entitle the holder to free admission to the "Shilling Reserved (Cushioned) Seats" at the Sunday lectures. The club began with an enrolment of more than three hundred and quickly rose to over a thousand. At the opening meeting Watts was naturally elected president, and Foote became vice-president, with R. O. Smith as manager. After the "numerous company of ladies and gentlemen" had disported themselves in a dance, instrumental and vocal music was dispensed by various members, and the affair ended auspiciously with short addresses by the old veteran, Charles Bradlaugh, and the new darling, Annie Besant.

Just before Bradlaugh left for America he prepared a general message for his flock, pointing out their past achievements and new goals, which could be reached only by unity, co-operation, and hard work. He saw the opportunity for much good in the new club, but he advised against allowing smoking in its rooms, since this failing was objectionable to most of the ladies and would give "an air of loose manners to the Club." Bradlaugh was always a stickler for propriety, as well as something of an ascetic. During a recent spirited discussion in his paper over whether flesh-eating was immoral, he had made it clear that he was a vegetarian; but he had also confessed with engaging candor to a correspondent that he was no longer a teetotaler, though he had been one for many years.

Before he sailed on the "City of Berlin," the club was tastefully decorated for his farewell lecture for the Freethinkers' Benevolent Fund by Mrs. Besant, Mrs. Watts, and two other willing ladies as an unexpected surprise. After presiding at his Birkenhead lecture "by request" and being "presented with a handsome bouquet" in gratitude, Annie went on with him to Liverpool, where they were both much upset by the behavior of the newspaper reporters at his talk. Not long before he left London, he

[2] *National Reformer,* September 12, 1875; *Secular Chronicle,* December 12, 26, 1875.

had raided his library, loaded two hansom cabs with all kinds of French and English books on the French Revolution, and brought them to Annie, who was preparing a series of six lectures on the subject. This she was to give at the South Place Institute of Moncure Conway, who was also temporarily absent in America. Then, after promising a weekly letter to the *National Reformer* from abroad and turning over the editorial control to Charles Watts with his "full confidence," Bradlaugh set sail in the middle of September.

Mrs. Besant had plenty to do, even without her mentor. Her lecture schedule was jammed; she had established a regular connection as contributor to an American Freethought periodical, the *Index;*[3] she had joined the Republican Club and was writing for the *Republican Chronicle,* a political arm of the N.S.S. edited by a member of its Executive Committee, George Standring; and she was pushing her "Monster Petition." She was also keeping up her interest in the problems of the agricultural laborer; in fact, she and Bradlaugh had participated in a meeting held in an open field at Upper Basildon and had departed "amid much cheering and waving of hats," even though they had refused to take sides in the dispute over whether a new union should replace Arch's old one, because, while disagreeing with some of his policies and tactics, they had never questioned his sincerity of purpose. She was still reviewing from one to five books a week, in addition to keeping up her "Daybreak" column and writing articles; but she was ready to drop her nom de plume of "Ajax" and use her real name. She brought out a collection of six of her lecture essays. Her articles on Comte were still running; Comte's Positivism had much to say to the Secularists. And she had to keep her eye on the Hall of Science.

This was a delicate job. Most of the veteran leaders of the N.S.S. had to swallow their pride and try to conceal their resentment at the airy way Annie had displaced them in the attention of the rank and file, who adored her. There had been a little trouble here and there, to be sure, as at some of her later meetings in Glasgow; but Bradlaugh had wrathfully reprimanded the dissidents, and the grumbles had died down. Mr. and Mrs. Watts in particular had to wreathe their latent jealousy in smiles. Charles, indeed, publicly praised the French Revolution lectures of "our very hearty and graceful co-worker . . . who is really working so hard at lecturing and writing"; and Mrs. Watts had taken the chair at one of them.

Kate Watts was a second wife, considerably younger than her husband, who had a grown son of his own; she was still pretty enough to have been regarded as the belle of the London group and as a sort of chief hostess at the Hall of Science. The daughter of two leading Nottingham Freethinkers, she had not been inside a church till she was over seventeen and

[3] D. M. Bennett, *The World's Sages, Thinkers, and Reformers,* pp. 1034–37.

had not read a line of the Bible till after she was married. She had some dramatic ability, which she developed on the Secularist platform, and was later to play some minor roles under Forbes-Robertson. Although she had just had a baby, which Bradlaugh had "named," she found an opening for her talents in the elocution and dramatic class which her husband had now turned over to another member.[4] Stimulated by the success of other women on the platform, she made her first public appearance just before Christmas—an appearance at which, according to the *National Reformer*, she received loud laughter and much applause for her humorous introduction of her husband and his speech entitled "Woman: What She Has Done, and What She Can Do." Not long before, Mrs. Besant, remembering her recent treatment by her own husband, had lectured to the largest Sunday-morning audience the Hall of Science had yet had on "The Marriage Question." Although she mentioned no personalities, she knew that the thoughts of the sympathetic audience were fixed on her own predicament.

Bradlaugh's weekly letters, in the form of a sort of diary, soon began to come in, to be read by the staff and then duly printed. Concerned solely with his reception in America, which was still enthusiastic, but apparently not quite so frenzied as before, they made no reference to affairs in London. Suddenly, disturbing news arrived. Bradlaugh was not well, though he was trying to complete his tour. Then, in December, word came that a bad case of pleurisy had developed into typhoid. Fortunately two American doctors and a good nurse treated him very skilfully, and he recovered, though he had come close to death. The Baltimore *Advertiser* praised him in print for his fortitude and patience in the face of danger, and the "Rev. Mr. Frothingham bore public and admiring testimony in his own church to Mr. Bradlaugh's perfect serenity" in his desperate illness. But while he made many friends, even in the ranks of the godly, he was prevented from making the money he had gone for and returned to England at the end of 1875 in bad health and pocket—a malady from which he suffered for many years.[5]

On the surface, all looked tranquil at the Hall of Science. But the name of James Thomson, the melancholic poet, had silently disappeared from the pages of the *National Reformer*. And when Conway, who had met Bradlaugh in America and had given him temporary financial help, got back to London, he discovered that in his absence there had been a stormy revolt against him led by a minority of his congregation—those more timid ones who disapproved his opening the South Place pulpit to

[4] See the *Secular Review and Secularist*, September 22, 1877; Gertrude Marvin Williams, *The Passionate Pilgrim*, pp. 62–63. But many of the picturesque details of Mrs. Williams' story are entirely the result of a creative imagination.

[5] This story is reconstructed from the accounts in the *Autobiography*, the *Sketches*, and the *National Reformer*. See also Hypatia Bradlaugh Bonner, *Charles Bradlaugh*, II, 7 ff.

Mrs. Besant. His firmness and loyalty to her, however, forced their secession, and the rest of the flock closed ranks behind him.[6] On the other
hand, Charles Voysey, another liberal on the Secularist fringe, once more
changed his mind and decided to make gestures of reconciliation toward
the Church. In so doing, he turned against his former Freethinking
friends, so that both Bradlaugh and Mrs. Besant felt called upon to reply
in the *Reformer* to his attacks. In a sort of ecclesiastical compensation,
however, young Stewart Headlam was drawing closer. He went even so
far as to lecture in the Hall of Science and at the East London branch of
the Society in April, but was welcomed cautiously by Bradlaugh as a
"good, kind-hearted man, somewhat confused with the theological riddles
his Church has propounded."

Most important of all, the venerable George Jacob Holyoake had recovered from his illness, was ready to return to his journalistic and lecturing activities, and seemed to be in a conciliatory mood toward Bradlaugh and the N.S.S.[7] Now, even though Bradlaugh still felt shaky and
had to cancel most of his lectures, it seemed as if he could relax and enjoy
the discussions, classes, and parties at the club. There was a "Freethinkers' Juvenile Party" on Twelfth Night, "sacred to children," with—of all
things—a Christmas tree donated by the president himself and gifts for
two or three hundred of "those little ones to whom we must look as the
mainstay of our cause when we ourselves are worn out." Mrs. Watts managed the affair, but Mrs. Besant was present in the early evening. In
March a special "Tea and Soirée," with dancing, recitations, and a concert, was given in honor of Bradlaugh's recovery from a relapse. This
time, though Mrs. Watts gracefully read and presented an address which
the committee had drawn up in tribute to him, it was Mrs. Besant who
presented him with a purse containing almost £170 which his affectionate followers had contributed. Mr. Bradlaugh thanked them all as impar-
tially as he could. All the ladies, however, probably recalled the special
paragraph of commendation he had directed to Mrs. Besant, individually enumerating each of her achievements in his annual "New Year's Address to Our Readers" in the *National Reformer* a few weeks earlier.

But the ground was beginning to quaver slightly. On January 23, 1876,
Bradlaugh in a "Personal" editorial reviewed his career as a leader in all
liberal causes, but ended with the challenge:

Are there grumblers? Let them be silent till their deeds for the cause speak
louder than their words! Are there rivals? Let their rivalry be honest, open
labour. . . . We claim no first place in these our armies. . . . We do not war with
traitors.

[6] M. E. Burtis, *Moncure Conway,* p. 156.

[7] Joseph McCabe, *Life and Letters of George Jacob Holyoake* (London, 1908), II,
78 ff.; *National Reformer,* January 16, May 7, 1876.

The traitors were to remain anonymous for several months to come, so far as the public was concerned. But the new disruption was again acknowledged, without naming names, by a prominent editorial entitled "Party Unity" by Holyoake himself on May 7. No longer, he announced with sorrow, would he write as a staff member of the *National Reformer*. He had decided to establish a daily paper of his own, the *Secular Review*, in the belief that he could do more for the cause of Secularism by expressing his views and policies independently. He was leaving on friendly terms and with only the pleasantest memories; but he was leaving. In his statement he admitted only by implication that during January and February he had tried to collaborate with G. W. Foote in founding still another journal, the *Secularist*, but had soon broken the connection, partly because he found Foote too hard to get along with and partly because Bradlaugh had remonstrated with him by mail.[8] Nor was he interested in associating himself with the *Secular Chronicle*, which had been bought by Mrs. Harriet Law on the death of the destitute Reddalls and was being used as her personal organ, and to which Mrs. Besant sometimes contributed.

He would go it alone; but first in his capacity as elder statesman he felt constrained to make some criticisms and give some advice:

It is not pretending to merit, but merely claiming the natural advantage of long and active experience in many movements, to assume that I may know some things that very young persons may not know, and that it may better serve the Secular party to edit a paper in its interests than leave it to be represented by those who cannot know its needs, and who indeed were not born when the struggle was raging out of which the new form of Freethought arose. . . . Therefore, when I saw advocates older and abler attacked, . . . it seemed to me a duty not to lend any countenance to it, and to relinquish a connection which implied concurrence in it.

Still veiling the object of his main allusions, Holyoake then pleaded for the necessity of courtesy and good will in the movement and concluded by naming his first names:

Had I commenced the *Secular Review* a short time ago, I should have given a very different account of the writings of the Editor of this journal and the work of Mrs. Besant than that which some may have seen. What encouragement may there be for any lady of grace and ability to stand on the side of Liberal progress if she may be assailed under the silence or consent of those she serves? Such criticism might easily be retaliated, the writers themselves not having yet excited any general belief in their own infallibility. It is for those who care for critical fairness, and who value unity and good sense, to discountenance articles which can only create ill-feeling and party passion, and give satisfaction only to adversaries. I, for one, disclaim concurrence of any kind with them, as being mostly untrue and entirely unfair.

[8] McCabe, *George Jacob Holyoake*, II, 78 ff.

The ungentlemanly attacker of Mrs. Besant, whom Holyoake so politely defended, was his own brief associate on the *Secularist,* the young G. W. Foote, who was sharpening his ax for use at the next big public opportunity. Foote was vice-president of Watts's Hall of Science Club and Institute and an aggressive, uninhibited speaker at Freethought meetings all over the country. Whether he was talking about Whitman, Shelley, or Jonah and the Whale, he pulled no punches, nor did he care whether they landed in vulnerable areas, proscribed by the laws of sportsmanship. Naturally, he had his own ideas about the leadership of the Society.

Everything was therefore pointed toward the annual convention, which was to take place at Leeds early in June. The contenders organized their forces. Bradlaugh and Mrs. Besant moved up into Yorkshire in advance, since there was unrest among the miners there, especially in the Cleveland district, where Bradlaugh led a demonstration in favor of the Trades Union movement; later, at Barnsley, Annie herself addressed the striking men, advising them to return to work and giving them the proceeds of her previous lecture. Freethought and labor reform continued to march hand in hand.

On Sunday, June 4, at Leeds, all seemed serene in the conference hall as the proceedings began. Seated on the platform were Bradlaugh and his two daughters, who guarded the proprieties by always accompanying their father when Mrs. Besant was along; Mr. and Mrs. Watts; Holyoake; Mrs. Law; and various other notables, with or without official titles. Mrs. Besant, as "Hon. Sec.," recorded the events for the *National Reformer.* Bradlaugh read his annual report, distributing praises as lavishly as possible among the stalwarts, from Holyoake and Watts to Mrs. Law and Mrs. Besant. The only ripple in the early smoothness came when he had to announce the resignation of Watts from his position as general secretary and special lecturer because of the increased demands on his printing press; Watts, however, would continue with his general propagandist activities. This all seemed natural enough.

But when Bradlaugh started to move on to the election for the new terms, young Foote quickly sprang up and moved that it be postponed till the constitution and bylaws could be revised "to make them acceptable to the general body of Freethinkers throughout the country." He did not get very far, for after a sharp procedural debate between himself and Bradlaugh, he lost by a large majority. Bradlaugh, supported by Watts, was then re-elected unanimously; his nomination of Holyoake and Mrs. Besant as vice-presidents was accepted by acclaim, Holyoake seconding her nomination fulsomely.

As in the previous year, Mrs. Law was next proposed. Harriet Law was a bluff, stout, loud-voiced woman, a female Boanerges, "whose violent declamations used to make themselves heard, and almost felt, far beyond the limits of the hall in which she spoke."[9] But her good-natured though rough humor made her popular with many Freethinkers, and her insistence on preserving her independence engaged their respect. She refused the nomination; she could serve the cause of Freethought better outside the Society than within it, she said. As in the past, whenever there was a hard task to be performed and others shrank from it, she would continue to respond; she knew she was a last resource. Then, as the audience laughed and applauded, she launched her parting shot: she deprecated the convening of a conference for the mere purpose of mutual congratulation and urged that if there was any dissatisfaction in the party they should all sedulously endeavor to remove it. Despite Bradlaugh's plea that he needed her advice on the Executive Committee, she sat down and refused to budge.

This was the signal for the nomination of Foote from the floor. He had a loud, if not large, faction behind him, especially from the dissident Glasgow branch. But Bradlaugh calmly put down the revolt. While Foote boldly challenged his leadership, he made a frank statement of the "extremely grave" reasons why he thought his young rival should not be elected. After Holyoake, Mrs. Besant, and others supported their leader, and a confused battle of proxies developed, Foote failed of election by a large majority.

But the Glaswegians continued to grumble. One of them even proposed that Foote should replace Bradlaugh as president and shouted out, amid much laughter from his cohorts, that for all he cared Mr. Bradlaugh, Mr. Holyoake, and Mrs. Besant might "all go to—the wall." Even the valiant efforts of Mrs. Law to act as peacemaker failed to quell the abusive interruptions from Glasgow. The skilful attempt of Mrs. Besant to play down the affair in her notes failed to conceal her worry over the schism. Perhaps her conscience worried her about her share in precipitating the situation. As a concession to the rebels, however, a committee to revise the principles and constitution was agreed on, with Mrs. Besant herself as secretary; and the conference dispersed.

Soon afterward, back in London, Foote was summoned to appear before the Executive Committee to answer various charges against him. He refused to appear and submitted his resignation instead. Rather than accept this, the Committee angrily voted to erase his name formally from the books. The first stage of the revolt was over, with a victory for the loyalists.[10]

[9] Quin, *Memoirs of a Positivist,* p. 53.

[10] See accounts in *National Reformer, Secular Chronicle,* and *Secular Review;* also, McCabe, *George Jacob Holyoake,* II, 79.

6

Christian Charity and
Secular Romance

Annie scarcely had time to get the somewhat polluted Leeds air out of her lungs before she plunged into the political maelstrom once more. For several months she had been prodding, pushing, and cajoling the antigovernment—that is, the anti-Disraeli—voters wherever she and her friends went to sign her "Monster Petition" against granting Prince Edward funds for his proposed imperialistic propaganda trip to India. Her perseverance was demonstrated when, on June 16, 1876, the petition, almost a mile in length, was rolled on a tough mahogany pole, encased in "American cloth," placed tenderly in a carriage, and driven with great public display to the House of Commons. Its arrival there caused considerable excitement and was duly recorded by the press. Its heading ran: "The petition of the undersigned Charles Bradlaugh, Annie Besant, Charles Watts, and 102,934 others," but its weight was insufficient to overawe the Tories, who put the bill through anyway. The Prince of Wales made his triumphal tour; "Dizzy" proclaimed Edward's mother empress of India; and the ground was prepared for the Indian independence movement led by Mrs. Besant, Mohandas Gandhi, and others many years later. Annie, however, continued unabashed her satirical attacks on the royal family in her "Daybreak" column.[1]

Rather surprisingly, Mrs. Besant was, on occasion, able to keep her political sympathies separate from her religious skepticism. While a Freethinker, she was a tremendous admirer of the pious but Liberal Gladstone and had been sickened by his recent defeat and temporary retirement into private life. The tense situation in the Near East, par-

[1] *Sketches,* p. 106; *National Reformer,* June 18, 25, July 30, 1876.

ticularly the new atrocities of the Turks against the Bulgarians, but including Disraeli's daring commitment of England to a staggering investment in Suez Canal stocks, could, it seemed to her, be met only through Gladstone's leadership. Her mounting fears, as well as her political acumen, reached such a point that in November she hurried through Watts's press an anonymous pamphlet entitled "Why Did Gladstone Fall from Power?" and dispatched a copy to the former Prime Minister at Hawarden. Apparently she could not resist divulging her authorship to him, since he promptly wrote her a very courteous note of thanks and approbation, praising the "very great ability" with which she had analyzed the points of the Eastern question, though being less pleased with her criticism of the new Liberal leaders at home. No one can blame her for treasuring carefully the letter in Gladstone's own hand which ended:

It is not my custom, for it is not in my power, to acknowledge so particularly tracts on public or other affairs which I may receive, even if they convey as pointed an appeal; but I beg you, Madam, to accept this note as a willing tribute to the ability and force, as well as the integrity and sense of justice, with which you have discussed a question of vital interest.[2]

The Eastern situation, which was to lead to war between Turkey and Russia within a few months, worsened so rapidly that a "National Conference" on the subject was called in mid-December, and Gladstone emerged briefly to address it. Mrs. Besant, who was the only woman in the body of the hall and had been roughly refused admission by the doorkeepers till they recognized that she was the companion of Bradlaugh, wrote acidly in her paper that it was neither national nor a conference and that the audience awakened only when Gladstone spoke. "When," she lamented, "will this man resume his rightful post?" But when he did return in 1879, she found that she could not agree with all of his policies and actions.

In Italy, too, the surge toward new conceptions of freedom of political and religious thought was rolling onward. In the wake of the political and military victories of Mazzini, Garibaldi, and Cavour had come the resuscitation of the memory of Giordano Bruno, whose martyrdom at the Roman stake in 1600 was now being used as a rallying point for the demand for freedom round the world. An Italian committee had been formed to raise funds for a statue of their hero in defiance of the opposition of the Papacy. It was to be an international memorial, and at the Leeds conference the support of the N.S.S. had been guaranteed and some sixty pounds had been raised.

Here was another chance for Annie's stabbing, glittering pen. Her leading article on Bruno for July 23 was to be widely reprinted and years later to have an entirely unanticipated influence on her own past.

[2] *Pedigree*, pp. 260–70. See also *National Reformer*, November 26, 1876.

"Who was Bruno?" she queried rhetorically and then went on to answer her own question by tracing his career as student, Dominican monk, and eventual skeptic of Christian and Aristotelian dogmas; his revival of Plato and Pythagoras; his disputations in France and England; his persecutions for heresy in Germany, Prague, and Italy; and his final burning as an atheist in 1600, after being imprisoned for eight years by the Inquisition. In a philosophy of martyrdom which she had long cherished for herself, Annie perorated:

They scatter his ashes to the wind, and boast that nought is left of Bruno save the remembrance of his execution, and they forbid any to read his books, and fondly dream that they have slain his memory; but now, in Rome, Bruno's memory lives, while that of his murderers only remains because their names are linked with his immortality, and on the base of the statue we are raising to him might fitly be engraven his own sublime words: "To know how to die in one century is to live in all centuries to come."

It was by a very strange coincidence that, only the Sunday before, Charles Bradlaugh had lectured on "Hypatia: Christianity and Woman" and had told his audience of this still earlier martyr to Christian bigotry, the beautiful Alexandrian teacher and intellectual who had been torn to pieces by a bloodthirsty mob in 415. How could Mrs. Besant have suspected in 1876 that within thirty years she would discover that Bruno, Hypatia, and she herself were one and the same—that she had once been Bruno, that she had once been Hypatia, had lived their lives and suffered their fates? But time works many wonders.

In 1876 Annie Besant was having her own troubles with Christians. Almost everywhere she went, with or without Bradlaugh, she found hecklers and tormentors arraying themselves against her. Sometimes they attacked in concerted, solidified groups, sometimes in solo performances; sometimes with words alone, sometimes with rocks and blows. But one thing they had in common: they all behaved in a most unchristian fashion. Early in the year Mrs. Besant, commenting on a series of *National Reformer* articles on "The Religious Condition of India," by "A Hindu Spectator," remarked that the English missionaries should look at home instead of wasting their time in India, so rowdy was the rioting against Freethought organized by respectable Christian citizens in such places as Congelton, Cheshire, and Llanelly, Wales. Certainly they had rejected Christ's command to love their enemies, his reminder that all men are brothers.

The hostile techniques were various. One, used by some of the clergy at Southampton in February, was first to try to shout down the heretical speakers and then to repeat the famous "watch story," which was to dog Bradlaugh's footsteps for years in spite of his vociferous and repeated denials and was later to be attached to Mrs. Besant as well.[3] This story charged that, some years before, Bradlaugh had brazenly drawn his watch from his pocket, laid it on the desk before him, and challenged the Deity to prove His existence by striking the blasphemer dead within five minutes. By the spring of 1877 the Rev. Dr. Joseph Parker, who had just opened his great Nonconformist City Temple in Holborn, ascended his pulpit and, according to the *Northern Ensign* for May 17, thundered forth into the shocked ears of his congregation:

There is a woman going up and down the country lecturing, and may be in London city at this moment; and she proudly cries out that there is no God, and she takes out her watch and says, "Now, if there be a God, I give him five minutes to strike me dead," and she coolly stands watching the hand of her watch dial, and because she is not struck dead by the time she stipulates, she cries out that there is no God; and working men run after this woman, and pay for listening to this ginger-beer blasphemy, and the ravings of a half-drunken woman.

Dr. Parker's informers had apparently failed to apprise him that it is difficult to get drunk on ginger beer and that whenever possible Annie Besant always put up at temperance hotels.

Nothing the Freethinkers could do was ever able to set at rest the horrified whispers of this scandalous tale which rippled before both Bradlaugh and Mrs. Besant whenever they invaded a new community. In fact, so widespread was the story that in 1878 young Bernard Shaw, recently arrived in England and already cultivating the brash irreverence which was to pay off so well in intellectual dividends, scared the members of a bachelor party of young professional men by remarking that if Bradlaugh had not actually issued the challenge he ought to have and that he, Shaw, would immediately try the experiment, since he "happened to share Mr. Bradlaugh's views as to the absurdity of the belief in these violent interferences with the order of nature by a short-tempered and thin-skinned supernatural deity." Shaw's producing his watch precipitated such consternation in the group that, in spite of his urging "the pious to trust in the accuracy of their deity's aim with a thunderbolt," his host hastily intervened and forbade the completion of the experiment. Shaw, however, could never understand how his evangelical friends' fears could be so easily allayed, since after all he had formulated the thought in his mind, even if he had not put it into the parlous words.[4]

Another effective technique against the Freethought speakers was exemplified in the north. Mrs. Besant did not so much mind the miserable

[3] *The Autobiography of Charles Bradlaugh* (London, 1891), pp. 28–29, reprinted from *National Reformer*, August 31, 1873. It was also attached to Mrs. Law (*Secular Chronicle*, October 27, 1878). See also Bonner, *Bradlaugh*, II, 70–71.

[4] Shaw, Preface to *Back to Methuselah*.

weather and wretched accommodations which she often suffered ("And people talk of the luxurious materialism of the atheists!"), the ruffianism of the crowds at Swansea and Bristol, or the violence of the language of such papers as the *Sun* in the great carpet-weaving center of Kidderminster, which advised Bradlaugh to look to his laurels because his colleague was "more venomous" than he.[5] Her real indignation was aroused by the spreading of renewed charges of immoral, rather than irreligious, teachings against herself and Bradlaugh. Led by "a primitive Methodist preacher named Hebblethwaite," this attack culminated in the little towns of Barnsley and Hoyland in September. Here Annie, as she put it in an article entitled "Wild Beasts at Hoyland," encountered what she described as "Christianity in its natural state, and a very ugly and savage state it is." During the week before her arrival two other Protestant missionaries had joined in inflaming the lowest and roughest elements of the populace by giving open sermons on the "most immoral and disgusting doctrines" which they put into Bradlaugh's mouth after reading certain medical books and deducing the "most indecent conclusions" from them about the opinions and practices of the Secularist party. These lectures, "garnished with invented stories," actually proclaimed, commented Mrs. Besant, the "foul thoughts" of the lecturers themselves, but they were supplemented with placards asking whether she would defend these teachings. At the same time, not very consistently, the leaders urged their followers to sweep her and all Secularists out of town.

But Annie was intrepid. She appeared as scheduled. She was used to the general heckling. There was, however, a diversion in a "very lively fight near the door, occasioned by an enthusiastic Theist." This led to a prolonged verbal squabble among Annie, Hebblethwaite, and another very "disreputable individual." The audience then joined in with equal enthusiasm—yelling, making faces, and shaking fists at her. There were even attempts to kick her as her Barnsley friends rushed her out of the hall between the angry rows of her enemies. Annie, concealing her fright by forcing herself to laugh in their faces, was saved by a sensible and quick-thinking cab-driver, who hurriedly drove his hansom away before the crowd could execute their threat to "Overturn it! Overturn it!" "The last we heard of Hoyland," she wrote in ironical retrospect, "was the yells of the pious," thwarted of their prey.

This little contretemps, faced by Mrs. Besant without the support of Bradlaugh, was only a preliminary to an even more dangerous riot in the silk-weaving town of Congelton three weeks later. There had been some trouble when he had joined her in the shipping city of Plymouth, and even more when they had chaired each other's lectures in the pottery town of Longton. But Congelton was the real test.

With the help of some local Secularists two lectures were scheduled

[5] *National Reformer*, March 26, April 9, 1876.

there in an old silk mill, since the city fathers had refused the use of the town hall. The first night, to an "accompaniment of broken windows," Bradlaugh spoke on the individual's right to think and speak for himself, and Annie was hit on the back of the head by a stone thrown by someone in the room. After the lecture, as they walked the mile and a half to their friends' house, they were accompanied all the way by a crowd which divided its time between throwing more stones, singing hymns at the top of their voices, and cursing the Secularists with good Christian curses. The next night, when Mrs. Besant lectured, the same stone-throwing crowd hospitably accompanied them from the house to the hall. In the middle of her talk a gentleman shouted, "Put her out!" and a well-known local tradesman and prize-winning wrestler stood up in front of the platform as a signal to his seven friends who were to do the putting-out.

But the pious defender of the faith did not know that Charles Bradlaugh was also a wrestler of some prowess. In fact, when the local man refused to remove himself and challenged Bradlaugh to eject him, he soon found himself being propelled through his awed friends and turned over to the police at the door, who had watched the encounter with impartial benevolence. Annie then finished her lecture peacefully inside, but when her party went out afterward her Freethinking hostess was cut over the eye by a particularly hard flint of the type indigenous to the neighborhood.[6] The York *Herald*, in writing up the disgraceful affair, suggested co-operatively that in future the prices at Mrs. Besant's lectures be raised "if the audience are to be entertained with a lecture and a battle on the same night."

The strain of these constant disturbances and the conditions under which she traveled finally proved too much for Annie. Her health again gave way in November, and she had to cancel several engagements because of a "severe indisposition" brought about by a congestion of her right lung. In making the announcement, Bradlaugh remarked that her condition probably had been aggravated by "the cowardly burning of Cayenne pepper by the Armsley Christians," who had, it seems, discovered still another method of interfering with lectures repugnant to them.

The repeated joint appearances of C. B. and A. B., as they soon were referred to by the Secularists, naturally gave rise to a flood of suspicions among the respectable concerning the exact degree of their intimacy; the unrespectable, with other standards of virtue, were unconcerned about such matters. In fact, on September 5, 1875, Bradlaugh had formally inserted in the *National Reformer* the following notice: "Mrs. Besant requests us to state that she destroys all anonymous letters unread." More-

[6] *National Reformer*, September 17, October 1, 8, 1876; *Secular Review*, October 6, 1876; *Sketches*, p. 102; *Autobiography*, pp. 296–300; Bonner, *Bradlaugh*, II, 54–55.

over, the *Reformer* frequently printed specimens of the published invectives. In Brighton one town councilor called her a "foul woman," and another hoped that "such an animal as Mrs. Besant would not be allowed to use the Town Hall." The Essex *Standard* labeled Bradlaugh a skunk and anathematized "that bestial man and woman who go about earning a livelihood by corrupting the young of England." The Cheshire *News,* quoting a local lawyer, asked where such people as Bradlaugh and others would be if there were anything on the statute books making the procurement of a miscarriage an offense. One enterprising publisher even got out a lurid pamphlet, *Wife or Mistress?*, implying that it was by Mrs. Besant herself. These racy speculations of the righteous scandalmongers were soon heightened when the two principals made a change of residence—a move which brought them personally much comfort and happiness at the same time that it plunged them into a maze of new troubles and problems.

Despite Mrs. Besant's frequent complaints about the straitened circumstances of the Secularist life, by June, 1876, her "improved means" as a result of her lectures, articles, pamphlets, and books enabled her to leave the cramped rented premises of Bayswater. She moved to a more commodious house of her own at 17 Mortimer Road—a name soon changed by the Metropolitan Board of Works to Avenue Road. The house, called Oatlands, stood in St. John's Wood, where she had lived with her family as a little girl. Since it was just north of Regent's Park and west of Primrose Hill, she and her friends had an opportunity for many pleasant strolls.

St. John's Wood at this period had both a suburban and a bohemian reputation. The un-Victorian morality of the faster circles demonstrated its temerity in the number of expensive mistresses with saddle horses and phaetons who were being set up there by discreet but wealthy gentlemen.[7] As Shaw wrote of it in his novel *Immaturity*, it was also well known for its "jollifying amongst all the artists and their models." As an exponent of the artist's life, Annie had her piano and her singing, but her son Digby, when he came to her on his allotted holiday visits, was even more impressed by her "tiny study, lined with books from floor to ceiling." She continued to rent rooms to some of her female friends, and gradually, with the slow improvement of her fortunes, she added more and more luxuries. After several years she had a conservatory with ferns and palms and dozens of tame birds flying about, well-tended gardens outside, and several dogs—one a large St. Bernard given her, appropriately enough, by Charles Bradlaugh.[8]

[7] Cf. Cyril Pearl, *The Girl with the Swansdown Seat* (New York, 1956).

[8] Affidavit, Chancery 2640; *National Reformer,* May 26, 1878; *Sketches,* p. 96; *The Annie Besant Centenary Book,* p. 218; Gertrude Marvin Williams, *The Passionate Pilgrim,* pp. 68–69, 152.

A few months after A. B.'s move C. B. discovered that his Turner Street quarters were far too minute, mean, and unsanitary to accommodate himself and his growing girls any longer. For some time during his first residence there Alice and the younger Hypatia had come to stay alternately with him, a month at a time. Then they had both been sent to school in Paris at the solicitation of his French Republican friends, but after a time, when in their late teens, they had had to return to England because of diverse domestic difficulties. Mrs. Bradlaugh's condition was deteriorating (she finally died in May, 1877), and their father's brother Robert had been imprisoned for embezzlement. On the positive side of the ledger, Charles had recently inherited almost £3,000 through the wills of two of his followers.[9]

On February 11, 1877, the following announcement appeared in the *National Reformer:* "On and after Feb. 12 Mr. Bradlaugh's private address will be 10, Portland Place, Circus Road, St. John's Wood, exactly opposite the St. John's West District Post Office, at which office all Money Orders should in future be made payable." Within a year the Board of Works had eliminated the name Portland Place and given Bradlaugh the simple Circus Road address associated with his name for many years.

These new lodgings, while a great relief from Turner Street, were not devoid of their peculiarities. As Hypatia later described the place, it was a queerly arranged house, in which they had the top floor and basement, with a bathroom on the first floor—the remainder of this floor and the whole ground floor being occupied by a firm of music sellers. The basement room, used for cooking, eating, and storing government reports, was dark and so large that their battered table and four chairs looked very desolate in it. Though they had "one little servant much given to fainting," Hypatia herself was appointed head cook and conducted her culinary education at the expense of the rest, her father being completely satisfied so long as the meals were served at the time he set. The top floor contained a large room given over to her father's library, which continued to expand so rapidly that in three years it had to be moved to the floor below; the bedrooms were all small and crowded with the old Turner Street furniture. Charles's room was about nine by ten feet, with just enough space for his bedstead, a chest of drawers, a washstand, and two chairs. His study, even after it had been moved below, did not have enough wall space for his books; they overflowed into three movable floor-shelves which obscured his desk, writing table, cane-seated chairs, two old oak armchairs, and the one easy chair in the house. The entire furnishings of the place would probably not have brought twenty-five pounds. Hypatia cited these details to refute such charges as those in the *Plymouth and Exeter Gazette* in April, 1878, that

[9] Bonner, *Bradlaugh,* I, 50, 346; II, 31–32.

Bradlaugh lived "in the most aristocratic style," or those in the Leeds *Daily News* for July, 1883, that he had a most enormous income, or even those of the American atheist, D. M. Bennett, who wrote back to his own paper, the New York *Truthseeker,* that "Bradlaugh travels like a prince, he had a first class coach reserved."[10]

It was probably not by mere coincidence that 10 Circus Road was only a few minutes' walk from 17 Avenue Road in St. John's Wood. Annie Besant bubbled over when she recalled those days in her *Autobiography.* For many years, when one or both were not out of London, Bradlaugh would devote the first hours of his mornings to legal work for charity and then would pick up his books and papers and hasten the three-quarters of a mile to her house. Hour after hour they would sit in her sunny study, each immersed in his own occupation, hardly exchanging a word, breaking off briefly for lunch and dinner and returning to their labors till about ten in the evening, when Bradlaugh would go back home to bed. Sometimes, for a diversion to break the monotony, which to them was no monotony, but a peaceful and contented communion, they would stop for an hour of euchre, their favorite game. And there were also times when they would forget the solemnity of their business and "make holiday" together. Then the great, grave Bradlaugh was transformed into a boy, "brimming over with mirth, full of quaint turns of thought and speech." The pair wandered everywhere around the London countryside. They tramped across the park at Richmond and sat under its mighty trees, which they contrasted with the bracken groves at Windsor; they had tea in a funny little room at Kew, with watercress ad libitum; they admired the "dishevelled beauties" of Hampton Court.

Charles Bradlaugh was happiest near a river. Whenever he needed rest and recreation, he went fishing.[11] He loved Maidenhead and Taplow; but Broxbourne was his favorite resort, for he knew every eddy of the little Lea River, haven of anglers from Izaak Walton's time on, and plied it with his rod. Laughing at his companion's shivers when she had to touch the fish she had caught, he taught her all the mysteries of the art. Interspersing his piscatorial lectures with talk of his ambitions, he told her of his hopes for the poor; his plans to sit in Parliament, where he could accomplish all his projects for reforming and improving the England that he loved and admired; and his love of India.

Such closeness of relationship could not help causing gossip. Nor was Annie always as circumspect as she might have been in publishing the state of her feelings. The two were obviously in love, and yet each was married to another, from whom there was apparently little or no chance

[10] Bonner, *Bradlaugh,* II, 31–32, 97–98; Williams, *The Passionate Pilgrim,* p. 75. p. 75.

[11] *Autobiography,* pp. 275–77; *National Reformer,* March 12, 1876.

of escape. All sorts of parallels and possibilities opened from this situation. Even her interest in French Positivism held its contribution. In the spring of 1875, just after Bradlaugh's return from America, Mrs. Besant had begun the serialization of her life of August Comte in the *National Reformer*. Tacitly she implied a resemblance between the unhappy marriage of the French philosopher and her own. Comte, after his marriage, had contracted his well-known friendship with Madame Clotilde de Vaux. From Mrs. Besant's lyrical pen came: "Those who are too base to believe in a true and noble friendship between a man and woman will alone try to cast any slur on the frank and noble love which bound these two great souls." She compared them in the purity of their passion and the reverence of their faithful love with Dante and Beatrice, Petrarch and Laura. One wonders how Charles Bradlaugh and the readers of the *National Reformer* reacted when they read the next paragraph:

To August Comte, this woman's friendship came as a revelation from heaven. It woke up all the music in his heart, silenced so long by care and toil and friendlessness; it unscaled the springs of tenderness, fast-closed by coldness and neglect; it revealed to him the beauty and grandeur of the human spirit; it crowned the cold white brow of Humanity with the rosy diadem of Love. The philosopher who had defined pure intellect now became the High Priest of the Heart.

Perhaps this was Annie Besant's earliest confession to her benefactor and protector, who with his old-fashioned sense of honor might have hesitated to speak first. It was open and public, yet it was discreet.

Such a romance might also have a special kind of appeal to the rank and file of the party. And perhaps the very preservation of the "purity" of the affair set Bradlaugh apart from Frank Besant in Mrs. Besant's mind and made her worship him with the kind of spiritual love which had once received physical expression in the biblical passages, prayers, and hymns against which she had revolted. There was, after all, a particular kind of titillation to be derived from such a situation. The newspapers, the preachers, the private and public gossips might vilify and abuse: they might speculate and hint all sorts of obscenities, as they did. But only Annie Besant and Charles Bradlaugh could know the truth.

Their intimates thought they also knew it, but not one of these ever suggested the slightest impropriety or extralegality in the relations between A. B. and C. B. Hypatia Bradlaugh Bonner, who should have known if anyone did, testified:

They were mutually attracted; and a friendship sprang up between them of so close a nature that had both been free it would undoubtedly have ended in marriage. In their common labours, in the risks and responsibilities jointly undertaken, their friendship grew and strengthened, and the insult and calumny heaped upon them only served to cement the bond.

The Honorable John M. Robertson, M.P., a Scotch protégé of Mrs. Besant, a Secularist, and the author of a memoir of Bradlaugh, wrote to the same effect. Many years later Theodore Besterman, who had once been a member of the inner Theosophical circles, asserted:

There is no doubt that if they had been free Bradlaugh and Mrs. Besant would have married. As it was they neither of them had the wish to indulge in an intrigue, which would, moreover, in their position, have been fatal to both. They remained devoted friends and colleagues and though Bradlaugh was in the end disappointed in her, she never had anything but praise and admiration for him.

Finally, from the Indian point of view, Sri Prakasa, a modified disciple of Mrs. Besant from his childhood and the present governor of Bombay, commented on Hypatia Bradlaugh Bonner's statement that her father and Annie Besant would have married if possible:

Personally, I think Mrs. Annie Besant was the one person who was capable of the deepest affections without any thought of sex; and she was a woman of such remarkable courage that when she was working with colleagues she did not care what the world thought of her personal attachment to those colleagues and her absolute abandon to the Cause for which they were working together.

As Gertrude Williams, usually ready enough to imply the worst, points out, even though Mrs. Besant was shadowed by Frank's detectives who interviewed everyone with any possible evidence against her, he and his advisers "never once attempted to attack her in court."[12]

There were to be many more men, some of them quite famous, in Annie Besant's life, and with some of these she was undoubtedly in love (she always formed closer associations with men than with women). But it is very unlikely that she ever took a lover.

[12] Bonner, *Bradlaugh*, II, 12–13; John M. Robertson, *Account*, in Bonner, *Bradlaugh*, II; W. T. Stead, "Annie Besant," in *Review of Reviews*, pp. 70–72; Theodore Besterman, *Mrs. Annie Besant*, p. 106; Sri Prakasa, *Annie Besant: As Woman and as Leader* (Adyar, India, 1941), p. 37; Williams, *The Passionate Pilgrim*, p. 97.

7

Birth Control and
"The Fruits of Philosophy"

As a matter of fact, there was little time for love, idyllic or otherwise, in the Besant-Bradlaugh schedule. It was a wonder that Bradlaugh even found time to transfer his family and belongings from Turner Street to Circus Road when he did.

The year 1876 had ended on what in other circles would have been described as a note of Christmas peace and harmony. Foote had departed, and Holyoake was back in the main flock exchanging compliments with its younger leaders. Plans were being laid for the annual children's "monster party" in January, and the organizers expected to exceed the previous year's record consumption of 180 pounds of currant cake, 900 oranges, 50 pounds of "sweets," and "gallons enough of lemon and raspberry syrup to float a fair-sized ark."[1] Then, suddenly, a new storm broke upon the National Secular Society.

There had already been dark clouds and rumblings in the refusal of the proper Victorians to drop their charges of the Secularists' sponsorship of *The Elements of Social Science*, a title that misled nobody about its medical contents and advice. But long before, in 1832, a Massachusetts doctor, Charles Knowlton, had published, anonymously, a work with a similarly innocent-looking title, *The Fruits of Philosophy*, the word "philosophy" being used even more loosely than "social science." Its subtitle, however, had somewhat guardedly given away its real content and purpose: *The Private Companion of Young Married People*.

The pamphlet itself was mostly factual, but Knowlton started off with

[1] Joseph McCabe, *George Jacob Holyoake*, II, 79; *National Reformer*, January 7, 21, 1877.

a "Philosophical Proem" and devoted his first chapter to "Showing how desirable it is, both in a political and a social point of view, for mankind to be able to limit, at will, the number of their offspring, without sacrificing the pleasure that attends the gratification of the reproductive instinct." His second chapter, "On Generation," contained a medical description of the reproductive organs and their functions, especially in the female. Next came a chapter entitled "Of Promoting and Checking Conception," dealing with both medicinal and mechanical devices. This was followed by another chapter entitled "Remarks on the Reproductive Instinct." The booklet ended with an appendix containing an article from the Boston *Investigator* supporting the spread of knowledge on "checks" to reproduction.

The problem of birth control, at first alluded to under such innocent-sounding phrases as "limitation of population," had first been popularly focused by the Rev. Thomas R. Malthus in 1798 with the first version of his upsetting *Essay on the Principle of Population.* Recklessly asserting that the world's population, if uncontrolled, would increase in geometrical proportion, whereas its food supply would increase only arithmetically, he predicted dire consequences for mankind, especially in England, if man himself did not quickly find means to decrease the birth rate. Plagues, famines, wars, vice, poverty, and the other catastrophes of civilization, which he presented as nature's remedies, could not alone be depended on to act as equalizers. It was birth itself that must be controlled. Man's incontinence was the fault; it must be curbed.[2]

Malthus originally saw no remedies other than individual "moral" restraint. Male and female must check their impulses. The poor in particular must do so, he thought, forgetting that the poor would find it hardest. And people must marry much later, so that children would not start coming so soon. After marriage, however, according to Malthus' first implications, no restraint was called for; continence then became the sin, discountenanced by God and the church. In the years of a young couple's probation before marriage, pure will power and moral determination were to be the only preventives. Physical preventives at any time were regarded as against the will of God; few people seemed to see any inconsistency between interfering with the course of nature by preventing or curing disease, or building houses against the elements, and yet refusing to interfere with the process of procreation.

Soon, however, a number of more realistic people began to point out the weaknesses of the Malthusian position. They insisted that it was psychologically and physically unsound for most normal people to postpone marriage. They insisted, too, that there was nothing inherently immoral in adopting and applying the knowledge of physical and material

[2] For one of the best discussions of the Malthusian and Neo-Malthusian controversies, see Field, *Essays on Population and Other Papers.*

preventives which mankind had possessed for immemorial ages. As early as the seventeenth century in France and England there had been books of sexual instruction, such as the anonymous *L'Escole des filles,* addressed directly to women and providing advice on matters of contraception, such as the use of a merkin. In the eighteenth century condoms were actually advertised in the English press, but only as a protection against infection, as Daniel Turner made clear in his book on syphilis in 1717.[3] The rock-ribbed Malthusians were horrified by the sacrilegious proposals of the Neo-Malthusians, such as Richard Carlile and Francis Place, to use physical checks after marriage. Some even advocated infanticide as preferable to contraception.

The first open appeal to the English public to use physical checks on the spread of population and the first source of exact and frank advice concerning the means was a small, elegantly printed pamphlet entitled "To the Married of Both Sexes" published in 1820. The authorship of this pamphlet, referred to as "The Diabolical Hand Bill" by its enemies, may never be known; but Francis Place, Richard Carlile, and Robert Owen have been suspected of playing at least contributing roles. In 1825, Carlile's *Every Woman's Book* appeared, and in 1830, Owen's son, Robert Dale Owen, gave further impetus to the movement with his well-known *Moral Physiology; or, A Brief and Plain Treatise on the Population Question.* Interestingly enough, when Bradlaugh had left his father's home at the age of sixteen, he had been taken temporarily under the roof of Carlile's widow, where he may well have heard his first stories of the old controversy and read some of its documents.

Knowlton's work of 1832 simply carried to America the kind of advice and instruction that had been established in England for some years. Knowlton, it is true, had been immediately prosecuted in Taunton and fined $50.00 and costs for publishing his book. He had then been tried again in Cambridge and jailed for three months, but the book was allowed to continue publication and went through nine American editions in the next seven years, respectable citizens of course still regarding it as obscene.

The eighteenth century had not been bothered much by what constituted obscenity, but in 1824 in England it became an offense to exhibit so-called obscene books and prints in public. In 1857 the Obscene Publications Act, sponsored by Lord John Campbell, chief justice, gave the police power to search for, seize, and destroy stocks of such publications after laying an information at a police court; and the Post Office Act gave the post office authority to open and impound packets of such a nature and to prosecute the sender. These bills passed Parliament only after the assurance of the Lord Chief Justice that they would apply only to works "written with the single purpose of corrupting the morals of

[3] G. Rattray Taylor, *Sex in History,* pp. 151, 187.

youth and of a nature calculated to shock the feeling of decency in any well-regulated mind." Not worried by the equivocal and relative terms in this statement, in 1868 Lord Chief Justice Alexander Cockburn "re-defined" the word "obscenity" so that literary works and even scientific studies might be banned under the act. The shockability of the Victorians reached such heights that John Stuart Mill in his youth had been ar-rested for even suggesting that the use of contraception might reduce the high rate of English infanticide.[4]

In spite of Victorian sensibilities, *The Fruits of Philosophy* found as great a popular demand in England as it had in America, whether the purchasers knew the work of Malthus and his successors or not.[5] The pamphlet had been quickly brought out in England by an early Free-thinker, James Watson, who had sold it without molestation till his re-tirement in 1853. It was then taken over and sold at a steady rate first by George J. Holyoake and then by his brother Austin till Watson's death. At this point, Charles Watts had bought the plates from Watson's widow and had continued to publish it over his own imprint. Again all went well till late in 1876, when a Bristol bookseller named Henry Cook, who had already acquired a minor police record for offering "obscene" works for sale, conceived the idea of interleaving his copies of Watts's publication with some illustrations of his own. These were called to the attention of the Bristol police, who adjudged them indecent and charged the whole book as indictable. Cook was sentenced to two years at hard labor, and one of the most sensational, important, and far-reaching cases in English legal history had begun. Prosecution was inaugurated under the highly elastic and infamous Lord Campbell's Act.

The initial, basic facts of the situation are clear, but any account of exactly what happened next depends on whether one is on the Brad-laugh-Besant or the Watts side of the controversy. Each accused the other of inaccuracy, misrepresentation, faulty memory, and deliberate perversion of the truth. There is no doubt, however, that when Mrs. Besant arrived at the N.S.S. publication office on December 14, Watts excitedly showed her a letter he had that morning received from Touzeau Parris, of Bristol, a former Unitarian minister who had recently come over to Freethought and had enthusiastically offered to organize the

[4] Williams, *The Passionate Pilgrim*, pp. 77–78; Taylor, *Sex in History*, pp. 151, 187, 207–209, 216, 222–23.

[5] Unless otherwise indicated, the remaining material in this chapter is drawn from the *National Reformer*, January 14, 1877–December 15, 1878, *passim; Secular Chron-icle*, January 7, 1877–March 1, 1879, *passim; Secular Review and Secularist*, June 9, 1877–December 29, 1878, *passim;* London *Times*, May 15–July 19, 1877, *passim; Autobiography*, pp. 302–35; *Sketches*, pp. 112–57; Bonner, *Bradlaugh*, II, 16–17, 20–36, 100; McCabe, *George Jacob Holyoake*, II, 80–85; Williams, *The Passionate Pilgrim*, pp. 78–93; Charles Watts, *A Refutation of Mr. Bradlaugh's Inaccuracies and Misrepre-sentations* (London, 1877); Mrs. Charles Watts, *Mrs. Watts's Reply to Mr. Bradlaugh's Misrepresentations* (London, 1877).

whole west coast in the cause. Parris' letter told of the arrest of Cook and its reason. According to Mrs. Besant, Watts asked her to do him the kindness of reading the book and telling him her opinion of its indictability; he admitted that he had merely glanced at it himself, since he was concerned only with the printing and not with the editorial side of his business. To her inquiry whether Bradlaugh knew the book Watts answered that when he had bought the plates he had shown a copy to Bradlaugh, who was in such a hurry that he had only glanced at it and opined: "Oh yes, it's indictable. I'll speak to you again about it"; but both had forgotten to do so. Watts, however, later denied that any such conversation with Mrs. Besant had occurred. He did agree that she had taken the pamphlet home with her and had telegraphed him her opinion that it was defensible as a medical work. Watts had immediately written Parris this opinion and had even cut out a passage, marked in red ink, as being the strongest part of the argument. The next morning Mrs. Besant repeated her opinion at the office and advised Watts to consult Bradlaugh on the matter when he came back to town. Watts did so, and Bradlaugh promptly asserted it was Watts's duty to go to Bristol and declare himself as the responsible publisher of the work.

Watts, having respect for his employer's legal ability and greater age, complied. Just before Christmas, when Cook had his first formal examination at the Bristol magistrate's court, Watts was examined as a witness and signed a deposition justifying the sale of the book as a medical work, with nothing morally wrong about it. Watts said that by this time he had read the book; Bradlaugh maintained that the other had stated in the hearing of another prominent Freethinker that he had not really read it even after he had made another affirmation concerning its essential morality, "if properly used," at the formal quarter sessions trial at Bristol on December 29. Watts now insisted that as soon as he had learned the "vile purpose" for which the book had been used, he withdrew from Cook's defense and informed the authorities that, whatever their decision regarding the book, he would publish and sell it no more—a decision that he adhered to in spite of the greatly increased public demand for it.

Nevertheless, on January 8 Watts was arrested in London without warning and arraigned before the magistrate at the Guildhall. Several well-known Freethinkers, among them the publisher Edward Truelove, who had good personal and business reasons for being interested in the case, were on hand to offer bail or enter into recognizances. Watts was released on surety, and the case adjourned for three days. In the meantime G. H. Lewis, of the law firm that regularly handled the business of Bradlaugh and the N.S.S., was engaged. Bradlaugh said he hired and paid him to defend Watts and *The Fruits of Philosophy*; Watts insisted he had hired and paid Lewis and that they had agreed from the first that the work was indefensible and they would not fight for it. After all, it was a subject that concerned not Freethought as such but only freedom of thought and the press. Bradlaugh, Watts reiterated, knew his attitude all along, but he suddenly pretended to be astounded by it when he heard the detective sergeant's evidence and Watts's answer.

When Bradlaugh, Watts, and Mrs. Watts returned to the office after the hearing, a lively but polite altercation ensued over whether Bradlaugh had advised Watts against selling the book when he first took over the business. Bradlaugh said he had; Watts said he had not. Mrs. Watts said she wished she had known that Bradlaugh objected to the book; if she had, she would soon have stopped it. Bradlaugh agreed that the Society could not be appealed to for funds for a possible defense and added that he hoped, since the case promised to be a nasty one, that he could get a hearing from the grand jury, so that perhaps "No bill" might be returned.

Up to this point Annie Besant's name had appeared only casually in the affair. After the above conversation, however, Bradlaugh apparently hurried to Oatlands to acquaint her with developments, and there he discovered that his colleague thoroughly disagreed with the others' decision. She thought the Freethought party could be appealed to; she was sure the book must be defended. Bradlaugh argued long, but in vain. Her logic, her fighting spirit, her feminine spell—one or all were too much for him. That evening the Wattses received an urgent summons to come to Oatlands at once. There, in the presence of his two daughters, Bradlaugh confessed that he had changed his mind and was thoroughly converted to the other point of view. So eloquently did Mrs. Besant talk that she persuaded even the Wattses that she was right. She actually had a circular all drawn up and read it to them. Entitled "Charles Watts's Defense Fund," it outlined the previous facts of the case, explained the reasons for the decision to fight it, and appealed to all Secularists for help. Here, as Mrs. Watts later admitted, came "the great mistake myself and husband made." Instead of demanding the night to think over the proposal, they at once agreed to print and distribute the circular. Mrs. Besant immediately wrote Truelove to that effect.

The Wattses went home in a sort of daze. The next morning Mrs. Watts realized she should have read the *Fruits* before committing herself. She remedied this error very quickly and concluded, as Bradlaugh and Mrs. Besant had stated all along, that the subject matter in general was good, but that the style was "very coarse." But whereas C. B. and A. B. were willing to waive the style for the content, Mrs. Watts felt that the presentation of such a delicate matter was of prime importance. Moreover, she concluded, "I believe that the evil portions of the book counterbalance the good it contains, and that it is not suitable to be put forward *in its entirety* as a work which we, as Freethinkers, believe." She told her husband her views, they discussed them nervously and excitedly the rest of the day, and in the evening they sent a note to their "dear old friend" Bradlaugh, informing him they had changed their minds.

In the meantime, Mrs. Besant had left for Plymouth to lecture, burning with zeal for her new cause. Though Bradlaugh telegraphed her that there was to be a change in the circular, she went ahead with her mission and pleaded so successfully that the Plymouth brethren contributed more than eight pounds to start off the new defense fund. While this was going on, Bradlaugh summoned the Wattses to Turner Street and angrily demanded their reasons for changing their intentions and planning to plead guilty. Finding neither their reasons nor their future plans for not defending the case acceptable, he wrathfully informed them, "If you do not defend the book according to this Circular, all business transactions between us shall cease, and I must request you to let me have my accounts by Tuesday next." Watts, equally angry, agreed that they should part. Bradlaugh accused him of being a coward, and Mrs. Watts begged them not to be rash, but to talk things over calmly. They tried again, but Mrs. Watts was unable to persuade Bradlaugh that if they should lose and her husband should have to go to prison, there would be no gain or honor for either them or the party. In fact, the Wattses were ironically unappreciative of Bradlaugh's assurance that he personally would look after the family while "Charlie" was in prison. Charlie was already ill enough.

The four-cornered wrangle was resumed at Oatlands after Mrs. Besant returned on Monday, and it was widened to include certain sections of *The Freethinker's Text-Book*, which she had written and now insisted were just as indictable as the *Fruits*. The Wattses expressed surprise at this extreme view, but agreed with her sarcastic remark that perhaps Watts's name as publisher should be removed and her own substituted. The quarrel soon reached such a pitch that Bradlaugh carried out his previous threat: he withdrew all the printing business of the N.S.S. from Watts's shop, even though Watts had just invested £120 in a new set of type to be used especially for the *National Reformer*, and dismissed him from his job as subeditor of the weekly. Soon thereafter Bradlaugh and Mrs. Besant announced the formation of their own new company, to be called the Freethought Publishing Company. They borrowed a few hundred pounds from personal friends and rented and remodeled a tumble-down little tenement in Stonecutter Street, just off Shoe Lane. W. J. Ramsey, a fellow atheist hired as manager, set up shop with a small staff and by February 25 was open for business.

Annie was both amazed and amused to find herself thus "in business" with absolutely no business knowledge. But she soon remedied this deficiency, and publishing, in all its aspects, remained one of her favorite occupations until the end of her life. Bradlaugh appointed her subeditor

113

of the *National Reformer* in Watts's place, though several older Secularists applied for the position. Watts's weekly "Summary of News" was turned over to the Bradlaugh girls. It was quite a family affair. Watts took himself off and started the *Secular Review and Secularist* with the disaffected Foote. Furthermore, Watts divulged bitterly that he had got only fourteen shillings a week from Bradlaugh as subeditor, and his myriad articles had been gratis.

While the business breakup was developing, personal discord reached new heights. Since the quartette could no longer meet safely face to face, they took to writing telegrams and letters, some of which found their way into print, calling forth from their writers pained protests against violation of confidence. Watts formed a Defense Committee for himself and started raising money; Bradlaugh formed another and did the same. Mrs. Besant returned the funds that she had raised at Plymouth under, she said, false pretenses. All three went out on their lecture circuits and were wildly applauded at Sheffield, Leicester, Nottingham, Bristol, Lincoln, Dundee, and the Hall of Science itself as they presented their respective cases. Kate Watts discovered that her own talents had not been given a proper chance and supplemented her husband's platform appearances by giving dramatic readings and recitations. Circulars and counter-circulars ran off the presses. Mrs. Watts rushed to her husband's aid with her *Reply to Mr. Bradlaugh's Misrepresentations,* since her husband and Bradlaugh had finally agreed to be silent until after Watts's trial on February 5. Bradlaugh rejoined with a *Plain Statement of Facts.* Watts met him with *A Refutation of Mr. Bradlaugh's Inaccuracies and Misrepresentations, As Contained in the* National Reformer *of Feb. 11 under the Title of a So-Called "Plain Statement of Facts."* And so it went.

The ordinary members of the N.S.S. were by now thoroughly confused. Many of the branches were reading and discussing *The Fruits of Philosophy* before making up their minds about which side to support. Some canceled lectures by Bradlaugh or Watts; others added new ones. Among the minor leaders, many did not know which way to jump, and some tried to jump both ways. M. C. O'Byrne was a notable example. O'Byrne, a former Roman Catholic, had been befriended by Bradlaugh and Mrs. Besant while he lay sick and alone, had joined the Freethinkers, and now had a wife and five children to support. In the fall of 1875 he had applied to the Executive Committee for a lecturing certificate. The committee, sensing an essential instability in him in spite of his speaking ability, had hesitated, but had finally given in. So O'Byrne had joined the lecturing corps, along with the ex-Anglicans, ex-Unitarians, ex-Theists, and undeviating atheists, and had built up a considerable following for himself with his talks on such recondite subjects as "Was; Is; To Be; Man and the God Opinion" and "From Rome to Freethought."

The Knowlton book, however, proved too "vile" for O'Byrne, with his Roman Catholic background. He offered his help to Watts, wrote a letter to Plymouth in his favor, and signed one of his circulars against Bradlaugh, along with two dozen other defecters. Then he began to get cold feet; he wrote Bradlaugh repudiating what he had signed. When Watts tried to persuade him to become subeditor of his new paper, he considered the offer for several days and then turned it down because he did not want to take sides in the affair. He wrote an article in the *National Reformer* on "What Is Truth?" and continued to seek it for several weeks in his usual lectures. But by the beginning of April he had had enough. He announced that because of the "pressure of literary work" he had "decided to withdraw from the advocacy of Secularism." A few weeks later the *Secular Review* noted with grim brevity that Mr. O'Byrne had become a Christian missionary and was writing for *The Shield of Faith*. A couple of years later he regained his faith in skepticism and tried to rejoin his former friends, who by then were too wary of this weathercock to accept him. On May 25, 1879, the *Reformer* excoriated him for his ingratitude and warned its readers against this apostate who had changed his creed four times in five years. Mrs. Law also asserted early that she refused to take sides, but she and her husband Edward continued their "advocacy" and lectures.

On February 8 Watts's case came up at the Old Bailey, and he altered his plea to "guilty in law." The judge accepted the defendant's story, in spite of the contradictory evidence about when he had read the book, and released him on his own recognizance of five hundred pounds, to return for judgment when called upon. By late April the case against him was dropped. He was let off with a payment of only twenty-five pounds in costs; the City assumed the rest. He had to destroy his plates and stock, as he was only too glad to do; and no official notes of his trial were preserved at the Old Bailey.

Before this happy ending, seeing that things were going their way, Mr. and Mrs. Watts felt free to open the floodgates and release the torrent of rancor that had been storing up within them—in the husband's case for weeks, but in the wife's ever since Annie Besant had invaded the N.S.S. and swept all before her. Watts in his *Refutation* reminded his readers that he had always been of a "peaceably disposed turn of mind," but that the same thing could scarcely be said of Bradlaugh. Never before had Watts had a serious difference with any of his co-workers, but Bradlaugh was chronically in trouble. One by one his colleagues had deserted him (Watts inserted all their initials), being unable to endure his overbearing manners, till only one, a comparative newcomer, remained, and even she, if faithful to her principles of independence, might soon be expected to follow suit. Watts was too gentlemanly to give this lady's name, but his wife felt bound by no such reticence. In her *Reply,* after admitting that Bradlaugh had done much for the party, she plunged on:

One by one he has swept co-workers from his path the instant they become obnoxious to him. . . . [He] evidently believes he is fully capable of guiding—I beg pardon, ruling the Secular party, with of course the assistance of Mrs. Besant, who, if she cannot lay claim to many years of service, has the gratification of finding that her brief connection with the movement and the *National Reformer* has resulted in her advancement to the post of sub-editor, which there are good reasons for believing she has long coveted.

Mrs. Besant, of course, had been Mrs. Watts's quarry all along. She had masked her growing annoyance and jealousy for over two years, but now she could no longer conceal them. They were both fairly young, attractive, and ambitious women; but Annie had immediately over-shadowed her rival. Mrs. Watts, naturally, felt the Society should realize the truth: Mrs. Beasant was the troublemaker. It was she who had twisted the redoubtable Bradlaugh round her finger, she who might

congratulate herself upon being the means of causing a break between two old and tried friends. . . . From her first entrance amongst us she has taken the rôle of champion of Mr. Bradlaugh, and general defender and ratifier of what he says or does. No matter what course he pursues, in her opinion it must be right, and she would more bitterly punish those who dared to deviate from it than even Mr. Bradlaugh himself.

Mrs. Besant's brief letter to Plymouth returning the money so badly needed by Watts for his defense, charged Kate Watts, "contains an amount of condensed spite, which but few women could use." Yes, concluded the aggrieved wife blackly, Mrs. Besant in her officiousness "acts as if she had a greater claim on Bradlaugh than any other person in the party." What the nature of this claim was she did not specify. Bradlaugh, of course, ignored the charges about Mrs. Besant and denied the rest, accounting individually for everyone who had been associated or dissociated with him for the past seventeen years.

So far as the outer world was concerned, up to this point the affair was only a small tempest in a tiny teapot of a peculiar and rather obscure sect. But the villain-hero and villainess-heroine were not willing to let the leaves settle. They wanted a much stronger brew. Charles Watts, having played his subsidiary but essential role, soon dropped out of the larger picture. A revolt against Mrs. Besant in the Executive Committee, led by W. H. Bull, secretary of Watts's defense committee, was suppressed there after several weeks of parliamentary jockeying; and when Bull found he could not impeach her and refused to apologize for an offensive letter and resolution, he and his supporters also withdrew from the Society.

Bradlaugh and Annie now agreed that the only way to test the right of an Englishman to publish information of a sexual nature would be to bring out a new edition of Knowlton under their own imprint and challenge the police and the courts to stop them. So they wrote a joint "Publishers' Preface" and had the booklet ready for sale by the end of March. The Preface reviewed the history of the case and gave the authors' reasons for questioning the application of Lord Campbell's Act. It also explained how, in order to be sure of their physiology, the publishers had submitted the text to an eminent, world-famous doctor, the author of *The Elements of Social Science,* who had composed the notes in this new edition signed "G. R." "G. R." of course turned out to be Dr. George R. Drysdale, who remained one of the pair's most loyal supporters throughout as well as a leader in the whole Neo-Malthusian movement, in which Knowlton's pamphlet played a conspicuous role. The publishers also pointed out that they had made some grammatical corrections and slight improvements in the original text. This proceeding soon brought them to a split with another of their old friends, G. J. Holyoake, the stages of which were lucidly revealed in a series of letters between him and Mrs. Besant.

Holyoake thought that the original pamphlet should be dropped and another written "without its coarseness." When he learned that the others had decided differently, he wrote begging them to keep his name and his dead brother's out of the matter, since they had never appeared as actual publishers of the book nor had it even been printed in their shop. If they did so, he promised not to oppose them. He then warned Mrs. Besant of his deep concern that if she persisted it would mean ruin to her "as a lady." He called Knowlton a quack, thought that such books had no place in Freethought literature, and reminded them that he had already carried "the flag" into prison. Mrs. Besant thanked him for his "most kindly meant" letter and for a later "nice little note" and described their intention to "revise carefully, publish matter, but refine style." No real revision was actually ever made, though some passages which their opponents, including Watts, charged them with omitting were restored in a later printing.

When Holyoake saw that no important alterations had been made, he refused to accept the invitation of Touzeau Parris to join Bradlaugh's defense committee. Parris by now had left Bristol and joined the growing colony in St. John's Wood, to be near his new comrades, the principals in the fight. Later, when she and Bradlaugh were brought to trial, Mrs. Besant named Holyoake as having once published the book, and Bradlaugh actually had him subpoenaed as a witness. Then the old man lost his usual good temper and wrote a letter to the *Daily News* and the *Times* explaining his side of the "truth." When the *National Reformer* refused to print the same letter, he could bear no more and soon seceded from the N.S.S.

In the meantime, the Bradlaugh girls had been having their own exciting experiences, first in Turner Street and then in Circus Road. One morning before they had moved, Hypatia was sitting on the floor in her father's study sorting some pamphlets when their landlady announced that a man was at the door to see Mr. Bradlaugh. A "thick-set man, of middle age, with a reddish beard," entered and asked to buy a copy of Bradlaugh's pamphlet, *Man, Whence and How,* which was Part I of *The Freethinker's Text-Book.* To Hypatia's surprise, her father obligingly dusted off a copy and sold it to the caller there in the house. The man was hardly out of the door before Bradlaugh broke into a hearty laugh. "Did you see his boots, Hypatia?" he asked and then explained, "Yes, he actually came in the regulation boots. That was a detective, and those who instructed him evidently think that 'Man, Whence and How' is a book upon the population question." If so, they were much surprised when they read the subtitle, "Revealed and Real Science in Conflict," and found the pamphlet dealt with Genesis and "the alleged creation of Adam and Eve."

A few weeks later, after the transfer to Circus Road, the large new edition of the Knowlton pamphlet had been printed in preparation for its imminent sale and stored in the Bradlaughs' home. Bradlaugh was away in Scotland, and the three women, resolute but filled with feminine trepidation, were left alone. Mrs. Besant's fear of the possibility of a police raid and seizure of the books finally reached such a pitch that she persuaded the girls to help her wrap them up in waterproof parcels and hide them in every conceivable place. Some were buried in her garden at night, some hidden behind the cistern, and others put under a loosened board in the floor. When Bradlaugh was informed of this female cleverness, he was greatly annoyed and sent word that there was to be no more hiding. Fully aware that a raid was perfectly possible, he had no wish to appear ridiculous; and as soon as he returned he initiated the reverse process, but found that the women had done their secreting so well that it was some time before even they could rediscover all their "treasure."

Bradlaugh came back from Scotland on March 22, in order to direct the opening of the sales campaign the next day. First, he dispatched a copy of the new *Fruits* to the Chief Clerk of the Magistrates at the Guildhall, accompanied by a formal notice that the book would be sold in Stonecutter Street the following day, Saturday, from four to five. A similar notice was sent to the Detective Department, with a polite request asking that they arrest him at some hour convenient to them both; the officer in charge replied in the same spirit. A third notice was delivered to the City Solicitor, J. T. Nelson, who was expected to lead the prosecution, but did not do so.

On Saturday, Bradlaugh and Mrs. Besant, accompanied by his daugh-

ters and Mr. and Mrs. Parris, marched on Stonecutter Street at the appointed hour. They found a crowd jamming the narrow way, though
there had been no advertising of the sale anywhere except in the *National Reformer*. Two policemen were calmly patrolling the area and
keeping traffic moving. Once inside, the girls eagerly wrapped up copies
of the book at sixpence each, singly or in packets, and counted out the
change; but their father would let no one but himself and Mrs. Besant
actually make the sales. Five hundred copies passed over the counter in
the first twenty minutes. Among the purchasers were several detectives,
one of whom bought two copies from Bradlaugh, gracefully retired, and
then, in a second role, returned to buy another from Mrs. Besant. Members of the Dialectical Society, in whose discussions and debates she had
recently been distinguishing herself and which was now scheduling debates on topics like "Physiology and Morality," dropped in to offer bail
if necessary. A rival bookseller was angry when charged full price; but
one of Watts's sons came in and was allowed to buy seven copies at the
trade price, while the sales force speculated about whether Watts intended to resell. By six o'clock about eight hundred copies had been
sold, and many parcels had been wrapped to be mailed to the rest of
the country. Yet, to the great disappointment of the participants, no one
was arrested.

The largest crowd in years turned out at the Hall of Science on Sunday
to hear their heroine lecture on "The Prison and the Crown," with their
hero in the chair; and his concluding statement on the Knowlton affair
was received with "vehement cheering" and assurances of support. Watts
was not present at this meeting, but the following Sunday he defended
his position before a divided audience.

No arrests having been made by the beginning of the next week, the
two lawbreakers again notified the police that they would be in their
shop to be arrested on Thursday. Upstairs they held a "bright party" of
a few insiders, including Dr. Drysdale; and a group of some "twenty
gentlemen" filled the shop downstairs. But the law would not be hurried,
so Annie and Bradlaugh impatiently took a cab to the Old Jewry to see
what was amiss. There they were told very courteously that the papers
would be ready early the next week and that the Home Office had received a delegation of two from the Christian Evidence Society and
another unidentified deputation asking that the Lord Chancellor himself
take up the matter. Pleased with the nature of their opposition, they
passed the intervening time printing a new defense fund notice and
congratulating themselves on the attention the affair was arousing in both
the city and the provincial press. They were deluged with news clippings
and letters; five thousand copies had been sold, and many orders had to
be left temporarily unfilled. The population question was now being
widely discussed everywhere. The two announced they would no longer

have any responsibility for any sections of *The Freethinker's Text-Book* other than those they themselves had written; Watts must look after the rest.

Finally, one warm, sunny morning in the middle of April, after Bradlaugh had again helpfully notified the police that he and Mrs. Besant would be at their office from ten to eleven, the officers appeared. Hypatia had been previously instructed by her father that when this happened she was to rush home and fetch his volumes of Russell's *On Crime and Misdemeanours*, while the older but less aggressive Alice was to stay with him for any other errands. So Hypatia dashed off to St. John's Wood, picked up the three bulky tomes of Russell, and ran to catch the next train back to the city. Hot and anxious, but feeling with nineteen-year-old innocence that she had the golden key to all legal problems in the three slippery volumes, she was the object of considerable curiosity and amusement from the other passengers. But when she and her sister reached the police court in the Guildhall, they found that their elders had not yet been arraigned. So they sat in shuddering disgust while "some of the lowest specimens of London low life" were tried for drunkenness or assault in the very dock which their father and Mrs. Besant were to occupy.

In the meantime, as Mrs. Besant recounted with proud but ironical relish in her lengthy running accounts of the affair in the *National Reformer*, the detectives had taken them in the friendliest fashion to the nearest police office, where they were examined, searched, measured, and generally put on the criminal records. Then, guarded by some sergeants, they were conducted to the Guildhall, where they were kept waiting for two and a half hours in separate jail cells, through the gratings of which they could dimly see each other. They passed the time by joking, reading the *Secular Review*, and correcting proofs for the next *Reformer*, shoving the sheets through the bars to each other. Finally they were taken to the dock before Alderman Figgins, "a nice, kindly old gentleman, robed in marvellous, but not uncomely, garments of black velvet, purple, and dark fur." Everyone was smiling and civil to everyone else, the testimony of the detectives was taken, there were many laughs in the testimony, subpoenas were issued for many witnesses, bail and recognizances were accepted, and, to partisan cheering, the case was adjourned until April 17. Afterward, they all went home to talk over their next strategy.

At the next hearing, reported verbatim in the *Reformer*, with additional comments by Mrs. Besant, Alderman Figgins was joined by two or three other aldermen, who had been instructed by the City Solicitor. Everybody was very fair, very polite, and mutually complimentary. When Bradlaugh began his defense of himself and Mrs. Besant, some of the officials wanted to exclude women from the room, since the testimony might prove embarrassing to them; but Figgins ruled they might remain if they insisted. The girls stayed the first day, but later waited outside.

Through a series of hearings and adjournments, Bradlaugh argued his case in his usual masterful manner, citing Malthus, Fawcett, and Mill, among others, but especially Acton. He inquired into the meaning of "obscene" under the terms of Lord Campbell's Act, examined the drawings and illustrations in other medical handbooks, and discussed "prudential checks" both before and after marriage. Mrs. Besant then took the stand to make her own statement and defense and impressed everyone by her self-control and grasp of the subject. In fact, her speech was printed in full in both the *Evening Standard* and the *Daily Telegraph* and was translated and telegraphed to Germany the same night. Figgins then adjourned the case until the Central Criminal Court's sessions of May 7.

This gave Bradlaugh his chance to show his mastery of the intricacies and opportunities of the law. He submitted an application to have the case transferred by a writ of certiorari to the Queen's Bench and heard by a special judge and jury. Lord Chief Justice Cockburn and Mr. Justice Mellor were both present at the hearing, and after examining all the records and affidavits, Cockburn decided that the case was of the type and importance to deserve this treatment. It was a tremendous triumph for Bradlaugh, and for Annie, too, since she was allowed merely to affirm and not to take the Christian oath on the Bible before the Commissioner, who could hardly believe that she did not have "a little private deity" of her own, "somewhere out of sight." To celebrate after the preliminary hearing they all went to see Henry Irving in *Richard III* at the Lyceum. She pronounced him "a really great actor," though she had not liked him before.

Before the new hearings opened, Bradlaugh and Mrs. Besant had the additional satisfaction of knowing that the Executive Committee was behind them and had refused to accept their resignations. There had, however, been a great deal of political maneuvering, and Holyoake and Watts, who had not yet departed, persisted in voting against them. The lines of battle were being drawn for the coming annual convention.

The post office, moreover, was making new trouble. Even though the sale of the new edition of the *Fruits* had now passed five thousand copies (and another printer had struck off a fraudulent imitation with a similar cover and top title), Bradlaugh charged in public letters that not only was his correspondence being opened, but copies of the *Fruits* and the *Text-Book* sent through the mails were being seized and impounded. The Postmaster General at first professed ignorance, but Bradlaugh finally forced him to a bland admission of the truth, as stated in the *Times* for May 15.

Worst of all, their old friend Truelove's shop was raided by the police, and its proprietor was arrested for selling not only their own pamphlet but also such similar self-help booklets as R. D. Owen's *Moral Physiology* and J. Y. Palmer's *Individual, Family, and National Poverty. Reasons Why in Every Family the Number Should Be Regulated.* The Society for the Suppression of Vice was openly behind this prosecution. Truelove was committed for trial in the Central Criminal Court, but was released on Bradlaugh's bail till the Bradlaugh-Besant case could be decided. The National Secular Society guaranteed that it would stand behind the defense of this member, too.

Another of Annie's old associates in her struggle for freedom of thought came off slightly better. Thomas Scott, after fifteen years of bold and liberal propaganda, was allowed to announce his retirement because of ill health without ever having been arrested. Almost simultaneously the Freethought Publishing Company brought out Mrs. Besant's *My Path to Atheism,* a collection of thirteen of her preceding essays on the subject, which she dedicated to Scott,

Whose Name Is Honoured and Revered Wherever Freethought Has Spread; Whose Wide Heart and Generous Kindness Welcome All Forms of Thought; to Whom I Owe Most Grateful Thanks, As One of the Earliest of My Freethought Friends, and As the First Who Aided Me in My Need.

The Knowlton incident also had political repercussions; in Northampton in February, Bradlaugh's clerical enemy, the Rev. Thomas Arnold, had founded a Liberal Association which was primarily an anti-Bradlaugh organization. At the other extreme, Annie and Bradlaugh had recently paid a very friendly visit to a well-known Radical agitator and Republican leader, George Odger, who, though on his deathbed, had praised their activities.

The most distracting interim affair, however, was the convention. C. B. and A. B. knew well in advance that they would have a fight on their hands as a result of the Knowlton business. The convention was scheduled for Nottingham toward the end of May. When Bradlaugh and Mrs. Besant had announced in the *Reformer* early in the month that they refused to hold any proxies at the conference and that each branch must select its own delegates, they had probably perceived a possible source of trouble. They just as probably failed to anticipate the full force of the confusion and rebellion which developed almost as soon as Bradlaugh called the meeting to order. It can scarcely be said that Annie, as secretary, preserved true impartiality in drawing up her account for the *Reformer.* No one disputed Bradlaugh's suggestion that Holyoake take the chair because he had been head of the Revision Committee, which had been appointed after the previous convention and which had held many meetings at Mrs. Besant's home. All moved smoothly as amendment after amendment was passed—smoothly, that is, till the topic of the "Executive" was reached on the agenda.

This was the signal for which the rebels had been waiting. A Nottinghamite sprang to his feet and moved that the offices of president and vice-president be abolished and that the Executive Committee simply elect a chairman. Another insurgent seconded loudly, and a heated discussion ensued. Watts, still a vice-president, and Foote, who had come in together with Mrs. Watts and had seated themselves in the audience, joined in; Mrs. Law, sitting among the notables on the platform, delivered her aggressive support. Bradlaugh kept his silence, fully aware that the motion was aimed not at the office, but at him as holder of the office. Mrs. Besant, though involved as a vice-president, had no such reticence and dropped a speech into the hopper. At last Holyoake, who received praise from both sides for the composure and impartiality of his conduct, succeeded in cutting off the debate and called for a show of hands. This proving indecisive, the voters proceeded to a division. Then all order disappeared. In the angry shouting and milling about, the tellers could not distinguish eligible from ineligible voters. As Annie related the story, over a hundred Nottingham people were present, only a few of whom were national members. But they all voted, just as if they were official delegates. Guests, visitors, free lances—all voted equally with the authorized voters. The Nottinghamites, whom Mrs. Besant suspected of having arranged the whole plot, inasmuch as they had refused to let Bradlaugh know anything about their local arrangements in advance, also opposed the use of the proxies of those who were absent. Nevertheless, she wrote in triumphant exasperation, the nefarious scheme failed. When the tellers had finished their job, they announced 110 votes for the amendment to abolish and 117 against it. Right and constituted authority had won again!

The insurgents knew they were beaten. After tea, Watts again led a feeble movement to oppose the acceptance of proxies, but it sputtered out and he withdrew it himself. Routine business once more prevailed. Bradlaugh took the chair again and read his annual report, which smoothly claimed new strength and progress everywhere along the Freethought line. When it came to the choice of president, Bradlaugh's only opponent, nominated without his consent, spoke in praise of the incumbent and withdrew. Bradlaugh was re-elected, with only four dissenting hands and amid cheers from his party. Mrs. Besant was re-elected. Holyoake was re-elected. Parris was elected. But when Watts was nominated from the floor, he refused to stand, "after the vote which had just been taken." Foote and Mrs. Law were again declared ineligible, since they were not national members. The list of officers being complete and the mutiny being suppressed, the meeting adjourned in exhausted orderliness.

Mr. and Mrs. Watts immediately sent in their resignations from the

N.S.S., which the Executive Committee refused to accept till they had paid up their back dues. Quickly, too, Watts's and Foote's new *Secular Review and Secularist* printed the bitter protest of the Nottingham group against Mrs. Besant's distorted picture of the convention, though they were unable to change its results. And Mrs. Law, in the *Secular Chronicle,* protested against the light in which her refusal to accept a vice-presidency had been put. She simply did not want to be an officer in the N.S.S. again. The British Secular Union, a rival organization, was silently developing apace.

The big news in London to Bradlaugh and Mrs. Besant was that the great Lord Chief Justice Cockburn had decided that their case had become of such national consequence that he would hear it himself. The Knowlton pamphlet had now sold over 133,000 copies of a printing of twice that number, the newspapers were full of the issues involved, and the preachers and public speakers could not keep it out of their addresses. Mrs. Besant started a new section in the *National Reformer* entitled "Prosecution Varieties," written in a light, jesting tone which continued to mark her commentaries and which suggested that at first she might not have realized the full gravity of the dangerous situation she had helped to create.

She declared that on the whole the press had been very fair, but that in a few quarters its treatment had been "foul and coarse." So great was the anticipated public interest that the *Reformer* announced a series of "Special Trial Numbers" to supplement the regular issues with a verbatim report of the trial—except for purely physiological details. This series continued to come out with inexorable thoroughness for several weeks after the trial was ended, so determined were the editors to get every scrap of the testimony before their eager readers. New "very handsome" cabinet photographs and less expensive *cartes de visite* of the two principals were prepared for sale.

In spite of the overpowering battery of official legal talent arrayed against them, the intrepid pair insisted that they would conduct their own case. The news that Mrs. Besant would again plead in person aroused many shocked protests against her unwomanliness.

Leading up to the opening of the trial in the Court of Queen's Bench on June 18, there were various hearings and legal preliminaries. Attempts to subpoena several prominent authorities like Charles Darwin and Henry Fawcett, M.P., professor of political economy, resulted in a courteous excuse in the one case and a rude rebuff in the other. Stewart Headlam, like other lesser notables, was happy to testify, even though he knew he would get into trouble with his bishop and his vicar if he did.

Annie, who had burrowed into Bradlaugh's library with her usual zealous thoroughness and had mined some rich veins there, was the first to be called. For two days she spoke fluently on the social and national problem of limiting population; and the special jury and the learned justices hung on her every word, with only Cockburn and Bradlaugh infrequently interrupting for a question or a comment. Her final sentence, "I ask you to give me a verdict of 'Not Guilty,' and to send me home unstained," was directed with such shrewd femininity at masculine hearts that the court officers had to suppress the applause. Then Charles Bradlaugh took over, with a defense which was almost an attack. He also spoke for almost two days, interrupted only by Cockburn and the Solicitor General, Sir Hardinge Giffard. Drysdale testified, too. Then Cockburn delivered his summing-up. It was judicious, unbiased, and often flattering, praising the defendants for their honesty, integrity, and courage, as well as their service to society, and reprimanding Giffard for his unprecedentedly ill-advised and injudicious proceedings. Everything looked delightfully auspicious to the defendants. They could not have had a fairer trial, Mrs. Besant wrote; the jury had been attentive and intelligent, the judges courteous and helpful, and only the Solicitor General had sometimes used "coarsely vicious" language.

When the jury went out, even the Bradlaugh girls were hopeful. Dressed in black because of the recent death of their mother and frightened for the possible fate of their elders, they had gone to Westminster every day. They had deferred to public opinion and stayed out of the courtroom, pacing up and down the great hall outside. Now their father summoned them in to join him for the verdict. The four, with their other friends, settled back happily to listen.

After an hour and thirty-five minutes of unexpected delay, the foreman delivered the decision: "We are unanimously of opinion that the book in question is calculated to deprave public morals, but at the same time we entirely exonerate the defendants from any corrupt motive in publishing it." As Mrs. Besant commented ironically, this amounted to saying, "Not guilty, but don't do it again."

Cockburn looked perplexed and confused, but stated that he would have to interpret the verdict as meaning "Guilty" and pass judgment accordingly. Almost everybody was equally surprised. Later Mrs. Besant investigated what had happened. The villain in the plot was Arthur Walter, a journalist and the son of the chief owner of the *Times*, which had been bitterly hostile in its editorial columns, though impartial in its lengthy "Law Reports"; it had also printed a letter from Holyoake protesting the introduction of his name into the trial. Walter and the foreman, a harshly religious man, had persuaded the jury to adopt the wording of the verdict, even though six of its members were against conviction. The jury had agreed that if its opinion were not accepted in this form, it would retire for further deliberation, but the foreman's acceptance of the Lord Chief Justice's translation into "Guilty" so overawed the rest that they did not have the courage to contradict him till it was too late. Cockburn then set the defendants temporarily free, upon Bradlaugh's recognizances to appear a week later for the judgment.

On Sunday evening, as the *Times* itself sorrowfully reported, the Hall of Science was "densely crowded, it having been announced that Mr. Bradlaugh and Mrs. Besant were to deliver addresses." Inside the hall were six hundred people, a third of them women, "many of them very young," all having paid from twopence to a half-crown for admission. Outside in the street were four hundred more loyal supporters who were unable to get in. Hundreds more copies of the *Fruits* sold briskly, "young women and lads purchasingly largely." The entrance of the two princi-pals, along with the equally beleaguered Truelove, elicited great cheering. From the chair Mrs. Besant announced that on Thursday Bradlaugh would move to quash the indictment on the ground that it was bad law; and on the same day, if his plea were rejected, she herself would move that the verdict should be entered as a real verdict of acquittal, since the word "Guilty" had not been used (*"non obstante verdicto,"* as she put it technically in the *Reformer*). If this device should fail, she would re-quest to get a clear finding one way or the other. In the event that all these expedients failed, they would of course have to abide by whatever punishment Cockburn inflicted, but they would never flinch from the cause. Following his codefendant's speech, Bradlaugh briefly confirmed her account of the situation and announced, to the accompaniment of prolonged cheering, that his old friend Joseph Garibaldi had just written him from Italy to add his name to the defense committee, which had al-ready raised over £900. As Mrs. Besant later commented, the office had been deluged with letters from high and low, domestic and foreign, but mostly from the poor and from the wives of clergymen of all denomina-tions, thanking and blessing them for the stand they had taken.

Thursday came. Bradlaugh had withdrawn £250 from the bank in an-ticipation of a possible heavy fine and had instructed Hypatia, business manager in his absence, to take the money back in case of an unexpected sentence of imprisonment. He and Mrs. Besant now stood up before the Lord Chief Justice and Justice Mellor to hear their fate. First, Cockburn refused to accept any of their several arguments. But he still did his best to save them. Since they were already acquitted of any attempt to violate the law, would they submit to the jury's verdict and promise not to sell the book again? Intending to free them without penalty if they agreed, the Lord Chief Justice found he had underestimated the resoluteness of the pair. Annie had always wanted to be a martyr, especially in a just cause. Now she knew she had it. She and Bradlaugh therefore main-tained their right to sell the book and stated that they intended to do so. The judge, balked in his merciful intentions, pleaded and argued in vain. Pitted against two such granite blocks, it was no wonder he finally lost his temper and sentenced them to six months' imprisonment and fines and fees of £1,400. Hypatia saw her father turn white, saw a court officer step forward to take the two into custody, and saw her father beckoning her to give him his pocketbook with the £250. But when Cockburn heard Bradlaugh calmly state that he would apply for a writ of error, the Justice also recollected himself and decided to liberate them on their recognizance of £100 apiece. The law would then resume its customary course.

This left the situation muddier than ever but gave everybody the opportunity to interpret it as he wished. The National Secularists spoke of it as essentially a victory. Watts and Foote in their paper exulted in the verdict as a complete justification of Watts's course and sarcastically commiserated with their former allies on their heavy sentence, which of course they claimed the others had deliberately brought on themselves. Mrs. Law in the *Secular Chronicle* tried to preserve her famed impartiality, but featured the dissident leaders in her lecture series in her new headquarters in Cleveland Hall. The Northampton *Mercury* chortled that Bradlaugh had now certainly ruined any hopes he might have retained to sit in Parliament from that district; yet when Bradlaugh attended an electioneering meeting there early in July, he was cheered roundly by his faithful adherents. Again when, early in August, Mrs. Besant was invited to speak there and, accompanied by Bradlaugh and the girls, did so, the *Northern Guardian* reported that "Hats, handkerchiefs, and umbrellas were waved in the air" for her. On a family trip to Scotland they were cordially received in Edinburgh and had special fun in touring all the famous buildings and landmarks. At Paisley and Loch Lomond they were not so well received, but they enjoyed the picturesque scenery in compensation.

Practically all the metropolitan and provincial papers, as well as many papers in America, took editorial sides, as did the N.S.S. branches, most of which remained loyal; but Dublin withdrew. Many authors and booksellers brought out special pamphlets to capitalize on the affair, featuring the names of Bradlaugh and Mrs. Besant in various specious ways. The two now decided that this was the time to revive Bradlaugh's old Malthusian League of seventeen years before. George Drysdale's brother, Dr. Charles R. Drysdale, senior physician of the Metropolitan Free Hospital, assumed the presidency; Mrs. Besant was secretary; and the membership soon reached over a thousand. The House of Commons was petitioned to make clear just how far the discussion of overpopulation might go, and plans were laid to agitate for a change in the law on teaching birth restriction. A clarification was also asked on censorship of the mails. Bradlaugh, moreover, boldly carried the war into the enemy's own country by suing the police for the recovery of some of his other pamphlets which they had seized. When he won his case, he stamped them "Recovered from the police" and thus gave them a special sentimental value for their purchasers.

Mrs. Besant wrote a series of articles entitled "Does Not the Bible Come within the Ruling of the Lord Chief Justice as to Obscene Literature?" (later condensed to "Is the Bible Indictable?"), and Bradlaugh wrote a report on the role played in the trial by C. H. Collette and other members of the Society for the Suppression of Vice. Then he went on to discuss "What Is Blasphemy?" at considerable length. The Freethought Publishing Company also started to bring out the first English editions of Colonel Robert Ingersoll, the most famous American advocate of Freethought.

Truelove was absolved of responsibility for selling the Knowlton pamphlet, but was condemned to stand trial for selling Owen's. At Manchester, Mrs. Besant was presented with a gold pencil case and pen, together with an "illuminated address." Crowds were turned away at Leeds and Glasgow. No longer did most of the provincial papers refuse to print notices of her and Bradlaugh's appearances. At the same time she found she was not too busy to resume her "Daybreak" column, suspended during the trial, and add a new department, "Second-Hand Bookshelf," in which she reviewed Swinburne, Charlotte Brontë, and Shelley. She also took Watts's place as coeditor of the N.S.S.'s annual *Almanack.*

In the meantime, all through the summer and fall, the Knowlton case was dragging on through the courts. Bradlaugh fought his appeal with every trick in his considerable repertoire. There were hearings and adjournments, writs of error, petitions, and subpoenas. While the appeal was pending, he agreed not to sell any copies of the *Fruits,* but Mrs. Besant took advantage of the opening to bring out her own booklet on the subject, which she said would be written in a less "coarse" style than Knowlton's and yet preserve its chief purposes. Entitled *The Law of Population: Its Consequences and Its Bearing upon Human Conduct and Morals,* it first appeared in the *National Reformer,* without the medical parts that were later added. So well did she know the English public that her work soon superseded Knowlton, Owen, and all the rest and proved a best-seller, with hundreds of thousands of copies all over the English-speaking world. Whatever the law and the church thought, all classes of people in Britain, America, Australia, and Holland, and the Parsis in teeming India, yearned to collaborate in limiting the population. Mrs. Besant was, of course, threatened with prosecution for her *Law of Population,* but was never summoned to court.

Just before the middle of February, 1878, the *Reformer* splurged with an extra "Special Trial Double Number" of thirty double-columned pages, containing the full transcript of the hearing of the appeal before the Lord Justices Bramwell, Brett, and Cotton. On February 12 Bramwell an-

nounced the unanimous decision of the three justices reversing the decision of Cockburn and Mellor on the ground that, in Hypatia Bradlaugh's
phrase, "the words relied on by the prosecution as proving their case
ought to have been expressly set out." It was a technicality, but it was a
grand victory. The government left the impression that it would try the
case again before another jury, but it had lost its taste for battle. Cockburn himself had ruled Bradlaugh and Mrs. Besant guilty against his
will. Consequently, the whole matter was allowed to expire quietly; it
was never revived. Various side issues were heard in other courts, but
most of them too were won by Bradlaugh.

Even Watts, who had been left as sole editor of the *Secular Review*
through the resignation of Foote, backed up temporarily and grudgingly
congratulated Bradlaugh on his success. Mrs. Law, whose journal was
putting up a bold front on a very wobbly basis, commented on the victory and published flattering biographical sketches of both Mrs. Besant
and Bradlaugh, with photographs, in a series of articles on the leading
liberal leaders of the day. A description of Annie was reprinted from the
North of England Review, written by "one of the most eminent literary
men in the country" (unidentified), who cited her beauty, education,
character, and humanitarianism. The newspapers and periodicals of more
general circulation, mixed in their attitudes, agreed on the importance of
the decision and the bravery of the defendants. It was a resounding triumph for the freedom of the press and a turning point in the history of
birth control.

It took supreme courage for Annie Besant to become the first woman to
dare to advocate publicly a cause which most men of the time feared to
support. As a result of her efforts, in the following year Dr. Aletta Jacobs
opened the world's first birth-control clinic in Holland. Both the birth and
death rates soon began to decline in England. Dedicated crusader or
would-be martyr, Mrs. Besant had demonstrated the wisdom of her resolve to fight the Knowlton case when Watts decided he wanted to be
neither.

No one ever was allowed to learn who had initiated the proceedings
against Mrs. Besant and Bradlaugh, in spite of Bradlaugh's persistent inquiries. Denials were issued by authorities all down the line: it was not
the national government, nor was it the City, though the city solicitor
played a prominent role and the City paid at least £700 of the considerable costs; it was not the Vice Society, which Mrs. Besant sarcastically
referred to as the Society for the Promotion of Vice; nor was it any other
public agency or organization. Bradlaugh, however, seems to have suspected an alderman named Ellis, who directed the strategy of the prosecution, of having been the mask used by the unknown enemy, probably
someone close to the Christian Evidence Society, though not in it.

Whereas a great financial deficit had been expected, though almost

£1,100 had been raised by the committee, there was a surplus of a few pounds when the reversal swept away £400 of recognizances. Unfortunately, there were also some casualties. The sixty-eight-year-old Truelove was not so lucky as his friends, though Bradlaugh also fought hard for him and got into another quarrel with Watts over which of their papers had the official right to raise money for this second defense. Watts assured his readers, however, that his essential attitude toward the *Fruits* had not changed. After several months of exhausting hearings, in which the Vice Society was the open prosecutor and Truelove was freed one day and recalled the next, he was found guilty of selling obscene literature, fined, and sentenced to four months in prison. His appeals were rejected, and he served his time, thus becoming a genuine Freethought martyr. Stewart Headlam also suffered for his participation, for at the instigation of the Bishop of Lincoln (whom Mrs. Besant had never ceased to torment in the columns of the *Reformer*), he was driven from his curacy in St. Matthew's, Bethnal Green, and forced to look for a more open-minded parish.

The Freethought Publishing Company resumed the sale of the *Fruits*, in a limited way because of the continued activities of the police and the post office, but Mrs. Besant's *Law of Population* naturally had her greater interest and support. To remind the world of the other work, however, she put out a little tract with the echoing title, *The Fruits of Christianity*.

As the immediate aftermath of the Knowlton hearings, with their interminable speeches, wranglings, arguments, and cross-examinations, Mrs. Besant came down with "so severe a cough" that she had to cancel or postpone her usual lectures. And James Epps & Co. through the whole affair continued their standing advertisement in the *National Reformer* of their "Glycerin Jujubes for Throat Irritation."

8

Husband Take All

Even before its climax the transformation of Annie Besant from a potential Freethought martyr to a birth-control heroine had been entangled with another plight of an even more personal and emotional nature—and a less happy outcome. From the remoteness of Sibsey, the Rev. Frank Besant had been observing the continuing debasement of his family name with more and more dismay. Since to him a divorce was out of the question, there was no way of preventing his wife from using that name, hateful as the association was. In 1877 the vindictive Watts had threatened to sue both Mrs. Besant and her husband for a professional debt of eighteen pounds which he said she owed him. But he admitted he knew that, being a married woman, she could not be sued directly and that, since the debt was not incurred for necessities, her husband could probably not be sued successfully either. Nevertheless, as Annie put it in the July 22 *National Reformer*, "rather than allow a gentleman, whose marriage with myself had been so long severed by formal deed, to be dragged by a legal fiction into the London Sheriff's Court," she had been willing to compromise and had settled for eight pounds. At the same time, in his *Secular Review*, Watts had retracted certain statements he had made about her, but had refused to retract certain others he had made about Bradlaugh. This refusal plunged him into a new and long lawsuit, in which Bradlaugh sued him for damages. To escape a verdict, Watts finally decided to emigrate to Canada and accept the "pastorate" of a Freethought "congregation" there.

Perhaps because of the Watts incident, but chiefly because of the Knowlton scandal, Frank Besant turned his attention to his children—or, rather, to his little daughter. On January 20, 1878, Bradlaugh printed the following "Personal" conspicuously in the *Reformer:*

Our readers will regret to learn, that Mrs. Besant has received notice from the solicitor of the Rev. Frank Besant, of Sibsey, that an application is to be made to the Chancery Division of the High Court of Justice, to deprive Mrs. Besant of the custody of her daughter, on the ground that the conviction for publishing the Knowlton Pamphlet disqualifies Mrs. Besant from being the guardian of her own child. The proceedings will be resisted to the uttermost, although the additional worry and cost might well have been spared until the pending appeal in error had been fully decided.

Since the separation in 1873, the Besant children had been brought up strictly within the terms of the agreement. Arthur Digby, however, instead of living continuously with his father, had been sent as a boarder to a small school, primarily for "young ladies," in nearby Boston, run by a spinster schoolmistress, Louisa Everitt. Soon outgrowing this kind of education, in January, 1876, he had been placed by his father in the charge of an old and dependable friend, the Rev. W. L. Childs, vicar of Alvingham, another tiny north Lincolnshire town. Digby was apparently quite happy here. Childs was starting a small boarding school, with the help of his wife, "the gentlest and kindest of women." There was a young son of Digby's own age, as well as an older daughter, Mary, who tried to teach Digby music; but he described this experience as a "nightmare." Just before the boy's seventh birthday, Childs, who was reputed to be a fine classical scholar, introduced him to the Latin primer. Childs also taught him the Scriptures, geography, history, reading, writing, poetry, arithmetic, and, later, Euclid. Digby, who was eventually to become a prominent London actuary, was not much impressed by his instructor's knowledge of the latter two subjects; he later remarked condescendingly, "Mr. Childs really knew nothing of mathematics." Here perhaps he reflected the views of his father, of the mathematical tripos. Digby was a good-natured, affectionate, and responsive boy, in spite of the generally Calvinistic atmosphere of the household. He confessed that he must have worried Miss Mary greatly by his questions on all sorts of subjects, especially religion, and he was sometimes depressed by the fear of hell-fire that the family taught him. On the whole, however, he felt so much a member of the Childs group that when Childs died a long time later, Digby brought to his own home in London the tall, enamel-faced grandfather's clock, dating from 1790, which had stood in the Alvingham house.[1]

During the holidays every year an exchange of children took place. Arthur Digby went to visit his mother in London, and little Mabel Emily was sent to Sibsey. When Mabel had reached the age of five, Annie felt she could no longer allow the child to grow up without more supervision than the press of her own activities would permit; the "care and affec-

---

[1] *Pedigree,* pp. 210–12. When I visited Digby Besant in August, 1954, he proudly showed me this clock, which, although it had been injured in the World War II bombing, was still running well, and inside the case of which he had posted its complete history.

tion" given Mabel by Mrs. Ellen Lumley Perrier, one of her Bayswater roomers, when her mother was away, was not enough.[2] So Annie called her Aunt Marion to her aid. Though "Co" was still a staunch member of the Church of England, her love and loyalty to Annie overcame her religious disagreement. From November, 1875, to September, 1877, she acted first as daily and then as resident governess to Mabel, whom she described as a very "delicate and sensitive child requiring great care in her treatment." Perhaps because Annie did not trust even this favorite aunt with anything very serious in the way of education and also because the Knowlton business was attracting so much attention, Mabel was then sent to a "high class school" in the St. John's Wood neighborhood, conducted by a Miss Fuller. Miss Fuller, like "Co," was expected to teach Mabel everything she thought proper, except religion.

But in the summer things changed. When Mabel arrived in Sibsey in 1876, she found that her father had engaged his friend Miss Everitt, the Boston "proprietress of a boarding and day school for young ladies" which Digby had attended, to look after her. Miss Everitt insisted that while the girl was under her charge she "always avoided alluding to any neglect on her mother's part in not affording her Religious Instruction." She soon found, however, that the poor child had not only had no such teaching and knew no prayers, but that her mother would not even let her say "God bless you." The next summer things were no better. In fact, to her shocked eyes, Mabel was a pitiful little thing, thwarted and frustrated in her natural religious desires, who at home sometimes got out of bed secretly and said her forbidden prayers alone, who was strongly interested in religion, and who was fond of reading the Bible. Who had taught Mabel the prayers or who had provided the Bible, Miss Everitt did not explain. Could "Co" have been playing the innocent traitor? But when Digby stayed briefly at Boston that summer after returning from his mother's in London, he told Miss Everitt that his sister had not even been allowed to accompany him to church there. According to Miss Everitt, Mabel was much worried about whether God would be angry with her because of her neglect of Him.

Frank Besant's actual petition to recover his daughter was not filed in Chancery till April. This gave Mrs. Besant time to prepare and serialize her widely read article, "Marriage. As It Was, As It Is, and As It Should Be." Even though she wrote impersonally and never mentioned her own experience or situation, it was obvious to any reader that she was analyzing the problem with herself in mind. As the *Reformer* informed a correspondent, "the law as to husband and wife and the custody of children" was "very carefully stated" in her series on the subject. In her pamphlet

[2] See affidavits of Mrs. Perrier, Marion Francis Morris, Louisa Everitt, and Annie Besant, Chancery 2640, 2641, 2642, 2974, and 2983; also, *National Reformer*, May 26, 1878.

she briskly reviewed the history of marriage laws from Hebrew and Roman times to the present, when woman was still regarded as a chattel; advocated the passage of a short act ordaining that marriage should in no fashion alter the civil status of a woman as an individual; urged equal rights for men and women in seeking divorce, on grounds of adultery, cruelty, or drunkenness; and took a positive stand against such anomalies as "judicial separation."

Mrs. Besant needed to know the law, past and present; she needed to know history; she needed to know sociology. She needed to know many things. For her court experience with the expert Bradlaugh in the Knowlton case had determined her to flout all precedent, outrage all decency, and challenge the judicial system and the English sense of propriety by fighting her case in person. Of course, she would also have the advice and counsel of Bradlaugh and the N.S.S. law firm, the Messrs. Lewis and Lewis.

A copy of Frank Besant's petition, filed in Chancery on April 9, was delivered to Annie as she sat by Mabel's bedside, nursing the child through an attack of scarlet fever which she had caught at her day school. The *Reformer* naturally did not fail to call attention to the callousness of this act on the part of the father, who had been informed of the situation.

The document began with various aggrieved allegations. Besant charged that his wife had been endeavoring to "propagate the principles of Atheism" by her addresses, lectures, writings, and especially by her book called *The Gospel of Atheism.* Moreover, she had also "associated herself with an Infidel Lecturer and Author named Charles Bradlaugh in giving lectures and in publishing Books and Pamphlets whereby the truth of the Christian religion is impeached and disbelief in all religion is inculcated." Even worse, in conjunction with Bradlaugh she had recently published "an indecent and obscene pamphlet," *The Fruits of Philosophy,* which had been the subject of legal proceedings, and in her public defense of its contents had "stated or inferred that in her belief it would be right to teach young children the physiological facts contained in the said pamphlet." She had even published her own work, *The Law of Population,* on the same subject. Finally, his request that Mabel should be kept from any association with Bradlaugh had been in vain. Consequently, believing that it would be detrimental to his daughter's "morals and happiness" to be left in her mother's charge, he asked that Mabel be either returned to his own care or given into the custody of "some proper person" as her guardian till she became twenty-one. He also pointed out that, some time before, he had set up a trust fund of over a hundred pounds in consols for Mabel, the income to be used for her benefit until she was twenty-one.

To substantiate these charges, Besant's solicitors, the Messrs. Scott, Jarmain, and Trass, had sent out three of their clerks to make purchases at

Truelove's shop, at the Freethought Publishing Company, and at 28 Stonecutter Street; these included copies of the *National Reformer*, of its printed records of the Queen's Bench trial, and of the *Fruits*, the *Gospel*, and the *Law of Population*, as well as the *Text-Book*. These were all carefully labeled and deposited as exhibits. Affidavits flew back and forth on both sides and were duly filed. Mrs. Perrier told her version of Mabel's upbringing, Auntie "Co" added hers, and Annie herself tied everything together—reviewing her life with her husband and Mabel, denying that she had ever said anything about teaching "physiological facts" to children, and insisting that Bradlaugh had had nothing to do with Mabel's education or religious training. Dr. Drysdale swore he had attended Mabel during her illnesses and insisted that, though she was "fairly healthy," she should have the "continued and affectionate care of her mother" for some time to come because of her "sensitive and nervous disposition." Dr. Philip John Hensley, of Cavendish Square, on the other hand, swore that when he was called in to examine Mabel in May she had made very good progress; and he found nothing that would endanger her health if she were removed from the custody of one person and given into that of another.

Before the hearings began, Annie announced that, in order to be ready when summoned, she might have to cancel her engagements without notice. Bradlaugh appealed to various workers' groups and to all the members and branches of the N.S.S. to help, since this at least was a matter on which all Freethinkers could agree. Some of the branches of the newly formed British Secular Union promptly pledged their support. Bradlaugh and Mrs. Besant prepared and circulated petitions to Parliament requesting the repeal of all the present laws on the expression of "heretical opinion," blasphemy, and so on. In 1876 the Leeds convention had tried to induce Freethinkers to work seriously for such a repeal, but the movement had had little effect, since people regarded the laws as generally obsolete and harmless. The new danger alerted them, and hundreds signed. But Parliament, when the twenty-five petitions were presented early in June, was not yet ready to abandon its guardianship over English souls.

As for the case itself, after the usual preliminaries and postponements, it was considered so important that it was to be heard by none other than the Master of the Rolls, Sir George Jessel. Sir George, while an able and esteemed lawyer, turned out to be very different from the Lord Chief Justice and the Justices of Appeal who had treated Annie so kindly. Jessel called the first meeting for May 4. Mrs. Besant, conscious of her sex and the role she intended to play in its demands for justice and equality, surrounded herself with a cohort of her closest woman friends—Mrs. Conway, Mrs. Parris, the Misses Bradlaugh, and a dozen other Secularist members and officers' wives—and descended on Chancery. Charles Bradlaugh and Moncure Conway also acted as attending strategists. Perhaps Jessel, subjected to this female invasion, was not to be blamed for expressing his disinclination to listen to Mrs. Besant defend her case in person rather than through counsel. Not only did he object in strong terms and a harsh voice to a layman's appearing before him in such a major role, but he was especially perturbed about a woman's thus exposing herself before lawyers, journalists, spectators, and the nation. Frank Besant, meantime, was willing to rely on his lawyers and on affidavits; he remained quietly at Sibsey to await the result of his suit.

Mrs. Besant's vignette of Jessel was bitterly etched in her *Reformer* articles and her autobiographies. He had been a Liberal member of Parliament, had had a very profitable practice as a lawyer, had risen rapidly in the judicial system, and was the first Jew who, in spite of the actual technical disqualification of his race, had been allowed to take an active part in the executive and judicial side of the British government. But in Annie's unforgiving memory he remained "a man animated by the old spirit of Hebrew bigotry, to which he had added the time-saving morality of a 'man of the world,' sceptical as to all sincerity, and contemptuous of all devotion to an unpopular cause."

Jessel's unconcealed hostility immediately placed him, not as the presiding judge, but as an adjunct to the prosecuting Queen's Counsels, Ince and Bardswell. Ince argued that Mabel, if educated by her mother, would be both "hopeless for good in this world" and "hopeless for good hereafter, outcast in this life and damned in the next," and Bardswell implored the judge to remember that the mother's custody "would be detrimental to the future prospects of the child in society, to say nothing of her eternal prospects." Only once did the Master of the Rolls and the Q.C.'s fall out even slightly—Bardswell, forgetting momentarily that Sir George was a Jew, reminded him with horror that Mrs. Besant had admitted taking the New Testament away from Mabel "because it contained coarse passages unfit for a child to read," and Sir George insisted sharply that in this opinion he concurred with the defendant.

Otherwise, nothing that Mrs. Besant, who had again been allowed to "affirm" rather than to take the usual oath on the Bible, could say shook Jessel's prejudgment in the slightest. She maintained that she had kept her husband fully informed from the beginning about the development of her religious doubts and her views on the necessity of limiting their own family. He knew about her writing and her association with Charles Voysey. He knew that Mabel had been carefully, even admirably, cared for. As for Miss Everitt's statements, most of them were "ridiculously untrue." In spite of these denials, the prosecution remained unshaken. The charge that Mrs. Besant had forbidden her daughter to say even "God bless you" seemed to stick especially in Ince's craw.

On May 18, after the defendant had completed her argument, Jessel, who was noted for the speed with which he reached his decisions, handed down his judgment. Admitting that Mrs. Besant had apparently been a careful and affectionate mother, he found for the plaintiff on two main grounds: first, the mere fact that she had deprived her child of religious instruction was enough to convince him "that this child ought not to remain another day under the care of her mother"; second, the even more heinous fact that she had promulgated what he bitterly and abusively regarded as an obscene and demoralizing Malthusian publication (Jessel himself was the father of five children, but he was a rich man) left no doubt in his mind that the terms of the original separation in regard to the disposal of Mabel should be abrogated. He refused to stay his order of restoration until Mrs. Besant's announced appeal of his judgment could be heard. The Revs. W. L. Childs and G. W. Lowe, Frank Besant's representatives at the trial and the directors of his trust fund for Mabel, were given permission to sell as many of their consols as necessary to pay for their share of the costs. It was probably one of them whom Annie described as the "messenger from the father" who immediately came to her house and carried away "the little child . . . by main force, shrieking and struggling, still weak from the fever, and nearly frantic with fear and passionate resistance." As a narrative writer, Mrs. Besant never failed to take full advantage of her dramatic opportunities.

Hypatia Bradlaugh later gave a slightly different version of this aftermath.[3] Since her father realized that Besant's advisers would not lose a minute in claiming their prize, he instructed his daughters to drive posthaste from the courtroom to Avenue Road, to carry Mabel off, and to deliver her to her mother at a nearby railway station which Mrs. Besant would pass through on her way to a lecture engagement at Manchester. Here, according to the *National Reformer*, Mabel's appearance on the platform with her mother was a signal for "loud and prolonged applause." In this manner Mrs. Besant not only procured a few hours for a more peaceful and private farewell from the perplexed little girl but she skilfully contrived a final use of her child as an instrument of propaganda against her Christian enemies. The hysterical scene of separation as she described it in her autobiographies must have come two or three days later.

The strain of waiting to hear the result of her appeal, wrote Mrs. Besant, was so great that she "nearly went mad, spending hours pacing up and down the empty rooms, striving to weary myself to exhaustion that I might forget." The loneliness and silence of the house, drained of the sunshine and music which her "darling" had brought it, weighed on her "like an evil dream." She listened in vain "for the patter of the dancing feet, and merry, thrilling laughter that rang through the garden." During her sleepless nights she "missed in the darkness the soft breathing

3 Bonner, *Bradlaugh*, II, 36–37.

of the little child," and each morning she longed uselessly "for the cling-ing arms and soft, sweet kisses."

Late in July she was attacked by rheumatic fever, which at least gave her "the rest of pain and delirium instead of the agony of conscious loss." And day after day Charles Bradlaugh, who was still involved in three lawsuits simultaneously, came and sat writing beside her, feeding her with the ice and milk which she refused from everyone else, and "behaving more like a tender mother than a man friend." Though Alice and Hypatia, who by now were practically like her own daughters, also came in to nurse her, Annie was sure that their father had saved her life.

The public reception of Jessel's verdict was somewhat mixed. The majority opinion, as might be expected, was with him. The influential *Daily Telegraph* and *Times,* which carried objective legal reports of the trial, were pleased and represented the prevalent view. An editorial in the *Times* even hinted openly that Mrs. Besant herself was leading an immoral life. The only London paper to say a word on her side was the *Weekly Dispatch,* but its circulation was small. In the provinces, the Bradford *Observer* and the Nottingham *Journal* surprisingly came out for her, but it was no surprise that the Secularist journals did so. Brad-laugh, who had publicized the whole trial by a series of verbatim reports in the special numbers of the *National Reformer,* as he had done in the Knowlton affair, indignantly rushed into print with an article, "Are Atheist Parents Outlaws?" and reprinted Shelley's "To the Lord Chancel-lor," written when the poet had suffered a similar deprivation by the state. Mrs. Besant came to speak in Liverpool in June and found its biggest crowd awaiting her; but on her departure from the hall her cab was besieged by a mob who spat on the windows and hissed, hooted, and groaned. She charged that the police themselves had tried to stop her from speaking, but the commissioner replied that he had sent his men only to preserve order and keep her from harm. All the Liverpool papers took sides in the controversy. Conway preached at South Place condemning the government's proceedings, and Mrs. Besant received a flood of sympathetic letters.

The annual conference of the N.S.S., held at Sheffield on June 9, re-elected its old officers, including Bradlaugh, Mrs. Besant, and Truelove (but Holyoake, Watts, Foote, Mrs. Law, and many other prominent Secularists did not even attend, as the *Secular Review* gleefully re-corded); adopted a petition to the Secretary of State backing up previous public demonstrations and demanding the freeing of the ailing Truelove from prison, where he had been set to picking oakum; and ended by adopting a unanimous resolution condemning Jessel's conduct and decision.

In her statement before Jessel, Mrs. Besant had suggested that if he wanted to put Mabel into the hands of some third person, she would transfer her allowance from her husband to the child under two trustees, one to be appointed by herself. Besant's attorneys had made no reply to this offer, but his monthly payments to his estranged wife stopped after the trial. Since that time she had not only seen nothing of her daughter, but her son had not been permitted to make his annual summer visit to her. Since the original indenture had never been canceled, she and her advisers insisted that its terms still stood. Therefore, on July 22, her husband still showing no disposition to comply with them, she instructed her solicitor to send Frank Besant a letter stating that because of her "anxiety and grief" about her children she had decided to come home to live with him again and asking on what day of the following week it would be convenient for him to receive her. Thus, she added darkly, it would not be necessary for her to file suit for "restitution of conjugal rights," a step which was legally possible in view of the terms of the original deed of separation.

If Mrs. Besant's real purpose was to scare her husband to death under the ostensible guise of seeing her children, she almost succeeded. His reaction was convulsive. Through a politely acrimonious and insulting interchange of letters between her and his lawyers, he testily refused to let her see the children, in either Sibsey or London, or to send them toys or clothes, and challenged his opponents to institute proceedings. When her lawyers again threatened him either with "cohabitation" or with observing the terms of the 1873 agreement, he applied to Chancery to have the document canceled. Early in August summonses were served not only on Mrs. Besant but also on the trustees of the agreement, Henry Trueman Wood and Cornelius Vincent Webster Neale, to appear in court within eight days to answer Besant's new petition. Besant also got out an injunction "to restrain the Defendant Annie Besant from molesting or annoying him by letter or otherwise and also from instituting any action or other proceedings for the purpose of compelling him to cohabit with her." In an affidavit to procure the injunction he swore that he did "verily believe" that Mrs. Besant intended to execute her "threat" to return to his home unless she were enjoined from doing so. This injunction and a writ were then served on her by the special permission of the Master of the Rolls.

Next, in true Chancery fashion, there followed a maze of claims and counterclaims, demurrers and defenses, and hearings and postponements, the first of which were occasioned by the defendant's painful attack of rheumatic fever which she swore prevented her from reading or even opening any letters till the middle of September. (Nevertheless, the bulletins in the *Reformer* had chronicled her convalescence, which allowed her to move around the house early in August and took her to the seashore in north Devon with the Bradlaugh girls at the end of that month.) Bradlaugh had already commented on the characteristic "inhumanity" of Frank Besant in serving his wife with an injunction at the height of her illness. When she was finally able to put in an appearance before Justice Sir Henry Hawkinson on September 25, he decided to postpone the case till all the relevant material could be brought together. This delay enabled her and Bradlaugh, accompanied as usual by the two girls, to reply to Professor R. Flint's widely discussed series of lectures on "Theism" in Edinburgh, where they found the Music Hall, the Artillery Hall, and the Hall of the Royal Scottish Society of Arts successively denied them. Bradlaugh's reply was to be entitled "Is Belief in God Reasonable?" but his colleague's was to be much more pugnacious: "Christianity: Immoral in Theory and Demoralizing in Practice." While the Edinburghers had always before been receptive to the appeal to reason, the charge of immorality was apparently more than they could endure, and they closed their minds as well as their public buildings to the invading pair. At the last place, as the *Times* put it, "They separated quietly, after a round of cheers and hisses had been given for Mr. Bradlaugh and Mrs. Besant." Flint, however, immediately wrote them a courteous letter deploring what had happened.[4]

The legal situation at home was further complicated by some new factors. Annie's brother Henry, who had married in 1873, was in the process of raising a good-sized family. He had continued to rise in office with the London Society of Arts and was by no means happy to be brought into his sister's unsavory affair. Digby always remembered his uncle Harry as "a tall man, gifted with a caustic tongue, which concealed a kindly heart," who enjoyed photography and mountaineering. But Henry had no kindly feelings toward his sister in her present predicament, though he later regained them. Realizing his discomfort, Annie requested that two new trustees be appointed, since for some time Henry had really ceased to act in that capacity and the other trustee, one of his associates, had emigrated to the colonies; but Henry nevertheless had to go through with the case and have it identified by reference to his name. In fact, in spite of his and Neale's officially filed disclaimer that they had had anything to do with any payments since June, 1875, and had had no control over anything that Annie Besant had said or done, Frank Besant insisted on including them as defendants. Albert Besant was also brought into the hearings; nothing was said of Walter.

The first real hearing of the case came up early in November before Annie's old enemy Jessel, who had lost none of his former gall. But as he examined the accumulated pile of affidavits, claims, and counterclaims before him and quizzed her and the opposing counsel about them, even he was forced to the public conclusion that Besant had gone too far in disregarding the original agreement. Consequently, when the second hearing came up on January 21, 1879, he made a proposal

4 In addition to the London *Times,* see Bonner, *Bradlaugh,* II, 156.

that startled everyone. This was that she file a new counterclaim for divorce or at least for a full judicial separation, which Jessel said he himself could grant without her having to go through the unpleasantness of the Divorce Court. Judicial separation would end her appeal, which she had all along insisted on calling only an "interim order," and she would be allowed "reasonable access" to her children. She jumped at the chance. Though she said later that from the outset she doubted Jessel's ability to do any such thing, his use of the phrase "a counterclaim for divorce or for legal separation" must have impelled her to think again of her possibility of marriage to Bradlaugh, now that his wife was dead.

At this time there were two kinds of divorce in England, established by a reform of the divorce laws and procedures about twenty years before: divorce *a vinculo matrimonii* and divorce *a mensa et thoro*, both more complete and final than the separation by mutual consent which Mr. and Mrs. Besant then had in force. The first type of divorce allowed remarriage, but was extremely hard to obtain; the second, known popularly as "judicial separation," severed all legal ties, but did not allow remarriage. To obtain either, adultery, desertion, or cruelty had to be proved. Since Mrs. Besant would be suing, she could scarcely charge her husband with either of the first two, though he might perhaps have tried to proceed against her on such grounds. In her self-defense before the Court of Appeals on March 24, according to the *Times*, she stressed "the fact that there was no sort of personal allegation against her," as there had been in the case of Shelley; nor did anyone attempt to contradict her, even though she was accompanied by Bradlaugh. But to prove the third ground for divorce, it was only necessary for the plaintiff to show that real danger to life, limb, or health had continued for at least two years. This was at least within the realm of possibility for Annie.

Two days later the opposing counsel argued that Jessel could not decree such a separation because Mrs. Besant had not made out a proper case for it: she had presented no facts. The courtroom was then treated to the comedy of hearing the Master of the Rolls, while frankly acknowledging his and the defendant's mutual dislike, instruct her on how she should go about amending her earlier counterclaim so that it would support a charge of cruelty on the husband's part. It would be a "painful case," he admitted, but worth her while. He would see that in accordance with the law in such cases she received suitable alimony till it was over.

So Mrs. Besant went hopefully away and dug down into her memory for all the cruel and hateful things her husband had done to her while they had lived together—how he had struck her, almost thrown her over a stile, pushed her out of bed, used violent language, shaken his fist at her, and even threatened to shoot her if she should ever divulge that she was the one who had obtained the living at Sibsey for him. Dr.

Winterbotham came up to town from Cheltenham to give his evidence concerning the earlier of these cruelties. These charges Jessel allowed Mrs. Besant to add in writing to her already lengthy, previously filed and printed defense; and these same charges Frank Besant in his amended reply denied categorically, one by one, but ended contradictorily by stating that if he had really committed any of these acts of cruelty he had done so "inadvertently under the provocation occasioned by the said Defendant refusing to comply with what the Plaintiff considered to be and submits was his reasonable request for her to discontinue her said correspondence[,]readings and writings." He therefore concluded that "the Plaintiff submits that the said Defendant is not entitled to have a decree for judicial separation but that her counterclaim ought to be dismissed."

Consequently, when the next hearing was called before Jessel on March 27, the great Master of the Rolls apologized for having given mistaken advice. He had thought that the other side would agree to such a separation. Now that it had refused, he could not grant it by himself. He implied that if Mrs. Besant had gone to the Divorce Court in 1873, she "might at least have obtained a divorce *a mensa et thoro";* now it was too late. Previously that day Ince had refused even to cross-examine her, nor would the plaintiff go into the witness box to deny her charges on oath. Though Mrs. Besant argued subtly that a husband cannot legally sue his own wife and that his bringing her into court had revived all her original matrimonial rights, Jessel stated that he could not decree a legal separation, since the separation had already taken place years before; he also ordered a perpetual injunction against her and her friends from instituting proceedings to compel her husband to cohabit with her; and he assessed costs of sixty pounds against her for her counterclaim, while her husband had to pay the expenses of his trustees. These expenses, coupled with the manifold others involved in such a suit, turned out to be much easier for the vicar to meet than for Annie, whose defense fund fell far short of the need. And although Besant's counsel brazenly stated in court that his client had no fund to draw on, the *National Reformer* had no trouble in proving that the Bishop of Lincoln and the dedicated members of his diocese had actually raised several hundred pounds for this very purpose.

The Appeals Court, which had been holding up its decision till Chancery acted, now politely dismissed Mrs. Besant's appeal and with the greatest of courtesy upheld the awarding of Mabel to her father. Bradlaugh was there to support Annie in this finishing blow, but he was in a highly nervous and excited state himself. After traveling all night on the train from Scotland in order to be present, he had had his cab stopped by a friend who told him that his daughter had been injured in a riding mishap. Early that snowy morning Hypatia had gone out riding alone in Regent's Park on Mrs. Besant's temperamental little mare Kathleen. At Clarence Gate, the mare had suddenly bolted and fallen with her rider, who had been knocked insensible. Hypatia had been carried to the nearest doctor, and Alice had been summoned by a passer-by who knew the Bradlaughs. When the frightened father reached the doctor's house, he found Hypatia still lying unconscious on the parlor floor with a cup of tea beside her, while the doctor and his wife were devoting their attention to a more important matter—the attempt to save Alice's soul. Under her father's ministrations, Hypatia, having no broken bones, finally revived. And that afternoon, after Bradlaugh had rushed off to court to hear the verdict against the woman he loved, Alice received a letter from the doctor's wife saying she would pray to her Heavenly Father that "in this great affliction you may be led to know Him as your Saviour and Comforter."[5]

In a final hearing in chambers on April 29, Jessel defined the terms of Annie's future relationship with her own children. They were to be encouraged by their guardians, the Childses, to write her once a week; she was to be allowed to see each of them alone once a month and to send them small presents, books, etc.; they were to be allowed to visit her twice a year in London for a week at a time; and once a year all three would be permitted to go to some seaside place, under the care of one or two persons selected by their father, who would be given daily access to the children at reasonable times by their mother.

This all sounded more promising than it turned out to be. The monthly visit so upset the sensitive Mabel, who, according to her mother, constantly fretted for her, that "in mercy to her" Annie soon felt compelled to relinquish it. Perhaps, too, the fact that the trip to Sibsey was a slow and tedious one by train and carriage had some bearing on her decision. Similarly, on the first visit to the seaside she found herself saddled with the cost of maintaining both the Childses, who treated her in the children's presence as though she were "a dangerous animal from whom they were to be protected." This reverent couple even refused to let Mabel go in bathing with her mother. After a time, following a vain appeal to have some sort of consideration shown her when she was merely exercising the rights of access granted her by the court, and having it mockingly suggested that she complain to the Master of the Rolls if she were not satisfied, she resolved neither to see nor to write to her children "until they were old enough to understand and to judge for themselves."

After the Childses left Alvingham for Portsea later in 1879, Mabel went as a boarder to another "dame school" in Boston under a Miss Adams, where she lived for a while in a house formerly occupied by Jean Ingelow, the popular Lincolnshire poetess. Still later, dissatisfied with the "fifth-rate teaching" her daughter was getting, Mrs. Besant offered

[5] Bonner, *Bradlaugh*, II, 37–38.

to pay the whole expense of her education at the Cheltenham High School or some London college, but her proposal was of course ignored. Digby was sent to the Boston Grammar School, which had a reputation for turning out fine scholars as well as for providing a somewhat severe life for its students. When he soon fell ill under the regime, his father packed him off to the Portsmouth Grammar School, which the Childses were now conducting, and where the boy was in close contact with the older Besants. Here Digby, whose boyhood impressions of the Childses completely belied his mother's, spent six "happy and uneventful" years, doing well in mathematics and the classics, but otherwise not distinguishing himself. On his holidays he went back to Sibsey.

Although Mrs. Besant did not write to or see her children, she found ways of knowing what was happening to them. She was sustained partly by a firm confidence that when they were free and intelligent agents they would leave their father and return to her—a mother's intuition that proved to be right: poor Frank Besant could instil love in no one; Annie could instil both love and hate. In the meantime, she determined that, robbed of her own children, she "would be a mother to all helpless children." Martyrdom once more led to humanitarianism.

This tragic chapter in her life was momentarily closed. Yet it left some significant results for society, as always seemed to be true of her adventures. Never again would the government take a child from a parent under similar circumstances, for it came to realize that giving a father absolute rights over his children meant essentially, as Mrs. Besant put it, "If you are legally your husband's wife, you can have no legal claim to your children; if legally you are your husband's mistress, your rights as mother are secure." The public, moreover, had been reminded of the heresy and blasphemy laws and would eventually modify them. And as an obvious aftermath to Mrs. Besant's skilful and spectacular performances as a laywoman lawyer before the highest courts and judges in the land, the Dialectical Society made her a member of a special committee to propose a new codification of the criminal law. At the same time the Association To Promote Women's Knowledge of the Law prepared a report on the abilities and disabilities of women in the practice of the law in any of its branches and pointed out that so far no woman had ever applied for admission as a student to any of the Inns of Court. It was a deficiency which within a few years was to be remedied with considerable success.

III. *Third Life:* THE MARTYR OF SCIENCE

1

Love and Science

Mrs. Besant's unflagging interest in all the new feministic causes had been reflected in her "Daybreak" column ever since she had started it; and she was fond of gloating over every new success, however small, such as when, in the London School Board elections of December, 1876, four women had won places on the Board. The Malthusian League, of which she was secretary, had prospered sufficiently to start publishing its little paper, the *Malthusian.* In February, 1878, she herself had helped to organize the International Labor Union and had been placed on its council, along with Bradlaugh, Headlam, Mrs. Law, and others. Her unionist sympathies had developed steadily, and as early as December, 1876, she had written an impassioned defense of two of the members of the National Union of Boot and Shoe Riveters and Finishers who had been imprisoned for "intimidation." Politically, she had continued to wield her pen boldly against the Disraeli government and its policies, and had of course supported the *National Reformer's* peace policy whether toward Russia, Turkey, Egypt, Afghanistan, or India. She joined with Bradlaugh's Radicals in supporting Gladstone's campaign against the Tories, was present in the outskirts of two or three "peace demonstrations" in Hyde Park in the winter of 1878, and accused Disraeli of hiring roughs to break them up who used such violent means that Bradlaugh's left arm was badly hurt in one of the riots. Her leaflets *Rushing into War* and *England, India, and Afghanistan* sold in the tens of thousands, and she lectured all over the country.[1]

In most of these matters she was, as usual, on the unpopular side, and the number of her enemies mounted. But so did the number of her

[1] See her autobiographies; the *National Reformer,* 1876–79; Lansbury, in *Annie Besant Centenary Book* (Adyar, 1947), pp. 25–26.

friends, even though she lost some old ones, like the revered Thomas Scott, whose death on the last day of 1878 elicited a black-bordered emotional obituary from her in the *Reformer*. One of her enemies was Lord Thurlow, a minor peer who in the spring of 1879 was persuaded to run for president of the National Sunday League, the anti-Sabbatarian organization of which Mrs. Besant had been a vice-president for several years. But Thurlow's liberalism did not extend to consorting with out-and-out Freethinkers. Nevertheless, when he and his clique attempted to force her resignation, the whole Freethought party, irrespective of faction, rallied so powerfully to her support that Thurlow was rejected by a large majority and Mrs. Besant and her friends took over the arduous task of trying to open the art galleries, museums, and concert halls on Sundays.[2]

Busy as she was with these multifarious concerns and omniscient as she seemed to her associates, Annie Besant was not satisfied with her training for her tasks. Though her private schooling under Miss Marryat had set her on the right path, she had been essentially self-educated. Never had she attended formal classes. But while the custody case was still in its last stages, she made an important decision which was to start her off on a fresh career.

Early in January, 1878, the convocation of London University had approved a new supplemental charter to admit women to its degrees. There had been angry opposition, led by Sir Henry Tyler, M.P., and supported by other champions of male supremacy like Sir William Jenner, professor of pathological anatomy and physician to Queen Victoria, whose arguments showed an extreme sensibility to women's delicacy and incapacity for rigorous and unpleasant work. But the progressives had triumphed, and the victory had been written up prominently in the *Reformer* in an article on "Women in Science" by a mysterious "D," whom Mrs. Besant regarded as one of the chief acquisitions from the Knowlton affair, but whose identity was never divulged in spite of his activity as one of her most esteemed contributors and friends.[3]

This new educational opportunity for women, coupled with her own recent researches in law and medicine, offered an irresistible challenge to Mrs. Besant. Consequently, early in February, 1879, Bradlaugh inserted a prominent announcement in his magazine:

Mrs. Besant, thinking that it may add to her usefulness to the cause, intends to try to take advantage of the opportunity afforded for women obtaining degrees in the London University. The necessary studies in preparation for the very severe

[2] *National Reformer,* March 12, 1876, February 9–April 6, 1879; *Secular Chronicle,* January 1–March 1, 1879.

[3] Though Dr. Charles R. Drysdale seems a likely possibility, he could not have been the man because he wrote many signed articles, in one of which he corrected a statement in one of that "accomplished writer" "D" 's preceding articles. But there was also a Dr. John Drysdale, one of whose books on scientific materialism was reviewed in the *Reformer*. See also *Autobiography,* pp. 327–28, and *Sketches,* p. 156.

146

examinations will occupy so much of her time that for many months to come she will be able to lecture only on Saturday and Sunday. Miss Hypatia Bradlaugh is studying with Mrs. Besant for the same object.

It was chiefly the new science which had captured the desires of the two women. For a long time Mrs. Besant had been audaciously reviewing books on chemistry, biology, and psychology. In a lecture at the Hall of Science in 1878, she had contended that the Darwinian theory was the only one which accounted for all the facts of evolution. Like all the Secularists, she had nothing but scathing contempt for everything mystical, supernatural, or unmaterialistic. The Freethought Publishing Company was selling *A Book for Children. The Gooroo Simple. A Satire on the Hindu Religion.* For years the *Reformer* had particularly recorded the attacks of Mrs. Besant, Bradlaugh, Mrs. Law, Foote, and the rest on the Spiritualists, whose proselytizing was having considerable success. Seances, tabletipping, clairvoyance, ghosts—Mrs. Besant's scorn for them all was unbounded. About the newly formed Theosophical Society in America and India she and Bradlaugh were skeptical, but hesitantly so, for Bradlaugh had met one of its founders, Colonel Henry Steele Olcott, in America and was grateful to him for "many courtesies." Though the Theosophists maintained that they were as opposed to institutional religion and Spiritualism as were the atheists, the latter, quite properly, refused to accept them as brothers-in-arms. In July, 1879, the *Reformer* quoted from an address of Olcott's in Bombay, where he had gone with Mme. H. P. Blavatsky, his partner in Theosophy and the author of *Isis Unveiled.* In this speech Olcott had spoken with approval of Bradlaugh's militant atheism, had claimed Tom Paine and others as essentially Theosophists, and had ended: "Follow the Theosophists whom Atheists venerate, and you will be the friends of Science and the enemies of religion." Nevertheless, the writer in the *Reformer,* though describing the mind of Olcott as "a fine one, but curiously twisted," had expressed his conviction that nothing permanent could be "formed out of such mixed elements." Mrs. Besant regarded herself as a friend of science and an enemy of religion, but she was as yet far from ready to accept Theosophy.

A month before Annie's intention to get a university degree had been publicly announced, the *Reformer* had printed a leading article entitled "Darwin and His Views" and signed "E.D. (D.Sc., Lond.)." Undoubtedly no one in the N.S.S. guessed the portentousness of this event; certainly Annie Besant could have had no notion of its crashing effect on her future.

"E.D." was the nom de plume behind which Dr. Edward Bibbins Aveling, lecturer on comparative anatomy at the London Hospital and teacher of science at King's College, London University, was temporarily concealing his identity, for reasons soon to be seen. When Annie, as she put it, "resolved to fill up the gaps" in her scientific education and at the same time seek recreation and resuscitation from her editorial work, her legal worries, her peripatetic lecturing, and her translating from the French, she first chose algebra, geometry, and physics. Among her journalistic acquaintances was a well-known political economist and newspaperman of "advanced" religious and political views, J. H. Levy, who was also seeking diversion from his daily occupations by taking lessons from Dr. Aveling at King's College.[4] Knowing that Aveling depended for much of his income on his fees from "coaching" or tutoring, Levy introduced his mentor to the celebrated Mrs. Besant. Impressed by his talents and personality, she first suggested that he try writing for her paper and then, in February, "became his pupil, with the view of matriculating in June at the London University." It was a very intensive course she had laid out for herself—one that put great demands in time, concentration, and personal devotion to her plan on both of them; in fact, they devoted every possible moment to it. As Mrs. Besant covertly described their relationship in a brief passage in her *Autobiography,* Aveling was

. . . a marvellously able teacher of scientific subjects, the very ablest, in fact, that I have ever met. Clear and accurate in his knowledge, with a singular gift for lucid exposition, enthusiastic in his love of science, and taking vivid pleasure in imparting his knowledge to others, he was an ideal teacher.

But science was not the only thing he taught her, though she never said so publicly.

Edward, or "E.D.," was four years younger than Mrs. Besant; he was now just past twenty-seven. Though she did not know it at first, he was already married, but—like herself—was separated from his spouse, who had left him with accusations of cruelty, but was unable to get a divorce.[5] He had been born at Stoke Newington, the son of the Rev. T. W. Aveling, a Congregationalist minister who had left his native Ireland. He had been a sickly and delicate child, for he had been dropped in nursing. The resultant injury to his spine, which gave him years of torment and harnessed him in an "infernal" machine for a time, still caused him to walk with a slight but perceptible stoop. Thus handicapped physically, he had taught himself to read the classics when he was very young, since his father had a splendid library. Tutored at home and in private schools through his childhood, he was finally judged fit to enter Harrow, where perhaps he heard stories of the Besant family who had been there before him.

Much as young Edward was addicted to literature, he apparently saw no living in it. Instead, he started off on a brilliant career in medicine. Having gone to Taunton College from Harrow, he next passed to Univer-

[4] The most complete sketch of the early life of Aveling is found in the *Republican* for December, 1881, with a photograph.

[5] For this fact, as well as some others not in the *Republican,* see Eduard Bernstein, *My Years of Exile: Reminiscences of a Socialist* (London, 1921), p. 160.

sity College, London, where he gained the top entrance scholarship in medicine and won medals in biology, physiology, anatomy, and chemistry. It was a talented family, for on the day that Edward took his degree in science, his elder brother took his in medicine, and his younger brother took his in the arts, while their parents looked on with pride. Cambridge was next, where Edward became a laboratory assistant to an eminent physiologist. He had already begun to earn a few extra pounds by tutoring and by writing two textbooks, *Botanical Tables for the Use of Students* and *Physiological Tables for the Use of Students*. On his return to London he obtained his first lectureship at—ominously—the North London Collegiate School for Girls; Aveling was always attractive to, and attracted by, girls. He had also been a consecrated Sunday-school teacher for many years. Sometime in the interim, having discovered a bent for acting, he had managed a struggling company of strolling players, which soon came to shipwreck; but his propensity for histrionics and oratory, cultivated by his preacher-father, never left him.

Obviously, Dr. Aveling was a versatile and precocious young man. He was also fascinating, and utterly undependable, if not worse. This discovery, however, Annie Besant and her circle were to make only some time later. To judge from his photographs at this period, he was not a bad-looking fellow. He had a rather narrow face, sloping upward; a straight nose, with curved nostrils; an ordinary mustache, drooping slightly around his sensuous mouth; and thin, dark hair, parted on the left, drawn back in a long theatrical curve over his ears, and curling up at the back of his neck. It was the kind of hair that women yearn to run their fingers through.

This, at least, was the man in the photographs. The descriptions of him, however, differ in various ways. Gertrude Williams, though on unstated authority, called him

handsome in a showy sort of way, as irresistible to women as he was susceptible to them. There was a fascinating touch of the diabolic about his handsome, intellectual face. He talked easily of the arts, the theater, the pictures at the Academy show, the newest books. His knowledge of the mysterious new sciences just then beginning their laboratory careers diffused about him an added glamour.[6]

People who knew Aveling personally, however, saw him rather differently. One called him "a repulsive creature"; another damned him as "a perverted character" and "a criminal"; still another warned, "Nobody can be as bad as Aveling looks."[7] But these reactions probably reflect him at a somewhat later stage of his career. Bernard Shaw, who knew

[6] *The Passionate Pilgrim*, pp. 109–10.

[7] See Felix Barker, in *New Yorker*, November 27, 1954, pp. 177–78. Mr. Barker has kindly given me his sources, omitted from his printed letter about Bernard Shaw: Joseph Clayton, *The Rise and Decline of Socialism in Great Britain, 1884–1924* (London, 1926), and Gustav Mayer, *Friedrich Engels*.

Aveling very well, painted a much more circumstantial portrait for his biographer-friend Hesketh Pearson:

Now Aveling was not a handsome man. He was undersized, had the eyes of a basilisk, and it was said of him that he would have been interesting in a Zoological museum as a reptile but impossible as a man. Short of actual deformation he had every aesthetic disadvantage except a voice like a euphonium of extraordinary resonance and beauty of tone.

Moreover, though Aveling had "an incorruptible integrity" in certain intellectual matters, according to Shaw's story,

as a borrower of money and a swindler and seducer of women his record was unimpeachable. On the same day he would borrow sixpence from the poorest man within his reach on the pretense of having forgotten his purse, and three hundred pounds from the richest to free himself from debts that he never paid. He had the art of coaching for science examinations, and girl students would scrape money together to pay him in advance his fee for twelve lessons. The more fortunate ones got nothing worse for their money than letters of apology for breaking the lesson engagements. The others were seduced and had their microscopes appropriated.

Shaw, at least, should know whereof he spoke. For Dr. Edward B. Aveling sat unconsciously as the chief model, through a process of aesthetic distortion, for the charming but unscrupulous young artist Louis Dubedat in *The Doctor's Dilemma.*[8]

Edward Aveling, however, aroused very different feelings in the beautiful and notorious Mrs. Annie Besant when she met him in 1879. Their mutual admiration, concealed for several months from all but insiders by Aveling's continued use of his pseudonym, unfolded like a tantalizing serial story before the readers of the *National Reformer.* What Charles Bradlaugh, to whom Annie soon introduced her new find, thought of the budding romance can only be guessed at, but his daughter recalled once seeing him stretch out his great muscular arm and say, "I have not a passion that I could not crush as easily as an egg within my hand if it were necessary for the good of the cause I love."

At this juncture the cause he loved demanded his attention even more than the woman he had loved. At the annual convention he had been able to point with pride at the 650 new members who had joined the N.S.S. as a result of the recent publicity, but as usual he listed no figures on the losses. And the breach with Foote was now sufficiently healed so that when this smoldering young firebrand found enough time left over from the editing of his own vulgarly irreverent magazine, the *Freethinker,* he sent over a manuscript on a subject like "Freaks of Revivalism" for his former leader to print.

No traces of Mrs. Besant's new feelings showed through her usual

[8] Hesketh Pearson, *G. B. S.: A Full-Length Portrait* (Garden City, 1946), pp. 102–3.

reviews of such technical medical books as Dr. D. Ferrier's *The Localization of Cerebral Diseases*, or of a series of tracts on "Science Lectures for the People," or even in her concurrent talks in the Hall of Science on such subjects as the physical formation of the brain and the nervous system. It was, in fact, "E. D." who first betrayed what was going on. Working up gradually to his theme through a series of relatively impersonal articles on "An Educated Woman," by the latter part of June he was no longer able to restrain himself in a long essay, "On Personal Influence." After a turgid introduction concerned with the debts of modern chemistry and astronomy to medieval alchemy and astrology, he argued that the myths and folklore of all nations had actually expressed the world's groping for some such science of the mind as was beginning to be found in the new study of psychology. He then reassured his readers ecstatically that though "Truly enough in this 'harsh world' we 'draw our breath in pain,'" still "for us all there is some comfort." There are, for instance, the beauty of flowers; woods, "still and fragrant as the thoughts of a maiden in whom love has just dawned"; music; moonlight on the sea; odors, sounds, sights, and thought; and books—"all these sink into the very being of the wanderers and give something of peace and strength." Then, recalling that the magazine was devoted to social and intellectual reform rather than to aesthetics, he slightly checked his soaring: "Oh to be able to show more of this to our poor brethren and sisters in any way—even the feeblest." So, he promised prosaically, "It is my intention in the present article and its successor to dwell especially upon the influence of human beings one upon the other." Nevertheless, his exposition and illustration of this theme remained relatively remote and ambiguous: "There are some few who leave indelible marks upon every life they encounter. Of these one hears such commonplaces as, 'He made a remarkable impression on me,' 'She is a most fascinating woman.'" He speculated on the possibility of the influence of the unspoken thoughts of one person on another, especially "when he remembers that some one woman holds him forever enshrined in the sacred temple of her heart, and breathes as she wakes from slumber and as she sinks to rest his name." Edward was beginning to tread on dangerous ground, but he shied off and drew all his remaining cases from Shakespeare, Henry Irving, and Sarah Bernhardt.

He was not yet ready to divulge his identity publicly, even in professional matters. But early in July, still signing himself only "E. D.," he laid before his readers his reasons for not going on with his application for the vacant chair in comparative anatomy at King's College. Ambitious to have his talents recognized by an official faculty appointment, he discovered when he received a copy of the "General Rules Laid Down by the Council Affecting Candidates for All Classes in King's College, London," that the requirements were "so humiliating, so insolent,"

151

that he felt he would suffer a "loss of dignity not to be atoned for even by the acquisition of a professorship." All candidates except those in oriental literature and modern languages (strange bedfellows!) must be members of the United Church and so declare; they must attend chapel regularly; and they must not engage "in public duty of any kind elsewhere than in the College" without special permission. On top of all this, when Aveling learned that the Council might change the regulations in regard to "emoluments" without notification, his conscience would not allow him to sign any such terms. His protest ended sadly, "How long, oh, Liberty, how long?"

Mrs. Besant and her sister crusaders, however, were still carrying high the standard of the new freedom. Two of her woman colleagues lent her encouragement by getting certificates in anatomy, practical chemistry, and surgery from the London School of Medicine for Women. Buoyed up by the knowledge that she had been tutored by an expert, Annie boldly tackled the severe five-day matriculation examination for London University, and on July 20 Bradlaugh was able to announce in a paternally proud "Personal":

Our readers will be pleased to learn that Mrs. Annie Besant is now an undergraduate at the London University. . . . We may now, without breaking any confidence, say that Mrs. Besant intends to win a Science degree, and we are sure that if hearty wishes can aid her hard work, she will command the heartiest from all our friends.

As a self-admitted sentimental humanitarian, a littérateur, a social entertainer, and an all-round good mixer, Aveling had no equal. But it was in his capacity as a dramatic entertainer that his real name first appeared in the *Reformer.* For some time the vocal talents of the various Freethinking groups had been channeled into an organization which called itself the London Secular Choral Union and gave quarterly variety performances for the benefit of the treasury of the Hall of Science. On July 20 Bradlaugh in his "Rough Notes" prophesied a particular success for the next performance, "as Dr. E. B. Aveling has consented to read on the occasion." Nor was the audience disappointed in Aveling's first appearance, for a "tumult of applause" broke out for him, as well as for Mrs. Besant, who also recited. Bradlaugh himself, not to be outdone, read from Shelley's "Masque of Anarchy," and the Bradlaugh girls, if they followed their usual custom, sang in the chorus, conducted by Herr Trouselle. The family group was being enlarged to five.

Aveling now threw off his incognito. He insisted on committing himself completely, in spite of the advice of some of his friends. So, on July 27 he published his manifesto under his own name. "Credo ergo laborare"—"I believe; therefore I work"—he proclaimed with a flourish.

I desire to make known in a manner as public as possible that I am a Freethinker. . . . The duty is mine, with especial plainness, because for some time past I have written for this journal under the initials "E.D." . . . No creed of which I have any cognizance is so full of unselfishness. . . . For many years I have held opinions such as I now hold. . . . But the years are gliding past. There is much to be done.

Strangely enough, this heretical avowal failed to disrupt Aveling's relations with his own family. His father remained as fond and proud of his middle son as ever; and when the youngest son, Frederic Wilkins Aveling, who had become the Congregational minister in Bradlaugh's hoped-for political constituency at Northampton, engaged in an extended correspondence with the *Reformer* on the merits of Christianity as representing the highest degree of self-sacrifice and unselfishness, he and Bradlaugh conducted their debate in the most respectful and courteous fashion. In fact, no direct mention at all was made of his renegade brother.

No one, except perhaps Frederic, as yet saw anything incongruous in Edward's implying his own unselfishness in his "Credo." Next, he promptly started off on a summary and review of W. H. Mallock's *Is Life Worth Living?* in eleven instalments. Arguing from his own Positivist point of view rather than from the author's Roman Catholic one, Aveling concluded emphatically that life was worth living. Certainly he had nothing to complain of in his new environment.

Up to this point, his little affair with Annie Besant had been quite one-sided so far as the readership of the *Reformer* was concerned. Her turn first came when her new friend gave his initial lecture before his new audience early in August. Mrs. Besant outdid herself in her account of the man whom she called "A New Soldier." In spite of the fine weather outside, she wrote, the loyal audience had filled the hall to hear the new convert, whose fame had long preceded him. "As is their wont, they gave kindly greeting to the stranger come to throw in his lot with theirs, and mindful that he came with warm, strong recommendation from the chief, they sent right brotherly greeting ringing round and round the hall as he stepped on to the platform." She spoke of her own pleasure in being able to take the chair in Bradlaugh's absence, feeling so confident of the speaker's ability to win his own way with the audience that he needed no pleading of hers in lengthy introduction. His talk consisted of a simple, loving, and personal account of the life and poetry of that hero of the Freethinkers, Shelley. She went on to congratulate the party on the acquisition of a man with such "exquisitely chosen" and "polished" language, such "music of speech," such "artistic charm," and such scholarship and wide knowledge, combined with "a brilliancy of brain I have not seen surpassed, and a capacity for work without which the intellectual power would be half wasted." Indeed, she concluded with all the pride of a discoverer, "our friends will not wonder that we, who know him, rejoice that our mistress Liberty has won this new knight."

It goes without saying that the new knight was promptly added to the list of certified N.S.S. lecturers and that his lectures were listed immediately under Mrs. Besant's own. He started off on the Leeds-Edinburgh circuit, where he was hospitably received, though his press notices did not compare in ecstasy with those that Annie had got on her early tours. After all, he was scarcely as beautiful as she.

But he continued to find life emphatically worth living. By the end of August, he had proceeded far enough in his comments on Mallock to analyze the affection of womankind in freshly rapturous terms:

Her life is as full of beauty as are her deep eyes. The loveliness of her face and form make a new joy in the world. The loveliness of her mind increases that joy a thousandfold; and whilst all around her may taste something of the happiness her presence diffuses, to me falls the deepest gladness, for her tenderest smiles are reserved for my eyes only; her inmost thoughts are breathed to me alone.

This purely hypothetical description of the effects of true affection naturally aroused in a man a purely hypothetical desire to be worthy of such a pure heart. "As I could not bear the thought that her love for me went hand in hand with a kindred love for another, she shall be the sole mistress of my life," Aveling confessed with disarming frankness, and concluded that, to him, "the most intense form of affection conceivable would be between a man and woman who both believed fully in the happier future of humanity and were both toiling to bring about that desired end." Charles Bradlaugh apparently did not want to understand or did not mind any longer; in his "Rough Notes" he continued to praise the new "knight" effusively for what he was doing for the cause.

Mrs. Besant's response was not quite so obvious or public as Aveling's invitation. When a journalist in Manchester, describing her appearance there in August, remarked, "We do not think her face had such a sad and melancholy expression as it had when we heard her previously," she quickly replied in the *Reformer* that on the earlier occasion she had been in the midst of Mabel's trial. Soon, however, she discovered that a science laboratory can provide a useful environment for experiments other than those dealing with chemical elements and cross sections of animal anatomy. So far the Hall of Science had deserved its name only through its cultivation of a scientific method of thought and procedure. But now the executive committee, of which Mrs. Besant was an influential member, saw a new and brilliant opportunity. What could be more appropriate than to start a series of actual science classes under the direction of the distinguished Dr. Aveling? Consequently, in the early fall, an announcement was made of the intended formation of one class in elementary chemistry and another in animal physiology, both of which were Aveling's specialties. If these were successful, courses in other subjects would be developed later. These would help students prepare for the examinations in the science and arts departments of the South Kensington branch of the university. Since the thirty weekly lectures in each course were offered for only five shillings (eight shillings for the pair— and half-price to members of the N.S.S. and the Hall of Science Club), it was necessary to ask for donations, which were contributed in generous fashion. Moreover, to stimulate enrolment, the Executive Committee decided to offer a prize of five guineas to the best student in each course. Since the regulations at South Kensington required that for such affiliated classes as these a sponsoring committee of responsible citizens, including at least one clergyman, must be formed, Stewart Headlam volunteered and was chosen chairman, with Drysdale and four others under him.

By October the classes had been formed, with forty-two (including six ladies) in chemistry and thirty-seven (with three bold females) in animal physiology. Bradlaugh was at hand to give the opening meeting his agnostic blessing. Mrs. Besant, however, was present in an official academic capacity. She had been appointed to assist the instructor "in the experiments necessary to illustrate Dr. Aveling's teaching." Bradlaugh was much impressed by Aveling's initial demonstration of his pedagogical powers, but also found it suitable to drop in informally every now and then—not as a chaperon, of course, but to keep an eye on how the students were developing. In November he was especially impressed by an experiment in the creation of carbon monoxide, which, as he put it, "seemed as hard to catch as an electric eel, but was ultimately produced with a sort of *feu de joie,* and general applause given most freely by those who had avoided any inhalation." Could it be that Annie Besant had had amateur trouble with her test tubes?

The year 1879 was coming to a triumphant close, though Mrs. Besant admitted that when she had seen little Mabel in the summer she was unhappily shocked at the change that had taken place. "The old fair frank innocence had passed away—for ever"; and all because the child had been subjected—apparently simply because she was now allowed to read the Bible—to the learning of such "filthy" tales as those of Judah, his daughter-in-law Tamar, and his son Onan, not to mention Lot and his daughters. On the public side of her career, she had been flattered by being made the subject of a poem by a popular poet, the mystical Christian Socialist, Gerald Massey. Massey's "Annie Besant—1879. A Greeting" was actually one of his feeblest works, but she prized it as a tribute from a widely read writer whom she had never met, but who was willing to waive her atheism in order to praise her championship of the cause of the oppressed. Her spine tingled when she read his opening line, "Annie Besant, brave and dear," and went on to his welcoming her to the fight:

> Though we stand not side by side
> In the front of battle wide.

His assertion that as long as there were people like Mrs. Besant, "Bruno lives!" was the final accolade. She and the Secularists were still collecting funds for the proposed Bruno monument in Italy.[9]

The lecture program was also going well. The N.S.S. shock troops, headed by herself, Bradlaugh, Aveling, and three or four other accomplished speakers, were making forays all over the land—sometimes alone, but sometimes together, chairing one another's meetings. Aveling now had a sporadic column of his own, "At Work," to go along with Bradlaugh's "Rough Notes" and Annie's "Daybreak." On the whole he seemed rather smugly satisfied with his success, though sometimes the attendance was not all he would have liked. Even then, however, his heart was always gladdened by the presence of many women: "With the softer influence of women upon us," he reflected, "comes not only the impulse to gentleness but a new strange strength to work."

There was a reciprocity in this impulse, too. The annual N.S.S. *Almanack* for 1880, published for the Christmas trade in 1879, reflected it. In previous years the contributions of Mrs. Besant, who had been made coeditor with Bradlaugh, had been restricted to such topics as "The Duty of Citizens to the Law" and "English Kings and Parliaments." But in 1880, in a lyrical allegory of her spiritual and intellectual life, with the unpromising title "Humanity and Its Teachers," the pseudopoetical note which had marked some of her earlier girlish writings reappeared. "A little child lay on the shore of an island in a mighty ocean," she began. "The child was very young, and she was all alone; in her eyes was a look of wonder, of inquiry, and of fear." But her heart was stilled as she looked at the shimmering water, the pine forests, and the blossoms about her; and she sank quietly into sleep. During her sleep the weather changed treacherously. Dark clouds came up, the thunder rolled, and the lightning flashed, till the child awoke and screamed with terror. Then came a rift in the clouds, the sun came back, and she prayed to it and thanked it, thinking that it "was living like herself." Then for a long time as she grew older, "all things fair and strange and terrible were to her living friends and foes," to which she gave names. In this way she became "strong, and wise, and lovely, but yet was proud and oft cruel and selfish in her strength." Finally, a new teacher came to her. He was, as she rather churlishly described him, gray and dull and unbeautiful, and he scorned all her pleasant dreams. Instead of roses, he

---

[9] Jinarajadasa, in *Annie Besant Centenary Book*, pp. 5–7.

wreathed thorns about her; but through him she learned some strange and useful lessons of work and sacrifice and "grew strong in the endurance of pain." Then this master too began to fade away into the past of her education, for the child was now a woman—lonely, but full-grown at last.

Mrs. Besant's final sentence dimmed away: "And the woman stood by the sea where the child had played; the wonder, the awe in her eyes had deepened, but the fear had passed away." Aveling immediately thereafter took up the story and continued her water metaphor in one of his own characteristically precious descriptive essays, "A Holiday Musing." This time, however, the setting was no abstract sea of life; it was a very tangible stream in north Wales (recently Annie's favorite resort spot), with a quaint old stone bridge spanning it, a little island in it, and mountains, dells, and glens all around it. Indeed, "One leafy tree on the edge of the green isle leans out over the rushing water and says: 'Kiss me.' . . . an underfoam half seen under the pellucid wave, as a maiden's love half reveals itself under her pure glance." At this point, however, Aveling's boldness failed him, and he too turned allegorical:

When the time of struggle, with its toil and its tumult, is over, . . . it flows on serene and strong. . . . And lo! from hills far asunder from those that had given it birth, another stream had been struggling to meet this. It also had had its seasons of wild fighting, with, for support and comfort, none but divine nature. It also has triumphed. For both the season of doubt and struggle is now over, and these twain . . . flow into each other—as two noble lives—and move onwards to the sea, making a new gladness and beauty in the earth.

▾

2

Love and Politics

If the *National Reformer* were ever going to justify its name, it was obvious that the nation must be reformed politically and economically as well as religiously and scientifically. The national reformers of course were to be allowed their lighter moments, but fundamentally their program was an intensely serious one. The new triumvirate of C. B., A. B., and E. A. might continue to disport themselves by giving readings and song selections for the Choral Union, and Aveling might even work up for himself a reputation as a comic entertainer, as well as a Darwin specialist. But these things were merely the raisins in the bread. There were meetings of all kinds to be attended—sometimes two or three in a single night. It was exhausting, but the trio turned everything into adventure. February, 1880, for instance, was such a foggy month in London that sometimes a person could scarcely tell where he was going. Once, two nights after Bradlaugh and Aveling had been trapped for hours in a wandering cab, the two men, accompanied by Mrs. Besant and one of the Bradlaugh girls, had decided to try their luck walking. But this way was no better than the other. London, if it could have seen anything at all, would have been diverted by the hilarious spectacle of the little party feeling its way from the central City all the way to St. John's Wood. Walls, lampposts, rails, and curbs finally ended the odyssey by guiding them to their misty destination. Such experiences gave them a fine sense of solidarity and interdependence.

One of the weighty problems they set themselves to solve was that of the Land Question. From her girlhood days when she had first learned of the devoted labors of Joseph Arch, Mrs. Besant had kept an observant eye on English agriculture. The supporters of Gladstone were now making a valiant effort to return to power. Mrs. Besant aided them by writing slashing articles and delivering speeches on such subjects as "The Story of Afghanistan; or, Why the Tory Government Gags the Indian Press." Aveling chaired one of these speeches at Middleton and pronounced ecstatically: "To read her book is a delight, but to hear the thoughts thereof spoken is like seeing a play of Shakespere acted after having read it in the study."

But Mrs. Besant's work in helping to organize and promote a great London conference on land reform occupied even more of her time. For months before it was held in February, committees met, discussions were held, and programs and speakers were arranged. All the liberal, radical, and progressive groups sent representatives. Among the delegates from the Tower Hamlets Radical Association in the East End slums was a recent Cambridge graduate named Herbert Burrows, who, along with Bradlaugh and others, was appointed to act on the Executive Committee. Burrows on this occasion apparently did not care for what he saw, for he did not return. Annie Besant, as usual a prominent figure in the discussions, hardly noticed him. But Burrows remembered her, and reminded her of this glancing meeting when he came into her new life a few years later.

The conference met on February 10 at St. James's Hall. Attended by more than five thousand delegates, it attracted much notice in the press. The Glasgow *News*, disregarding the fact that Bradlaugh, its moving spirit and chairman, had always carefully dissociated himself from any sympathy with socialism because he thought it impractical in England— though in the name of freedom of speech he had allowed Socialist writers to express their views in his columns—went so far as to label the meeting communistic. The speeches by Arch, Headlam, Parris, Aveling, Mrs. Besant, and others who sat on the platform struck fear into the Tories. George Standring's *Republican*, supplementing the accounts in the *Reformer*, told how a certain "Dr. Aveling, hitherto unknown in the front rank of the advanced movements, startled and delighted the audience by his eloquence." And when Mrs. Besant got up to second Bradlaugh's motion that the conference set up a Land Law Reform League, her "graceful words" precipitated an ovation almost as great as Bradlaugh himself got. It was no wonder, then, that when she and Aveling went out on the lecture road again, they brought in new members for the League by the score.

The stage was now set for Bradlaugh's supreme political effort. For twelve years he had been exerting every nerve to get one of the seats in Commons from Northampton. Try as he would, however, and in spite of the increasing number of his votes, he had not been quite able to make it. Since his last try, his name had become even more widely known and was more likely to appeal to the rough-and-ready electorate of the city. His enemies there were also violent and legion. It would be an unruly campaign, but he had been raising funds and friends for some time. And his preliminary printed address "To the Electors of the Borough of Northampton" had made some impression.

His very departure from London for the north early in March was symptomatic. As he and Mrs. Besant were driving to the railway station, their cab was caught between two coal wagons and overturned. She was somewhat bruised and shaken, but he was unhurt. She gallantly went on with him to the train, but then remained in London for a fortnight, "watching from afar." She wrote an article, "Shall England Vote Tory?" and Aveling supported her with an ironic essay, "Upon the Value of the Publican," for one of the heated issues of the campaign bore on the conduct and licensing of "public houses" and their operators. It was about this time, too, that she first injured the knee which was to be so troublesome to her all during her life and which, as one of her later Indian Theosophical friends was to put it, seemed to be "the most vulnerable part of her body for the Dark Powers to work on." This injury came while she was "tackling with a travelling trunk in a train long long ago while she was working with Bradlaugh."[1] Perhaps in her memory the traveling trunk in the train became confused with Bradlaugh's trunk in the overturned hansom cab, and the two accidents were really one and the same.

By the end of March, 1880, Bradlaugh's two colleagues could no longer stay away from his campaign. Neither could his daughters. All four joined him in Northampton. He kept a diary for printing in the *Reformer;* Mrs. Besant and Aveling sent back their own stories. The Northampton *Evening Mail,* the *Reporter,* and the *Herald* all gave them big write-ups. At one meeting, two thousand people crowded into the hall, and another thousand were turned away. To the accompaniment of "loud and prolonged cheering," Aveling spoke first, then Mrs. Besant, and finally the crowd's hero, Bradlaugh. As the worshiping Aveling described it, "It was a goodly sight to see over two thousand people, many of whom were women, listening intently to the lightest word that fell from the lips of her who has made the name of Woman more sacred to everyone across the path of whose life she has moved." But, truth conquering devotion, he had to admit that the voice of Bradlaugh had more power in Northampton than even Annie's.

The five plunged into the campaign in other ways, too. Aveling got to work on the polling tickets. The four Bradlaughs—Annie had long ago been adopted as, to all intents and purposes, a Bradlaugh—drove in an open carriage through the various wards, where, in her words, they were repaid by the happy faces of mothers with babies in their arms "pointing out to the children clinging to their skirts the man whose work

---

[1] W. L. Chiplunkar, "Annie Besant, My Mother," *Theosophy in India,* XXVIII (October, 1931), 213.

will, they hope, make the young lives gladder than their own have been." The five were also joined by the celebrated Henry Labouchère, whose distinguished career as the crusading editor of the weekly magazine *Truth* and as a diplomat and a Liberal leader made it practically certain that he would retain the other Northampton seat in Commons which he already held.

At last, on April 2, the voting was over. The ballots were counted as the anxious crowds stood in the darkening village square outside the George. The two progressives had won: Labouchère had exceeded his colleague by about three hundred votes, but for the Bradlaughites it was an almost incredible victory. "Beer and Bible," their ironical slogan, had defeated the Tories domestically, and the attacks on Disraeli's foreign policy had defeated them internationally; "priest and publican" had gone down with Dizzy under "Charlie's" attack.

Bradlaugh promptly went fishing in his favorite river retreat, from which he issued a bulletin that he loved his friends and had no hard feelings against his enemies—one of whom was the Rev. Charles Voysey, who had walked out on an attempt of Conway, Huxley, Tyndall, and others to found an Association of Liberal Thinkers two years before,[2] and whose later career had more and more disappointed the Freethinkers; Voysey, indeed, went out of his way to preach a sermon asserting his shame and disgust that the voters of Northampton had made such a mistake.[3] When Bradlaugh had had his rest, he returned to the Hall of Science, where he received ovations at two overflow meetings which were so crowded that the police could hardly open a way for him through the street outside. Mrs. Besant, however, was so exhausted from her Amazonian efforts that she had to cancel two lecturing engagements because of a bad sore throat, which developed into pleurisy. Aveling contracted a sympathetic cold.

The annual convention in May was turned into a sort of victory celebration of this first resounding political success of a Freethinker in England. Bradlaugh was unanimously re-elected president; and on his grateful nomination, Dr. Aveling was swiftly voted into a vacant vice-presidency. Mrs. Besant of course retained hers and was presented with a large bouquet by the members, while Bradlaugh and his girls had to be content with buttonholes. In his report he singled out for special comment Aveling and his devotion to the cause, as evidenced by his 116 lectures and 60 evening science classes since his accession. Mrs. Besant's labors on her studies at the university, of which the whole N.S.S. was so proud, had also not prevented her from averaging three lectures a week. It is true that of the seventy students who had started in the Hall of Science science courses, less than a third had finished; but of these

2 M. E. Burtis, *Moncure Conway*, pp. 171–72.
3 Bonner, *Bradlaugh*, I, 136.

twenty-one, Mrs. Besant had taken honors in animal physiology, Hypatia had done the same in chemistry, and Alice had taken a first class in each. At the close of the meeting, Bradlaugh, Mrs. Besant, and two others were chosen to go as delegates to the International Conference of Freethinkers to be held at Brussels in August. Finally, on the last evening, three hundred of the London Freethinkers, of assorted brands and views, got together to give a banquet for their victorious hero, and Foote and other secessionists were once more to be seen breaking bread with their old friends. Bradlaugh was presented with a silver salver, and Mrs. Besant, Dr. Aveling, and others made speeches which were received with "Laughter" and "Cheers."

As Bradlaugh had secretly suspected, these festivities turned out to be quite premature. Aware of the implications of the situation, immediately after the election the newspapers had started speculating on what would happen when this famous atheist had to appear in Parliament to take the oath which always preceded the assumption of a new seat. The requirement of swearing on the Bible as a preliminary to public office or the giving of legal evidence had been under fire for some time and had been modified to allow the substitution of a solemn affirmation almost everywhere except in Parliament, the last fortress of the Conservatives. As for himself, Bradlaugh would have preferred to be allowed to affirm; but at the same time, attaching no importance to the oath on the Bible, he was willing to swear if necessary. At first, when he appeared with the other new members, knowing that his enemies would center their fight on his very right to be sworn in, the process was halted just before his turn came. On May 3 he appeared again, but, after being allowed to make a short speech stating his position, he was asked to withdraw from the House without any public discussion of his case. Instead, a Select Committee was appointed to decide whether precedent could be shattered by permitting him to affirm.

On May 20 the Select Committee surprised nobody by announcing that it could not. Next day Bradlaugh faithfully appeared, saying he was ready to take the required Bible oath. This move having been anticipated by his enemies, Sir Henry Drummond Wolff immediately rose to object, whereupon another committee was appointed to hear his side of the case. It too was not impressed by Bradlaugh's arguments and reported against him.

In the meantime, he was being attacked from the flank. The Tory *British Empire* was so lacking in ingenuity as to revive the old watch story as a proof of Bradlaugh's disrespect for the Bible, whereupon he promptly filed suit for libel in the Bow Street Police Court. In their zeal to prove their case, the officers of the paper produced so many witnesses who swore they had been present at the watch episode at so many diverse places and times that the justice was dazed by their contradictions and held the defendants for trial for publishing "a false and defamatory libel." This gave Mrs. Besant a chance to trace the history of this popular generic tale through the eighteenth and nineteenth centuries in France, Great Britain, and America and to suggest that Bradlaugh could scarcely have been Protean enough to have defied the deity in such a variety of times and places. But the gossipmongers could not be stopped. They now applied the story to Mrs. Law, whose husband issued an angry denial. In July, when the Central Criminal Court found a true bill against James Edgcome, editor of the *British Empire*, he decided to discontinue publication. The story, however, lived gaily on.

Though Mrs. Besant was obviously not personally concerned in this struggle for the seat, some of her Tory and Anglican enemies could not resist the opportunity to blacken Bradlaugh's name by introducing hers. Sir Henry Tyler was one of these. In an "Extra Special Number" of the *Reformer*, Mrs. Besant told how at a hearing of Commons on oaths and affirmations (Bradlaugh not being present), the ungentlemanly Tyler had brought up her name in referring to a pamphlet written by Bradlaugh on the obscenities in the Bible, but had been interrupted by cries of "Order, order!" from other members. Bradlaugh had by now been temporarily allowed to sit but not to participate and had always chivalrously maintained that he was getting perfectly just and considerate treatment from his Parliamentary colleagues. But when he was allowed to make another speech at the Bar of the House on June 23, he was skilfully able to draw many rounds of applause from the more gentlemanly members who agreed with him that Tyler had used expressions against his comrade which were "wholly gratuitous in such a quarrel." But when it came to a vote, his enemies still outnumbered his friends.

There had been meetings everywhere—public meetings and private meetings, committee meetings, Parliamentary debates, and behind-the-scenes lobbying. Annie continued to supervise "Extra Special" numbers, with verbatim reports of the transactions. Aveling, turning himself into a gallery reporter, wrote floridly indignant descriptions of what he had seen and heard. Labouchère introduced an Affirmation Bill for its first reading. Old John Bright, a powerful figure in the new government, rose to speak in Bradlaugh's favor. Naturally, a new Defense Fund was started. Many of the lectures of the triumvirate were canceled because of the press of business. Crowds followed Bradlaugh whenever he approached Westminster.

When affairs reached their first climax in the adverse vote on June 23, Bradlaugh in his most respectful manner refused to obey the decision that he must leave the House. The members, equally polite and correct, then proceeded to a division, leaving him and the Speaker alone together in the chamber. When the members returned, it was announced that they had voted to enforce the withdrawal of the representative from

Northampton. Bradlaugh still refused to budge. The House waited, in a mixture of tension and tittering, to see what would happen when the sergeant at arms, little Captain Gosset, attempted to remove the defiant Hercules. There was no cause for alarm, however, for, as Mrs. Besant later explained in her *Autobiography*, Bradlaugh's respect for the law was always so great that "he gravely accompanied his small captor and was lodged in the Clock Tower of the House as prisoner until the House should further consider what to do with him." By now it knew it had a tartar on its hands.

Annie immediately got out another extra, featuring Aveling's vivid description of the afternoon's debate and climax and displaying prominently her own dramatic "Stop Press" announcement: "As the paper goes to press, I go to Westminster to receive from him his directions as to the conduct of the struggle with the nation into which the House of Commons has so recklessly plunged." Aveling of course accompanied her; and on their return in a hansom close to midnight, she rushed back to the office and penned her pamphlet, *Law Makers and Law Breakers*, which was printed in the *Reformer* and distributed by the thousands. The next morning she was back in the Clock Tower—the "prison room," as she preferred to call it—as soon as possible, only to find the table there already covered with the calling cards of many visitors, including several foreigners, who had come to express their sympathy over Bradlaugh's treatment and their support of his stand. In fact, so violent was the reaction that the authorities decided to release him that same day.

The fury of his sympathizers, however, could not be so easily disarmed. As Aveling summarized it in an article, "The Voice of the People," hundreds had assembled at Westminster Hall on Monday, thousands on Friday, and ten thousand came together in a "mass indignation meeting" which Bradlaugh addressed in Trafalgar Square the following Monday. When he mentioned the name of Gladstone, the crowd burst into spontaneous cheers. The forces of progress were highly optimistic, but they still continued to exert pressure. Letters and telegrams were dispatched to influential people. Some two hundred mass meetings broke out in protest all over the country. On July 1 the House rescinded its resolution of expulsion and the next day allowed Bradlaugh to affirm and take his seat. He and Annie crowed over their victory in their respective columns; he had recently started a new one, "Parliamentary Jottings," in which he proposed to give a frank and intimate account of his political experiences. Here he recounted how he immediately made a brief speech in Commons, how he asked Gladstone an important question there, how he voted in nine divisions, sometimes not getting home till four in the morning, how he addressed miners' meetings at Northampton and Durham and was cheered to the echo, and how he marked time for many weeks waiting for the next move of his enemies to mature.

As soon as he had taken his seat after affirming, he had been served with a writ for having voted without taking the oath. Thus the scene of battle was to be transferred to the law courts once more—a familiar battleground for him, but one on which his rich and powerful enemies thought they could bankrupt him, knowing that he must both support himself and pay his legal expenses from the proceeds of his writings and lectures, which would be greatly interfered with by this perpetual harassment. They knew, too, that his health had already been undermined and that he was still burdened with debt.

The respectable scandalmongers also continued their assault on him by attacking Annie. This attack reached its dingy peak in July and August. In various by-elections several newspapers had circulated what Bradlaugh called "exceeding wanton and coarse personal slanders" against him, and he had had to extend his legal lines still further by starting suit against them for libel. The most reverberating of these attacks was made in an electoral campaign at Wigton by Sir John Hay, M.P. and a vice-admiral in Her Majesty's Navy. This "infamous, most cowardly and utterly uncalled for" speech had been printed in the Glasgow *News* and had contained a passage referring to Mrs. Besant which was so offensive that the Glasgow *Herald* and the Edinburgh *Scotsman* had refused to print it; in fact, the editor of the *Scotsman* had described the language as "so coarse that it could hardly have dropped from a Yahoo." Consequently, Bradlaugh twice wrote the Admiral asking for a confirmation or denial of his "infamous" allusions, threatening that if Hay did not apologize he would place copies of the speech and his letters before the Speaker of the House. Knowing, however, that the rules of the House and the law itself afforded him no real remedy, and feeling himself so physically superior to Hay that personal chastisement would be unfair, he contented himself at first by submitting his letters in print to the public.

Mrs. Besant was even more affronted and expressed herself more vociferously in a printed letter to Hay about the newspaper accounts, "in one of which you, in the coarsest language, accuse me of conduct which would entitle Mr. Besant to a divorce, and in the other you admit the language and make a sort of clumsy apology. You are aware that a man is not legally punishable for slander, however vile, provided he do not impute an indictable offense." Accusing Hay of cowardice in attacking a woman who had not wronged him in any way, Mrs. Besant promised to bring him before the bar of public opinion and asked him whether, if Bradlaugh had alleged that Lady Hay was guilty of the same crime, he would hesitate to brand the slanderer as a coward and a liar. "Yet," she swore, "the accusation would have been as justifiable as the one you have made." But though the *Reformer* continued to pitch into Hay for some time, he preserved an undignified silence throughout. He had contributed his share to the denigration campaign.

In the meantime, the dogged Bradlaugh faithfully performed his

Parliamentary duties, in the full knowledge that his actions might be ruled unconstitutional. Though he felt that Gladstone, as prime minister, inclined toward his side of the controversy and would have liked to see the Affirmation Bill pass in spite of his strongly Anglican opinions, he and Mrs. Besant nevertheless felt justified in opposing many of the government's stands. In the autumn she even stumped up and down England in what she regarded as the defense of Irish freedom, showing by figures that life and property were far safer in Ireland than in England under present conditions and that Ireland was singularly free from crime except in some agrarian disputes. Charles Parnell and his Irish insurgents were taking almost as much time in Parliament as was Bradlaugh; but while she wrote against him and his methods, she agreed with Bradlaugh when he spoke against the Irish Coercion Bill. A few months later she wrote a widely reprinted article on "Coercion in Ireland and Its Results," which she claimed helped to persuade the government to send Lord Frederick Cavendish to Ireland to try to straighten out the situation. Unfortunately, this contribution to the cause of "the Irish land so dear to my heart" had an ironically tragic conclusion, for one day when she was lecturing at Blackburne on "The Irish Question," she was horrified to hear that Cavendish had been assassinated—according to one account by some Irish who were unwittingly aiding the English policy by trying to prevent friendship between the two countries in this violent way. Mrs. Besant and Bradlaugh also started a campaign against what they dubbed "Perpetual Pensions" for members of the aristocracy and the royal family and collected large bundles of petitions in their cause. Consistently opposing British expansionism, they likewise attacked the annexation of the Transvaal.

The opening months of 1881 saw the action to compel Bradlaugh to give up his seat coming to a head. It was brought in Queen's Bench by a comparative unknown, H. L. Clarke, who, it was discovered later, was a mere front, a "man of straw," for Charles Newdigate Newdegate, long-time Conservative M.P. from North Warwickshire, who was paying the costs. Bradlaugh's libel suit against Edgcome was still pending, and he was also engaged in a third suit brought by a solicitor named Taylor for a debt which Bradlaugh was able to prove he had paid thirteen years before. On March 19, as a sort of foreshadowing, John E. Gorst, soon to become solicitor-general, walked across the floor of the House to warn Bradlaugh that he intended to take steps to vacate his seat and call for a new election in Northampton, though he knew the other had recently addressed his constituency there and been assured of their support. A few days later the verdict was handed down from the Court of Appeal, where the case had landed. Aveling, who was there with Mrs. Besant, told of the unhappy scene in another extra issue of the *Reformer* and praised his chief for his philosophical behavior. The verdict, he pointed out ironically, meant substantially that a man who would be allowed to affirm in any of the courts at Westminster must nevertheless take the oath for his veracity, trustworthiness, and loyalty if he found himself in the House of Commons.

In spite of this incongruous ruling, few expected Bradlaugh to lie down without a fight. His seat had been vacated, it is true; but he would go back to Northampton and ask his constituents to defy Parliament and the courts by electing him again. He was tired and out of funds, but he would never give in. In an article entitled "Fair Means or Foul," Mrs. Besant exposed the silliness of some of the Tory charges, such as that Bradlaugh kept liveried servants and a carriage and pair. The Tories, she jeered, should see him at work in his "modest rooms" in Circus Road and watch him driving home from Parliament "these cold nights in a chilly hansom cab." A little later in the campaign she apparently surreptitiously attended a meeting for the Conservative candidate at the Carlton Club in London and maliciously revealed how its leaders had decided to change the date of the meeting on the records to April 2, since it had actually been held on "All Fool's Day." Labouchère entered the contest to help his colleague. All these things helped to consolidate Northampton sentiment so successfully that when the votes were counted, it was found that, as Annie put it, "The solid Radical vote outweighed the united ballots of the Tories, the moderate Liberals, and, as it is stated in many journals, their new allies, the Irish."

Bradlaugh, in his "Rough Notes," told the public that he would go to the House again on April 26 to take his legitimate seat; moreover, since he had been refused the right to affirm, he was still willing to take the conventional oath. So, again, with the nation watching, he marched down to Westminster and into Commons. Mrs. Besant watched the proceedings from a "perch" in the gallery, from which she could barely see and could hear almost nothing. The vote went against him, though both Gladstone and Bright spoke in his favor. And again, when he was instructed to withdraw, he refused to go, because, he maintained, "the resolution . . . is against the law." Once more the Speaker called on the sergeant at arms to remove the offender, who once more refused to go. The following prolonged debate on what to do made the assembly look so ridiculous that Bradlaugh finally allowed himself to be conducted to the door.

The national hubbub was tremendous. Bradlaugh issued an "Appeal to the People." Mass meetings broke out feverishly. The House debated, and the press, national and international, raged, pro and con. It was announced that the verdict of the Court of Appeal in the Clarke case would be fought on a technicality and that the Lord Chief Justice, Sir John Coleridge, who had succeeded the dead Cockburn, would hear the proceeding. The title of "Parliamentary Jottings" was changed to "Jottings out of Parliament." Bradlaugh's partisans formed a "League for the Defense of Constitutional Rights," and Mrs. Besant, Dr. Aveling, Dr. Drysdale, the Rev. Moncure Conway, Joseph Arch, and even Foote were elected vice-presidents. Alice Bradlaugh and other Secular ladies seized their scissors and needles to cut out and sew rosettes of mauve, green, and white, the Northampton colors, for the League members to flaunt. At the Congress of French Freethinkers in Paris, the N.S.S. delegate reported that toasts were drunk to Garibaldi, Bradlaugh, and Mrs. Besant, and the memory of Giordano Bruno. There was an Antiatheistic meeting at Exeter Hall, which Aveling described in "The Church and the Prize Ring," and which he, Foote, and others infiltrated and defied from the floor.

By the end of May, Mrs. Besant's indignation had reached such a peak that she made two impetuous proposals. The first she headed "Stop the Supplies" and proposed the pledge:

I solemnly promise that if by August 15th 1881 the said Charles Bradlaugh, M.P., has not been duly permitted to take his seat, I will wholly abstain from the use of beer, wine, spirits, tobacco, and snuff, until justice be done and the law obeyed. . . . These articles all pay heavy duty.

Then, in case this proposed boycott (which of course would bring little deprivation to the abstemious like herself and Bradlaugh) failed to make enough converts among the more unregenerate, she had a second idea: Bradlaugh's friends should withdraw all but a token shilling from their savings bank accounts. Such measures, she thought, would hit the Tories where it hurt.

The more levelheaded members of the League, however, foresaw the new troubles such boycotts would start, and her proposals were allowed to drop silently after she had been soothingly praised for making them. But, at the annual conference at Bury in June, she gave a long report proposing the censure of G. J. Holyoake for his attack on what he regarded as Bradlaugh's lack of integrity in declaring his willingness to take the Bible oath; her motion, seconded by Aveling, was carried unanimously, with great cheering. The old officers were unanimously reelected, after the Huddersfield branch had created a brief discordance which ended in its withdrawing its premature intention to urge Mrs. Besant herself for the presidency. Bradlaugh's treatment by Parliament had so altered the Huddersfield plan that, along with the other branches, it enthusiastically supported Foote's resolution that the convention approve all of Bradlaugh's actions at Westminster.

The League for the Defense of Constitutional Rights was rapidly gaining strength and respectability. At a "magnificent" mass meeting in St. James's Hall, the crowd not only responded to the urgings of the acknowledged extremists like Mrs. Besant, Aveling, Foote, Headlam, and

Bradlaugh himself, but it was addressed by Labouchère and Admiral Frederick A. Maxse, who thus helped to counterbalance the operations of his brother admiral, Sir John Hay. At the close of the meeting the Marquis of Queensberry, of pugilistic fame and the father of Oscar Wilde's too-close friend, Lord Alfred Douglas, rose to propose a vote of thanks to the chairman, Councillor Adams. As a result, all over England people were circulating petitions for Bradlaugh and against Bradlaugh. The cartoon warfare in the papers and magazines also waxed more and more lively, one drawing in particular selling in large numbers from the office in Stonecutter Street.

By July 4 Bradlaugh had determined his next step. Gladstone, on account of the Tories' opposition, had been forced to withdraw the government's Affirmation Bill. Bradlaugh wrote formally to the Speaker of the House that, notwithstanding his former ejections, on August 3 he would again present himself at the table of Commons in order to fulfil the duties of his elected position.

The night before that fateful day he called for a mass meeting of all friends of constitutional liberties to join him in Trafalgar Square to protest the actions of the majority of Parliament. It was a crowded and sympathetic meeting, with delegates from all over England, especially the North Country, and some even from Edinburgh, though the spirits of its leaders had been somewhat dampened by a verdict against Bradlaugh which the jury in the Clarke-Newdegate case had just handed down. With his own cry of "Courage, brave hearts!" echoing in his head, he went down to the House, which all through July had been heavily guarded by police, who had kept the great gates tightly closed against all but officials.[4]

Just before leaving home, Bradlaugh had said to Mrs. Besant, "The people know you better than they know any one, save myself; whatever happens, mind, whatever happens, let them do no violence; I trust you to keep them quiet." Bradlaugh and Aveling had gone on ahead, but Aveling had of course dropped back at the door of the House. Mrs. Besant, Alice and Hypatia Bradlaugh, and some other friends had followed by train. At Westminster Station they were astonished by the masses of men and women who were waiting there in orderly fashion and who, recognizing them at once, passed them through their ranks to the Palace Yard. Here they were challenged by the police, but because they were carrying the petitions which had been so widely circulated, they—seven to a petition—were allowed to squeeze through the gate into Westmin-

[4] Accounts of the ensuing events are to be found in the National Reformer; Autobiography; Bonner, Bradlaugh; and John M. Robertson, "Account of [Bradlaugh's] Parliamentary Struggle, Politics, and Teachings," in Bonner, Bradlaugh. But they differ, and are sometimes contradictory in several details; Bonner seems to be most circumstantial and reliable.

ster Hall, where they were again stopped on the steps leading to the lobby passage. Little groups of Bradlaugh's followers had already managed to penetrate the thin line of police. An inspector ordered them all away. Mrs. Besant intimated that they were within their rights. The inspector called for four more officers to help him. Mrs. Besant suggested that he consult Chief Inspector Denning before using violence to put them out. The chief inspector sustained her and rebuked his subordinates.

So both sides waited, wondering what was going on behind the silent doors. The crowd, feeling they had been improperly kept out of the lobby, grew restive, curious, angry. Suddenly their irritation boiled up into a roar: "Petition, petition, justice, justice!" Then a fearful rumor swept through the Hall. "They are killing him, they are killing him!" Next the angry cry arose, "To the House!" and the crowd surged up the steps toward the policemen at the door. Their command to "Fall back!" went unheeded. Annie, remembering that moment years afterward in a glow of pride, recalled how, mindful of her chief's admonition, she instinctively flung herself forward so that she was between the advancing police and the menacing crowd. She heard an officer laugh at her temerity, her female defiance. She did not blame him. But, planting her tiny figure at the top of the flight of stairs, she held off the crowd alone, the police behind her. Calling on all her vocal powers, she pleaded with the crowd, for their leader's sake, to keep the peace which he had bade them not to break.

Muttering, the men sullenly drew back. The peace had been preserved outside, and by a woman. As one historian summarized the situation, if Mrs. Besant had not quieted the mob, then might "the multitude have taken its own way, sacked the House, and thrown, if not the Speaker and his wig, at least Lord Randolph Churchill, and Sir Stafford Northcote, and Sir Henry Woolf, comrades three, into the Thames, that ancient river and unclean."[5]

But if the crowd had known what simultaneously was going on inside, they would never have stopped—as some of them stated later—until they had "carried him into the House up to the Speaker's chair." As the watchers and the police waited in a mutual truce, they heard a crash of breaking glass and splintering wood inside. Then nothing, till soon afterward a man came with a message for Annie: "He is in the Palace Yard." She and her friends were allowed to enter. Bradlaugh was standing there, white and motionless, with his coat torn and his "face set like marble, . . . as though carved in stone, facing the members' door."[6]

The shameful story was quickly spread through the newspapers. As Bradlaugh had entered the House alone and endeavored to take his seat,

[5] Geoffrey West, *Annie Besant,* p. 76.

[6] Bonner says this meeting took place in Stonecutter Street,

fourteen ushers and policemen,[7] directed by Mr. Erskine, Captain Gosset's deputy, had flung themselves upon him to force him to leave. According to some witnesses, Alderman Fowler had immediately yelled, "Kick him out!" when he saw Bradlaugh, but the Alderman later piously denied any such orders. At any rate, Bradlaugh did not fight. He would commit no violence in such precincts. He simply resisted, with all his great passive strength. As the others pushed, pulled, and shoved, he contested every inch. Every muscle was strained and racked. His clothing was torn. He gasped, turned pale, and seemed almost ready to faint from the tension and his exertions. But the fourteen hauled him down the stairs, breaking the glass and wood of the passage door in their haste and anger, and threw him into the Yard.

"I nearly did wrong at the door," he confessed afterward. "I was very angry. I said to Inspector Denning, 'I shall come again with force enough to overcome it.' He said, 'When?' I said, 'Within a minute if I raise my hand.'"

But he did not raise his hand, though the hundreds outside had now increased to thousands. "No man will sleep in gaol for me tonight," he told Annie later that day when they had all gone back to Stonecutter Street; "no woman can blame me for her husband killed or wounded, but ——" The "wave of agony" which swept over his face told Mrs. Besant that he would never again be the same man, even though he would eventually win his fight.

That night he limped onto the platform of the Hall of Science with his arms swathed in bandages. The muscles of his left arm particularly were so badly wrenched and bruised that for weeks he could use it only with great pain. The wooden shell of the hall echoed with the cheers of those who could crowd in. He told them he was returning at once to Northampton to report. Some opposition newspapers hinted that he was only shamming illness, and some callous M.P.'s expressed private pleasure at the way he had been treated. Shaw so relished the story of the "intelligent member of Parliament" who supported the exclusion on the ground that "a man ought to believe in something or other" that he retold it at least twice.[8] But most of England and the outside world was horrified at the way brute force had thus for the first time been used in England to keep a legally elected man from his Parliamentary seat.

[7] Shaw, Self Sketches, p. 120, sets a smaller number: "Bradlaugh was thrown out of the House of Commons with such violence that John Bright, who arrived just in time to see him dragged down the stairs by six policemen, was horrified." There is also some disagreement about the source of the roughness: Aveling and Mrs. Besant blamed Erskine and his ushers and praised the police for their politeness and discipline; Bradlaugh himself applied at the Westminster Police Court to charge Inspector Denning with having assaulted him, but had his application dismissed.

[8] Our Theatres in the Nineties, II, 22; and the 1921 Preface to Back to Methuselah.

Mrs. Besant was thoroughly aroused—and few could be as thorough when aroused as she. When she took Bradlaugh's place on the Hall of Science platform the following Sunday, she expressed her plans for economic and political revenge so fantastically that the next day another M.P. rose in Commons to ask Gladstone whether the government was taking the necessary steps to prevent the threatened Besant riot; but Gladstone temperately replied that he was not worried. When Bradlaugh returned from the north, his little family decided they should take him to the Sussex seaside town of Worthing to recuperate. On their way they heard a clergyman, who had passed the open cab and stopped to stare hatefully at Bradlaugh in spite of his bandages and the erysipelas that had developed, remark loudly so that all could hear, "That's Bradlaugh; I hope they'll make it warm for him yet."

Aveling, however, was not included in this family trip.

3

Botanists and Chemists
in Opposition

All through 1880 and 1881, Annie Besant and Edward Aveling had continued to be close comrades. They had fought Bradlaugh's
battles in politics together, they had lectured and led meetings together,
they had studied science and taught classes together. So inseparable were
they that it seemed surprising to their circle to find them apart, except
when their professional schedules demanded their division.

It is temptingly possible, however, to press these implications too far.
Gertrude Williams, for instance, manufactured "a mysterious hiatus during the second summer of the Aveling intimacy," in which the *Reformer*,
"usually full of Annie Besant's doings, made no reference to her whereabouts for two full months" in the summer of 1880. As a matter of fact,
the columns of the paper were crammed as usual with accounts of the
activities of all the N.S.S. leaders during June, July, and August, though
it is true that apparently two or three of Mrs. Besant's and Dr. Aveling's
lectures were temporarily canceled. To cap the implications of this nonexistent "hiatus," however, Mrs. Williams continued:

In the autumn, Aveling, with his air of swallowing a canary, wrote, "Long,
happy, never-to-be-forgotten days . . . stretched lazily on beaches made of
myriads of shells smoothed and polished by the sea so delicately and fantastically that each might be the bridal bed of a sea goddess; peaceful, dreamless
nights, the rarest of companionship make certain August days in 1880 as moments
in the passing, as years in the remembrance of them." It was his final rhapsody.
With the autumn a change in their relation became apparent. His articles in *The
National Reformer* trailed off to sophomoric essays. His New Year's greetings reflected a melancholy, contrasting with the exhilaration of previous years: "Each
day follows another with the relentlessness of Fate. We name them Christmas day

or New Year's day, our birthday or hers, that whereon her lips met ours for the first or last time. A thousand memories and pains cluster round this date and that."[1]

Though the first passage seems to be written in Aveling's best style, I have been unable to locate it anywhere; the second, however, comes authentically from his New Year's greetings in the *Reformer* for January 2, 1881.

If the couple took a secret holiday together in August, 1880, it must have been a very brief one in the middle of the month. During the first two weeks of the month, either one or the other was clearly in London attending meetings of the House or the Executive Committee of the N.S.S. But on August 20, neither one attended the regular meeting of the latter. On August 27, however, Mrs. Besant was present; Aveling was in the north, having lectured at Manchester on August 22 and having planned to move on from there to Edinburgh. On August 29 the *Reformer* carried a brief story explaining that because Mrs. Besant was "out of town unwell," it was doubtful whether she would be able to go as delegate to the International Conference of Freethinkers at Brussels from August 29 to September 1—a conference she had been looking forward to for a long time.

Whatever the explanation of the sequel—whether conscience or duty—she made a rapid enough, though temporary, recovery to be in London on August 27 and Brussels on August 29. Hypatia Bradlaugh went with her, and other London Secularists also attended; but Charles Bradlaugh himself could not go. Freethinking delegates from all over the world were present, including the famed Dr. Ludwig Büchner, "the great German scientist, a man with a noble head and strong, gentle face," and De Robigne Mortimer Bennett, better known as simply D. M. Bennett, next to Colonel Robert Ingersoll the leading American atheist, whose writings and whose editing of the New York *Truthseeker* the English group had long admired. Mrs. Besant immediately took her usual prominent place at every meeting, providing a brief English translation of the Belgian president's welcoming speech, reading a letter from Bradlaugh, and delivering a speech in French on the status of Freethought, particularly in England. Later, when one of the delegates moved that the congress recommend that the two English Freethought societies join hands, she whispered to the president that she would be forced to oppose the motion. The motion was dropped. Statutes were adopted, routine business was accomplished, and plans to found an International Federation of Freethinkers were made. Since the next meeting was to be held in Paris, a Frenchman was elected president; Mrs. Besant was chosen vice-president to represent England, and Bennett received the same honor for the United States. She then gave the closing remarks and later lost the addresses of

[1] *The Passionate Pilgrim,* pp. 131–32.

many of the delegates when she had her pocket picked while leaving the Brussels boat.

The international association never came to much, but as the result of a controversy between the two rival English groups over the election of a joint delegate, G. W. Foote, never happy for long in any group not headed by himself, returned to the fold of the stronger N.S.S., carrying its approval of his plans to publish his own new paper, the *Freethinker*. Bradlaugh and Mrs. Besant were chosen to represent the N.S.S. at the next annual meeting. The B.S.U. elected Holyoake.

Annie's meeting with Dr. Büchner had more permanent results. She had long admired him and had often referred to his ideas in her own writings. Now she promptly set up a steady correspondence with him and received permission to translate some of his works into English. Three or four months after her return to England, following another bad sore throat, she had an operation which kept her in bed for three weeks, but which cleared up her ill health for a time. While recuperating, she taught herself to write while lying on her back and in this way translated much of Büchner's *Mind in Animals* for quick publication. After recovering and regaining her health, she went on to the enlarged new edition of his *Force and Matter* and two or three pamphlets on *The Influence of Heredity on Freewill* and similar topics. Büchner was much struck with this intrepid little Englishwoman who was undaunted even by German science and scientific style. The Freethought Publishing Company announced a new series, "The International Library of Science and Freethought," to begin with *Mind in Animals* and go on to Aveling's *The Student's Darwin*, based on his series, *Darwin and His Works*, which was eventually to run to twenty-nine instalments in the *Reformer*. Soury's *Jesus and the Gospels* and "a work of Dr. Ernest Häckl, of Jena," were to add further distinction to the list.

At this time, too, D. M. Bennett—who, after being imprisoned in America for his heretical ideas, had gone to India, where he had been sponsored for admission into the Theosophical Society by Mme. Blavatsky and her Master, Koot Hoomi[2]—stopped in England to meet his new English Secularist friends, whose sympathies as fellow martyrs impelled them to give him a supper in the newly remodeled Hall of Science in recognition of his defense of Freethought. Though Bradlaugh was to be in the chair, and Mrs. Besant was to give the main tribute and address, Bennett's reputation did not prove strong enough to draw more than a handful to the affair—mostly speakers. He was more impressed later, however, when he dined several times at Oatlands with Mrs. Besant, the Bradlaughs, and Aveling. The last of these made the deepest impression of all; Aveling treated him to an hour-and-a-half dinner at the glittering

---

[2] *Vahan*, October, 1907, quoting from Mrs. Besant's speech to the American Theosophical Society convention in that year.

Criterion and later to a box at the theater. So overawed was Bennett at this display of foreign "swank" that he wrote back to his American subscribers that, "to a casual observer, it could hardly have been known that we were not of the aristocracy of the city." Commenting discreetly on his three chief hosts, he also divulged that they were known locally as "The Trinity."[3]

Perhaps the achievement of which "The Trinity" was proudest, because it was the newest and because they stood to it in the somewhat anomalous role of triple parents, was the establishment of the Hall of Science classes for popular education. Here the prosecution of Mrs. Besant's own studies at the University of London and her tutoring by young Aveling formed a vital contributing factor to the ultimate success of the work.

At this time, in her mid-thirties, she made the sort of figure which, standing in front of a class, would attract students by its natural ease and grace. Her face was oval, soft, and gently rounded. She wore her hair cut in short bangs at the front, with long plaits wound around her head at the back so as to reveal her small ears. She was fond of ribbed, tightly buttoned dresses which showed off her slim figure, topped off with closely fitting white collars fastened with a cameo brooch or some other piece of simple jewelry.[4] And if her appearance did not command attention, her deep, rich voice would.

As a student she must have been a pleasure to her examiners at the South Kensington branch of the university. Her studies were not only of remarkable diversity, but of a most unfeminine nature. In the examinations in 1880, for example, she was rated "First Class" in inorganic chemistry, mathematics, theoretical mechanics, magnetism and electricity, botany, general biology, animal physiology, and acoustics, light, and heat. At the Christmas examinations at the Hall of Science, she took top honors in botany, advanced physiology, mathematics, and advanced chemistry. She must have repressed her rightful pride when she saw that though the Bradlaugh girls ranked high, they did not rank so high as she. Perhaps she might have suspected some favoritism on the part of Aveling, if she had not been able to demonstrate her mastery of these scientific subjects objectively at the South Kensington examinations.

So impressive were her attainments that she herself was listed to offer the course in elementary animal physiology in the fall. Aveling announced a "daring campaign" to add botany and mathematics to the Hall of Science curriculum, to be taught by himself; and when it was found that the music master, Herr Trouselle, could not handle both the choral

[3] *National Reformer,* October 24, November 7, 1880; Williams, *The Passionate Pilgrim,* pp. 117–18. For Mrs. Besant's own overglamorized account of Bennett's visit and her speech, see her *Autobiography,* pp. 329–34. Bennett died in 1883.

[4] See the cover picture on the *Republican,* October, 1881.

and dramatics classes announced for him, Aveling airily assumed the dramatics work also. Alice Bradlaugh, the less scholarly and scientific of the two girls, undertook to start a class in French. It was an ambitious program that the Secularists planned, in spite of the previous year's deficit. At first the new registration did not rise to their hopes, stopping at a little over two hundred. There was also for a time a disturbingly high degree of absenteeism at both lectures and examinations. To improve the *esprit de corps,* therefore, the directors started a Hall of Science Students' Association, which aimed to bring the students together socially as well as intellectually, and of which Dr. Aveling was elected president. The social and intellectual combination was effectively illustrated when Aveling announced that a large group had requested to be taken out on botanizing expeditions into the country on Sundays. Bradlaugh was of course present at the first organizing meeting; he congratulated Aveling on his initiative and the students on their teacher.

People like Mrs. Besant and Dr. Aveling inevitably sought a place in all the liberal controversies of the day. Vaccination and vivisection were still new and unsettled enough to precipitate violent arguments all over the world. Sir Eardley Wilmot had introduced into Parliament a bill for the "Total Suppression of Vivisection." The pages of the *Reformer* echoed with the doughty but cautious defense put up by Mrs. Besant and the two doctors, Aveling and Drysdale. A third doctor soon came in, but on the other side. Mrs. Anna Kingsford, after studying medicine at the University of Paris, had astonished and upset most professionals and laity by earning her M.D. in this very year, 1880. It was one of the landmarks in the English feminist movement. Dr. Kingsford, who was a leading vegetarian as well as an anticlerical, did her best to wean Mrs. Besant from her theoretical acceptance of vivisection—"theoretical" because the latter had to admit that so far the only dissection she had practiced had been on dead animals. Yet only a few years later, under circumstances which neither lady at this time would have predicted, Mrs. Besant spectacularly adopted Dr. Kingsford's anti-flesh platform in both particulars.

The fight against orthodox religion also went on. The N.S.S. for some time had backed the right of parents to withdraw their children from religious education classes in the public schools and had persistently kept this agitation alive. Aveling joined Mrs. Besant's old Sunday League and spoke at its opening meeting in the fall. When Conway returned to America for a time, Aveling conducted a popular series of lectures on "Biological Discoveries and Problems" at the South Place Chapel. Mrs. Besant inveighed against "Christianity in the Hospitals." Literature itself could not escape their eager predatoriness. When the skeptic George Eliot died, Mrs. Besant in an obituary predicted that she would never be forgotten, "as woman and genius." On the death of Carlyle, Aveling pronounced the dour Scotsman an "unconscious Radical." Nor did they confine their writings to the *Reformer;* the advanced magazine *Modern Thought* printed Aveling's famous lecture on Shelley, the atheist.

Mrs. Besant's triumphant career continued into 1881. But its perfection was now marred slightly by two "second divisions." In the South Kensington examinations she made "first divisions" in advanced botany and advanced animal physiology but only "seconds" in advanced mathematics and advanced chemistry. Nevertheless, it was announced that she would teach new Hall of Science courses the next term in advanced chemistry and light, heat, and sound. Aveling was branching out into natural philosophy, practical chemistry, and geology. They were an omnivorous and omniscient pair. In his "Rough Notes" for August 7, Bradlaugh issued public congratulations to Annie on her success in her examinations and reminded their friends that "Dr. Edward B. Aveling has been Mrs. Besant's sole tutor in preparation both for the matriculation and for these examinations."

Unfortunately, this happy mood was not to last. Two or three days later Bradlaugh was forcibly thrown out of Parliament, as previously described. The news a few days afterward that Annie had passed her botany examination with honors was only a partial counterbalance, for now their enemies in high places had discovered a new quarter from which to attack. In August, Sir Henry Tyler, the wealthy and influential M.P. who sat on railway directorates, church vestries, school boards, and hospital committees and who a little over a year before had aroused the wrath of Bradlaugh by dragging the name of Mrs. Besant into a Parliamentary debate, reopened his righteous assault by raising a formal objection in the House to South Kensington's approval and acceptance of the courses taught in the Hall of Science by Mrs. Besant, Dr. Aveling, and Hypatia Bradlaugh. In his opinion, no atheist, especially one who had expressed in print the view that the findings of science undermined religion and the Bible, should be permitted to teach science to anyone.[5]

Temporarily discomfited after two speeches, largely because of the vigorous and skilful opposition of Anthony Mundella, a Radical M.P. with a progressive attitude toward modern education, Tyler withdrew from the skirmish, growling that he would bring in a later motion to prevent further subversion of the schools. His skill as a strategist was soon demonstrated, however, on another flank. He had friends on the board of the London Hospital; and Edward Aveling taught a class in comparative anatomy at that hospital. In Mrs. Besant's perhaps prejudiced words, quoting the opinion of one of the chief visiting physicians there, Aveling was "the most painstaking and the most successful lecturer in that insti-

---

[5] For the ensuing episode, see the *National Reformer,* 1881–83, *passim;* Robertson, "Account of [Bradlaugh's] Parliamentary Struggles, Politics, and Teaching," in Bonner, *Bradlaugh,* II, 291–344, *passim;* Bonner, *Bradlaugh,* II, 92–93; *Autobiography,* pp. 344–49; C. Jinarajadasa, in *Annie Besant Centenary Book,* p. 4.

tution" and had taken over the most disgraceful class in the hospital and made it the "best-conducted and most orderly." Nevertheless, when at this crucial moment Aveling laid himself open by requesting that the day of one of his class meetings be changed, Tyler saw his chance and influenced his colleagues to dismiss Aveling because of insubordination and incompetence. Though for several weeks there continued to be arguing on the governing board and indignation among the students, Aveling, who probably realized that an investigation might reveal his vulnerability on other scores, accepted his dismissal and announced his intention to give the same course (apparently a sort of cramming course) at 142 Old Street, i.e., at the Hall of Science. He already had a private "Practical Laboratory" in Newman Street, just off Oxford Street, where he could take care of his personal tutoring cases and where—he seemed to be in perennial need of money—he asked to have special subscriptions to his work delivered. He had also recently moved his residence up to St. John's Wood, where he could be close to his two great friends, Bradlaugh and Mrs. Besant. He was a man of many addresses.

In the meantime, Mrs. Besant, who was very proud of the fact that she was the only student in all England who had been given honors on her botany examination and that none other than the great Thomas Huxley had been one of her examiners, had applied through Dr. Aveling for permission to use the Royal Botanical Gardens in Regent's Park for her further studies. The curator, however, rejected the application in horror, on the ground that his daughters often used the gardens and he did not dare let them be exposed to Mrs. Besant's presence. Though it is hard to see how her investigations of pistils and stamens could have corrupted the girls, the board in charge of the gardens sustained its secretary. As soon as Sir J. D. Hooker, another famous botanist, heard of this act of bigotry, he dispatched a ticket admitting her to the Kew Gardens—but with the cautious provision that she must use them before the public visiting hours. After all, there were now 50,000 copies of her *Law of Population* in print; in Australia her name had just been forged to a pamphlet called *Wives or Mistresses;* and she had been engaging in a lengthy correspondence with the Bishop of Manchester on Knowlton and the true attitude of Secularists toward marriage.

A little later the Birkbeck Institute, where she had attended a class in electricity, omitted her name from the list of its successful students at the South Kensington examinations. When Mrs. Besant, thinking the omission accidental, inquired about the error, she was told that members of the committee who were collecting money for a building fund feared that some of their contributors would withdraw if they realized she had been allowed to attend one of its classes. Stung by the unfairness and seizing the chance for reprisal, Mrs. Besant quickly printed and distributed a circular on the matter and found most of the press on her side.

Nevertheless, in spite of these hostilities, by December, 1881, the Education Department officially accepted both Bradlaugh girls as "authorised teachers, qualified to earn payments"—that is, state grants for the institution where they taught. All through 1882 the sniping continued, directed by Tyler. In March he again brought the case of the four Hall of Science teachers before the House. Mundella answered calmly that Aveling had now also been approved, but that Mrs. Besant's name had been withdrawn by her own board. Here he was in error, and thus in April he rose to defend the qualifications of all three women to teach, irrespective of their theological views. Early in May, Tyler warned that he was now ready to fix the date of his motion to have all four removed; and in "Daybreak," Mrs. Besant assailed this "champion of religion and director of companies (not always remarkable for their success so far as shareholders are concerned)" for having prevented her from earning the government grant she was entitled to. He had succeeded, she maintained, only because she had decided not to fight the point for fear of jeopardizing the status of the Bradlaugh girls. She was at the same time proud that her students had presented her with a "very beautiful illuminated address" in token of their support. During June and July, Mundella pointed out that the policy of grants to science teachers had been started by the previous administration and that, since he was simply carrying it out, he felt more than ever that Tyler had no case. Mrs. Besant entered the editorial fray by asking ironically why Tyler and his "Christian bloodhounds," such as the editors of the ultra-Christian *The Rock*, did not demand the removal of Huxley himself from the South Kensington staff and reported five more personal successes of hers at the most recent examinations.

By this time Tyler was making a bore and an ass of himself, even in the eyes of the Conservatives. He went so far as to obtain from the Lord Mayor a writ to examine the private business banking account of Bradlaugh and Mrs. Besant, but found so little that the Mansion House itself rebuked him. His desperate persistence culminated on August 10, when he finally brought forward an express motion in the House to the effect that the Hall of Science was not a proper place, nor the teachers there the proper persons, to teach science in connection with the Science and Art Department at South Kensington. When he adduced his old argument about the undermining of religion by science, Mundella pointed out that no fewer than thirty-five clergymen of all denominations were teaching science under the department (Stewart Headlam's bishop, however, was soon to deprive him of his curacy because of his support of the classes) and that even a religious visitor who made surprise visits had given highly satisfactory reports on the teaching at the Hall of Science. He therefore ended, as Labouchère had previously done, by censuring Tyler for his malice. Before the ignominious affair was over, all Tyler's own Tory benches had emptied themselves, leaving the Liberals to express their emphatic disappointment over the desertion, but to crow over the victory.

There were celebrations, of course, at the Hall of Science, though Tyler, as will soon be seen, had not yet surrendered. Few could excel him in obstinacy and ingenuity. At the fall prize-giving ceremonies, Mrs. Besant told the happy crowd that well-wishers had also donated some much-needed equipment: two pairs of steel bar magnets, an electromagnet capable of raising two hundred pounds, a small "dynamo machine (lent)," anatomical diagrams, a skeleton, and various plants and minerals. Her own pamphlet on vivisection was being used by a resident surgeon in a large hospital as the best thing yet written on the subject (she still had some reservations, however, on vaccination). In October, Aveling described a visit he had made to Darwin in 1881 in the company of the great Dr. Büchner. Science and Freethought were advancing hand in hand.

But the battle of the botanists was not yet really won. Mrs. Besant, it is true, belatedly applied for and received her grant. Tyler, a director of fifteen public companies, was investigated for "misconduct" in some of them, and under pressure resigned the chairmanship of the Anglo-American Electric Light Corporation. Under the new stimulus a higher proportion than ever of the students in the Hall of Science and Aveling's Practical Science Laboratory took and passed their examinations. On the other hand, Aveling, who had been persuaded by the Radicals to run for the London School Board and to their surprised delight had won the election, found that the controlling conservative membership of the Board was doing a fine job of freezing him out of any important committees. In March, 1883, when the Misses Bradlaugh summoned up courage to apply for membership in the Somerville Club for women, their application was denied on the ground that their name alone was enough objection. And early in May, when Mrs. Besant and Alice applied for admission into a practical botany class at University College, they were refused. The winner of the only honors award in botany in England was refused!

The pair had sent in a letter of application and had thereupon been asked to present themselves in person. Suspecting nothing, they did so and were then informed insultingly by the secretary and the "lady superintendent" that they could not be admitted because "There was some prejudice against them." Their hope that this was only an eccentric personal reaction was quelled when a few days later the Council itself indorsed the rejection, nullifying the very purpose for which the college had been founded: to dispense with religious qualifications. Now fighting mad, they circulated a petition, prepared by Aveling, asking the Council to summon an extraordinary meeting to reconsider its action, and got several important professors and doctors, including Huxley, to sign it; but other presumed liberals, like John Tyndall and Henry Morley, refused. Huxley remarked that Mrs. Besant had been "a very hard-working student" in his class and he would be "very glad to be of any use to her." In the meantime, the University College Senate took action in support of the position of the Council. Mrs. Besant wrote a long letter to the *Inquirer* on the matter, blaming Professor Morley particularly for his leadership against her.

When the extraordinary meeting of the Council was held late in July, however, it was Mr. Justice Denman, who had presided at many of her previous brushes with the law, who led the opposition. Again she faced a solemn and unfriendly male jury, which this time contained some of the greatest scientists and teachers in England, but which reminded the irreverent Aveling, as they sat there in a stiff semicircle, of "a pale edition of Christy's minstrels." Nevertheless, the Council listened attentively and politely to Mrs. Besant's resolution proving that their recent action was contradictory to the fundamental principles of the college. But the medical graduates, who made up a great percentage of the Council and were not interested in any silly radical ideas, had come out in large numbers; and they voted against her. In fact, only nine members voted for her. Her supposed friend and teacher Huxley, recently elected president of the Royal Society, was not one of these. Huxley abstained from voting at all.

In a footnote on the whole disillusioning affair, Mrs. Besant thanked Aveling for his unflinching aid and then commented ruefully: "They have probably made it impossible for me to take my degree this year, but they have not the power to shut me out altogether." She consoled herself by reflecting that she could still graduate from London University, a "more Liberal institution." Hypatia Bradlaugh, she reminded herself, had just concluded her special chemistry course for science teachers at South Kensington—the only lady to do so that year.

But it was chemistry that was to prove Mrs. Besant's own undoing, to prevent her from achieving the ambition that had activated her for the last four years to earn her B.Sc. degree. She passed her First B.Sc. and Preliminary Science Examinations at London University with no trouble. Then three times she came up for the examination in practical chemistry; and three times she failed. At first she could not understand this failure, since she had passed a much harder examination in the same subject at South Kensington. Then she recalled that there "was one examiner in the University who told her beforehand that however brilliantly she might do the papers which were set, he would not pass her, because he had a strong antipathy towards her atheism and to certain of her activities for the masses, which he considered immoral."[6] She never took her degree.

Rejected by the orthodox academic world, she would in the future have to make her own. Some day she would found her own college, where she could make her own rules, apply her own principles, and be granted an even higher degree. She could, and she would!

[6] Jinarajadasa, in *Annie Besant Centenary Book,* p. 4.

4

Blasphemy and Theosophy

The policy of the *National Reformer* was still, as it announced at its masthead, "Republican, Atheistic, and Malthusian." In addition, Bradlaugh had recently changed his own personal editorial slogan to "Thorough." The Malthusian objective, however, was not being strongly pushed at the moment, and the contributions of the editors were largely confined to such token support as Mrs. Besant's speaking at the annual meeting of the League in 1883 and a series of articles on the subject by Bradlaugh's favorite contributor, the mysterious "D." Bradlaugh was much more thorough in his steely determination to attain his Republican objectives. This was to be done, primarily, by forcing Parliament to recognize his right to his seat, regardless of his religious opinions, and, secondarily, by preaching his own Radical political philosophy on such matters as land reform, Irish home rule, and Egypt and the Suez, and by opposing the newfangled ideas of the young and militant Socialists, whose creed was fundamentally repugnant to his own deeply rooted individualism. In these aims he was of course firmly backed by Mrs. Besant, who frequently spoke at the hot-tempered Dialectical Society on such topics.

By September, 1881, the fiery young intellectual, Henry M. Hyndman (later the partial model for Shaw's John Tanner), with his pronouncedly Marxist new Democratic Federation, could no longer be ignored, though he could scarcely be accepted. In one of his "Rough Notes," Bradlaugh took a skeptical attitude toward its future, since it could offer no better-known names than those of such embryo Socialists as Herbert Burrows and Helen Taylor; but he tolerantly suggested that a public meeting should be held to discuss its program. Two weeks later he found he was able to say a kind word for Hyndman's new *Text Book of Democracy,* though in various problems such as agriculture he thought his own Land

Law Reform League was sounder. He was quite sure that Hyndman and his colleagues wanted the state to do too much. But when these new zealots refused to be dampened, and Burrows was invited to speak in the following June on such subjects as taxation before various branches of the N.S.S. itself, Bradlaugh decided to turn "D." loose against the new heresy in a series of articles on socialism. By February, 1883, when the argument was merrily under way in the columns of the *Reformer,* the Rev. J. L. Joynes, Jr., a clergyman and house master at Eton who had lost his job the year before because of his advanced views, was allowed to begin his rival series, "Socialism: A Reply," which enabled "D." to rejoin in "Mr. Joynes's War Dance." Bradlaugh was also broad-minded enough to welcome the new organ of the socially militant Anglicans, the *Christian Socialist,* which started off auspiciously with articles by Joynes, Canon H. C. Shuttleworth, and Headlam. (The latter two were to contribute notably to Shaw's conception of Candida Morell's Christian Socialist husband.)

Neither Bradlaugh nor Mrs. Besant was happy, however, when in October, 1883, the London School Board, which was still extremely cool toward its new member, Dr. Aveling, voted down the latter's proposal that compulsory elementary education be made free to all, as it was in America. Mrs. Besant's own rebellious impulses during this year were concentrated largely on the French Revolution. Her popular lectures on this subject, after being delivered orally and then serialized in the *Reformer,* were republished in her widely selling book, *A History of the Great French Revolution,* which she maintained was different from other treatments of the theme because it was written "from the standpoint of the people" and because part of its purpose was to present Robespierre as "one of the great pathetic figures in history, for he saw an ideal to accomplish, but had not the strength to do it."[1] Thus, as a martyr to a great cause, he had a powerful appeal to Annie Besant.

After his violent ejection from Parliament in 1881, Bradlaugh found himself entangled in a mesh of lawsuits—some brought by himself against his persecutors, some brought by his persecutors against him. At first beaten in the Court of Appeal in the Clarke case, but nevertheless complimented by the judges for his handling of his own argument, he was at the end of the year granted a new trial, all written up with verbatim transcripts and ironical or exultant comment by the persistent Aveling. The suit for assault which Bradlaugh started against little Captain Gosset and his deputy Erskine dragged along. At one time in 1883, he was involved in five lawsuits simultaneously, for any one of which he might expect to be summoned to court at any time. A favorable decision in the House of Lords in the Clarke case in April, 1883, however, saved him, as he put it, from bankruptcy and enabled him to go fishing again.

[1] Jinarajadasa, in *Annie Besant Centenary Book,* p. 10.

The most important of these suits had to do with his Parliamentary seat, which he both occupied and did not occupy.[2] Several times Mrs. Besant turned up in the gallery of the House to hear her friend argue his case before its Bar, always without success. To show his popular backing, he called for 100,000 signatures on petitions that were being circulated in his favor. In February, 1882, he presented 1,008 petitions with 241,970 signatures, but Commons was not impressed. It refused to declare his seat vacant, but also refused to allow him to fill it. Labouchère —as dapper, sophisticated, and skeptical as Bradlaugh, but temporarily controlled in his utterances—did all he could in Parliament and in his magazine, *Truth*, but was blocked. So, on February 21, Bradlaugh stunned everyone by carrying his own pocket Testament to the House, taking both an oral and a written oath on it, and then voting in a division. As Foote delightedly described the scene in his *Freethinker*, all the Conservative members "who were unprovided with cotton wool, thrust their thumbs into their ears 'lest they should hear the profanation. Newdegate, Sam Morley, 'Randy Pandy' [the as yet unreformed Lord Randolph Churchill], and Baron de Worms all rent their garments and howled blasphemy." Bradlaugh had already voted 91 times in 1880 and 129 times in 1881, in spite of the shrieks of unconstitutionality. Now he had renewed his crime. The Conservatives, therefore, insisting that such an action by an atheist was not only blasphemous but invalid, expelled him; even Gladstone, who was fair-minded enough to be generally sympathetic with this rebel's Parliamentary fight, this time refused to do anything about it. The *Reformer*, in an extra special number, accused the Prince of Wales himself of being present and using his influence against Bradlaugh.

Labouchère demanded a new election, which after a bitter campaign Bradlaugh won from his Tory opponent by a majority of 108—a slight increase over the previous count. But there was still a majority of 15 against him in the House when he tried again to take his seat, after receiving the congratulations of his friends and listening to the undisguised epithetical remarks of his enemies. Tyler, with the real view of prosecuting the junior member from Northampton and his coeditor, Mrs. Besant, threatened to refer a new series of articles by Aveling, sardonically entitled "The Christ of Dr. Aveling," to the Public Prosecutor. One Joseph Gurney, a Conservative voter from the Northampton constituency, and some of his friends started a new lawsuit to unseat Bradlaugh, arraigning the House of Commons itself and praying for judgment from the High Court of Justice. At the end of September, 1882, Bradlaugh addressed an announcement "To the Electors" stating that, having been charged with cowardice for not pressing his right to sit in the House and

[2] For this story, see *Autobiography*, pp. 365 ff., and *National Reformer*, 1882–83, *passim*.

vote during the current season, he now intended to assert that right anew and asked for their help. At first, when he fell back on his favorite technique of legalistic procedures and tried to present a petition to the House in accordance with his own interpretation of Sir Thomas Erskine May's *Parliamentary Practice,* he was refused by the Speaker. Then a public demonstration was "spontaneously" organized in Hyde Park. Mrs. Besant wrote that it attracted over 80,000 demonstrators; but the newspapers scoffed and estimated much less. Joseph Arch, whose National Agricultural Labourers' Union had been prospering, journeyed up to London to help plan this "indignation meeting" in the cause of his friend and supporter Bradlaugh, and it was in the room where the committee had gathered to make the necessary arrangements that he first met Mrs. Besant, who had so often spoken for his cause.[3]

All this time the Affirmation Bill, which had been proposed by Labouchère, with Gladstone's support, and which would have modernized and equalized the House with other English legal and political institutions, had been stormily debated. The liberals had high hopes for it, but in May, 1883, Bradlaugh sat in his old seat, after making a speech, and watched bitterly while the government's own bill went down to defeat by three votes on its second hearing. All the Tories crowed triumphantly that they had "beaten Bradlaugh," and one M.P. diagnosed the case as "The Irish have beaten Bradlaugh."

Stung by these defeats, Bradlaugh sent a warning to Gladstone in July that he intended to make another try for his seat "at an early date," whereupon the House ordered Sergeant at Arms Gosset to exclude him from the floor unless he "engages not further to disturb its . . . proceedings." A few days later Bradlaugh applied to the High Court of Justice for an injunction to prevent the sergeant at arms from keeping him out of the House. Tension in London again mounted. More mass meetings were held. In August four police were alerted when Bradlaugh scared the authorities by driving to the Palace Yard in a cab. But it was only a test. He was not yet ready to move to a new front of attack. Too many other webs entangled him. But he found time to travel with Mrs. Besant and other Freethinkers on special invitation to the International Freethought Conference in Amsterdam at the end of August. At this meeting Mrs. Besant was particularly honored by being the only woman to be given a seat on the lecturers' platform, and at the final banquet, after she had had a paper cheered, by being seated at President Roorda's right hand, with famous men like Büchner and Müller further down the table. Where Bradlaugh sat, she did not say in the story she sent to the *Reformer;* but just before Christmas he went alone to Paris, where he had dinner with some of the chief French political leaders. So resilient and optimistic was he about the future that just before the New Year in his "Jottings out of

[3] Joseph Arch, *The Story of His Life,* pp. 123–24.

Parliament" he exulted that all the twelve judgments against him during the year in the Divisional Courts and the Court of Appeal had been "swept away" and that all his law cases, at least, seemed to be moving in his favor. Neither he nor Mrs. Besant could have been displeased, either, with the news that Sir George Jessel had died.

But the *National Reformer* was not only Republican and Malthusian; it was also intended to be primarily—as many of Bradlaugh's followers continued to remind him—atheistic. It was their atheism that, in addition to its sidewise effect on their Republicanism, plunged A. B. and C. B. into still more trouble.

If there was one thing of which the Secularists were thoroughly convinced, it was the power of the press as a weapon, both propagandistic and personal. They seemed to feel that no one could really establish his claims to leadership unless he had his own journal, weekly or monthly, in which to offer his individual revelations and convictions. Bradlaugh and Mrs. Besant of course had the *National Reformer*, the oldest and solidest of all. Holyoake had had his *Secular Review;* the independent Mrs. Law had had her *Secular Chronicle*, later taken over by George Standring, a young, thin-faced, intellectual-looking member of the Executive Committee of the N.S.S.;[4] Foote had had his *Secularist;* he and Watts had had their amalgamated *Secular Review and Secularist.* Standring had also had his *Republican,* to supplement the political program of the *Reformer.* These and others like them had started off with high ambitions and confidence, had attained circulations of a few hundreds, or perhaps thousands, had struggled desperately, undergone transfusions of new editorial or managerial blood, languished, and in most cases ultimately died. Mrs. Besant was so bitten by the journalistic bug that in 1882 she decided to start her own monthly literary magazine, which was to contain departments that would appeal to every taste, age, and occupation. It was to be called *Our Corner,* and the *Reformer* pushed and advertised it for several months before its first number came out in January, 1883, only toward the end divulging the fact that Mrs. Besant was to be its editor.

This sixty-four-page magazine, published by the Freethought Publishing Company, had a corner to which everybody could retire comfortably. Besides its fiction, original and translated, serial novels or short stories (some by A. B. herself, in her best *Family Herald* style), its essays and travelogues, and its poetry, it had its "Political Corner," conducted by Bradlaugh; its "Science Corner," all about comets, eclipses, spectra, ultrared rays, falling dust, speaking dogs, diseases of beetroots and corn, and appointments to professorships at Oxford, conducted by A. B. herself; its "Art Corner" on drama, music, and painting, usually conducted by Aveling; its "Gardening Corner"; its "Inquisitorial Corner,"

[4] See photograph and biographical sketch in *Republican,* May, 1885.

containing answers to questions; its "Prize Puzzles" corner; its "Young Folks' Corner"; its "Publisher's Corner"; and even its "Chess Corner." This Annie-Wants-a-Corner magazine, all for sixpence, gave the restless and ambitious Mrs. Besant another outlet for her energies and during its six-year course was to play a significant role in her history.

But it was the free-swinging, mercurial Foote who pulled down the whole wasps' nest of the guardians of respectability around the ears of the godless. In 1882 Foote was a good-looking young widower of thirty-two—sporting a full, curly beard and mustache; hair parted in the middle and flowing back over his ears; broad coat lapels surmounted by a velvet collar; and a small black bow tie tucked under a pointed, white, stiff neckpiece.[5] A happy-go-lucky rebel, with respect for nobody's opinion but his own, Foote had been in and out of the B.S.U. and the N.S.S. (he was now in and soon to be one of its vice-presidents). Mrs. Besant, at once repelled and fascinated by him, had argued with him many times at the Dialectical Society. In May, 1881, he had embarked on a new journalistic venture, the *Freethinker,* a small, ribald weekly, featuring articles with titles like "Cracked for Christ," "The Bible and Bung," and "On the Advantages of Going to Hell." It was enlivened by a series of crudely drawn "Comic Bible Sketches," such as "Samson and the Foxes," depicting a repulsive Semite in striped bathing trunks, dipping the foxes' tails in a bucket labeled "Petroleum," setting the animals afire with a box of Bryant and May matches, and turning them loose in the Philistines' cornfield. It ran one series of yellow-tinged stories about the woman characters in the Bible from the Virgin to the Magdalene, implying a sisterly relationship between the two; and another series of burlesque "Biblical Romances," like "Righteous Lot & Co." It had departments labeled "Profane Jokes," "Acid Drops," and "Sugar Plums," under which confectionery terminology Foote dutifully recorded the effect his magazine was making on his enemies and his friends. As he put it in his "New Year's Address" in 1882, his very successful paper had only two kinds of ill-wishers, the Christians and the "mealy-mouthed Freethinkers," who objected to ridiculing people who say that twice two are five—this being a slanted reference to Holyoake and his middle-way followers. Among Foote's main contributors were *Reformer* stand-bys like Dr. Aveling and J. A. Symes, and he thanked the editors of that rival periodical for "their continued and unvaried generosity."

It was obvious that such a sheet could not long escape the angry attention of men like Tyler in Parliament. In February, 1882, he attacked it on the floor; by May the rumblings of charges of blasphemy to be brought against Foote were heard in the *Reformer;* and in July the hurricane broke. As Mrs. Besant recounted the story in "Daybreak," the situa-

---

[5] See *Republican,* April, 1883.

tion was much worse and more widespread than they had expected. Not only had the editor Foote, his publisher Ramsey, and the printer Whittle been summoned for blasphemy, but Tyler and his associates were attempting to include Bradlaugh and Mrs. Besant in the indictment because the *Freethinker* was published by Ramsey from 28 Stonecutter Street, the address of the Freethought Publishing Company. As Mrs. Besant pointed out indignantly, the *Freethinker*, like the *Malthusian*, was printed on Ramsey's presses, with the same type and general format as the *Reformer*, but it was a paper "over which we have no kind of authority, no sort of control, and which we never see until it is on sale." In fact, as she retold the story in her *Autobiography*, she and Bradlaugh had refused to have anything more to do with the *Freethinker* as early as November, 1881, because of its "comic Bible illustrations." For the information of the readers of the *Reformer*, the traditional verbatim transcriptions of the hearings began and were soon supplemented by the usual extra special numbers. Naturally, she and Bradlaugh intended to fight.

Bradlaugh's command of all the devices of the law again came to his rescue. Moreover, he skilfully handled these matters so that—for a time—Foote bore him no ill will. Watts's son, Charles, Jr., writing under the pseudonym of "Wasp," made some scurrilous attacks in the *Secular Review* on Foote, Whittle, and the defense; but Mrs. Besant, who had recently refused to accept its advertisements any longer because of its new editorial policy under Watts and its "prurient indecency," replied with her usual cleverness. First, the court freed Whittle because he was only a printer, and Mrs. Besant's name was also dropped, leaving Foote, Ramsey, and Bradlaugh to face the charges. To make sure that their publishing business would no longer be thought to be associated with the *Freethinker* crowd, Mrs. Besant with her usual optimism persuaded Bradlaugh to take a bold step, which later proved to be a stumble. Always a believer in aggression, she determined to expand the business and move into larger quarters. Consequently, a shop at the corner of Fleet and Bouverie Streets—just across from 62 Fleet Street, where Richard Carlile had once conducted his fight for Freethought—was leased at a much higher rent, leaving the other premises entirely to Ramsey and his printery. Annie and the elder Bradlaugh girl, Alice, undertook the responsibility of the publishing side of the business, but, being inexperienced, had to burden Bradlaugh further as referee for all their problems. The situation was not improved when, two years later, because of the financial difficulties of his landlord, Bradlaugh was compelled to take up the lease for the entire building, and he and Mrs. Besant, as partners, soon had to issue several thousand pounds' worth of debenture stocks to keep afloat. It was here at 63 Fleet Street, however, that Annie Besant spent most of her working hours in London until her partner's death.[6]

The case of the Queen *vs.* Foote, Ramsey, "and others" (which chiefly meant Charles Bradlaugh) dragged through the courts. At the earliest signs of trouble, Mrs. Besant was the first to write Foote what he described in his paper as "a plucky little note," quite characteristic of her fighting spirit, offering to do everything she could for the *Freethinker* if its editor should be gagged. Aveling did the same, and Bradlaugh of course gave his legal advice. The paper came out with a big new black scarehead on the front page, "PROSECUTED FOR BLASPHEMY."

Foote's ebullience was not to be dampened easily. In fact, in January, 1883, he offered London a new general monthly magazine, *Progress,* edited by himself, contributed to by the usual inner circle, and featuring Dr. Aveling. Shortly afterward, Mr. Justice North, "a bigot of the sternest type," as A. B. described him, rendered his "harsh" decision; and Foote, Ramsey, and H. A. Kemp, a subordinate and printer, found themselves in Newgate jail, Bradlaugh having luckily been able to get his case tried separately. He and Mrs. Besant promptly called on the prisoners, had trouble shaking hands with them through the bars, and promised their undying support. Annie immediately started a Prisoners' Aid Fund in the *Reformer* and began a series of articles, "The Christian Creed; or, What It Is Blasphemy To Deny," pointing out the absurdities of belief which the complete Christian had to swallow. This series, she asserted, helped to awaken the public to the realization that the blasphemy laws were not mere dead letters on the books, as the reactionaries tried to maintain.

Aveling, who had found a kindred spirit in Foote, enthusiastically volunteered to help edit both the *Freethinker* and *Progress* during the incarceration and was as enthusiastically accepted. He soon took over the entire responsibility, for Joseph Mazzini Wheeler, Foote's subeditor, collapsed mentally under the strain and the notoriety. For several months the Freethought magazines carried sympathetic but horrified bulletins of his alternating recoveries and relapses, but finally his case was deemed hopeless and he was committed to an asylum. Aveling was also ready to become a martyr to the cause, but he did temper the policy of the *Freethinker* slightly, especially in the matter of the comic Bible illustrations. A managing committee was chosen to keep Ramsey's business going, and aid to the wives of the prisoners was voted by the executive of the N.S.S., which also issued a cautious warning to its branches not to circulate or sell any literature such as the *Freethinker* unless they were prepared to go to jail for their temerity.

Only in the middle of April, however, was Bradlaugh freed from the

---

[6] *Autobiography,* pp. 383–84; Bonner, *Bradlaugh,* II, 100; *National Reformer,* September 17, October 1, 1882.

fear of joining his friends in prison. "The verdict of the jury," he wrote gratefully, "saves me from the bitterness of gaol and convict dress." Most of the London papers had been on his side all along. Annie, present in court when Lord Chief Justice Coleridge himself read the findings and verdict, wrote exultantly of the victory in "How They Tried Charles Bradlaugh for Blasphemy." She had sat between Bradlaugh and Foote during the trial, charged with having all Bradlaugh's references ready for his use and marking off each point on a duplicate brief as he made it. On occasion she was also called as a witness in the case, and, in spite of her personal involvement, delivered her testimony in her usual convincing style. Coleridge, she decided, was another of the few judicial officers she could admire—a truly Christian judge. Tyler and his crowd were again defeated.

Foote and Ramsey, however, were transferred to Holloway jail, where their friends were allowed to visit them at times. Annie came frequently, especially after the prison chaplain had stopped, having abandoned hope of saving the souls of the prisoners. The experience was harder on the stern-faced Ramsey than on the younger Foote. Ultimately, after what Mrs. Besant in her *Autobiography* remembered as "a noble charge to the jury" by Coleridge, the jury disagreed in their case, a nolle prosequi was entered, and they were freed.

They were triumphantly met as they left the prison on February 24, 1884. A composite description of the scene by the *Reformer*, the *Freethinker*, and the *Echo* (a reactionary paper which claimed a circulation of 15,000 more than all the other London evening papers combined) told how at eight in the morning Mr. Bradlaugh, Mrs. Besant, and the new Mrs. Foote were admitted on foot within the prison gates, while twenty-five or thirty "brakes" or carriages drew up outside, filled with an unusually large number of highly enthusiastic ladies, several of them waving flags. Later, two carriages were allowed inside, the first carrying Foote and his wife, Bradlaugh, and Mrs. Besant, with Aveling sitting proudly "on the box." A large procession, including a new clerical recruit, the Rev. Mr. Sharman, escorted them back to the Hall of Science for breakfast, at which Annie was paired off with Foote, Bradlaugh with Mrs. Foote, and Aveling with Miss Bradlaugh. Speeches were made, and Annie announced that she had over £332 in her testimonial fund. She had wanted to hire a brass band, but Foote had vetoed this idea as a little too ostentatious and refused to leave the prison if "any such folly was perpetrated." He did, however, thank her in his paper for showing all the way through "the finest womanly tact and sensibility with the temper of a hero." He also thanked Bradlaugh for his legal aid. A month later, the breakfast having been adjudged slightly inadequate for the magnitude of the occasion, a more formal banquet was laid at the Hall of Science. Annie and Aveling were as prominent here as Foote, who by

191

now had taken back the editorship of his paper, with profuse thanks to Aveling for his magnificent substitution.

The two trials, as Annie summed them up, had exactly the opposite result from that which their backers had intended: they brought many new members into the N.S.S., they increased the circulation of the *Reformer* and other Freethought literature, and they raised Foote "for a time to a position of great influence and popularity" and placed "his name in history as a brave martyr for liberty of speech." Mrs. Besant admired martyrs; but she was not long to continue to admire Foote's particular methods of martyrdom.

But not even Annie could enjoy martyrdom when it was forced on her thirteen-year-old daughter Mabel, still in Miss Adams' school in Boston. In May, 1883, according to custom, Miss Adams took Mabel to church. The preacher, the Rev. W. Mitchinson, a visitor from London, wishing to spice his sermon for the provinces by working in the latest sensation from the capital, launched into an angry attack on "vile trash" like Mrs. Besant and her friend Bradlaugh. When the girl heard her mother referred to by name as one who was living "without hope of heaven or fear of hell," she was "so much affected" that Miss Adams had to remove her from the church in the full gaze of the congregation. Whether correctly or not, Mrs. Besant was convinced that this example of "Christian Humanity" was planned and premeditated. In fact, the Boston *Guardian* wrote up the incident as one of "an exceedingly painful nature" and printed her letter of protest, in which she informed Mitchinson of the purity, respectability, and industry of her life and reminded him that if it had been otherwise, her husband would have been able to get the divorce which he now craved. For even though her house had been watched, private detectives had followed her to hotels, and landlords had been questioned, no evidence of ill conduct had ever been turned up against her. She sarcastically suggested, however, that Mitchinson's technique of cruelty would probably rouse great envy in the breasts of relatively clumsy practitioners like Sir Henry Tyler. All this could have afforded little consolation to the sensitive Mabel, especially when the Boston *Herald* supported the sermon. Nevertheless, as Mrs. Besant admitted in the *Reformer*, other papers and individuals joined in the condemnation of Mitchinson's callousness and discourtesy, even though they were far from approving of Mrs. Besant herself.

A good professional irreligionist must know a great deal about religion and religions and often knows more about these subjects than a good religionist does. One of the responsibilities of the Freethought leaders, as conceived by Bradlaugh, Besant, Aveling, and company, was to keep their constituency acquainted with the new as well as the old in religious or mystical thought; to examine, analyze, and evaluate; and finally, to accept or reject. Normally, of course, the process ended in rejection—

sometimes after serious and dignified reflection, more often after comic or sardonic mockery.

For a long time the staff of the *Reformer* had shown an immense interest in the East, particularly in India—not only in its politics and economics, but in its religious and other sacred books, which on the whole they treated much more respectfully than they did Christianity. As early as August, 1879, Edwin Arnold's popular and poetical treatment of the life and philosophy of the Buddha in *The Light of Asia* had come to Mrs. Besant for review, and she had nodded at it as "a pleasant book of verse," not a poem; still, she found its contents useful. The *Reformer* was becoming especially interested in Buddhism, which one contributor approached in an article on "The Indebtedness of Popular Christianity to Buddhism," but which Aveling in his long review of Mallock's *Is Life Worth Living?* preferred to examine as a form of Positivism. By the end of 1882, the interest had extended to a series of unsigned reviews of works on the Upanishads, the Vedantas, etc.

By the time Mrs. Besant began *Our Corner* in 1883, her concern with the Orient had definitely crystallized. In the first number—along with a minor contributor's travel sketch of Egypt and one Chunder Labul's "A Hindu Poet to Alfred Tennyson," attacking "In Memoriam" in rhyme, one quatrain of which was devoted to the "miracles" of modern "spiritists" and mediums—Mrs. Besant started off her "Young Folks" corner with her own story, "A Hindu Legend." This began, significantly enough: "Far away, in the vast range of mountains that close Hindustan against the barbarians of Thibet, the great God Siva lay asleep." Then followed Annie's very un-Secularist version of the tale of Ganga, the daughter of King Himavat and "his fair wife, Menaka, a nymph of the air," and of how Ganga finally turned into a great river, bringing fertility to the starving land. The danger of such a myth to youthful minds was immediately balanced by a biographical sketch of Tom Paine. But the next issue started a story, "The Three Caskets," by Mrs. Besant's old friend, Moncure Conway, in which he had much to say about the influence of Buddha on modern Christendom. In the following months came other children's stories in which Mrs. Besant mixed another "Hindu Legend" ("after Sir William Jones," the great Orientalist) with "A Christian Legend," "A Jewish Legend," and "A Greek Legend." This impartial approach to mythology was extended to more historical tales of religious martyrs like Hypatia and Giordano Bruno, not to mention an essay on the mythological history of the legend of "The Christ-Child."

In the latter half of the nineteenth century, the Spiritualists were very active and were arousing world-wide curiosity with their "phenomena" of seances, clairvoyance, telepathy, table-rapping, levitation, manifestations of material objects, and all the rest. Societies, nicely balanced between scientific skepticism and an only half-repressed will to believe, were organized to scrutinize and evaluate the claims of the various mediums, seers, and other practitioners of the art. Back in 1869, following up an interest that had begun twenty years earlier, Bradlaugh had taken part in such an examination into alleged Spiritualist phenomena conducted by the Dialectical Society, but the results had been unsatisfactory.[7] His interest, however, had not abated, especially when the Society for Psychical Research, graced with many noted names such as those of Professor F. W. H. Meyers, Gladstone, Ruskin, Tennyson, Arthur Balfour, Crookes, Lodge, Wallace, and William James, was founded in London in 1882. Mrs. Besant had published a contributor's article on "Clairvoyance" in an early issue of *Our Corner*, showing the fakery of many mediums, mesmerists, etc. But only a few months later she herself had vouched for the authenticity of "A Curious Ghost Story," according to which a prisoner, as a result of solitude and fasting, had a series of "mental hallucinations" in which he became aware of someone walking around his cell and passing his hand over the prisoner's arms or face. Sometimes the visitor's own face, pleasant and smiling, would appear, late at night or after daybreak. Of course, when the prisoner attempted to grasp the figure, it melted away, and when his mind was relieved and his strength returned, the phenomena all vanished. But after this experience he—and by implication Mrs. Besant—could understand why many people believe in the "divine manifestations" they have received.

Strangely enough, Spiritualism and other forms of occultism had a strong attraction for a certain type of Freethinker. In March, 1881, when John Holmes, a well-known member of the N.S.S. branch at Leicester, turned Spiritualist lecturer, he was expelled by the Executive Committee for "disgraceful conduct." The same thing had happened some years before to another Secularist, George Sexton. C. B. and A. B., however, did not worry till reports began to arrive from India telling how many members of the N.S.S. branches there, particularly in Bombay and Madras, were also joining a mysterious new occultist group calling itself the Theosophical Society. When one of their own vice-presidents, P. Murugesa Mudaliar, editor of the *Philosophical Inquirer and Freethought Journal* of Madras, announced publicly that he had become a Theosophist as well as a Freethinker and suggested that they do the same, they realized they must look fully into the matter.

The two leaders of this new mystical movement, which had started in New York in 1875, were the enigmatic Russian émigrée, naturalized American, and former Spiritualist with the overpowering hypnotic eyes, Mme. Helena Petrovna Blavatsky,[8] and Bradlaugh's old American acquaintance, Colonel Henry Steele Olcott, former lawyer, Civil War in-

[7] Bonner, *Bradlaugh*, II, 248; *National Reformer*, December 7, 1884.

[8] The two main books on Madame Blavatsky are the popular, journalistic, and somewhat sensationalized biographies, *The Mysterious Madame: Helena Petrovna Blavatsky: The Life and Work of the Founder of the Theosophical Society, with a Note on Her*

vestigator of funds for the army and navy, and "President-Founder" of the T.S., as its members liked to call the Theosophical Society. After four years of trying to establish their Society in New York and London, unsuccessful in spite of the publication of H.P.B.'s first book, *Isis Unveiled*, they had gone to Bombay in 1879. There they made an affiliation with the society for religious reform, the Arya Samaj, leaving the other member of the original triumvirate, William Quan Judge, a clerk in Olcott's office, to carry on the propaganda in the United States. After a few months in India, the pair met and soon made converts of two very important leaders of Anglo-Indian society, A. P. Sinnett, editor of the Allahabad *Pioneer* and already a Spiritualist, and A. O. Hume, who was to become the inspirer and first chairman of the Indian National Congress.

With the Theosophical movement thus under way on the mainland, the two founders moved down to Ceylon in 1880, where they both "took pansil" in a temple at Galle and became Buddhists, though for a time after his arrival in Bombay, Olcott had assumed certain Hindu manners of dress and thought. The Arya Samaj soon thereafter dissolved the connection. Both Buddhists and Hindus, however, as well as some Europeans, began to join the Theosophical Society in fair numbers, and Olcott and Mme. Blavatsky returned to India well satisfied with their work. Through the help of a wealthy and fanatical new young Indian disciple, Damodar K. Mavalankar, they were able to buy at a bargain a beautiful property on the Adyar River, Madras, where they settled down to consolidate their cult. Hume, it is true, had by this time become disillusioned and had cut loose completely. Sinnett, on the other hand, had had his faith in occultism and Theosophy so strengthened and had pushed these beliefs so strenuously in his paper that he had been relieved of his job by its skeptical owners; he had then gone back to London to write about his communications with the Mahatmas or Masters, in *The Occult World* and *Esoteric Buddhism*. But the loss of Hume and Sinnett was made up for by the accession of new recruits such as the brilliant young Brahmin lawyer and Sanskrit scholar, T. Subba Rao, who was to become the leading Theosophical writer and mystic until he, too, broke away. It was here at Adyar that Moncure Conway, on his trip around the world, renewed the acquaintance he had first made with Mme. Blavatsky in London through a member of his Unitarian congregation. He found her amusing, pungent, vulgar, apparently sincere, and quite frank—when she was alone with him and there were no witnesses to her confessions of how she cast a "glamour" over her followers.[9]

Bradlaugh was quite unaware of the inner history of this remarkable

Successor Annie Besant (New York, 1931), dedicated to H. L. Mencken and written by the English and Indian journalist, C. E. Bechhofer-Roberts ("Ephesian"); and Gertrude Marvin Williams, *Priestess of the Occult: Madame Blavatsky* (New York, 1946).

[9] Conway, *My Pilgrimage to the Wise Men of the East* (New York, 1906), p. 194.

group when his eye was caught by the name of his American friend Olcott. Mrs. Besant knew even less, but she was the first to express fear of its influence. On June 18, 1882, she devoted a considerable portion of her "Daybreak" column to the attention the Theosophical Society was attracting in India and mentioned Olcott by name. Her knowledge of the subject being slight, she contented herself with criticizing its "vagueness" of doctrine, its belief—as she thought—in "apparitions" of the dead, and its general "other-world-ism." She trusted that the Hindu Freethinkers would not be led astray, though she granted that, in spite of the contradiction of their beliefs, Theosophists might become Secularists if they wished. Mme. Blavatsky, who knew how to handle people and had had her eye on this conspicuous feminist for some time, replied gently and forgivingly in the *Theosophist* for August, suggesting that her opponent was laboring under a complete misconception of the true nature and objects of the Society. "For one so highly intellectual and keen as that renowned writer," she flattered, "to dogmatise and utter autocratic ukases, after she has herself suffered so cruelly and undeservedly at the hands of blind bigotry and social prejudice in her lifelong struggle for freedom of thought seems, to say the least, absurdly inconsistent." Though H.P.B. added some other kind remarks about Mrs. Besant's superiority of speaking powers over those of some "modern trance-speakers," Annie speculated later about what would have happened if she had met the other woman at this juncture, but concluded that she was still too much dazzled by the triumphs of Western science to have been moved.[10]

Bradlaugh too was at first rather complacent. In April he had noted a lecture Olcott had delivered on the spirit of Zoroastrianism, which had caused a sensation there. He had gone on to point out that Olcott and the Theosophical Society had been "publicly assailed" in India by Joseph Cook, an American Christian evangelist—whom Bradlaugh himself had often vainly challenged to debate, and whom he expected to back down similarly before Olcott—who "is not a man easily silenced and publishes the whole truth about 'The Theosophical Society' and its founders" in a new pamphlet by the Industrial Press, Bombay. On July 2 Bradlaugh announced the receipt of the current issue of the *Theosophist*, a new monthly journal conducted by H. P. Blavatsky from Bombay (soon to be moved to Adyar) and devoted to "oriental philosophy, art, literature and occultism, embracing mesmerism, spiritualism and other secret sciences." Being much easier on Olcott than he had been on other occultists, he found this number especially interesting because of its exposure of Cook. Their common antipathy to Christianity was one of the chief early bonds between Theosophy and Freethought. In fact, as Foote's *Freethinker* pointed out, the Hindus who had left Hinduism

[10] *Autobiography,* p. 380.

seemed "far more ready to accept the Buddhist Theosophy of Colonel Olcott and Madame Blavatsky than the Christianity of the missionaries or Joseph Cook." By August 20 Henry J. Atkinson, who had for some time been the *Reformer's* chief crusader against ghost stories, Spiritualism, and the occult, threw himself into the controversy. But Bradlaugh was satisfied in his "Crowded Table" to acknowledge the receipt of three more issues of the *Theosophist* and to remark that "Those who desire to learn something of the curious mysticism now being pressed in India by the energy of Colonel Olcott, formerly of New York City, and now President of the Theosophical Society, will find in the *Theosophist* a record of this semi-spiritualistic movement." After all, every other week he was accepting advertisements of the *Theosophist* for the *National Reformer* and exchanging N.S.S. literature with it.

Within the next two weeks, however, Bradlaugh had received so many letters from Madras and Bombay concerning converts to Theosophy that he reluctantly issued a statement. Having heard from so many Indians that Theosophy was organized partly to counteract the drift of society toward materialism, atheism, and science, he felt he must take the stand that "Theistic opponents of Scientific Materialism" ought not to belong to the N.S.S.:

Theosophists possibly understand their own meaning, but it is not quite clear to us how they can at the same time reasonably profess friendship to, and desire alliance with, us as a Freethought society, and yet declare their efforts to be in the direction of neutralizing and contradicting our work. We believe Colonel Olcott and Madame Blavatsky to be both very earnest and sincere. Our disagreement with their theologic teaching is not intended to imply personal hostility or antagonism to their independent work.

The Theosophists themselves then joined the debate—trying to explain the aims and objectives of the Society; quoting its rules; pointing out that according to the standard Theosophical principle, the ideas of even such leaders as Olcott and H.P.B. were merely their own and not necessarily those of the T.S.; and ending with the assertion that Theosophists are not really opposed to true science, but only to its modern dogmatism. Olcott wrote from Bombay to compliment Mrs. Besant on the influence of her *Free-Thinker's Text-Book* in Ceylon. Bradlaugh was being forced into a corner. By the end of the year he was declaring to his correspondents that their letters had not changed his opinion, correcting Olcott on the question of belonging to both groups, commenting on the "curious movement" to promote Buddhism which the Colonel was then conducting in Ceylon, and trying to understand the motto of the Society and its magazine: "There Is No Religion Higher than Truth." To him Theosophy had become only a "strangely mingled" movement of skepticism, mysticism, and Hinduism.

The case of a South Indian named Rangapalli Jagannathiah was a typical one. Having come into contact with the followers of materialism in 1875, being dissatisfied with his own Hinduism, and being also impressed by the writings of Bradlaugh and Mrs. Besant, he joined, first, the English N.S.S. and then the Freethought Union of Madras. But when, in 1882, he heard of Theosophy through Damodar and H.P.B., he accepted it and raised the question "Can a Secularist Be a Theosophist?" in the *Reformer*. Besides her public reply in June, Mrs. Besant also wrote him a strong personal letter against joining the Theosophical Society. He replied to Bradlaugh, asking whether Freethinkers were bound by the dictates of Mrs. Besant. Bradlaugh answered no, and Jagannathiah retired from the Freethought Union and thereafter devoted all his spare time to Theosophy.[11]

By November, 1883, relations between the two groups had become so strained that, when Atkinson sent a brief letter to the *Theosophist* expressing his position, it was printed with an editorial note, running: "Our respected correspondent is a Materialist and a Freethinker, while we are Occultists and Metaphysicians. We can hardly understand each other." Bradlaugh, recalling certain scandalous revelations of occult trickery that had recently emanated from Simla and Adyar, added sourly: "We hardly wonder at this note, for we see that Theosophy includes miracle working, even to the extent of restoring a broken china plate to its perfect state without cement or patching. A Theosophical housemaid ought to be a desideratum in a household where there are so many breakages." By this time the Society for Psychical Research had issued its call for ghosts that deserved special study and had held its investigation of the celebrated medium Daniel Dunglas Home, whom Browning had unflatteringly immortalized as the remarkable Mr. Sludge.

Under this publicly conducted surface-fishing in one another's ponds, hidden lures and baits had also been dangled—at least in Mrs. Besant's case—deeper down. For all her apparent hardness and cocksureness in her skepticism, the beauties of the old faiths and rituals and the yearning for the power to believe in a spiritual, non-material world still exerted a secret pull. One winter evening in the late seventies, as she related in "Daybreak" after a lecture to a group of freethinking laborers at Barrow-in-Furness, where there was as yet no regular N.S.S. branch, she had felt so lonely and distraught that she had struck out alone across the moonlit snow to walk to the ruins of the famous Cistercian Furness Abbey two miles away. As she stood silently among the broken walls, her imagination conjured up a vivid picture of the past—of phantom processionals winding through the ancient transepts, of white-robed choristers and scarlet-cassocked acolytes, of priests in cloth-of-gold chasubles, of incense and candles, of the peasants bowing before the host, and of the rich benediction which finally floated out over the kneeling worshipers.

11 *The Path*, December, 1894. See also *Autobiography*, pp. 378–79.

Standing in the crisp snow, she fell into a sympathetic reverie. Forgetting her heartache and loneliness, she returned for a few moments to the beautiful spiritual certainties of her girlhood. As she ultimately confessed to Bradlaugh over a decade later, she had for many years been secretly dissatisfied with their materialistic teaching, even while she stood haranguing on the platform beside him.[12]

Mme. Blavatsky, a skilled amateur psychologist, must have guessed that something of this nostalgia for a belief in the other world still hovered in Mrs. Besant's soul. Or, if H.P.B. did not guess it herself, her Mahatmas did. By this time she had two of these beings from Tibet—men who had evolved onto a superhuman level—in direct communication with her, speaking their messages and directions or writing them down on exotic rice paper in colored inks or crayons and "precipitating" them to her and her specially honored associates in all sorts of unexpected places. These two Masters, who had undertaken to be the particular guardians of the Theosophical Society, were Master Koot Hoomi and Master Morya—abbreviated to Master K.H. and Master M. by their intimates. A. P. Sinnett was another lucky recipient of these missives (which some rude disbelievers thought were written by H.P.B. herself), and when the controversial *Mahatma Letters to A. P. Sinnett from the Mahatmas M. and K.H.* were published in 1923,[13] it was discovered that Annie Besant had figured prominently in two of them and Charles Bradlaugh in one.

The first of these, No. XXXIII, undated and unlocated, but probably received by Sinnett in London in the summer of 1883 after he had been dismissed from his job with the *Pioneer,* is labeled "K.H. Letter received through M. shown to A.B." In it K.H. first tried to smooth out a few apparent discrepancies between some notes received by Sinnett from "my brother M.—and myself." Moving next to Sinnett's "dream of establishing a nucleus of honest scientific enquirers of good repute, who would give weight to the T.S. organisation in the eyes of the multitude," the Master pointed out that even among English men of science there were some who "are already prepared to find our teachings in harmony with the results and progress of their own researches." Hinting mysteriously that "the situation shall be more fully explained to you by and by," he concluded significantly:

Meanwhile use every effort to develop such relations with A. Besant that your work may run on parallel lines and in full sympathy; an easier request than some of mine with which you have ever loyally complied. You may, if you see fit—show this note to her *only.*

Sinnett's inscription on the letter indicates that he did show it to Mrs. Besant—with unrecorded but imaginable results.

[12] Bonner, *Bradlaugh,* II, 14.

[13] "Transcribed, Compiled, and with an Introduction by A. T. Barker."

The second letter, No. LXXXVI, is more specific, since Sinnett marked it "Received Jan. 1884."—just about the time Mme. Blavatsky and Colonel Olcott had reached England. As usual, Master K.H. ran H.P.B. down as an imperfect medium for conveying his ideas, but, again as usual, their ideas showed a surprising similarity. The letter began:

I am sorry you took the trouble of posting me about Bradlaugh. I know him and his partner well. There is more than one trait in his character I esteem and respect. He is not immoral; nor could anything that might be said against or for him by Mrs. K[ingsford, the vegetarian-Spiritualist-doctor who had now become president of the London Lodge of the T.S.] or even yourself, change or even influence my opinion of both him and Mrs. Besant.

On one matter, however, Master K.H. was firm. Like H.P.B., he regarded *The Fruits of Philosophy* as "infamous and highly pernicious." He disclaimed ever having read the book, or ever intending to, but "its unclean spirit, its brutal aura" were before him; and in his sight "the advices offered in the work are abominable. . . . The sooner we leave the subject—the better."

Perhaps to help herself withstand these temptations and to reassert her firm faith in doubt, during the middle eighties Mrs. Besant made a new onslaught on religion, and especially on Christianity. But whereas there had previously been some constructiveness in her approach, she now turned bitterly destructive. A few titles in the ceaseless torrent of pamphlets that poured from her untiring pen between 1884 and 1887 seem to indicate a special animus on her part: *Is Christianity a Success?; The Natural History of the Christian Devil; Woman's Position According to the Bible; A World without God; The Sins of the Church; Life, Death, and Immortality; The Myth of the Resurrection;* and *The World and Its Gods.* To prepare for the last-named work she collected a special exhibit of specimens, which she put on display in the Hall of Science. Culminating all, in 1887 she summed up the reasons for her un-creed in *Why I Do Not Believe in God.*

Only in 1888 did she fall into a portentous silence.[14]

[14] Cf. Theodore Besterman, *Mrs. Annie Besant,* pp. 131–33.

5

The Triumph
of Eleanor Marx

During the hectic blasphemy trials, the strange trinity of Annie Besant, Charles Bradlaugh, and Edward Aveling had offered a strong and united front to the world. There were intimate little domestic scenes involving all three, such as when, early in 1881, she had lectured at the Hall of Science on "The Physiology of the Home," Bradlaugh had presided, and Aveling had operated the magic lantern. In the New Year's issue of the *Reformer* for 1882, Aveling began a series, written in his old ecstatic style, to prove "A Godless Life the Happiest and Most Useful." One of the chief reasons, he found, was that such a life makes for a greater and purer love between man and woman. Religionists, he pointed out, should not want to know that God sees all their secret doings and knows all their most private thoughts. "But the lovers who are godless have a holy of holies into which they alone quite withdraw." In such a relationship, too, there can be no division between sacred and profane love. His readers must have lifted their eyebrows knowingly.

As usual, Aveling was in need of money. He therefore announced the expansion of the Hall of Science classes to include, at an exceedingly low charge, a weekly class for preparing students for the Matriculation Examination at London University. He was to be helped by Hypatia Bradlaugh, even though she did not pass her own examination till the following year. But within six weeks a special bulletin appeared in the *Reformer* to announce the serious illness of Dr. Aveling, who had finally broken down under the strain of overwork and—probably—overplay. The Secularists' favorite physician, Dr. Ramskill, found it desirable to issue a special certificate on the breakdown and to recommend a ten-day holiday at the seaside after recovery from the illness, which proved to be typhoid. So, Hypatia carried on the classes alone, and a series of lectures on "Electricity" by Mrs. Besant was substituted for the one the sick man was to have given on *Macbeth.* A month later, still weak, he returned from Bournemouth, where he had stayed with a Freethinker whom he had never known before. While there, he informed his readers, he had also had an inflammation of the membrane of his shinbone because he had ridden a tricycle sixteen miles. He thanked his two daughters and Mrs. Besant for their help and sympathy, but he was still unable to return to work immediately. Annie, coincidentally, had had to cancel some of her own lectures because of a bad cold. By fall, however, they were both completely recovered. Aveling was able to announce the new schedule of science classes for the coming year, and in October he was again writing his "At Work" column in his old, long-absent lyrical style.

He was so fully occupied with his work on the *Freethinker* and *Progress* that for several weeks at the beginning of 1883 he gave up his lectures entirely. When they were resumed, their announcement was relegated to the small type at the end of the *Reformer* along with similar notices of the secondary lecturers; Mrs. Besant's, however, stood boldly alone in their old place. He was able to contribute a series of articles on "Ernst Haeckel, the German Darwin" to the *Reformer,* to keep his "Art Corner" going in *Our Corner,* to do a series on "Shakspere the Dramatist," and to work up some odds and ends on scientific subjects. On *Progress,* however, he lavished all his incredible versatility and industry. He wrote on the advances of science, and especially on his favorite, Darwin; he wrote on the blasphemy prosecution; he reviewed Henry Arthur Jones's sensational new melodrama, *The Silver King;* he wrote light, humorous little familiar essays; and he wrote poetry by the ream. It was in his poetry that he really expressed his soul. The subject was invariably the same: thwarted and unhappy love, treated lyrically and usually tragically, though without despair.

In the meantime, a new name had begun to appear with considerable frequency in the pages of *Progress* and in some other advanced magazines of the day. It was that of Eleanor Marx, youngest daughter of the recently deceased author of *Das Kapital* and other Communist works, Karl Marx. Aveling seemed to be much impressed by the abilities of his new find and let her write for him about her father, about Russian Nihilism and the Underground, about "The Irish Dynamiters," and about philosophy and religion. Bradlaugh even thought her article about "Underground Russia" worth mentioning in the *Reformer.* She had long been well known, of course, in Socialist circles, but only as an interesting child; now she was an interesting and intellectual young woman.

Suddenly, on December 23, 1883—possibly angered by an article in which Miss Marx twitted the Secularists with the decline of their party from upper-class intellectualism to its present status as a refuge for mal-content workers—Mrs. Besant, in her newly revived "Daybreak" section, inserted the following acrimonious notice:

My name is being used by a Miss Eleanor Marx, daughter of the late Karl Marx, to give authority to a gross and scandalous libel on Dr. Edward Aveling. She invented the libel, and then promulgated it, giving me as the author of the statement, hoping thereby to create a breach, and to hinder and impede the Free-thought cause by introducing discord and quarrel among co-workers in the ranks. So far, fortunately, the attempt has failed, for Dr. Aveling brought the statement to me when it reached his ears. As, however, it may reach many privately who will not have heard of the private exposure of the lie, I warn all London Free-thinkers, and especially those of the North West London branch, against accepting any statement made in my name by Miss Eleanor Marx, or by any of her friends. We have enough open enemies around us; warning should be given of strangers who try to creep into our movement with the object of treacherously sowing discord therein. Irremediable mischief may be caused by such persons, and they are the most useful tools employed by the Christian foe.

These somewhat reckless imputations of far-reaching motives to her enemies were always characteristic of Mrs. Besant when personally aroused. This time, at all costs, she intended to protect against depredation her favorite protégé, Dr. Aveling, president of the North West London branch of the N.S.S., now in danger of being weaned away both from his personal devotion to her and from his Secularism by the new Socialist menace.

The exact nature of this "gross and scandalous libel" against Aveling remains obscure. There were so many charges that might have been brought against the sinister, fascinating scapegrace. His classes afforded him plenty of opportunity for extracurricular flirtation, innocent or otherwise. His unreliability in money affairs was by now notorious. More lurid rumors about his personal habits and conduct were circulated later. Probably, however, Eleanor Marx's rumor had something to do with a letter from Aveling inserted in the ultra-advanced Socialist weekly, *Justice*, on September 27, 1884:

I shall be glad if I may use your columns for a brief personal explanation, rendered necessary by statements and rumors, more or less vague, that are being made about myself. I am at the present time indebted in many sums to many persons. I am using every endeavour to clear myself of this indebtedness. But I wish to say that to the best of my knowledge and belief all monies received by me as funds in trust for others have been fully accounted for. My monetary difficulties have to do with my poverty and my want of business habits alone.

He was sick at the time he wrote this veiled allusion to a collection he had made for Mme. Olga Novikoff, an aged Nihilist refugee who had recently come from Russia to London and who had placed her affairs in his friendly but sticky hands. He later described her as "a Russian adventuress."[1] But in the meantime, by a peculiar process of inverted attraction, he would also come into much more intimate contact with Eleanor Marx. Annie Besant would lose her desperate gambit.

In 1883 Eleanor Marx was twenty-seven years old. That year Beatrice Potter (still a long way from becoming Mrs. Sidney Webb and still merely a humanitarian Liberal striped with some Tory streaks) met her in the "refreshment room" of the British Museum, went home, and recorded her impressions in her diary for May 24. She found Eleanor in general a comely person, though "dressed in a slovenly picturesque way," and with "curly black hair flying in all directions." Her fine black eyes, which were full of life and sympathy, redeemed her otherwise "ugly features and expression" and her bad complexion, which Miss Potter attributed to her "unhealthy excited life, kept up with stimulants, and tempered by narcotics." Though the latter comment lacks substantiation—Eleanor's narcotics were chiefly cigarettes—this anomalous description nicely sums up her contradictory character. It is corroborated by the much more detailed picture of her appearance and life drawn by Eduard Bernstein, the intimate French Socialist friend of the Marx group.[2] The tiny, vivacious, emotional "Tussy," as her father had liked to call her, had been much more interested in the Socialist movement and the heated discussions than had her two older sisters, the only survivors of an original family of six. In fact, her father was in the habit of remarking, "Jenny is most like me; but Tussy *is* me." He tried to discourage her overweening interest in the theater: she would have liked to be an actress, for she had a very musical voice and a talent for impersonation; instead, she confined herself to recitations and readings, dramatics classes, and amateur theatricals. She kept a little Shakespeare museum in her bedroom and walked miles with the family to Samuel Phelps's productions at Sadler's Wells. Her father, just before his death, had consented to her taking a course of dramatic lessons from Mme. Jung as a means of curing the "mental discord which is quite undermining her health."

At the age of sixteen, Eleanor had had a brief affair with the French political exile and revolutionary writer, P. Lissagaray. With girlish but undismayed pride, she confided to a friend that his courtship technique was highly compromising, but her father eventually sent the Gallic adventurer on his way. Until Aveling came along over a decade later, there had apparently been no other real-life romance in Eleanor's career; love had been all in books and in the theater. Meanwhile, she had devoted herself to earning a living by corresponding for Socialist newspapers, doing free-lance writing, and holding a well-paid job teaching literature in one of the better-class boarding schools for girls.

[1] *National Reformer,* July 12, 1885.

[2] Beatrice Webb, *My Apprenticeship* (London, 1926), pp. 301–2 n.; Bernstein, *My Years of Exile,* pp. 159–71, *passim;* also Barker, in *New Yorker* (November 27, 1954), pp. 177–78.

She and Aveling had remarkably similar characters and interests. Aveling had continued his popular "Readings, Grave and Gay" and never lost a chance to read plays and visit the theater. He was also becoming interested in the new socialism, and she, as a dedicated Marxist, was naturally skeptical of religion. Both were brilliant, erratic, and emotionally unstable. At least, Eleanor was unstable until she met Aveling, but from that point on he became the one firm focus of her life. The attitude was not reciprocal. Shaw reflected the disparity in his depiction of the relationship between Louis Dubedat and Jennifer in *The Doctor's Dilemma*. However, he denied the story that he had said he preferred Eleanor's ankles to her political speeches. In the mid-eighties he participated in a private reading of *A Doll's House*, in which Aveling played Helmer, the hypocritical husband; Eleanor played Nora, on her way to emancipation; and Shaw himself enacted Krogstad, the villain. They were all very fond of Ibsen and *Madame Bovary*. Bernstein also saw Eleanor and Aveling do a dramatized one-act version of *Enoch Arden*, in which, "wavering between love and loyalty," she chose the latter "with great warmth of emotion."

Beatrice Potter made her first acquaintance with Social Democracy, scientific materialism, and Eleanor Marx all at the same time. The reading room of the British Museum was a sort of clubroom for the impoverished intellectuals who could afford no club of their own. In fact, it was in the same May that Aveling contributed one of his delightful little sketches, "Some Humors of the Reading Room at the British Museum," to *Progress*. Mrs. Besant had always frequented the place, searching for and verifying references for her voluminous writing. No one, however, has recorded what happened when she first met the young and exciting Eleanor Marx. The same lacuna occurs for the first meeting between Eleanor and Edward Aveling, but it is easy to trace by indirection, through the pages of *Progress*, the *Freethinker*, the *Reformer, Our Corner*, and *Justice*, the sharpening of the angles of the Marx-Aveling-Besant triangle during the fateful year of 1884. In March, Aveling was fulminating against "The Rottenness of the Press" because of the failure of the *Times* and other papers to print a letter from Miss Marx refuting an attack on her father by Sedley Taylor. In the *Freethinker*, whose contributing editor he had become on the return of Foote to his old place, he pushed the "stirring" articles by Eleanor Marx which he was printing in *Progress* as its joint-editor. Both journals also called attention to her articles on international socialism in the new Socialist monthly, *To-Day*, edited by J. L. Joynes and E. Belfort Bax.

But it was, as before, in the poetry which Aveling printed in *Progress* —sometimes signed and sometimes not—that he revealed his sentimental soul. "A Nocturne" told of a brief, sadly idyllic experience by the sea with "Idalie." "In Articulo Mortis" presented the dying words of an unbeliever who had taken his stand on science: "Oh, yes, my life's been a failure, and fortune has not been kind." "Melodies" preached the "quiet of a simple life" in the country as a "stay to human misery." "From the South"—the "sad, sweet trysting-place again"—dealt with another triangle in which the male lover righteously upbraided and rejected his sweetheart who had not been honest either with him or with her husband-to-be. In August he reached his climax in "Song and After Song," beginning and ending with the couplets:

> The song of a lark; the sound of the sea;
> Green grass growing on a salt-sown lea.
>
> The voice of a maid; a man's heart-strife;
> Strange hopes growing in a storm-tossed life.

In the middle section of the poem he confessed to bursting forth in song like a lark, which "Rings out the old and new" and fully quiets the ache in his heart.

The series came to an abrupt stop in November with the following editorial announcement:

For private reasons of no public interest, I am leaving the editorship of *Progress* in the hands of its founder alone. This I do without any quarrel with my colleague or any dissatisfaction with the conduct of the magazine, to which I hope to contribute as before. Edward Aveling.

His contributions now, however, consisted of such prose articles as "The Death of Socrates" and "Astronomical Problems."

Annie Besant's side of the affair was revealed primarily in the *Reformer,* of which Aveling was still one of the mainstays in the fields of art, science, and politics. At the New Year's season, in the annual N.S.S. *Almanack,* she had written on "The Aim of Life" from the materialistic and monistic point of view and had concluded that life was very good. Bradlaugh and Aveling had also contributed leading articles. For over half of the year, too, the three continued to chair one another's lectures; and Aveling dropped in every now and then at N.S.S. Executive Committee meetings. The January 13 number of the *Reformer,* however, disclosed that the old triple harmony was sliding into a dissonance. The Socialist invasion was making such inroads that Bradlaugh was forced to plan a series of lectures on it in the Hall of Science the following month. Moreover, *To-Day* not only featured an article on the subject by Henry Hyndman, but, as Bradlaugh put it, ". . . it is much to be regretted that the editors should pass a line signed 'Eleanor Marx,' in which it is stated the 'individual acts,' recently perpetrated, and intended to destroy human life by violent means, 'seem to us useless, and at times even harmful.'" This callous, inhuman reference to recent bomb-throwings and dynamitings by the energetic revolutionaries was more than Bradlaugh could digest: "If this is scientific socialism, we are glad not to have any part in it." Continuing in only a very slightly softer vein, he decided that "Dr. Aveling is a little impractical in his essay on 'Christianity and Capitalism.'" In fact, he found him positively "embarrassing" when he stated that "Socialism has nothing to do with religion or irreligion" and yet at the same time asserted that socialism must be entirely irreligious. He was slightly worried, too, when he found Aveling attacking "the bourgeois feeling," and he queried whether "bourgeois" really meant anything worse than "middle class."

In succeeding issues Mrs. Besant quickly joined in by denouncing the doctrine that any means is justifiable to gain a desired end. She remarked that at a recent meeting of the Democratic Federation there must have been at least two members present—Aveling and Headlam—who detested this opinion of a "foreign school," represented in England by the late Karl Marx, but certainly not English. Aveling—according to *Justice,* he had attended the organizing meeting of the Democratic Federation with Eleanor Marx, had identified himself as a "Scientific Student," and had said he therefore felt at home in a group of scientific Socialists—was promptly stung into replying in the same paper that the meeting Mrs. Besant had referred to was "conversational rather than formal" and that no resolution had been put. Admitting that the assumption had been that "the changes desired by Socialism" could come only by revolution, he disclaimed any intended program of arson and assassination; but the "Eds. N.R." were politely incredulous. In fact, though Mrs. Besant herself was just concluding a new series of lectures at the Hall of Science on the French Revolution, the *Reformer* found itself too pressed for space to be able to print Aveling's "long defence of Mr. Morris's position, and of the scientific side of Dr. Marx's Socialism." In William Morris, one of the editors of *Justice,* Aveling had apparently found a kindred spirit who possessed his own combination of abilities as a poet and advanced thinker. Still, the forgiving Annie desired to be fair; and when Ramsey found it necessary to write *Justice* to correct a statement about the *Freethinker,* she added magnanimously in the *Reformer:*

It is due to Dr. Aveling to say that he also wrote, contradicting the falsehood, but the Socialist editor, in pursuance of his silly attempts to injure Dr. Aveling in the eyes of the Freethought party, did not insert the rebuke.

She was still hanging on three weeks later when she thanked Aveling for "able literary assistance, . . . freely and courageously rendered," in preparing an article on the Foote case.

Where Eleanor Marx was concerned, however, the situation was quite different, and Annie could be quite femininely waspish. Finding a short passage in a scientific review by Aveling to be a little obscure, she inserted a footnote: "These sentences are, I fear, unintelligible, but Dr. Aveling is not in town, and the copy is written by such a slovenly aman-

uensis that I have had to make the best of it throughout." Only the insiders realized that the "slovenly amanuensis" was Eleanor Marx. Aveling was still gentleman enough to explain mildly that the whole passage
would become perfectly clear if "past" were substituted for "part." One
commentator has since suggested that Miss Marx had committed a
Freudian slip because she wanted Aveling to part with his past.[3]

The situation was rapidly getting out of control. Aveling delivered a
series of out-of-town speeches on his new mission, beginning at Ball's
Pond, by stating that he was a Socialist first and an atheist afterward,
and culminating in April at Birmingham in a talk on "Socialism and Freethought," where, according to the report in *Justice*, he rashly asserted:
"It took seven years before I declared my adhesion to Freethought and
five years of deep study and close reading before I became a Socialist."
Even without his gratuitous attack on Bradlaugh for his attitude on labor,
surplus value, etc., this would have been too much for Mrs. Besant to
endure. She snapped back scornfully in "Daybreak":

> I am sure that Dr. Aveling never said anything so untrue. It is less than five
> years since Dr. Aveling joined the Freethought party. . . . As his friends closed
> their doors on him, I opened mine, and save for the time that he was with his
> pupils and night time, he made my house his home. All his work was carried on
> with me. During all that time he never uttered a word on Socialism, nor studied it
> in any way. He and Mr. Bradlaugh and myself were constantly discussing politics,
> and he was quite at one with us, though his political knowledge, like that of most
> scientific and literary men, was very small. He had not a single Socialist book
> in his library. . . . In fact, he never touched Socialism in any way or knew any-
> thing about it until in 1882 he took to reading at the British Museum, and un-
> fortunately fell into the company of some of the Bohemian Socialists, male and
> female, who flourish there. Supposing that his was a "sudden conversion," Karl
> Marx acting as a Socialist Moody and Sankey, it could only have taken place two
> years ago. It is a pity that reporters of *Justice* do not study dates before making
> wild assertions.

Her sarcasm had no effect. Aveling elaborated on his remarks at Liverpool and, after a full month's reflection, brought his lecture into the Hall
of Science itself, where, crowed *Justice*, "it is very remarkable that a declared Socialist should have been so warmly received." Following his
usual line of comparing *Das Kapital* with *The Origin of Species*, Aveling
arrogantly refused to argue with a heckler who had not read Marx. He
himself had done so, he bragged, though the work had not yet been
translated into English; "but in a short time it will be laid before the
English public." (As a matter of fact, Aveling and Joynes were the earliest to start rendering *Das Kapital* into English, in 1886.) Neither Bradlaugh nor Mrs. Besant was in the audience to judge the applause; Bradlaugh was engaged, and Mrs. Besant was ill. All during the year she was

[3] Williams, *The Passionate Pilgrim*, p. 147.

falling ill of "congestion of the lungs" and losing her voice. The *Free-thinker* as well as *Justice* and the *Reformer* commented on "the silence which her doctor has recently imposed on her."

She was well enough, however, to attend the annual conference of the N.S.S. at Plymouth early in June. Aveling, returning from the funeral of his youngest brother Ernest, was present and spoke frequently. In signing her secretarial report, Mrs. Besant commented: "I have to thank Dr. Edward Aveling for help in the above report; he did for me my own speeches and some others." They were both re-elected vice-presidents; Bradlaugh naturally continued as president; but Murugesa Mudaliar, the Indian who had turned Theosophist, was dropped. The next month she attributed the success of the science classes in their examinations largely to "the admirable method of tuition introduced by Dr. Aveling." In the fall she was elected president of the Hall of Science Students' Association; the name of its former president, Aveling, was not mentioned. In July his lecture schedule was dropped even from the advertisements of the *Reformer*. A series of his articles on Drummond's "Natural Law in the Spiritual World" abruptly disappeared after the announcement that they would continue. In August he conducted his last "Art Corner" for *Our Corner*, and his "Insects and Flowers" series was discontinued. When Mrs. Besant's lectures at the Hall of Science recommenced in the autumn, a newcomer, the bright young Scotsman, John Robertson, presided. He also, instead of Aveling, became the *Reformer's* reporter for Bradlaugh's latest appearances before the Queen's Bench and the Court of Appeal. Mrs. Besant and Bradlaugh announced that neither of them would go to lecture in the United States, though they had received some very urgent invitations. In August, too, Bradlaugh went fishing in the western Highlands. Annie Besant and his daughter Hypatia went with him.

All these events had been publicly recorded in the Secularist and Socialist press of 1883–84, but the papers had all remained close-mouthed about what had actually happened. The truth was that in July, 1884, Eleanor and Edward had run off to Derbyshire together.[4] They took a cottage at Bole Hill, near Wirksworth, letting a few selected friends know what they had done. On August 6, Friedrich Engels, who took a semi-paternal interest in his former colleague's daughter, wrote to another member of the inner circle, Eduard Bernstein:

Aveling and Tussy, without the aid of officials, &c., are married, and now bathed in bliss in the mountains of Derbyshire. *Nota bene:* about this there must be no public report. The fact is that Aveling has a legal wife whom he cannot

---

[4] Havelock Ellis, "Eleanor Marx," *Adelphi*, X (September, 1935), 345–46; Barker, in *New Yorker*, p. 178. Ellis gives contradictory dates for the following events—naming 1884 for the year when Eleanor "joined herself" to Aveling, but dating the letters of Bernstein and Olive Schreiner in 1883. The facts and events cited above make it obvious that the year was 1884.

get free from *de jure* although he has for years been so *de facto.* This is a fact fairly well known and even among the literary Philistines it is fairly well accepted.

Havelock Ellis, who recorded the story, was soon able to observe these goings-on for himself, for early in August he joined Olive Schreiner for a week at Bole Hill. Miss Schreiner, Eleanor's closest friend—whose naturalistic novel, *The Story of an African Farm,* was setting the advanced critics on their heads even though it had been published under the male pseudonym of Ralph Iron—had taken rooms near the Avelings and had written to Ellis on July 24:

> Dr. Aveling and Miss Marx have just come to see me. She is now to be called Mrs. Aveling. I was glad to see her face. I love her. But she looks miserable.

Such a comment, felt Ellis, made during the honeymoon itself, was significant and prophetic. A week later Miss Schreiner wrote again:

> I am beginning to have such a horror of Dr. Aveling. To say I dislike him doesn't express it at all. I have a fear and a horror of him when I am near. Every time I am near him this shrinking grows stronger. . . . I love her, but he makes me so unhappy. He is so selfish, but that doesn't account for this feeling of dread.

One lonely night, when her lover had marched off alone to a dinner party, the deserted girl sat up writing pages to her friend, confessing how she still longed for real love.

What Ellis's own reactions were upon his arrival he failed to record. But anyone who could arouse such a feeling of repulsion in a woman of Olive Schreiner's strength of character must have been a paragon in his own field. Aveling, however, not foreknowing what Miss Schreiner's opinion of him was to be, had written a long encomium of *The Story of an African Farm* for *Progress* in September, 1883, heading it "A Notable Book."

The Avelings returned to town about the same time as Olive did, Edward having conveniently forgotten to pay his drinking bill at the inn. The couple had decided not to try to keep their liaison a secret any longer, but to announce it openly and defiantly as a "free marriage." Such things were looked on tolerantly, if not enviously, in their bohemian circle, and Eleanor was soon to be referred to everywhere as Mrs. Aveling or Mrs. Marx-Aveling. Inevitably, however, she was promptly discharged by the principal of her boarding school. There was, in fact, an almost universal condemnation of the match—not so much because of its nature but because of her partner. As Bernstein summed it up in retrospect, "His reputation in the Radical and Democratic world of London was already very bad, and it became worse year by year."[5]

During all this mental and emotional torture, Annie Besant never condemned—or even mentioned—this "free marriage," though early in the

[5] Bernstein, pp. 160–63.

same year in the *Reformer* she had angrily reminded the editor of the *St. James's Gazette* that Bradlaugh had never taught free love. However, soon after the pair had returned to Aveling's lodgings in Bloomsbury, Eleanor had an exciting story to tell Ellis and Miss Schreiner of an incident which had happened that morning: Bradlaugh had driven up in a cab and demanded the return of all Mrs. Besant's letters to Aveling. His mission was duly accomplished, Aveling having apparently saved the letters. "Of Mrs. Besant's more intimate relations with Aveling," commented Ellis primly, "I know nothing."

Bradlaugh by this time, it seems, had accepted his role as a father substitute—or at least as an elder brother. Nevertheless, the old rumors about himself and the deserted Annie would not die down; and in May, 1884, the *Freethinker* told about how a Secularist who was staying a hotel at Bury overheard "some of the company in the coffee room charge Mr. Bradlaugh and Mrs. Besant with the most disgusting immorality." Angered at this unjustified attack on his idols, he objected and was thereupon cut in the face by a "sugar basin" wielded by one of the defamers. He sued for damages, and the attacker was fined forty shillings "as ample compensation" for his injury in such a cause.

Nevertheless, Annie refused to surrender to these blows of fate. In her annual editorial article for the 1885 N.S.S. *Almanack*, she chose "The Future Life" as her subject, saying that heaven was still to be built in a happier world on earth. Dr. E. B. Aveling had no contribution to make to this volume. In fact, his name was nowhere mentioned.

IV. *Fourth Life:* THE SOCIALIST LABOR AGITATOR

1

Enter Bernard Shaw, Grinning

The upsurge of the new socialism in England had precipitated a battle royal. It was the focus of interest among the bohemian intellectuals and even found its way at times into the august and dignified halls of Parliament.

One day early in May, 1884, Mrs. Besant found herself in the South Place Institute, listening to her friend Bradlaugh open the second discussion of a series of lectures on the burning topic. Hyndman had delivered the first. His missionary championship was as well publicized as Bradlaugh's antagonism. Her eyes wandered about the audience, and, as she put it in "Daybreak":

> I was struck by the significant character of the opposition. There were four speakers, a Russian Pole, a German, an Englishman who described himself as a "loafer," and a foreign Jew. . . . The "loafer," a Mr. Shaw, is pretty well known on the platform, but accustomed to him as I was, I was fairly astounded at the audacious confession that he led so shameful a life. The only fair answer would be: "Go and work, before you set yourself up to teach workers."

Mrs. Besant then proceeded to expose the Socialist party, and Shaw in particular, in her most schoolmarmish manner:

> Mr. Shaw's description of himself is, I am inclined to think, pretty accurate, and explains a thing that has often puzzled me, why he should be so marvellously shrewish and "crooked" in discussion. It must be a very sad thing to be a "loafer" in a world where there is so much to be done, and the self-discontent (which ought to spur to exertion) is certain in a nature devoid of sympathy to turn into mere bad temper.

After this acute but somewhat inadequate analysis of one of the most conspicuous of the young Socialist leaders, she turned her guns on the group as a whole: ". . . the opposition was a fair sample of the Socialist party in England. It is made up of discontented foreigners, and of a few clever men playing on the suffering that exists. . . ."

This clash between the Freethought (or, more properly, the Individualist) and the Socialist groups was a minor one in the history of the Socialist movement but a major one so far as Annie Besant was personally concerned. It was but a tiny sequel to the first great public collision of the two widely talked about leaders, Charles Bradlaugh and Henry M. Hyndman—the famous debate which had been held on April 17 at St. James's Hall. Interest in this debate, to be focused on the topic "Will Socialism Benefit the English People?" had been building up for some time; and Bradlaugh felt that he could no longer avoid it, though he was continuing to struggle in the web of his personal affairs.

As an outgrowth of his battle to take his seat legally in the Commons, the High Court of Justice had decreed a penalty of £1,500 against him. Declaring that he would fight all the way up to the Lords if necessary, in February he had again taken his seat under the Peers' Gallery to "observe," but as the result of a final "disgraceful scene" had resigned and gone back to Northampton for the fourth time, to be re-elected with a larger majority than ever. But on his return to the House in March he was again refused the right to speak or record his vote.

It was in the midst of these battles that he prepared to settle Hyndman and socialism once and for all. He and his opponent, who was later to be immortalized by Shaw as the basic part of John Tanner, had been tuning up by delivering independent lectures on the subject in such places as the Cambridge Union Debating Club and the Hall of Science, and by contributing articles to their respective party organs. It was in early February that Mrs. Besant first learned about *Justice: The Organ for the Social Democracy,* edited by a board consisting of William Morris, J. Taylor, and Henry Mayer Hyndman. The extreme Marxism of its advocacy of violent means and a "bloodier revolution" than that of France, her own favorite topic, so angered her that she carried on a feud with it in "Daybreak" until she could boast of provoking the other paper into "a sensible paragraph, condemning the advocacy of violence as long as free agitation was allowed." Mrs. Besant was always a free agitator, whatever the cause she took up.

In the second issue of *Justice,* hoping to shine in the reflected light of Bradlaugh, the editors challenged him to a debate. In the fourth issue, after they had launched their Democratic Federation with the additional aid of Bax, the Avelings, Burrows (a Secularist hanger-on of long standing), and Headlam (who stayed for only one meeting and left to become warden of the Christian Socialist Guild of St. Matthew),[1] Hyndman was

---

[1] Eduard Bernstein, in *My Years of Exile: Reminiscences of a Socialist,* says that Shaw used Headlam for the partial model of his Rev. James Mavor Morell.

able to proclaim that the great Bradlaugh had accepted his challenge. He was very magnanimous about his opponent, calling him "undoubtedly the most formidable and imposing platform figure in the country."[2]

As for the debate, Hyndman admitted that on that night, according to the reaction of the audience and most of the newspapers, Bradlaugh had the better of him. But he maintained that eventually he himself was the victor, since his simple, clear, logical statements of the issues remained in the minds of the listeners after Bradlaugh's emotionalism, dogmatism, and "squelching" tactics had been forgotten. He was impressed by the deference paid Bradlaugh by his followers and worried by the "deep draught of cold claret" his opponent drank afterward in spite of the great heat. He was also impressed by the skill and impartiality with which Professor E. S. Beesly, the well-known and well-liked Positivist follower of Comte, presided over the meeting.

Mrs. Besant, commenting on the sidelights of the affair in the *Reformer* —a Special Extra number was devoted to a verbatim transcript of the text—took a more womanish and partial approach. First of all, though she had a good view from the side of the hall where she was seated with friends, she was irritated because she and Bradlaugh's daughters had not been allowed seats on the platform, whereas, she charged, the Democratic Federation had put chairs there for Hyndman's party. Moreover, she complained, most of the Socialists present were Germans, many of whom she generally found insolent and intolerant. As for Hyndman himself, her verdict was that he was "very clever, very fluent, very shifty, and very shallow in his knowledge of the English working class movements." Socialism, she concluded, was just then a fashion, as aestheticism had been a little while before.

The landslide sale of the debate edition helped to bolster the shaky finances of the Freethought Publishing Company but not sufficiently to avoid the necessity of offering £5,000 worth of debentures at 5 per cent interest for public sale. A printing office was also set up on the second floor, to be managed by Hypatia's fiancé, Arthur Bonner, the son of the Rev. W. H. Bonner, for whom Bradlaugh had great respect in spite of his profession and who had been one of the original vice-presidents of the National Reform League in 1866.

Soon afterward came Annie's exasperated comments on the "crooked" Mr. Shaw and—within two weeks of her initial complaint—a complete retraction and apology to him. The Irish charm of Mr. Shaw had overpowered the Irish charmer, Mrs. Besant. In "Daybreak" she told her readers of her mistake. The word "loafer" was only an ironical, self-deprecatory term. He was really "very hard-working" and quite poor. In her *Autobiography*, she looked back on the episode with a soft but blurred nostalgia. Leading up from a description of her first reaction to the fiery young So-

2 Henry Mayer Hyndman, *The Record of an Adventurous Life* (London, 1911), pp. 334–39.

cialist speakers, their violent and sometimes inaccurate speeches, and their determined efforts to educate themselves and learn the truth in spite of their scanty means and pay, she finally pardoned the "faults which grew out of the bitter sense of injustice" and unreservedly praised the essential nobility, self-sacrifice, self-denial, and brotherly affection of the Social Democrats, as they soon came to call themselves.

At this time I also met George Bernard Shaw, one of the most brilliant of Socialist writers, and most provoking of men; a man with a perfect genius for "aggravating" the enthusiastically earnest, and with a passion for representing himself as a scoundrel. On my first experience of him on the platform at South Place Institute he described himself as a "loafer," and I gave an angry snarl at him in the *Reformer*, for a loafer was my detestation, and behold! I found that he was very poor, because he was a writer with principles and preferred starving his body to starving his conscience; that he gave time and earnest work to the spreading of Socialism, spending night after night in workmen's clubs; and that a "loafer" was only his amiable way of describing himself because he did not carry a hod. Of course I had to apologize for my sharp criticism as doing him a serious injustice, but privately felt somewhat injured at having been trapped into such a blunder.

This was all Annie Besant wished to salvage from her long intimacy with Bernard Shaw. She had been similarly reticent about her intimacy with Edward Aveling. In both cases, however, much more had gone on than met the general reader's eye. But her intimacy with Charles Bradlaugh, of which she remained very proud to the end, was more adequately treated.

Shaw himself, in a reminiscent mood many years later, recollected his first impression of Annie Besant on the platform at a South Place meeting, "at which nobody seemed incredulous, when hopes were held out by her chairman that the production of what would now be called synthetic protoplasm might shortly be expected from an Edinburgh laboratory."[3] In his ensuing tribute to Besant and Bradlaugh, he failed to mention the fact that in his first speech before the Zetetical Society in 1879 he had defended the action of the state in taking Shelley's and Mrs. Besant's children from them on socialistic grounds.[4] But he did describe Annie as "a woman of swift decisions," who "always came into a movement with a bound, and was preaching the new faith before the astonished spectators had the least suspicion that the old one was shaken."

Mrs. Besant herself, however, always discovered that her real roots had been growing for a longer time than the world realized. For in-

[3] Shaw, "Mrs. Besant's Passage through Fabian Socialism," in *Dr. Annie Besant: Fifty Years in Public Work* (London, 1924).

[4] R. F. Rattray, *George Bernard Shaw: A Chronicle* (New York, 1951), p. 34; Archibald Henderson, *George Bernard Shaw: Man of the Century*, p. 92; St. John Ervine, *Bernard Shaw: His Life, Work, and Friends*, p. 130.

stance, she found that her attention had first been drawn to socialism at a pitifully small meeting in Steinway Hall on January 12, 1883, at which she and Alice Bradlaugh had heard the dedicated fanatical French social reformer and anarchist, Louise Michel, "la vierge rouge de Montmartre," touch on the subject.[5]

Shaw had been tempted to attend his first Besant meeting when, shortly before, in a mood of mixed truculence and depression caused by his complete failure to establish even a toehold in London after his departure from Dublin in 1876, he had walked several miles to the Hall of Science to listen to Bradlaugh expound Shaw's own favorite topic, atheism. Nevertheless, with his customary spirit of perversity, he had asked Bradlaugh a question which had seemed to imply that the questioner was as fearful of the dangers and superstitions of science as the speaker was of those of religion. As a result, Shaw had not only been informed that Bradlaugh's daughters were taking lessons in biology without any fears of its dangers but had also heard his own name spoken in public for the first time. Bradlaugh's assertion that to his mind the two greatest forces for good in the world at that time were science and birth control caused Shaw to go to hear Bradlaugh's coadjutor, Mrs. Besant, advocate the principles of Malthus, denounce the "miserable subterfuges" women were forced into when they found themselves pregnant, and, as he summarized it later, state that "Because birth control was not an open and honoured thing the knowledge of it had to be conveyed by gossip, and sexual intercourse was made the occasion of great anxiety instead of a pleasure." Shaw came away from the meeting convinced that Annie Besant was the personification of greatness; and when she and Bradlaugh were later brought to trial in the Knowlton affair, Shaw attended the trial. Horrified at the verdict, he had immediately offered his help in distributing the banned book but had been rebuffed because the others regarded him as an Irish Catholic because of his peculiar question at the Bradlaugh meeting. But he kept buying copies of the *Reformer*, in spite of the fact that his favorite uncle, Dr. Walter Gurly, kept sending him papers like the Essex *Standard*, which referred to Bradlaugh and Mrs. Besant as "that bestial man and woman who go about earning a living by corrupting the young of England."[6]

After the "great debate" between Bradlaugh and Hyndman, and—probably even more important—Mrs. Besant's new friendship with Shaw, who, like Aveling, was several years younger than she, a new theme crept into her speeches and articles and soon dominated them. It did not replace her concern with Freethought and science, for this continued

[5] *National Reformer*, January 21, 1883; *Autobiography*, p. 398.

[6] Stephen Winsten, *Jesting Apostle: The Private Life of Bernard Shaw*, pp. 34–35, 50; based on "the story of his early days in London from his unpublished records."

powerfully for some time, but it paralleled it.[7] *Justice* was gleefully pleased to detect the new trend and to twit Mrs. Besant about it in its section named "Tell-Tale Straws." On June 21, 1884, it commented, "Mrs. Besant is finding it necessary to turn Socialist; but does not like anyone to tell her so," and proceeded to analyze her recent lecture before the Cromwell Club at Plaistow on "Social Reform or Socialism?"

> The lecture, regarded from the Radical point of view, was extreme; the lecturer made various blood-stirring allusions to the injustice of amassing immense wealth at the sacrifice of labour. Mrs. Besant used the arrows of Socialism very freely . . . , but then suggested the curious paradox that the State could not bear the responsibilities proposed by the Democratic Federation.

Following the Bradlaugh line further by calling socialism un-English, she ended by proposing a Social Reform League which could send members to Parliament. Unrelenting, *Justice* pursued her even to Edinburgh, where in July she spoke on "Social Reform, Not Socialism, the Need of the Times," advocating such extreme measures as cumulative taxation upon rent and capital and the fixing of an eight-hour working day, especially for children, with five hours on Saturday. When she inveighed against the "foreign" methods of inculcating socialism by dynamite, the Austrian Socialist, Andreas Scheu, who had followed her all the way from London to continue his heckling and conscience-prodding, demanded in vain that she name one Austrian or German who had proposed such a policy. William Morris was especially delighted by Scheu's performance, for he wrote him a letter praising him for the way he was knocking the Freethinkers about and ending: "What a game for Mrs. Besant to see you jump up at Edinburgh after having had the last of you in London: she must have thought it a sort of nightmare."[8] Shaw had supported Scheu in his heckling of her and Bradlaugh at the Hall of Science in London.

Mrs. Besant's reason for going to Edinburgh, however, had not been primarily political or economic. For some time she had been looking for some young writer who could replace the omniscient Aveling on the staffs of *Our Corner* and the *Reformer*. She had found him in the able young Scotsman, John Mackinnon Robertson, ten years her junior. For over a year Robertson had been sending familiar essays on subjects like

---

[7] Williams's statistics (*The Passionate Pilgrim*, pp. 149–53) on this matter are completely unreliable. For instance, she states that Mrs. Besant, because of her new social interests, was unable to finish even Part I of her study of *The Christian Creed; or, What It Is Blasphemy To Deny* and that the promised Part II never appeared. Actually, Part I was completed between March 11 and August 19, 1883; and Part II was begun on July 27, 1884, and carried through to December 14, though with some irregularity. Theodore Besterman (*Mrs. Annie Besant*, pp. 131–33), who is Mrs. Besant's bibliographer, gives a true presentation of the proportions of her writing at this time.

[8] *Justice*, July 12, 1884; *The Letters of William Morris to His Family and Friends* (London, 1950), p. 201.

literary plagiarism, diary-keeping, literary style, the orthodoxy of women, Keats, Burns, Shelley, Browning, Tennyson, and George Eliot to both *Our Corner* and *Progress*. A leading member of the Edinburgh branch of the N.S.S., he had come down to London to listen to Bradlaugh in the "great debate" and had written his impressions at some length in *Progress*. He had ranged himself generally at Bradlaugh's side, but because he had described himself as both "a Socialist and a Pessimist" he had been attacked in a friendly way by "D" in the *Reformer*. Mrs. Besant, however, had traveled up to Edinburgh a little later to persuade Robertson to move permanently to London. They went sight-seeing together around the city, as she had previously done with Bradlaugh and Aveling, but this time she paid special attention to its slums, as an object of social reform. Her trip had proved so persuasive that in "Daybreak" in August she was able to announce that Robertson had joined the staff as a regular weekly contributor.

Her confidence in Robertson was not misplaced. His sharp wit, wide-ranging mind, and nicety of taste eventually made him editor of the *Reformer* when, for various reasons, A. B. and C. B. found it desirable to withdraw. He also later became a highly regarded historian and literary critic. He moved into one of the extra rooms in Mrs. Besant's large house, where she already had two woman lodgers. The first real scholar she had known, and an open-minded and analytical supporter of the principles of socialism and Freethought, Robertson helped further to break down the inhibitions which had been instilled in her mind by the revered Bradlaugh.

Annie Besant, John Robertson, and Bernard Shaw were now moving in orbits rapidly approaching one another. Her increasing attraction for Shaw was something that the young Irishman had trouble understanding and diagnosing even to himself. Only after his death did it become publicly known that he had begun to keep a diary on January 5, 1885, and that he had kept it going more or less scrappily until October 12, 1897.[9] During the first week in March, 1885, he set down a cryptic entry which indicated that his intimacy with Annie Besant had reached such a peculiar crisis that they were embarrassed before other people by each other's presence. Learning that she was returning from a trip to Northampton, Shaw and his new friend Robertson went to the railway station to meet her. They found her in the company of an eccentric and aggres-

[9] This diary, along with Shaw's other papers, on his death passed into the possession first of the Public Trustee and then of the British Museum. The papers are still being catalogued and will not be open to public inspection for some time. The diary (whose entries for 1892 are unfortunately completely missing) was kept mostly in Shaw's peculiar shorthand, but was later transcribed by his secretary, Blanche Patch. Before the transcription was withdrawn, it was inspected by a very few persons, among whom were Winsten and Ervine, who drew on it for *Jesting Apostle* and *Bernard Shaw*, respectively.

sive young man, Horatio Bottomley, whose current radical political interests gave not the slightest hint that within a few years he was to become the founder and editor of the ultra-chauvinistic *John Bull* and during World War I was to spend a term at penal servitude because of his ingenious victory-bond scheme, which defrauded guileless gambling investors out of hundreds of thousands of pounds. According to a current malicious but completely unfounded story, Bottomley was reputed to be Bradlaugh's bastard son. Shaw and Robertson met the other pair and saw them into a cab. But, recorded Shaw in his journal, "Mrs. B. and I did not speak or bow. She did not know how we stood with one another."

There were various possible reasons for this constraint, as will soon be seen. At any rate, their misunderstanding did not last long. In April the eyes of the readers of *Our Corner* were caught by the first instalment of a new novel, *The Irrational Knot*, by George Bernard Shaw, "Author of 'An Unsocial Socialist,' etc." This identification was for the benefit of those few devotees who had been following the strange fortunes of Shaw's other hero, Sidney (Webb) Trefusis, in the rival Socialist monthly, *To-Day*. In other words, Annie had discovered that her "loafer" friend possessed a considerable flair for literature, and art in general, even though dozens of commercial publishers had as yet refused to admit it. In fact, in some ways he excelled even Edward Aveling in his versatility with his pen. Soon afterward, consequently, Shaw took over the "Art Corner," then exercised his coruscating wit on contemporary music, and finally turned to his ultimate love, the drama. Mrs. Besant had started him on the career of universal art critic which a few years later was to astonish and dazzle all of London.

Not only did Mrs. Besant give her new protégé an opportunity to see his work in print; she also paid him for the privilege. Considering that in this year his total income was £117, Shaw could never forget her generosity. Many years later in the preface to a new edition of *Cashel Byron's Profession*, which in its serial form had helped *To-Day* to its obsequies in 1886 and to which Mrs. Besant had called special attention in her competing *Our Corner* as a "very original tale," Shaw termed her "an incorrigible benefactress." He also told how, when he became "novelist in ordinary" to her "little propaganda magazine" (as he described it in a later preface to *The Irrational Knot*), he discovered that she had the "singular habit" of paying her contributors. This habit, he speculated, was to some extent a device of hers for "relieving necessitous young propagandists without wounding their pride by open alms-giving."

The public culmination of this phase of the Shaw-Besant affair came abruptly at a meeting of the Dialectical Society in January. The progressive political world had long been watching to see which way Mrs. Besant would jump. As far back as May, 1884, Foote had written an article, "Freethought and Socialism," for his paper in which he asserted that the destruction of religion was still more important than any schemes for social reform, no matter how useful these might be. In October, in making a vinegary remark on how Christian socialism was becoming a "canting dodge," he had ended, "If Socialism be true, let us accept it, but let us do it with our eyes open, and not be carried away by cheap sentiment and plausible catchwords." He then advised a correspondent to read Mrs. Besant on "Free Trade and Fair Trade." But veiled warnings like these did not deter her, and her indorsement of *Justice's* program of free breakfasts and lunches for Board School children in her Christmas "Daybreak" column brought agonized protests from many Secularists who thought it sounded more like the idea of an illogical and unscientific Socialist than of a sound Individualist. A new, loud voice, that of W. P. Ball, led the attack, which was only a preliminary to his slashing pamphlet, *Mrs. Besant's Socialism,* a year later, in which he cut her to pieces as an economic and political thinker. As she confessed in her *Autobiography,* she was hesitating to acknowledge her new allegiance because she did not want to hurt Bradlaugh, who could see no difference between the new socialism and the old.

By January 21, 1885, she had made up her mind, though the world did not know it. As usual, she showed her flair for the dramatic. Shaw told the story, for he was at the center of it. He had gone to the Dialectical Society to make an address advocating socialism and had found the members upset because Annie Besant, who had ceased to attend meetings some time ago, had unexpectedly put in an appearance in the company of Robertson. Shaw explained modestly:

I was warned on all hands that she had come down to destroy me, and that from the moment she rose to speak my cause was lost. I resigned myself to my fate, and pleaded my cause as best I could. When the discussion began everyone waited for Mrs. Besant to lead the opposition. She did not rise; and at last the opposition was undertaken by another man. When he had finished, Mrs. Besant, to the amazement of the meeting, got up and utterly demolished him. There was nothing left for me to do but gasp and triumph under her shield. At the end she asked me to nominate her for election to the Fabian Society, and invited me to dine with her.

This, according to Shaw's diary, was the first time he had actually made the acquaintance of Mrs. Besant. On January 31, he spent his first evening at her home.

From this time on, to Mrs. Besant's regret, her relationship with Charles Bradlaugh changed. Though their private friendship remained as firm as ever, he never thereafter felt the same confidence in her judgment, "nor did he any more consult me on his own policy, as he had done ever since we first clasped hands."[10] Bitter attacks were made on her by some Radicals in the Freethought party like Ball, who in the

[10] *Autobiography,* pp. 404–6; Hypatia Bradlaugh Bonner, *Charles Bradlaugh,* II, 14–15; John W. Robertson, "Account of [Bradlaugh's] Parliamentary Struggles, Politics, and Teachings," in Bonner, *Bradlaugh,* II, 383.

Freethinker dubbed her a "St. Athanasius in petticoats," said she possessed a "mind like a milkjug," and referred to her as "our lady of the pinafore," perhaps in reference to the red skirt she had taken to wearing in token of her Socialist affiliation. But she stoutly defended herself against his charge that he "had heard Mrs. Besant described as being, like most women, at the mercy of her last male acquaintance for her views on economics." No, she asseverated, she had always thought her way into new opinions absolutely alone. "I did not make the acquaintance of one of my present Socialist comrades, male or female, until I had embraced Socialism." Here is certainly an interesting specimen of equivocation!

She chose the Fabian Society rather than any of the other Socialist groups because it was "less hotly antagonistic to the Radicals." Hyndman's claim after describing the "great debate" that it "is a fact that within six months . . . Annie Besant, Dr. Aveling, Heaford and several other of Bradlaugh's ablest supporters joined the Social Democratic Federation" is a manifest exaggeration. It took Mrs. Besant much longer than six months to trip that far down the Marxian primrose path. In fact, she confessed candidly in her autobiographical tribute to Hyndman: "Personally, my debt to him is of a mixed nature; he kept me from Socialism for some time by his bitter and very unjust antagonism to Mr. Bradlaugh," even though his argument in the debate, when she read it over calmly, convinced her that there was more in "practical Socialism" than she had realized. She also paid tribute to "the devotion of that noble and generous genius," William Morris.

The news of the prodigious conversion soon got out. The lynx-eyed *Justice* first told it in a report on a meeting of the Fabian Society early in July: "Mrs. Besant made her first speech as a member of a Society avowedly Socialist, and at once made the Fabians feel how much they have already been strengthened by her accession." Herbert Burrows, however, the mild-looking but stubborn young Cambridge visionary who was soon to run an unsuccessful race for the London School Board, got up and pointed out that the particular political policy recommended by Mrs. Besant had actually been carried out for years by the Social Democratic Federation, the sect to which he belonged. The various brands of Socialists at the time were always turning up annoyingly at one another's meetings, or even, more co-operatively, exchanging speakers. On August 1, under the caption "Conversion," *Justice* announced Mrs. Besant's official joining of the Fabians and told how at a recent meeting she had advocated the abolition of wages, of production for profit, and of classes. "That," it crowed, "is about as far as Collectivism can go." In *Our Corner* she had also published a paper, "in which she is as socialistic as the most revolutionary Socialist could desire." And yet, less than a year before, *Justice* reminded her, she had been classing Socialists with dynamiters! Its further speculation that "Mrs. Besant will soon find that the individualism of the *National Reformer* and collective socialism are, to say the least, somewhat incompatible" so provoked her that she wrote an angry reply saying that this kind of "wild and wicked language" was still repugnant to her and had delayed her own conversion. The alliance between her and the "chief champion of individualism," she assured her hecklers, will last "as long as we live"; and as late as October, Bradlaugh assured an S.D.F. heckler at Manchester that he did not know one point on which he differed from Mrs. Besant's political views—this in spite of the fact that in the previous month she had remarked in her column that the Fabian Society had a good autumn program, which included Webb, Walter Crane, and herself as speakers.

It was not, however, till December 13, while ridiculing an "imbecilic" letter in the *Pall Mall Gazette* maligning socialism, that Mrs. Besant told her own republican constituents of her conversion. The Fabian Society, "the Socialist body to which I belong," had—she was glad to say—issued a public protest against the scandal of the S.D.F.'s accepting money from the Tories to defray the expenses of Socialist candidates. She also added that she had been made a member of a Fabian subcommittee "to report on the advisability of holding a conference of advanced reformers to decide on the steps to be taken to improve social conditions" and to draw up proposals. Not long afterward, with Shaw and others, she was made a member of the Executive Committee itself.

Hyndman soon had too many problems of his own to ridicule Annie further. The Social Democrats had been having trouble all year. A schism in their ranks over "arbitrary rule" versus "fraternal co-operation" resulted in the secession of seventeen members, led by Morris, both Avelings, Scheu, and Bax. The name of Edward Aveling was greeted with cries of "Shame!" by the old-liners like Hyndman, Burrows, Champion, Harry Quelch, and John Burns.[11] The seceders, who later occasionally added Friedrich Engels to their number, soon formed their own little clique, which they named the Socialist League and which, through its badly printed new monthly magazine, *The Commonweal*, issued vociferous but largely ineffective bulletins and manifestoes from its tiny headquarters in Bloomsbury. Morris, however, felt enough encouraged to start printing his *Chants for Socialists*, which *Justice*, seconded by Bradlaugh, promptly derided as poetry.

Justice was having trouble, too. In spite of its reduction of price, it failed to find many takers. "Comrades" (they were always "Comrades" in the S.D.F.) paraded down the main London streets, through railway stations, and past sweatshops hawking copies in the cold and fog. By March it announced that it was now "in the hands of the workers" and,

11 See Arthur H. Nethercot, *Men and Supermen*, pp. 248, 300, and *passim* for Shavian associations.

because it had taken a new format on cheaper paper (and showed it!), was "in great part distributed gratuitously." The woman workers were called upon to make red flags and banners for an unemployment demonstration. Parades were planned with great ostentation; but at one of these the only five to turn up were the organizers. A "paste-pot brigade" was formed to stick up bills. Walter Crane, the well-known illustrator, contributed a full-page cartoon, "The Vampire," showing socialism rescuing labor from the dragon-vampire of religious hypocrisy, capitalism, and party politics; and a few more copies were disposed of.

Success came, however, in September, when Burrows, John Williams, and two or three others were jailed for preaching socialism in the streets. The Socialist League magnanimously joined with the Social Democrats in a protest meeting, which drew some 60,000 orderly people. Annie Besant, of the Fabians, offered to speak on her favorite subject, the right of free speech, at the corner of Dod Street the next Sunday. Since she was just recovering from another of her bad throat congestions and, in spite of her famous organ voice, hated to speak out of doors (she was often forced to do so because the Fabians had no other place to meet), this was a great concession. Aveling, who wrote up the affair, recounted how the police "rushed ferociously" at the standard-bearer and arrested him. Mrs. Eleanor Marx-Aveling and Morris were roughly treated in the process. This meeting, which drew only one-tenth as many as its predecessor, made Aveling more detested than ever among the Social Democrats, since he committed what *Justice* called "a gross breach of faith" in promising not to speak at a certain place and time and then going ahead and speaking anyhow. He denied that he had ever made the commitment, and Mrs. Besant, for the Fabians, signed a statement issued by various Radical clubs against *Justice*'s charges.[12] As for her speech, it was apparently not given after all; nor was Bradlaugh's, though in the *Reformer* he had questioned the legal right of the police to interfere. Both of them had come down with incapacitating colds. By December, however, he had recovered sufficiently to win re-election at Northampton for the fifth time, with his largest vote yet; and Mrs. Besant lectured for the Fabians at the South Place Institute.

It was the Fabians, with their policy of patient economic reform, gradualism, "Evolution, not Revolution," who commanded her allegiance. The total membership of the group was only forty, but it included such upper-middle-class intellectuals as Shaw, Sidney Webb, Sydney Olivier, Hubert Bland, Graham Wallas, and its secretary and historian, E. R. Pease.[13] Their somewhat abstract utopianism and usual gentlemanly conduct did not bother Mrs. Besant at first, though *Justice* scoffed at

[12] Henderson, *George Bernard Shaw: Man of the Century*, pp. 176–77, calls Aveling "the hero of the occasion," even though Morris had expected the honor of making the speech.

[13] Mary Agnes Hamilton, *Sidney and Beatrice Webb* (London, 1933), p. 23.

such milk-and-water behavior. It is true that, as Shaw expressed it in his famous Fabian Tract No. 41, *The Fabian Society: What It Has Done and How It Has Done It,* in 1883 the Society was content with nothing less than the prompt "reconstruction of society in accordance with the highest moral possibilities." In 1884 "we were discussing whether money should be permitted under Socialism." A few months later:

We were joined by Mrs. Wilson, now one of the chief members of the Freedom Group of Kropotkinist Anarchists, and a sort of influenza of anarchism spread through the Society. . . . In short we were for a year or two just as Anarchist as the Socialist League and just as insurrectionary as the Federation.

But there was a vital difference: the Fabians were middle-class; the other groups were "proletarian."

Mrs. Charlotte Wilson's group, calling itself the Hampstead Historic Society ("Hampstead" because it met at her cottage on Hampstead Heath, while her husband Arthur kept in the background; "Historic" partly to conceal its true nature and partly because, as Shaw explained, it was a "systematic history class in which each student took his turn at being professor" in the study of Marx and Proudhon), had comparatively little appeal to Mrs. Besant, although along with some others of the Fabians she attended a meeting or two. She went far enough in support of the revolution in Russia, however, to hold a meeting at her home on August 7, 1885, to form a Society of Friends of Russia to help such Russian exiles as Prince Kropotkin and Sergius Stepniak, who were present; so was Shaw, who in his diary called it her "Russophile party." She always continued this interest in Russian political emancipation.[14]

Her role among the Fabians remained vivid to Shaw many years after she had slipped away from them. Recognizing her as "the greatest orator in England, and possibly in Europe," he told how she "swept ahead with her accustomed suddenness and impetuosity," in spite of the necessity of her tragic opposition of Bradlaugh, who "was quite simply a hero; a single champion of anti-Christendom against the seventy-seven champions of Christendom." At the moment of her joining, the Society had just what she needed to complete her equipment: administrative machinery for a practical program on constitutional lines (which had always been Bradlaugh's principle). She therefore

became a sort of expeditionary force, always to the front when there was trouble and danger, carrying away audiences for us . . . , forming branches for us throughout the country, dashing into the great strikes and free speech agitations . . . , forming on her own initiative such *ad hoc* organisations as were necessary to make them effective and generally leaving the routine to us and taking the fighting on herself.

[14] Margaret Olivier, *Sydney Olivier: Letters and Selected Writings* (London, 1948), pp. 76–77; William Irvine, *The Universe of G. B. S.* (New York, 1949), pp. 78–79; Henderson, *George Bernard Shaw: Man of the Century,* pp. 224 ff.; George Lansbury, in *Annie Besant Centenary Book,* pp. 31–32; *Autobiography,* p. 411.

Any attempt to keep pace with her on the part of a mere man, Shaw somewhat ruefully concluded, generally wrecked the man; "those who were unselfish enough to hold out to the end usually collapsed and added the burden of nursing them to her already superhuman labours." He was much kinder than the ribald writer in *Justice* who referred to her as "the Joan of Arc of the proletariat, chastening herself by prayer and fasting for her great mission." The Social Democrats, warned this writer, had been watching her progress for the last eighteen months with interest and satisfaction, but her performances on the platform at the end of 1885 filled him with some doubt. "There is more joy, etc.," he quoted.

There were really, however, no halfway measures for Annie Besant. The publication of penny pamphlets such as *Why I Am a Socialist*, blazoning her belief in social as well as biological evolution, and presenting herself as a member of the new "educated proletariat" and a champion of the downtrodden and poverty-stricken workers, was not sufficient. She had conceived *Our Corner* as a sort of general family magazine rather than a personal organ. True, she had serialized her own *Autobiographical Sketches* in it, beginning in January, 1884; and when the series had reached the Knowlton episode and her separation from her children, she had found that such papers as the *Times* and the *Westminster Review* had not forgotten their old animosity, whereas even *Justice* called attention to the special interest of these numbers. But though *Our Corner* had been far from uninterested in economics and politics, as seen by its reviews of Henry George's *Poverty and Progress* and the editor's own series on "Modern Socialism," which she had submitted to Shaw in advance for his criticism, it was not till March, 1886, that she determined to take the risky step of turning it into a propaganda machine. In that month she introduced a large new department with a special title-page: "The Fabian Society and Socialist Notes." The first issue explained the origin of the name "Fabian," with due reference to the Roman general, Fabius Cunctator, "The Delayer"; discussed the basic theory of production for use rather than profit; offered ideas on method; printed the minutes of the last meeting in detail; appealed to all trade societies and Radical associations to join the crusade; and, in general, overwhelmed its readers with an avalanche of propaganda. Later issues continued in the same vein.

In June the Fabians sponsored a great three-day conference of fifty-three liberal organizations at the South Place Institute on the grandiose subject "The Present Commercial System, and the Better Utilization of National Wealth for the Benefit of the Community" (later simplified to "Nationalization of Land and Capital"). So far did Mrs. Besant identify herself with the cause that a writer in *Progress* referred to her sarcastically as the "head janitress" and jeered condescendingly at the efforts and speeches of such reformers as herself, Shaw, Webb, Morris, Robertson, and even Bradlaugh, who attended. Aveling and Foote fared somewhat better.

Such political propinquity between Annie Besant and Bernard Shaw inevitably resulted in an ever deeper personal propinquity. In the short digest of the year's important events with which Shaw prefaced each annual volume of his diary, he summed up the development of his relationship with her during 1886 as follows: "During this year my work at the Fabian brought me into much contact with Mrs. Besant, and towards the end of the year this intimacy became a very close and personal sort, without, however, going further than friendship."

At this stage in his career, Bernard Shaw, at the age of thirty, was perfecting himself in the relatively new role which seven years later he was to project into dramatic form under the title *The Philanderer*. It was an exciting, time-consuming, and nerve-racking pastime, not without its dangers as well as its pleasures. By this time, indeed, he had involved himself in at least six love affairs, the initiative in most of which had come from the female side and each of which he was trying his best to keep secret from the participants in all the others. How many of the rest Annie Besant suspected, there is no knowing, but she must certainly have realized that she had rivals. After all, she herself had been caught on a sort of double rebound from Bradlaugh and Aveling. On the other hand, Shaw was probably guilty of a slight exaggeration when, in reply to Hesketh Pearson's speculation that Mrs. Besant had been one of the first women to fall in love with him, he bristled and corrected him: "Good heavens! . . . About the tenth, I should guess."

From these early rivals for Shaw's love, Annie Besant by 1886 no longer needed to have any serious fears of Alice Lockett, a strawberries-and-cream young nurse from an Essex hospital; the handsome Mrs. Hubert Bland, wife of his Socialist friend, with her nice poems and attractive fairy stories for children, written under her maiden name of Edith Nesbit; the dark, strong-featured, yet somewhat ethereal Lesbian, Mrs. Kate Salt, wife of his Socialist friend Henry Salt and sister of his friend Joynes; or May Morris, with whom he had once reached what he described as a tacit state of "Mystical Betrothal," and whom he might have married if he had felt he had enough to offer her financially.[15]

But the woman from whom Shaw first learned fully about women was another of his mother's pupils and a friend of his sister Lucy, Mrs. Jennie

[15] For the story of Shaw's love affairs, particularly that with Annie Besant, see, in addition to the diary and the passages in Winsten's and Ervine's biographies: Hesketh Pearson, *G. B. S.: A Full Length Portrait*, pp. 92–94, and *G. B. S.: A Postscript*, pp. 31, 74; Frank Harris, *Bernard Shaw* (London, 1931), pp. 234–38; Winsten, *Days with Bernard Shaw* (New York, 1949), p. 143; Rattray, *Chronicle*, p. 55; Williams, *The Passionate Pilgrim*, pp. 153 ff; Shaw, "Mrs. Besant's Passage through Fabian Socialism," in *Dr. Annie Besant: Fifty Years in Public Work;* Nethercot, "G. B. S. and Annie Besant," *Shaw Bulletin*, September, 1955; Henderson, *George Bernard Shaw: Man of the Century*, p. 108. But Henderson is profoundly and strangely silent about this intimate aspect of the Shaw-Besant relationship.

Patterson. Mrs. Patterson was a wealthy widow, several years older than he and also older than Annie Besant. She was clever, accomplished, idle, passionate, and experienced; and she was captivated by the fascinating, red-headed son of her music teacher. For several months she unrelentingly pursued the fastidious and as yet sexually innocent young man, who described himself in his diary as "an absolute novice"; and on the morning of July 26, 1885, his twenty-ninth birthday, he succumbed. His initial flattery and pleasure little by little turned to a horrified dismay when he realized he was caught in a lovely boa constrictor's toils. His eventual escape he preserved in pickle in the mortifying, knock-down-and-drag-out battle between Julia Craven and Grace Tranfield over Leonard Charteris in *The Philanderer.* The original of Grace Tranfield, however, was not to impinge on his life—or Annie Besant's—till some years later.

When Shaw penned a long letter to his new patroness, Mrs. Besant, on July 24, after having taken coffee with May Morris at the Ludgate Hill Station the day before, he undoubtedly had some inkling of what might soon occur between him and the tempting Jennie. Mrs. Besant certainly did not. Perhaps it would not have mattered. During the rest of 1885, while Charles Bradlaugh was assuring the world that he and Mrs. Besant had no differences of opinion on socialism or any other matter and the insatiable Mrs. Patterson was pursuing Bernard Shaw to exhaustion, Bernard and Annie were also seeing more and more of one another. Their intimacy increased through the next year, as Shaw sought some respite and relief from the active pursuit of Jennie, Edith, and Kate and the more passive waiting of Alice and May. In his diary he recorded long walks with her as they slummed through the East End, and even dropped into a music hall in Poplar. In December, as he walked her to the bus in Piccadilly Circus after a Fabian meeting, she told him she had just learned she had heart disease. It must have been of the romantic rather than the physical type, since nothing further was heard of it.

The culmination came in 1887. Between January 19 and 26 he wrote Annie no less than five times, and early in February sent her his photograph. By now the two had discovered that their mutual fondness for music was a further tie between them. He had early acquired from his musician-mother and her eccentric Irish teacher, George John Vandaleur Lee, not only a knowledge of the history, technique, and meaning of music but some proficiency in its performance. The use of his tenor voice gave him a great deal of satisfaction at home gatherings and sometimes even at Salvation Army meetings. He had worked hard to improve the dashing, rough-and-ready style which marked his command over the piano. Annie Besant, ever since her girlhood days at Harrow, had loved music in her more Victorian way, though in recent years she had had little opportunity to practice it. She of course had a piano of her own at Oatlands. So they formed the pleasant custom of meeting there frequently on Monday nights to play pianoforte duets, mostly from Haydn's symphonies. Shaw always came in, sat down at the piano, and plunged ahead, but Mrs. Besant whenever possible practiced for hours to perfect her parts in advance. The neighborhood resounded with their efforts to keep in time. Thrown to the winds were the uncompromisingly high standards for performance, both amateur and professional, which Shaw preached in his novels and later extended to his music criticism. In the periods between these goings-on there was naturally time for more personal interludes. In fact, as he candidly confessed to his diary, "The intimacy with Mrs. Besant alluded to last year reached a point in January at which it threatened to become a vulgar intrigue, chiefly through my fault. But I roused myself in time and avoided this."

After they had appeared together on the platform of a public meeting or at a session of some Socialist or other reform organization, he would walk home with her. Once, about a week after he had had an unpleasant scene with Mrs. Bland when warning her not to visit him alone at Fitzroy Square for fear the visit would compromise her, Mrs. Besant in an affectionately protective mood bought him an umbrella, which Shaw (who maintained that she had no taste, though his own as manifested by the décor of his later house at Ayot St. Lawrence scarcely qualified him as a connoisseur in such matters) described as "so ugly that I wouldn't be seen at a funeral with it." So, on a walk through Regent's Park, he politely returned it to her, whereupon in a pet she threw it over a fence. The episode gave him a chance to display his ability as an amateur artist by doing a drawing of the field "with lots of little umbrellas coming through," like dragon's teeth.

Sometimes he would insist on carrying the handbag which, womanlike, she had always with her. He would then mischievously complain of its weight and hide it behind his back when, misunderstanding his teasing, she would try to snatch it away. These tantalizing experiences resulted in a revival of Annie's poetic impulse, dormant since its application to theistic and philosophical themes a decade or two before; and she composed a number of somewhat fervent poems to him, which, perhaps fortunately, have not survived. One morning toward the end of July she telegraphed him to come over to see her, but when he arrived he found she had no business of any real importance. It was, he said, "Sentimental nonsense only."

Becoming panicky over this entanglement, Shaw now tried to make his meetings with Mrs. Besant "almost entirely in public." Jennie Patterson, nevertheless, had got on the scent. Once, coming away from a Fabian meeting with both ladies, he left Mrs. Patterson in Piccadilly, expecting her to go home, while he escorted Mrs. Besant to a bus stop. Looking back, he found that "J. P." had been following them. So he had to take his jealous mistress to her door, but he did not go in.

The conclusion of such an association was more or less predictable, though Shaw's account of it to Hesketh Pearson (the only one extant, except for the diary, inasmuch as Mrs. Besant was utterly silent on the theme) is somewhat open to question, since it is so much at variance with her character and general attitude toward such relationships. It may be, however, that she was still clinging to her hopes toward G. B. S. when she dropped a telltale remark into the middle of a discussion of the economic position of woman in the *Reformer* for August, 1887: "The closest of human ties may be the noblest or the basest of relationships; fully and graciously given, it crowns friendship with its last perfection. Life has nothing fairer for its favorites than friendship kissed into the passion of love." Is there an echo here of certain similar sentiments expressed in the same periodical soon after she had met Edward Aveling?

It is possible that, told through the romantic haze of elderly recollection, Shaw colored his side of the story. Nevertheless, as he reminisced to Pearson many years later, the legalistic Mrs. Besant finally drew up a formal contract in which she set down the terms on which the two of them were to live together as man and wife, perhaps à la Aveling and Eleanor Marx, and presented it for his signature. "Good God!" Shaw reported himself as exclaiming after reading the document. "This is worse than all the vows of all the churches on earth. I had rather be legally married to you ten times over." But Mrs. Besant already had a legal husband and would settle for nothing less than her contract. Shaw would not listen but only laughed. In despair she demanded her letters back. He collected what he could find and at an interview just before Christmas returned them to her. (Shaw's diary, however, records that he dropped them off at Avenue Road during a walk with Sidney Webb, but that Mrs. Besant was out.) At any rate, she thereafter "produced a casket in which she kept all his letters, and, convulsed with suppressed tears, handed them to him. 'What! You won't even keep my letters!' he said. 'I don't want them.'"

But he took them and, according to his diary, carelessly left them on his table. "Reading over her letters before destroying them," he recorded, "rather disgusted me with the trifling of the last 2 years with women." Once while he was absent from his workroom, Jennie Patterson entered, found the letters there, and took some of them away. Early Christmas morning, he was wakened by Jennie's knocking at his door. She had come to upbraid him about the letters. After another scene, he succeeded in getting them away from her and put them into the fire along with the rest.

Thus posterity was deprived of another romantic Shavian episode to take its place alongside the stories of Alice Lockett, Ellen Terry, Florence Farr, and Stella Campbell, who avariciously preserved the letters which their capricious cavalier wrote them. One can only speculate on the line he took with Annie Besant and the line she took with him. Nevertheless, when Pearson boldly inquired whether she had ever attracted Shaw physcially, the other informed him brutally, "She had absolutely no sex appeal. . . . Did I ever tell you that she is Raina in *Arms and the Man?*" (At another stage and in some respects she was also Mrs. Clandon, the twentieth-century woman before the twentieth century, in *You Never Can Tell.*)

These somewhat unchivalrous confessions present quite a different picture of the intimate relations between G.B.S. and A.B. than he allowed the world to see during her lifetime. In his public tribute to her in 1924 he began:

... my personal feeling towards Mrs. Besant remains as cordial after a long period of years during which I have hardly seen her half a dozen times as it was when her association with the Fabian Society brought me into daily intercourse with her. . . . I attracted and amused Mrs. Besant for a time; and I conceived an affection for her in which I have never wavered; but in the end the apparently heartless levity with which I spoke, and acted in matters which were deeply serious . . . must have made it very hard for her to work with me at times.

Looking back kindly on those old days, he analyzed their association with some self-deprecation:

The chief fault of her extraordinary qualities was that she was fiercely proud. I tried, by means of elaborate little comedies, to disgust her with beneficence and to make her laugh at her pride; but the treatment was not . . . very successful. I would complain loudly that I wanted something I could not afford. She would give it to me. I would pretend that my pride was deeply wounded, and ask her how she dared insult me. In a transport of generous indignation she would throw her present away, or destroy it. I would then come and ask for it, bare-facedly denying that I had ever repudiated it, and exhibiting myself as a monster of frivolous ingratitude and callousness. But though I succeeded sometimes in making her laugh at me, I never succeeded in making her laugh at herself, or check her inveterate largesse. I ought to have done much more for her, and she much less for me, than we did.

In fact, he ended, paraphrasing the old saying, his feeling toward her could be summed up in " 'Love me lightly, love me long!' And that is how I loved and still love Annie Besant."

But Annie, Pearson reported later, could not take the affair so lightly. Through her lecturing, journalistic work, and campaigning she had become stouter and coarser every year, but her hair now suddenly turned gray. She even thought of suicide. "But nothing private could hold her down for long. The Trafalgar Square business coming just then took her quite out of her private self."

The sardonic Shaw, like Frank Besant, "Mr. D——," Charles Voysey, Moncure Conway, Edward Aveling, and even Charles Bradlaugh, began to fade into the background as her restless character found a new outlet.

2

Bloody Sunday
in Trafalgar Square

In the mid-eighties England was building up to one of her worst economic depressions. At the annual conference of the N.S.S., held at Glasgow in June, 1886, Bradlaugh admitted unhappily that the "continued dullness of trade" had decimated the usual acquisition of new members, though the organization was still in the black. The Hall of Science classes (perhaps influenced by the defection of Aveling) were neither as large nor as self-supporting as could be wished, and sometimes Bradlaugh and Mrs. Besant, who was still teaching three courses, had to make up the deficit out of their personal pocketbooks; but the quality of achievement, as shown by the examinations, remained as high as ever.

The situation, however, penetrated much deeper than merely to the fortunes of the Secularists. Labor conditions were deplorable. Unemployment stared gauntly from every side. Mills and factories were shutting up. Wages, for those who were lucky enough to have jobs, were sliding down. These conditions gave all the little radical and reform groups, which had never had the responsibility of controlling legislation in Parliament, the chance to exploit their panaceas. Kropotkin and the gentle-spoken Mrs. Wilson with their Anarchism; Stepniak and Madame Novikoff with their Nihilism and Terrorism; Engels with his Communism; Morris and Aveling with their Socialist League; Hyndman with his Social Democratic Federation; Webb, Shaw, Besant & Co. with their Fabianism; Headlam and Shuttleworth with their Christian Socialism; Henry George (who had by then been rejected by most Socialists in England, though in his unsuccessful campaign for mayor of New York he was regarded as a Socialist by most Americans) with his Single Tax; Arch with his agricultural reform; Frederic Harrison and Professor Beesly with their Comtist Positivism; Bradlaugh and the aristocratic renegade Auberon Herbert with their Individualism; Foote with his Freethought; even Dunglas Home with his Spiritualism, and Olcott and Blavatsky with their Theosophy—all believed that, if the world would listen, they could lead it to the New Jerusalem.

In the meantime, the jobless slouched listlessly through the streets, crouched over tiny fires in their damp homes, or thronged to mass meetings in Hyde Park and Trafalgar Square to hear inflammatory speeches by the revolutionaries. From the beginning of 1886 these meetings began to multiply in number and attendance. The Social Democrats were the most vociferous, to the fury of the Tory press, and *Justice* duly recorded their feats. In February, Hyndman, Burns, the former military officer H. H. Champion, and a minor member named John Williams received summonses to appear at the Bow Street police court for disturbing the peace. The Socialist League, unwilling to be left out, promptly passed a strong resolution of sympathy, and Morris and the versatile littérateur E. Belfort Bax appeared to offer bail. A few months later Mrs. Besant herself, after twitting *Justice* in the *Reformer* for its difficulty in raising a defense fund, organized a Socialist Defence Association composed of well-to-do men and women who promised to obey a telegraphic summons, day or night, to bail out (as she put it in her *Autobiography*) "any prisoner arrested for exercising the ancient right of walking in procession and speaking." This was the first of the many groups she was to form which were sworn to accept her sole word as their guide to action. By the middle of April the rebels were able to celebrate the acquittal of the four defendants for sedition, though the jury condemned the "inflammatory language" of Champion and Burns and, contrary to the judge, expressed the opinion that the proceedings had been rightly instituted. The rebels immediately organized more open-air mass meetings. Herbert Burrows was ubiquitous and indefatigable. In August, Williams and Mainwaring, a hopeful Socialist League martyr, were brought to trial for speaking without permission at the corner of Bell Street, and the sentencing of Williams precipitated another huge public demonstration in Trafalgar Square.

Naturally, in this same revolutionary vein, it was not only the official Anarchists who were aroused by the Haymarket Riot in Chicago and the trial and sentence of the accused. Like most of the Socialists, Mrs. Besant continued to utter protests against their conviction on what seemed to be insufficient evidence and to speak at various London protest meetings against their execution.

The Avelings, on the invitation of the Socialistic Labor party, actually went to America on a lecture tour in August, which in spite of its brevity enabled him later to write a book, *The Working Class Movement in*

America, and to utter an immediate denunciation of anarchy there. This provoked Henry Seymour, editor of the *Anarchist,* "A Revolutionary Review" which soon announced its paradoxical policy of accepting communism as well as anarchism, to vituperate the pair as "Lying lickspittles!" and to call attention to the fact that not only had the man been publicly repudiated by the Social Democratic Federation, though still claiming to belong to it, but he had been "kicked out" of every society he joined, "and in one case, for rather disreputable reasons which had to be hushed up. . . ." *Justice* soon entered the fray by summarizing a battle of circulars which had taken place between different Socialist factions in America. It also printed Aveling's letter in which he categorically denied that he had indulged in high-living and unjustified expense accounts; that he had recommended that members of the Socialistic Labor party, his sponsor, join the Knights of Labor instead; and that he had called all those who disagreed with him "God-damned fools." Though the *Commonweal* quickly leaped to the defense of its emissary, *Justice* politely suggested to "the Socialist League, of which Dr. Aveling is an original member, and to Mr. Frederick Engels, his close friend," that more than a mere personal denial was desirable against charges which impugned not only his own character but also the good name of all English Socialists. A few weeks later Aveling resigned from the editorial board of the *Commonweal,* because, he said, he was overworked.[1]

Annie might well look with silent sympathy at "Mrs." Eleanor Marx-Aveling when she met her in the basement rooms of the picturesque and bohemian Democratic Club in Chancery Lane, where both ladies were members along with May Morris, daughter of the poet-Socialist; John Burns, Tom Mann, and Ben Tillett, soon to become notorious labor leaders; and various journalists, artists, and unattached ladies who were getting a foothold in their professions.[2] On the Avelings' return from America, they had moved into a block of cheap flats at the north end of the Lane, where they lived a hand-to-mouth existence doing literary hack work. Eleanor, in fact, candidly wrote to Havelock Ellis saying, "I need work much, and find it very difficult to get. 'Respectable' people won't employ me. . . ."

In fact, it was the intimacy of Engels with Eleanor and her common-law husband which kept almost all callers except Belfort Bax away from

[1] For this episode, see *Justice,* October 12, November 13, 1886, April 30, May 14, May 21, 1887; *Anarchist,* September, November, 1886; *Commonweal,* September 4, 1886, January 29, May 1, 1887; *John Swinton's Paper,* September, 1886. H. R. Fox Bourne also cast further insinuations against Aveling's "antecedents and present occupations" in *Commonweal* for June 5, 1886.

[2] Joseph Burgess, *John Burns: The Rise and Progress of a Right Honourable* (Glasgow, 1911), p. 34. See also Felix Barker, in *New Yorker,* November 27, 1954, pp. 178–79.

Engels' home on Regent's Park Road—some of the women writing him flatly that they would not come while the Avelings came but refusing to give reasons for their abhorrence. It was clear, however, that it was Aveling and something in his past rather than Eleanor and hers that kept them away. The mystery was to deepen and even after its tragic climax was never to be fully resolved. Certainly Mrs. Besant never darkened the doors of Engels' home, though she was the Fabian for whom he had the greatest respect, because of her influential pamphlets. Though closest to Morris and his Socialist League, Engels never backed any of the English Socialist groups because he felt that in none of them could be found the basis of a real proletarian movement.[3]

As one of the chief Radical leaders, much was expected of Bradlaugh in the cause of the workers, who had supported him so faithfully in the north. In January, 1886, the Tory and Cabinet opposition to his officially taking his seat could no longer hold out against the general clamor. After six years, Mrs. Besant exulted in "Daybreak," the long struggle was over. Bradlaugh went to the table in Commons, was formally presented to Speaker Peel, who spoke some welcoming words "in defence of law and right," and received congratulations from his supporters. At a special "soirée" at the Hall of Science, Mrs. Besant presented him with a trout rod, suitably inscribed, as a memento of his triumph. A few months later, at a general election, he held his seat with a greater majority than ever and even somewhat cut down the lead which his colleague Labouchère still maintained over him. Mrs. Besant attributed the defeat of the Gladstone government in part to its refusal to take an unequivocal stand behind Bradlaugh.

In his usual aggressive fashion, he pitched in on his new program. He moved in committee for the extending of Parliamentary suffrage to all women, including married ones. He renewed his battle against perpetual pensions. He pressed his fight on the constitutional rights issue and thanked those friends who had raised several hundred pounds to help him with it. He appealed to all Secularists and other believers in freedom of speech and thought to push harder for the Affirmation Bill and the repeal of the Blasphemy Laws, which were soon coming up. Within a year, to his pleased surprise, Lord Randolph ("Randy Pandy") Churchill, the bantam chancellor of the exchequer whom he had regarded as his particular enemy, came out in support of his modified Affirmation Bill; it eventually passed and established another milestone in Parliamentary history, even though the irreconcilable Foote called it a "miserable abortion." When Bradlaugh began his fifty-fourth year, in October, 1886, he was able to write that at last, on the completion of his suit in the House

[3] Eduard Bernstein, *My Years of Exile*, pp. 200–201; Gustav Mayer, *Friedrich Engels*, p. 251.

of Lords, he was free of "the worry and harassing strain of litigation," though he was still weighted down with debts. He ended the year with an article in *Our Corner* entitled "Who Shall Be the Radical Leader?"

Yet success and middle age both have their penalties, as Bradlaugh was soon to find. Both are likely to mellow the more extreme views of one's youth. All parties were keeping sharp eyes on his every speech and action, and the progressive press had especially keen-eyed reporters on the watch. *Justice* started the carping as soon as it became public knowledge that he would be seated. A month or so after his seating it turned its guns on " 'the huge self-idolator,' as Marx called him," and it announced that all the workers were already jeering at him. It especially wondered why, though he was trying to save himself in Parliament by maintaining that socialism had no roots, all his ablest supporters had turned Socialist. By May, Bradlaugh himself was forced to take notice in the *Reformer* of the "hopelessly inaccurate" and "pettishly spiteful" attacks which Herbert Burrows had been making on him and his views on Land Law Reform, and he refused to print Burrows' reply. Bradlaugh's shifting views on landownership and private property continued to preoccupy *Justice,* which took pleasure in reminding him that he had once been in favor of land nationalization. Even Mrs. Besant, when Bradlaugh brought a motion on the subject into Parliament in July, found it necessary to defend her friend's position in an article on "The Rights of Private Property in Land" in "Daybreak."

The chorus of denunciation for treachery grew more and more angry all through 1887. "The workers," yelled *Justice,* "never really supported this overrated bully, but they now hiss and hoot him publicly as a cowardly office-seeker and a traitor to the cause of the people." The *Commonweal* referred to Bradlaugh's "canonization" by the Tory Earl Wemyss, which resulted in the old Radical's being classified by the *Daily News* among "thoroughly sound and modern politicians." Earlier, another reporter had stated:

Mr. Bradlaugh is getting more popular than ever, and . . . what he loses in the opinion of the working-class he gains ten times over in that of the middle-class. . . . I don't wish to say that Mr. Bradlaugh is consciously going against the people, but that his fierce and enthusiastic defence of the propertied class . . . is rapidly getting him the reputation of a respectable Whig.

Even Foote, the echoes of his vows of gratitude and loyalty in the blasphemy case having hardly died away, began in the *Freethinker* to voice his increasing distrust. His friend, he charged, was not taking his old interest in "destructive Freethought." His views on education, the raising of children, property, etc., were all open to serious question.

Mrs. Besant herself could not have been merely amused, as she pretended, when in July she told her readers how the York *Post,* Bradlaugh's ancient enemy, had come out with an article in his praise. She must have felt some suppressed worry when such a source could refer to him as a "kindly, cheerful soul," a "charming companion," with a "roystering, jolly laugh, like some Titanic schoolboy," and praise his "manly beneficence."

But it was the relationship between Annie Besant and Charley Bradlaugh, the tried-and-true old comrades, which really commanded the attention of the press and the public. While speaking in Parliament in March, 1886, Bradlaugh made an unfortunate slip which, though he promptly made a partial apology, may have betrayed what was really in his mind more fully than he was ready to admit. The English Socialists, he asserted, consisted entirely of "a few poets, a few idiots, and some for whom he could not use such kindly words." Naturally, the press immediately tried to fit Mrs. Besant into one of these categories. *Justice*, under the headline "Iconoclast Assaulting His Partner," decided that since she was obviously neither a poet nor an idiot she must fall into the third group and inquired hopefully, "How long will the partnership last?" The *Anarchist* quoted *Justice*. Burrows, lecturing at Hackney and Shoreditch, quickly improved on the situation by lecturing on "Bradlaugh and the Socialists; or Poets, Idiots, Traitors, and Madmen." He tried to show by Bradlaugh's votes that he had proved himself to be a traitor to the people and also "by his designation of his more sincere co-worker, Mrs. Besant, as a traitor and madwoman, to be unworthy the esteem of all honest men." Papers like the Ipswich *Free Press* also took up the cudgels for Mrs. Besant.

Bradlaugh's series of explanations in the *Reformer* that his remarks could not possibly be taken to apply to his good friends such as Headlam, who was really more of a social reformer than a Socialist, or to his "most loyal and devoted co-worker" Mrs. Besant, who had served the cause of the poor ever since the Malthusian affair in 1877, were too mild to throw the baying pack off the scent. Still, in calling attention to Mrs. Besant's articles on socialism in *Our Corner*, he was now ready to admit that there was "a radical difference between that lady and the present writer," but maintained that it was something gained to have these various questions clearly and calmly stated. Their desperate and touching loyalty to each other was demonstrated at Northampton, where in the summer Bradlaugh first spoke against socialism and a few weeks later Mrs. Besant spoke for it with great eloquence, which was unfortunately marred, reported *Justice*, by her "fanatic efforts to save her dear friend and co-worker from the effects of his own foolishness." But when, in an interview with the Tory *Evening News* in November, Bradlaugh again repeated his opinion of all Socialists except Headlam, *Justice* trumpeted:

Now then, fair "partner" of the illustrious Charles Bradlaugh, Annie Besant of the Fabian and other Socialist Societies, how many more of these resounding slaps in the face do you mean to take peacefully? We call it nothing less than brutal assault.

Yet the two continued to chair each other's largely attended lectures at the Hall of Science and other meeting places and to debate the merits and demerits of socialism, Radicalism, and social reform in the pages of the little magazines.

Still the gadflies kept stinging, in spite of Bradlaugh's erysipelas and neuritis; and the irritation increased, till on January 16, 1887, both partners were impelled to issue separate statements in their columns denying the truth of a paragraph going the rounds of the press, such as the Manchester *Evening News,* to the effect that at last they had fully parted company. Said the *News,* in wondering why Mrs. Besant did not engage in an open platform debate with her opponent, "When she does speak there is a notion that she will be very aggressive and that Mr. Bradlaugh will have to take some hard knocks." Cried Mrs. Besant indignantly: "The whole statement is a deliberate falsehood, invented in the hope of giving pain, a hope which has entirely failed of realisation, for Mr. Bradlaugh and myself laughed heartily over its absurdity. A comradeship of thirteen years is not so easily to be broken." This personal note continued to mark their public exchanges; and in March, Bradlaugh appealed to his colleague not to work so hard and predicted, "Persistence by her in her present labors can only end in her entire breakdown." As always, Annie Besant was working too hard, but her hard work indicated that she was also running away from unpleasant things—several things. Bradlaugh was one, Bernard Shaw was another, her relationship to the Social Democrats was a third.

The alert reader of the *National Reformer* for October 23 would have noted immediately that the masthead on the first page had changed. Instead of being "Edited by Charles Bradlaugh and Annie Besant" the paper was now being "Edited by Charles Bradlaugh." Then came a "Personal" by Annie Besant announcing her resignation as coeditor because of the increasing number of complaints being made by subscribers on account of "the divided editorial policy of this paper on the question of Socialism." Tacitly confessing that the rumor she had so indignantly denied earlier in the year had been correct, she revealed that she had offered to resign several months before, but that Bradlaugh, "with characteristic liberality," had persuaded her to stay on to see if matters would not readjust themselves. But instead their differences had only become greater. Taking the entire blame because of her own shift to socialism and stating that over the greater part of their spheres of action they remained substantially agreed and likely to stay so, she announced that she was resuming her former position as contributor only, though of course full legal responsibility for everything appearing in the paper still rested on them both as its publishers. In a brief paragraph, Bradlaugh expressed the deep regret and "real grief" he felt in accepting the break, reiterated his gratitude for Mrs. Besant's long enriching the paper by her "never-ceasing and most useful work," and commended her for her self-sacrifice in resigning.

It was only after Bradlaugh's death that Mrs. Besant in her *Autobiography* asserted that she had actually resigned because she realized that she was looked on as a clog and a burden to his political career by his new Liberal friends. Her use to him in public was over. She ended the episode with "I never loved him better than when I stood aside."

Nevertheless, in *Our Corner* in November began *Love among the Artists*, a novel by George Bernard Shaw, which both Mrs. Besant and Bradlaugh said they hoped would add a few hundred subscribers to the magazine. Unfortunately, Shaw as a novelist did not have a wide appeal to English readers in 1887 and 1888. He had just made his first and only contribution to the *Reformer*, a long, serialized review of the new two-volume translation of Marx's *Capital*, made by Edward D. Aveling and a new collaborator, Samuel Moore, and edited by Frederick Engels. Mrs. Besant, in spite of her own need, continued to pay Shaw quietly out of her other earnings.

Not all of Mrs. Besant's checkered career during the last two years had been concerned with Bradlaugh and Shaw. Foote and Ball were giving her plenty of trouble in her old Freethought circle, and Hyndman, Burrows, Quelch, and the rest of the Social Democrats were pestering her from their side of the political fence. But she still stuck to her Fabian allegiance.

In *Progress* for June, 1886, Foote, in reviewing the publication of her *Autobiographical Sketches* in book form, had called her a "born enthusiast," with too meager an acquaintance with the real world of the poor, but with a great deal of personal charm. Mrs. Besant had indignantly rejoined by reproaching him with using her sex against her and by insisting on her long-continued closeness to the workers because of the necessity of earning her own living. The increasingly ungrateful Foote, in a six-page "Reply," maintained that he had far from a "mean opinion" of his erstwhile champion, as the length and care of his review should show, but that her interest in the common people was still that of a dilettante. Besides, he added, he had never seen her traveling third-class with them, as she claimed, but always first-class. The ostensibly friendly feud between the two built up through a series of minor tiffs until a continued weekly debate between them on the whole question of Socialism vs. Freethought was arranged for the Hall of Science in February, 1887. Morris and Shaw were among those who chaired these meetings, and Bradlaugh walked onto the patform for the final session, to the accompaniment of much cheering. Mrs. Besant admitted that she knew most of her audience was against her, but she could not understand why some people would not let other people change their minds. The *Echo* referred to the whole affair as the "well-known case" of "litigation" between her and Foote.

239

Her defense of socialism against other ism's went on in a well-publicized debate at South Place between herself and Corrie Grant, Q.C., who defended individualism, and in a printed debate between herself and the Rev. G. F. Handel Rowe, who defended Christianity. At an International Freethought Congress in September, at which she occupied the chair during one session and was presented with a basket of flowers, she had, however, to agree with the final resolution, backed by Foote and others, that "Freethought cannot be indifferent to the question of social amelioration, but that it should not be identified with a Socialist or anti-Socialist solution." All this time Foote was also consolidating his position as the rising young leader of the rock-ribbed Freethought party by organizing all the London branches of the N.S.S. into a single federation.

The *Freethinker* acted not only as a recording board for Foote's covert tactics, but as a sounding board for the undisguised contempt of the other rising young Secularist, W. P. Ball, whose "vulgar abuse" Mrs. Besant found it even harder to stomach. Yet, wrote Ramsey the publisher, after gloating over the way a pamphlet by Ball had pulled Mrs. Besant's *Modern Socialism* to pieces "in the most merciless fashion," "may difference of opinion never alter friendship." The more opinions are knocked about, opined Ramsey, the better, so long as persons are spared.

One of Mrs. Besant's causes for which many of the Secularists as well as the leftists could find no excuse was her persistent Malthusianism. When, in May, 1886, she attended and addressed the annual meeting of the Malthusian League on "The Law of Population and Its Relation to Socialism" and gave her blessing to the middle-aged Dr. Charles R. Drysdale, who was still directing the organization,[4] Burrows promptly gave a talk on "The Malthusian Delusion." The *Anarchist* also excoriated her by deriding her theory in *Our Corner* that there is a necessary relationship between socialism and the "neo-Malthusian nonsense of the orthodox political scientists" and by sneering, "We simply laugh to scorn the ridiculous idea that the reconstitution of Society depends upon the poenis."

But though Mrs. Besant maintained her support of the Malthusian League, of which she had been one of the founders, she apparently found that another of her early causes, the National Sunday League, was too minor to command her time, even though it was headed by Shuttleworth and Headlam. Though its organ, the *Free Sunday Advocate*, mentioned Dr. Aveling's "humorous recital" at its Annual Soirée and Ball, Mrs. Besant was never listed as attending any of its meetings.

The Fabian Society was of course the focus of her activities. She brought it up on all occasions. When she went out on the road to propagandize for Freethought, she talked about the Fabians. When she talked about socialism, she urged her audiences to join the Fabians. She started branch groups in such diverse places as Sheffield, Nottingham, Deptford,

[4] *Republican,* June, July, 1886.

and Edinburgh; but, as Shaw admitted with rueful good nature, most of these soon withered away and died, for the provincial cities had little interest in such an esoteric, intellectual group. Always fecund in ideas, she soon conceived the plan of organizing the Fabians into a political party. In January, 1886, she was empowered to form a subcommittee to investigate the matter, and by September, at a meeting at Anderton's Hotel at which representatives of the Social Democratic Federation and the Socialist League were also present, she read a paper on "Socialism and Political Action," culminating in the easy passing of her resolution that "Socialists should organize themselves as a political party." The debate, in which Shaw, Morris, Burns, and many others participated, waxed so hot and noisy that the manager of the hotel told them they could no longer be accommodated there. After trying a chapel in Wardour Street, Sydney Olivier calmly applied to the ultradignified and conservative Willis's Rooms, St. James, which admitted them without quibbling, having inferred from their classical name that they must be some learned society. There were many Fabians who bitterly opposed the conception that the Society should be anything else than a hotbed for the forcing of political ideas; but the main opposition came from the members with anarchistic leanings, like Mrs. Wilson and Morris, who rejected the idea of any political parties or government at all.[5]

To avoid a complete break with the dissidents, Mrs. Besant next proposed the formation of an inner group, which she called a Fabian Parliamentary League, and invited it to her own house, as she often did in similar cases, to discuss it. Seconded by Bland and supported by Shaw, her motion carried with only one dissenting vote. By April, 1887, it had become sufficiently oriented to pass rules and issue a manifesto, which Shaw, according to his diary, helped her to revise. But even though Mrs. Besant continued to be on the Council, nothing much ever came from this group, except the publication of one or two Fabian tracts, which Shaw also recorded having a hand in. Mrs. Wilson and her friends soon faded away.

In the meantime, Mrs. Besant came up with another idea: as a bit of preliminary training for the time when the Fabians would take over the government of Great Britain, why not form a mock Parliament, to be called the Charing Cross Parliament, in which the Fabians could get practice in parliamentary rules and procedures and learn the duties and privileges of Cabinet officers by assuming these offices themselves? This plan was adopted, under the pressure of her enthusiasm, and by July, after the "Tories" had been unable to form a Cabinet and the "Liberals" had failed to get a vote of confidence, the "Socialists" took over the "government." H. H. Champion (who with characteristic flexibility had left the Social Democrats) was prime minister and first lord of the treasury,

[5] Shaw, *Fabian Tract No. 41.*

Annie Besant was home secretary, Shaw was head of the local government board, Webb was chancellor of the exchequer, Bland was secretary of foreign affairs, Headlam was secretary for Ireland, and so on down the line. In her Fabian section of *Our Corner,* Mrs. Besant duly chronicled all the activities of her "Parliament," noting especially the many speeches and motions by herself and Shaw, all of which she summed up in her *Autobiography* by saying:

Some amusement turned up in the form of a Charing Cross Parliament, in which we debated with much vigour the "burning questions" of the day. We organized a compact Socialist party, defeated a Liberal Government, took the reins of office, and—after a Queen's speech in which Her Majesty addressed her loyal Commons with a plainness of speech never before (or after) heard from the throne—we brought in several Bills of a decidedly heroic character. G. Bernard Shaw . . . and I . . . came in for a good deal of criticism in connection with various drastic measures.

William Morris wrote to his daughter May from Kelmscott House, his famous arts and crafts center, that he had dined with Touzeau Parris in September and that Mrs. Besant, Shaw, and Scheu were also present: "The two latter had so fierce a debate on parliamentarism that I could barely get a word in edgewise. As we were all very good tempered it was most amusing." In the famous *Fabian Tract No. 41,* Shaw confessed that his part in this "amateur Parliament" made most of his friends think him madder than ever.

The Fabians also, as Shaw put it, collared the *Star* newspaper "and before the year was out had the assistant editor, Mr. H. W. Massingham, writing as extreme articles as Hyndman had ever written for *Justice.*" They were later caught and run out by the conservative proprietors, but by this time they had encouraged a morning daily, the *Chronicle,* to take up the struggle.

There obviously was considerable fraternization among the members of the various Socialist splinter groups, as well as some shifting from one to another. The Social Democrats, still regarding themselves as the only real champions of the ill-treated and oppressed worker and seeing how valuable an asset Mrs. Besant was to any group who could claim her, continued their sweet-sour tactics—now wooing her with compliments, now spurning her with denunciations. "How long is Mrs. Annie Besant going to run with the hare and hunt with the hounds?" demanded *Justice* in April, 1886, after laughing at her patronizing attitude toward Marx in March. It then went on to assert that though "the worthy lady" was always personally friendly with the Social Democrats, she never lost an opportunity to asperse them as a group. Yet she was not above cribbing from Hyndman's *Historical Basis of Socialism in England* in her own book on *Modern Socialism;* and she knew perfectly well that if it had not been for the work Hyndman, Burrows, and Williams had done in the debating and discussion clubs, no Fabian would be listened to there now. In September, *Justice* regretted that she was unable to attend the dinner it had given for a committee of Parisian workingmen sent to investigate the condition of the English laboring classes and remarked that this was a pity, since she had done plucky and valuable work for the cause. Next, it asked when she was going to apologize to Comrade Tom Mann for the *Reformer's* attack on his pamphlet against Malthusianism. But in her controversy with Foote, *Justice* felt that the cause of socialism was quite safe in that "able lady's" hands: ". . . the change that has taken place in her attitude towards us since the summer of 1884, the careful study which she has manifestly devoted to Socialistic literature as well as the ever-increasing perspicacity and outspokenness of her utterances on the questions of the day are so many reasons for congratulation for the whole Socialist party."

On the other hand, *Justice* joked about the "most dolorous tone of appeal" in the Fabian circular signed by her, Shaw, Webb, and the rest in their desire to found "a great Socialist organization which shall *not* be the Social Democratic Federation." As a matter of truth, it maintained, all other Socialist organizations have been "dead failures." But when Walter Besant, her brother-in-law, temporarily deserted his more literary pursuits to propose a conference on "Women's Labor" in the autumn, it expressed the hope that Mrs. Besant and other women who had studied the economic robbery of women would attend "and speak up for their slave-driven sisters." The *Commonweal* and the *Anarchist* also indulged in the same tactics in the hope of inveigling this prize catch in their direction. But neither of these could have much hope, since the Socialist League was already beginning to move in the direction of anarchism and had recently announced that it would "deprecate all meddling with parliamentary methods of reform" and would endeavor to educate the people for "Revolution and the abolition of artificial restraints on life." Mrs. Besant had been too thoroughly indoctrinated in the Bradlaugh school of political science ever to abandon her faith in parliamentary and constitutional methods of social reform.

The appeals of all these groups were to the "people," the masses, labor, the workers—and the workers were out of work. All through 1886 and 1887, the grievances accumulated against the government, which seemed to be unable to do anything to ameliorate conditions. When the agitators took over, the police made arrests. When the agitators cried "Free speech!" the police, deaf to the ancient English cry, made more arrests. The newspapers wrote editorials—the respectable papers of wide circulation defending the government's actions, the revolutionary papers of small circulation attacking them. Tension mounted so high that when the S.D.F. called for a mass demonstration in Trafalgar Square on November 9, 1886, to ask the workers to picket the annual Lord Mayor's Show, the

243

shopkeepers in the vicinity boarded up their shops, the streets were blockaded, all forms of transportation were suspended, troops and police were massed in the squares, and the whole city was in a virtual state of siege. However, as *Justice* reported, everything was well ordered, though plenty of hisses, boos, and groans were heard and red flags were seen.

Sir Charles Warren, the police commissioner, was the nub of the attack, and the slogan arose, "Defeat Sir Charles Warren!" Edward Carpenter wrote his famous Socialist marching song, "England, Arise!" and the protesters memorized it and sang it as an English "Marseillaise." Mrs. Besant lectured to a crowded, appreciative audience at Battersea on "Slums and the Men Who Made Them." Another tremendous demonstration was slated for November 21. The "capitalist press," wrote *Justice* scathingly, told its readers that the rally was a failure, but it was really the "greatest working-class demonstration ever seen in London," with over a hundred thousand people in and near Trafalgar Square. The Social Democrats were overwhelmed by the avalanche they had started. *Justice* introduced a special section entitled "The Unemployed Agitation."

Novel methods of attracting publicity were devised. A Social Democrat named Edward Morris interrupted a sermon in church by hissing the preacher and was arrested for "brawling." Late in February, 1887, plans were laid for an "Unemployed Church Parade," in which the jobless were to demonstrate outside and inside St. Paul's during a Sunday service. The parade was headed by two bands, which competed successfully with the choir and organ. Mrs. Besant had nothing to do with this unmannerly demonstration, but about this time the Salvation Army put out a tract accusing her of throwing a Bible on the platform during a lecture and stamping on it. The perennial "watch" story was also resuscitated and applied to her as well as to Bradlaugh and others. (The *Freethinker* not long before had explained the tardy opening of a convention by saying that the chairman did not have the advantage of using Bradlaugh's watch.)

In April the scene of one of the rallies was shifted to Hyde Park. Since the subject was free speech, one of Bradlaugh's specialties, he was universally missed; some even denounced him for cowardice, not knowing he was on tour. Again the police caused some disturbances. In August, *Justice* proudly described a Sunday demonstration back in Trafalgar Square which had been organized and controlled entirely by Social Democratic workingmen without any "middle-class" assistance. Not all of the S.D.F.-backed rallies were equally successful, however, and in the same month a correspondent wrote to suggest that they "join the aspiring and aristocratic body of Fabians and direct the movement. . . . Mrs. Besant is willing, she states, to give us £300 a year. . . ." Tom Mann came up with a suggestion that the Socialists take advantage of Edison's new phonograph to "send round the country a varied assortment of Burns, Morris, Burrows, Annie Besant, Fielding, &c., with a life-size photograph of each." At this time the Freethought Publishing Company was offering large-size photographs of Mrs. Besant, "for framing," at ten shillings sixpence, and cabinet size for two shillings.

Justice grew more triumphant and hysterical and doubled its size. It wrote about the "outcasts of Trafalgar Square," and the S.D.F. issued another manifesto. The demonstrations in the Square on Sunday, October 23, were "simply magnificent." A week later, when Burrows and Henry George attempted to speak at another mass meeting and a black flag was unfurled, the police were distinctly hostile; and when a second procession, headed by a red flag and bands, started to march toward the Square, it was charged by the police, and a man named Burrell was arrested. The next day, after a meeting in the rain addressed by Headlam and others as a deputation of the Land Restoration League, Mrs. Besant joined in voicing her views. She wrote a letter to the papers, "The Police and the Public," concerning the right to hold public meetings in Hyde Park without their being charged by mounted and foot police. She and Headlam constituted themselves a committee to raise funds to see that one of those "little people" who had been arrested, a poor unemployed painter named Oldland, would get a fair trial. The trials in the police courts continued.

The government finally decided to close Trafalgar Square, the traditional forum for free speech, to all meetings. A howl of protest went up. As things turned out, it was not unemployment which precipitated the catastrophe after all. When an agitator for Irish independence, William O'Brien, an Irish M.P., was arrested and imprisoned for protesting the government's Irish policy, the Metropolitan Radical Federation resolved to challenge the decree and call a protest meeting in the Square on Sunday, November 13. The home secretary, Henry Matthews, at first backed down and promised that "bona fide political meetings" might be held, but Warren refused to listen. On Saturday the irresolute Matthews issued an order forbidding processions within a designated area, including Trafalgar Square. That evening delegates from the various Radical clubs, the Fabian Society, the Social Democratic Federation, and the Socialist League met together and decided to defy the edict. They would march on the Square the next day as intended.[6]

[6] For the details of this and the ensuing story, see *Autobiography*, pp. 423–28; *Justice*, November 19–December 24, 1887; *National Reformer*, November 20, 1887–January 15, 1888; *Our Corner*, December, 1887, January, 1888; *Freethinker*, December 25, 1887; *Commonweal*, November 12–December 24, 1887; Henderson, *George Bernard Shaw: His Life and Works*, pp. 112–13, and *George Bernard Shaw: Man of the Century*, pp. 233–34; Pearson, *G. B. S.: A Full-Length Portrait*, pp. 62–65; John M. Robertson, "Account of [Bradlaugh's] Parliamentary Struggles, Politics, and Teachings," in Hypatia Bradlaugh Bonner, *Charles Bradlaugh*, II, 382–83; W. T. Stead, "Annie Besant," *Review of Reviews*, pp. 81 ff.; Frederic Whyte, *The Life of W. T. Stead* (New York, 1925), pp. 249–54; William Kent, *John Burns: Labour's Lost Leader* (London, 1950), pp. 30–32; Shaw, *Fabian Tract No. 41*; George Lansbury, *My Life* (London, 1928), p. 88, and in *Centenary Book*, p. 26; Arthur H. Nethercot, "G. B. S. and Annie Besant," *Shaw Bulletin*, September, 1955; and Shaw's diary.

The plan was to have four separate nucleuses of the organizers start from four different points in London and converge on Trafalgar Square. It was expected that they would pick up supporters as they marched along. In one of these groups were Shaw and Annie Besant, who asked him whether they might march together. He strongly objected, on the score of her risking an open conflict with the police, but she insisted. So, after he had warned her that she must look after herself in case of trouble, they trudged on side by side. The expected accretion of adherents did not materialize, but the police carried out their orders anyhow and charged the columns. Shaw cried to Annie, who was marching right behind the banner at the head of the procession with him, "You must keep out of this!" She "immediately vanished and made for the Square." He himself dissolved into the crowd and pretended he was just another curious sightseer. This was the only time in his life that Shaw ever made even an attempt to mount the barricades and take part in an actual physical revolution.

But with Annie it was different. She rushed on to the Square, climbed up on a wagonette, and tried to persuade the driver to pull it across one of the roads to break the charge of the mounted police and to get others to do the same. But the driver was afraid and drove away as fast as he could. So she jumped out and made her way back to the Square. While she had been thus elevated for about ten minutes above the heads of the crowd, she saw the police come up at a hand-gallop, brutally "rolling over the people against whom they charged." By the time she had returned, the Life Guards and the Scots Guards had come up to help the police. So, since she and the rest of the paraders were unarmed, she went home. Later, she learned that the police had made no distinction between the sexes. Mrs. Taylor of the Socialist League had been knocked down, and Mrs. Marx-Aveling of the same militant organization had been struck severely on the arm with a truncheon. A score or two of men were badly bruised and bloodied, and one died later of his injuries.

Contrary to Pearson's statement that Shaw "saw no more" of Annie Besant that day, Shaw's diary records that, after he had got separated from her in the "scrimmage" and at 5:15 had gone home to have some tea, he then went to Avenue Road to "get news" of her. Finding that she had gone to the Hall of Science, he went there to pick her up, since she was to chair his lecture at Farringdon Hall on "Practical Socialism." Whether the demonstration that afternoon had proved socialism practical or not, Shaw did not say. But he drove home with her after the lecture that night.

Also among the demonstrators was W. T. Stead, crusading editor of the *Pall Mall Gazette;* absent was Charles Bradlaugh, who was again charged with cowardice by his enemies, though he was actually out of town fulfilling two lecture engagements he had made months before.

As a matter of fact, he had warned all along that such a thing might happen. George Lansbury, who had not yet been converted from liberalism to socialism, was in the crowd of onlookers, as he had been in the Palace Yard affair, and he always remembered Mrs. Besant's courage and determination on both occasions. *Justice*, in "The Tory Terror in London," congratulated her on her appearance in the Square and on her "advocation of those measures for the relief of the unemployed which we have been pressing forward for the last four years. We shall be curious to see whether Mr. Bradlaugh will be consistent enough to denounce her as he has denounced us." She was, as Shaw acknowledged, the heroine of Trafalgar Square and its aftermath.[7]

The two heroes, as Shaw also acknowledged, were John Burns and Robert Bontine Cunninghame Graham, "who charged, two strong, at the rampart of policemen around the Square and were overpowered and arrested." They were prominent Social Democrats. Burns was just starting the career which made him famous as "The Man with the Red Flag"; he later, because of his conflict with Keir Hardie, a Fabian, deserted his early friends and became an M.P., a Liberal, and a cabinet minister. Graham, the "hidalgesque," as Shaw described him when he used him as a partial model for Sergius in *Arms and the Man*, had just started on his own Parliamentary career.[8] No other two arrests, even if Mrs. Besant had been one of them, could have rallied the rebels to their cause as quickly and solidly as these. Other less conspicuous demonstrators were also jailed. It was really not a very bloody affair, but it offered the rebels a new rallying point and soon became known as "Bloody Sunday in Trafalgar Square." The new cry was "Remember Trafalgar Square and Bloody Sunday." Mrs. Besant claimed a circulation of 100,000 copies of a leaflet she got out with this slogan, called *The Police and the Public*.

Mrs. Besant scarcely slept that night. The next morning saw her rushing about London visiting the prisoners and arranging bail for as many as possible through her Socialist Defence Association. "Here," she recorded magnanimously, "Mrs. Marx-Aveling did eager service." She herself invaded the police courts, browbeat the stunned magistrates, argued with the police, and contradicted the witnesses. An open meeting to decide what to do next was called by the sponsoring societies. Thoroughly roused and knowing no compromise, Mrs. Besant made an impassioned motion to return immediately to the Square and fight to the bitter end for free speech and assembly. No one was willing to back such a measure officially, and her motion was badly beaten. In fact, Shaw noted in his diary

[7] In his account of the affair in Stephen Winsten's *Salt and His Circle*, p. 13, Shaw tells what happened to himself, Salt, Carpenter, Burns, and Graham but never mentions Mrs. Besant. By this time his memory was failing.

[8] Strangely enough, in neither of the biographies of Cunninghame Graham (H. F. West, *Robert Bontine Cunninghame Graham* [Hanover, N.H., 1932], and A. F. Tschiffley, *Don Roberto* [London, 1937]) is Mrs. Besant mentioned.

that he "spoke in opposition" to her. But another disorganized attempt to return was made on the following Sunday, against Bradlaugh's frantic plea, with the expected results. Mrs. Besant heeded Bradlaugh and did not witness the fray. A well-known South London Conservative, Feargus O'Connor, had his nose crushed, his forehead cut open, and was knocked senseless when he tried to take the number of a policeman who seemed unnecessarily zealous. He and several others had to be taken to hospitals. Most notable among these was an innocent bystander named A. Linnell, a non-political "indigent law copyist," who had come out to watch the fun. He died a short time later.

Bradlaugh issued a statement in the *Reformer* condemning the action of the Tory government as completely illegal and promising to bring the whole matter up in Commons when it reconvened. He and Burns got into a public wrangle in the *Reformer* and the *Pall Mall Gazette* over whether or not he had agreed to participate in the demonstration and whether or not he had agreed to lend Burns some law books dealing with the situation before the demonstration occurred. Burns artfully twisted the facts to make Bradlaugh look as bad as possible, but even *Justice* commended the latter for his clear and logical analysis of the legal aspects of the case and his spending two days in the Bow Street police court giving evidence for the defense in the pending case of Burns and Graham. Mrs. Besant, who had invited Mrs. Burns to stay at her house during her husband's imprisonment, sided with Bradlaugh in the affair. He rewarded his colleague with the following tribute in the *Reformer:*

> As I have on most serious matters of principle recently differed very widely from my brave and loyal co-worker, . . . it is the more necessary that I should say how thoroughly I approve, and how grateful I am to her, for her conduct in not only obtaining bail and providing legal assistance for the helpless unfortunates in the hands of the police, but also for her daily personal attendance and wise conduct at the police stations and police courts where she has done so much to abate harsh treatment on the one hand and rash folly on the other.

This was bravely done, he told the world, particularly since it was not woman's work and the weather had been so inclement.

The chief instrument of Mrs. Besant's defense activities was a new organization called the Law and Liberty League, which she formed in co-operation with her new friend William T. Stead and for which she gave him more credit than she took for herself because of the use to which he put the columns of his newspaper in publicizing and advancing the cause. Stead was a canny crusading journalist, sensational and unstable at times, but a man of great energy and many ideas. He used his *Pall Mall Gazette,* inherited from John Morley, for various good causes, but his methods were often those of the yellow journalist. For instance, in 1885, in order to provoke action on a long-pending Criminal Law Amendment Bill prohibiting traffic in young girls for immoral purposes, he had himself purchased a girl from her mother and brought her to a brothel, of course keeping her under careful protection. Then he had shipped her off to the Continent into the hands of one of the lieutenants of General Booth of the Salvation Army, who had been in the plot all along. Both Mrs. Besant and Bradlaugh in the *Reformer* had joined the outcry against such extreme devices, which brought Stead himself three months in prison for acting as a procurer. He had nevertheless stood up for Mrs. Besant in his earlier paper, the *Northern Echo*, during the *Fruits of Philosophy* affair and had attempted vainly to meet her after he came to London, "knowing by a sort of instinct that whenever we did meet we should be good friends." This opportunity, however, came only with Trafalgar Square.[9] He conveniently forgot that during the first years of his editing of the *Gazette*, Mrs. Besant had accused the paper of falling into a slough of "mawkish religious sentimentality" and even imbecility. It was another instance of her changing her mind about a man after she had actually met him.

The Law and Liberty League was formed at a meeting on November 18, with the Liberal M.P. Jacob Bright, brother of John Bright, in the chair and Mrs. Besant herself, William Morris, and other notables in the audience. Speeches by Stead, Headlam, Burns, Hyndman, Foote, and Dr. Pankhurst showed such unanimity among diverse interests that the League was organized without trouble and quickly started operations. It helped to obtain the release of several of the minor prisoners, but suffered a blow in the unexpected collapse of its case against the constables who had presumably been responsible for the injury of Linnell. Mrs. Besant, however, consoled herself and her readers by saying that the open verdict of the jury in the case was as much as could be expected, since the argument still went on over whether he had died as a result of being ridden down by the police or from other causes. But, she demanded, why had his deposition not been taken down while he was still conscious?

Simultaneously she conceived a grandiose scheme for making a martyr out of the unknown Linnell and capitalizing on his death. "London," she informed her readers in "Daybreak," "has not seen in a generation a public funeral given to a poor man killed by violence of the police." She resolved to give London that edifying spectacle. "How We Buried Him," she headlined her story in the *Reformer* on Christmas Day. "Sleepers Awakening," hoped *Justice;* "Funeral of Linnell," announced the *Commonweal* more soberly; the *Freethinker* had no headline, but it had plenty to say.

The hearse bearing the corpse started from Windmill Street. Heading

[9] *National Reformer,* September 6, 1885; Stead, "Annie Besant," *Review of Reviews,* October, 1891, p. 81; Whyte, *The Life of W. T. Stead,* pp. 249–54; G. Rattray Taylor, *Sex in History,* p. 218.

the procession was a small group of wand-bearers, bald and white-haired veterans of the old days when Chartism represented what socialism now stood for. Next came Burns, out on bail; Dr. and Mrs. Richard Pankhurst, the new suffragette leaders; and other notables in advanced causes. Mrs. Besant, Stead, Morris, Burrows, Cunninghame Graham (also out on bail), and the three honorary pallbearers followed. Headlam, to officiate at the final rites, marched before the coffin, which was piled high with flowers over a crimson pall and bore the inscription, "Died from injuries inflicted by the police." "Killed in Trafalgar Square" was the legend on the hearse itself. A band played the "Dead March" portentously. Then came the various sponsoring organizations—the Irish League, for O'Brien, the cause of it all, with its green banner bearing an uncrowned harp; the Socialists with their red flags; and the Radical clubs with their various yellow pennons.

To Hyndman, as the procession started, the whole scene looked rather mean and even grotesque. There were few watchers, partly because Warren's police diverted the marchers to Wellington Street before they reached the Strand. But suddenly people began to emerge from all sides —jamming the street as onlookers or falling in behind the hearse. The *Scottish Leader* estimated the crowd at a hundred thousand, spread out over a distance of a mile and a half. All hats except the "chimney pots" of the rich, wrote Annie, were doffed; and the cry, "Murdered by the police!" rang out as the body went past—"the victim of the Blue Terror." Reeves, the Radical bookseller in Fleet Street, had hung out a red banner, which was cheered. When the office of the *Daily Telegraph* was reached (the "favorite profit-monger's print," jeered Hyndman), a light-haired gentleman and a tall lady in black were seen on the balcony, and the crowd burst into howls and groans—more at the expense of the newspaper, thought Hyndman, than of the couple, who were much embarrassed nevertheless. From St. Paul's to Mile End it was practically a Social Democratic demonstration, he claimed, since many more branches, with their red flags draped in black, came in at that point. At the terminus the crowd good-naturedly cut the traces of a tramcar whose driver had obstinately persisted in moving it along in their way. Hyndman clambered up on its roof and looked out, awed and hopeful of the mob's potential power, over a sea of heads which he now optimistically estimated at two hundred thousand. Headlam then read the funeral service, Morris declaimed a new poem, and several people delivered obituary addresses.

The misanthropic Foote reported that the ceremony was a "grotesque performance," with the rain falling so fast that Headlam had to read—or rather mumble—by the light of wax matches held in a hatbox. To him, Morris' "Death Song: In Memoriam" was a "miserable affair," really dull as death. And Foote wondered how Mrs. Besant, standing among the

Socialists around the grave, felt as she had to listen to the Lord's Prayer and attend to what Stead in his *Gazette* referred to as Stewart Headlam's "religious expression" of the intense feeling of the London demonstration. But Mrs. Besant had created her martyr—a poor sort, after all, thought Foote, for the funeral was not really a mark of respect for him but a protest against political tyranny.

Two weeks later another unknown man died. He was William P. Curner, a poor, unemployed painter but a member of the N.S.S. from Deptford. He really should have been the beneficiary of the great demonstration, since he had actually and incontrovertibly received his mortal injuries on "Bloody Sunday." But he died too late. Mrs. Besant and her friends gave him another public funeral, but it had nothing like the success of that of "poor Linnell."

Several months later, when a correspondent wrote to the *Star* to complain that Linnell's grave was insufficiently marked, Mrs. Besant replied that the Law and Liberty League had more important things to do with its money.[10]

[10] *National Reformer*, January 15, 1888; *Commonweal*, January 14, 1888; *Star*, June 9, 1888.

3

"The Link" and the
Strike of the Match-Girls

Stead and Annie Besant were so encouraged by the triumph of the Law and Liberty League in organizing and directing this momentous record-breaking funeral that they resolved to start a new magazine to be the League's mouthpiece. It was to be called the *Link* because it was to act as a link of communication between the newly forming units of the expanding L.L.L., and it was to have a subtitle, "A Journal for the Servants of Man," based on a phrase from Victor Hugo. It was to be printed and published by Arthur Bonner, who had married Hypatia Bradlaugh some time before.

For a long time, as a result of her turbulent experiences in social reform and the general unrest of the time, Mrs. Besant—as she gushingly put it in her *Autobiography*—had been wondering whether a new humanistic "religion" (and she was not afraid of the word!) based on a "common ground of faith in and love of man" would not be possible. In "The Army of the Commonweal" in *Our Corner* for February, 1888, she related how she had been talking the matter over with two of her Christian friends, the Rev. Stewart D. Headlam and Mr. William T. Stead, who supported her views. In that same month came out the first issue of the *Link*, with its two strangely assorted editors—one of them described herself as "an uncompromising and aggressive atheist," whereas the other "has constantly affirmed that 'to be a Christ' is to him the command of God." To be published weekly for a halfpenny in the interest of no sect or party, theological or political, the paper would work "simply and solely as the helper of the helpless, the friend of the oppressed, and the advocate and champion of the cause of the Disinherited of our race." In other words, its dauntless editors would seek no less than "the Temporal Salvation of the world" and the establishment of a "New Church dedicated to the Service of Man." But the editors had the grace to admit that the complete attainment of this high goal would probably be slow.

In the interim the previously announced work of the Law and Liberty League, especially as it affected the victims of Trafalgar Square, was to be carried on. An Executive Committee, including Mrs. Besant, Stead, Headlam, Burrows, Morris (who wrote proudly that he had "little life now outside the movement—which is as it should be"),[1] and others, was chosen. There was also a general council, including Mrs. Besant, Headlam, Burns, Mrs. Josephine Butler (another feminist leader), Cunninghame Graham, Jacob Bright, and several other progressive M.P.'s and notables. But when Annie approached her cooling friend Shaw with an invitation to join, he laughed and reminded her that he was rather "just the person to call the *righteous* to repentance."[2] But, as shown in his diary, he did contribute one article, on an "Eight Hours Bill," to her magazine. In August, when calling at Mrs. Besant's, he found Geraldine Spooner, in whom he had been somewhat romantically interested, addressing copies of the magazine for the mails.

Always inventive, the editors of the *Link* created several special departments with catchy names: "The Lion's Mouth," into which, as in the Doge's Palace in Venice for the information of the Council of Ten, complaints and suggestions could be dropped—anonymously; "The Watchman," who would keep a sharp lookout from his tower; "The War-Chest," for financial contributions to keep the battle going; "The People's Pillory," which undertook to place offenders in business, industry, and government in the stocks for public scorn; and even an "Honour Roll," where would be displayed the names and actions of those benefactors of humankind who deserved public gratitude. Unfortunately, it was the "Pillory" which flourished and the "Honour Roll" which languished. Shortly there also appeared a new section, with a mandatory tone in its very title: "To Be Done. By Order of the Executive. Law and Liberty League."

The core of the philosophy of the League lay in this last section, combined with "The Pillory" and "The Lion's Mouth." They looked innocent at first, but sharp-sighted critics like Bradlaugh and Hyndman quickly saw their potential dangers of totalitarianism and dictatorship, of subornation, and of misuse by anonymous and unproved accusation. But Mrs. Besant was always so convinced that she was right that she felt she could do no wrong along the way. The philosophy, moreover, was to be instrumentalized through the organization itself. The total membership of the League was to be divided into "Centers" and "Circles." A

---

[1] R. Page Arnot, *Unpublished Letters of William Morris* (Labor Monthly Pamphlet, 1951 Series, No. 6), p. 12.

[2] Stephen Winsten, *Jesting Apostle*, p. 71.

complete Center was to consist of 240 persons, divided into 20 groups of 12 each, called "Vigilance Circles," in communication with the "Local Center." Heading each group was to be a "Captain," who would keep the names and records, collect money, and give orders. The Vigilance Circles were soon renamed, more dramatically, "Ironside Circles." Each Circle had a name and a number, as well as four "Duties." Each member was pledged to watch for and report to the proper hierarchy cases of police violence, industrial exploitation, bribery in elections, persecution of the poor, extortion, etc. There were also twelve general "Objects" and a Constitution of twelve "Planks."

Fascistically, the Executive promptly ordered that a circle be started in every Parliamentary borough and division. By the end of March there were eighteen Local Centers of Circles in or near London; early in June there were twenty-two. But the organization never grew much beyond the London radius, though the original announced intention was to extend it all over the land, "from John O'Groats to Land's End." Forty-six organizations sent delegations to the first general meeting of the re-organized League, but many of them, notably the Metropolitan Radical Federation and the N.S.S., seeing which way the wind was blowing, soon dropped out. Hyndman criticized the lack of democratic procedure, but otherwise approved. The Fabians appointed Mrs. Besant and Bland as their delegates.

At a meeting of the Executive of the N.S.S. in January, Mrs. Besant had pushed over a motion that the organization temporarily affiliate with her new "baby." But after Bradlaugh had had time to study its principles, he called a special session of his committee to consider some of the objectionable features, especially of the Ironside Circles, a name which in itself he considered most inappropriate and ominous. Consequently, the affiliation was temporarily rescinded; but to allay the expected hurt feelings of Mrs. Besant, who was not present, a resolution was also adopted assuring her of their "deep feeling of respect and personal regard." Not only were Mrs. Besant's feelings hurt, but she was moved to such anger that, as she wrote in the *Reformer*, she seriously considered resigning her vice-presidency. She desisted, however, because of Bradlaugh's mediation and her hesitation to split the movement any further (Foote's London Secularist Federation, with himself as president, was growing stronger every month). Bradlaugh, while refusing to budge from his disapproval, then apologetically explained his fears that the activities of the Ironsides might lead to attempts at boycotting offenders, which was illegal because it involved conspiracy, or to blackmail, or even to "the possibilities of gross immorality." Summing up his attitude, he repeated that he objected to asking people to pledge in advance that, on the orders of a leader, they would carry out undefined directives against persons as yet unnamed. He also voiced a doubt of the ability of the *Link* "to defend the general interests of the poor . . . from John O'Groats to Land's End." Mrs. Besant missed her next lecture because of illness.

She and Stead, her new coeditor, were, however, getting along beautifully. He was two years her junior, although his nervous, boyish, impulsive manner and his light blue eyes and reddish beard made him look still younger. During the first four months of their editorial intimacy in 1888, she wrote him a whole flood of notes—sometimes two in a day—on her little square sheets of note paper, with a big "ANNIE" in gold letters in the upper left-hand corner, which gave them "a jolly school-girlish look, quaintly incongruous with the desperate earnestness of *The Link*." Addressing him playfully or informally as "My dear Head Centre" or "My dear Sir Galahad" or simply "My dear friend," she ended her remarks on editorial matters and policies, atheism and religion, associates and friends, or personal affairs, with phrases like "*Addio*, A. B." or "Yours always, dear friend, St. George." When, in April, Stead decided to go off to Russia to interview the tsar (he shook hands with him like a democratic Englishman), she wrote him of the blank that would be left in her life and the calming effect his presence always had on her. "I suppose it is because you are so good," she explained, "that your presence is like the 'Peace, be still' of the Christ, and there is 'a great calm.' "[3] Yet, strangely enough, neither of their lives was ever calm for long.

There were so many things that needed cleaning up. There were, for instance, the Burns-Graham trial and the O'Brien imprisonment. The new "Radical journal," the *Star*—edited by Massingham, owned by T. P. ("Tay Pay") O'Connor, and taken over surreptitiously for a time by Shaw and the Fabians—joined the smaller sectarian papers to give full coverage to these events and, with its gossipy, personal style and its record-breaking evening circulation, helped keep London fully aware of developments. It told how Louise Michel had been shot at and seriously, though not mortally, wounded at an Anarchist meeting in Havre. It made fun of Sir Charles Warren and his "Latest Captures." It told of the entrance of the Law and Liberty League onto the scene and joined with the *Pall Mall Gazette* in printing pleas for its support. It described in great detail the trial of Burns and Graham in January and railed against their sentence of six weeks in jail in spite of the best efforts of Bradlaugh and other legal talent, both in the courtroom and on the floor of Parliament. When the two were convicted of unlawful assembly in the middle of January, Bradlaugh wrote in the *Reformer* that he feared the sentence was due in part to "the foolishly boastful evidence" of Hyndman and others. He had already indicated that he felt Mrs. Besant's indignation against real injuries at times led her to immoderate general denunciations.

As soon as it was announced that the terms of Burns and Graham had

[3] Frederic Whyte, *The Life of W. T. Stead*, pp. 250–54.

been reduced and that they would be released on February 18, Mrs. Besant and the L.L.L. planned a great mass meeting of welcome for them, O'Brien, and the others who had gone to jail over Trafalgar Square. The vast hall of Allen's Riding School in Seymour Place was engaged in anticipation of a tremendous turnout; but first, two days earlier, a smaller tea for the inner circle was given at Craven Chapel, Regent Street. This was mobbed, and it degenerated into what *Justice* called a "veritable tea fight," with, according to the *Link*, May Morris, Eleanor Marx-Aveling, and other ladies pouring, Annie "shovelling out plates of cake into outstretched hands," and Stead "grabbing" at the plates as they passed by. Of course, speeches were made. The jam here, however, was nothing to that in the Riding School, where the hall overflowed with nearly five thousand Irish, Radical, and Socialist sympathizers. The *Star* reporter, who wrote up both affairs with plenty of colloquial dialogue, saw Mrs. Besant rushing about with her hat off, but slighted her and the L.L.L. so that she wrote to protest that even the *Times* and the *Daily News* had been less unjust. Nevertheless, both meetings more than paid expenses, and the speeches were inspiring. Michael Davitt, the Irish patriot, was in the chair; Mrs. Besant's "forcible" words were received with "loud and continued cheering"; O'Brien made his first address at a public meeting in England; Stead spoke; and Hyndman uttered some "injudicious" remarks which brought the meeting to an abrupt end before Morris got a chance to deliver the lines he had prepared.[4] The heroes of the occasion, Burns and Graham—the latter was still somewhat weak from his injuries—were almost forgotten in the enthusiasm.

In spite of these satisfying events, however, Mrs. Besant could not forget that Trafalgar Square was still forbidden for public meetings. She had various schemes to express defiance and force its reopening. In the *Link* she serialized a long, detailed account of "The Story of Trafalgar Square, 1887–88," stuffed with names of the injured and imprisoned. She lectured at such places as the Ball's Pond Radical Club and the South Place Chapel on subjects like "Trafalgar Square and the Right of Public Meeting" and "The Service of Man." At a General Council meeting of the League she proposed a plan for what she at first called "guerrilla warfare" by means of small open-air meetings which would harass the police by their mobility. This idea developed into a really novel stratagem, exotically called a *"conversazione,"* and the Square was renamed an Open-Air Town Hall. Every Saturday afternoon for several weeks hundreds of the faithful congregated in the Square, but broke up into constantly moving and shifting small groups so that the police could not accuse them of unlawful assemblage. There were no set speeches, but everyone talked animatedly on the topic which was nearest his heart.

[4] See the newspapers mentioned, and Arnot, *Unpublished Letters of William Morris,* p. 12.

The *Link* described a May meeting in which four or five hundred, including Mrs. Besant, Graham, Headlam, Burrows, C. A. V. Conybeare, M.P., and others participated, and a row of interested spectators lined the northern parapet three deep. Everyone walked about chatting and discussing, and when any group remained too long on one spot, a line of policemen lounged up and gradually, but not roughly, "moved it on."

Although, as the *Star* said, the *Daily Telegraph* poked "feeble fun" at the whole thing, the authorities were learning a lesson. Encouraged by the lack of molestation, at the next *conversazione* the League decided to put three resolutions to each small circle simultaneously. Large numbers attended, but a young Socialist lecturer named Underwood climbed up the plinth of the monument and waved a red flag, whereupon help was called from Scotland Yard, and the police charged the demonstrators and dispersed them. Other minor disturbances continued in the following weeks, even though two judges announced their decision that there was no right of public meeting in the Square because it would interfere with the right of free passage. In one fracas Graham was knocked under a cab, a *Star* reporter took the numbers of the constables involved, and the hawkers of *Justice* made big sales.

Mrs. Besant defied the authorities in another way, too. The government had issued an order against the taking-up of collections of money at public meetings. So, after Annie had spoken in June on Clapham Common at the request of the S.D.F. on "Why Mr. Matthews Meddles," she took up a collection amounting to one pound, nine shillings, and sixpence. She announced she would take more at her next meetings and offered to go to jail for breaking the new bylaw of the Metropolitan Board of Works. A police inspector and the keeper of the Common respectfully wrote down her name and address just as if they did not know them—and no action was ever taken. Annie continued to take up more collections in the parks, till finally the rule was rescinded.

Relatively few of the rebels, however, were as belligerent as she. In the middle of April the Metropolitan Radical Association convened a meeting at the offices of the Irish National League to decide what to do next in the Trafalgar Square impasse. The *Star*, whose news pages and correspondence columns had for weeks devoted more space to this question than to any other, headlined its long account of the affair: "To the Square! To the Square! But Radicals Are Divided. Down on the Liberal Members." When one Aeneas Smith of the Radical Federation had proposed mildly that the Square merely "be made a test case at the next election," Mrs. Besant had risen so indignantly and spoken with such fervour that Smith's motion lost by 92–37. Maintaining that bolder measures must be taken, she moved to organize a new public meeting in the Square. Stead supported her, but Foote, who was now to be found in opposition wherever Mrs. Besant or Bradlaugh was concerned—at the annual N.S.S. convention he had vainly demanded reorganization because Bradlaugh was devoting too much time to Parliament and Mrs. Besant too much to socialism—moved an amendment against such a proposal, to the effect that such a meeting be held only if the Liberal members of Commons from the Metropolitan district agreed to attend and speak. Everyone knew that such a miracle was impossible to expect. But Bernard Shaw, apparently with no qualms of disloyalty, seconded Foote's amendment; and when the division was counted, it was found that Mrs. Besant "was in a minority of one, deserted even by her seconder."[5] *Justice* and the *Star* in their somewhat distorted stories made Mrs. Besant out to be the real heroine and Foote the discomfited villain, but future events proved him to have won the fray. The public meeting was not held, since the Liberal members refused the invitation. Mrs. Besant, however, went down fighting, for after a lecture to the Marylebone Workmen's Club in June on "Remedies for Poverty," she took the names of an unannounced number of volunteers to join her in going to prison for speaking in Trafalgar Square.

There was considerable surprise in advanced circles, therefore, when in November she refused to participate in a meeting which was organized to commemorate simultaneously the anniversaries of "Bloody Sunday" and the execution of the Chicago Anarchists. In the spring she had been scheduled along with Burns, Morris, Eleanor Marx-Aveling, Charlotte Wilson, and Prince Kropotkin to speak at an anniversary celebration of the Paris Commune, organized by the various Socialist societies but especially by the *Commonweal;* but when the papers came out with their accounts of the meeting, her name was not mentioned. Now, when her name was again included, she openly withdrew it. It had been used without her permission, she wrote the *Star:* "I will never commemorate Trafalgar Square until I commemorate it in Trafalgar Square, and I have no sympathy with loud talk about our liberties which is not translated into action." She thought it bad strategy, moveover, to play further into the hands of Warren, who was already in bad odor with his superiors. She was also completely out of sympathy, as she wrote in a long manifesto in the *Link*, with the attempt to bring the "Chicago Massacres" and "Bloody Sunday" together by those who, like the Anarchists and the Socialist League, advocated the use of dynamite in social reform; and she condemned the "mad talk" in which Mrs. Parsons, widow of one of the Chicago Anarchists, had recently been indulging in London. Mrs. Parsons, the Anarchists, and the Socialist League promptly reciprocated by condemning Mrs. Besant, but the *Star* and *Justice* staunchly came out in her support. The meeting, with or without Mrs. Besant, did not succeed in reopening the Square, but shortly afterward Sir Charles Warren resigned.

[5] Pearson, *G. B. S.: A Full-Length Portrait,* pp. 64–65; *Star,* April 19, 20, 23, 30, June 12, 1888; *Justice,* April 28, 1888.

Annie's refusal did not betoken any lessening of her interest in the cause of the downtrodden, for on Christmas Eve she was one of the speakers at a midnight "monster meeting" of the unemployed held on the Thames Embankment. In spite of the early rain, the cold, and the mud, and against the eerie background of yellow torches, red flags, and Cleopatra's Needle, *Justice* estimated that several thousand persons turned out to hear the first-class speakers and start the New Year with undiminished spirit and determination. But when several hundred hard-core enthusiasts marched singing toward the Victoria Station afterward, the mounted police dispersed them.

One of the causes for labor's hope was the growing strength of the unionization movement, to which Annie Besant and the *Link* had largely contributed. To the reformers, a prime instance of capitalist exploitation of the working classes for private profit was the Bryant and May string of match factories, which employed hundreds of girls. Working conditions at Bryant and May's were notorious; and as early as October, 1885, the *Reformer* had noted that the girls had gone out on strike because of the lowering of wages and the undermining of their health, particularly the loss of their teeth, through the constant inhaling of chemicals. Without the backing of the British Trades Union, which had confined its activities to the organizing of male labor, the strike had failed; and the company had felt safe in going along its old road.

Wherever they went, a favorite subject of Herbert Burrows and H. H. Champion in 1888 had been the intolerable treatment of the unskilled woman workers in London. One day in June, Champion suggested that Bryant and May be posted in the "Lion's Mouth," which had been pretty full ever since, in the second issue, it had roared about the cases of the free porters and of some costermongers from Battersea. Mrs. Besant therefore journeyed to Bromley, where she quietly talked to three unsuspecting girls, whose harrowing experiences and complaints she described in detail in a sensational article entitled "White Slavery in London." A few days later, under big black front-page headlines, she appealed to the shareholders of the company, pretending to assume that they were ignorant of what was being done to earn their dividends. In her most eloquent sentimental style, and perhaps with her daughter Mabel in mind, she cried:

Do you know that girls are used to carry boxes on their heads until the hair is rubbed off and the young heads are bald at fifteen years of age? Country clergymen with shares in Bryant and May's, draw down on your knee your fifteen year old daughter; pass your hand tenderly over the silky, clustering curls, rejoice in the dainty beauty of the thick, shiny tresses. . . .

Mabel was then about eighteen, and there is no way of knowing whether the Rev. Frank Besant held any Bryant and May stock, but the implication is suspicious. Of course, at this time Mrs. Besant did not know that women in India carry heavy burdens on their heads from childhood without rubbing any bald spots in their hair. Still, it was effective journalism, as the more open-minded London papers, especially the *Star,* promptly recognized. Best of all, it was a thoroughly sound and justifiable exposé.

While the iron was hot, Mrs. Besant returned to the factory, taking Herbert Burrows and John Williams with her. They distributed copies of the *Link* article and also some roses Mrs. Besant had brought. At the gift, one girl "literally danced for joy," for life had brought her not roses but thorns, as Annie freshly put it. The news spread, and the girls flocked around her during their lunch hour; but the foremen were angry, and the girls feared "the sack." In fact, Mrs. Besant had to undertake the temporary support of the original guilty three, who were threatened with discharge unless they would sign a paper saying they were satisfied with conditions. The *Pall Mall Gazette,* the *Star,* the *Echo,* and the *East London Observer,* as well as the *National Reformer, Justice,* and the *Commonweal,* took up the hue and cry. Bryant threatened legal action for libel, which Annie said she awaited "placidly."

A protest meeting of employees was called on Mile End Waste; and the avid, excited girls, no longer listless and dull-eyed, drank in exhilarating speeches by Annie Besant, Burrows, Burns, Graham, and Conybeare. Deputations were appointed. Follow-up meetings were held. The company threatened to import new girls from Glasgow or to move its factory to Norway or Sweden. The matchmakers voted to go out on strike, and stopped work. Fifty of the more daring were entertained at tea in the Fleet Street office by Mrs. Besant and Burrows and then, with Bradlaugh's guidance, marched off to Commons under police escort to interview Graham and Conybeare in a House committee room; both M.P.'s promised their help. Officers of the company made lame explanations, and Mrs. Besant magnanimously granted that perhaps they had not known all that was really going on. She could scarcely go along, however, with Frederick Bryant's ironic query whether they would all want champagne dinners next. The newspapers were full of letters and editorials on both sides, but Mrs. Besant and Burrows were both generally commended for the orderly conduct of the strike. *Justice* at first gave Mrs. Besant full credit for planning and organizing the whole affair, but then tried to steal it away for one of its own "comrades," H. W. Hobart, a member of the London Society of Compositors, who interviewed some of the girls, helped make collections, and collaborated on strategy: "The strike of the match-girls at Bryant and May's, so ably organized by our comrade, H. W. Hobart, and so earnestly and fearlessly supported by his fellow-Socialists, Annie Besant and Herbert Burrows, has done still more to awaken the conscience of the people at large."

To keep the girls fed while they were out of work, the contributions that had been raised through newspaper appeals and private solicitations were distributed publicly. The *Gazette* sent one of its draftsmen to draw a picture of the scene. First, the girls were registered by Burrows and Hobart in the little hall that H. W. Charrington, a sympathizer, had lent for the purpose. Then John Robertson, from the *Reformer* staff, seated the strikers in sections according to the type of match factory they came from. Sydney Olivier and Headlam acted as general assistants. Burrows presided, and Mrs. Besant spoke to the entranced audience. Then the strikers filed up to the platform to receive from her hands their shares of the weekly "take," which were counted out by Graham Wallas and Bernard Shaw, who had entered the fray rather late. There was a temporary disorder when a few boys who were also employed tried to crowd in before the girls, but this discourtesy was soon repressed. Later, Shaw, together with Burrows, Hyndman, Headlam, Burns, etc., spoke from different platforms at a great general Anti-Sweating Demonstration one Sunday. The match-girls were there with banners, and Mrs. Besant dealt in her "usual impressive and eloquent manner . . . with the limitation of child labor. . . ."

The relief funds had to be spread so thin that some five hundred girls decided to go fruit- and hop-picking to supplement their income, but they found that rural conditions and wages were no better than urban. Only two more distributions, however, had to be made. The end came quickly. It did not come because a man named J. A. Elliott wrote a poem, "The Match-Maker's Complaint," for the *Link* or because the *Commonweal* urged a boycott: "Get your matches from Wilson and Palmer!" More important, papers like the *Financial World* recommended that Bryant and May improve conditions in their company, and the *Star* not only appealed to the owners in their private capacity to stop the strike, but suggested that the London Trades Council should undertake to arbitrate. This it did, and by July 18 the *Star* and the *Times* were able to announce the terms of the settlement. A two-day conference had been held among a delegation from the Trades Council, a deputation of eight young women from four different match factories, and the directors of the company. The directors made seven important concessions and guaranteed there would be no reprisals. The girls said they were satisfied with the terms and wished to return to work. Even though the wage gain was trivial, the improvement in working conditions more than offset this lack.

So a crowded mass meeting of woman and girl workers was called in the great Assembly Hall in Mile End Road to hear the results of the conference, while relatives and friends waited anxiously outside. Mrs. Besant, "amid great and enthusiastic cheering," said that the terms far exceeded her expectations and urged acceptance. A resolution to accept the terms and return to work was made and adopted unanimously, with a vote of thanks to the Trades Council and Annie Besant, who said that "she was only too glad that her humble efforts had been of such service." A correspondent to the *Star*, however, immediately wrote in to assert that all the credit for the victory should not go to an atheist, because God and some Christians helped. Mrs. Besant and Herbert Burrows, who maintained that he was a Christian, thereupon provided a fete for all the girls at Mile End Waste, and Bryant and May's declared a 15 per cent dividend. Wilberforce Bryant delivered himself of some "coarse abuse" of Mrs. Besant and Burrows at a shareholders' meeting; but after only a short period of grumbling resistance, Bryant and May became, and have remained, one of the most successfully and co-operatively run firms in England.

Mrs. Besant in "Daybreak" thanked everybody in sight for their aid—the editors of the *Pall Mall Gazette,* the *Star, Reynolds' News,* and even the *Echo;* the London Trades Council; the Social Democratic Federation in Glasgow; the Fabian Society; Bradlaugh, Graham, and Conybeare in the House; and even the aggrieved Hobart, who was still fighting for more recognition of his role in the affair. She also praised "the brave Mr. Headlam" for a speech accusing those who pay starvation wages to young women of forcing them into prostitution and for pointing out that "Many of the rich church and chapel people [who] build refuges for fallen women out of the profits of their business [have] previously provided inmates for them from among their underpaid employees"—a theme that Shaw was later to use in *Mrs. Warren's Profession* and to some extent in *Widowers' Houses.* Robert Mitchell has also recently written a successful play, *The Matchgirls,* for the Unity Theatre in London about these events; both Annie Besant and Shaw are prominent members of the dramatis personae.[6]

The new team of Besant and Burrows, however, was not content to end its efforts here. Their gains must be consolidated at once. They determined to form a Matchmakers' Union, on the most advanced modern model. The girls agreed, the Union was organized, and Mrs. Besant was unanimously elected Hon. Sec. Early in September she was able to announce that there were over six hundred members, paying their dues with commendable regularity—and more coming in every day. A balance sheet of the strike was issued and printed by the *Star,* which congratulated Mrs. Besant, the Law and Liberty League, and itself, because through its participation it had been forced to formulate its own future labor policy. A strike in a branch factory was quickly settled after she and Burrows had spoken; and they claimed that, as a related result, fining in adjacent factories, such as one manufacturing confectionery, had been stopped. They started a building fund to erect a home for their union and backed a benefit performance of a popular melodrama at the Princess's Theatre. The *Link* asked for some philanthropist to devote £1,000 to provide the home with a large sitting room, a library, a piano, and similar items.

The pair came to be more in demand than ever as speakers at meetings

---

[6] *Shavian,* December, 1957, p. 26.

of all kinds—gigantic Anti-Sweatshop meetings in Hyde Park, where drastic resolutions were passed and the "Marseillaise" was sung; Socialist meetings at Norwich, where ten thousand enthusiasts passed a resolution to abolish private property and sang "No Master," the popular new workman's song; a smaller meeting, presided over by the hard-working Morris, at Carrow, close to the Coleman Mustard Works, whose owners took proper warning; and a meeting at Birmingham, which voted for the establishment of an eight-hour working day by Parliament.

Mrs. Besant was so busy that, after nine years, she had to give up teaching her classes in the Hall of Science. Since Alice Bradlaugh had recently died of typhoid fever, and Hypatia had had to resign for various reasons, Bradlaugh announced the closing of the school soon afterward. This meant the end of an important phase of Annie Besant's educational activities.

So proud were the match-girls of their new patron and champion that they chose her and the president of their Executive Committee, Edith Simcox, to represent them at the new International Trades Union Congress in London in November. The Standing Orders Committee made an abortive attempt to challenge their right to sit because they were not operatives, but the Congress showed no disposition to interfere with the duly exercised rights of the newly organized Women's Trades Unions. The *Gazette* pointed out that this indicated an important gradual broadening-out of the trades-union concept to all those "who honestly earn their bread." This first meeting of this International Congress, though not Socialist in makeup, was organized largely by Adolphe Headingley, a Socialist interpreter, and brought together 112 delegates from England, France, Belgium, Holland, Denmark, and Italy. This time Mrs. Besant, who attended as frequently as she could, was content to listen quietly to the speeches of the other more seasoned labor representatives like John Burns, Tom Mann, and J. Keir Hardie and put in only an occasional comment of her own. Foote, however, in his short-lived *Radical Leader*, conceded that she had "given utterance to some sensible strictures on the conduct of Trade Unionists" and that her remarks would undoubtedly do some good.[7]

The reason for Mrs. Besant's sporadic appearances was that she was already deeply involved in a new project. She was running for public office. But she never lost interest in the match-girls and in the next few months was to plunge even deeper into strikes and union organization. In her leadership of the matchmakers she had accomplished enough to make G. M. Trevelyan many years later in his *British History of the Nineteenth Century* refer to the episode as the "first skirmish of the new Unionism."

[7] *National Reformer*, November 11, 1888; Frederick J. Gould, *Hyndman* (London, 1928), p. 110; Joseph Clayton, *The Rise and Decline of Socialism in Great Britain, 1884–1924*, pp. 36–37; *Star*, November 6, 1888; *Radical Leader*, November 17, 1888.

4

Diggle and the
London School Board

Annie Besant's new male *attaché*, Herbert Burrows, had long been one of her most vocal antagonists, as a leader of the extremist group of the Social Democrats. He was at this time, as a *Star* reporter saw him,[1] a tall, well-made man of about forty, with a mustache and a closely shaven chin; he usually wore a tweed suit over the conventional Socialist flannel shirt and crushed strawberry necktie. Since his period of study as an unattached student at Cambridge, he had resided at Norwich, Barnet, and Blackburn. At the latter place he had acquired his pronounced Socialist views, when "he went over the chain factories and collieries with Mr. Henry George" and saw the contrast of the workmen's lot with that of their aristocratic employer, the Earl of Dudley. Sometime during this career he had married an American woman, who was in bad health.

Annie herself, just over forty-one, was no longer the slim, sweet woman she had been. Everything about her had coarsened. She had broadened out considerably, and her slight stoop made her look shorter than she was. Her hair, cut close in order to be more easily taken care of, had begun to show silver streaks. Her skirts had been shortened to keep them out of the mud when she was trudging through the East End, and she wore thick, laced boots for the same reason. And always she marked her costume with something red, a neckerchief or a tam-o'-shanter, to denote her Socialist coloration. She looked, indeed, like a genuine woman of the toiling class, or, as Colonel Henry Olcott was soon to put it, an "Annie

[1] *Star*, October 9, 1888. See also *Justice*, April 6, 1889.

Militant."[2] In this role she was the subject of some savage caricatures in *Punch*.

Herbert and Annie now became practically inseparable. They were crusaders together. Many years later when she was making her jubilee speech to commemorate her fiftieth year in public life, she recalled that one winter night when they were tramping through the snow and mud along a London street, returning after midnight from a meeting of omnibusmen who had no other time to meet and plan for a union, she turned to him and said, "Herbert, I wonder why on earth we go on doing this." He thought and rendered his only answer, "We can't help it!"

A rash of strikes now began to break out in London and all over England. Early in August the *Link* invited the "heads of Circles and all correspondents everywhere" to send in their suggestions for a symposium to decide on "The Next Point of Attack." Annie and Herbert pitched in wherever they thought their services could be of use, whether the workers were male or female. When the woman weavers at Leeds and Aberdeen went out on strike, Mrs. Besant's Matchmakers' Union helped them with money. The wooden-matchbox–makers of London were notorious for their methods—"Twopence-farthing per gross of boxes, and buy your own string and paste," as Mrs. Besant described it and went on to tell how she and Burrows, tramping through the lanes and alleys of Bethnal Green Junction to note the condition of those who had been thrown out of work by the match strike, were nauseated by the sight of children lying on shavings, rags, anything but beds, and famine staring from the faces of babies and the eyes of men and women. The answer: unionize!

Then the L.L.L. decided to post Messrs. Lloyd, manufacturers of tin boxes, in the "Lion's Mouth," for their operatives in South London complained of how they were illegally fined and often "grievously mutilated by the non-fencing of machinery." Mrs. Besant complained to the Chief Inspector of Factories, who started an investigation; and many copies of the *Link* were sold outside the plant. After a visit from Besant and Burrows, the employees struck and got rid of an obnoxious foreman. Moral: unionize!

Other employers were black-listed and attacked. The shop assistants, the Cradley Heath chainmakers, the fur-pullers, the gas-workers, the capmakers, the hairdressers, the printers' laborers, the tailors, the stokers, the furriers, the house painters and decorators, the cigarette-makers, the tramwaymen—all these and other forgotten workers all through the latter part of 1888 and the whole of 1889 received the help of the tireless couple in the form of speeches, advice, organization, publicity, and money-raising.

[2] Clayton, *The Rise and Decline of Socialism in Great Britain, 1884–1924*, pp. 36–37, quoting Keir Hardie in the *Miner;* Theodore Besterman, *Mrs. Annie Besant*, p. 168, quoting Olcott, *Old Diary Leaves*.

Just at the time Mrs. Besant was beginning her exposure of Messrs. Bryant and May, she had been put—or had put herself—on a new L.L.L. committee to draw up proposals for the coming London School Board election. On the successful conclusion of the unionization, she issued a program of objectives and analyzed the desired qualifications for candidates. Edward Aveling some years before had passed through the Board like a meteor—or a falling star! Herbert Burrows, after an instructive campaign, had sat on it, but had been defeated for re-election in the spring because of his radical views. At the end of August he announced in the *Star* and *Justice* that he would not try again, being convinced that he could do more for the cause of education from the outside. At one time Mrs. Besant had tried to persuade Shaw to run for the Board, arguing that school was at least warm and dry and would keep the children off the streets, but Shaw, remembering his own hatred for school, had ejaculated pithily: "So is prison!" She dropped the point.[3]

Now Mrs. Besant began a speaking campaign on the election. She had already withdrawn from the Marylebone election committee because it had adopted a status quo attitude toward religious education in the schools, especially in respect to the activities of Arthur B. Moss, a teacher in the system who had got into trouble because, as a member of the N.S.S., he had written and lectured on atheism after hours, particularly on Sundays. She published a fighting manifesto on "Secular Education" in the *Reformer*, insisting that, unlike some Radicals and Freethinkers, she believed in sticking to principle and would thus win sooner or later. At the end of August she spoke to the London Secularist Federation on the general subject of the School Board, reiterated her belief in free secular education, but granted that atheists should not expect their antitheological views to be actually taught in tax-supported schools. These views she uttered again at a meeting of delegates from the Marylebone Radical associations, presided over by Foote, who had been quarreling with Bradlaugh in the *Freethinker* over the policy that should be pursued with Moss. This meeting was addressed also by Burrows, Wallas, and Quelch. All of them, agreed Foote in his other paper, the *Radical Leader,* made stirring speeches on the necessity of reforming both education in general and the School Board in particular.

The objective of Mrs. Besant's educational activities had been covert up to this time. It took *Justice* to make it overt on September 1 and at the same time to reveal with studied casualness to its readers that at last, undoubtedly under the influence of Burrows, she had capitulated in her long fight against the Social Democratic Federation: "We should gladly see Annie Besant, whom we heartily hail this week as our collaborator in JUSTICE, on the board if she can spare the time to contest a district and sit for it." Immediately in her public speeches she began to acknowledge

---

[3] Winsten, *Jesting Apostle,* p. 71.

that she was a member of the S.D.F. She continued to belong to the Fabians also, but she reduced her Fabian section in *Our Corner* to almost nothing.

The first to rise to the bait was a delegates' meeting from the "democratic bodies" in Finsbury, who picked a preliminary panel of six nominees for the Board, including Conybeare, Mrs. Besant, and Helen Taylor. Shortly afterward the East London Working Women's Radical Association issued an appeal to place women on the Board. The London Secularist Federation had already voted to push Secularists and Radicals for a place, and it eventually asked Mrs. Besant to stand as one of its candidates. But the East End, where all of her recent life had been focused, won her. A joint committee from the Tower Hamlets Division, including the Radical Association, the East London Branch of the N.S.S., and certain Liberal groups, asked her, with two men—one a clergyman—to stand for their section, and she promptly accepted. She had been building up to such a candidacy through her many speeches and articles all along. She later admitted, however, that she had really wanted to run for the newly authorized London County Council, but had discovered that women were not eligible.

Her circle quickly rallied around her and her program of free secular education, free meals for poor school children, new contracts for all types of School Board employees which would make the government subject to the same principles of employment and purchase of supplies as other employers, and other advanced measures. All her friends, from Burrows and Shaw to the match-girls, pitched in to help by making speeches, organizing meetings, writing campaign propaganda, and soliciting votes and money. Burrows, in fact, became her campaign manager, and R. Forder, an old-time Secularist officer, her main assistant. It was the general opinion, expressed in the *Link*, the *Star*, etc., that she stood a good chance. In her district her socialism was not regarded as a disadvantage, though her Secularism was; the latter, however, was balanced by the fact that she was a woman, and good women were wanted on the Board. Bradlaugh asked his friends to "plump" all their votes for her, as well as to send in money to her campaign fund. *Justice* did the same. The *Star* advised its readers to divide their votes among the three running on the progressive ticket, three others having withdrawn in her favor, but added that "Mrs. Besant's return at the head of the poll would be a well-deserved reward for her untiring work in the cause of the poor in the East-end."

Annie campaigned as she had never campaigned before. Tower Hamlets was a huge, sprawling district, but she spoke from Stepney to Bromley, from Poplar to Bow, from Peckham Rye to Old Ford and Mile End Waste. At first the electorate was apathetic. Frederick Rogers, a minor liberal in Labor politics and literature and a man with a low opinion of the efficacy of feminine "charm" and "glamour" on an audience of tired

267

workingmen, recalled her walking out on a meeting of the Tower Hamlets Radical Club one morning when only a dozen people turned out to hear her.[4] Gradually, however, interest built up so that her assemblies were well attended and the contributions almost kept pace with the expenditures, which ran to about ninety pounds. A "Central Democratic Committee," from the *Link* address, issued a circular and a statement of principles in favor of her, Bland, Headlam, and other approved candidates, signed by the Metropolitan Radical Association, the London Secular Federation, the Fabian Society, and the Social Democratic Federation. "Canvass! Canvass! Canvass!" urged *Justice* in favor of its new "comrade." There were outdoor meetings and indoor meetings, daylight meetings and torchlight meetings.

Excitement was soon injected into the campaign from several quarters. The racial issue was introduced when the Jews in Tower Hamlets determined that there must be a Jew on the Board and decided to back Claude Montefiore, a Conservative but a good educationist. The *Star*, in an article headed "Yiddish against Jewish," while admitting Montefiore's ability, urged its Jewish working readers to heed the manifesto written in Yiddish by Lewis Lyons and vote for Mrs. Besant.

Next, one of her fellow Fabian, Bland's, committee accused Burrows of using unfair tactics in invading the Finsbury district to get workers to help in Tower Hamlets; but Burrows and Mrs. Besant denied the accusation to a *Freethinker* reporter. Bland was not convinced. Mrs. Besant also failed to take advantage of Foote's offer to speak for her candidacy. He predicted some "shindies" at certain of her open-air meetings, especially when a pair of Christian Evidence representatives, "Edwards, the black preacher, and Goodship, the white," got to work on her and her *Law of Population.*

Foote's prediction was justified. It could scarcely be expected that the churchmen would forget Mrs. Besant's past at such a crucial juncture. In November the two Christian Evidence members appeared at one of her Sunday assemblies and urged her rejection. "This," reported the *Reformer*, "was defeated by an immense majority, with great enthusiasm." Nevertheless, the next week Mrs. Besant herself complained: "The clergy are straining every nerve to defeat me, and are using against me all the slanders that the disreputable Christian Evidence street lecturers can invent. . . ." *Justice* was even more specific in describing the last stages of the campaign, which was "raging rather hotly in consequence of the clerical and Tory attacks on our comrade, Annie Besant. Mothers' meetings, district visitors, and all the weapons of the Church are being used against her."

Her two chief clerical opponents were two Anglicans, the Rev. Edwyn Hoskyns and the Rev. Mr. Dundas. In the last stages of the campaign

4 Rogers, *Labour, Life and Literature* (London, 1913), p. 72.

both circulated handbills against her. Dundas was the less offensive, though he had come to talk with her in a friendly fashion and had then "hypocritically" gone away to make false statements in his leaflet. Hoskyns, a thirty-eight-year-old graduate of Jesus College, Cambridge, and the son of a Tory clergyman who was also a baronet, was the vicar of Stepney. In order to warn his parishioners against voting for such a pernicious woman, he listened to some of the old stories about her Malthusian views and then, without reading any of her books, flooded his parish with thirty thousand anonymous handbills which contained such passages as the following: "A Freethinker thus describes the practical outcome of her teaching: 'Chastity is a crime; unbridled sensuality is a virtue.'" Actually, as Mrs. Besant said at the end of the campaign, when she announced that she intended to sue Hoskyns for "grossly defaming" her, he had "attributed to her 'some vile passages' from a book which was not hers" and used them to try to beat her.[5]

It was all in vain. When the votes were in at the end of November, Mrs. Besant stood at the head of the poll in her district, with slightly under sixteen thousand votes. Only a very small percentage of those eligible had voted, but those who had had placed her far above her Tory, Jewish, and churchly opposition. Among the candidates from her circle, only she, Headlam, and Mrs. Ashton Dilke had won; Bland had been defeated. Moreover, except for one candidate in Tynemouth, she and Mrs. Dilke were the only Freethought candidates elected anywhere in England. Foote, congratulating them while noting ruefully that his own favorite Secularist Federation candidates had been beaten, attributed her victory partly to her Socialist support but even more to the activity of the Radical clubs, the backing of the *Star*, the *Pall Mall Gazette,* and the *Daily News;* her womanhood; and her personal popularity. George Lansbury felt that the Radical clubs had been much more responsible than the Socialists.[6] Annie herself issued a statement in the *Link* and the *Reformer* thanking her "election agent and colleague, Herbert Burrows," who had undermined his health in her cause; her Fabian colleagues, Headlam, Shaw, and others, who had volunteered to speak at her meetings; her Secularist friends like Forder; and many others. Bradlaugh she did not mention. Shaw recorded in his diary late in November that he had had quite a passage at arms in the *Justice* office with H. H. Sparling, who accused Mrs. Besant of having attacked the Socialist League only to catch votes in the election.

At the same time she announced the demise of both the *Link* and *Our Corner.* There had been warnings several months before in both cases.

[5] *Autobiography,* p. 460; *Link,* December 1, 1888; *Star,* November 14, 26, 1889; John M. Robertson, "Account of [Bradlaugh's] Parliamentary Struggles, Politics, and Teachings," in Hypatia Bradlaugh Bonner, *Charles Bradlaugh,* II, 395.

[6] Lansbury, in *Centenary Book,* pp. 26–27.

Neither publication had ever paid for itself. It seemed as if she had kept the *Link* going only long enough to see her successfully through her campaign; but she merely said in small type under "To Be Done" that her funds had given out and that she knew her little paper had during its brief existence "put an end to many wrongs inflicted on the poor." The Law and Liberty League, with less vast objectives in the new religion and the brotherhood of man, lasted a few more months, but it too ended in debt. As for *Our Corner*, it seemed as if she had kept it artificially alive, mainly to present her friend Shaw's "A Refutation of Anarchism" and "The Transition to Social Democracy" and to complete the serialization of his *Love among the Artists*, which filled most of the last two or three numbers. In fact, toward the end of May, Shaw made an entry in his diary saying that he had written to Mrs. Besant offering to let her have the rest of the novel for nothing because the magazine was entailing a loss to her. For the first time in years she was no longer editing any magazine. But she now had another duty and occupation: the reform of the London school system and the amelioration of the condition of its impoverished and underprivileged children.

One of the main issues of the campaign had been the defeat of what the *Star* called "Diggle and Diggleism." The Rev. J. R. Diggle, who had for some time been chairman of the London School Board, in its eyes stood for "crude individualism" and Church-of-Englandism; and it editorialized on the necessity of turning him and his supporters out of their majority on the Board, knowing it was impossible to defeat him at the polls. It was "Diggle & Co." (as the *Freethinker* named it) who, with religious Fundamentalists like H. H. Raphael as leaders, were persecuting Moss for his atheism. The voters failed to defeat the Diggle party (and their leader eventually became a powerful bishop), but they at least reduced their majority to only 30–25; and the reformers took courage. At the first meeting of the new Board early in December, Mrs. Besant, Headlam, Conybeare, and an adherent named Cook formed a "democratic corner" on labor principles, and, led by Mrs. Besant, won their first vote on a key question of labor contracts for supplies. Great things were expected of her, and she immediately pledged her unswerving devotion to her campaign promises. In the *Reformer* she started a diary of her doings on the Board, paralleling Bradlaugh's on his Parliamentary actions, and promised a "fighting minority." The *Gazette* and the *Lady's Pictorial* ran drawings of her and Mrs. Dilke in their current issues. Mrs. Besant reviewed and lectured on Bellamy's American romance of the utopian future, *Looking Backwards*; wrote an editorial for *Justice* on "Socialism and Administration"; supported the successful campaign of John Burns, as a Socialist, for the County Council; and when aldermen for the new Council were elected in the following February, received one vote herself.[7] Mrs. Cunninghame Graham sent her list of the twelve greatest

[7] William Kent, *John Burns: Labour's Lost Leader*, p. 37.

women in history to the *Pall Mall Gazette*. It included Mrs. Besant and the Virgin Mary.

Annie was placed on the committees she had asked for: school management, works, and bylaws. At Christmas time she filled her "Notes" column with harrowing case histories of starving families, exploited boys and girls, absenteeism from school because of child labor, and infinitesimal wages, all of which mocked at the idea of "A Merry Christmas" celebrating the birth of the Christ Child. In the eyes of later labor leaders like George Lansbury, her big contributions to social reform at this time lay in her exposing the absurdity of the idea of trying to educate half-starving children, in her laying the foundation of the later system of medical examination and treatment in elementary schools, and in her destroying the strangle hold that sweaters had on public contracts. By the end of 1889 she herself boasted proudly that she had been the means of raising £185 to provide some thirty-six thousand lunches for needy children, and Lansbury praised her as "a 'Pioneer' on behalf of organized Labour" in the way in which she cut across the practices of the sweaters by inducing the School Board to insert into all its contracts a clause that all goods it purchased should be produced under trades-union conditions in respect to rates of pay and hours of labor. This news electrified the whole world of labor.[8]

Mrs. Besant and her advance guard also indulged in various other skirmishes and full-fledged battles in the Board, all duly recorded in the *Reformer*, or written up in the *Star*. When she proposed that the time of meetings be changed from three to six o'clock so that wage-earners might run for the Board, she was accused by "irate orators" of "playing to the gallery"; she replied that if that were the case, she would have chosen a larger gallery. There were run-ins about the teaching of science and religion, that old bugaboo; the free use of Board schools for public meetings; the abolition of compulsory fees as a step toward the ultimate goal of free education; Board schools vs. Church and sectarian schools; the annual budget; the payment of decent wages to the Board's own printers, which precipitated a suit for libel by the accused printing company; sectarian training schools; "kid-glove" parents who sent their children to charity schools; the restriction of Board employees to the male sex; revision of the bylaws; etc. When she learned that the firm which provided Bibles for use in the schools employed a special, paid chaplain, while the girls who folded the paper sheets were paid a miserable pittance, she scornfully told the Board, "They may well employ a Chaplain for the girls they have driven to prostitution."

Sometimes she complained that the meetings were "not altogether a bed of roses," sometimes that they were "so very dull," though she and Headlam did their best to keep them unsettled. Their engagement with

[8] Lansbury, in *Centenary Book*, pp. 27–28; *National Reformer*, February 10, June 24, 1889.

the Diggle forces which resulted in Moss's being not only reinstated but allowed to lecture on Sunday was one of their better efforts. When she proposed the appointment of a "peripatetic magistrate" to go around hearing cases against delinquent parents at homes instead of forcing the parents to make long trips to come to court, the *Star* reporter, who almost alone among London reporters covered all the Board meetings, remarked: "It is very comical to watch the expression of the Rev. Diggle's countenance whenever he has to call on Mrs. Besant. The full moon of his face goes under an eclipse, and he looks as if the name stings his lips as he utters it."

On only one prominent occasion did Mrs. Besant and Stewart Headlam fall out. It came early, and it was over a question of aesthetics vs. child labor. Mrs. Besant, to her horror, suddenly discovered that many theaters which gave pantomimes employed children in them at sweatshop wages and without providing any means of education—a "cruel thing," she cried. Headlam, who had previously had trouble with his bishop because he had permitted and encouraged aesthetic dancing in his parish house as a form of spiritual education, thought this was carrying matters a bit too far. After she had agitated the case for a month, the Board decided to drop the matter, having been informed that Augustus Harris had opened a regular school for his child-dancers; and both she and Headlam were happy. A few months later they successfully fought a further aesthetic battle side by side when they persuaded the Board that, wherever possible, children should have pianos in their schoolrooms.

It was no wonder that when, at meetings like that of the Bow Reform Club with Headlam in the chair and Burrows as a fellow speaker, she defended her work on the School Board, she was cheered to the rafters. Her reputation as a militant champion of the victimized was also enhanced in October when Diggle tried to declare Conybeare's seat on the Board vacant after he had been released from a prison term for making a disturbance in Donegal in the cause of Irish freedom. Though Diggle's action was eventually sustained legally, Mrs. Besant put up her usual valiant fight in his defense and used the case as a sounding board for her perennial advocacy of the Irish cause. (She had never yet been in Ireland!)

Solidly as she had consolidated her Board position with the progressives, she, unlike her colleague Bradlaugh, had failed utterly to alter the attitude of the conservatives toward her. Their persistent animosity was again demonstrated when her threatened libel case against Edwyn Hoskyns, rector of Stepney, came up in November. All the papers, but notably the *Star,* the *Pall Mall Gazette,* and the *Daily Chronicle,* followed the trial and the verdict with avid attention, and some in unusually great detail. Hoskyns, with the backing of his Church and Tory friends, retained no less than Sir Edward Clarke, the solicitor general, and the case was tried before a special jury, with Baron Huddleston, the author of a book called *Libel and Slander,* as presiding judge. Mrs. Besant, as always, conducted her own case "and never," said the *Star,* "put anything more logically and clearly." Many young members of the bar attended to hear the arguments.

Mrs. Besant's charge was based on the single sentence in Hoskyns' anonymous handbill concerning the Freethinker who asserted that she taught that chastity was a crime and unbridled sensuality a virtue. Although he had previously written in a parish newsletter that her teachings tended toward "gross immorality," this statement was not included in the suit. Hoskyns admitted the authorship of the leaflet, but maintained that he had intended it (all thirty thousand copies of it!) only for his own parishioners. All the old charges about Knowlton, *The Elements of Social Science,* and *The Law of Population* (which had recently been the basis of a criminal prosecution of a bookseller in Sidney, New South Wales, who had finally won vindication on an appeal to the Supreme Court there) were raked up, though Hoskyns admitted he had never read any of these works himself.

As usually happened to Mrs. Besant, the judge in the case was violently prejudiced against her from the start, perhaps because he had already sat on a similar libel case against Bradlaugh, which he had decided for the plaintiff. In fact, the *Star* reported the rumor that Huddleston intended to summon the editor of the *Gazette* for contempt of court because Stead's paper had written: "No judge on the whole bench could have been more of a partisan than Baron Huddleston was." The same reporter also speculated whether there was any significance in the fact that the name of Mr. Hoskyns' curate was also Huddleston. John M. Robertson, of the *Reformer* staff, wrote a caustic analysis of the casuistic summing-up made by His Lordship in his instructions to the jury,[9] which were based on the remarkable principle that "the question was not whether Mrs. Besant's books were obscene," but rather on "the defendant's honesty of belief at the time he had published the handbills." Since he made it quite clear to the jury that in his opinion Hoskyns believed the truth of the hearsay and brought his charges without malice and in the interest of and out of his duty to his parishioners, and since the judge himself cited and vilified passages from Mrs. Besant's works, the jury members were pretty thoroughly baffled. As Robertson pointed out, Huddleston was now influencing the jury to act on a principle which, in the case of *Peters* vs. *Bradlaugh,* he had stated "would never do." The priest was adjudged free to do what a layman was never allowed to do— make libelous charges without himself investigating their truth.

Under these circumstances the jury naturally disagreed and was dis-

[9] Robertson, "Account of [Bradlaugh's] Parliamentary Struggles, Politics, and Teachings," in Bonner, *Bradlaugh,* II, 395; *National Reformer,* November 24, 1889.

charged. As Foote learned from a Freethinker who had somehow been allowed to sit on it, two jurors were strongly in favor of giving the verdict to the plaintiff, with damages; four maintained that Mrs. Besant should not be held for the costs; two thought the action should not have been brought at all; and four were for the defendant. Though Mrs. Besant pretended that this split decision had vindicated her innocence, she nevertheless immediately announced that she would bring Hoskyns into court again. But she never did so,[10] having apparently listened to the advice of her friends who maintained that no English jury would ever give a unanimous verdict against a clergyman for libeling a Freethinker. She therefore had to be satisfied with a bouquet presented her by lady members of the Socratic Club of Croydon as an expression of sympathy for the many persecutions she had suffered and with a letter signed by several prominent women thanking her for her contributions to the public welfare.

Hoskyns preached immediately to a crowded church, filled predominantly with ladies, and handled the verdict in the case "without gloves." According to the ubiquitous *Star* reporter, "One of the hymns sung was that appointed for times of trouble." Perhaps this choice was made because the *Times* was soon to print an appeal signed by Hoskyns' friends asking for contributions to meet his costs of three hundred pounds in the trial. A solicitor general comes high; Annie had conducted her own case.

[10] *Freethinker*, March 30, 1890. For another strange episode in these studies, see Appendix, pp. 399–403.

5

Possibilists versus Impossibilists

Shaw, in his "Mrs. Besant's Passage through Fabian Socialism," airily overlooked her virtual desertion of the Fabians for the
Social Democrats during the final stages of her socialistic career, but his
diagnosis of her character and her relationship with Fabianism was
nevertheless acute. As he saw the situation, Fabianism could no longer
hold her when she had quickly learned what it could teach her "to
complete her equipment." For Fabianism was too unheroic in its outlook and methods for a woman who, like her friend Bradlaugh, was
essentially heroic in her "power, courage, and oratorical genius." She
was therefore wasted on work which did not have a strong element of
danger and extreme arduousness in it. On the Shakespearian stage of life,
concluded Shaw, Mrs. Besant was

a player of genius, . . . a tragedian. Comedy was not her clue to life; she had a
healthy sense of fun; but no truth came to her as a joke. Injustice, waste, and the
defeat of noble aspirations did not revolt her by way of irony and paradox; they
stirred her to direct and powerful indignation and to active resistance. Now the
Fabian view was largely the vein of comedy, and its conscience was a sense of
irony. . . .

Perhaps, by implication, Shaw was suggesting that the approach of
the Social Democratic Federation to life and reform was essentially
tragic, like Mrs. Besant's. In any case she clung to her socialistic outlook
for some time longer before she let it be superseded, though not completely replaced, by a new philosophy which to her searching mind held
out even stronger hopes of attaining the brotherhood of man and a new
world—or rather two new worlds, one on this earth and the other outside

it, yet in it. For some time there was an overlapping between her two utopias, and it was only unwillingly that she surrendered the first in favor of the second.

In January, 1892, Stewart Headlam read a paper to the Fabian Society in which he referred to a sermon "by the good old Archdeacon of London who was called up on a memorable afternoon to preach to the Socialists in St. Paul's Cathedral" and noticed that on the Socialist banners were quotations only from Christ and his apostles and not from Marx, Lassalle, Hyndman, Champion, or Mrs. Besant, "who were then supposed to be leaders."[1] At that time even Headlam would have failed to predict Annie Besant's eventual attitude toward Christianity, but he knew that she would be a leader wherever she went. After she had electioneered in January, 1889, in favor of Social Democratic candidates for the London County Council, she had to write a letter to *Justice* protesting against the increasing habit of the Federation's branches in billing her as a speaker without consulting her first. A few weeks later Hyndman printed an editorial to the effect that there were some persons in the organization "who are so well-known and so closely identified with our movement, Herbert Burrows, Quelch, myself, Annie Besant, John Burns, for example, that if they take an active part in canvassing for any candidate without protest it is taken for granted that the S.D.F. as a whole approves of the policy."

There were still many unfinished pieces of business in Mrs. Besant's program for 1889. There was, for instance, the matter of Trafalgar Square which was still hanging fire. In March the Socialists held an exploratory midnight meeting there, with speeches, and when the police—perhaps being too drowsy—did not interfere, the Radical clubs quickly called a conference to plan new tactics. Although, as usual, the uncommitted M.P.'s refused to attend, a planning committee of twelve, consisting mainly of Socialists, was elected. Among its members were Burrows, Burns, Conybeare, and Foote. Mrs. Besant received the second highest vote, just after Cunninghame Graham. Bernard Shaw, who was just starting a new career as "Corno di Bassetto," "the *Star's* 'Own Captious Critic'" of music, was twelfth on a committee of twelve. Even though the Square remained closed for some time to come, perhaps Mrs. Besant felt a slight stir of selfish gratification when she recalled how he and all the rest had deserted her on the former occasion when she had wanted to march back to the Square and capture it from the troops by force of moral indignation. At a later meeting in April, in fact, she reported that she was not now prepared to take it by force, since the committee was recommending that it be put under control of the County Council.[2]

All this time Mrs. Besant's conscience had not ceased to trouble her

---

[1] *Fabian Tract No. 42.*

[2] *Star,* February 21, March 15, 1889; *Pall Mall Gazette,* March 15, April 12, 1889.

about her desertion of Bradlaugh and his fellow Radicals, who had so often come to her own political assistance. She could not forget how, when R. B. Haldane, M.P. for Haddingtonshire and future lord chancellor, had come innocently to a Fabian meeting on March 16, 1888, to prove that "Radical Remedies for Economic Evils" were better than Fabian proposals, he had—as Standring put it in the *Radical*—been "butchered to make a Fabian holiday." Not only had Mrs. Besant joined with Webb, Shaw, and others "to shake the life" out of him, but she had turned her back on him during most of her extemporaneous attack, showing him her face and her emphatic forefinger only when she wished to stress a clinching point.

So, in April, 1889, after lecturing to the Socialist Co-operative Federation and not attending the annual Fabian soirée, Mrs. Besant sent a letter to *Justice* which Hyndman published with some reluctance. This letter, headed "Socialists and Radicals," took the position that since there were some advanced Radicals whose views had been so much influenced by socialism, the Socialists might as well join with the Radicals in the war against their common foe. Since *Justice* had never stopped its battering at Bradlaugh, Mrs. Besant's suggestion was not very well placed or timed, even though it had been precipitated by a long article in the *Star* (an officially Radical paper that had been much influenced by socialism) discussing the new Radical program. Consequently, she took a spanking from both sides—most of the members of both groups seeing too many differences in policy and methods to justify such close collaboration. Hyndman, Bax, Quelch, Shaw, and others joined the epistolary controversy—Shaw taking both sides but leaning toward Hyndman's firm opposition. Massingham, of the *Star*, was the only one who editorially saw some virtue in Mrs. Besant's proposal. Bradlaugh remained discreetly silent. The *Star* thought he talked too much anyhow, showing "too much of the impartial statesman" and not enough of the "people's advocate." H. H. Champion's new paper, the *Labour Elector*, "The Organ of Practical Socialism," summed up the fiasco by comparing the reckless Annie with "the young lady of Riga" who took a ride on a tiger and ended up inside the beast.

The excitement was all building up to a great International Socialist Congress which was to be held in Paris in July and which was nicely timed to coincide with the opening of the Paris Exhibition. Though the general subject was to be the strengthening of the labor movement by planning and co-operation, bad feeling between the Socialist factions began mounting early. "Adolphe Headingley," whose real name was Smith and who was described by the *Labour Elector* as a "worthy colleague on the *Times* newspaper of Mr. Richard Pigott [the forger of the letters in the Parnell case] and contributor to Parisian Anarchist journals," started it off in March by writing a new report on the activities of the recent International Trades Union Congress in London. In it he made so much of the contributions of himself, "Comrade" Mrs. Annie Besant, and one or two others that, as the *Elector* complained, no one would guess that John Burns and Tom Mann were also present. Four weeks later it announced its discovery that "Adolphe Smith-Headingley" was the agent of the Parisian Socialists and "Possibilists." At the same time an argument was developing in *Justice* between Eduard Bernstein, described as the editor of the German *Sozial Demokrat,* and Hyndman, who concluded that the French Possibilists were coming closer to socialism in their Marxism.

By early May, however, the *Star* was able to headline a split between the down-the-line Marxists and the Possibilists, who wished to bring about the new society by means which they considered within reason and who labeled their opponents "Impossibilists." The latter group soon organized an International Congress of Workers, which was to meet in Paris simultaneously with the other. The Social Democratic Federation, in an angry manifesto published in *Justice,* cried:

> The chief promoters of the Hague Caucus and of the rival Congress in Paris are Lafargue, Guesde, Mrs. Eleanor Marx Aveling (whose sister, a daughter of Karl Marx, Lafargue married), Bernstein . . . , Bebel, and Liebknecht. Friedrich Engels is in full accord with their proceedings.

Since their return from America, the Avelings had been under something of a cloud and had been supporting themselves largely by expressing in print and on the lecture platform their not very flattering opinions of the condition of American labor. As the *Star* phrased it in February, following a news story in which it told how Eleanor, a beautiful Jewess, had valiantly championed the cause of an inebriated woman against a policeman, "As Socialists, by the way, the Avelings have rather fallen to the rear, and they seldom, if ever, nowadays either take part in the Socialist League lectures or contribute to the *Commonweal.*" There was something very strange about the Avelings, which not even Bernstein ever got to the bottom of. He told how, in that very year, he and his wife, recently arrived in England, received a social invitation from the Blands, who were inner-circle Fabians. Bernstein having incidentally mentioned the Avelings, there was suddenly a suspiciously unanimous chorus of praise for them, for their cleverness, their great service to the movement, and so on—so concerted, in fact, that Bernstein was sure there was something in the air. Diplomatically he diverted the conversation to politics, but he went away feeling that "a judge of human nature might have blurted out the question: 'What's the truth about them, really? Have they murdered their children, or what?' " Though he concludes with an observation on the hypocrisy of thus evading a definite accusation, he leaves the reader with the impression that there might have been some truth in his question.[3]

[3] Bernstein, *My Years of Exile,* pp. 201–2.

Whatever the Avelings' crime, Bernstein was apparently willing to associate himself with them in the International Congress of Workers. After all, they were not ostracized, and they were accustomed to mingling with the other advanced thinkers who gathered at such places as the Central Democratic Club in Gray's Inn Road. (Bax, Champion, Burns, Bernstein, and assorted minor novelists and feminists, as well as Herbert Burrows and Mrs. Besant were often seen there by the reporter of the Sunday *Sun.*) Indeed, special meetings of the Club at the end of June were devoted to discussions of the coming rival congresses in Paris.

In the I.C.W. the Avelings saw an opportunity to rehabilitate themselves, even at the expense of Socialist unity, but with the plea of the workers' good. Mrs. Besant, who was one of the delegates from the S.D.F., and the backers of the original convention were of course furious. Declaring that the representatives of the other group, which stemmed from a knot of German exiles, represented nothing but themselves, they demanded to see their credentials. The rather naïve William Morris, whose Socialist League and its magazine were being stolen away from him little by little by the anarchistically inclined members of his board and who would have done better to stick to his medieval epics and his Morris chairs, reported to his readers: "We have therefore offered to let them see our mandates, but we have no obligation to them." Champion, who had been read out of both the Social Democratic and the Fabian groups, was more scathing in the *Labour Elector*, in connection with a rumored offer of peaceful fusion:

Meanwhile Mrs. Besant does her little best to secure that such a petition from the "Possibilists" will be rejected, by declaring, in the name of the "Brotherhood of Man" and "the Future of the Workers," that the Congress of which the convocation is signed by thirty-three well-known Austrians, Germans, Russians, Italians, Frenchmen, and Englishmen is "the shameful outcome of the petty jealousies of a few middle-class Socialists belonging to no serious organization."

This was in reply to a war cry of "Solidarity" in the *Pall Mall Gazette* by Mrs. Besant; *Justice* had praised it and asked whether anyone could believe that people like Graham, Champion, Morris, and Mann really represented the workingman, although Keir Hardie did have some influence with the Scotch miners. Soon after this exchange John Burns resigned from the S.D.F., but he attended the Possibilist convention nevertheless; and Stepniak, the former Nihilist, announced that he was joining the "Marxists." The *Labour Elector* charged that Mrs. Besant was really the dupe of Adolphe "Smith-Headingley" and "probably derives her knowledge of the 'Brotherhood of Man,' &c., mainly from that gentleman and he, as we all know, has gone about this country saying that KARL MARX was 'himself dishonest.'"

So the "respectable" newspapers of Paris and the world laughed at seeing the two rival revolutionary organizations at each other's throats— the Marxists led by Jules Guesde and the Possibilists by Paul Brousse, of the Paris Municipal Court.[4] Mrs. Besant sent her reports of what transpired to the *Reformer* and the *Pall Mall Gazette;* Edward Aveling sent his back to the *Sun.* Even though the latter two accounts were originally anonymous, each writer immediately accused the other of twisting the facts. When the true authorships were revealed, the amity between them was not improved.

The residue of truth from the conflicting recriminations of the two parties seems to be somewhat as follows. The question of credentials continued, and the Marxists offered to co-operate; but Mrs. Besant, leading the credentials committee, insisted that only Socialist and Radical organizations and trades-union groups in existence in 1888 were authorized to attend. On this basis, 612 delegates from 396 societies in 14 European and American nations came to the Possibilist convention. The Marxists did not issue similar figures, but their attendance was much less. The groups met simultaneously between July 15 and 20, but spies from each slipped into the other's meetings, as Cunninghame Graham of the Marxists did, even though he had to sit in the gallery. On the nomination of Smith-Headingley, who acted as interpreter, Hyndman was elected chairman for the first meeting of the Possibilists. At the final meeting Mrs. Besant was elected a vice-president, was put into the chair "by acclamation," and gave an applauded speech in French which was purely English in style. Both groups pretended to enough harmony to attend a banquet given in their honor by the mayor of Paris, and at the end both groups adopted almost identical sets of resolutions in favor of the proletariat. Shouts for "the Social Revolution, for the Commune, for the Brotherhood of Man" ended the final emotional scene of the Congress. After it was all over, many of the delegates, including Mrs. Besant, Hyndman, and Burrows, went to the cemetery of Père La Chaise to lay wreaths on the graves of the "martyrs of the Paris Commune" in 1871, though Mrs. Besant had for some time been absent from the London anniversary celebrations of this event.

But though Mrs. Besant went home and described the convention as the "grandest International Labour Congress ever held," completely harmonious and businesslike in every respect, its cacophonous echoes lasted for some time in other quarters. Not only did Burrows and Aveling prolong their acrimonious controversy in the Sunday *Sun;* but the Italian, Cipriani, who had just been released from twenty years' imprisonment, attributed the failure of the two groups to coalesce entirely to Annie Besant's hypocritical and vindictive waspishness, calling her "une petite femme aigrée" and quoting the *Parti Ouvrier,* the official Possibilist organ, to the effect that she had called all the British members of the other group "bogus." "That," sneered the *Labour Elector,* referring to her supposed perpetuation of the cleavage, "will be something for her

[4] Gould, *Hyndman,* pp. 112–13.

to take—a sort of peace offering—when next she pays a visit to her old friend in St. John's Wood. . . ."

Mrs. Besant was missing from the British Trades Union Congress held in Dundee in September. Beatrice Potter, who was not to meet her personally for another year, commented with some surprise on the absence of this Socialist leader. Because neither she nor John Burns was present, the presentation of the Socialist viewpoint depended on "two somewhat foolish young men, delegates of the London compositors," and the Socialists' strength dwindled to only 11 votes, while the old-guard opposition, led by Broadhurst, received 177. Nevertheless, shortly afterward, Mrs. Besant lectured on "The Trades Union Movement" in a series on "A Century of Social Movements" conducted by the Fabian Society.[5]

It was toward the end of this year, too, that Shaw edited and published his influential collection of *Fabian Essays*, one of which, "Industry under Socialism," was by Annie Besant. It, like some of the others, had appeared in preliminary form in *Our Corner*. Urging the reformers to "Capture the County Councils" so that socialized production could be initiated by the municipalities, co-operative societies could be formed, and gradually the land and most of the instruments of production could be bought up—with the exception of mining and a few other natural resources, which should be developed by the central government—she laid the foundations for some of her later basic ideas on the fundamental importance of village councils in India. Though Sidney Webb later spoke of her scheme for ending the unemployment problem as one of the follies of Fabian youth, her inclusion in this significant volume showed the respect in which she was held as an authority on labor, industry, and trades unions. In fact, her name was the only one of the whole panel of later famous authors to be at all known outside the pale of the small circle of her revolutionary associates. Yet the public sale of the volume was astounding.[6]

When the dock-workers' strike broke out in August, paralyzing shipping and industry and almost developing into that bête noire of capitalism, a general strike of all workers, Mrs. Besant did not participate, though she had been in the midst of a dozen or two strikes all through the year, including one of the male matchmakers. Her women's Match-makers' Union now had over seven hundred members; young Frederick May had died, leaving a fortune of £272,321; she and Burrows were still secretary and treasurer of this Union; and Sweden had formed a similar organization, its first for women.[7] But, though Mrs. Besant had written an article

[5] Beatrice Webb, *Our Partnership* (London, 1940), pp. 23, 403–4; *Justice*, September 14, 1889; October 5, 1889.

[6] *Fabian Essays* (London, 1950), pp. 140–58; Clayton, *The Rise and Decline of Socialism in Great Britain, 1884–1924*, p. 214; Irvine, *The Universe of G. B. S.*, p. 99; *Star*, March 21, 1889; St. John Ervine, *Bernard Shaw*, p. 203.

[7] *National Reformer*, February 10, December 7, 1889.

on "Dockyard Labor" for the *Reformer* in January, based on a paper in the *Lancet* entitled "The Dangers Attending Labor in the Docks," the S.D.F. had never quite approved the dockyard strike, perhaps because it was being led chiefly by such labor leaders as Mann, Burns, Champion, and Tillett, who had "ratted" from the Federation and the Red Flag. Even Burns, "the Man with the Red Flag," no longer waved it, especially when he accepted a compromise after first backing the later withdrawn manifesto demanding a general strike. As *Justice* put it, ". . . the moment the White Feather is allowed to supplant the Red Flag our cause is lost."

Eleanor Marx-Aveling, however, was in the midst of things, speaking and helping the families of the strikers. She, Edward, and a tiny number of other dissidents had recently broken away completely from the Socialist League and formed their own little cell, which they called the Bloomsbury Socialist Society and which met at the Communist Club.[8] Mrs. Besant's role in this greatest of all the year's many strikes was confined to signing a long, privately circulated document which tried to dissuade "all the men who have any brains and courage from leaving the S.D.F." She also wrote an editorial in *Justice* on "The Lessons of the Strike," wherein she reminded the workers how for years the S.D.F. had gone to the docks to preach their rights and attacked the ill-conceived proposal for a general strike. Instead, she ended, all must prepare for the great "uprising which will come ere long."

The last months of 1889 were marked by another shattering event for Annie Besant. Charles Bradlaugh, who had remained her unswerving and devoted friend for fifteen years and, though flinching now and then, had loyally absorbed all the heavy blows she had been dealing him, caught a fever in the rain and collapsed with consumption. After four weeks in bed, nursed by his daughter Hypatia and visited by Mrs. Besant whenever possible, he announced his intention of resigning as the head of the fading N.S.S. By February, "pale, dreary, and dejected," he had recovered sufficiently to sail for India, partly to recuperate on the long voyage and partly to participate in the annual meeting of the National Congress party at Bombay, where he was generally acclaimed as the "Member for India," a title he had long held in the House because of his advocacy of Indian causes.[9]

His illness had undoubtedly been aggravated by Annie's latest step in her fanatical quest for what she felt she could call "Truth"—a step which was to involve her in more public obloquy and derision and in a new kind of martyrdom.

[8] Morris, *Letters,* December 15, 1889; *Star,* September 23, 1889.

[9] *Autobiography,* p. 458; Bonner, *Bradlaugh,* II, 13–14, 107–8; Robertson, "Account of [Bradlaugh's] Parliamentary Struggles, Politics, and Teachings," in Bonner, *Bradlaugh,* II, 407; *National Reformer,* November 24, December 8, 1889.

V. *Fifth Life:* THE CHELA OF THE MAHATMAS

1

Madame Blavatsky
and Her "Secret Doctrine"

One day late in June, 1889, Bernard Shaw dropped in at the office of H. W. Massingham, editor of the *Star*. Inquisitively glancing at a set of proofs lying scattered about the table, he noticed that one was headed "*Sic Itur ad Astra;* or, Why I Became a Theosophist." Knowing that everybody who was anybody in London had been talking about Theosophy for the last four or five years, he looked for the signature. It was that of Annie Besant.

Staggered by this unprepared blow, which meant to me the loss of a powerful colleague and of a friendship which had become part of my daily life, I rushed round to her office in Fleet Street, and there delivered myself of an unbounded denunciation of Theosophy in general, of female inconstancy, and in particular of H. P. Blavatsky, one of whose books—I forget whether it was "The Secret Doctrine" or "Isis Unveiled"—had done all the mischief.

Resorting to all the old tricks by which he had puzzled, teased, or moved her in the past, Shaw found that this time he had met his match. Mrs. Besant listened to him with kindness and amusement and then remarked that since she had become a vegetarian (as he was), perhaps the diet had enfeebled her mind. "In short, she was for the first time able to play with me: she was no longer in the grip of her pride: she had after many explorations found her path and come to see the universe and herself in their real perspective." In other words, Shaw went on, introducing one of his own favorite themes, she had "lost her illusions, if she had **any,** as to the impudent idolatry of the voter which we call democracy." Consequently, he concluded, after a short time he dropped out of her "saga," though he never forgot his part in it—or his affection for Annie Besant.[1]

Shaw's recollections of his stupefying discovery are probably correct in most details, though the fact that he says he was unprepared for the blow shows how far he had already dropped out of Mrs. Besant's "saga" before the revelation came. His ignorance of her developing mysticism is especially surprising in view of his own long-continued interest in Spiritualism, prompted by his mother's faithful devotion to it—even though this interest led to complete skepticism, which revealed itself inversely through his later confession that he attended many seances simply in order to "cheat" mischievously at them.[2]

Some of Shaw's biographers,[3] however, tell a somewhat different and even more circumstantial story, presumably based on Shaw's later (and probably retouched) recollections. In 1888, according to one version, Annie had asked him to get her some reviewing work on Stead's *Pall Mall Gazette* (though why she had to use Shaw as an intermediary is hard to understand, since she had already become close friends with Stead through their association on Bloody Sunday and in the Law and Liberty League). And it was Shaw himself (who had already reviewed certain of the *Proceedings of the Society for Psychical Research,* as well as a life of Mme. Blavatsky) who had passed on to her the copy of *The Secret Doctrine* which the *Gazette* had given him for review. When he saw the results of his rashness in the *Star* proofs, he

. . . instantly rushed round to her office in Fleet Street and asked her whether she knew that Blavatsky had been exposed at a meeting of the Psychical Society at which he had been present, as having worked a miracle at her shrine in Adyar by a conjuring trick? She knew all about it, and, rightly, did not consider that it made any difference to theosophy even if she believed in the exposure, which she didn't. Shaw played his last card. "Why need you go to Thibet for a Mahatma? Here and now is your Mahatma. I am your Mahatma." But the charm was broken. They remained good friends; but the rest of her career was Shawless.

But in the version of the story told by Annie herself as well as by Stead and his biographers, the review episode itself was Shawless. In these more immediate and authentic versions, in fact, Shaw was never even mentioned.[4] In a way, said Stead, it all went back to Mme. Olga

---

[1] Shaw, "Mrs. Besant's Passage through Fabian Socialism," *Dr. Annie Besant.* For an attempt to show how many essentially Theosophical ideas Shaw himself was to hold, see H. B. Hyams, "Bernard Shaw and Theosophy," *Theosophist,* November, 1915.

[2] Archibald Henderson, *George Bernard Shaw: Man of the Century,* pp. 77 ff.

[3] Notably R. F. Rattray, *Bernard Shaw: A Chronicle,* p. 63, and Hesketh Pearson, *G. B. S.: A Full-Length Portrait,* pp. 94–95. Cf. also Arthur H. Nethercot, "G. B. S. and Annie Besant," *Shaw Bulletin,* September, 1955.

[4] *Autobiography,* pp. 438–45; Frederic Whyte, *The Life of W. T. Stead* (New York, 1925), p. 249 n.; W. T. Stead, "Annie Besant," *Review of Reviews,* October, 1891, pp.

Novikoff, the peculiar "unofficial Representative of the Russian Nation," whom he had first met in 1877 and at whose salon in the next year he had found Gladstone, Froude, Matthew Arnold, Carlyle, and other notables. Mme. Novikoff had written Stead in 1888 asking whether he would like to meet Mme. Blavatsky, her countrywoman, who had just arrived in London. After hesitating for a while, even though he had been somewhat interested in the occult since he had attended his first seance in 1881, he finally went and "was delighted with, and at the same time somewhat repelled by," this strange, unconventional, masculine woman. H.P.B. soon gave him her photograph and told him that, whatever he might call himself, he was still a good Theosophist.

Consequently, when the two thick volumes of *The Secret Doctrine* reached his office for review, Stead felt an obligation to notice them, though he himself "shrank in dismay" from the task of mastering their contents. Knowing that Mrs. Besant had for some time been interesting herself in the other world, and even investigating seances, he took the tomes down to her and asked if she would tackle them, saying (perhaps with reference to Shaw), "My young men all fight shy of them, but you are quite mad enough on these subjects to make something of them." She did so, was fascinated by their contents, wrote her review, and asked Stead to give her a letter of introduction to their author. Thus, through Mme. Novikoff (with whom, in fact, Stead had recently had a "tiff"), Annie Besant became a Theosophist. During the course of her fiercely determined study of the book, she wrote one of her little "Annie" notes to Stead: "I am immersed in Madame B.! If I perish in the attempt to review her, you must write on my tomb, 'She has gone to investigate the Secret Doctrine at first hand.' "[5]

On March 15 she sent Stead's note to Mme. Blavatsky and asked permission to call. On receipt of a cordial and flattering reply, inviting her to come and bring Herbert Burrows and anyone else she wished, she and Burrows, who had been her constant companion in her new studies and investigations as well as in her work in social reform, walked "in the soft spring evening" from the Notting Hill Station to the door of 17 Lansdowne Road, wondering what they would meet behind it. According to her own story, Annie, at first sight of the strange, corpulent, rough, compelling woman, confined to a wheel chair and waiting in the drawing room, was conscious of a sudden leaping forth of her heart—"was it

91–92; Estelle W. Stead, *My Father: Personal and Spiritual Reminiscences* (New York, 1913), pp. 61, 72, 155–56; Annie Besant, "Stages in My Growth toward Theosophy," *Daily Chronicle*, November 16, 1891; *Theosophist*, September, 1930, pp. 779–80; October, 1931, pp. 56–57; January, 1932, p. 377; February, 1932, pp. 509–13. Mrs. Besant's own accounts often contradict one another in minor details of time, order, etc.

[5] Whyte, *The Life of W. T. Stead*; Gertrude Marvin Williams, *The Passionate Pilgrim*, p. 179; *Star*, January 10, 1889.

recognition?"—and then of a "fierce rebellion, a fierce withdrawal, as of some wild beast when it feels a mastering hand." She told Mme. Blavatsky she was interested in her work and would like to know a little more of her sources of knowledge, but the other merely started to tell about a visit she had once paid to Egypt and then turned the conversation into even more general channels. It was very disappointing, for not a word was said of occultism. But at the end of the meeting, as the callers rose to go, "for a moment the veil lifted, and two brilliant, piercing eyes met mine, and with a yearning throb in the voice: 'Oh, my dear Mrs. Besant, if you would only come among us!'" But Annie, though feeling a "well-nigh uncontrollable desire to bend down and kiss her, under the compulsion of that yearning voice, those compelling eyes," hardened her heart to the hypnotic power and turned away with a commonplace goodbye.

As soon as her review came out in the *Gazette*, she sent the author a copy and was quickly invited to call again. Annie went, and this time asked tentatively about the Theosophical Society, "wishful to join, but fighting against it," realizing the new "vortex of strife" and ridicule into which she would be plunged, after she had largely conquered public prejudice against her atheism, Malthusianism, and socialism by her work on the School Board. Inwardly tortured, she went away without committing herself, but soon returned a third time. Now she was ready to join, but H.P.B., who had been astutely reading the minds and estimating the attitudes of both Mrs. Besant and Burrows all along, as she admitted later, asked whether Annie had read the damning report made by Richard Hodgson for the Society for Psychical Research about her "phenomena" and about the Coulombs, her servants and "accomplices," who had turned against her and made their disclosures and charges during her absence from Adyar. Mrs. Besant said she had not even heard of the report (a statement which is extremely hard to believe; but years later she also said she was not even familiar with the name of the author of *The Secret Doctrine* when Stead offered it to her—two lapses of memory which, together with Shaw's, show how fallible the human mind is). So she borrowed a copy of it (plenty of her friends could have lent her one, since the "exposé" had been widely read in London) and read and reread it for two days. It did not change her mind, which obviously was made up to accept her new martyrdom. She rejected all the S.P.R. evidence as built on too slender a foundation, especially on the treachery and previous lying of the Coulombs (to which even Bradlaugh had called attention in his own comments on the matter in the *Reformer* in 1884). She simply could not believe such trickery and hypocrisy of a woman like Mme. Blavatsky. Besides, she asked herself, even if the accusations of the fake occult phenomena were true, how could they affect the basic truths of Theosophy?

The next day she went to the office of the Theosophical Publishing Company in Duke Street and asked the Countess Wachtmeister, one of the earliest and "lealest" (a favorite word of Mrs. Besant) of the many titled converts to Theosophy, for an application blank, which she promptly made out. Now ready to become a "Fellow of the Theosophical Society," or an "F.T.S.," as its members all signed themselves, she hastened to Lansdowne Road to report what she had done. There, with tears in the eyes of both, she knelt before H.P.B. and received the blessing of "Master K.H.," who had chosen Mme. Blavatsky to be his agent. Annie would become his own chela or disciple and would study under H.P.B. From that day, May 10, 1889,[6] she never wavered in her public faith in Theosophy or in her conviction that it held the key to her long-sought brotherhood of man. Nor was her faith in H.P.B. ever shaken, though she did not always have the same confidence in various others who claimed to have been chosen as vehicles by the Mahatmas. It was a sort of repetition of her first experience of religious skepticism, which she had rejected with "Credo quia impossibile."

As a matter of fact, Mrs. Besant was simply following in the footsteps of Herbert Burrows, who had made up his mind before she had. With the exception of Mrs. Thornton Smith, who had done valiant editorial and lecture work for the N.S.S. for several years, Burrows was the only important member of any of her old circles to join the Theosophical Society, though Stead was eventually to become a prominent Spiritualist. Burrows, who emphasized his own spirit of skepticism mixed with a dissatisfaction with the materialistic life he had been living, had been drawn back, after his first visit with Annie, to this "stout, unwieldy lady, playing Russian 'Patience' "; and, though he neither saw nor expected any miracles of levitation or materialized teacups à la Adyar, he was convinced and became an "F.T.S." a few days before Mrs. Besant. His spirit was heavy, for his wife had died early in April, and Mme. Blavatsky had helped him when "the wheels of my life ran so heavily that they nearly stopped." (Many people became Theosophists under somewhat similar circumstances.) Burrows later wrote a note to the Press Association, asking it to correct a slightly erroneous report in the *Manchester Guardian* concerning how and when he and Mrs. Besant had joined the T.S.; thus the world no longer had any excuse for not knowing the facts of the immediate conversions.[7]

But the world could not yet know how long this process of transformation had been going on or what a hypocritical life (if that is not too strong a term) Mrs. Besant, according to her own later confession, had

---

[6] She was formally admitted, however, on May 21 (see *The Golden Book of the Theosophical Society* [Adyar, 1925], p. 102).

[7] *Pall Mall Gazette*, September 9, 19, 1889; *Lucifer*, June 15, 1891; *Justice*, April 6, 1889.

been leading, though most of London had for many months been observing the development of her astounding conversion. Hypatia Bradlaugh Bonner, with sad reproachfulness, in describing the effect of the announcement on her father, dated the beginnings of Mrs. Besant's doubts back some ten years:

For thirteen years she had stood upon the same platform with him; and when she one day said that for ten years she had been dissatisfied with her own teaching, he felt it very keenly, but he neither uttered a word of blame himself, nor would he allow anyone else to blame her in his hearing.[8]

Mrs. Besant herself, more specifically, dated the beginning of the final phase of her loss of faith in doubt at the year 1886. Acknowledging no effects from her disappointments in her relations with individual persons such as Shaw and Bradlaugh, she described only a growing feeling that her philosophy was not enough. The Socialist position had sufficed on the economic side, but it did not furnish the motive and inspiration to lead to the brotherhood of man. Her efforts to organize "bands of unselfish workers" in the L.L.L. had failed; people, she found, did not work for love—they wanted to take, not give. Certainly—though she did not mention it—Freethought did not furnish this altruistic inspiration either. Despairing, she turned to the study of the new psychology and the revelations of hypnotic experiments—the "obscurer sides of consciousness, dreams, hallucinations, illusions, insanity."

All these feelings and new interests revealed themselves in the subjects of her reading, her reviews, her articles, and her lectures during this period, alongside the ambivalent attitude of herself and her friends toward the peculiar new doctrines of Theosophy. Ostensibly she still supported the opinion that Bradlaugh had stated in the *Reformer* of November, 1884, toward Mme. Blavatsky and his old friend Olcott, together with their beautifully printed magazine, the *Theosophist:*

. . . to our untutored mind the bulk of the last two or three years' declarations of Madame Blavatsky and Colonel Olcott are so startlingly at variance with the possible that we hardly read the *Theosophist* as a serious publication, nor can we treat the Theosophists as serious persons. Many of them are very respectable, very good, and very mad. Some of them are less mad and less good.

In respect to the Coulomb affair, "we can only acquit Madame Blavatsky by regarding her as an enthusiastic semi-spiritualist who has managed to get fairly crazed in dabbling with the wonderful in company with many simpletons." Exactly three years later Mrs. Besant herself in her "Publisher's Corner" of *Our Corner* remarked:

Very strange are some of the publications of this last quarter of the nineteenth century. What is to be said of such a magazine as *Lucifer,* "a theosophical

---

[8] *Autobiography,* pp. 438–40; Bonner, *Charles Bradlaugh,* II, 13.

monthly"? It has a very effective cover, but the contents are mere ravings; it may suffice to say that during the perusal of one story the reader is requested to accept "the theory of the reincarnation of souls" as a living fact.

An article, however, of which Mrs. Besant was more disposed to approve was one exposing the fallacies of Spiritualism and the jugglery of most mediums. In the next month she published a contemptuous review by "Fabian Bland" on the popular novelist, Rider Haggard, and his use of witchcraft, astral bodies, and a belief in eternal life in his highly popular stories. Her own viewpoint was presumably more faithfully reflected in a digest she wrote in October of a paper by her admired old contributor, Dr. Ludwig Büchner, "Freethought and Philosophical Doctrines: Considerations on Spiritualism, Materialism, and Positivism." In it he opposed Spiritualism to materialism in a general sense, but did not deal with the psychic except in connection with the theory that "Force and matter (Stoff) or Spirit and matter (Materie) are . . . only two sides of different phaenomena of one and the same unknown something or fundamental principle of all things." From this point of view, he concluded, "Supernatural or extra-natural things . . . cannot exist, since all things are included in Nature."

In view of her later editorship of *Lucifer* and acceptance of reincarnation and astral bodies as basic elements in her own Theosophy, it is amusing also to find her continuing her previous contempt for Edwin Arnold's poetry by ending her review of his "Lotus and Jewel" in the *Reformer* for December with a protest against its "magniloquent absurdity" and a generous permission, "By all means let anyone who wants to do so say Om." Within three years she herself was saying "Om" with the best of the Hindus and presumably benefiting from all the mystic advantages accruing from the proper repetition of this reverberating monosyllable.

During 1888 and the first half of 1889, however, most of the attacks on mysticism in the *Reformer* came from the pen of its chief editor. Bradlaugh admitted that because of his long-standing prejudice he was probably incapable of doing justice to the undoubtedly talented exponents of Theosophy and did not blame the Archbishop of Canterbury for having difficulty in following their expositions. He hoped H.P.B. was right in asserting that Theosophists had helped to break down caste in India, and he thought they might be right in predicting that 1888 would be a bad year; but he did not consider their reason—that 1888 was a "dark number"—to be very convincing. And all the time he continued his campaign against Spiritualism, its mediums, its seances, and its heartless exploitations of credulous poor people.

During the same period, however, the tone of Mrs. Besant's references to religion, and especially Oriental religion, began to change. Early in 1889 she began her series of articles called "Primitive Religion"—her first on such a subject for some time. In it she made certain significant observations: how "The belief in spirits, which always accompanies developed fetichism, has its chief origin in dreams," evil spirits coming first, good later; how widespread in savage tribes is the notion "of the dream-life being a spiritual existence"; and how "from wonder, divorced from fear, has been born Knowledge; but fear and ignorance have only given birth to Superstition; of Knowledge, Science is the radiant child; but Religion is the offspring of Superstition." Soon she herself would be teaching that all the happenings in the world were the result of the conflict between the Dark Brotherhood and the White Brotherhood and accepting the existence of Black and White Magic. At the same time she was reading articles in the *Reformer* by the faithful N.S.S. member, George Standring, on "Esoteric Buddhism" and reports on the lectures by A. P. Sinnett on the same subject, leading to his lucid explanation of the principles of Theosophy. By May 5, 1889, she herself was talking to a Hall of Science audience on "Buddha: His Life and Teachings." She also, it is true, lectured on "The Value of Unbelief" and "Problems of Mind" and commented happily on the announcement that at last the long campaign in which she and others had engaged to erect a statue of Giordano Bruno in Rome had come to a successful conclusion, in spite of the Pope's horror. After all, though to Freethinkers Bruno was a skeptic and a martyr, to Theosophists he was essentially a Theosophist. In fact, some years later, she would "remember" that she herself had once been Giordano Bruno.

Although she had participated in a debate on "Buddhism and Christianity," with herself the exponent of Buddhism, and had eloquently defended the scientist W. K. Clifford and his "Unseen Universe" because to him science was a sacred thing, she also attended services at St. Paul's, to hear her old friend Canon Liddon preach, and at St. Nicholas Cole-Abbey to hear Canon H. C. Shuttleworth. In both cases, though reflecting on the waste of eloquence and power in their "useless casuistries," she came away impressed by their sincerity and the beauty of their services. At the same time, she commented sarcastically on the theistic church run by her one-time mentor, Charles Voysey, in Swallow Street, Piccadilly.

In fact, as the *Freethinker* sarcastically told its readers in September, 1888, at this time Mrs. Besant was actually requesting permission from the Church Congress to address it on socialism, and Foote wondered whether she had changed her attitude toward the church and whether perhaps she might be converted by the bishops. He need not have worried, however, since her offer was not accepted. Annie could have read in the same paper some innuendoes about a past affair in the life of the Rev. Charles W. Leadbeater, who was then an Anglican curate in Hampshire and later received an enthusiastic reception in Ceylon as a Buddhist and a Theosophist. Likewise, she could have learned how happy

Olcott was over the success of Theosophy in France and America and how he had just left for Japan to convert the people there. And she could have found more about the opinions of Sinnett, Blavatsky, etc., on the existence—or rather the lack of existence—of a personal God and about a poem in *Lucifer* by Gerald Massey, who in spite of his mysticism was always highly regarded by the Freethinkers.

In the meantime, the other London papers were keeping up a running fire on Theosophy. In the *Star* she could have read how the elderly Lord Crawford, Earl of Crawford and Balcarres, who had belonged to Edward Bulwer, Lord Lytton's, Rosicrucian set when he was a boy, was now investigating Theosophy; how the Brahmin, Mohini Chatterji, the Theosophical emissary who had been such a social hit in England and America, denied that he had been converted to Catholicism by a Jesuit; how, surprisingly, the first edition of *The Secret Doctrine* had sold out in October, 1888, and a new one was being printed; how the amiable Colonel Olcott, who had just departed for Ceylon, could "describe minutely the future career of the astral body of a confirmed theosophist—himself to wit"; how H.P.B.'s "great heavy Blucher shoes" were an interviewer's "only hold on reality"; how the house of the Dutch Baroness de Pallandt in Bryanston Street was the center of many Theosophical activities; how the Theosophical movement, including Lord Crawford, Lady Caithness, "and other distinguished persons," had been thrown into confusion by the withdrawal (actually the forced resignation)[9] of Mabel Collins, coeditor of *Lucifer*, but how the Countess Wachtmeister had assured the *Star* that her departure would have no important effect; and so on.

Against this general background, what had actually happened to Annie Besant herself after she had decided to discard her previous materialism? In her popular lecture, "Stages in My Growth toward Theosophy," delivered in Camden Town on November 15, 1891, with Herbert Burrows in the chair, Mrs. Besant explained that after giving up Christianity she had first been attracted to Spiritualism, but that at that time she had been working too hard for her living to follow it up. Strangely enough, this was her first mention of such a phase, since previously it had been an interest in theism, through Voysey and Scott, that had supplanted her allegiance to Christianity. Her deprivation of her daughter had next turned her to Secularism, because she thought it would make her more useful to society. This period trained her powers of observation and took away her cocksureness. Then her study of psychology, aided by Bradlaugh, brought out many facts which puzzled her. At this point a report on Spiritualistic phenomena issued by the Dialectical Society from the experiments conducted by J. H. Levy and ten other people, all above suspicion, impressed her greatly. In this "fluidistic condition of mind," one of the members of her science class brought her a copy of Sinnett's *The*

[9] See W. B. Yeats, *Four Years* (Churchtown, Dundrum, 1921), pp. 74–75; Joseph Hone, *W. B. Yeats* (London, 1942), p. 71.

Occult World, which at first repelled her. Knowing that Sinnett's famous London Lodge of the Theosophical Society had been built on a purely social and intellectual appeal to the upper-class members of society, she concluded that the T.S. was only a "fashionable, dress-coat affair." Nevertheless, she persisted. The famous Mahatma letters contained in the volume, "expounding not the supernatural but a nature under law, wider than I had dared to conceive," appealed strongly to her. So, with Burrows, she made a careful study of Sinnett's *Esoteric Buddhism,* which sent her back to Spiritualism again.[10]

Experimenting privately, as she confessed in her *Autobiography,* she found the phenomena themselves indubitable, but the Spiritualistic explanation incredible. Having thus accepted the reality of such things as clairvoyance, clairaudience, and thought-reading, she was convinced by the spring of 1889 that there was "some hidden thing, some hidden power," which she resolved to find. Among these preliminary private experiments was a seance held early in October, 1888, at her home in St. John's Wood. This was duly reported in the *Star,* which added ironically, "Unlike the French clerics described in Blackwood's Magazine, she has not yet succeeded in calling up the Prince of Darkness." Foote was even more derisive in the *Freethinker,* which quoted the *Star's* phrase, "an interesting seance," and then queried:

We should like to know how the seance was "interesting." How many spirits turned up, and did they say anything worth listening to? Perhaps we shall find the particulars in "Daybreak"—no connexion with the *Medium and Daybreak* [the title of a leading Spiritualist paper].

As late as March 9, 1889, the Hon. Auberon Herbert, son of the Earl of Carnarvon, former Liberal M.P., trustee of Herbert Spencer, author of *A Politician in Search of His Soul,* and a former member of the anti-Sabbatarian movement along with Bradlaugh and Mrs. Besant, had not lost hope of converting the latter to his hobby of Spiritualism. Early in January, indeed, he had entered the lists against the great Thomas Huxley himself by replying doughtily to Huxley's long article, "Spiritualism Unmasked," in the *Pall Mall Gazette.* On March 10 Beatrice Potter wrote in her diary:

Auberon Herbert dropped in for lunch yesterday. He was excited with the prospect of converting Mrs. Besant to spiritualism; she had written to him about his article in the *Pall Mall* and it will probably end in a visit to the Old House. Strange will be the intimacy between these two natures: Mrs. Besant, with her rabid Socialism, embittered, by personal suffering, against the morality and the creed of Christendom; and Auberon Herbert, with his idealistic individualism, a character softened and perhaps even weakened by perpetually dwelling on spiritualistic influences.[11]

[10] *Daily Chronicle,* November 16, 1891; *Autobiography,* pp. 439–40; *Golden Book,* p. 103.

[11] Beatrice Webb, *My Apprenticeship,* p. 187.

Herbert of course was to be disappointed, though Mrs. Besant and Burrows did associate themselves temporarily with a group of Spiritualists and asked Stead also to join. At first he refused, but joined later after they had left. Probably he was disillusioned by such episodes as that in which a table tapped out a circumstantial story about the death of one of their members, a clergyman, while traveling in Ireland, only to have the seance interrupted by the arrival of a latecomer, the clergyman himself. With such an interest in Spiritualism, it is indeed surprising that Mrs. Besant attended none of the meetings of the Society for Psychical Research, which had its first office in the Dean's Yard rooms of Frank Podmore, an original Fabian. Through him and Edward Reynolds, another Fabian, Shaw had been brought into touch with the activities of the S.P.R.; and on one exciting evening, after attending a Fabian meeting, he had gone on to hear the end of a Psychical Research seance "and ended by sleeping in a haunted house with a committee of ghost-hunters," where he was mortified by having a nightmare and waking up to find himself struggling in a corner with the ghost.[12] Since the scene of this encounter was perhaps the Old House of Beatrice Potter's diary, it is all the more surprising that Shaw knew nothing of Mrs. Besant's similar investigations.

Shortly after this, as she was sitting alone at her desk in the *Reformer* office, just after the sun had set, and was immersed in a deep but nearly hopeless longing "to solve the riddle of life and mind," she heard a Voice speaking to her. It was much like her experience when, as a young, despairing wife, she had almost taken the chloroform, but had been forbidden by the same Voice. Again she could see nobody, but the Voice said, "Are you willing to give up everything for the sake of truth?" She made what she later realized was a curious answer for a Radical and a Freethinker. She said aloud, "Yes, Lord." Then the Voice informed her quietly, "In a short time you will know it." That was all.

But in a few days the Voice spoke to her again, and she became His pupil. She recollected over forty years later, with a much more vivid memory for detail than she had shown in her revised *Autobiography* only four years after the event:

I did not challenge Him or ask questions. I had this intense feeling in me. He had the knowledge. I had not. I wanted the truth; that was the fact. I was longing to have it intensely. So I went head over heels into it, and I have never wavered since. I was forty-two years old when I first read *The Secret Doctrine.*[13]

The Voice was of course that of her Master, who directed Stead to give her Mme. Blavatsky's volumes a fortnight later.

[12] Williams, *The Passionate Pilgrim*, pp. 183–84; Henderson, *George Bernard Shaw: His Life and Works*, p. 127 n., and *George Bernard Shaw: Man of the Century*, pp. 77 ff.

[13] *Theosophist*, October, 1931, pp. 56–57, quoting from *Hollywood Theosophist; Autobiography*, pp. 440–41.

2

Annie among the Occultists

Shaw could hardly be blamed for not recognizing Mrs. Besant's review in the *Pall Mall Gazette*, since like all *Gazette* reviews it was unsigned. Entitled "Among the Adepts. Madame Blavatsky on the 'Secret Doctrine,'" it appeared on April 25, 1889, and ran to a column and a half. It opened thus:

It would be difficult to find a book presenting more difficulties to the "reviewer with a conscience" than these handsome volumes bearing the name of Mdme. Blavatsky as author—or, perhaps, it would be more accurate to say, as compiler and annotator. The subject matter is so far removed from our Occidental fashion of envisioning the universe; the lore gathered and expounded so different from the science or metaphysics of the West, that to ninety-nine out of every hundred readers—perhaps to nine hundred ninety-nine among every thousand—the study of the book will begin in bewilderment and end in despair.

She then went on to comment on and summarize the book very sympathetically and concluded:

The wild dreams of one generation become the commonplaces of a later one, and all those who keep an open door to Truth will give scrutiny to any visitant, be the garb of Asia or of Europe, be the tongue of Paris or of India. If this counsel be of folly or of falsehood it shall come to naught, but if of Truth ye cannot overthrow it. Passing strange is it. Of the truth in it our superficial examination is insufficient to decide.

The missionary—almost the Christian Evidence—style and purpose of this review stand out all over it!

Nor could Shaw be blamed for failing to notice the first appearance of his former comrade's name in print with a Theosophical label, since the magazine *Lucifer* was scarcely within his ordinary purview. In its issue for June 15, however, it had rushed into print an article by the new prize convert, signed "Annie Besant, F.T.S." Its topic was the logical one for a writer with her immediate antecedents—in fact, it was one of her main reasons for entering the Theosophical Society. Entitled "Practical Work for Theosophists," it promptly gave a new turn to the whole Theosophical movement in England, for it offered humanitarian and altruistic advice to members, including names and addresses of people who would be glad to accept their "duteous service to Man" through Consumer Leagues, leisure-time service in hospitals, buying shares in companies that needed reform in working conditions and hours, and such practical matters. There was nothing in the slightest degree mystical in Annie Besant's first contribution to the Theosophical movement, even though her paper was stuffed with abstractions such as Love, Service, Brotherhood, Intellect, Ignorance, Altruism, and Humanity.

Shaw, however, might well have come upon Mrs. Besant's third acknowledgment of her new allegiance, since it was made in the *National Reformer*, a weekly that he generally kept up with, particularly because, as he asserted later, he had once been considered as a possible successor to Foote as president of the London Secularist Federation. Luckily, his address to them on "Progress in Freethought," being of "a somewhat mystical and even Catholic nature," so froze the marrow in the bones of the Fundamentalist atheist members that the idea was never revived.[1]

On June 9 the annual convention of the N.S.S. had been held in the Hall of Science. Bradlaugh had been unanimously re-elected president, though he confessed in his address that he had thought of resigning because he feared he did not any longer have the "full confidence of the Freethought party." Mrs. Besant and the rest of the old slate had been re-elected vice-presidents, and her speech in the evening, advocating Freethought and humanism, had been welcomed with "loud and long applause." Her work on the School Board was praised; but not a hint was passed, by herself or anyone else, of her new Theosophy.

Then, in the issue of the *Reformer* for June 23, appeared another long review of *The Secret Doctrine*, this time signed simply "Annie Besant." First explaining, without apologizing, why she thought such a work should be interesting to the "more or less liberal-minded" readers of the *Reformer*, in spite of the difficulty and the unfamiliar views expressed, she attested to the honesty and reliability of Mme. Blavatsky, the depth of her Oriental learning, and her "access to rare and recondite sources of information." Then she launched into an even more detailed analysis of the contents of the work than she had made for the *Gazette*. Starting with the Book of Dzyan, "which is claimed as one of the oldest MSS. in the world" and which Mme. Blavatsky said she had examined and copied

---

[1] Shaw, "What Is My Religious Faith?" in *Sixteen Self Sketches* (New York, 1949), p. 121.

during her sojourn in Tibet (but which no one else has ever seen; nor does anyone but Theosophists accept her claim that she spent ten, seven, or three years—the period varies—there in the Himalayas studying under the Masters),[2] Mrs. Besant went on to her task of summation.

Much of the difficulty of the book, she felt, lay in the difference between the scientific approach of the West and the East—the West interrogating Nature and looking for the tangible in facts; the East exploring the Mind, cultivating faculties unknown to the West, and regarding all the rest of life as Maya or illusion. As a matter of fact, she pointed out, many psychical faculties previously unrecognized and certainly beyond the range of the normal were now revealing themselves to many persons in the West: "clairvoyance, mesmerism, hypnotism, point to the existence, under abnormal conditions, of an inner vision that transcends the eye-power, and of faculties not yet understood." Her digest of the work before her, based on the Book of Dzyan and its commentaries by "The Wise Men of the East," then continued as follows:

First in the evolution of the universe came the "Absolute Be-ness" (sometimes called the "Logos"), before the visible universe came into existence. The visible universe consists of seven stages, or hierarchies—the first three concerning the crystallization of Spirit into Matter and the fourth concerning the turning of Spirit upward again and its beginning to rid itself once more the grossness of Matter as seen in the physical body of man. The last three stages are devoted to the completion of this process and the eventual emergence of the spirit into Nirvana, or perfection. Man himself is also a sevenfold being—the first four parts being animal or material, and perishing at or soon after death; the other three, which are immortal, forming the Ego, or higher self. Mrs. Besant's synopsis ended with a brief description of the mental and physical evolution of man and each race of men. Throughout, adopting Mme. Blavatsky's approach, she stressed the confirmation of the Eastern teachings by the new scientific discoveries of the West, emphasizing especially the recent conclusion by biologists that the mysterious pineal gland in the brain is simply the vestigial remains of a "third eye" which man once possessed. (Strangely enough, a few weeks earlier the *Reformer* had published a long article, citing modern scientific authorities, on the pineal gland of vertebrates as "the stalk on which once rested an invertebrate eye.") With her own background as a student and teacher of science, Mrs. Besant called special attention to Mme. Blavatsky's section on "Science and the Secret Doctrine Contrasted," as "though Science were standing on the very threshold of knowledge which shall make all her past seem small." Most of this knowledge was already available through Theosophy. It had

[2] See C. E. Bechhofer-Roberts, *The Mysterious Madame: Helena Petrovna Blavatsky* (New York, 1931), and Gertrude Marvin Williams, *Priestess of the Occult* (New York, 1946). Both these books are vigorously and angrily decried by Theosophists of all sects.

a vast potential if used properly, after "the social order has been transformed," but was very dangerous in the hands of mere Selfishness and Greed. "Hence the wisdom of those 'Masters' in whose name Mme. Blavatsky speaks, has ever denied the knowledge which is power until Love's lesson has been learned, and has given into the hands of the selfless the control of those natural forces which, misused, would wreck society."

With such a promising prospect before him, what intelligent person would not join the Theosophical Society? As the publicity officer for the Besant centennial celebration in 1947 wrote of this review: "For she, agnostic of agnostics, had become gnostic."

Charles Bradlaugh, however, felt quite differently about Mme. Blavatsky's secret doctrine, which had now become public. He was particularly hurt by the fact that Annie had neither asked his approval of the review in advance nor informed him that she had turned Theosophist—almost the worst thing, in his opinion, that a good Freethinker could become. He had learned about it only from reading the review and a personal note in a newspaper. Consequently, the next issue of the *Reformer* carried a large box entitled "Some Words of Explanation," in which the editor told of the letters he had received, asking for an explanation of Theosophy and an explanation of Mrs. Besant. First, he replied: "An Atheist certainly cannot be a Theosophist. A Theist might be a Theosophist. A Monist cannot be a Theosophist. Theosophy must at least involve Dualism. Modern Theosophy . . . asserts much that I do not believe, and alleges some things that to me are certainly not true." Admitting that he had not had the opportunity to read Mme. Blavatsky's two volumes, he maintained that he had read enough of her work and that of her associates during the last ten years to know that they "have sought to rehabilitate a kind of Spiritualism in Eastern terms." Then he came to the crux of the matter: "I very deeply regret that my colleague and co-worker has, with somewhat of a suddenness, and without any interchange of ideas with myself, adopted as facts matters which seem to me as unreal as it is possible for any fiction to be." Knowing how earnestly Mrs. Besant always devoted herself to any cause she believed in and remembering the pain caused both of them by his having to disagree with her publicly on her adoption of socialism, he looked to "possible developments of her Theosophical opinions with the very gravest misgiving" but assured his readers that the editorial policy of the paper would remain unchanged.

Mrs. Besant replied in a brief paragraph printed below Bradlaugh's. She could not, she said, now give the full reasons for her joining the T.S., but she listed its three main official objects, which were the only requirements to which a Theosophist actually had to subscribe. These were: "to found a Universal Brotherhood without distinction of race or creed; to forward the study of Aryan literature and philosophy; to investigate unexplained laws of nature and the psychical powers latent in man." (The

second of these tenets was later modified to commit the member to a belief in the study of comparative religion.) Mrs. Besant then continued:
"On matters of religious opinion, the members are absolutely free. The
founders of the Society deny a personal God, and a somewhat subtle
Pantheism is taught as the Theosophical view of the Universe, tho' even
this is not forced on members of the Society. I have no desire to hide the
fact that this form of Pantheism appears to me to promise solution of
some problems, especially problems of psychology, which Atheism leaves
untouched." As a matter of fact, the views which Mrs. Besant and her
closest adherents, particularly Charles W. Leadbeater, were eventually
to develop came even closer to polytheism than to pantheism.

Only once more, a month later, did Bradlaugh use the pages of his
magazine to state his position further. After all, he said, he was not willing to let his correspondents devote space to a belief which "has only a
very minor place among the world's delusions," not being comparable
even to Mormonism.

The great religions of the world are properly debateable in these columns,
because the editorial position is one of universal challenge; . . . but my interest
is small in "General" Booth, except when his musical followers annoy me. . . .
The "Masters" in Thibet are to me as the "inhabitants" of the planet Mars, and
equally fall into the category of romance, whether vouched by Mme. Blavatsky
or by M. Jules Verne.

Little did he realize that, according to the beliefs of the Theosophical occultists, there had been a constant interchange of souls, or Egos, between
the Earth and Mars, and also the Moon—not to mention Venus and other
planets.

H.P.B. countered by writing an editorial in *Lucifer* for July, suggesting
that she knew it was useless to try to convert as thorough a materialist
and atheist as Bradlaugh to Theosophy, but pointing out that if he came
over he would not have to give up "one iota of his Secularistic ideas" and
would find there even greater atheists than himself—"namely, Hindus belonging to certain all denying sects." Bradlaugh was not much tempted.

The newspaper reference which Bradlaugh had alluded to had been a
brief personal in the Sunday *Sun* on June 16, announcing not only that
Mrs. Besant had turned Theosophist but also that she had been admitted
to "the Esoteric Section of the famous Blavatsky Lodge." The Esoteric
Section was an inner group, almost a cult, within the Theosophical Society, which had already caused a great deal of dissension and was to cause
more. The *Sun* reporter, a predecessor of the modern gossip columnist,
was overwhelmed by Mrs. Besant's sonorous presentation of the future
potentialities of Theosophy and tried to reproduce it in his story: "Mrs.
Besant seems to recognize that under the mask called Theosophy lies
hidden a something which the world must sooner or later receive as a

revelation of the greatest value in connection with that true knowledge leading to the intellectual—and thus moral—progression of humanity."

The next day Annie Besant made a sort of public debut into the aristocratic social group where her conversion had taken her. The *Sun* and the *Star* sent their society reporters to the grand opening of Mrs. Isabel Cooper-Oakley's first restaurant for West End working girls.[3] As they saw the affair, it was a sensational success, with social luminaries, especially ladies, everywhere: Lady Dorothy and Miss Neville, Lady Colin Campbell, Lady Mary Hope, the Hon. Mrs. Bevan, the Hon. Miss Borthwick, Countess Wachtmeister, the Baroness de Pallandt, and Mrs. Oscar Wilde. The *Star* singled out two "fair Theosophists, the pretty Misses Chambers," for special notice, whereas the *Sun* was attracted to Lady Colin Campbell, who, "of course, looked charming, as she always does, and all the other women looked charming likewise." And in the midst of them all were the two lionesses of the hour, Mme. Blavatsky, smoking cigarettes as usual and telling how she did not approve of mesmerism, and her newest acquisition, Mrs. Annie Besant. In fact, most of the ladies were smoking cigarettes, and a crowd promptly gathered outside, pressing their noses against the window, to see the shocking sight and get a glimpse of the latest goings-on in high society. "The faces in that crowd were a study!" burbled the *Sun*. Whether or not Mrs. Besant was dressed in her "Annie Militant" costume, the reporter did not mention; but Colonel Olcott was soon to remark that there was some trepidation among his clientele when it was learned that such a rough outsider as Mrs. Besant was to come among them.

Among this select gathering were also a few males, particularly Mr. Oscar Wilde, whose aesthetic doctrines and doings had already made him a marked man in advanced circles. So, while discussing their coffee and cigarettes after luncheon, the guests clustered around Wilde and Mme. Blavatsky to listen to a spirited argument on the relative merits of aestheticism and Theosophy. The entranced dictum of the reporter was that the general conversation was also "fully up to the standard and truly entertaining"—as excellent as the food. In a follow-up note in the correspondence column, the paper informed a Secularist who had written in to protest the previous week's announcement of Annie's conversion as part of a vile plot to injure the cause of Secularism, that in a special interview Mrs. Besant had said that she wished it to be stated that it was neither her desire nor her intention that her conversion should not be known. The reporter added gratuitously that Mrs. Besant was "too loyal a woman to the cause of truth to wish for any secrecy"—especially since Theosophy, "the science of the highest wisdom, and which is synonymous

[3] For this episode, see *Sun*, June 16, 23, July 21, 1889, which was much more flattering than *Star*, July 19, 1889. See also Olcott, *Old Diary Leaves; Our Corner*, August, 1888; *Star*, July 7, 1888; and *Australian Theosophist*, August, 1928.

with Universalism, combines all known and unknown advanced thoughts, tenets, methods, policies and actions within itself." The *Star* a month later was not quite so kind; in fact, its reporter was dumbfounded to hear a woman of Mrs. Cooper-Oakley's intelligence, keenness, and practical ability "talking of Mahatmas and cycles, of new births, and all the rest of the jargon which the Theosophists mistake for thought." It ended by commenting on the "terrible pity" of the news that Dr. Rose Bryant, an American specialist in the treatment of the insane, was another convert recently arrived in London.

Oscar Wilde never became a convert, though his notorious desire for new experiences and sensations had been bringing him into contact with Theosophists for some years. As far back as 1884 he had attended a large reception given by Sinnett for Olcott and the young Calcutta lawyer, Mohini Mohun Chatterji, who had come abroad as an emissary of Theosophy. Among the two hundred guests being introduced to the T.S., including the famous pundits, Professors William Crookes and F. W. H. Meyers, was Charles Webster Leadbeater, who always preserved his impressions of that memorable meeting. Oscar Wilde, giving, as usual, the impression of wishing to be bizarre in both manners and dress and wearing his black velvet knee breeches and white stockings, was introduced to the dark-skinned Mohini. He bowed gracefully and in retiring remarked in a very audible stage whisper to Mrs. Sinnett: "I never realized before what a mistake we make in being white!" Mohini looked very sick over the whole experience of this introduction to the culture of English society. Wilde could not have met Mrs. Besant at this time, for she was still holding out against Mme. Blavatsky's early advances. But at the first meeting of the Fabian Society in July, 1888, when the artist Walter Crane read a paper on "The Prospects of Art under Socialism," Wilde had been present and taken part in the discussion along with Shaw, Burrows, and Mrs. Besant, who had made a particularly eloquent plea for music as "the supreme form in which the art of the future would develop itself."

Another promising young author, just beginning to get a foothold in the London literary circle in 1889, did not hold out against the seductions of Theosophy—nor did he want to. William Butler Yeats and his family had come over from Dublin in 1887.[4] H.P.B. had reached London a month earlier, and Yeats, having dabbled in Theosophy in Dublin and being especially interested at the moment in Ahasuerus, the Wandering

---

[4] For the full story of Yeats and his Theosophy, see especially Richard Ellmann, *Yeats: The Man and the Masks* (New York, 1948), pp. 56–69, 86–91; also Joseph Hone, *W. B. Yeats*, pp. 69–71; Yeats, *Four Years*, pp. 69–80, *Autobiographies: Reveries over Childhood and Youth* (London, 1926), pp. 109–13, 127–30, and *The Trembling of the Veil* (Churchtown, 1924), pp. 214 ff.; Katherine Tynan, *Memories* (London, 1924), pp. 280–81; Yeats, *Letters of William Butler Yeats to Katherine Tynan* (Dublin, 1953), p. 111; P. L. Pielou, "The Growth of the Theosophical Society in Ireland," *Theosophy in Ireland*, July–September, 1927.

Jew, and knowing that the Theosophists believed in him too, immediately called on her. Impressed by her personality—"a sort of old Irish peasant woman with an air of humour and audacious power"—he at once joined her new Blavatsky Lodge.

In Ireland, Theosophy had strongly appealed to the mystics and advanced thinkers—all "the queer people, the Fenians and Socialists and Theosophists, and worst of all Papists," as the poet Katharine Tynan called them. They gathered at such places as the home of William Johnston of Ballykillreg, the mild-eyed old Orangeman, who could not understand what his son Charles and his other children were thinking of to bring such strange characters into his house. Charles Johnston, who had been a schoolfellow of Yeats, was the leading spirit in the group, which he was soon to startle by breaking his vow of celibacy (usually regarded as a very helpful condition by occultists) and marrying the niece of Mme. Blavatsky. The brilliant young Johnston, at the advanced age of eighteen, had read a paper, published as an article in the *Dublin University Review* in 1885, on the Theosophical theories of spiritual evolution, and Yeats had heard it at the Dublin Hermetic Society. He also became acquainted with Sinnett's *The Occult World* through Johnston and another schoolfellow, Claude Falls Wright, and soon afterward, at the home of the famous critic and teacher, Edward Dowden, learned about Sinnett's next book, *Esoteric Buddhism*, which provided an exegesis of the first. The whole group engaged in experiments with mediums, seances, table-rapping, etc., at one of which Yeats himself went into a sort of fit, which the medium attributed to his having been attacked by an evil spirit. These experiences were all very exciting, but, though Johnston, Wright, and some others obtained a charter to form a Dublin lodge of the T.S. in 1886, Yeats hesitated to join it. So did another young mystical poet, George W. Russell ("AE"), who was to become a dominating factor in Irish Theosophy for a great many years.

But when Yeats got to London, the inexplicable attraction of Mme. Blavatsky was too much for him. He was self-conscious, unsure of himself, but determined to find a philosophy and an aesthetic which would give him the inspiration against the materialism and skepticism for which —in spite of his reverence for the opinions of his father, the painter John Butler Yeats—he was searching. At the same time, however, he maintained a much more questioning attitude toward his new doctrine and his new associates than most of them did themselves. This was perhaps partly suggested and supported by H.P.B. herself, who often, when in one of her depressed and impatient moods, would ejaculate in her usual salty phraseology about the stupidity and easy credulity of many of the hangers-on about her. "Oh, you are a flapdoodle, but then you are a theosophist and a brother," Yeats once heard her exclaim to an unfortunate member who had displeased her. He never doubted her sincerity and the genuineness of her essential power, though he admitted that she sometimes used mere trickery and chicanery in her demonstrations. In two diaries, one written in 1887 and the other, a scribbled, often incoherent record he started keeping as soon as he was admitted to the Esoteric Section, about Christmas time, 1888, he speculated a great deal about the explanation of Mme. Blavatsky and her Masters. Rejecting the theory of pure, conscious fraud, he wavered between the beliefs that they were real, living occultists, as she maintained; that they were spirits, as the Spiritualist mediums asserted; that they were "possibly unconscious dramatizations of H.P.B.'s own trance nature"; or that they might be the trance principle of nature, "expressing itself symbolically." He inclined, however, to the belief that they were "trance personalities":

. . . but by "trance personalities" I meant something almost as exciting as "Ahasuerus" himself. . . . I thought that her masters were imaginary forms created by suggestion, but whether that suggestion came from Madame Blavatsky's own mind or from some mind, perhaps at a great distance, I did not know; and I believed that these forms could pass from Madame Blavatsky's mind to the minds of others, and even acquire external reality, and that it was even possible that they talked and wrote. . . .

Yeats maintained a similarly analytical and critical attitude toward the devotees and habitués of the Blavatsky menage. Some, he thought, seemed intellectual, one or two cultural, and "the rest the usual amorphous material that gathers round all new things." There were cranks "from half of Europe and all of America," but, whatever their origins or classification, all were marked by their zeal and many by their fanaticism. And everyone wanted to talk. The Esoteric Section, he thought, would not in any way influence educated thought, largely because its present type of propaganda repelled many people, and it had neither the right type of members nor the method to attempt a different kind. He himself had some difficulty in signing a sort of pledge approved by the E.S. (as it was usually referred to, according to the Society's fondness for using only initials) at the end of October, 1889, swearing faith in and obedience to H.P.B. and her teachers and guaranteeing to "defend her, subject to our own conscience." But although one member, Mlle. Zambuca, walked out rather than sign, Yeats persuaded himself at first that his conscience could be reconciled to this wonderful opportunity to learn something about occultism and magic—for they were what he was really interested in—at first hand.

One member of the Esoteric Section, a comparative newcomer, had no qualms about signing such a pledge. To judge from the entries in his journal, Yeats was no more impressed by Mrs. Annie Besant than by any other member of the E.S., but he apparently soon persuaded her to participate in his own demands on H.P.B. to demonstrate some of the phenomena of the occult world. Mme. Blavatsky had played down the occult aspect of Theosophy ever since she had got her fingers burned at Adyar; but she had yielded to pressure and, while warning her followers against the great dangers of black magic, had formed the E.S. especially for those who would not be satisfied with the merely metaphysical and religious aspects of Theosophy. Yeats had once taken Katharine Tynan to a Spiritualistic seance where he had been so overwhelmed by the supernatural phenomena that he lost control of himself and beat his head on the table. When H.P.B. learned about this, she severely reprimanded him for his disobedience, for she had a great antipathy to Spiritualists, having once been one herself. Yeats's lost love, Maud Gonne, who was predisposed to a belief in reincarnation, also once accompanied him to a meeting of the general lodge, where nothing was said about the occult; but Mme. Blavatsky pleased her by saying that the Dublin Theosophists were talking nonsense when they said that underground political activities need not preclude one from becoming a Theosophist.

At a Sunday meeting of the E.S. a week before Christmas, 1889, the whole question of the pledge had been reviewed by the group, including Mrs. Besant, Burrows, and G. R. S. Mead, who was to become a leading officer and the chief scholar of the English Section, but whom Yeats summed up as a somewhat overrighteous individual, with the "intellect of a good size whelp." Warning himself against taking part in the kind of propaganda work the general section was planning, he was disappointed when no occult experiments were forthcoming and proposed a scheme for organizing and pressing occult research. Seeing that the general interest in such investigations was irresistible, H.P.B. yielded, and a committee was formed for this purpose, with Yeats as secretary.

The resuts were not very fruitful. He had been present when some very mysterious things had happened in Mme. Blavatsky's presence. And he remembered how a young Theosophist had complained loudly when an insensitive materialist had sat down unexpectedly on his astral body, which was lying on a nearby couch. But Yeats himself never succeeded in getting even a feeling of the presence of the Masters, though everyone else around spoke as if they were "more important than any visible member of the house." He made an experiment in burning a flower and then trying to reincarnate it—or its ghost—in the moonlight under an air pump, but the ashes would not respond. He also tried placing indigo under his pillow at night to induce special dreams, but the dreams failed to come. There was also an experiment in clairvoyance, with one Mr. Mouser as the medium, Yeats himself as the mesmerist, and Mrs. Besant and others as observers; Mrs. Besant set down a detailed account for the committee. Another experiment consisted of suspending a needle by a silk thread under a glass case and then watching it move to and fro in answer to the will of the members of the group. Yeats wrote to Katharine Tynan that he was considering publishing the results of some of these experiments; but his fear of being called "impostor, liar, and the rest" proved too strong, and he desisted. It was just as well, since he was not very confident of them himself.

It all ended rather quickly. Yeats's final public appearance in the Theosophical Society probably occurred in August, 1890, when he lectured on "Theosophy and Modern Culture." Mrs. Besant was in the chair. Shortly afterward, the secretary, "an intelligent and friendly man," asked him to come into his office. When Yeats complied, he was informed that his presence and conduct were causing disturbance in the Society and a certain important lady had been discovered "red and tearful" after talking with him. The secretary, therefore, feeling that Yeats was "not in full agreement with their method or their philosophy," requested him to resign. He said tolerantly:

I know that all these people become dogmatic and fanatical because they believe what they can never prove; that their withdrawal from family life is to them a great misfortune; but what are we to do? We have been told that all spiritual influx into the society will come to an end in 1897 for exactly one hundred years. Before that date our fundamental ideas must be spread through the world.

Yeats had heard of this prophecy of Mme. Blavatsky—or rather of her "trance personality"—and speculated about the fear of heresy after her death being the reason for it. At any rate, he resigned from the Theosophical Society and devoted the next phase of his occult experiments to the Hermetic Students of the Golden Dawn, whom he had joined a few months earlier and who based their proceedings on the European tradition of cabalistic magic, with its debts to Rosicrucianism, Freemasonry, Eliphas Levi, Macgregor Mathers, etc., rather than on Oriental sources.

Mrs. Besant's own first mystical experience had come in July, in the midst of the International Labour Congress in Paris, at which she had had to absorb many gibes from both parties about her recent spiritual transformation. H.P.B., who had been in poor health, had gone abroad for a few weeks' rest at Fontainebleau, whose forest just outside Paris provided the restful haven she wanted for working on her new book. Here in this quiet shelter she was joined by both Annie Besant and Herbert Burrows for a day after the conference, and here she showed them the latest passages of her "translations" from a mysterious book which she called *The Book of the Golden Precepts,* but of which she had no "material" copy before her. Of these "fragments," which she later entitled poetically *The Voice of the Silence,* Burrows remembered best those parts which described the "toilsome ascent of the pilgrim-soul." Madame was a tremendous worker, sometimes laboring for twelve hours a day at her writing with scarcely a stop, but this time she declared a little vacation for discussions and Spiritualistic demonstrations. For instance, she showed her new guests, and also a staunch American Theosophist, a Mrs. Ida Candler, how the famous "taps" of the seances were produced, without the help of any spirits. She also told them all about "collective hallucination," "elementals" (rudimentary spirits of the elements—earth, fire, air, water, trees, rocks, etc.), "astral light," and all the rest of the theological terminology, of which Annie and Burrows were to write a *Glossary* before the end of the year.[5]

That night Mrs. Besant, still tense and emotionally highly keyed from the day's experiences and from her reading aloud to the others passages from *The Voice of the Silence,* went to bed alone in a small room near H.P.B.'s. After she had been asleep for a while, she was suddenly awakened by the consciousness that something unusual was happening. Startled, she sat up, "to find the air of the room thrown into pulsating waves, and then appeared the radiant astral Figure of the Master, visible to my physical eyes." Her memory of this remarkable manifestation became more detailed with the passage of time, for six years after the event she told an interviewer from the *Westminster Gazette* that she had seen the figure, "shadowy at first, but growing more substantial," with all her senses. Not only did she see Him with her eyes, hear Him with her ears, and touch Him with her hands, but she smelled the odor of sandalwood and other Eastern herbs and spices which marked all the Mahatmas. Apparently, however, the Figure did not affect her taste. She recognized him at once as Master Morya, partly by intuition and partly from a portrait which had long hung in Mme. Blavatsky's room (and copies of which, showing his heavily bearded, Christlike face, are owned by many Theosophists today). Mrs. Besant seemingly gave credit for this manifestation to the nearby H.P.B.; for in November, according to the Nottingham *Guardian,* she told a large audience there, in talking on the brain as simply the tool of the mind, that "she had seen appearances such as she had mentioned, she knew persons who could produce them, and she meant to be able to do so herself some day."

From this time on, she found that these psychic experiences came more easily and frequently. A close colleague wrote many years later that, during the two-year period of Mrs. Besant's "physical plane" association with Mme. Blavatsky, she "remembered her Self, remembered that great body of Superhuman Men, the Men beyond Mankind. . . . During those two years she remembered Theosophy, the Wisdom of God, the Science of Life, the Theosophy she knew she had known before, and which she was now to know more deeply than ever before." Nevertheless, in Au-

[5] For the Fontainebleau episode, see *Autobiography,* pp. 453–55; *Lucifer,* June 15, 1891, pp. 301–2; *Westminster Gazette,* April 24, 1895; Williams, *The Passionate Pilgrim,* p. 197; Geoffrey West, *Annie Besant,* pp. 109–10; Theodore Besterman, *Mrs. Annie Besant,* pp. 169–71.

gust, 1893, when she published the revision of her *Autobiography* called for by the new insight and understanding which had come through her conversion, she still spoke of herself as "a pupil of low grade, as it were in the infant class of the Occult School." But she anticipated a far more wonderful future when her powers were properly trained. Since she could hardly have anticipated the wonders which would be eventually revealed to her, even with the help of the raja yoga (i.e., royal or major yoga) which she had begun practicing, it is surprising to find H.P.B. writing a somewhat qualified appraisal of her friend's psychic potentialities to the American Theosophical leader, W. Q. Judge, just before her death in 1891. "Judge," she wrote, "she is the most wonderful woman, my right hand, my successor when I will be forced to leave you, my sole hope in England as you are my sole hope in America." But she felt it necessary to warn him about Annie's utter soberness and lack of humor on serious subjects. He was never to let her hear any light or irreverent talk about occultism and was never to indulge in the slightest exaggeration or deviation from fact in her hearing. "It is only a few months that she studies occultism with me in the innermost group of the E.S., and yet she has passed far beyond the others. She is not psychic nor spiritual in the least —all intellect; yet she hears Master's voice when alone, sees his light and recognizes his voice." Emphasizing that A.B. was "the soul of honor and uncompromisingly truthful," she closed with a comparison of Annie's heart to "one single unbroken diamond, transparent . . . and filled to the brim with pure, unadulterated Theosophy and enthusiasm."[6]

Immediately after the Fontainebleau visit, H.P.B. went to stay with another friend at St. Helier on the Channel island of Jersey, while Annie returned to London. Their relationship was already reversing itself, and Madame was not ashamed to admit her dependence on her new friend, who had practically taken over the running of the Lodge in her absence. In fact, she had to keep in close contact with her by correspondence— sometimes writing twice in a single day. "You are my only hope and ray of salvation in the London fogs," she wrote on July 26 and asked her to investigate the "Coues 'conspiracy'" (a case in which a long-time American supporter had turned against her and was publishing "revelations" in the newspapers). She addressed Annie in suspiciously fulsome and endearing terms: "Dearest," "My Dearest," "Dearly Beloved One," and signed herself "Very adoring." "I see your big lotus-eyes peeping into mine, and *I* do see and visit you if you don't," she once wrote. After her return to Lansdowne Road, she dispatched missives to Annie on various organizational problems and addressed them to "My Darling Penelope" from "Your . . . female Ulysses." Mingled with these remarkable endear-

[6] G. S. Arundale, "Annie Besant," in *Autobiography*, pp. 18–19; *Theosophist*, November, 1929; Countess Wachtmeister, *H.P.B. and the Present Crisis in the T.S.* (London, 1895); Williams, *The Passionate Pilgrim*, pp. 196–97.

ments, however, she usually sent love and kisses to Herbert Burrows, though she sometimes reprimanded him for his handling of certain matters involving trades unionists and matchmakers.[7]

The problem of the nature of the relationship between Annie Besant and Helena Petrovna Blavatsky is an intricate one. Certainly Mme. Blavatsky was the only woman in Mrs. Besant's life whose intimacy of influence compared with that of many men. There were several women in her later career, it is true, who lived closely and affectionately with her for long periods of time, but never was their association expressed in the peculiar terms of that with H.P.B. The masculinity of Mme. Blavatsky's appearance, manners, and conversation has already been commented on. An early acquaintance, Princess von Racowitza, described her as

. . . far more ugly than beautiful. A Russian type, with a wide forehead, a short thick nose, prominent cheekbones, a small clever mobile mouth with little fine teeth, brown and very curly hair . . . almost like that of a negro's; a sallow complexion, but a pair of eyes the like of which I have never seen; pale blue, grey as water, but with a glance, deep and penetrating, and as compelling as if it beheld the inner heart of things.

With these hypnotic eyes, which in her well-known portrait are made to pursue one wherever he goes, and with her long, beautiful hands and flowing dark robes, Mme. Blavatsky cast a spell which was hard for a susceptible person to escape.[8]

Colonel Henry Steele Olcott, who knew her even better, though at a later period in her life, had an even more remarkable theory, which he expressed in his usual jocose style in a private letter to some friends just before the inauguration of the Theosophical Society in New York in 1875:

I say her, because it is a habit, but dear lord! boys, in my opinion she is no more a *she* than you or I. Putting aside her actions, habits of thought, masculine ways, her constant asseverations of the fact (which while made to third parties in badinage, nevertheless are deeply significant to one who has learned to read her subcutaneously)—putting these aside, I have pumped enough out of her to satisfy me that the theory long since communicated by me to you was correct—she is a man, a very old man, and a most learned and wonderful man. . . . I say Isis is a man. Let me add that *she* is (in my opinion) a Hindu man.[9]

Of course, at this time perhaps Olcott did not know enough of the facts about his new friend's previous marital experiences, her medical exam-

---

[7] *Theosophist,* January, February, April, May, 1932, pp. 377–80, 509–15, 19–23, 125–28; *Freethinker,* July 28, 1889.

[8] *Autobiography of Princess von Racowitza* (1910), quoted by Josephine Ransom, *Madame Blavatsky as Occultist* (London, 1931), pp. vii–viii.

[9] Besterman, *Mrs. Annie Besant,* pp. 148–54, quoting a long, previously unprinted letter to C. C. Massey and the Rev. Stainton Moses, now in the archives of the Society for Psychical Research.

inations, and doctor's certificates, as unearthed by her later skeptical bi-ographers, to realize that his theory could be applied only symbolically; but his speculation is significant, especially since almost every commentator who knew her remarked on the maleness of her personality. The Lesbian overtones of the situation in 1889–91 cannot be overlooked.

Nor can the theories about the source of her power over others and the mystery of her own character be overlooked. For there can be little doubt that, however secret and shady her past, ultimately she was completely sincere and convinced of the genuineness of her revelations and teachings. As Aldous Huxley in his own mystical phase put it in *The Devils of Loudun,* discussing the trickery, fakery, lying, and general dishonesty that went on on both sides of this famous case of diabolical "possession," "The history of spiritualism makes it very clear that fraud, especially pious fraud, is perfectly compatible with faith." At the outset, Mme. Blavatsky may have been a clever charlatan, but finally she became one of her own victims and in the process came close to successfully founding a new religion. But Theosophists always refuse to call Theosophy a religion, although their official motto is, "There is no religion higher than Truth." They have, however, suggested no better word.

Yeats's somewhat mystical theory of the "trance personality" has already been presented. The theory most generally offered, however, has to do with some aspect of hypnotism. Everyone commented on H.P.B.'s hypnotic eyes. For many years the Theosophists themselves experimented with hypnotism; and some remarkable examples of a Danish practitioner's powers, involving handkerchiefs suspended in mid-air with the holder completely invisible to the subject, and identifying cards seen through a human body, were participated in by Mrs. Besant herself. H.P.B., however, pretended to frown on these practices, and they were largely abandoned, though the many Theosophical journals continued to write on the subject at considerable length, as did Mrs. Besant herself. Though the London *Daily News* wrote that hypnotism had been an "avowed factor" in Mrs. Besant's conversion, Theosophists like Burrows specifically rejected this explanation when applied to their own cases.[10] Nevertheless, the theory of posthypnotic suggestion perhaps comes the closest to explaining the relationship between Mrs. Besant and Mme. Blavatsky and, later, between Mrs. Besant and C. W. Leadbeater. Theodore Besterman, Gertrude Williams, and others have remarked on the extreme suggestibility of Annie Besant; and Besterman tells how, in one of her later lectures, she related how she had first discovered she had the gift of clairvoyance. Once, when she was deploring her apparent lack of occult faculties to Mme. Blavatsky, Madame innocently inquired whether, in giving a public speech, she did not visualize the various ways of

[10] Olcott, *Old Diary Leaves,* IV, 199; Annie Besant, "Hypnotism," *Lucifer,* October 15, 1889, pp. 93–102, 151, June 15, 1891, p. 300.

expressing what she intended to say and then select the best alternative. When Mrs. Besant agreed, H.P.B. triumphantly announced that that was clairvoyance. Leadbeater later expressed somewhat similar theories about the psychic reliability of the creative visual imagination. As Besterman phrased it, Mrs. Besant "ever after, no doubt, gave forth as clairvoyant visions all the memory-images, hypnogogic and hypnopompic hallucinations, day-dreams, etc., which are so vivid in persons who belong to the visualizing type."[11]

This Galtonic theory of visions like Joan of Arc's is at least suggestive in an attempt to explain Mrs. Besant's experiences. As for posthypnotic suggestion, another former Theosophist (like Besterman) has told me of an instance, when he himself was present, where Mrs. Besant informed a curious group before a lecture that she had not been in communication with her Master the night before, but, after a few minutes in private with Leadbeater, went on the platform and delivered a message which she said had been communicated to her on that very night.

At the same time, it must be remembered that to give a name to a phenomenon is not necessarily to explain it. There are many experiences in the world that are, as yet, inexplicable, though namable. The Theosophical Society is at least justified in stating, as its third principle, its willingness to explore the unknown and latent psychic potentialities in the mind of man.

[11] Besterman, *Mrs. Annie Besant,* pp. 169–70, 171–73.

3

Annie among the Secularists

Bradlaugh, of course, was not the only one of Mrs. Besant's old friends who were stupefied by her conversion. Even he, however, apparently thought it necessary to confirm his opposition, for in his "Sick Room Notes" in the *Reformer* for November, 1889, he declared that his illness had in no way altered his theological opinions. John M. Robertson became more perplexed than ever when he tried to examine her new arguments against materialism and the relationship between matter and mind in the light of her former principles based on Bradlaugh and Büchner. Labouchère cynically ridiculed Theosophy and its leaders in *Truth*. Hyndman, from the Social Democratic point of view, had trouble in reconciling his admiration for Annie's remarkable talents and her services to the cause with his risibility when, after Annie had gone to India, "one of the best-known Secularists" showed him a picture in an Indian newspaper of her walking between two white bulls in a religious procession. Even years later, when she returned and took part in a Fabian meeting, "those two white bulls, dear things, would persist in poking up their flat, moist noses in front of her." But when Margaret Harkness, a feminist with whom Mrs. Besant had worked in the S.D.F., accused her of deserting the Federation, the latter indignantly replied that her Theosophy had in no way slackened her work for socialism. She refused to admit that the three were incompatible.[1]

The religionists, on the other hand, could not quite make up their

[1] Robertson, "Account of [Bradlaugh's] Parliamentary Struggles, Politics, and Teachings," in Bonner, *Bradlaugh*, II, 136–39, 383; *Star*, August 22, September 25, 28, 1889; Henry Mayer Hyndman, *Further Reminiscences* (London, 1912), pp. 3–8; *Freethinker*, September 1, 1889, quoting *Weekly Times* and *Echo*.

minds.[2] They were equally stunned by the news, but many could not decide whether it was good or bad. The *Star*, having printed its two instalments concerning Mrs. Besant's rise to the stars, or "Why I Became a Theosophist," with her exposition of Initiates, Adepts, Mahatmas, Planes, and the Brotherhood of Man, was naturally committed to keeping the story alive as long as possible. So it printed approving letters from Theosophists like Herbert Coryn and Arthur Desmond, "late Colonel, Madras Engineers," together with disgusted ejaculations from people who liked to use such sarcastic signatures as "Uninitiated." *Lucifer* reprinted its favorite, Gerald Massey's, earlier tribute to Mrs. Besant in very minor verse, beginning "Annie Besant, brave and dear." The *Indian Mirror*, noting the "wonderful phenomenon" of Mrs. Besant's coming over, predicted a great future for Theosophy in England; but the *Indian Spectator* was content to comment on the surprising nature of the transformation.

Stewart Headlam, almost the only one of Annie's old friends who, with no mystical tendencies of their own, remained loyal and understanding, devoted an article, "My Soul Is Athirst for God," to her in his paper, the *Church Reformer*. Though it is true that here he remarked, "There is but little now to hinder her from again making her communion at a Christian altar," and suggested facetiously that she might find herself even more at home two flights up (his Guild of St. Matthew was located that distance higher in the same building as the T.S.), Mme. Blavatsky welcomed his article as "unprecedented in the annals of clerical publications," since he proclaimed that there was still much good in Theosophy. In the annual report of the Guild he called special attention again to this conversion. The popular "Parson of Puddleston" in his column in the *Church Times* found Foote's attempts at refutation of Mrs. Besant quite clever and amusing. The *East Anglian Daily Times*, in fact, went so far as to suggest ironically that the "Fathers at the Brompton Oratory will soon have to look to their laurels," so rapidly were the Theosophists making converts. Many of Mrs. Besant's own older friends, indeed, were already predicting that she would herself end as a Roman Catholic.[3] The *Methodist Times*, perhaps recalling her many earlier run-ins with the evangelists, editorialized against her and her "new teacher." The Unitarians, on the other hand, were optimistic of a further conversion—to their own group. In Belfast a popular Unitarian preacher featured her conversion in a sermon; another, in Oldham, welcomed her as "a sister in the faith"; and a sectarian paper, the *Inquirer*, hoped she and Theosophy would do for the Freethinkers what atheism could never do—"awaken them . . . to

[2] For the following allusions, quotations, and incidents, see, *passim, Star, Path, Freethinker, National Reformer, Lucifer, Church Reformer,* and *Theosophist* for the last half of 1889.

[3] C. Jinarajadasa, in *The Annie Besant Centenary Book,* p. 11.

a beginning of a spiritual life." A "pious little Christian monthly," the *Light of the World,* exulted over "Mrs. Annie Besant's conversion from Atheism to God," but *Lucifer* quickly set it right on that subject.

The news spread rapidly abroad. In the United States, Judge's little magazine, the *Path,* while expressing amusement over the way the English religious papers had announced the conversion of this hardheaded unbeliever, carried a story about how two Theosophists in Chicago, "having passed through the fire of abuse," could now take heart and renew their labors to lift some of their heavy karma, or fate inherited from their past incarnations. The New York *Truthseeker,* while admitting that she was "the ablest woman in England," deplored her "new fad." J. T. Symes, a former close associate of Mrs. Besant as a Secularist lecturer and leader, denounced her from Australia in his new paper, the *Liberator.* On the other hand, her quondam enemy, Charles Watts, now a Secularist lecturer in Canada and the United States and editor of a paper called *Secular Thought,* in which he was assisted by none other than M. C. O'Byrne, assured a crowded audience in Toronto of her sincere character and great abilities in spite of her new aberration.

The Christian Evidence lecturers of course still hounded her, but the *Christian Commonwealth,* after denouncing the "Buddhist craze" and "that astounding imposture called Theosophy," found consolation in the discovery that she was "after all not utterly opposed to supernaturalism." The Spiritualists, who attached quite a different meaning to supernaturalism, were at first divided. One of their papers, the *Medium and Daybreak,* thought that her "apostasy" should have been treated with "silent contempt" by the Freethinkers; but another, *Light,* rejoiced in her conversion as "a dash out of the Sahara in which she has so long wandered." By December, however, the Spiritualists were all flocking around her effusively after she had lectured to one of their meetings on the advantages of Theosophy over Spiritualism. Almost simultaneously, Stuart Cumberland, editor of the *Mirror,* issued a challenge and a wager of one thousand pounds to Mme. Blavatsky that she could not produce any occult phenomenon which he could not explain and parallel.

The general journalistic reaction in Great Britain and the colonies by November, 1889, was reflected by Colonel Olcott himself in his magazine, the *Theosophist,* which he published from Adyar—and to rival which Mme. Blavatsky had decided to publish *Lucifer,* "The Light-Bringer," from London. The T.S. in India subscribed to a clipping bureau, which after one of Olcott's lectures at the South Place Institute, with Mrs. Besant in the chair, sent in over a hundred cuttings, "the prevailing tone of which is chaff or bitterness" and only a very few of which showed the slightest respect or desire to learn. The very number of the clippings, however, showed the prodigious interest in the subject.

As might have been expected, the most steady and virulent stream of attack came in the *Freethinker,* from its editor, G. W. Foote, and from his assistant, the now recovered J. M. Wheeler. Mrs. Besant herself in her *Autobiography* singled out Foote as having "especially distinguished himself by the bitterness of his attacks." For Foote regarded himself as the last remaining bulwark of atheistic Fundamentalism, and he had long had his eye ambitiously on Bradlaugh's presidency. In his attacks he was ably seconded by Wheeler, who considered himself a much greater authority on Oriental religions, and especially on Buddhism, than Mrs. Besant was; but at first the two maintained a fairly respectful exterior, until they could see just how far and how fast she was going. Thus, when, early in July, Foote aimed one of his "Acid Drops" at the "jargon" of Mrs. Besant's Theosophical confession in the *Star,* Wheeler partly counteracted it by declaring that Mme. Blavatsky must have at least some smattering of science, some acquaintance with the literature and religions of the world, and "much penetration into human nature" to have secured the adhesion of such a person as Mrs. Besant. Consequently, Wheeler, feeling that she had claims on the sympathy of Freethinkers which no alteration on her part could obliterate, announced his own forthcoming review of *The Secret Doctrine.* This, unfortunately, did not turn out to be very flattering to H.P.B., and Mrs. Besant resented it, just as she resented a twopenny pamphlet, *Mrs. Besant's Theosophy,* which Foote quickly got out to take advantage of popular curiosity in the subject and also, as he said, to prevent her from further misleading Freethinkers, members of whose provincial branches were already writing to him to have their perplexities resolved. He feared—and rightly—that she intended to use her old, well-established, Freethought circuit to propagandize her new ideas on Theosophy.

In the same issue of the *Reformer* that carried her long report on the Paris labor conference, Mrs. Besant announced that because of the many statements being made about herself and her views, "some of which are absurdly, and some of which are maliciously, untrue," and also because of her unwillingness to ask Bradlaugh to devote any more space to the controversy, she planned both to issue a condensed pamphlet and to give two lectures in the Hall of Science on the subject "Why I Became a Theosophist." In the meantime, she asked her old associates to wait before they judged. The versions of the reception of her lecture vary considerably according to their source. *Lucifer* pictured the packed audience, consisting mostly of Freethinkers, listening with intense interest and now and then interrupting with "vociferous and prolonged applause," while the "Hindu gentlemen who were present, conspicuous by their quiet mien, nodded their frequent approval in silent but significant manner." At the end of the second lecture, on August 11, a long debate followed, touching transmigration, mesmerism, Sinnett, Olcott, Blavatsky, the Coulombs, the Hodgson Report, and allied matters. In the course of the debate Mrs.

Besant remarked concerning the slanders which Christian missionaries had passed on herself and H.P.B., "I have been accused of the vilest life a woman could lead. Have I prosecuted? No. A strong woman and a good woman knows that her life is enough to live down slander."

Foote and Wheeler were not so kind as *Lucifer*. In fact, Foote felt that his former friend's reaction to his pamphlet had so insulted him, in spite of his care not to pick a quarrel, that he felt compelled to answer her from the same platform. This he did in two lectures on "Freethought and Theosophy" and declared his views had been received with "almost universal sympathy," though there had been some "curious opposition." Bradlaugh was content to print the brief facts about the rival lectures and pamphlets, including the names of the rival publishers. After all, the Freethought Publishing Company, which still brought out all of Mrs. Besant's writings, had just been forced to form a limited liability company, selling shares for one pound, most of which were being absorbed by the unlucky investors who already held debenture bonds on the venture.

Foote and Mrs. Besant then took their respective cases out to the country, repeating their essential lectures at Plymouth, Portsmouth, Birmingham, Manchester, Rochdale, Nottingham, Liverpool, and the rest of their favorite stands. Arthur Moss, for whom Mrs. Besant had fought so strenuously on the School Board, also ungratefully entered the attack, though chiefly at the expense of Colonel Olcott.

As a result of the publicity, some of the N.S.S. branches announced their intention to devote some study to Theosophy; others said they would have nothing to do with it. To her Secularist audiences, Mrs. Besant played down the exploits of the Mahatmas; and despite her best efforts, she failed to convert many Freethinkers. Her successes were rather at the lectures she gave to the general public, but both antagonists continued their anti-Christian attacks. (Mme. Blavatsky could find less to admire in Christianity than in almost any other religion.)

As Annie traveled from place to place, in railway carriages and waiting rooms and cold hotel-bedrooms, on tramcars and busses, she expended every spare moment on her study of Theosophy, just as fifteen years before she had done for Freethought. She was an extremely fast reader and with no difficulty remembered virtually everything she read, but she still had much to learn. Almost all her contributions to the *Reformer* now were short notes taken from something she had read or heard.

Lansbury always prided himself on the fact that Mrs. Besant had asked him to preside at her first open meeting after her conversion. This was held in his own bailiwick, at the Bow and Bromley Institute, before a turbulent crowd of over two thousand people, who, however, "under the magic of her voice and personality," soon listened in absorbed silence to "her first public confession of faith in positive religion and away from negative agnosticism." This speech, which preached the unity of religion with everyday life and asserted that there could be no division between religion and politics, made such a great impression on Lansbury and his family that he eventually embraced Theosophy and carried its social precepts into his career as Socialist labor leader and Cabinet officer. This meeting, which apparently occurred in August or September, was followed by a series in October and November, culminating in a gathering at the St. Pancras Reform Club which filled the "large marquee" to bulging with an "eager and intelligent audience." The *Star* reporter, who by this time was becoming so well known to Mrs. Besant that, as he stated, she always kept a suspicious eye on him as she talked, headed his story prophetically "The Coming Priestess of Theosophy."[4] By this time the *Star* was virtually treating Mrs. Besant as two separate characters, reserving one style for her Theosophical manifestations and using quite a different one for her normal civic activities.

The battle was enlivened by a side encounter between Foote and Mme. Blavatsky, she—recalling Homer's blustering braggart soldier—attacking him under the title "Thersites of Freethought," and he—recalling the famed eighteenth-century magician and charlatan—retaliating under the heading, "The New Cagliostro." A second exchange took place between H.P.B. and Wheeler, supported by Major Arthur Lillie, on the old topic of the name and history of her special guru, Master Koot Hoomi, or "K.H." Lillie, in a pamphlet, *Koot Hoomi Unveiled,* parodying the title of her *Isis Unveiled,* accused her of gross ignorance of the Tibetan language. However, during the Society for Psychical Research investigations, Mohini Chatterji had informed F. W. H. Myers that the name was mentioned in the *Vishnu Puran* as belonging to a Rishi, or holy and semidivine sage, and that there was a school of Sama-Veda students founded by him and called Kauthoomi. Since Brahmins who belong to this school were entitled to call themselves "Kauthoomis," and since Master K.H. was a Brahmin of this group, who had been partly educated in Europe and had attended Professor Fechner's lectures before he had become an Adept and settled in Tibet, the Theosophists maintained there was sound authority for his use of such a name. Some time later, Moncure Conway, who had traveled in India and was much disillusioned by Mrs. Besant's straying from the path of what he regarded as reason, spread the theory that Madame had compounded the name from the last syllable of the name of her colleague, Olcott, and the full surname of the early Theosophical renegade, A. O. Hume.[5]

[4] Lansbury, *My Life,* p. 78, and in *Centenary Book,* p. 30; *Lucifer,* December 15, 1889, p. 342; *Star,* September 18, November 27, 1889.

[5] *Freethinker,* August 4, October 6, 1889; *First Report of the Committee of the Society for Psychical Research, Appointed To Investigate the Evidence for Marvellous Phenomena Offered by Certain Members of the Theosophical Society* (London, 1885), p. 15; *Pall Mall Gazette,* October 23, 1891.

The rise of Mrs. Besant in the T.S. was as meteoric as had been her rise among the Secularists, and it took similar forms. Just as she had quickly become Bradlaugh's closest and most trusted colleague and a vice-president of the N.S.S., within a few months, on January 17, 1890, she was elected president of the Blavatsky Lodge, after the "resignation" of William Kingsland. Madame herself had never officially been anything more than corresponding secretary of the Society, having little speaking or organizing ability and preferring to control affairs from behind the scenes anyhow. Similarly, just as Mrs. Besant had quickly joined Bradlaugh on the editorial staff of the *Reformer,* so in September, 1889, she became coeditor of *Lucifer* along with H.P.B. The latter had run the heavily subsidized London magazine alone since the forced disappearance of the gifted Mabel Collins, author—or rather "transmitter," through her Master—of that "Theosophical gem, *Light on the Path,* and the exquisite romance, *The Idyll of the White Lotus.*" Soon after her departure, Miss Collins had become Mrs. Kenningdale Cook and had started a libel suit against Mme. Blavatsky, who had declared publicly that the idea for the novel, instead of coming from Miss Collins' own imagination, as she had claimed, had been stolen from a Mahatma who had lived in Tibet some four hundred years earlier. Since the truth of the case was difficult to establish either way, the suit was dropped just as it was called in court, after Mme. Blavatsky's counsel had shown a mysterious letter to Mrs. Cook's counsel.[6]

Yeats had watched the episode with sardonic amusement. He wrote his friend John O'Leary early in May:

Madame Blavatsky has expelled Mrs. Cook . . . and expelled also the president of the lodge for flirtation; and expelled an American lady for gossip about them. Madame Blavatsky is in great spirits, she is purring and hiding her claws as though she never clawed anybody.

Later, in *Four Years,* Yeats supplemented this tidbit: "When I first began to frequent her house, . . . I noticed a handsome clever woman of the world there, who certainly seemed very much out of place, penitent as she thought herself." But soon gossip and scandal began to circulate because of her behavior with two young men, "who were expected to grow into ascetic sages." H.P.B., discovering what was going on, quickly put an end to the double affair by calling the young woman and lecturing her on the beauty of living in chastity in thought and act, concluding with unexpected tolerance and understanding, "I cannot permit you more than one." Rumors of these family dissensions and upsets were not slow in reaching the outside world, and Foote gleefully called the attention of the non-elect to the admission in *Lucifer* that at the most only one or two influential members of the Society had left it within the twelvemonth:

⁶ *Star,* July 10, 1890; *Path,* August, 1890, p. 154.

"Of rows, it is true, we have had plenty, and we may expect more, so long as human nature is the same among Theosophists as elsewhere." Mrs. Besant meanwhile continued to contribute to *Lucifer* articles such as "Karma and Social Improvement." After all, according to Theosophical belief, everything that happens to an individual in this life is the outcome of karma.[7]

Though Bradlaugh's warning of his coming resignation had been only provisional, no one—Foote least of all—seemed inclined to try to dissuade him. He returned from his Indian trip late in January, 1890, after a stay of only two weeks. His health was somewhat better, he had made a few public speeches and given a few interviews, and he had had his proposals for a draft bill for reforming and improving the Indian legislative councils discussed, amended, and adopted by the Fifth Indian National Congress. While in Bombay he had met A. O. Hume, the former Theosophist who had been responsible for the idea of founding such a representational Indian assembly for discussional and advisory purposes (as yet it had no official or legislative power). Bradlaugh's right to the title, "Member for India," even though the imperialists in Parliament usually used it sneeringly, was vindicated by the farewell given him at the final meeting. There an address was read by Sir William Wedderburn, who had also come from England and had been elected president, and the platform was piled from end to end with copies of other addresses in carved wooden and engraved silver caskets and with rugs and mats and carvings and shawls brought as gifts from all over India. His modest speech of thanks and his promise to present the bill to Parliament at its opening session were met with great applause. There was a large turnout of Hindus, Parsis, and even Mohammedans to say goodbye at the wharf to the two Englishmen; but the only Europeans present besides Hume were a couple of reporters and some policemen. The cause of Indian nationalism was still not a safe one with which to associate oneself in 1890.[8]

Mrs. Besant, who had temporarily returned to her position of editor of the *Reformer* in Bradlaugh's absence, had carefully abstained from even mentioning Theosophy in it, with one exception. She had announced that she was emphatically not a candidate for the presidency herself, since her running would necessarily divide the party: "As a Socialist, I am in a minority—so far as the older members of the Society are concerned—and as a Theosophist I am in antagonism to the vast majority of members." In the meantime, Foote had announced that he would not even campaign; he had had private assurance from enough of the branches that they would support him. So, in mid-February, Bradlaugh arrived at the

[7] *Lucifer*, August, September, 1889, January, 1890; Besterman, *Mrs. Annie Besant,* pp. 168–69; *Golden Book*, p. 104; Hone, *W. B. Yeats*, p. 171; Yeats, *Four Years*, pp. 76–77; *Freethinker*, August 4, 1889; *Theosophist* (Supplement), December, 1889, p. 1.

[8] *National Reformer*, January 5, February 9, 1890; *Commonweal*, August 27, 1915.

Hall of Science, accompanied by Mrs. Besant and followed shortly by Foote. Sadly he told the crowd that he could not remain even as nominal president, as some had suggested; he reviewed the history of the National Secular Society and the Freethought Publishing Company under his leadership, mentioning Mrs. Besant several times along the way; listened to speeches of gratitude from several members; and himself nominated Foote as his successor until the annual conference could act. Robertson, who was nominated by a small group which did not care for Foote's somewhat raucous methods, declined to run, and Foote was chosen by acclamation. In a note of thanks in the *Freethinker,* he called Bradlaugh a "mighty leader" who could still be counted on to give legal advice, but added invidiously that though he himself was now forty years of age and "past the heats and effervescence of youth," he was still "not old enough to be useless." The Shelley Society apparently agreed with him, for, according to the *Star,* it promptly invited him to address it on Shelley's religion.

Two weeks after the election the Executive Committee received a communication from Mrs. Besant announcing her resignation as vice-president and member of the committee. It appointed a deputation to try to dissuade her, but she replied that she was sure that she and Foote could not work harmoniously together. Characteristically she inserted an incidental remark to the effect that she was glad to find that her Theosophy did not disqualify her for the position. The board refused to commit itself on that question but passed a resolution thanking her for her fifteen years of past work. Foote's paper pointed out churlishly that she had been absent from committee meetings for a long time anyhow, but she replied that it was only during Bradlaugh's illness that she had been away. The *Freethinker* added that presumably, when she had resigned as an officer, she had also resigned from the Society, but that this did not really matter, since she had actually resigned many months ago when she joined the Theosophists. At the annual convention at Manchester in May, Foote—who was of course re-elected by acclamation—commented on the absence of "two famous figures," Charles Bradlaugh because of illness, and Mrs. Besant, "who has resigned her connexion with the Society." Hypatia Bradlaugh Bonner and R. Forder also resigned their offices—for reasons of health, they said. Later it transpired that they also, like Mrs. Besant, had left the N.S.S. for good.

In order that the liquidation of their connection with the Society would be complete, Bradlaugh and Mrs. Besant transferred to the N.S.S. the shares they owned in various of the Secular halls around the country, to be sold for the benefit of the group. They also withdrew from their joint editorship of the annual *Almanack.* Most important and difficult of all, they announced the breakup of the Freethought Publishing Company and their desire to clear off the debenture debt as fully and quickly as possible. The publishing part of the business was to be transferred to Forder, and Arthur Bonner would continue the printing. The Fleet Street shop would be let, including the insolvent Vegetarian Restaurant which it had housed, and there would be a great clearance sale.

At the end of December a formal joint notice informed all who might be concerned that "the partnership heretofore subsisting between Annie Besant and Charles Bradlaugh under the title of Freethought Publishing Company is dissolved by mutual consent" and that Bradlaugh, carrying on the business, would assume all the assets and discharge all the liabilities. Immediately underneath, he printed a pathetic appeal "To My Friends" to help him out of his desperate financial straits: "My only means of livelihood are my tongue and my pen." In spite of the opposite charges of his enemies, he said he had never been rich and never would be. In fact, he would like to give away all his "assets" except his library to anyone who would also assume his liabilities. There were no takers.

The incoming leaders of the N.S.S. were elated over their new unity. In July none other than Charles Watts reappeared from Toronto and was heartily forgiven for his sins of thirteen years past. Not only was a big reception given at the Hall to celebrate his return, but the venerable G. J. Holyoake, who had fallen upon evil days but had had a subscription raised for him by Mrs. Besant and others, came in from Brighton to preside at the meeting. Watts, wrote Foote, was as jolly as ever in his skepticism.

Mrs. Besant, however, was still hanging on to her memberships in her Socialist societies. She was one of the speakers representing the S.D.F. in the vast May-Day demonstration in Hyde Park; she spoke from the same platform at the Marble Arch with representatives of the Lithographic Artists, the Amalgamated Engineers, the Society of Compositors, the Philanthropic Coopers, etc. She had somehow or other maintained an active participation in labor movements, strikes, and unionization. She had worked for the fur-pullers, the jam-makers, the envelope-makers, the Irish female factory-workers, and the dockers; and when the match-girls from the Bell factory went out on strike, she addressed them early one November morning "in a white fog," wrote to the *Star* about the trouble, and tried to persuade the dock-workers to refuse to load the Bell barges until the girls had won.

But she failed to be present at the annual Fabian soirée in June; and at the end of November the *Star* carried a personal note as follows:

A Fabian writes us:—Mrs. Annie Besant has just resigned her membership of the Fabian Society, and theosophy gains at the expense of social democracy. . . . By way of compensation for the loss, the Fabians have, during the last fortnight, recruited three times as many members as ever in the same time before. The essays are still selling at the rate of about three hundred a week.

Annie Besant's contribution to the *Fabian Essays* still remains as one of the chief evidences of what Shaw called her "Passage through Fabian Socialism."

4

The Building of the Kingdom

During the years 1889 and 1890 Annie Besant had broken,
either wholly or partially, most of her ties with her past life. At the same
time she was forming many new ones, some of which were to last for a
relatively short time, others for the remainder of her now half-finished
and still unpredictable career. Two of these new intimates brought to her
by her conversion by Mme. Blavatsky were Colonel Henry Steele Olcott
and the Rev. Charles Webster Leadbeater, both of whom she had been
hearing about for some time, but had not yet met.

Early in September, 1889, Olcott returned to London from his proselytizing trip to Japan and parts between and immediately headed for
H.P.B.'s house on Lansdowne Road—actually the house of Bertram
Keightley, a well-to-do young neophyte. It was a pleasant place in a quiet
neighborhood, the back of it giving onto a small private park common to
it and the surrounding houses. Because H.P.B.'s huge size and feebleness
made it difficult for her to walk up and down stairs, her rooms were on
the ground floor. Most of her work was done in the library at a desk in
front of a large window which looked out over the green of the park. The
room was provided with tables and chairs and crowded with book-racks
filled with reference works. After all, the Masters could not be expected
to provide her with all the knowledge she needed in her writing. The
room was also littered with Indian souvenirs, bronzes, mats, carpets,
plaques, and images of all kinds of gods. But the heterogeneous clutter
of her room in New York at the time she and Olcott had founded the
T.S. fourteen years ago had disappeared. Here there were no stuffed owls,
stuffed monkeys, stuffed snakes and lizards, stuffed lionesses' heads, or—
least of all—stuffed baboons, with white collars and cravats around their

necks, spectacles on their noses, and bundles of manuscripts under their arms labeled *The Decent* [*sic*] *of Species*. The volumes on magic, Spiritualism, and comparative religion were still present, together with the stale effluvium of cigarette smoke and the playing cards laid out for the perpetual game of Russian solitaire; but, generally speaking, Madame had gone respectable. Her titled ladies and professional gentlemen would not have been impressed by a collection from the corner taxidermist's shop.[1]

Here in this small menage in Holland Park, where the Countess Wachtmeister was acting as a combined housekeeper, nurse, and counselor, Olcott found Annie Besant, who had moved in "bag and baggage," leaving her St. John's Wood residence for a few weeks in order that she might be close to her guru. She was still dressed in what Olcott called her "Annie Militant" costume, but in spite of his dubiousness about her appearance he felt that here was a "natural Theosophist," even before her conversion was mentioned. He took her by the hand as they parted and said solemnly: "I think you will find yourself happier than you have ever been in your life before, for I see you are a mystic and have been frozen into your brain by your environment. You come now into a family of thinkers who will know you as you are and love you dearly."[2]

The next day he and Annie went to call on Bradlaugh at his home, for Olcott wished to pay his respects and renew their acquaintance. He found the other aging fast, "yet full of the virile strength which made him stand like an oak among men." Knowing how Bradlaugh must be feeling about the situation, he remarked on his regret that the Theosophists' gain of Mrs. Besant had been at the other's expense and reminded him that she had come over through no solicitation on their part. Bradlaugh replied sadly that it was a great and deep loss to him, but that Mrs. Besant was a woman who would always act according to the promptings of her conscience. Even if he had anything to say, which he did not, he knew it would be useless. Olcott at this meeting was wise enough not to try to convert Bradlaugh too, though in the *Theosophist* he had dropped hints in this direction, along with reprintings of the *Pall Mall Gazette*'s "Among the Adepts" and Mrs. Besant's review of *The Secret Doctrine* from the *Reformer*. Most of the Theosophical magazines were doing the same thing, though at the same time they were frankly skeptical of their success.

The friendship between A.B. and H.S.O. ripened rapidly. He immediately began to attend her lectures on subjects like "Memory" to learn

[1] Olcott, in *Theosophist* (Supplement), October, 1888; Bechhofer-Roberts, *The Mysterious Madame*, pp. 7-10; *Freethinker*, August 31, 1890.

[2] For the story of Olcott's first meeting with Mrs. Besant, see his *Old Diary Leaves*, IV, 171 ff., 190-91, 203; *Theosophist*, July, 1889, pp. 598, 675-76; January, 1890, p. 286.

from her oratory and was properly impressed by what he regarded as the greatest Theosophical acquisition since Sinnett and Hume. He was not an inspiring speaker, as she was; but his dignified, genial bearing and his great, soft, silvery beard, like that of a benevolent Santa Claus, impressed non-Secularist audiences with confidence. Within less than two weeks, when he gave his first public lecture in London at the South Place Chapel, where Stanton Moses Coit had replaced Moncure Conway, Mrs. Besant took the chair. The hall was packed with an assemblage which, according to the *Gazette,* demanded immense respect "by reason of its mental capacity and ability." It was made up of "bronzed Anglo-Indians, Easterns in fez and goggles, medical, theological, and secular students and teachers, representative South Place people, agnostics, freethinkers, and spiritualists"—all come together to hear Olcott tell in undramatic but convincing terms of "The Theosophical Society and Its Work." Olcott basked in the paper's praise. This was but the beginning of many occasions on which he and Mrs. Besant supported each other from the platform.

He also saw a great deal of her private life. When a noted palmist, Mrs. Louise Cotton, came to read H.P.B.'s hand, and read his and A.B.'s very accurately at the same time, he saw the "infinite tenderness and unselfish compassion" of which Annie was capable when she took into her house and nursed "like a sister" an old friend, "a fellow-reformer and a very well-known man," who "was utterly prostrated by overwork of the brain, and his life in peril." But this same man (his identity is not clear; he may have been Holyoake, Truelove, or Wheeler), after she had cured him of his ravings and perhaps saved his life, "turned upon his gentle nurse and said cruel things against her in the press." Olcott was sure the man must have had "another access of nervous debility" to show such ingratitude.

Before Olcott left England to return to India early in 1890, he issued another presidential order designed both to pacify Mme. Blavatsky and to safeguard the T.S. from what he had long considered to be her lack of judgment and organizational ability. In fact, for some years there had been a weakly patched-up rift between them, and a sort of division of territory had been tacitly agreed on, whereby he was to maintain his headquarters in Adyar and she was to do her missionary work from London. After the events of 1884 and 1885, Olcott had wished to minimize the doctrine of the Masters and of occultism in general. H.P.B., realizing that it was through this aspect of Theosophy that the "Wisdom-Religion" had its greatest appeal and attracted the most attention, could not agree; and in 1888 she reverted to the 1876 organization of the Society by reviving its Second Section, consisting of those members who had proved by their conduct that they not only believed in brotherhood as the guiding factor in life but also in the reality and immanence of the Masters of the Wisdom. Thus she had formed her Esoteric Section, comprising the most reliable and devoted members, but within them she had added an Inner Group, made up of those select few who had displayed the greatest talents for discipleship and occult training. So strong had been Olcott's objection to this sort of fragmentation and favoritism that only a "precipitated" letter from Master K. H. himself, received miraculously on shipboard on his way to London, reconciled him to these orders from the hierarchy; and he signed a joint communiqué with his colleague establishing the "E.S. of the T.S." and declaring the friendship and unity between himself and H.P.B. in spite of the "mischief-makers."

But he was still not fully convinced of Madame's wisdom in this matter. Consequently, at the end of his 1889 tour, to make it clear to everyone that the Esoteric Section still had no official or direct connection with the Society, its name was not only changed to the "Eastern School of Theosophy" but he issued a new presidential order, couched diplomatically as follows:

> In compliance with the unanimous request of the British Section, and to obviate the inconvenience and delay of reference to Headquarters of current local questions requiring my official adjudication, I hereby appoint H. P. Blavatsky as Chairman, and Annie Besant, William Kingsland, and Herbert Burrows as Members, of an Appellate Board, to be known as "The President's Commissioners" for Great Britain and Ireland.

He added that this board should also have all the proxy executive powers conferred on him by the constitution but that all orders and decisions on his behalf must be unanimous. Thus, as he admitted later in his *Old Diary Leaves*, he got around letting H. P. B. alone be responsible for decisions, since he had more respect for the good sense of the other three.[3]

Madame, however, though old and ill, had plenty of fight left. The feud between her and Olcott had been carried into their respective magazines, and she had, for instance, written a note about Adyar entitled "Muddled Meddlers." Now, early in July, as duly reported in *Lucifer*, she called an Extraordinary General Meeting and, with her "Penelope" in the chair, manipulated a resolution demanding that she accept the "duty of exercising the Presidential authority for the whole of Europe," with the London headquarters becoming the European headquarters. To avoid the appearance of autocracy she appointed a council which would, unlike its predecessor, be merely advisory. It was enlarged to seven members, all from London, including the original three and Sinnett, Mead, E. T. Sturdy, and H. A. W. Coryn, president of the Brixton Lodge. In December, Mrs. Besant followed this action with an article entitled "The T.S. and H.P.B.," warning that "it is time that some

[3] *Golden Book*, pp. 119–21; Annie Besant, *The Theosophical Society and the Occult Hierarchy*, pp. 8, 13, 15; *Theosophist* (Supplement), December, 1888, p. xxvii; Olcott, *Old Diary Leaves*, IV, 182; *Path*, March, 1890, pp. 387–88.

protest should be made against the constant petty criticisms levelled at H.P.B." and concluding that, if the Society meant anything at all, there must be Masters, and H.P.B. was their messenger. Two months later, however, H.P.B. corrected her and pointed out that all Theosophists did not have to believe in the Masters.

Olcott knew when he was beaten. In his next annual report on the year's events, he told how, because of age, exhaustion, and bad health, he had tried to retire, although he had been elected president-founder for life, and how he had asked Mme. Blavatsky to take his place. She, however, fearing that the Society would collapse because of the disaffection of the Indian and American sections if he withdrew entirely, refused to agree. Olcott therefore modified his intention: he would withdraw for a rest and place affairs in the hands of a committee for one year, beginning in April. The only non-Indian on Olcott's committee was William Quan Judge, head of the American Section. It was a decision and a situation destined soon to plunge the whole Society into a morass of trouble.

"Colonel," as he was familiarly known, was considerably older than Mrs. Besant, and their association, though close, was to last for only a few years. But C. W. Leadbeater had been born in 1847, the same year as she, and their friendship—or perhaps it should be called their alliance—was to last until their deaths, which occurred within a few months of each other. Little by little, as Leadbeater's occult faculties burgeoned, so grew his ascendancy over Annie Besant, who in her aspirations for occult development had the same ambitions as he.

Their first face-to-face meeting occurred some time in the year 1890—neither of them could remember the month—at a meeting of the London Lodge in Sinnett's drawing room in Ladbrooke Grove.[4] But he had known her by sight and hearing from 1876 or 1877; for as he was fond of pointing out, he had gone to hear her many times at her Freethought lectures in the Hall of Science, without daring to speak to her. Though he was at that time scarcely prejudiced in her favor, being a young curate in the Church of England, he was so impressed by her power, fearlessness, and knowledge that he was led to examine the works of the renowned American atheist, Colonel Robert Ingersoll, and this experience opened his eyes to "the impossibility of the whole orthodox system as it was commonly explained."

[4] For this autobiographical sketch of Leadbeater, see his letter quoted by G. S. Arundale in *Autobiography*, pp. 34–35, and the revised version in Jinarajadasa, in *The Annie Besant Centenary Book*, pp. 159–60; Mrs. Besant's sketch of him in *Theosophist*, November, 1911, pp. 306–10, and Arundale, in *Autobiography*, pp. 38–40; Ernest Wood, *Is This Theosophy . . . ?* (London, 1936), pp. 197–98; *Australian Theosophist*, October, 1907, and *Theosophy in Australia*, July, 1922, and August, 1923; *Adyar Bulletin*, March, 1912; *Secular Chronicle*, June 1, 1873; Besterman, *Mrs. Annie Besant*, pp. 204–5. The present author also had an interview with B. P. Wadia at Bangalore, India, January 12–13, 1957.

He had come into the Church by a somewhat roundabout route, through a family that was inclined toward mysticism and adventure. He remembered that in his parents' home when he was a child he had seen the "great Occultist," the novelist and politician Bulwer-Lytton; and he recalled "seeing a letter, lying on a table, drop to the floor and flutter along it to his hand, untouched by aught visible." From this incident Mrs. Besant later supposed that the boy's parents "were in contact with occult thought." Some reason unexplained by Leadbeater next took his father (in some versions Leadbeater says both his parents), himself, and his younger brother to Brazil, where they lived "a life of manifold adventures." Actually, his father was a railway contractor there. Here occurred a fatal episode (otherwise unauthenticated) of the kind that Leadbeater later liked to weave into his stories of past reincarnations: his father "was killed by rebels, refusing to trample on the Cross, and he himself endured horrible torture and was tied to a tree half dead at night; he felt arms come around him, his father's arms, and his bonds were cut and he was carried away by him and by a Negro servant, who loved him." Since the father by this time must have been in a ghostly state and the Negro very much alive, their collaboration must have been a queer one, but it became the basis of a story, "Saved by a Ghost," which Leadbeater wrote and published in a collection called *The Perfume of Egypt and Other Weird Stories.* Finally returning to England, he entered Oxford, but was soon compelled to leave it by the financial smash of Overend, Gurney and Company on the historic "Black Monday," which swallowed up the family fortune. Despite this blow, he succeeded in taking orders in 1878, though where and how are not recorded.

It was in his seminary days that he learned certain sexual teachings and practices that were to bring him into continuous trouble for the rest of his life. He became a High Church curate in the little parish of St. Mary's Bramshott, in the south of England, where his interest in young boys first displayed itself; there he earned the devotion of his head choirboy, J. W. Matley, and his elder brother, who spent all their spare time in his company for twelve years. Though the dates Matley gave hardly concur, since Leadbeater had left England for India long before twelve years had elapsed, the young man later became an F.T.S., went to Papua, and corresponded with his mentor for over thirty years, finding his advice "the purest and noblest." During this parish period, while decorating his church with holly one Christmas season, the young priest fell from a ladder and injured his back. The pain from this accident sometimes recurred, so that he frequently had to lie down to recover from it; but the injury did not prevent him from indulging his fondness for tennis, which he kept up until he was a hale and hearty septuagenarian.

During the period of his active priesthood, which lasted until 1884,

Leadbeater developed a strong interest in Spiritualism and "carried on a series of careful experiments" himself, though as yet he showed "no signs of any psychic faculties." Perhaps, though the initial is wrong, a note in the *Secular Chronicle* for June 1, 1873, may reflect a still earlier interest in the subject, for it told how a "Mr. J. Leadbeater . . . very effectually presided at the request of the joint committee" at a debate on "Spiritualism" at Hickmondwike between the Freethinker Reddalls, editor of the paper, and J. Burns, editor of the *Medium and Daybreak.* By the strange route of Secularism and Spiritualism, then, the young priest had his attention drawn to Theosophy. He joined the Society in 1883, though his diploma bore the date 1884, when he left the Church. He had read the books of Sinnett and, unable to escape their fascination and appeal, struck up a close friendship with their author. The arrival of H.P.B. in England at this juncture clinched his determination. He threw up everything—church, family, and friends—to accompany her back to India. On the way they paused for a time in Egypt. One day as he was sitting alone with her, "a third Person suddenly appeared, and he started violently. 'A nice Occultist!' quoth H.P.B. scathingly, and there was no more starting at unusual appearances," many of which quickly followed without her help.

At first Leadbeater did not expect much in the way of progress and was willing to do anything he was told, from sweeping floors to addressing envelopes; but soon "His Master stretched out his hand," and he was given work on the *Theosophist.* In 1885 he became recording secretary of the T.S. in India. Damodar K. Mavalankar, the idolized, sensitive young Theosophist saint and mystic and the previous holder of the office, had been swept away by his studies and his astral meetings with the Masters. Nothing would suffice but that he must go to Tibet himself, as H.P.B. said she had done, and find them in the flesh. Leaving everything and wrapped mostly in his devotion, he started out on the lonely road to Tibet from Darjeeling in the midst of winter. A few days later a frozen corpse, stripped of most of its belongings, was picked up only a short distance from the border. The authorities identified it as that of Damodar, but the Theosophists refused to accept the identification. They were sure that a dedicated believer like Damodar could not fail to find his Masters. For over forty years many of the older members, including Annie Besant, waited in the expectation that he would return with a new message from Tibet.[5] But in 1957 a memorial statue of him was set up in the library at Adyar, not far from the triple group of Mme. Blavatsky, Colonel Olcott, and Annie Besant. From another angle, a bronze bust of Bishop C. W. Leadbeater gazes benignly at them all.

The neophyte Leadbeater, after a short proselytizing trip to Burma, was soon sent to Ceylon to help with the missionary work there and,

[5] *Theosophist,* October, 1910, pp. 281–84.

since he had become a Buddhist, to look after the Buddhist schools for poor children that Olcott had so successfully started. It was there that he met a young Ceylonese boy named Jinarajadasa, who showed tremendous promise. In 1889, Sinnett, who had kept watch over the development of his convert, wrote to ask Leadbeater to return to England as tutor to his son and another young English boy, George S. Arundale, the nephew and adopted son of a wealthy Theosophical spinster, Francesca Arundale. Leadbeater accepted on the condition that he might bring his Ceylonese protégé with him. There are conflicting stories of what happened next. One version has it that, using his powerful influence over the boy and knowing that the father was against the plan, Leadbeater practically kidnapped the lad. The father, discovering his son's absence before the ship sailed, pursued him on shipboard and, breathing curses and sinister accusations against Leadbeater's suspected relations with the boy, brought him home at the point of a gun, only to let him go later when he received proper assurances from friends that all would be well. Jinarajadasa himself, however, vigorously denied this story over and over again, giving corroborative evidence of its implausibility; but it has persisted nevertheless.[6]

Leadbeater's own story of the affair, as told by Mrs. Besant, casually revealed another sensational detail concerning the tragic tale of his family's history in Brazil: "From then to 1889, when he returned to Europe—bringing with him the little brother whom he had lost in South America, for whom he had been persistently searching, having been told by his Master that he was reincarnated there—he spent about three months each year in India and the rest of his time in Ceylon." For about a year in London, he tutored the two white boys and his newly discovered Indian "brother." Then, according to one scandalous story, Francesca Arundale learned about Leadbeater's reputation with boys and removed her nephew-son from his care. Sinnett did the same with his son; but he apparently did not mind the former tutor's becoming secretary of his London Lodge at the same time. Mme. Blavatsky, according to the same gossip, had already lost faith in the man she had taken to India with her five years before. She refused to admit him into her Esoteric Section and, with a grimace in the direction of the European connotation of "W.C.," delighted to refer to him as "W.C." Leadbeater.

All these details in the past history of her new acquaintance Mrs. Besant was certainly not familiar with at Sinnett's reception in 1890, and when she learned of them later she scornfully rejected the disreputable portions. Not until four or five years afterward would her friendship

[6] B. P. Wadia gave me a slightly different version of it in 1957, on the authority of Hevavitarana Dharmapala, whose diary is now in the process of being published by the Mahabodhi Society in Calcutta.

with the Rev. Mr. Leadbeater begin to ripen into perhaps the most far-reaching influence in her whole life.

One thing that may have struck her early in the acquaintance was his surprising resemblance to Bernard Shaw. The color of their hair was different, it is true, but they wore their beards in the same cut, their noses and ears had a sharp Mephistophelean conformation, and in their eyes was the same quizzical expression. Ironically enough, the final twisting of the sword in the relationship between Annie Besant and Bernard Shaw occurred just about the time she first met Leadbeater. It happened on July 18 when she was presiding at a meeting of the Fabian Society at the St. James's Restaurant.[7] As Shaw tells in *The Quintessence of Ibsenism*, it was the final lecture in a series devoted to "Socialism in Contemporary Literature," and he was giving the paper on Ibsen which he later developed into *The Quintessence*. (Eleanor Marx-Aveling would have been a much more appropriate chairman, since she had just begun a series of translations of Ibsen's plays.) But Shaw preserved a gentlemanly silence about everything except the paper itself. The *Star* and *Justice*, however, were not so reticent. As the *Star* reporter saw it:

. . . the fun of Mr. Shaw's lecture came when, after a really wonderful analysis of Ibsen's plays, he came to turn his guns against Mrs. Besant, Mr. Herbert Burrows, and the Social Democratic Federation in general, and upheld the Fabian Society as embodying true Ibsenism. . . . Naturally this set a lively flame a-blowing and probably Mr. Shaw's defiance will be resented elsewhere than in the Fabian Society's rooms.

In fact, Shaw's "anti-idealism" and his "anti-red-flag waving" made even his own Fabians' "flesh creep," inured as they were to his unpredictable forensic forays.

The talk not only aroused much argument and discussion in the correspondence column of the *Star;* it also provoked *Justice* to take a hand, and Burrows wrote an editorial entitled "Socialism of the Sty," prompted by Shaw's paper. After he had sneered loftily at Shaw's "intellectual gymnastics" and at the typical Fabian's lack of concern to "help his brother man or elevate his sister woman" (though, just two weeks before, Shaw himself had written the lead editorial in the paper), Burrows went on to deplore Shaw's attitude toward idealism:

Annie Besant, who was in the chair, which we could all perceive was anything but a bed of roses, and which some of us would not have been surprised to see her vacate, of course protested strongly against doctrines which cut at the root of everything she holds dear, but Mr. Shaw's answer to her was applauded more than her protestation.

---

[7] Arthur H. Nethercot, "G. B. S. and Annie Besant," *Shaw Bulletin*, September, 1955, pp. 13–14. Stephen Winsten (*Jesting Apostle*, p. 75) ludicrously states that Mrs. Besant was responsible for the series of lectures because of her admiration for Ibsen and adds that she listened to Shaw as if she were "listening to an oratorio"!

Burrows then concluded his revealing behind-the-scenes glimpse of the background of Shaw's first book on the drama by complaining about the harm of his "Jokism" and his unidealistic approach to life. Shaw's own conscience bothered him sufficiently so that when he wrote his *Fabian Tract No. 41*, he was impelled to insert a sort of embarrassed apology: "Those who have read this book and followed Mrs. Besant's subsequent career will understand at once that she must have felt as she listened to it that this was not her path."

Yet even this contretemps did not spell the end of Annie's loyalty. The *Star* recorded how, during the brilliant maiden speech of Grant Allen, the biologist-novelist, at the Fabian Society in October, an unidentified young man got up and tried to lay down the law to G.B.S. about just what "we hold." Mrs. Besant, who had been cospeaker with Allen, rose and, in a "remarkably eloquent and able" reply, gave the rash young fellow "beans." The piling-up of such events, however, proved too much for her to endure, and a little over a month later she resigned from the Society. Even then, Shaw persisted in his needling. At one of her heavily attended propagandizing lectures in the Theosophical cause toward the end of December, he seemingly got up in the audience and delivered a "little speech," which, said the ubiquitous *Star* man, "caused such a sensation." This incident marked the end of the Shaw-Besant public relations for some years.

The year 1890 was a big one for building and rebuilding. Two projects in the tangible form of wood, brick, and plaster were to occupy much of Mrs. Besant's attention during the year—one to contribute heavily to the psychic improvement of mankind, the other to its physical improvement. The first was a new headquarters building for the T.S., with all the necessary equipment and paraphernalia for expanding the latent powers of the human mind and soul; the second was a much more prosaic and practical Home for Working Women.

Mrs. Besant had soon realized that if the T.S. were to become all that she wanted it to become, it would have to find larger and more suitable quarters than the house in Lansdowne Road. Consequently, in the *Theosophist* for February and also in a special circular, she issued an appeal for a "Theosophical Building Fund" to procure "a house in a garden where there would be room to build, and then to add to it a large room for meetings and, over this, rooms for the accommodation of the staff." By a remarkable coincidence, this description exactly fitted her own premises at 19 Avenue Road. Counting on the well-proved generosity of some of the wealthy members, she and the committee started the necessary remodeling and new building even before the fund was completed. One anonymous donor was meeting almost the entire cost. Soon Mrs. Besant felt safe in announcing that the transfer would be made in June or July, although actually this estimate proved overoptimistic. Arrangements were also made to take over the remainder of Mrs. Besant's eighteen-year lease in the name of the T.S. in Europe.[8]

Nineteen Avenue Road, as Olcott and Digby Besant remembered it, consisted of a spacious detached house, standing within its own high brick-walled grounds and surrounded by a pleasant garden, with flower beds, bits of lawn, shrubbery, and a few tall trees. Much of this garden was to become the site for the new building. The original house could be transformed with only a minimum of reconstruction. On the ground floor, opening on the left from the vestibule, were two connecting rooms; the one which had been Mrs. Besant's study now became H.P.B.'s workroom, the other became her small bedchamber. On the right of the hall was the artistically furnished dining room, which was also used as a reception room for visitors; and behind it was another small room, originally used by Annie as a general workroom, but later turned into a bedroom-study for Leadbeater. The upper stories were sleeping apartments, one of which Mrs. Besant retained as a bed-sitting room for herself. But some additions had to be made also. A door had to be cut through the south wall of Madame's workroom to lead into the office of the general secretary of the European Section, while another was cut through the north wall of the dining room to afford direct access to the entirely new hall of the Blavatsky Lodge.

There was no secret about any of these rooms. Anyone might inspect them. But leading from H.P.B.'s bedroom there was a short secret passage ending in a rather spacious chamber built especially for and occupied by the Esoteric Section. Even more hidden was a small place for the Inner Group, called the Occult Room. Though it was never satisfactorily completed, it had mirrors instead of windows, a blue-glass ceiling, and a ventilating system which gave some trouble. Nobody except the inner circle knew what went on in the Occult Room, but there was talk among the common members of all kinds of mysteries, including seances and hypnotism. The Inner Group were sworn so solemnly to secrecy that even after forty years, G. R. S. Mead, who by then had long split from the Society, felt himself so bound by his oath that he would not divulge their rites or occult experiments.

It was the new meeting hall in the garden that excited the most curiosity from the public at large. Externally it was not in the least attractive or mysterious. It was originally planned to be one hundred feet long, but this size was reduced. The outer shell was of corrugated iron, which was sheathed inside with unpainted wood. The artist R. A. Machel, of whom the Theosophists were very proud, had covered the two sloping

[8] For the story of this construction, see *Lucifer, Theosophist,* and *Star, passim,* for 1890; Olcott, *Old Diary Leaves,* IV, 246–48; *Annie Besant Centenary Book,* p. 218; *Golden Book,* p. 225; *Autobiography,* pp. 462–65; Besterman, *Mrs. Annie Besant,* p. 172.

halves of the ceiling with intricate designs in blue, consisting of symbolic representations of the six great religions of the world and of the twelve zodiacal signs which to the astrologers have such a controlling influence over human character and action. At the south end of the hall was a low platform for the presiding officer and the speaker of the meeting. At the back of the platform stood a large mirror bearing the six-pointed Theosophical star, made of two interlocking triangles surrounded by a serpent. Above were painted a lion's head, a winged scorpion, and other occult emblems. On the walls were hung portraits of several Indians, together with "pictures of a strange-looking, many-handed individual," whom the ignorant *Star* reporter mistook to be Buddha. Finally, on the second floor of the hall were the sleeping quarters for the staff—eight large bedrooms and eight small, which would be occupied according to one's importance. It was a community group and a community life which were to be established in St. John's Wood, and a set of communal regulations was at once drawn up for the behavior of the members.

In July eleven persons moved together for the first time under one roof—a band of devotees whose unity under H.P.B. they were confident could never be shaken.[9] There were the two Keightley cousins, Archibald and Bertram, now in their early thirties—both educated at the Charterhouse and Cambridge, and both soon afterward converted to Theosophy by Sinnett. Bertram, ascetic-looking, with rimmed glasses, scraggly beard and mustache, deeply parted heavy hair, flat square bow tie, and stiff white waistcoat, was a lawyer. Archibald, less ascetic-looking, with a rounder face, fuller beard, and less conspicuous glasses, was a doctor—a member of the Royal College of Physicians and also of the Royal College of Surgeons; he later was to pass the medical examination of the state of New York and practice there. They had joined H.P.B. in her early days in England and were devoted to her. Dr. Archibald was regarded as the steadier of the two, whereas Bertram, though he was soon to become secretary of the Indian Section and hold other high offices, was regarded by many of his colleagues as unreliable, backbiting, and treacherous.

There was also the middle-aged Countess Wachtmeister, whose full name was Constance Georgine Louise de Bourbel de Montjunçon and whose parents had been the Marquis de Bourbel, formerly in the French diplomatic service, and Constance Bulkley, an Englishwoman. Born in Florence in 1838, she had been left an orphan early, had been educated in England, and in 1863 had married her cousin, Count Wachtmeister, the Swedish and Norwegian minister at the Court of St. James. After the birth of their son Axel, who inherited the title, and the Count's death in

[9] For the following sketches, see *Autobiography*, pp. 462–64; *Path*, July, September, November, 1893, January, June, July, 1894; Esther Bright, *Old Memories and Letters of Annie Besant* (London, 1936), p. 101; interview with B. P. Wadia.

1871, the Countess had first dabbled in Spiritualism. She had joined the T.S. in 1881 and had become a close friend of H.P.B. Though holding no official position, she was noted as a hard worker; and her pleasant voice, blond hair, blue eyes, sweet face, and fluffy, beribboned clothes and hats made her a popular lecturer of the second rank.

George R. S. Mead, to whom Yeats had taken an instant dislike, was Madame's private secretary—"an earnest disciple," as Mrs. Besant described him three years later, "a man of strong brain and strong character, a fine scholar and untiring worker." His father had been a colonel in the Ordnance. He himself had taken honors at Cambridge after shifting from mathematics to the classical tripos. He had taught school and, after reading *Esoteric Buddhism*, meeting Bertram Keightley and Mohini, and reading Hindu philosophy, had entered Oxford to undertake the study of philosophy in general, supplementing his Oxford work by reading in Spiritualism at the French university at Clermont-Ferrand. His complete conversion to Theosophy had taken place after his meeting with H.P.B. in 1887, and he had quickly become one of the leading chelas in her household. Physically, he was of medium height; with a rather heart-shaped face; bright, almond-shaped eyes under straight eyebrows; a narrow nose; thin auburn hair, "like some sunset afterglow"; a long, curved mustache; and a clipped, pointed beard which gave the final punctuation to a sharp, intellectual face.

Isabel Cooper-Oakley of New Bond Street, advertising herself to the public in *Woman* for April 26, 1890, as agent for Félix, Pasquier, Virot, and Reboux for "The Latest Models in Dresses, Mantles, Bonnets, &c. . . . First-Rate Fit Guaranteed," was known as "Madame Isabelle." Also the proprietor of the two Dorothy Restaurants, one for West End working girls and the other for ladies only, she was to her intimates "intuitional and studious, a rare combination, and a most devoted pupil in Occult studies." Her interest in Indian mysticism came naturally, since she had been born at Amritsar in the Punjab in 1854, the daughter of Henry Cooper, C.B., commissioner of Lahore, whose services to the Indian government and to education, especially that of women, were rewarded by his being made governor of Delhi on his deathbed. At the age of twenty-three—she had lived much of her early life on the Continent—she had had a severe accident and was unable to walk for two years, during which time she studied *Isis Unveiled*, Spiritualism, women's suffrage, and the Social Purity Alliance. Entering Girton in 1882, she met both Archibald Keightley and her future husband, A. J. Oakley, there in Cambridge; two years later, just after her marriage, the three entered the T.S. on Olcott's arrival in London. During that summer the new Cooper-Oakley combination joined H.P.B.'s establishment and went to India with her. They were at Adyar at the time of Hodgson's investigations and were incensed by their "unfairness." Besides traveling between England and India, and being in frequent ill-health, Mrs. Cooper-Oakley succeeded in being not only an active Theosophical worker and lecturer but also a highly successful businesswoman. She had a rather masculine-looking face, with a prominent nose, broad lips, and flat hairdo. She often wore a silk polka-dot dress, adorned with a gold swastika, a cameo brooch, and a feather boa over one shoulder.

These were the major figures, but there were lesser ones too. Claude Wright had come over from Dublin, "most lovable of Irishmen, with keen insight underlying a bright and sunny nature, careless on the surface." Walter R. Old, vice-president of the Lodge, was "dreamy and sensitive, a born psychic, and, like many such, easily swayed by those around him." Still less known and important was Emily Kislingbury, "a studious and earnest woman."

A little later came James Morgan Pryse, an independent, amusing, and erratic American, "than whom," wrote Mrs. Besant, "none is more devoted, bringing practical knowledge to the help of his work, and making possible the large development of our printing department," the H.P.B. Press, a separate building for which was soon to be set up on the grounds. Pryse was a real American dandy. He affected a broad-brimmed, black sombrero, a coat with braid edging buttoned close around his neck, a rose in his buttonhole, and a large black bow tie. His waxed mustache set off his narrow face and thick eyebrows. He was of Welsh blood. His father had been a Presbyterian minister in Wales before he came to Ohio, where James had been born in 1859. The young man proved to be a rolling stone and headed for the frontier at Red Cloud, Nebraska, at the age of seventeen. From then on there were few places and occupations in the New World that he did not try. He went from frontier tintype photography to printing and journalism with his brother John in Anaconda, Montana; in Prescott, Michigan; and in St. Paul, Minnesota. He went from Florida to LaCrosse, Wisconsin; from journalism to the law and then to a socialistic colony in Mexico—and he became disgruntled with them all. Next, after studying Spiritualism and rejecting it as being too narrow, he got into correspondence with the American Theosophist who became the wife of Dr. Archibald Keightley, and he and his brother joined the T.S. in Los Angeles in 1887. Eventually, by way of Peru, Panama, and New York, he landed in London, where he had heard that an expert printer was needed to take charge of the Theosophical press there.

Mrs. Cooper-Oakley's younger sister Laura and Herbert Burrows were also integral parts of this core group, but "other obligations" prevented them from always living as parts of the household. Such were the characters of this inner circle as Mrs. Besant, the thirteenth member (of course including H.P.B.), knew them at the time and later set them down in her *Autobiography*. Perhaps the number was prophetic. At least,

333

she would later have reason to revise her estimate of the devotion of all of them.

This very devotion rather worried the easygoing Olcott, who remarked that their constant high pressure tended to destroy the atmosphere of geniality and welcome which visitors from outside London hoped to find in the European center and which was always apparent at Adyar and New York; in fact, there was an inhuman chill about the place which actually drove some people away from the Society. There were even more, however, who were fascinated and drawn to it by its bizarreness.

H.P.B. herself, in spite of her position at the focus of such a crusading order, frequently had her black moments. In April, while the construction was going busily forward, she wrote to Annie that she was "profoundly miserable" and that "I believe in one person in England and this is *YOU.*" In May she was worried about the unbusinesslike operations which were going on in preparing to move to the new headquarters. She complained about how "Arch and Bert and Mead and the Countess and all—even Edge" (Sydney V. Edge, a young attorney) had been protesting against the way she had been spending the Society's money without sufficient guarantee, and she therefore requested "Penelope," who for some reason had been holding off, to transfer the lease of her house to the trustees of the T.S. within twenty-four hours.

The dedication of the new Theosophical temple on July 3 was a resounding success.[10] Two hundred and fifty people jammed into the hall meant for two hundred, many others crowded outside to look in through the windows, and more were turned away. *Vanity Fair,* in a description of what it called a typical Theosophical Society meeting in its cabalistic Gothic chapel, not very kindly summed up the audience as consisting merely of "human curiosities." But the observant society reporter from the *Star* was more specific: blond-complexioned, spectacled Germans; two dark-hued gentlemen from the East; young women with stern features, short hair, and the suspicion of a mustache; young men with abundant locks and highly colored neckties; a little lady in red, a famous chiromancist; a dark gentleman who studied astrology; a pale-faced seer; and a haggard-looking poet—all were "strange and wonderful to behold." Neither of these reporters spotted in the front row a woman whom H.P.B. herself, in a letter to her sister, identified as Mrs. Edward W. Benson, wife of the Archbishop of Canterbury, to whom a recent *Lucifer* had impudently addressed a "brotherly message."

Mrs. Besant of course presided, as president of the Blavatsky Lodge,

[10] For the following account, see *Star,* July 4, 8, 16, August 22, November 4, 12, 17, December 19, 1890; *Lucifer,* July, 1890, pp. 431–36, October, 1890, p. 164, December, 1890, pp. 344–45; *Path,* August, 1890, pp. 166–67, November, 1895, pp. 269–70; *Theosophist* (Supplement), August, 1890, pp. cliii–iv; (Supplement), November, p. xii; Bright, *Memories,* p. 19; *Golden Book,* p. 225.

and held out a sisterly hand to A. P. Sinnett, as president of the London Lodge. Both spoke eloquently and enthusiastically of the prospects of Theosophy, as well as of its bitter trials in the past; their cultured British voices contrasted strangely with the peculiar accents of the female representatives from America, Holland, Sweden, Belgium, and Spain. Young Brother Bertram Keightley, just back from America (where he had been connected in newspaper reports with the mysterious death of a medium but of course had indignantly denied any knowledge thereof), brought things back to the proper level, and Mrs. Besant finally declared the hall officially open. There was some newspaper controversy over where Mme. Blavatsky sat during the inauguration. Some saw her on the platform, some only in the audience. But all admitted that, consonant with her invariable custom, she did not speak—she only reclined in a large armchair. Yeats had previously noted her remarkable achievement in making herself one of the most talked-about women in Europe by only listening to other people talk. *Vanity Fair* commented on the adoration accorded her as she reclined in state at a later meeting, speaking only in short asthmatic sentences and then uttering only commonplaces.

Once open, the hall was kept busy, especially for its regular Thursday evening lectures by the best speakers it could put forward. Once a *Star* man confused these with a special high-society reception given on a Thursday by Countess Wachtmeister at her home, but he was quickly set right by Old and others. There was an insatiable appetite for publicity in the Society, and almost every journalistic reference to its doings, factual or satirical, was quoted or mentioned in its papers. As a result, the attendance mounted so rapidly that a new system of admission had to be introduced whereby, through a card signed by a member or an associate, a visitor might attend three lodge meetings, but after that had to become either a member or an associate himself. Reminiscent of the days of Trafalgar Square, *conversaziones* were also held every Tuesday evening. The last formalities of the transfer of headquarters to the new location dragged out till just after Christmas. At the previous meeting, Mrs. Besant stood at the door to sell Theosophical Christmas cards for threepence.

Two of the most important converts as a result of these activities were Mrs. Jacob Bright, the wife of the well-known M.P., and her daughter Esther. Mrs. Bright had known and backed Mrs. Besant in the early days when she "was gallantly fighting against terrible odds, . . . against nineteenth century respectability, false modesty and hypocrisy," and her curiosity had been aroused by the other's sudden alteration. So, one day in the fall, she and her daughter drove to Avenue Road in a hansom to hear the famous woman lecture and to meet H.P.B. Though they had not come to scoff, they remained to pray. Mrs. Bright, a wealthy woman, became one of the great benefactresses of the T.S., and her daughter, though her full conversion took longer, became one of the most faithful and hard-working of its members.

A small offshoot of the major building construction was the opening of a Theosophical Lending Library in the East End. A zealous T.S. member, inspired by these upper-class activities, became convinced that the lower middle classes needed help even more. He therefore converted a shed at the back of his house in Mile End Road, once used as an engine-house for his electrical experiments, into a free library—whitewashing it, furnishing it neatly, and lighting it extravagantly with both gas and electric light. So impressed were they by Brother Chapman's devotion, that Mrs. Besant and Mrs. Cooper-Oakley, together with Burrows, Old, and Mead, came and spoke at the opening and urged other members to contribute books and pamphlets.

The ministrations of these two buildings were primarily to the mind and the soul, but Mrs. Besant's program of brotherhood and humanitarianism also demanded care for the body. She had always had a special interest in the East End, perhaps because she had been born "within the sound of Bow Bells." As it happened, another wealthy but anonymous Theosophist had given H.P.B. one thousand pounds early in 1890 to be expended as she thought best for the interests of the Society, but, if possible, especially to benefit women. Mrs. Besant speedily persuaded her to devote most of it to the establishment of the Home for Working Women and to put herself and Mrs. Cooper-Oakley in charge of the project.

Across from Bow Church they discovered a large, old-fashioned house that had recently been used by the celebrated "Dr." Thomas J. Barnardo. (Barnardo's Homes for Boys and Girls had attracted international attention to him as a philanthropist and social worker, though at first both his motives and his methods had been under question and investigation.) This Elizabethan red-brick building, once a country house, with spacious rooms, large window seats, enormous old fireplaces, and oak beams and staircases, was skilfully remodeled within a few weeks' time. All the work was done on socialistic principles and handed over directly to the men themselves. When it was thrown open in the middle of August, the *Star* found no dreary, whitewashed, forbidding-looking place, but rather a private home, with bright and prettily furnished rooms, the beds in the sleeping rooms even being separated from each other by gaily colored Japanese screens. The club also contained a library, a workroom, sitting rooms (which could be rented to trades-union committees), and a dining room. By an egregious slip, the *Star* first announced that Bryant and May had generously donated five hundred pounds for this last room—a figure which Mrs. Besant hastily and somewhat sarcastically corrected to fifty pounds, with a plea for more subscriptions from the public. The club could accommodate about a dozen roomers and take care of several score more for meals and meetings. By the end of December, Mrs. Besant was able to announce that the membership had reached over one hundred and fifty names and that Mrs. Kitty Lloyd, the matron (of course, a devoted Theosophist), had her hands full serving about the same number of meals every day. But though the project had an initial success, the T.S. was never able to open a parallel one in North London, as it hoped to do, in furtherance of Mrs. Besant's declared object of making brotherhood a reality rather than only a word. Every Monday evening found her at the clubrooms, signing contribution and membership cards, counseling the girls, carrying out her duties as secretary, and about midnight trudging bravely back alone over Primrose Hill to Avenue Road.[11]

At the August opening, attended by about fifty girls, Madame had recovered sufficiently from her chronic illness to be present with her whole staff. There were tea, cakes, and even some dancing and singing, climaxed by speeches from Mrs. Besant and Herbert Burrows. Madame merely beamed happily. An arresting postscript to *Lucifer*'s proud description of the affair ran as follows:

Since then a subscription to *Lucifer* for the Reading Room has been received; Digby Besant has subscribed to the *Daily Graphic* for six months; Annie Besant supplies *Punch and Judy*. . . . Books should be sent direct to the Club, addressed to the Librarian, Miss Besant.

In this casual way did the coeditor of *Lucifer* herald to her readers the return of her two children, who had been taken away by their father and the law eleven years before.[12]

To those who had been present at Mrs. Besant's Sunday evening lecture at the Hall of Science late in June or to those who had read the account of this meeting in the *Freethinker*, this announcement would not have been news. For at the close of her lecture, Annie—who must have been waiting all evening with a full heart for the opportunity to make a public statement—turned confidentially to her audience and, recalling the support which Freethinkers everywhere had given her a dozen years ago when proceedings had been started to take Mabel away from her, told her "friends" that she thought it would please them to hear "that her son, who was now of age, had returned to her of his own free will, and that her daughter, although not legally free until next August twelve months, was again with her." Mabel, in fact, had asked to be allowed to

[11] *Lucifer*, January, 1890, p. 436, March, 1890, p. 68, September, 1890, pp. 79–80; *National Reformer*, August 17, 1890; *Theosophist*, October, 1890, p. 61; *Star*, April 29–December 27, 1890, *passim*; *Autobiography*, p. 461; *The Annie Besant Centenary Book*, p. 218.

[12] For the following account of this story, see *Freethinker*, June 29, 1890; *Autobiography*, p. 225; W. T. Stead, "Annie Besant," *Review of Reviews*, October, 1891, p. 74; Arthur Digby Besant, *The Besant Pedigree*, pp. 140–41, 216–26, 264–65; *The Annie Besant Centenary Book*, pp. 217 ff.; *Star*, September 21, 1891. Also interviews in London with Digby Besant, August 12, 1954, and Esther Bright, September 9, 1954.

come to the meeting that evening, but her mother, desiring to avoid any unpleasant complications, had advised her not to do so. "My daughter," ended Mrs. Besant triumphantly, "notwithstanding her training and surroundings, and without a practical knowledge of Freethought, already expresses her detestation of the religion that separated her from her mother, marring the happiness of her childhood, and causing her mother such poignant sorrow."

Digby had long ago made up his mind that as soon as he came of age he would go to see his mother and judge matters for himself. This he had decided in spite of his grateful and affectionate loyalty to his Uncle Walter, who, simultaneously with his own highly successful literary career, had put his brother's son through Portsmouth school, had sent him for a few months to France to perfect his conversational French, and then, in lieu of a Cambridge education, had given him two years at University Hall, a hostel attached to the University College, London. There, by diligence and a good head, and with the encouragement of Professor Henry Morley, Digby had passed his B.A. at the age of twenty and was ready to start off on his career as an actuary. Even while he was laboring as a clerk in a life-insurance office, Walter had supplemented his meager pay with a continuing allowance.

Anticipating his coming of age, Digby wrote his father to inform him of his intention. Frank Besant replied in a long and angry eight-page letter, warning his son against the proposed step. Then, guessing his decision, he refused to have any further interchange with his son and returned all his personal belongings that were still at Sibsey. Looking back at these events afterward, it seemed almost inconceivable to Digby that "the Vicar" (as he always formally referred to his father) could have acted so drastically; but many years later a little of the sting was taken out of the situation when he learned that his father's conscience must have troubled him, since sometime before his death he called in a lawyer and made his banished son a coexecutor of his will.

In the meantime, Mabel, or "Mab," who had been visiting her mother surreptitiously ever since she became eighteen, as Digby told me, informed her father that she intended to follow the same course as her brother. The vicar sent her a similar reply and severed all relations with her, though she was just over nineteen and he could have held her. Nobody, it seems, could love poor, lonely, austere, self-righteous Frank Besant, who continued to live out his life seeking solace from his parish duties in his study of antiquities. Ironically enough, Digby proved to have a great deal of his father in him, attested by his great proficiency in mathematics and his later indulgence in antiquarianism and genealogy. Many years afterward, Mab, who was a frail but lighthearted girl in spite of her dour upbringing (too lighthearted sometimes to please her mother) and who liked to play jokes on people, went back to visit Sibsey without announcing her coming. Her father, who must have been quite nearsighted by this time, showed her all around the church and gardens without recognizing her, and she only divulged her identity when leaving. How the vicar reacted to the revelation, Esther Bright, who told me the story, did not know.

Annie Besant's influence, personality, and fame were so overwhelming that both children, after holding out for some time, became Theosophists too. Their love and this vindication transported their mother so that three years later she wrote in her *Autobiography:* ". . . both are treading in my steps as regards their views of the nature and destiny of man, and have joined in their bright youth the Theosophical Society." Both continued to work for it all their lives—Mabel with her heart, and Digby with his head. Mabel was to cause her mother some worry and grief as she grew older; Digby, however, was always the perfect son, who could write in his reminiscences of her in *The Annie Besant Centenary Book* in 1947 that his whole memory of her was summed up in the single word "Mother." In 1954, when he was in his middle eighties and a proud and contented grandfather, still alert and hale, he admitted to me that he still called himself a Theosophist, but that, though retired from business long before, he did not have time enough to practice his belief very seriously.

In this same year 1890, so full of promise for Annie Besant, her brother, Henry Trueman Wood, was knighted for his services as British commissioner for the Paris Exhibition of the previous year; three years later he was to perform similar services for the great Chicago World's Fair, in connection with which his sister was to make such an international impression. Of all the family, only the Rev. Frank Besant remained neglected and alone in his little country parish in the diocese of the Bishop of Lincoln, toward whom Annie Besant had continued to launch barbed little arrows in her various papers and magazines all through these years.

5

Exits and Entrances

The year 1890 had been vital for Annie Besant, but 1891 was to be still more critical. There were several incidental events in 1890 which presaged what was to come, as she divided herself between her civic and her psychic labors.

Her work on the School Board remained one of her pet causes; and when the Board was in session, her speeches and investigations blazed a broad trail through the papers, especially the *Star*. This journal, which had undergone an editorial convulsion when its owner finally realized where Massingham, Shaw, and the rest had been heading, continued to admire Mrs. Besant for her valiant crusading, but turned a little kinder toward Diggle and Diggleism. (The *Commonweal*, similarly, had been stolen from Morris by the Communist Anarchists on his staff; and Stead had started a highly successful magazine venture on a completely new principle, the *Review of Reviews*.) On the School Board the Besant bloc took some hope from the parson's announcement at the end of May that his friends had persuaded him to resign from the Board after his term had expired and to suspend his parochial appointment in order to run for Parliament.

The public were most grateful to Mrs. Besant for her exposure of various scandals in the award of contracts, especially in her specialty of printing, where sweating and child labor were still practiced. Her own involvement in building construction also led her to turn her attention to the employment of architects and the erection of school buildings. These and similar exposés led to her writing a much noticed article in *Time*. Her persistent agitation for free education at last resulted in a favorable vote in the Board, though of course the reform did not spring full grown into being. She also got some attention from her opposition to the teaching of the Bible in the schools, where she lost, and from her objection to employing young mothers as teachers. The Board felt better when she explained that she had no objection to older mothers functioning in this capacity. In preparing her cases in all these and similar matters, she was helped by an anonymous annual gift of £150; and she used the money and her own talents so well that, at the end of her first year, her constituents held a large meeting in her honor to express their gratitude and their hope that she would run again.

In one important matter—the boiling question of the eight-hour day— she found herself clashing once more with Charles Bradlaugh.[1] He had further alienated himself from labor and endeared himself to the Tories when, consonant with his individualistic philosophy, he had opposed in Parliament any attempt to legislate for the limitation of hours of work unless by mutual agreement between employer and employed. Mrs. Besant had disagreed strongly with him on this issue; and, dressed in a dark woolen dress, high to her throat, with long sleeves, and with her short, almost-white hair flying in the May breeze, she had joined a detachment of S.D.F. Sunday speakers in Hyde Park to advocate the reform. She continued to support the S.D.F. for some time after she left the Fabians. In fact, her extremism increased to the extent that she rejoined the group which had been speaking every year on the anniversary of the Paris Commune; and she spoke so forcefully in Hyde Park on Russian Nihilism and the terroristic government of the tsar that she earned the praise of Stepniak himself. (Mme. Novikoff, as the reputed agent of the tsar, was now in complete disfavor in advanced circles.)

The eight-hour-day controversy finally culminated in a second Bradlaugh-Hyndman debate, held in St. James's Hall in July. It attracted considerable attention, since Hyndman and the other leftists had been unremitting in their verbal persecution of Bradlaugh; but the latter's series of illnesses had deprived him of much of his old fire. Nevertheless, some papers like the *Star* thought he had the better of the argument, even though the sympathies of the audience were with Hyndman. In this audience were Cunninghame Graham, whose *Labour Elector* was on the verge of collapse, representing one extreme, and Colonel Howard Vincent, Tory M.P., representing the other; Herbert Burrows and John Robertson in velvet coats; and Hypatia Bradlaugh Bonner—but Mrs. Besant's name was not mentioned. Perhaps she thought it kinder to stay away.

Bradlaugh was becoming more and more puzzled over the way he was being treated. He complained that most of the English papers either neglected his speeches or misquoted him. But he felt he had never deviated from his original principles; and he fought on, even when he continued

[1] *National Reformer*, August 3, 1890; *Star*, July 24, 1890; *Freethinker*, August 3, 1890; *Justice*, May 24, August 2, 1890; *Commonweal*, August 2, 1890; *Theosophist* (Supplement), July, 1890, p. cxlix.

to lose on such policies as perpetual pensions. He redeemed his promise to bring up his bill for greater self-government in Indian communities and supported the delegation from the Indian Congress, consisting of Wedderburn, Hume, and S. N. Bannerjee, when it went around England to make the cause of the Congress known. *Justice* made fun of him because of his imputed ambition to become undersecretary of state for India. (There was a rumor that Annie Besant and Mme. Blavatsky also intended to go to India and Ceylon very soon.) He continued to lecture on Freethought whenever he could find the time, but his voice was weaker and he was always catching cold. He had to take holidays to go fishing to recuperate. In September he announced pridefully in the *Reformer* that in spite of the very rainy Scotch weather, he had caught 668 fish, weighing 503.5 pounds. At the end of November he came down with a cold and had to cancel a tour. He had just written an article on "Secular Funerals" and how to conduct them from a legal point of view.

Ireland was one of the problems with which Bradlaugh and Mrs. Besant had been concerned almost from their first meeting. It was astonishing that, considering her pride in her Irish blood and her fierce defense of the Irish cause, she failed to visit that unhappy country until she was forty-three years old. As a matter of fact, it was not until the second and Theosophical half of her life that she turned into the world traveler who left all her companions gasping. In October, 1890, at last came her opportunity to cross the Irish Sea. The Theosophists, the Socialists, and the Freethinkers all wanted her; her anomalous new fame, indeed, had made her more wanted than ever. So, early in the month, she descended on Dublin, accompanied by Herbert Burrows, who had spent half his vacation in London organizing the fur-pullers' strike and the other half in Suffolk addressing the silk-weavers and mat-makers.

It was a mixed lecture schedule that she had engaged for, aiming at appeal to all three audiences. The first evening was spent in a private *conversazione* with ninety members and guests of the Dublin Lodge of the T.S. The second night she lectured in the Antient Concert Rooms before an audience of several hundred on "Why I Became a Theosophist," her lecture which was in most demand everywhere. The discussion period afterward was enlivened by a gentleman from Kerry who wanted to ascertain whether, by the theory of reincarnation, "the spirit which animates a Moonlighter to-day might possibly fill the body of a policeman, who would put a bullet in him, forty years hence." To the delight of the audience, Mrs. Besant quickly put the facetious Kerryman in his place—though her retort is not recorded. To another inquisitive individual in a back seat, who wanted to know whether her feelings toward Christianity had changed since she had been a materialist, she replied that she did not now feel as bitterly against it as she had at the time when it robbed her of her child and broke up her whole life. Christ and Buddha, she said, taught the brotherhood of man. As a result of this meeting, wrote *Lucifer*, the average attendance at Lodge meetings immediately jumped from forty to sixty-five. Dublin had not responded in this way to Olcott's visit the year before.

The Theosophical papers said nothing about her lectures on secular subjects; the secular papers did not mention her work for Theosophy. *Justice* told how after she and Burrows had addressed the New Society of Female Factory Workers on the organization of labor, she had delivered a well-applauded talk on "The Class War" and had predicted optimistically that when the home-rule question was settled, there was every reason to hope that socialism in Ireland would advance with giant strides. It also quoted an Irish paper which predicted that, on first hearing, people would not like her, for she had a "strong masculine type of face" and dressed in plain gray Jaeger clothes (a type of woolen stockingette that Shaw was also experimenting with at the time). "But, by degrees, her intense earnestness and refined type of rhetoric compels your attention and admiration," and you forget the face and the clothes. "Disabuse your mind of your old prejudices against Mrs. Besant," it advised. "Personally she is one of the most womanly women of the nineteenth century." The *Commonweal*, in commenting on the same lecture, noted how one of its supporters had gone after it from the Anarchist point of view and thus was given an occasion for distributing several dozen *Commonweal* papers and leaflets. Even *Woman*—its prize contest and poll on "Who is the most eloquent, convincing, rational, and powerful speaker among women of today?" had been won by Mrs. Besant against two suffragist leaders, Mrs. Henry Fawcett and Lady Aberdeen—reported on the "Class War" lecture, though it found some of the speaker's theories on such subjects as landlordism and the use of safety lamps in mines "rather startling" and not always to be taken seriously.

From Dublin, Mrs. Besant traveled north to Belfast, where she gave three lectures in a single Sunday for the Ulster branch of the N.S.S. Since there was some difficulty in obtaining a hall, only five hundred—including some of the most important citizens of the city—could get in to attend "three of the largest meetings of a skeptical character ever to be held in northern Ireland." Fortunately, everyone behaved well, although the subjects were "Can Christ Atone for the Sins of Man?"; "Is the Bible Impregnable?"; and "Why We Preach Socialism." Only the *National Reformer* and the *Freethinker* reported these "skeptical" lectures. The *Theosophist*, however, commented that the Irish press, with one notable exception, gave very fair and impartial résumés of Mrs. Besant's talks there; and *Lucifer* listed, with excerpts, ten or a dozen papers in Ireland, England, and Scotland which had reported them.

In none of her lectures did she refer to the episode which had dealt the greatest blow that the cause of Irish freedom had suffered in two or three centuries. The scandal of the divorce suit filed by Captain William H. O'Shea against his wife Kitty, with the great Irish political leader Charles Parnell as corespondent, had been filling the newspapers of the world for months with palatable tidbits and angry moral and political tirades. Mrs. Besant, who discovered that she was a second cousin of Kitty O'Shea through their mutual relationship to the now dead Lord Hatherley, did not allow herself to be influenced by this kinship. After reading countless articles, editorials, and letters on the morality of the situation and on Parnell's political future following the granting of an unconditional divorce to O'Shea in November, she wrote her own long letter to the *Star* to the effect that "a man cannot be cut into two halves, one labelled *public* and the other *private.* . . . The man who deceives in private life will deceive in public, and he who betrays the trust of a friend will betray the trust of a nation." It was not so much the immorality of such a liaison which troubled her, in view of the present unsettled state of the marriage and divorce laws, as it was Parnell's continued pretended friendship with the husband while seducing the wife. Mrs. Besant would not condemn the tie between George Eliot and G. H. Lewes, for example (and perhaps she might have mentioned the similar one between Aveling and Eleanor Marx, except that she did not want to open old wounds), because it was acknowledged publicly and the marriage bond had been broken in all but the legal formula. She was confident, finally, that the movement for Irish freedom did not depend on any one man and that other leaders would come forward. This was one of many instances in which Annie Besant's predictions for the future took so much longer to be realized than she intended that they were not true predictions at all.

This letter set her off from many of her friends. Shaw was for Parnell, as at first was the *Star.* Mrs. Jacob Bright, who was on the verge of joining the T.S., was for Parnell and postponed her decision to join because of her friendly disagreement with Annie. In fact, she wrote a long letter to Annie herself and another to the *Star* on the subject. For the first time, the Bright family, like so many other English and Irish families, was divided within itself. Although Parnell himself had confided the whole truth to Jacob Bright, Bright stood by Gladstone and the Liberals. Mrs. Bright, womanlike, was more concerned with the man than with the party and regarded the "Grand Old Man" as a bit of a hypocrite, since she knew of a similar case within his own Cabinet at the time. Hardest of all for Annie to bear, however, was her discovery that even her darling "female Ulysses," H.P.B., was against her and regarded her attitude as "untheosophical." Analyzing herself, Mrs. Besant concluded that she was probably swayed too much by her "old feeling of the injustice of making the woman an outcast while society welcomes the man with open arms."

Shortly after Mrs. Besant's and Mrs. Bright's letters, which provoked many replies in the *Star*, Gladstone declared that either Parnell would resign or he would. The *Star* changed its stand, the Irish M.P.'s and the Liberals expelled their disgraced hero, he went back to Ireland to try to rebuild his support, and within a few months after marrying Kitty O'Shea he was dead.[2]

Before Parnell's death, however, there occurred a tragedy which struck much closer to home. The winter of 1890–91 was early and severe. Charles Bradlaugh, confident that he could still rely on his early strength, rushed about the country in the cold and fog lecturing whenever he could escape from his Parliamentary duties. On January 18 the *Reformer* carried a "Special Notice" signed by him: "A rather severe attack in the middle of Tuesday night, affecting heart and lungs, compels me with great regret to cancel my Tyneside lecture." The next week's bulletin, however, was signed by Hypatia. There had been two more heart attacks, and her father had been sleepless, with the exception of one short nap, for six days. Still, his patience and his fortitude were marvelous. Bradlaugh himself issued a short, incoherent postscript, admitting that one attack had almost finished his "chequered life." He was fighting hard, as always; and the next week's issue carried a series of bulletins by Hypatia, based on the reports of three physicians, headed by Dr. Ramskill, telling of relapses and recoveries and the bursting of a blood vessel in her father's head. Two things worried him: the wretched and confused state of his finances, and a motion he was supposed to make in the House on January 27. No one was supposed to be allowed to see him except his daughter, his doctors, and the nurses. Foote, as the *Freethinker* informed its readers, tried to make a duty call on his old leader and was very sad to be turned away. Even the " 'gentlemen' of the press" (or "vultures," as Hypatia preferred to call them) were denied admittance, despite their "delicately worded inquiries." Annie Besant was the only exception to the order. She was twice allowed to see the only man, except her husband, she ever admitted to her friends she would have married if the law had permitted. In her first "long chat . . . after the first terrible heart attack," she wrote in the *Weekly Dispatch*, he faced death simply and bravely, fearing it only because it would leave his work incomplete. At the second talk, a brief one, when his voice was "low and broken," he could still think only of the fact that there was no one who could quite do his work; and he gasped out, "No one understands how that market business affects the food supply of the poor. It is a dull-looking thing, and no one will take the trouble to work it out." He also muttered about the "inarticulate, misunderstood" millions of Hindustan.

The *Reformer*, with a black-bordered front page and a heavy line drawn through the name of Charles Bradlaugh as editor, brought out a

[2] *Star*, January 9, November 22–December 3, 1890, *passim*; November 12, 1891; Bright, *Memories*, pp. 22–23.

345

"Memorial Number" on February 8, carrying Hypatia's final bulletin: "On Friday, January 30, at half past six in the morning, my father died from Uremia, following on chronic Bright's Disease," which was the cause of the hypertrophy of his heart. Except for one professional nurse, she had been the only one at his side; during his last days he had been delirious and only partly conscious. He had died as he had lived, she declared, "a consistent and conscientious atheist." Nowhere in her many bulletins did Hypatia mention Mrs. Besant. She could never quite forgive her for the blows she had given her father in his last years.[3]

Annie, however, in her "In Memoriam," made her unchanging feelings toward Charles Bradlaugh quite clear. Through their unbroken friendship of sixteen and a half years, "as she knew and loved him," despite their differences of opinion, she had always admired him for his three main characteristics of strength, justice, and tenderness. No one, she knew, could replace him as leader, "one of those royal natures which leave the world poorer for their loss."

All over Great Britain, from Robertson in the *Reformer* to the editors of the Northampton *Mercury* and the London *Times,* from Foote and Hyndman to the churchmen, the papers burst forth with obituaries. Not all of them were kind, especially those from the clergy, though the Nonconformists usually found something to praise (some of the chapels in Northampton had even offered prayers for his recovery; but the *Baptist* wrote that he was buried "like a dog"); some, like *Justice,* which still pursued him to his grave as "our enemy," could not overlook his courage, loyalty, discipline, and devotion to the principles of free thought and pointed out that in a Radical or Liberal Cabinet he might well have become secretary of state for India; even the *Times,* while not forgiving him for his entire past—in an obituary it recalled that at one time, with Mrs. Besant, he had published an "obscene book," *The Fruits of Philosophy*— devoted a full-column editorial to deploring his loss to Parliament and the country and maintaining that, despite the obsoleteness of some of his ideas, by the end he "had ranged himself by conviction, at no small sacrifice of political influence and personal susceptibilities, on the right side." The *Pall Mall Gazette,* next to the *Star,* was probably the most unstinting of the large-circulation papers in its eulogies, into which it introduced some admiring references to "his faithful co-worker, Mrs. Besant."

[3] For the story of Bradlaugh's death, see Bonner, *Bradlaugh,* II, 108; *National Reformer,* January 18–March 1, 1891, *passim; Weekly Dispatch,* February 1, 1891; *Pall Mall Gazette,* January 30–April 27, 1891, *passim,* June 24, October 9, 1891; *Freethinker,* February 1–April 19, 1891; *Justice,* February 7–28, 1891; *Star,* January 20–February 19, 1891, *passim;* London *Times,* January 7–March 25, 1891, *passim;* John Morley, *The Life of William Ewart Gladstone* (London, 1903), III, 11–21; Bernard Shaw, *Quintessence of Ibsenism,* pp. 9–10, 185–87.

The acute Mr. Shaw had his own individual comment to make when he published his *Quintessence of Ibsenism* later in the same year:

Yet when the obituary notices appeared, with the usual string of qualities: eloquence, determination, integrity, strong commonsense, and so on, it would have been possible, by merely expunging all names and other external details from these notices, to leave the reader entirely unable to say whether the subject of them was Gladstone, Lord Morley, William Stead, or anyone else no more like Bradlaugh than Garibaldi or the later Cardinal Newman.

Yet the most conspicuous tribute of all came from Gladstone himself, as the result of the intended House resolution that was preying on Charles Bradlaugh's mind as he lay dying. For years, apparently, he had been brooding over the action taken in June, 1881, expelling him from the House; and he had discussed with his friends the possibility of having it expunged from the records, now that he was firmly established and in good standing. He had intended to make the motion himself; instead, his friend Dr. William A. Hunter, M.P. and editor of the *Weekly Dispatch*, had to make it for him. Bradlaugh at this time was unconscious and was fated never to know that, with Gladstone's support, it was passed without a dissenting vote and actually with cheers. A few days later, debating a bill to "discard a lingering case of civil disability attached to religious profession," Gladstone spoke solemnly of his dead colleague in these words:

A distinguished man, and an admirable member of this House, was laid yesterday in his mother-earth. He was the subject of a long controversy in this House. . . . We remember with what zeal it was prosecuted; we remember how summarily it was dropped; we remember also what reparation has been done within the last few days to the distinguished man who was the immediate object of that controversy. But does anybody who hears me [the "Grand Old Man" looked challengingly around the House] believe that that controversy, so prosecuted and so abandoned, was beneficial to the Christian religion?

The whole long and unsavory episode, as John Morley described it, made a landmark in Gladstone's own development of religious toleration, which he had not previously possessed.

The funeral was held on February 3 at the Woking Necropolis, in the country twenty-five miles outside London. There had been a preliminary memorial service at the Hall of Science, the scene of so many of Bradlaugh's triumphs. There, with Holyoake, Truelove, Forder, Standring, Moss, and many others of the Secularist old guard on the platform, speeches, resolutions, and condolences had been read, culminating in a long eulogium by Foote. Mrs. Besant perhaps knew he was to make it, since she did not come to the meeting.

The throng at Woking was unexpected and astonishing. No efforts at advertising had been made, and yet three special trains were jammed at

347

Waterloo Station with some two thousand passengers, and hundreds more came directly to the cemetery. Even Bradlaugh's most intimate circle would not have believed he had so many friends who would make such sacrifices to show their love and admiration. They came especially from London and Northampton, but they also came from all over England, Scotland, Wales, and even Ireland. There were Freethinkers; miners and other laborers; political leaders like John Morley of Newcastle, Dr. Hunter, Labouchère, and J. O'Conner; delegates from Bradlaugh's Parliamentary committees and from the Indian National Congress; ministers; suffragettes; Hindus; and even a few red-coated soldiers. Hypatia proudly listed over forty organizations that sent official representatives. Many ladies, disregarding the wishes of the family, wore mourning, but the men were more casual. Some of them rather shocked the *Pall Mall Gazette* reporter by smoking cigars and wearing rosettes of green, white, and mauve (the old Northampton fighting colors) on their coats or gaily colored ribbons around their hats.

The fact that there was no ceremony, not even a speech, impressed everyone but the carping Foote, who found the proceedings a "lost opportunity"—too cold and inhuman for his taste. Although her father had left no instructions in his will, Hypatia knew he wanted everything to be simple and inexpensive. The coffin was plain and covered only with a black cloth. Whereas it had been intended to cremate Alice Bradlaugh's body, next to which her father's was to be laid, at the time of her death the apparatus of the Necropolis had been out of order; and so Hypatia decided to use a simple "earth to earth" interment for her father as well. She chose as pallbearers four of his original Northampton supporters, a representative of the Indian Agency, and John M. Robertson. The family funeral party included herself and her husband, her father's two sisters (his Christian brother sent a card with a verse from Job on it), his late secretary, one of his doctors, several members of the N.S.S., and Annie Besant. After the wicker-encased coffin had been lowered into the unbricked grave, circled with wreathes, the mourners filed past, some casting in flowers as they went. Finally, the dead man's staunchest supporters took the spades from the hands of the gravediggers, and themselves, one by one, heaped the earth upon the coffin.

Mrs. Besant must have been conspicuous among the immediate mourners, though the *Star* did not mention her name, because she alone, neglecting Bradlaugh's dislike for crepe and all "badges of grief," came heavily veiled. In her own characteristic style she described her feelings at Woking: "As I walked at his daughter's side behind that simple and unadorned coffin, unadorned save for her last gift to him of pure white blooms and laurel-leaves, I felt the irony of human life as I had never felt it before." Recalling her own uncertainty during all his struggles that his day must sometime come, she placed herself among the many others who had "loved and honored him" and ended with the reflection that, after all his troubles, he had "carved his name deeply into the history of his times." Then, with a heavy heart, she resumed her daily life, resolved to do any service that still remained for her dead chief and colleague.

Several of the newspapermen at Bradlaugh's funeral had been impressed by a small knot of Indian students who had come to pay their last respects to their champion; but none of the reporters paid any particular attention to one tiny, frail figure that hid shyly among the crowd. He was an insignificant-looking, dark-skinned Indian, a twenty-one-year-old law student, who was almost ready to take his examinations. He had been a father at the age of eighteen, having been married at the age of fifteen to a thirteen-year-old wife; and he had come to London somewhat dubiously to learn something of Western culture and prepare himself for a career. His name was Mohandas K. Gandhi. Nobody had ever heard of him, but everybody had heard of Bradlaugh and Besant. Fifty or so years later, everybody had heard of him, and Bradlaugh and Besant were almost forgotten.[4]

When Gandhi, like every Indian residing in London, as he said, went to Bradlaugh's funeral, he had already met Mrs. Besant, but was sure she did not remember him. He had also met Mme. Blavatsky, but felt himself unworthy to touch either her garments or those of "her distinguished disciple." Toward the end of his second year in England, he had come across two unmarried brothers, both Theosophists; and through their influence and enthusiasm, he for the first time read the *Bhagavadgita* and Arnold's *Light of Asia*. The brothers soon took him to a meeting at the Blavatsky Lodge and introduced him to both Mme. Blavatsky and Mrs. Besant, whose recent conversion he had been following with great interest in the papers. This meeting he described as an ordeal—partly because of his sense of boyish inferiority, and partly because he was still having trouble understanding British English.

After the meeting his friends advised him to join the Society; but he politely declined, saying that with his meager knowledge of his own religion he did not feel ready to join any religious body. Nevertheless, at the brothers' instance, he read Mme. Blavatsky's *Key to Theosophy*, which stimulated in him the desire to know more of his native Hinduism and disabused him of the notion which the Christian missionaries had fostered that "Hinduism was rife with superstition." As a further result, he learned more about Christianity and the Bible, preferring the New Testament to the Old, and read Carlyle's *Heroes and Hero Worship*, especially the chapter on "The Hero as Prophet." In this way he came to

[4] M. K. Gandhi, *The Story of My Experiments with Truth* (Ahmedabad, India, 1927), pp. 164–70, 437; also Jinaradasa, in *The Annie Besant Centenary Book*, p. 94. Eleanor Morton (Mrs. Elizabeth Gertrude Stern) in *The Women in Gandhi's Life* (New York, 1953), pp. 37–39, etc., tries to tell something of the story of Gandhi and Annie Besant, but is wildly inaccurate in almost every particular.

realize that when he had finished with his examinations he should learn more about the world's principal religions. Because "Every Indian knew Bradlaugh's name and his so-called atheism," he also read something about it, but without effect, since he had already crossed that "Sahara." The fact that Mrs. Besant had turned to theism from atheism, as he somewhat inaccurately put it, and that he had read her "How I Became a Theosophist" also strengthened his aversion to atheism.

Thus, though Gandhi never accepted Theosophy, he always retained a respect for it as being "Hinduism at its best" and as preaching the brotherhood of man; Islam, to him, though preaching the same doctrine, was a brotherhood of fanatics. Many years later, when he emerged into Indian politics, he was impressed by the fact that in the beginning the top Congressmen were Theosophists. In 1891, however, he could never have guessed that one day he would be writing: "When Dr. Besant came to India and captivated the country, I came in close touch with her and, though we had political differences, my veneration for her did not suffer abasement."

6

Cremation at Woking

Bradlaugh's death left both his Secularist and his business affairs very much in confusion. Foote, it is true, bragged that in the past year more people had joined the N.S.S. than during any similar period in its history; but though he gave special lectures and wrote articles eulogizing the memory and career of his dead leader, he managed to intrench himself more securely in the process. The editing of the *National Reformer*, under the control of Hypatia, her father's only heir and executrix, was soon taken over entirely by Robertson, after he discovered that his rational Scots mind could not co-operate successfully with Mrs. Besant's new mystical one. But within three years the paper had lost so many subscribers and he had gained so many new interests that it was allowed to expire. Foote's *Freethinker*, on the other hand, became the chief voice of atheistic thought in England and remains so to this day, bearing the proud caption, "Founded 1881 by G. W. Foote."

There were many plans to honor and preserve Bradlaugh's memory, none of which worked out very successfully. At first it was proposed to build a new Secular Hall in his name, since the Hall of Science had never belonged to the N.S.S. and was rented out to all sorts of organizations for lectures and meetings. Two or three times in previous years attempts had been made to get an independent building, but they had all failed. Nor was this one fated to do better. A Bradlaugh Memorial Committee, with Foote as chairman, was quickly formed and drew up its prospectus to raise the necessary funds, but Bradlaugh's followers were much less eager to contribute money than when he had been alive. Some Indian Freethinkers and Nationalists suggested that Indian marble be used, but could produce no means of paying for it. Foote also made the mistake of ruling Annie Besant off the organizing committee, on the ground that she was no longer a member of the N.S.S. and this was an exclusively N.S.S. project. Since he had already announced that any Freethinker who had the money to buy a share could join the group, a hot little controversy raged for a time in the pages of their respective magazines and even burned up two or three hours at the annual convention, till Foote confessed that he simply refused to work in any group containing Mrs. Besant, because of her public attacks on him. Hypatia Bradlaugh Bonner and her husband also withdrew their names from the central committee, which dragged along for some months and finally used the funds it had collected to take over the Hall of Science itself.

At one time it was proposed to place a stone bust of Bradlaugh in the new hall, but nothing came of this idea either. However, Hypatia, with the help of some of Mrs. Besant's lectures, raised her own fund of £125 for a tombstone for her father, which carried a one-word legend, his favorite motto, "Thorough." As narrated by the London *Times*, members of the National Liberal Club like Earl Russell, Canon Wilberforce, and the Rev. H. C. Shuttleworth also subscribed to a fund to purchase Bradlaugh's portrait for the clubrooms. Another portrait by the well-known portrait painter Walter Sickert was hung in the rooms of the Manchester branch of the N.S.S. in October; Mrs. Besant apologized for not being able to be present.

She had more than sufficient to do without attending such nostalgic affairs. The financial situation alone was involved enough to take up many weary hours. As Robertson pointed out in a special appeal to Freethinkers in the February 22 *Reformer*, which was reprinted in some other papers like the *Pall Mall Gazette*, when Bradlaugh died the liabilities which he had assumed on the dissolution of the partnership reverted to Mrs. Besant. Though the company had paid 5 per cent regularly on its debentures, some £5,600 still remained due. Though Robertson believed that probably Bradlaugh's whole estate, including his library, his Indian gifts, the printing plant, the stock of books and pamphlets, and his and Mrs. Besant's copyrights, might be worth that much, he was sure that at a forced sale they would bring considerably less. Moreover, such a liquidation would not only deprive Mrs. Besant of some of her best copyrights, such as that of *The Law of Population*, but it would leave Hypatia practically destitute, since her husband's income depended on the printing plant. Besides, Robertson added, Mrs. Besant now had a child of her own dependent on her, for Mabel was living at Avenue Road.

A month later, after the estate had been probated for a gross value of a little over £4,500 and a "nominal" net value, Robertson and Foote temporarily ignored their differences and made a joint appeal, since the fund was not swelling rapidly enough. At first, Robertson had suggested buying Bradlaugh's library and keeping it intact as a suitable memorial, but this idea had not then seemed grandiose enough to the committee. Now it was decided to sell the library, still intact, for £1,000, but there were no takers. Hypatia then sadly agreed to let it go piecemeal, and the sale began with an auction at the Hall of Science. Mrs. Besant also decided to part with most of her old library, including particularly her volumes in science, theology, history, and many marked volumes from the Knowlton trial, and listed them for sale. These drastic methods finally produced results, especially when the holders of the debentures agreed to settle for ten shillings on the pound. By October, Hypatia was able to announce wearily that with the receipts from all sources she could now settle with all her father's creditors on this reduced basis.

In the meantime, Edward Aveling had been trying to capitalize in his own peculiar way on Bradlaugh's death. Within less than a week he declared to the press that he had been asked by the Northampton branch of the Social Democratic Federation to stand as a labor candidate from that constituency in Bradlaugh's place. *Justice* was left sputtering, but not speechless. It had already been pursuing Aveling, now a leading member of the small extremist Bloomsbury Socialist Society—which included his wife, Engels, Mann, Burns, Hardie, Champion, Liebknecht, Bebel, and at times Graham—for writing for the *Chronicle*, *Time*, and other capitalist papers. Now it was not content till it had exposed Aveling's invitation as having come from an unauthorized, dissident group in the branch who admired him for having become a member of the Gas Workers' and General Labourers' Union, even though he had never done any gas-working or general laboring. Therefore, in order to black-list him forever among labor groups, *Justice* cited the following charges, in the form of questions, against its onetime favorite:

1. Why was he forced to leave the National Secular Society? 2. What were the proceedings in regard to his classes in Newman Street, Oxford Street, which occasioned so much talk? 3. What sort of bills did he run up for Mrs. Eleanor Marx Aveling and himself when the Socialist workers of the United States (all poor men) paid the expenses of his tour? What was the effect of his conduct on the movement in America? 4. What did he do in relation to the money collected to send a cable despatch, with signatures of well-known Englishmen, to the Governor of Illinois, when the fate of Chicago Anarchists was trembling in the balance? 5. What was his action in regard to a certain family whose children he undertook to educate?

As it happened, *Justice* did not need to worry about Aveling's candidacy, since he was unable to raise even the necessary deposit money. The *Star* now chimed in with a story of how he had been seen standing outside the town clerk's office in Northampton with a volume of Ibsen under his arm, waiting for the delivery of the security money of one hundred pounds, which the Tories were rumored to have offered him if he would run against their candidate, thus creating a reverse support for themselves. At any rate, he returned from Northampton empty-handed except for the book on his wife's favorite Ibsen. As a consequence of this fiasco and *Justice's* questions, the German Communist Club in London withdrew its invitation for him to address them, and the official who had invited him resigned. Nevertheless, perhaps because of the claim of the Bloomsbury Socialist Society that it was responsible for originating and maintaining the eight-hour-day issue, "Brother" and "Sister" Aveling were chosen officials of the Gas Workers' Union in Dublin soon afterward. Two months later the hot-headed doctor was arrested for assaulting the man who had denounced him at the Communist Club, after warning him in Liebknecht's *Vorwärts* that he was going to do so. He was fined two pounds and costs and told *Vorwärts* it was worth it. Two months after that, to show its balanced judgment, *Justice* praised him for the completion of his *Student's Marx.*

In the meantime, Mme. Blavatsky had been growing more feeble and more remote from the world around her. She therefore intrusted more and more of her mundane affairs to her new adjutant, Mrs. Besant. In the City, Annie buzzed from Steinway Hall, where she rebuked the skepticism of her old teacher, Professor Huxley, to the newly organized Christo-Theosophical Society, to the Bedford Park Club, to the Socratic Society of the Free Christian Church at Croydon, and to the South Place Institute; in the country she flitted from Leicester to Manchester. She put "poor young Mr. Hodgson" in his place by contributing a long exposé of "The Great Mare's Nest of the Psychical Research Society" to *Time.* She announced that, because the facilities of Blavatsky Lodge were already growing too cramped for the expanding membership, the T.S. had purchased the adjoining property at 17 Avenue Road, to which the British Section was transferred. Not long afterward she was able to add that, through the generosity of an anonymous Swiss donor, the mortgage on the lease of the main property had been paid off, so that the Society could enjoy its quarters, valued and taxed on the rate books at two hundred pounds per annum, for a mere fifty pounds' annual rental till 1905.[1]

Then, on April 1, 1891, Mrs. Besant set sail from Liverpool on the "S.S. City of New York" for her first ocean trip and a new responsibility. She was to attend the annual convention of the American Section at Boston as the personal representative of H.P.B., as well as the delegate from the British Section. Dr. Archibald Keightley was to represent the European Section. Both were from the Inner Group of the Esoteric Section. Madame, too infirm to go herself, was secretly dubious about Mrs. Besant's ability to carry it off, for she wrote to Mrs. Bright, who was now a full-fledged member:

[1] *Lucifer,* January, February, August, 1891; *Path,* March, April, 1891; *Theosophist,* January, April, 1891.

I share your anxiety for Annie and feel quite nervous about it; but what can we do? She has to be at the Annual American Convention of the T.S., her failing to be there being likely to produce a regular disaster. Moreover, we Theosophists—I mean the really devoted ones—have no right to make public good subservient to our personal comfort or discomfort. . . . Thus we have to "risk the thing," as the Americans say. Yet I have a strong hope that our friend will return unscathed from the ordeal, her eloquent and devoted head crowned with fresh and well-earned laurels.[2]

H.P.B. and Ursula Bright had no cause to worry, although Annie was stepping into a lion's cage. Professor Elliot Coues, a well-known naturalist and a recently lapsed member of the T.S. in Washington, had recently been publishing a series of sensational exposés of the T.S. and attacks on the leading Theosophists, including H.P.B. and A.B., for which Mme. Blavatsky and William Q. Judge had instituted a libel suit against the New York *Sun*, the publisher. Annie also had the American reporters, a sharp and rather rowdy lot, to face. The *Sun*, after prolonged hearings, eventually retracted, but the reporters never withdrew. Moreover, besides the address she was to give at the convention, she was scheduled for ten lectures on religious, social, and political subjects all along the American northeastern seaboard. Remembering that she was still officially a Freethinker, she issued a statement just before she left that she would be back with her friends at the Hall of Science on May 24.[3]

As she stepped off the boat in New York on April 3, she was almost knocked down by the swarm of reporters and photographers awaiting her. Judge, who had planned the whole trip and whom she was now meeting for the first time, was in the front rank. The results, in the *Evening Sun*, the *Recorder*, the *Daily Tribune*, the *World*, etc., were all carefully but ironically described in the *Path* and *Lucifer*, which commented:

> The newspaper man evidently imagines he can give a better account of Annie Besant than she can of herself, but we have no doubt that she will speedily undeceive the Press of the East Coast. The descriptions of life at Headquarters as filtered through the irresponsible brains of the New York reporters have aroused the Homeric laughter of our breakfast-table, but as it is all apparently intended in good part we suppose that the utter absence of truth in all the accounts is a matter of minor importance.

One can scarcely blame the dazed reporters for being bewildered by the visitor's versatility and exuberance, for she hopped from New York to

---

[2] *Lucifer*, April, May, 1891; *Path*, May, June, 1891; *Pall Mall Gazette*, March 18, 1891; *Theosophy in Australia*, May, 1924; *Theosophist*, August, 1931.

[3] *Freethinker*, September 21, 1890; *Star*, August 26, 1890, June 1, 1891; *Lucifer*, August, 1890; *National Reformer*, March 22, 1891; Bechhofer-Roberts, *The Mysterious Madame*, p. 283. Dr. G. Encausse at the same time was attacking H.P.B. and A.B. in his French Theosophical magazine; cf. Olcott, *Old Diary Leaves*, IV, 245.

Washington to Brooklyn, satisfying the thirst of Theosophical groups at the Aryan and Blavatsky Lodges with inspirational talks on "Why I Became a Theosophist" and allied subjects and gorging the curiosity of non-Theosophical groups on "Dangers Menacing Society," "London, Its Wealth and Its Poverty," and "Labour Movements in the Old World." She met publishers and Theosophical leaders and spoke at the funeral of one of the latter, leaving not a dry eye in the room. Dr. Keightley, who had gone on to the West Coast, had nothing like her reception there.

Then, accompanied by Judge and other New Yorkers, she repeated her triumph at Boston, where, in addition to making some remarks of her own at the convention, she read the message intrusted to her by Madame Blavatsky. In this message Madame praised the contributions of both Mrs. Besant and Judge; the convention then took a vote of thanks to H.P.B. for sending Annie and also passed a vote of confidence in Judge. Annie's coming had been heralded for weeks in advance by the Boston papers, and she was given a party there by the powerful New England Woman's Press Association, whom she regaled with a talk on "Women and Journalism, from a Theosophical Standpoint." At the conclusion of the two-day convention, she lectured thrice in Tremont Temple to overflow audiences, took a side trip to Springfield, and returned to New York, whose appetite had been whetted for more talks, after one of which a Women's Working Club presented an address to her. Early in May she sailed for Queenstown on the "City of Chicago," accompanied by Dr. and Mrs. J. D. Buck of Cincinnati, who were to play an important role in her coming drama. Dr. Buck, a tall, curly-bearded gentleman with light hair and complexion, was dean of the small Pulte Medical College.[4]

A few of what the *Freethinker* liked to call "Acid Drops" remained behind her. The Boston *Liberty* had described her "Message of Theosophy to the Western World" as "pitiable lunacy from beginning to end," and the Freethought *Investigator*, commenting sourly on her announcement that her next subject at the Hall of Science would be "Freethought in America," remarked that the only attention she had paid to Freethought while there was her short visit to the Tom Paine Memorial in company with another Theosophist. But even the *Investigator* was charmed with her oratorical powers.

All the way across the Atlantic, Annie quietly reveled in her conquest of the American Section. Buck wrote a long letter back to the *Path* describing the voyage. When a clergyman on board volunteered to hold a Sunday service and preach a sermon, the captain said he might if the passengers invited him. No service was held. But the same passengers requested Mrs. Besant to give them a talk on Theosophy, which she did, to their mutual pleasure. In her own long report on her trip to the *Star* in June, she told how "the editor of one of the most widely circulated

4 *Path,* January, 1893.

New York dailies," after hearing her, said that he was going to write a book about Theosophy. Whoever he was, he never did.

When the ship docked at Queenstown, Herbert Burrows was there waiting for them. He had bad news. Mme. Blavatsky had died on May 8. Neither clairvoyance nor the Masters had warned Annie of the disaster. Olcott, who was far away in Australia in search of his health, had more time to think it over and finally declared that he had had a message. He said he scented trouble, and, after receiving confirmation by telegram, he immediately started back to England. Judge took the next boat from America, cabling ahead, "Do nothing till I come."[5]

At the time Annie left her, Madame had actually been gravely ill from a combination of acute rheumatism and Bright's Disease (which by an ironical coincidence had also removed Bradlaugh from this world—forever, he was sure; only until her next incarnation, Madame was equally sure). She had recovered long enough to write an article, "My Books," for *Lucifer*, in which she assured Mrs. Besant and the other eleven leading Theosophists who had signed a statement of complete faith in her and all her works that, with the aid of the Masters, she had truly written them all without any plagiarism. On April 25 she had also attended a meeting of her chelas, many of whom had been absent because of an epidemic of influenza. Three days later she fell ill of it herself. Refusing, as usual, to give up, she sat at night propped up in an armchair so that she could breathe, with a nurse in the room and the faithful Laura Cooper within call. On the night of May 8 the nurse called Miss Cooper to warn her that the end was near. Isabel Cooper-Oakley was in the house but not in the room; while H.P.B. was still conscious, she had given Mrs. Cooper-Oakley her last message. Two male members of the headquarters staff, one of whom was Walter R. Old, hurried in, and all four tried to ease her agony till a doctor could be summoned. But she died in their arms.[6]

Like Bradlaugh's, her funeral was at Woking, but the circumstances were otherwise different. After three days her body was put into a hearse and driven to Waterloo Station. At Woking it was cremated, in the presence of about a hundred persons, some of them Indians. There was a simple ceremony, capped by an address by her secretary, Mead. (He later was to marry Laura Cooper.) Madame's ashes were placed in an urn, which was brought back to her room, but which later had other travels.

There were many obituaries, most of them—except those in the Theosophical magazines, which of course reeked with adulation—satirical.

[5] *Theosophist*, July, 1891; Bright, pp. 20–21; Williams, *The Passionate Pilgrim*, p. 204.

[6] *Lucifer*, May, June, 1891, November, 1894; *Theosophist*, June, September, 1891; Bechhofer-Roberts, *The Mysterious Madame*, pp. 285–86.

The leading editorial on page one of the *Pall Mall Gazette*, for instance, was headed "The Prophetess of the Buried Tea-Cup," referring to one of her Indian exploits; but it nevertheless admitted that she was "one of the most remarkable women of our generation" and that she herself was sincerely "possessed by the ideas with which she succeeded in possessing others." Theosophy, it pondered wonderingly, had "won the embraces of several not unintelligent men among us, and at least one remarkable woman, Mrs. ANNIE BESANT. . . ." The *Star*, also referring to Mrs. Besant as H.P.B.'s "greatest convert," predicted that her successor in the T.S. leadership must be either Mrs. Besant or Colonel Olcott. Mabel Collins-Cook, in the *Sunday World*, revenged herself on Madame with half-praise and predicted that strange revelations were to come now that she was dead. "Acid Drops," assuming that the very "able" Mrs. Besant would now take the lead in the T.S., remarked that unless she could "make people believe that she possesses miraculous, or as the Theosophists call it, abnormal powers," she and Theosophy would fail.

That was the great question: who would take Madame Blavatsky's place? Nominally, as everyone knew, Olcott was president-founder for life, but his resignation was pending—although he was beginning to hedge. Three years later, while the squabble over the succession was still going on, Mrs. Cooper-Oakley wrote a letter to a friend in which she asserted that H.P.B. had always told the inner circle to "look to Annie Besant, and that she would be in direct communication with Master. . . . She has told me often that Annie was her successor, and that Annie had been 'watched' by Master for years." To make the situation still more emphatic, Mrs. Cooper-Oakley then went on to quote Mme. Blavatsky's written order verbatim: "I hereby appoint in the name of the Master, Annie Besant, Chief Secretary of the Inner Group of the Esoteric Section and Recorder of the Teachings." To H.P.B. this was the highest position she could name. Orally, she also made her the Outer Head of the E.S., the Masters being Inner Heads. But other people had other ideas about the succession, though Annie soon appeared wearing H.P.B.'s great cameo seal ring; and Olcott himself, in his presidential address later in the same year, stated of the Blavatsky papers, whose location had aroused some rather angry speculation: ". . . she has left a large body of them, and in the custody of her chosen depositary, Mrs. Besant, who in the proper way and at the proper time, will give them out to the world." Mrs. Besant also immediately assumed the single editorship of *Lucifer*, which, to Mead's great pleasure, she had been running with much greater efficiency than Madame ever since her accession.[7]

On the very night of Judge's arrival, Mrs. Besant scheduled the first public meeting at Blavatsky Lodge since Madame's death. To this came a

[7] *Theosophist,* June, 1922, p. 318, September, 1891, p. 705; *Autobiography,* pp. 465, 472a, 474a; *Lucifer,* June, 1891, p. 297; *Golden Book,* pp. 22–23.

curious reporter from the *Pall Mall Gazette*, together with many other representatives of the London papers. The *Gazette* man had a card of admission from Burrows, whom he had met on the train coming back from Woking, where Burrows had tried in vain to explain Theosophy to him. Consequently, he had come to this meeting to learn all he could. The result he described as "The Theosophist at Home. By an Enthusiastic Outsider."

Surprised to find Blavatsky Lodge not a "musty, dusty" place but one of the prettiest, trimmest, and most substantial houses on Avenue Road, he discovered the lecture hall, with its symbolical decorations, to be even more delightful. Machel had continued to disport himself with triangles, snakes, flamingos, ibises, swans (one black), lotuses, reeds, and a frog. The large pier glass behind the platform, about which a reporter in the *St. Stephen's Review* complained because it reflected the light into his eyes, the *Gazette* reporter enjoyed because in it he could see the effect of the speakers on the rest of the audience. And before it, almost life-size, was the famous portrait of Madame, painted by H. S. Schmiechen in 1883, together with his portraits of Masters K.H. and M.[8] The face of Madame gazed so hypnotically that one almost expected the firm mouth to open and say, "Have a cigarette!" But that could not be, because on the platform also stood a little grayish urn, and all who had been at Woking knew what that meant.

The program was likewise a revelation. The just-returned Annie Besant began it by introducing the "picturesque, grave, fluent, and scientific" Herbert Burrows, who spoke on "Theosophical Ethics." The group of reporters who gathered afterward at the Underground Station agreed generally that even though most of his ideas had been lost on them, their curiosity had been aroused and they—even the one whose editor had instructed him "to be funny"—had been involuntarily attracted. The special features of the evening, however, were speeches by the eminent American visitors, Judge and Buck. Judge was something of a puzzle because he took such a "light, jesting approach" before he turned serious. When he told how an able editor collared him on the boat, informed him that he and his son were going to become Theosophists, and explained how Theosophy could really be made to "go" by "selling" it properly to the public, he had his audience in convulsions of laughter—even a Russian in sky-blue trousers and a purple belt, who did not know a word of English. Thus the audience was softened up for the serious words of Judge and Buck which followed. But though each of the speakers, in his own way, had interested and excited the audience, it was Mrs. Besant, in the black dress which she was now affecting everywhere, with a curious silver clasp at her waist, and "a tiny glistening cross at her throat," with her "fine dark eyes and gray hair," and her face so deep-lined and yet so

[8] *Golden Book,* pp. 81–82.

childlike, who dominated the evening. She dismissed the audience with a ringing plea to make the universe "a fit temple for the dwelling of man."

A few days after this public meeting, a Consultative Emergency Council meeting was called, consisting of the European Advisory Council and the British Section Council. Judge, the vice-president of the T.S. as well as the American secretary, was in the chair. Mrs. Besant made a statement on the affairs of Mme. Blavatsky; various resolutions were passed and tributes approved; and, in preparation for the coming convention, she, Judge, and Kingsland were appointed as a committee for drafting a new constitution for the proposed amalgamation of the European and the British Sections.

Since Olcott could not be expected back from Australia till early in July, Mrs. Besant and William Judge, who had made a very pleasant impression on her, went out barnstorming together, talking on Theosophical themes, particularly reincarnation, at well-known places like Bradford, Manchester, Liverpool, Sheffield, and Birmingham, with an average attendance of between eight and fifteen hundred persons. Judge's companionable, humorous, casual American ways made friends everywhere, and Mrs. Besant gained more and more respect for him.

When Olcott arrived in London on the evening of July 4, he was met at the train by Judge and taken immediately to headquarters, where he was given an affectionate greeting by the residents, especially by Mrs. Besant, "so sweet, so characteristic of her own loving temperament." He and Annie then proceeded to H.P.B.'s bedroom, where, after they had sat for a time in solemn meditation, they pledged themselves "to be true to the cause and to each other." Olcott was growing more and more conscious that the death of his "co-founder" had left him "as the recognized sole center of the movement." He was not so sure about resigning.[9]

The first annual convention of the Theosophical Society in Europe was held on July 9 and 10 and was duly described by all the Theosophical and many of the London papers, including even the august *Times.* At the first meeting, held at Blavatsky Lodge, Olcott presided and, as the *Gazette* admitted, made "a most venerable chairman." The meeting was dedicated mostly to Mme. Blavatsky; and, after various resolutions and plans had been approved, Olcott read a short paper proposing that her ashes be divided among Adyar, London, and New York. Mrs. Besant made the motion, Judge seconded it, and it was passed by acclamation. The incident was fraught with omen; it was like dividing the robe of the Saviour. The remainder of the two sessions, the second being open to the public in the Portman Rooms, was completed in loving harmony—Mrs. Besant, "who looked pale and tired," closing with her usual eulogy of Theosophy.

[9] Olcott, *Old Diary Leaves,* IV, 290, 303; "Biographical Notes" in *Autobiography,* pp. 306–8.

Annie had good reason to look pale and tired. A few days before the convention opened, she had notified the newspapers that she would not present herself for re-election to the School Board. The death of her "honoured friend and chief, Madame Blavatsky," she wrote, threw so many new duties on her that, believing that in Theosophy lay the main hope of a better religious, moral, and social order, she had resolved to leave "the more popular work in other hands." In April she also announced her withdrawal from the Malthusian League and her abandonment of its principles. Mme. Blavatsky had shown her that "however justifiable Neo-Malthusianism might be while man was regarded only as the most perfect outcome of physical evolution, it was wholly incompatible with the view of man as a spiritual being, whose material form and environment were the results of his own mental activity." In less abstract terms, "Theosophists should sound the note of self-restraint within marriage, and the gradual—for with the mass it cannot be sudden—restriction of the sexual relation to the perpetuation of the race." Obviously, the problem of providing enough bodies for the reincarnated souls was partly responsible for this qualified permission. To be consistent with her present position—if she had reached it ten years earlier, she would not have temporarily lost her daughter and been dragged through the muck of the courts—Mrs. Besant withdrew the remaining copies of her best-selling *Law of Population* from sale, refused two offers to buy the copyright, and destroyed the plates. But in spite of her articles, such as "Theosophy and the Law of Population," attacking her own former position, and the fact that she had ceased attending its meetings soon after she came under H.P.B.'s influence, the Malthusian League continued to thrive. Many years later she was to change her mind once more and return to it.[10]

To make the list complete, *Justice* informed its readers shortly after the convention: "We regret to report that the retirement of Annie Besant from active work in the Socialist movement has led to her resigning the treasurership of the Central Election Fund." The *Commonweal* had peevishly commented on former "Comrade" Besant's evident reaction against all three Socialist groups as early as February. Indeed, *Justice* wrote in November, the entire new trades-union movement which she and Burrows had helped to foster in 1889 now seemed on its way out because of a new business cycle.

This whole change in Annie Besant's orientation had been occasioned by H.P.B.'s removal from the scene. In January she had written a front-page article for the *Star*, defending herself from the charge that in becoming a Theosophist she had ceased to be an active humanitarian and maintaining that Theosophy as taught by Mme. Blavatsky "imposes on

[10] *Autobiography*, pp. 318, 335–42; *Lucifer*, July, 1891, pp. 395–99; Bonner, *Bradlaugh*, II, 19; *Freethinker*, May 19, 1889; *National Reformer*, August 2, 1891; *Pall Mall Gazette*, August 31, 1891.

its disciples a life of the extremest altruism." She had then begun a long series on "Women Workers in London," dealing with the matchmakers, the matchbox-makers, the fur-pullers, the washerwomen, and the India-rubber-girls. But soon after Madame's death she perceived she had a higher mission. When the bewildered editor of the *Gazette* sent another reporter to interview her in July to get her reasons for leaving the public work she had adorned for so long and to quiz her about H.P.B., she met each of his sharp questions with an equally sharp but polite answer, and he went off to end his article: "We talk of Mme. Blavatsky's 'miracles'— surely the 'miracle of miracles' is here."

Disappointed as were all her colleagues in social work from Stead to Headlam and Lansbury, her constituents in the Tower Hamlets accepted her decision without reproach. Instead, they organized a great mass meeting in Poplar Town Hall to which thousands came—"all that was most active and earnest in the public life of East London," as the devoted George Lansbury recollected it—"to thank her for her splendid work." There were many speeches from the civic leaders of East London, to which Mrs. Besant responded with a new "clarion call to service" by those whom she was forced to leave behind. When Lansbury joined the Bow and Bromley branch of the Social Democratic Federation in 1892, it held its meetings for a time in the Working Women's Club, where they often met Mrs. Besant, who had not yet, at least, abandoned it to its fate.[11]

[11] Lansbury, *My Life,* pp. 73, 77–78; *Centenary Book,* p. 29.

7

Farewell and Hail

Although Foote had succeeded in forcing Mrs. Besant out of the National Secular Society, he had not yet succeeded in forcing her out of Secularism and off its lecture platforms, especially the one in the Hall of Science. In his paper he reported how all the church sects were still hoping to get her and how the *Church Times* had somewhat inaccurately remarked: "Mrs. Besant began as a Catholic, and, if she retains her reason, will no doubt end as one." The *Medium and Daybreak* announced that Bradlaugh's ghost had appeared to a Birmingham Spiritualist and told of his finding a God and a life beyond the grave, little as he wished to admit it. Foote himself rashly predicted that now that Mme. Blavatsky was dead the world was likely to hear no more of Koot Hoomi. But he complained in August, 1891, that Mrs. Besant had again used the Newcastle branch of the N.S.S. as a platform for dealing out her "moonshiny" doses of Theosophy. He recollected that in June he had asked editorially: "Would it not be braver and better (and we say it without any trace of bitterness) for Mrs. Besant to set up her own Theosophical platform and advocate Theosophy there?" He announced that he would again lecture on "The Follies of Theosophy" and its "most distinguished follower."

In July the N.S.S. completed arrangements for renting the Hall of Science for a year for its popular Sunday-evening lectures and a few others. It asked Mrs. Besant, a valuable drawing card, to participate by giving some lectures, strictly on Freethought subjects, as she was still frequently doing in the branches. Irritated by Foote's persistent proddings, she declared that he was trying to throttle her freedom of expression and that she would not serve under his dictation. She even cried that she was being excluded from the Hall. Foote retorted that he and his committee thought it only fair to restrict lectures under Freethought auspices to

Freethought themes and pointed out that there was no restriction of subject for the Sunday-morning lectures. This rather reasonable explanation did not satisfy Mrs. Besant, who apparently felt that her long identification with the N.S.S. and the Hall should give her a privileged position. Seizing the opportunity offered, she therefore made a dramatic announcement: on the night of August 30 in the Hall of Science she would deliver her farewell to the Secularists and the Hall. It was an electrifying statement and virtually every London paper sent a reporter to cover the event. The public fought to get tickets. Her formal title would be: "1875 to 1891: A Fragment of Autobiography."

On the historic night, Colonel Olcott, just returned to London from a trip to France to take a look at the new schools of hypnotism at Nancy and Salpêtrière, called for Annie at her home and escorted her to the Hall. He later wrote in his autobiography that he sat with her on the platform, but the *Star* reporter, on the spot, wrote that Olcott, sitting at the foot of the stairs, "rose and bowed with patriarchal grace" as she swept by with her party. First in this party was Mrs. Thornton Smith, a "slim, girlish figure, whose close-cropped hair surmounted the handsome, intellectual face of the vice-president of the Society." Mrs. Smith, who was to preside at the meeting and who had often acted as a sort of understudy to Mrs. Besant on Secularist platforms, was almost the only important Secularist who had not broken with her since her conversion. Then came Mrs. Besant, "dressed in black, as her custom now is." Following her walked Mabel Besant, whom this time her mother was glad to have with her in the Hall, and last of all Herbert Burrows. Touzeau Parris, her old battle comrade, also came onto the platform. Foote and John Robertson, both of whom had written furiously against her for the way in which they asserted she had distorted the actions of the Executive Committee in enforcing its rules, looked up at her from the audience. Olcott, wherever he sat, could not help reflecting that a few years ago she herself had taken a similarly antagonistic attitude when some Freethinkers from Madras had written to ask whether they might simultaneously be members of the Theosophical Society. In the audience also was young Esther Bright, whose father's objections to Theosophy had so far kept her from joining the Society in spite of her increasing worship of Mrs. Besant; not long after the meeting, though still with some reservations about Theosophical doctrine, Esther joined her mother in the T.S.

Mrs. Besant looked down into the rows of faces—some hostile, some sympathetic, but all tense and curious—and began. Someone, Esther Bright remembered, shouted, "Shame!" Others cried, "No, no!" Then the audience cheered wildly for several minutes. There were also audible hisses. Finally she was allowed to go on. She spoke of Bradlaugh and reviewed her years of association with him, indicating that he would never have treated her thus. She stated, to the accompaniment of cheers and hisses, according to the report in the *Daily Chronicle,* that she was speaking from this platform for the last time—because "your Society sends me off it." When the Hall passed into the hands of the N.S.S., she said, she would not be permitted to say anything against its principles and objects.

(Hear, hear!) Now I shall never speak under such conditions. I did not break with the great Church of England and ruin my social position in order that I might come to this platform and be told what I should say. (Cheers.) Our late leader would never have done it. (Cheers.) I do not challenge the right of your Society to make any conditions you like. But, my friends and brothers, is it wise?

She assured her audience she was now no nearer the profession of any form of Christian belief than when she had joined the N.S.S.; in fact, she was farther from it. The concept of a personal God outside nature was as impossible as it had ever been. Olcott speculated that, to judge from the applause, if only some friend had taken advantage of this psychological moment to beg her to remain, the motion would have passed with acclaim.

Then, according to the *Star* and the *Pall Mall Gazette,* she launched into her lucky meeting with Mme. Blavatsky and soberly defended her against all charges of charlatanism and chicanery, especially in her maintaining that she was getting letters from the Masters in the "unseen world." Then, pausing portentously but casually, Mrs. Besant remarked that if such a claim made Mme. Blavatsky a fraud, so was she herself. As the implication became clearer, in a mere half-dozen sentences which were to occupy the press, pulpits, and dinner tables for weeks, she added:

You have known me in this hall for sixteen and a half years. (Cheers.) You have never known me to tell a lie to you. ("No, never," and loud cheers.) My worst public enemy has never cast a slur upon my integrity. ("Never," and cheers.) I tell you that since Mdme. Blavatsky left I have had letters in the same handwriting as the letters which she received. (Sensation.) Unless you think dead persons can write, surely that is a remarkable feat. You are surprised; I do not ask you to believe me; but I tell you it is so.

Without a pause she hurried on to her usual peroration, summarizing her reasons for bidding her old friends farewell and begging Freethinkers not to exclude from their minds the possibility of receiving new knowledge. Her last words, delivered with a breaking voice, were heard in a deep but ambiguous silence. Quickly, she walked down the steps. The courtly Olcott offered his arm, but, though she momentarily closed her eyes, she declined it with a slight wave of her hand. Mrs. Smith, Mabel, and Burrows followed her; and as they left the Hall, the crowd burst into tumultuous cheering. It had been a marvelous performance—with melodrama and mystery, it is true, but with perfect sincerity, too. The Colonel drove her home in his carriage.

As Mrs. Besant had hurried from the rostrum, she had scarcely noticed that Parris was coming toward her and that Forder was climbing onto the platform. Later, she was told that they had wanted to correct her picture of Bradlaugh's attitude toward Theosophy and Secularism and of her last months on the *Reformer;* in fact, they and Foote had addressed most of the audience for some time afterward on this theme. Apologetically, she later wrote to the *Reformer* to explain that she had not intended to hurt anyone's feelings or to cause any annoyance by her failing to remain to answer questions, as was the habit at Freethought meetings. The truth was, as she told Mrs. Thornton Smith, that it was as much as she could do to get through her closing sentences without breaking down. Besides, she had no idea that anyone wanted to end her association with the N.S.S. in a wrangle. She thought Parris and Forder had only wanted to speak to her as old friends.

Mrs. Besant's valedictory was a nine days' wonder. Parris, Watts, Foote, and others took to the road against her. But she was still asked by some of the branches, particularly the one in northwest London, to give her popular lectures on "The Place and Work of Mahatmas in Human Evolution" and "Crucified Saviours." Even such a strong instinct for martyrdom as hers was soon to be appeased, but the pain was neutralized by her conviction of the coming salvation.

Newspapers and magazines all over the world immediately exploded into reports, gossip notes, editorials, speculations, jeers, satires, and burlesques. What had Mrs. Besant meant? What had happened to her? Most of the stories scoffed, but two or three writers (in addition, of course, to those in the Theosophical magazines) tried to be open-minded enough to let her prove her case. The *Gazette* headed its lead editorial "A Theosophical Trèves?" in reference to a recent Roman Catholic "miracle" of a holy coat in that city, and asked, "Are we on the eve of a posthumous BLAVATSKY boom?" Recalling the interview which his reporter had had with Mrs. Besant in July, in which she had asserted she was getting letters of advice and instruction from the Mahatmas by ordinary post, the editor speculated on whether she had now experienced some new method of delivery or whether she was enjoying tête-à-têtes with Koot Hoomi in the Himalayas. As yet, however, he refused to swallow the bait as his colleagues on the *Daily Chronicle,* the *Clerkenwell News,* and other papers had done by raising the question, "Can it be that there are things in heaven and earth which philosophy and science have not yet dreamed of, and which the Psychical Research people have failed to probe to the bottom?" Though willing to answer an unqualified yes to the *Chronicle's* question, he was not yet willing to admit that the mantle of Mme. Blavatsky the thaumaturgist as well as that of Mme. Blavatsky the prophetess, the philosopher, and the neo-theosophist had fallen upon the shoulders of Mrs. Besant. He ended mournfully: "It will be a strange culmination indeed to the career of a keen and devoted intelligence if it is found supplying the Theosophists with their Holy Coat of Trèves."

The *Chronicle* was the leader of the "Give her a chance" school, though lamenting that Mrs. Besant had not found a "much older" book than *The Secret Doctrine* on which to found her new faith.

She is a singularly able woman, and therefore not likely to be herself the victim of imposition. . . . In the proportion in which people respect the talents and character of Mrs. Besant they will suspend their judgment until further evidence is forthcoming.

The enterprising editor immediately sent out a reporter to obtain that evidence. He hurried to the "Theosophical colony" with a long set of questions and printed Mrs. Besant's answers in a full column of small type. Then the editor wrote another full-column editorial, attacking her because she had refused to give any real proof of the sort she herself had always demanded for Christian miracles when she was an atheist. All she would do was plead for faith in herself and repeat that she had known Mme. Blavatsky, while her critics had not. The editor, though admitting he could easily understand her revolt, as a "noble, restless, and conscientious" modern woman, from the aridity of skepticism, concluded by wondering how her pursuit of "the retired gentlemen of Thibet, living on a kind of unearned increment of ideas" on the astral plane, could help the "woes of the young girls in the East-end" who had found in her a second mother.

The *Gazette*, not to be outdone, sent its own reporter for its own interview and gloated when Mrs. Besant informed him that the *Gazette* had been right and the *Chronicle* wrong about the method of delivery of the controversial letters. They had not arrived through "postal communication with the other world," but had been "precipitated." In other words they had been delivered by genuine occult means. She had found them in all sorts of unexpected places: they had dropped from the ceiling, they had appeared suddenly when no other human being—at least, no other normal human being, since the Masters were not spirits, but supernormal humans—was around. She herself, she averred quietly, was the pupil of one of these Mahatmas; and she had made her statement at the meeting deliberately, because she knew there were some people present who would accept her word on the subject, whereas they would reject Mme. Blavatsky's.

The battle of the correspondence columns then opened up, and literally hundreds of letters swamped the mails. Not all of them, of course, could be printed, but scores of them were. Almost none challenged Annie's sincerity, but most of them, except those from Theosophists like Burrows and Mrs. Cooper-Oakley, questioned her reason and good sense. Mrs. Besant, herself, in fact, contributed one of the first to the *Chronicle*, maintaining that she was right in refusing to submit her letters to a committee of handwriting experts or even to expose them to the gaze of any outsider, since Theosophy was after all not founded to start a new school of occultism, but to inaugurate a movement of international brotherhood. Mrs. Cooper-Oakley, however, did not quite share the parsimonious attitude of her friend, for she wrote letters to both papers to swear that she had seen and examined the letters herself. She told the *Chronicle* that they were written in red or blue crayon on a peculiar kind of rice paper and inclosed in an unusual type of envelope, all corresponding exactly with the communications which H.P.B. herself had been accustomed to receive from Master K.H.

Here the *St. Stephen's Review*, a weekly miscellany featuring gossip notes on the affairs of the day, as well as stories and plays, went somewhat astray, from the Theosophical point of view, since it reported that Mrs. Besant had stated that she was "now in the habit of receiving autograph letters from Madame Blavatsky, who, tho' dead, is still apparently hard at work letter-writing." The Theosophists, of course, had always indignantly denied that Madame had ever been in the habit of disguising her hand and writing letters to herself. The *Review*, not satisfied with Mme. Isabelle's information that the paper was "leaf-like" and that the Mahatmas "occasionally, but not always, avail themselves of Her Majesty's mails," wanted to know more about the language they wrote in, the quality of the paper they used, and such matters. A little later it offered its readers advice on "How To Become a Mahatma," by "Mahatma 342J," with reference to the correspondence now bulging the pages of the *Chronicle*. The *Review* also devoted its weekly cartoon in full color to the same topic and was very unkind to Mrs. Besant by referring sarcastically to various episodes in her past of which the conservative editor could hardly approve. It later waxed similarly sarcastic about the conception of "evidence" demonstrated by such Theosophists as Burrows and Mrs. Cooper-Oakley.

In the meantime the *Gazette*, in a lead editorial, "A Word for Religious Impostors," had implied a parallel between Mrs. Besant and two other current "seers," the English Laurence Oliphant and the American Thomas Lake Harris, both of whom it had been exposing and whom the *Contemporary Review* had been vindicating. However, still convinced of the sincerity of Mrs. Besant, it concluded that all such seers had probably added something to human aspiration. The *Chronicle* was still devoting columns and columns to letters on both sides about the Mahatmas, including one from Foote, whose opinions there and in the *Freethinker* about "the lady who carries charms and exhibits them to audiences, the lady who receives messages by electricity without the aid of wires, and letters from Thibet by 'supernormal' agency" were minor masterpieces of sarcasm. It was, indeed, as most of the papers except the *Chronicle* were pointing out, the height of the "silly season," in which some editors were desperate for news. The *Chronicle* did not mind, for it was setting new records in its circulation. Foote, however, proclaimed Mrs. Besant either "the victim of a hallucination or of a practical joker, or else . . . the statement of her receiving the letters that used to come from the Mahatmas to Mdme. Blavatsky is a deliberate bid for Theosophical leadership." Wheeler joined in and in "The Humbug" predicted that in the coming struggle for power, Judge would take America; Olcott, Japan and Ceylon; Mrs. Besant, India or Tibet; Burrows, England; and the Countess of Caithness, France. (The Countess of Caithness, or the Duchesse de Pomar, will re-appear later.) The reason the *Chronicle* was giving so much space to Mrs. Besant, proclaimed the *Freethinker*, was that she had "a friend in the office, a Pantheistic gentleman, cut out by nature for a curate, who has strayed into politics." The name of this gentleman the paper did not divulge, but he had an excellent nose for sensational news.

Everybody was enviously twitting the *Chronicle*. It printed a letter from an Indian calling himself Sat Bhai, who revived the old charge that Mme. Blavatsky was simply a Russian spy and added that Mrs. Besant was a "dupe of Russian and Indian intrigue." It published a long inter-view with Olcott in, as the *Gazette* put it, "the Colonel's very best man-ner," telling of his own interviews with the Mahatmas (perhaps six—his memory was not clear); their fine appearance (of course they were all men); his letters from them; the miracles of H.P.B.; and so on. It com-mented editorially on Mrs. Cooper-Oakley's assurance that two of the Mahatmas were residing on an oasis in the Gobi Desert and gave her sug-gestions about the difficulty of getting there and the names of some ex-pert Englishmen who were competent to take the trip. And it ran more letters from people ranging from Frank Podmore of the S.P.R. to "Num-ber Five, Fellow of Calcutta University." Mrs. Besant herself could not resist replying to Podmore and assuring everybody that her letters, "all brief ones, deal with private matters," but that all came from the same hand as wrote the communications printed in *The Occult World, The Se-cret Doctrine,* and other places. On one day alone, September 9, the *Chronicle* printed full or partial letters from forty people.

Even the *Westminster Gazette* was attacked by the infection, and ev-ery evening it embarrassed Esther Bright by its devastating and unpleas-ant assaults. For that was the paper which her family, and especially the skeptical Jacob Bright, always carefully read. The *St. James's Gazette* suggested that the publication of only one or two letters in facsimile would bring thousands of converts. Even Stead, in a long biographical article in the *Review of Reviews*, in which he listed Mrs. Besant, Mrs. Evangeline Booth of the Salvation Army, and Mrs. Josephine Butler, the feminist leader, as the three most remarkable and "apostolic" women of the time, confessed that he could not quite understand the "spiritual nutriment" which his friend derived from "the somewhat misty, mystical system which is the natural child of the marriage of Christianity and Buddhism." At last Gladstone himself was sucked into the maelstrom when the founder of a workingmen's club made a query about his attitude toward the subject of Theosophy and Mrs. Besant. Gladstone informed the *Chronicle* and the Press Association benignly that he could not absolutely deny the possibility of such things as Spiritism, Spiritualism, and Theosophy but that he could see no reason why such matters should be discussed in workingmen's clubs anyhow; besides, Christians would always apply the principles of Christian belief to these questions.

While all this battle was fiercely waging in the press, spread by some of her own epistolary contributions, Mrs. Besant was also taking her case to the public on the lecture platform, where the reporters, Theosophical and non-Theosophical, all followed her. The fourth night after her farewell speech, she, Mead, and Burrows devoted the whole lodge meeting to the recent publicity and new public interest, stressing the difference between "Theosophy and Occultism" and reiterating that occultism was not really important; universal brotherhood was the significant doctrine. The *Star,* commenting on the fashionableness of the audience, wondered who would design a new style of dress to fit the new fad. Soon a modish hatter was to announce a new Mahatma hat for only three shillings, eleven pence.

Attendance at lodge meetings was tremendous wherever Mrs. Besant went, in London or outside; but there was no doubt that people, even good Theosophists, went to hear her talk about her letters and the Mahatmas rather than about universal brotherhood. She also had a fat lecture schedule outside the T.S. At the United Democratic Club she gave a simple elucidation of the tenets of Theosophy, defended the letters, and assured her audience of her continued interest in the poor. She was still attending meetings of the School Board (where Diggle was also holding on). Though the crowd overflowed into Chancery Lane and even broke windows to get in, it learned nothing more about the nature of the letters. She next talked at Kentish Town in spite of a bad cold, caught from lecturing under an open window at the Democratic Club; and into her originally Freethought talk about "Crucified Saviours," she introduced a new passage on Mahatmas, their existence and localization. She also told the audience how a Mahatma had visited London in 1851 as a member of the Indian embassy and had revealed himself to Mme. Blavatsky in Hyde Park.

At a lecture at the Athenaeum Hall, in which she touched, as often, on the opposition between Theosophy and Spiritualism, she was challenged by Allan Montgomery, editor of the struggling new magazine, the *Key.* A

Monthly Journal Devoted to the Science of Spiritualism, Mesmerism, Clairvoyance, Occultism, and All Other Branches of Spiritualistic Science. Montgomery was simmering because, when he and a colleague had been invited to Mrs. Besant's home to give a demonstration of their powers and had succeeded far better than the Theosophists, Mead had asked them to resign from the T.S., which they had actually never joined. Consequently, when, at the meeting, Montgomery asked Mrs. Besant some pointed questions about mediumship and Spiritualism, she only flared up indignantly against him. He was even more pained when she had a collection taken up after it had been announced that the lecture was to be free.

Perhaps her most impressive performance was at St. George's Hall, Langham Place, where, in spite of the audience's "unusually earnest and intelligent" character, the previous mob scenes were repeated and she was warmly cheered; but she still refused to show the letters, though the *Star* informed her again that her listeners were not so much interested in her expounding the similarities and differences between Christianity and Theosophy as they were, frankly, in "spooks." She went from the London Fine Arts Club to Brixton, where, according to the *Commonweal,* she told the gaping crowd that it was actually the Masters and the Rishis who had "been at the bottom of all the great revolutions that have happened in the world's history"; from Croydon to Glasgow (three times); and even back to the Antient Concert Rooms in Dublin. They were all "monster meetings."

Finally, in October, the *Times* itself was for the first time forced to yield to the furor and sent a man to report her talk in St. James's Hall, which seated close to three thousand persons and therefore showed a nice profit. Burrows was in the chair, as he had been for all her recent talks; she wore Mme. Blavatsky's ring, "or one of similar form"; she spoke of the principles of Theosophy and of the Mahatmas; and at the end there were questions from both sides. One of the speakers "seemed to be well known as No. 5 and a Christian student of Theosophy" and was "applauded heartily." "No. 5" soon turned out to be the Rev. J. J. B. Coles, a brash young minister who had perceived his opportunity to cash in on all the publicity, since he had studied at Calcutta. Soon afterward he challenged Mrs. Besant to debate with him on "Theosophical Symbols" at St. George's Hall, with Professor Rhys David in the chair. Mrs. Besant was willing, but found Coles a foe unworthy of her mettle. Even the Christian press, including the *Times,* which had accused Theosophy of "absolute sterility," admitted that it had trouble in following the young man's arguments and diagrams; and when he tried to enliven his stumbling remarks with a bamboo pole and pictures thrown on a rumpled sheet from a magic lantern he got so badly confused that the audience laughed in his face. It was here that Maud Sharpe first heard Mrs. Besant and was converted at once into one of the few supporters who stuck with her to death.[1]

But it was all good "copy." Everything Mrs. Besant did, lamented Foote, was "copy." The *Christian Commonwealth* felt equally sad about the situation. *Black and White* wrote her up as its "Woman of the Hour." The Theosophical publications, somewhat shamefacedly, exulted over the number of press cuttings that were coming in—over a thousand a month, and at first a hundred a day, gloated *Lucifer,* the *Path,* and the *Theosophist.* Mrs. Alice Cleather's Press Bureau had a terrific time keeping track of it all, especially since headquarters was also being deluged with a hundred letters a day. Private members did not escape the flood either; one reported receiving two hundred letters in a week. Even with the restriction of visitors, meetings at Blavatsky Lodge had to be held twice weekly to meet the demand. Naturally, in October, Annie was re-elected president of the lodge, and Burrows' meritorious services were recognized with a vice-presidency. A third edition of *The Secret Doctrine* was called for. The controversy was referred to in sermons at the Roman Catholic Church of the Sacred Heart, Camberwell, and at the Anglican Church of St. Bride's, Fleet Street. The Prebendary of St. Paul's announced a whole series of lectures in "rebuke and correction of Theosophytes." Voysey the theist also denounced Theosophy before a large congregation and expressed his sympathy for Mrs. Besant in being hypnotized by "magnetic power." Annie's visit to Canon Wilberforce started a rumor that she had gone back to the church, but she quickly killed it by saying that she had been to see him on purely personal business. Mabel Collins' new serialized novel, *Morial the Mahatma,* was bringing increased circulation to *Short Cuts.*

Even a hoax which set all London laughing could not hinder the incredibly rapid development of what a pseudonymous writer named Sylvester Tomkyns, Jr., called the new "Besantine Empire." Immediately after Annie's farewell address at the Hall of Science, Colonel Arthur Desmond wrote to the *Star* to recall his letter of over two years earlier on his own advanced Theosophical powers. In view of her new claims, Desmond maintained that he had passed far beyond her in achieving knowledge of the mastery of mind over matter, having studied in both India and China and passed all the karmatic divisions and sevenfold stages, but that he was no longer bound by secrecy as she was. Therefore, he declared, he was ready to take his place on any public platform "and demonstrate the possession of powers beyond the grasp of materialistic capability." He would also like to give a series of lectures in London about Theosophy, but would especially like to debate with the president of the N.S.S. or any other leading materialist. Foote promptly accepted the challenge, if the Theosophists would put Desmond forward

[1] *Theosophy,* October, 1922.

as a "representative champion." While the public was waiting to hear from the Theosophical Society, Stuart Cumberland, editor and F.R.G.S., wrote to the *Chronicle* to offer to give one thousand pounds to any charity named if a genuine "manifestation" could be produced before a committee of scientific experts. The next day Desmond accepted the challenge, but Burrows also wrote to make it clear that "the object of Theosophy is not to decide wagers of £1000 by performing so-called 'miracles,' but to teach people generally to be better men and women."

Three days later Burrows soberly reported that investigation of the T.S. records had failed to discover any real "Colonel Desmond" entered there, and Mrs. Besant wrote to the *Gazette* to charge that Cumberland had made his wager in this knowledge. Consequently, Desmond, described by the editor of the *Chronicle* as "evidently a humorist," replied briefly, saying that he had had a "precipitated communication" forbidding him to demonstrate, though he could easily move pianos through faith in the Mahatmas. Cumberland then repeated his challenge to any Theosophist, since he had been disappointed by Desmond. There were, however, no takers; but there was a response from the famous music-hall "magician," J. N. Maskelyne, who had been saying all along in the *Gazette* that he could duplicate any of Mme. Blavatsky's feats, and many more, without claiming any superhuman means. Now, in order to ridicule the precipitation of letters, which he said was done by confederates through cracks in the floor and similar devices, he put on an "extraordinary" performance at the Egyptian Hall, in which, among other things, he made a young man vanish while tied by ropes, the ends of which were held by members of the audience. Olcott went to one of Maskelyne's later performances, after the "magician" had "told all" in a book entitled *The Supernatural?* and came away greatly puzzled. As he admitted in his autobiography, Maskelyne had done everything he had seen H.P.B. do, and more; and yet he was sure her "phenomena" were genuine, whereas Maskelyne's must be false.

Through Sylvester Tomkyns, Jr., even Walter Besant found his way back temporarily into his sister-in-law's saga. Walter, too, had become temporarily interested in ghosts and in his weekly letter to one of the papers had told a rather dull story, illustrated, of a ghostly experience he had had in a Northumberland inn with three phantom ladies in Queen Anne costume.[2] Tomkyns, to take canny advantage of both the Walter Besant reputation and the Annie Besant mystery, as well as an "Up to Date Ghost Story" which had recently been printed in the Liverpool *Post*, decided to bring them all together, along with his own burlesque introduction and commentary, in a small catchpenny pamphlet entitled *The Ghost-Mystery at Knotty Ash, Liverpool! or The Mysterious Midnight Funeral!* In this satirical performance Tomkyns interviewed, "after the

[2] *Pall Mall Gazette*, August 10, 1891; also note July 22 and October 12.

373

most approved fashion" of the Besant interview, "Solitarius, the Ghost-Seer and Theosophist," shown in a sepia sketch as a low-browed, large-nosed, big-mouthed, long-necked, Adam's-appled, pince-nezed, sloping-headed gentleman, who had suddenly turned from a profound skeptic into an "earnest seeker after Occult Truth," by means of a mysterious midnight vision.

After a learned introduction referring to Occult Phenomena, Esoteric Buddhism, Böhme, Swedenborg, the Neo-Platonists, Schelling, the Mahatmas, and Brotherhood; to mysteries which "defy not alone the Post Office Authorities, but also the handicraft secrets of the Crockery-Ware Mender"; and to the great contribution of the T.S. to society through its information on the occult nature of cigarette papers and the practice of "Aerial Precipitation," Tomkyns finally came to his somewhat Tam O'Shanterish ghost story from the *Post* and to Walter Besant's tale. The point of the burlesque, however, was found in the mock interview, where Solitarius and Tomkyns conversed impressively about Mme. Blavatsky, a "modern Hypatia," about German metaphysical writers, pundits, astral forms, the S.P.R., the T.S., Spiritualism, Vaughan, Plotinus, Porphyry, the Bhagavadgita, Yoga, Wave-Thoughts, and Materialization. In the course of the interview Tomkyns learned that Solitarius had already made the acquaintance of one Master, "Tooti Fruhti Fal Lal Lah" (according to one account Koot Hoomi's surname was Lal Singh), who had precipitated a poem to him on cigarette paper from Mount Everest, but whose real name was Jones, since Mahatmas are of all nationalities. All these revelations proved too much for the common-sensical Tomkyns, who parted from the seer at the Rocket Hotel, from which Solitarius planned soon to leave for India, via Jericho, "going direct to the Himalayas to commune with TOOTI FRUHTI, prior to his commencing a course of Initiatory Occult Induction, in the neighborhood of Thibet." His entire expenses, he boasted, were to be defrayed by two of the most eminent Theosophists of the day, Colonel Occult and Mr. A. P. Linnet.

On October 1, just a month after it had begun its circulation booster, the *Chronicle* decided it was time to call a halt and at the end of a column of letters wrote: "This correspondence must now cease." Then, to justify his conduct, the editor undertook a defense. If Theosophy and Mrs. Besant, he said, were not better understood now than a month ago, it was not the fault of the paper. "Our interests have been purely those of truth." He assailed her acceptance, in *Black and White*, of Mme. Blavatsky's demonstrations with gold rings, teacups, and showers of roses, all on second- or third-hand testimony, and asked what value such things were in comparison with her tangible social work. After all, the only Theosophical doctrine that had made any public impression was simply a revival of the Pythagorean notion of the transmigration of souls, orientalized as "reincarnation," which is a "poor excuse for immortality."

What good did it do for Mrs. Besant to tell the agnostic and worried Marquis of Queensberry, as she had recently done, that all his sorrows in this life were simply the result of karma? (Little did she then know of the problem which karma would soon create when the scandal of his son, Lord Alfred Douglas', relations with Oscar Wilde were to come out!) So, concluded the *Chronicle*, we cannot accept Theosophy as enriching the world, and we must regard Annie Besant and Herbert Burrows as merely deluded. Perhaps someday they will be driven from Mme. Blavatsky to the truly great mystics like Plato, Swedenborg, Blake, and Emerson.

Yet the *Theosophist* was to sum it all up, somewhat smugly, in December, by concluding that in spite of its lurid sensationalism the journalistic publicity had on the whole been good for the Theosophical Society because it had called it as never before to public attention. Judge's *Path* agreed. Judge had returned to America sometime before, where he had continued to build up the idea that he had broached in his article "Are We Deserted?" in the August issue, holding up the importance of contact with the Masters and hinting that he was receiving messages from them himself. Some time was to elapse, however, before it became clear to all but his devoted followers that the whole puzzle was simply an illustration of the ancient warning, "Judge not that ye be not Judged."

But the *Chronicle*'s temporary retirement from competition could not stop the avalanche, either in the press or on the platform. In fact, the great meeting in St. James's Hall, which Burrows pronounced to be a "milestone in the history of Theosophy," followed this event by a few days. At this meeting the reporter of the *Pall Mall Gazette*, commenting again on Mrs. Besant's "platform figure," noted also a strange fact: "Until quite recently her hair was dark, and now it has turned almost white within a few months' time."

8

No Passage to India

Sylvester Tomkyns, Jr.'s, gibes about trips to India and Tibet were no fabrications of his imagination. Even before Mrs. Besant's recessional, Olcott had caused to be inserted into his *Theosophist* a note to the effect that both his physical health and his mental fatigue had been cured by his holiday and that after the convention he hoped to be able to induce Mrs. Besant, the greatest speaker of her sex in either Europe or America, to display her splendid talents in a short cold-weather tour of India. It was confidently hoped that the generous Hindus there would provide the money for her expenses, as they had done for Bradlaugh's; in fact, a circular letter had already been sent out by a prominent committee, setting up a "Besant Travelling Fund." A little later he wrote from Paris in jubilation over his success in persuasion, although actually the thing had been prearranged for some time; but he admitted that, even though she would lecture free, according to the Indian custom, some £250 must be raised for her trip. She would be accompanied by Miss Henrietta Müller, a recent recruit to Theosophy from the women's suffrage movement. Olcott would have liked Mrs. Besant to do some propagandizing work for his Buddhist schools at Galle in Ceylon, since his adjutant there, Dr. J. Bowles Daly, had reported a considerable falling-off of interest in both the schools and in Theosophy; but her trip was to be too short, having been scheduled from November 7 to some time in January.[1]

Both the Indian and the Western papers soon picked up the news of her plan. The Bombay *Gazette*, though somewhat dubious about Theosophy, asked for an unprejudiced hearing of her case; the *India Times*

[1] Daly, *Report of the Convention for the Organization of Buddhist Schools* (Galle, Ceylon, 1891); *Vahan*, September, 1891; *Pall Mall Gazette*, October 24, 1891.

advised her to stay home if Theosophical propagandizing were her purpose; and the *Indian Spectator* suggested that her posing as a real teacher of Theosophy was premature and that she, and also Olcott and H.P.B., should have studied first under Indian instructors. The *Cosmopolitan* of Calcutta wondered at her daring in coming to India, the land of occultism, to teach occultism. The *Indian Mirror*, however, as reported by the *Pall Mall Gazette*, announced that the walls of incredulity were ready to fall before the blast of Mrs. Besant's trumpet.

The English papers were even less kind and in September picked up the rumor that she would also go to Darjeeling, where she would be met by one of the Masters from just over the Tibetan border. The *St. Stephen's Review* reported that she had already engaged the services of a Moonshee to teach her Hindustani and Sanskrit and suggested that the less Moonshee the better for her peace of mind; it also sent a reporter for an interview, who reported seriously enough on their exchange of questions and answers until he related how, on leaving, he must have had a visitation of karma when he stepped out into the garden in the pelting rain and found that his umbrella had seven slits in its octagonal form. This was the time when it was the rage in smart society to greet one's friends with the question, "How's your karma today?" The same *Review* also quoted the passage in the explorer Rockhill's book, *The Land of the Lamas*, in which he asked several Tibetan lamas whether they had ever heard of Theosophy or Mahatmas, only to have them laugh and imply that the "Neo-Buddhism of Theosophy was some kind of fraud."

Annie's ticket was bought, even though all the necessary rupees had not yet been raised, and it was arranged that Mrs. Thornton Smith was to take over much of her lecture and editorial work while she was gone. Then the announcement was abruptly made that she would not go after all. Her physician, Dr. Mennell, had declared that her health was too much impaired to stand the rigors of a passage to India, even in the cold weather (the temperature in southern India never goes below 65 degrees!). Instead, he recommended a brief holiday, which she decided she would spend by going back to America for ten or twelve days and giving only four lectures—two in New York and one apiece in Philadelphia and Fort Wayne, Indiana. It was reported that there was also an important difference of opinion among American Theosophists which she wanted to discuss with her old friend, William Judge. Olcott regretfully announced that the money raised for her trip would be refunded or held in the hope of a later visit.[2]

Annie was probably really overdoing things. On November 13 Esther Bright wrote in her diary: "A.B. lecturing every night up and down the

[2] *Theosophist* (Supplements), November, December, 1891; *Star*, October 26, November 16–17, 1891; *Chronicle*, November 18, 1891; *Vahan*, December, 1891; *Freethinker*, November 22, 1891.

country; she does look fagged out." She then told of going to a "tremendous meeting of the unemployed" in Trafalgar Square, which had
just been reopened to public meetings after four years, and of her talks
with Mrs. Besant, who told her about her personal interviews with the
Mahatmas and proved "the bread of life" to the girl.[3]

But few swallowed the story that bad health and overwork were really
the reason for Mrs. Besant's going to America rather than to India. Once
more the speculators took the field. The Adyar correspondent of the *Path*
wrote of the daily bulletins which had been appearing in the Indian
papers about her arrival and of how some now said that the cancellation
would be good for the political interests of the country, whereas others
thought that the Indian leaders had decided that she would become
disgusted at the apathy and degradation of the Hindus and leave the
whole concern. But the *Hindu* wrote that the Indian vernacular newspapers were referring to her as "Sannyasini Srimati Beshante," that is,
"the holy female ascetic Besant." The *Chronicle* reporter in England at
first implied that her visit to Canon Wilberforce had something to do
with it, but the next day withdrew his suggestion. More sensational
was a story in the *Pall Mall Gazette,* quoting the *Civil and Military
Gazette* of Bombay, that the irrepressible Mme. Coulomb was threatening to revive her old charges and prove to any committee of unprejudiced
judges that Mme. Blavatsky was the author of "the most extraordinary
delusion ever known in the world." Later, Olcott corroborated the rumor
on the authority of a woman-doctor in Bombay who told him that she
had "come to know that Madame Coulomb and the missionaries had
arranged a scheme by which Mrs. Besant was to be dragged into court
on a pretext, so as to reopen the old scandal about H.P.B." The *Freethinker* offered an alternative between fears that "the new High Priestess
of Theosophy" would hear too much about Madame in India and that
her stumping trip would be a "frost." These printed explanations, it transpired later, were all wide of the mark. The inside story was much more
sensational.

Mrs. Besant made her usual hit with the American public, especially
at Fort Wayne, "near Chicago"—which she did not reach.[4] Here the interest was so great that a thousand copies of Sinnett's *Esoteric Buddhism*
were sold, and the two T.S. branches merged into one and called themselves the Annie Besant T.S. When Mrs. Besant stepped off the "City of
Paris" at Liverpool on her return on December 16, she was met by a
single reporter, from the *Daily Post,* instead of the hordes she had been

[3] *Memories,* November 6, 13, 24, 1891.

[4] For this American trip, see Liverpool *Daily Post,* quoted by *Pall Mall Gazette,*
December 17, 1891; *Daily Chronicle,* December 18, 1891; *Path,* December, 1891;
Theosophist, January, and Supplement, February, 1892; *Lucifer,* January, 1892;
Vahan, January, 1892; Whyte, *The Life of W. T. Stead,* II, 62–64.

used to in America; but she chatted pleasantly with him and told him all about her trip and her views on the country. She had an agreeable impression of American audiences, since they liked lectures up to an hour and a half in length (but her Chickering Hall lecture, according to the New York *Herald*, was two hours long) and were willing to pay as much as a dollar for them (in England seats had been selling for one, two, or three shillings). Theosophy, she found, was most freely accepted on the West Coast, where people were more liberal and receptive to new ideas. (Dr. Archibald Keightley had been lecturing in the West, had recently married an American wife, and had decided to stay in America.) She herself had had her least success in Philadelphia, with its old-fashioned Quakers and Presbyterians. Being a vegetarian, she admitted with a smile, she had had some trouble with American meals.

But, the reporter discovered, the thing that had impressed Mrs. Besant most was that on the return voyage she had given an evening lecture on Theosophy, that "Almost the whole of the saloon passengers were there," and that no one less than Lord Aberdeen had taken the chair—he and his wife being on their way back to England from Canada. Lady Aberdeen, who apparently bore Annie no ill will for having been defeated by her in the *Woman* poll, wrote her friend Stead soon after Christmas that now that she and her husband had actually met and heard Stead's heroine, they could understand why he had wanted to put her name in the forefront of the authors he wished to contribute to his new *Review of Reviews*. "I think," wrote Lady Aberdeen of the lecture, "that all present felt that they had but rarely heard so powerful a sermon, uttered too with so unmistakable and intense a conviction of the message to be delivered to be divine." In fact, Lady Aberdeen herself was now ready to accept its inspiration as being from God.[5]

Apparently again in good health, Annie worked her way back to London, lecturing as she went. She was also concerned with a new project for social work, called the League of Theosophical Workers, which had got under way just before she departed and which was intended to be a reply to the critics who had accused her of abandoning her humanitarianism, although the T.S. handout which was printed by several London papers attributed it to the wish of Mme. Blavatsky. The announcement admitted that in the past the T.S. had been widely criticized for recruiting its followers mostly from the wealthy and educated

---

[5] Commenting on this episode, Whyte, Stead's biographer, remarked that "Stead had Mrs. Besant on the brain most of the time" and told how, at the height of the popularity of the *Review of Reviews*, Stead had thought of founding a religious *Review of Reviews*, to be entitled *Gesta Christi*, but Mrs. Besant had not liked the title. Stead had her listed to do the labor department but apparently had not been able to get the co-operation of the Pope, which he thought was also indispensable. Stead's collection of *Real Ghost Stories*, however, was enjoying a considerable success, and Mrs. Besant soon drew much of the material of her popular lecture on "Ghosts" from it.

classes but that this reproach would soon be removed by the new Workers' League.[6] The League was announced as the outgrowth of the working girls' club at Bow and was to be supported by donations from well-to-do Theosophical ladies and by small fees for such services as the crèche on St. John's Wood Terrace, where children of working mothers were cared for at threepence a day. Through the crèche it was hoped that mothers could be taught "hygiene and morality, cooking and cleanliness." A Free Labor Bureau and Registry was also opened at the Bow club, and "Friendly relations have been established with the Church and Salvation Armies." The value of a weekly sewing class was not overlooked. Ambitiously, the plan also looked forward to starting a club for workingmen somewhere in St. Pancras, which would be "of a recreative and instructive character," especially for the study of Theosophy through a debating class.

It was a kindly and altruistic idea, but most of the T.S. members were more interested in occultism. Shortly after her return, Mrs. Besant had to issue an appeal for old clothing, materials, and money for her Working Women's Club. There were not enough gifts like Esther Bright's five shillings which she donated every week during the winter when her mother raised her annual allowance from sixty to one hundred pounds. Still, there was enough money at times to take the girls on a holiday; it poured rain on two hundred of them when they went to the country in October. About a year later, in August, 1892, the Club celebrated its second anniversary, at which, following the clatter of teacups, milk jugs, and jam jars, and a program of glees, solos, and a dramatic sketch, Mrs. Besant made a speech in memory of H.P.B., whose death-day was being remembered and memorialized on every May 8 as "White Lotus Day."

It was in these clubrooms that Lansbury and his Social Democratic friends found a hospitable haven under Mrs. Besant and Mrs. Lloyd for their discussions of self-government for India and such matters. There is no doubt that Mrs. Besant was still sincerely interested in the bettering of the conditions of the poor. In September, 1892, she focused attention again on the problem when she addressed an immense meeting in one of the South London music halls on "Theosophy and Labour." However, unlike a few years earlier, there was always a Theosophical slant to her approach. The correspondent for Judge's *Path* perhaps had this in mind when he wrote that after the lecture and an hour's questioning, "The applause seemed to show a good deal of sympathy, though it is always hard to say if applause means assent or only some momentary pleasure in listening to a fluent speaker."

6 *Pall Mall Gazette,* November 3, 1891; *Chronicle,* November 3, December 30, 1891; *Lucifer,* October, 1891; *Vahan,* June, 1892; *Path,* October, November, 1892; Bright, *Memories,* pp. 25, 27; Lansbury in *The Annie Besant Centenary Book,* pp. 29–30.

MANIFESTO

OF THE

FABIAN PARLIAMENTARY LEAGUE.

THE FABIAN PARLIAMENTARY LEAGUE is composed of Socialists who believe that Socialism may be most quickly and most surely realised by utilising the political power already possessed by the people. The progress of the Socialist party in the German Reichstag, in the Legislatures of the United States, and in the Paris Municipal Council, not only proves the possibility of a Socialist party in Parliament, but renders it imperative on English Socialists to set energetically about the duty of giving effect in public affairs to the growing influence of Socialist opinion in this country.

The League will endeavor to organise Socialist opinion, and to bring it to bear upon Parliament, municipalities, and other representative bodies; it will, by lectures and publications, seek to deal with the political questions of the day, analysing the ultimate tendencies of measures as well as their immediate effects, and working for or against proposed measures of social reform according as they tend towards, or away from, the Socialist ideal.

The League will take active part in all general and local elections. Until a fitting opportunity arises for putting forward Socialist candidates to form the nucleus of a Socialist party in Parliament, it will confine itself to supporting those candidates who will go furthest in the direction of Socialism. It will not ally itself absolutely with any political party; it will jealously avoid being made use of for party purposes; and it will be guided in its action by the character, record, and pledges of the candidates before the constituencies. In Municipal, School Board, Vestry, and other local elections, the League will, as it

Manifesto of Fabian Parliamentary League

→ Fabian Society. ←

MEETING AT ANDERTON'S HOTEL, FLEET STREET,

On Friday, 17th September, 1886, at 8 p.m.

MRS. ANNIE BESANT

WILL DELIVER A LECTURE ON

"SOCIALISM AND POLITICAL ACTION."

AND WILL PROPOSE THE FOLLOWING RESOLUTION:

"That it is advisable that Socialists should organise themselves as a political party, for the purpose of transferring into the hands of the whole working community full control over the soil and the means of production, as well as over the production and distribution of wealth."

ALL SOCIALISTS ARE INVITED TO BE PRESENT.

Card to one of Annie Besant's Fabian Lectures

Fabian Society.

A CENTURY OF SOCIAL MOVEMENTS.

COURSE OF LECTURES

TO BE GIVEN AT

WILLIS' ROOMS, KING STREET, S.W.,

ON FRIDAY EVENINGS AT EIGHT O'CLOCK.

1889			
Oct. 4.	I.	EARLY RADICALISM	WILLIAM CLARKE.
„ 18.	II.	EARLY SOCIALISM	FRANK PODMORE.
Nov. 1.	III.	THE CHARTIST AGITATION ...	GRAHAM WALLAS.
„ 15.	IV.	THE PROTEST OF LITERATURE AND SENTIMENT— HUBERT BLAND.
Dec. 6.	V.	THE TRADES UNION MOVEMENT.	ANNIE BESANT.
„ 20.	VI.	THE NEW POLITICS	G. BERNARD SHAW.

ADMISSION FREE.

Card to 1889 Fabian Lectures

Cover design of *Fabian Essays*

Meetings.

Sept. 16th (Ordinary)	...	**Willis' Rooms,** King Street, St. James' Sq., S.W. HUBERT BLAND, "The Need for a New Departure."	
Oct. 7th (Public)	...	**Eleusis Club,** 180, King's Road, Chelsea, S.W. ANNIE BESANT, "Why we work for Socialism."	
Oct. 21st (Ordinary)	...	**Willis' Rooms,** WILLIAM SAUNDERS, "Ground Rents."	
Nov. 4th (Public)	...	**Hampstead,** Vestry Hall, Haverstock Hill. GEORGE BERNARD SHAW, "Some Illusions of Individualism."	
Nov. 25th (Ordinary)	...	**Willis' Rooms,** H. H. CHAMPION, "How to make Converts."	
Dec. 2nd (Public)	...	**Hatcham Liberal Club,** Portland House, New Cross Road, S.E. SIDNEY WEBB, "Socialism and Coöperation."	
Dec. 16th (Ordinary)	...	**Willis' Rooms,** CHARLES BRADLAUGH, M.P. "The Limits of Legislative Duty."	

Fabian meetings in 1887

THE FABIAN SOCIETY.

SESSION, 1886–1887.

Executive.

ANNIE BESANT.   G. BERNARD SHAW.
HUBERT BLAND.   SIDNEY WEBB.
EDWARD R. PEASE.   CHARLOTTE M. WILSON.
FRANK PODMORE.

Hon. Treasurer.

HUBERT BLAND, Bowater Crescent, Woolwich.

Hon. Secretaries.

(General), EDW. R. PEASE, 17, Osnaburgh Street, N.W.

(Assistant), ALICE M. HOATSON, 1, Pelham Road,
Wood Green, N.

(For Lectures), SYDNEY OLIVIER, 150, Portsdown Road,
N.W.

The Meetings are held on the 1st and 3rd Friday in the Month.

Fabian leaflet for 1886–87, with officers

Annie Besant, Herbert Burrows, and the strike committee of the match-girls

Members of the Matchmakers' Union

Helena Petrovna Blavatsky

ANNIE BESANT IN 1889

I am immersed in Mrs Blavatsky! If I perish in the attempt to review her, you must write on my tomb, "She has gone to investigate the Secret Doctrine at first hand."

Annie Besant and her note to Stead on *The Secret Doctrine*

H.P.B. and Colonel Henry Steele Olcott

London headquarters workers in the Theosophical Society in 1892. *Standing:* Claude F. Wright, Bertram Keightley, Walter Old, E. T. Sturdy, John Pryse, Sydney Edge, Dr. Archibald Keightley, G. R. S. Mead. *Seated:* Herbert Burrows, Laura Cooper, Mrs. Besant, Countess Wachtmeister, Mrs. Cooper-Oakley, Emily Kislingbury, James Pryse. *Standing at back:* Colonel Olcott

Annie Besant in the *Sun* supplement

William Q. Judge

Rev. Charles W. Leadbeater

"How To Become a Mahatma,"
from the *St. Stephen's Review* in 1891

The attacks from the churches, of course, had continued. In March the Bishop of London forbade "an unusually broad-minded and enterprising Vicar, the Rev. H. L. Cart," to allow Mrs. Besant to lecture to his flock; and a Jesuit, Father Clarke, assailed Theosophy in the *Month*. The latter onslaught was the cause of one of Mrs. Besant's lectures which the *Theosophist* said "marked an era in the T.S.'s life and progress" and in which the papers said she was "never heard to greater advantage." Her talk on "Roman Catholicism and Theosophy," later reworked into her tract, "Theosophy and the Society of Jesus," showed that in her attitude toward the Jesuits at least she was still as anti-Christian as even Mme. Blavatsky could have wanted her to be. The most temperate and polite of all these churchly attacks was from a Congregationalist, the Rev. Walter Wynn of Sandy Lane, Bradford, who in an address in November first apologized to Mrs. Besant (for whom he had "no other than the kindest feelings of respect") for making it, but then, after enumerating twelve points in favor of Theosophy, amassed an even greater number against it and in favor of Christianity.[7]

Naturally, when Mabel Besant decided to get married in May, she did not have the ceremony performed in any church or chapel but in the Marylebone Registry Office—this in spite of the fact that her husband, Ernest Scott, was the son of Clement Scott, the Roman Catholic dean of London dramatic critics. Mabel was now officially a Theosophist and had been speaking at small meetings. There was a little wedding breakfast at headquarters and an at home in the afternoon, but within a week the bride and groom, who was like his father a journalist, left for Australia, where young Scott had accepted a position on a Melbourne newspaper. There five years later, after Scott had become a Senate reporter in the Victoria Parliament, Olcott visited them and found the newly domestic Mabel making clothes for her little daughter Muriel. On the wall of the sitting room hung many photographs of her "idolized mother."[8]

The strange Indo-American goings on of 1891 were further obfuscated so far as the common F.T.S. or the general public was concerned by the even stranger maneuverings of the leading officers and the national conventions during 1892. In the first number of *Lucifer* for the latter year, Mrs. Besant wrote an editorial, beginning:

Mystics and Theosophists think that the world will be living for the next decade over a volcano. For the year 1891 is the eldest son of the last Septenary

[7] *Theosophist*, May, December, 1892; Wynn, *Theosophy: A Criticism* (Bradford and London, 1892).

[8] *Theosophist*, July, 1892; *Path*, May, 1892; Olcott, *Old Diary Leaves*, VI, 217; Arthur Digby Besant, *The Besant Pedigree*, p. 229. Collecting and hanging photographs of Annie Besant was a family trait. Digby did the same thing and even when he was a very old man covered the walls of his whole house at Hampstead Heath with pictures of his mother and all her famous friends. He showed me these photographs on my visit to his home in September, 1954.

in the said cycle. On February 17th next [she cited H.P.B.] will commence the last series of seven years which will close the first cycle of five thousand years of Kali Yuga—the "Black Age" of the Hindu Brahmins.

But in spite of all the tragic evidence, such as the deaths of Bradlaugh, Parnell, and H.P.B. herself, supporting these conclusions, Mrs. Besant exhorted her readers to trust in the Masters, who were guiding the course of the world. Until the year 1898, however, the ordinary mortal could hardly tell what would happen. She renamed her leading editorial section "On the Watch-Tower." Annie Besant was always on the watch. Mead was to help her as associate editor. He was also now editing the *Vahan* (the Sanskrit word for "vehicle" or "messenger"), the new English-speaking organ of the European Section, of which he had become the general secretary. All over the world, in their proliferating magazines, the Theosophists were on the watch.

Colonel Olcott had jockeyed himself into a bad spot in relation to his proposed retirement. He realized that his position was weak, except in impoverished India. In the *Theosophist* for March he began the serial publication of his autobiography, entitled *Old Diary Leaves*. But its subtitle, *The True History of the Theosophical Society*, gave a better conception of its real intention, which was to justify his policies in the conduct of the Society, especially in regard to the intrigues of Mme. Blavatsky and W. Q. Judge. Here Olcott confessed that in January he had gone through another emotional crisis, ending in his again tendering his official resignation, in a letter which was very humble about his own deficiencies, but very insistent on his constant attempts to "work his way upward" and help his fellow men. "Exaggerated reports" (of an unspecified nature), he wrote, had been circulated about him; the Judge influence was paramount in London; a scheme had been launched to send C. F. Wright to Australia to undermine him there; in fact, "Every other possible thing was done to reduce my position to that of a sort of cipher or figurehead." So, he met the situation halfway by reiterating his resignation, on the score of renewed bad health and a strong desire to write. There were certain obstacles, such as the legal procedure of transferring his authority as president-founder to the vice-president and the complications in the will of a dead Australian benefactor named Hartmann; but they did not seem insuperable. Judge wrote him officially in January and February that he was sorry to learn his decision, but that, in his capacity as vice-president, he would notify the Sections about it and the choice of a successor.

Olcott in his magazine had nothing but praise for both the main candidates. In Europe, he said, Mrs. Besant, by her integrity, blameless life, unselfish enthusiasm, and exceptional abilities, had come to the forefront of the movement almost at a single rush; in America, "under Mr. Judge's firm and able management, the Society has spread over the length and breadth of the land." The Indian Section, under the probable leadership of Bertram Keightley as general secretary, would be in safe hands. All this sounded very magnanimous and sincere.[9]

The Colonel's mind, however, was not yet at rest. For a long time he had been receiving no help from his guru who, H.P.B. had implied, was displeased with him. Now, in his crisis, his guru came back to his aid. Early in February he received a clairaudient message (which left no traces as precipitated letters and those he had been getting through the mail from the United States would do). The Mahatma was disappointed in him. For the good of the Society he must hold on till death. There would soon be more orders "by messenger" from an indisputable source. Olcott immediately concluded that this was a hint that Damodar could be expected back from his mission in Tibet; not long afterward Henrietta Müller actually proceeded to the border to welcome him. He did not arrive. The Colonel, however, his will to fight revived by this supernormal assurance, promptly wrote Judge from Adyar by "overland mail" to tell him he had changed his mind because of this message. Two weeks later he wrote again to Judge and the General Council to say that he could not agree to Judge's being both acting president of the T.S. and general secretary of the American Section, since this would give him control of the votes in the Council. Olcott should have spent a little more money and cabled. He continued to get letters from New York on his retirement and on his previous thoughtless nomination of Judge as his successor for president-for-life. Finally, about a month after Judge should have had his letter, he got a cable from Judge telling him to remain in office, since the other had important news from the White Lodge itself, and that he would therefore announce a great change in policy on April 24—the date of the American convention in Chicago.

When the convention met, however, Judge said nothing about Olcott's change of mind and allowed himself to be chosen as the next international president by the American Section, with Bertram Keightley as vice-president. Someone else presented a resolution, which was passed, asking Olcott to reconsider; but Judge did not inform the convention that the other had already done so. In fact, though Judge had notified Olcott in a letter written just before the convention that his Mahatma had instructed him to sway the European convention to request him to remain, Judge still said nothing when in August he went to England for the convention himself. There, with great enthusiasm, he was elected to the chair on Mrs. Besant's nomination and then, on the basis of the mail vote already taken, was again unanimously elected as Olcott's successor. Burrows proposed a vote of confidence, and Mrs. Besant seconded it.

[9] Alvin B. Kuhn, *Theosophy* (New York, 1930), p. 309; *Theosophist, Lucifer, Path,* and *Vahan, passim,* through 1892; Olcott, *Old Diary Leaves,* IV, 323–35, 423, 427–36.

Judge allowed the convention to take note of the resolution of the American Section asking Olcott to reconsider; but he himself made no recommendation, and no action was taken. Mrs. Besant was extremely quiet during the convention, but she made the closing speech. She had written in *Lucifer* in May that it would be well to delay Olcott's retirement as long as possible, but that "It is clear that Brother Judge will be the next President, whether now or at some future date, but whether he will take office at once or not will remain doubtful for some months." In June she had added that no more loyal, strong, and true hands than his could be found in which to confide the destinies of the T.S.

The issue of the *Path* containing Olcott's letter concerning the postponement of his retirement did not reach England till after the convention. In the meantime, the Indian Section had voted not to have the office of president filled during Olcott's lifetime, but to empower the vice-president to act in that capacity.

Apparently on the best of terms, the president-elect and Mrs. Besant, the joint Outer Heads of the Eastern School (or Esoteric Section), again went out on the lecture circuit—sometimes separately but usually together. The "Society of Brotherhood" must show its unity to the world. Not only did they cover England from London to Birmingham to Liverpool, but they crossed over to Ireland and spoke to the lodges at Dublin, Limerick, and Cork. They apparently did not reach Belfast, where George W. Russell had recently become corresponding secretary. Finally, the back issues of the *Path* and the *Theosophist* reached England, together with an official executive circular from Olcott revoking his resignation, but simultaneously declaring Judge his "constitutional successor, and eligible for duty as such upon his relinquishment of any other office in the Society which he may hold at the time of my death." In the October *Vahan*, Mead published this circular, together with letters on the subject from Olcott to himself and to Judge, and commented succinctly: "Every member of the Society will rejoice in the restoration of the President-Founder to vigorous health, and to learn that we shall not only have his counsel but also his continued active services in the future."

Mrs. Besant from her watchtower declared her happiness in Olcott's restored health and rejoiced that the Society now had a successor so that there would be no further worry over the leadership of the movement. Simultaneously, she told of a recent gathering at South Place to celebrate the birthday and work of "the nearest and dearest to me of all my old-time friends." Brahmin and Parsi, Theosophist, Hebrew, Christian, and atheist had all stood together to recognize the public services of Charles Bradlaugh, and she ended by wondering what would be the next "life-story, when the Ego that dwelt in the personality called Charles Bradlaugh comes back once more to earth."

Judge had already gone back to America. Annie was going back to

America, too. She had promised her new friends that she would make a really extended tour, as far as the West Coast. She knew that the Indians would feel badly used, to be rejected once more in favor of the Americans—and in so short a time. So she wrote them a letter, published in the *Theosophist* for December, repeating her previous reasons: the same doctor who had attended H.P.B. assured her that if she went to India and lectured as proposed, she would not return alive, because of the strain and the climate; she could not afford to go, since only Rs. 2,578 of the necessary Rs. 5,500 were in the Besant Travelling Fund, and this would certainly not cover her expenses, let alone the amount which she could contribute to headquarters if she lectured in Europe or America. After all, India still had Colonel Olcott, as well as its new secretary, Brother Keightley, not to mention Brothers Edge, Sturdy, and Old, all of whom had yielded to the call of the East and were being gladly lent by England.

But she made a promise:

Ere long I hope to stand face to face with you, I to whom India and the Indian peoples seem nearer than the nation to which by birth I belong. . . . When Karma opens the door, I will walk through it.

She was already thinking of India in private as her "Motherland"—a term which she was soon to begin using everywhere in public.

9

Chakravarti and the
Parliament of Religions

Mrs. Besant's American lecture schedule was a heavy one.
Starting in New York late in November, 1892, after a rough Atlantic
crossing, it was to take her all through the Middle West, the Northwest,
the West Coast, and the Plains States, and back to New York and Boston
by the end of February. The Southwest and the South were apparently
not yet considered ripe for Theosophy by her managers. As usual, the
Theosophical magazines in London, Adyar, and New York carried full
accounts of her experiences, embellished with anecdotes and comments,
and eked out by her own articles, "Speeding the Message." The highly
personal approach of American journalism continued to amuse, astound,
and anger the more conservative Britons, who nevertheless had to admit
that their compatriots were learning fast.

Certain episodes in the tour stood out against the routine. In Chicago
she found that the headquarters room was decorated with pictures of
H.P.B., Olcott, herself, and Victor Hugo. Fort Wayne, which had been
counted on for a tremendous turnout because of her highly successful
penetration there a few months earlier, was a disappointment, for the
clergy, having been forewarned, made house-to-house visits to caution
their flocks not to expose themselves again. In fact, Mrs. Besant's two
worst enemies on the trip proved to be clergymen and cold weather.
Because of the latter, she several times lost her beautiful voice and on
Christmas Day was actually snowbound in the Rocky Mountains ninety
miles from Portland. In spite of the snowsheds and snowplows, her long,
comfortable train was able to move only seven miles during the night;
the snow broke through the windows of some of the cars; and food ran

short. In order not to disappoint the children, a Christmas party with a Santa Claus was arranged; and in order not to disappoint the adults, Annie lectured on Theosophy to all that could crowd into her car.

Finally, the train broke into the big forests and fire-blackened clearings of the new state of Washington. There, with fifteen passengers on a boat going to her lecture, she was delayed for an hour or two in the middle of a lake near Tacoma. Next, she went to the Golden Gate and to Los Angeles, with their maelstrom of meetings, their judges, politicians, professors, teachers, doctors, and, "generally, the leaders in all departments of thought." At Oakland, however, something special was in store. There the hall of the Y.M.C.A. had been hired for the lecture. But when its president learned that Annie was not a London singer, as he had thought, and, upon consulting his janitor, heard that she had something to do with Spiritualism, he panicked and canceled the contract. But the Masters were looking out for Theosophy: the newspapers, especially the Oakland *Morning Times*, burst out into scorching editorials with titles like "Is Ignorance Bliss?" and when the Opera House was hired instead, many hundreds turned out who "might otherwise have remained indifferent to the philosophy of Karma and the delightful Nirvana."

Back along the Rio Grande, without stopping for lectures, Annie traveled to talk amid the frigidities of Kansas City, St. Louis, Indianapolis, and Cincinnati, where Dr. Buck quickly cured her of her lingering cold and sore throat. Mrs. Besant's grand tour ended in New York; its "suburb," Harlem; and Boston, "the Hub of the Universe." After being seen off by Judge, who had himself been in bad health, she sailed for Southampton on March 4 on the "City of New York," "the first trip of that vessel under the American flag." It was another rough voyage, but she stood the trip well, though the English reporters detected more white in her hair than when she had left. Only in the "Black Country" around Pittsburgh, of all the dozens of American cities she had visited, commented Mrs. Besant, had she found "the same types of working-class depression so familiar to us in the old countries." There were misery and starvation in the other big cities, it is true, but "not the type of worker who is anxious all his life." Even the natural picturesqueness of much of America was not enough to dazzle the eyes of Annie Besant, the social reformer, but she had been especially observant of the perfections of California; for there, according to the foreseeing eye of H.P.B., a new and improved order of mankind, the "Sixth Sub-Race," would soon put in its appearance.

Mrs. Besant's foreign travels were not over on her return from America, for the Dutch branch in Amsterdam had long been waiting for its chance to get this most effective of Theosophical propaganda weapons. In June, accompanied by Mrs. Thornton Smith, she paid a four-day visit to Holland—speaking in English, but speaking so feelingly that even those who could not understand her words understood her meaning. All the Dutch papers carried appreciative reports. For a short time during the summer Annie even considered emulating Olcott and going to Japan; but more important countries drove the idea out of her mind, and she never recovered it.

She was occupied also in bringing her *Autobiographical Sketches* up to date. The book had long been out of print, and enough vital things had happened since its composition to demand a complete change in viewpoint. T. P. O'Connor, publisher of the *Weekly Sun* as well as the daily *Star*, had persuaded her to make the revision and was serializing it under the title of *Through Storm to Peace: The Story of My Life.* Republished in book form in October by Unwin for sixteen shillings, under the strangely prosaic title *Annie Besant: An Autobiography*, the book got a rather mixed press but a much larger sale than its predecessor, even though it ended abruptly with Annie's own account of her conversion. Gladstone wrote a long and kindly review in the *Nineteenth Century*, disagreeing especially with her views on the Atonement but affirming his faith in her honesty, even though "at the expense of her intellectual pretensions." Young Digby Besant, however, stung by the former Prime Minister's implication that perhaps "his mother was not exempt from the general law of human kind, and consequently had human imperfections," wrote him a polite note of protest and was much flattered to receive a personal and sympathetic reply.[1] Mrs. Besant entitled her final chapter "From Storm to Peace"; stressed her new happiness in her "inner peace" despite the "troubled sea of outer life"; and ended the book, not with the conventional "Finis" but with the tailpiece, "PEACE TO ALL BEINGS."

But there was no peace. Or rather there was peace for only a brief moment. G. J. Holyoake, indeed, while praising Gladstone's review, had suggested that a more fitting title would have been "From Peace to Storm."[2]

During the summer of 1893, Thomas Muse, an otherwise unknown F.T.S. and a Fabian, published his *Popular Introduction to Theosophy*, with the motto of the T.S., "There Is No Religion Higher Than Truth"; A.E. came back to Dublin and lectured on "First Steps in Occultism," and Yeats talked to the lodge on "William Blake on the Symbolism of the Bible"; Shaw produced and published his first play, *Widowers' Houses*, through the Independent Theatre, and sent his former inamorata a copy, signed simply "To Annie Besant" and still preserved at Adyar; Gandhi, setting up his law office in South Africa after becoming convinced that he could not succeed in Bombay, hung a portrait of Mrs.

[1] *Nineteenth Century Magazine*, September, 1894; Besant, *Pedigree*, pp. 271-72.

[2] Joseph McCabe, *Life and Letters of George Jacob Holyoake*, II, 172.

Besant on the wall; and Stead began to publish his new psychic and occult—but not Christian—magazine, *Borderland*, with Mrs. Besant's article, "Theosophy and Its Students," in the first issue. She also wrote some amusing notes for *Lucifer* on a "Theosophical van" which had been touring the "hop-covered Kentish land," pulled by a horse so "inadequate to his duties" that he died after two months and cost the T.S. twenty pounds. News reached England of the embezzlements of the late Pandit Gopalacharlu, the treasurer of the Society in Madras, who had committed suicide, and it became necessary to take up a collection to remedy the shortage; Judge, Mead, and Mrs. Besant were of course put on the committee, and she sent Olcott a fifty-pound gift she had just received.

Judge had come back to London at the end of June, looking "none too well" but bringing with him an original "precipitation" by H.P.B. made on a piece of white satin in Philadelphia in 1874. He was just in time for a big debate in St. James's Hall on the subject of Buddhism vs. Theosophy between Mrs. Besant and a Mrs. Frederika MacDonald. Over three thousand persons attended, but the newspapers rather sarcastically declared a draw between Mrs. MacDonald's logic and Mrs. Besant's eloquence. In fact, the *Pall Mall Gazette*, quoted by the *Theosophist*, finished its account with: "and the women said it had all been 'so lovely' and that they had 'enjoyed themselves so much.' The men with the 'nice' faces doubtless said the same." But the receipts, which were split between the new H.P.B. Home for Little Children and Days in the Country for Poor Girls, were at least something tangible.

Although it had been expected that Judge's voice would be in no condition to be heard in public, he recovered sufficiently to preside at the European convention in London in July, where it was announced that Mrs. Besant had delivered 223 lectures during the past year. It was a "harmonious and interesting" convention, so far as all could see, and Judge and Mrs. Besant attended a meeting of the Society for Psychical Research to hear the famous banker and classicist Walter Leaf read a paper on the Russian occultist Solovioff's recent attacks on H.P.B.

But Judge had come back to London for other reasons. One of these was the great proposed World's Parliament of Religions to be held in conjunction with the coming World's Columbian Exposition in Chicago.[3] When the Theosophists had heard it mentioned the year before, they knew they must be represented. Through the help of Judge, an American committee under George E. Wright drew up an application, explaining the claims of Theosophy to representation at such a convention (forgetting, as so often happened, that Theosophists always insisted officially that Theosophy is not a religion). Their application was finally accepted,

---

[3] For this episode, as well as for some of the foregoing material, see *Theosophist, Path, Lucifer, Vahan, passim,* May–December, 1893, but especially *Lucifer* for October.

but was first sent up to the Psychic Committee, of which their former friend, Professor Coues, was the chairman. When this error was rectified, the application was transferred to the Committee on Moral and Social Reform, of which Coues' sister, Mrs. Flower, turned out to be the chairman.

At this critical juncture, Mrs. Besant fortunately arrived in New York for her long lecture tour, and she and Judge called on Mrs. Flower and C. C. Bonney, president of the World's Congress Auxiliary, to prove that the assignment of Theosophy to the Committee on Moral and Social Reform was scarcely appropriate. In this endeavor they were successful, but still no new classification to fit them had been found. They were then referred to the Rev. Augusta Chapin, chairman of the Woman's Branch of the Religions' Committee, and all parted friends; but the matter dragged on until just before the American T.S. convention in New York in April. Wright was then elated to hear from Bonney that, rather than group the T.S. with the Ethical Society or the American Philosophical Society, it had been decided to grant it a convention all its own. No one had expected such largesse and such recognition, but from then on everything worked "as if by magic"—the white magic of the White Brotherhood, of course. By this time Mrs. Besant was back in England, soon to be joined by Judge.

When Colonel Olcott in far-off Adyar—his two lame feet were bothering him, his general health was insecure, and his emotional condition was unsettled—heard the gratifying news, he immediately issued an official ukase, appointing Judge as his direct substitute and representative, Mrs. Besant as "a special Delegate from the President" and the chief speaker in behalf of the Society, and a brilliant, thirty-year-old Brahmin mystic, Professor Gyanendra Chakravarti, to represent the Indian Section. Another Indian Theosophist, Hevavitarana Dharmapala, decided to go along on his own, to represent Buddhism along with Chakravarti's Hinduism. Judge, indeed, had recently issued a letter "To the Brahmins in India," calling their attention to his own sound belief in the Vedas, but warning that if the rumor was true that the T.S. in India was losing its impartial character and becoming distinctly an instrument of Buddhistic propaganda, the Brahmins would certainly not sustain it.

Chakravarti and Dharmapala reached London in August, took up their residence in Avenue Road, and were at once invited to address the Blavatsky Lodge, where they caused a sensation by their suaveness, poise, and eloquent English. Chakravarti, a light-complexioned, rather fat-faced, sleepy Brahmin, originally from the sacred city of Benares, with a small, drooping, pointed black mustache, a "black, observing eye," a shiny black turban and a flat white necktie, had taught physical science and mathematics at various Indian colleges and now held the chair of mathematics at Allahabad University. He had also just passed the bar examination there and had a great reputation as a mystic, a student of the great Indian religious literature, and a skilful hypnotist. He spoke a soft, classical English, with a slight accent but with much expressiveness. He had gentle, dignified manners, and yet withal looked rather contemptuously at those about him. Annie Besant was at once fascinated by both his manner and his words. She knew immediately that she would gladly become a chela to this new guru, even if she was old enough to be his mother.

Dharmapala was quite different—tall, dark, very spare, and ready in English. In spite of his friendliness, Mrs. Besant was not so much drawn to him, though when she heard he had traveled second-class all the way from India at his own expense, she at once ordered him to join her and Henrietta Müller and go first-class the rest of the way. Money was already being raised by individual subscription on both sides of the Atlantic to pay their way; in the meantime, Bertram Keightley was advancing much of the money as a loan.

Burrows, treasurer of the European Section, would also go along, but primarily to attend and address a labor convention being held in Chicago at the same time. He had just corrected a statement in the *Path* to the effect that Mrs. Besant was his "friend and teacher"—"friend" he was happy to admit; "teacher," no, since he had been a materialist long before he had ever heard of her, a Socialist long before she was, and a member of the T.S. before she had joined. Burrows, it seems, was tired of being eclipsed by his old comrade. He had also had a little squabble with Mead in the *Vahan* over what he called the grave danger of the tendency to take H.P.B. as a divinely inspired prophetess and her works as an orthodox bible. Mead was having trouble in keeping his question-and-answer section filled; and he, Judge, and Mrs. Besant were providing far too many of both the questions and the answers.

Just before she left on August 26 for her fourth trip to the United States in a little over two years, Mrs. Besant paid a goodbye visit to her working girls at Bow. The Club had been running into monetary difficulties. She had recently had to make up a deficiency of £120 out of her own pocket; and Esther Bright, who had been admitted to the Eastern School even if she could not subscribe to all its beliefs, told of an oriental bazaar recently organized to raise money. About one hundred girls turned out for the farewell party, and Mrs. Besant showed her democracy and good sportsmanship by cutting the cake, giving another talk about H.P.B., and reciting "Molly" by G. R. Sims and "Arthur's Farewell to Guinevere" from *The Idylls of the King*. The girls liked Tennyson better than Sims, but perhaps more of them would have come if they were not always being reminded of H.P.B. Olcott, who prided himself on being a bit of a *bon vivant*, thought that the absence of male members kept many girls away. A few months later, at any rate, Mrs. Besant regretfully announced the cessation of the East End Club; there were not enough members and money to keep it going. In fact, she at last candidly admitted, her match-girls had made only a very limited use of it, and it had been kept going by the girls in other trades, notably in the mackintosh industry, which was now badly depressed. Besides, the health of Mrs. Lloyd, the matron, broke under the strain, and she was being sent to Ceylon. The some sort of trouble hit the H.P.B. Home for Little Children. After a time, too, nothing further was heard of the Theosophical League of Workers, though an attempt was made to start it in other cities.

The sessions of the Parliament of Religions in Chicago were not held on the grounds of the Columbian Exposition on the Midway (the fair was having its own troubles because of the financial panic which had suddenly hit the country), but in a large gray-stone building, christened the Art Palace and intended for permanent use as an art gallery. The building had an unfortunate location: although it was situated in a small park on the shore of Lake Michigan, it was also only a few feet from the snorting, bell-ringing engines and rumbling freight trains of the Illinois Central Railroad. But it had two large lecture halls, patriotically named Columbus and Washington, to be used for the general assemblies of the Parliament, as well as several smaller chambers for the individual "congresses."

The Chicago newspapers, especially the *Tribune*, gave the Parliament a big play, with large headlines, special reporters, and side gossip. Mrs. Besant had not arrived when the first session opened, though several days earlier Burrows had sat on the platform at the opening meeting of the Labor Congress, devoted to a discussion of labor and religion. In spite of her absence, her name was listed among those attending a large reception given for foreign delegates by the Rev. Dr. John Henry Barrow, chairman of the Executive Committee; contrariwise, after her arrival she was not named among those who were entertained by Northwestern University at an evening party at Mrs. Potter Palmer's famous residence. Mrs. Besant's delay, on account of certain business which detained her in New York, prevented her from participating in any of the early publicity, but Chakravarti more than compensated for her absence. Not only did he sit on the platform at the opening morning session, conspicuous in his picturesque costume, but he was among those selected to give short preliminary addresses to the packed crowd in the afternoon. His remarks and personality provoked an ovation, and he was accorded special mention, with a drawing, in the *Tribune*.

Mrs. Besant's arrival was properly heralded in the papers as the due of such a famous speaker. People jammed into the T.S. headquarters in the Athenaeum Building on Van Buren Street to meet her. The sessions of the Theosophical congress, addressed by herself, Chakravarti, Dharmapala, Judge, Miss Müller, Dr. Buck, and others, including Mrs. Cooper-Oakley, who had come back from an Australian trip for the purpose, burst out of their quarters; and the brotherly Lutherans exchanged their hall, seating fifteen hundred, for that assigned to the Theosophists, seating five hundred. The American public was seemingly athirst for the message of Theosophy, and Mrs. Besant expressed herself as highly gratified, but not surprised.

There were two climaxes yet to come. The first, but smaller, one happened on Saturday evening, when a vast audience of three thousand persons flooded into one of the two large halls to hear "the exposition of Theosophy by its accredited representatives," as Mrs. Besant put it in her own notes to *Lucifer.* So overwhelming was the response to her presentation that the managers of the Parliament themselves suggested holding an extra session on Sunday, to which they assigned the great Hall of Washington, where an extra wooden gallery had been erected so that it could accommodate thirty-five hundred auditors. Even this was not enough, and hundreds more stood in the aisles and along the walls. There was no suppressing the exultation in the stories which the various Theosophical correspondents sent back to their journals, for in the midst of a preliminary speech by Judge, the Rev. Dr. Barrow, a Presbyterian and the most important leader in the convention, came into the hall and asked for permission to make an announcement. There had been a mistake, he said. The Presbyterians had originally been assigned to the Hall of Washington, but were now convened in Hall VII next door. Since there were only a hundred persons present, he was sure the rest must have come to the Hall of Washington in error. He asked, therefore, that they all follow him to Hall VII. But no one moved; in fact, twenty-five more outsiders squeezed in. As Dr. Barrow retreated in embarrassment, "a smile passed over the broad sea of upturned faces," and the audience started to clap. Judge, sympathizing with the Presbyterians' discomfiture, quickly resumed his speech, and the meeting went on to the end, with another ovation for Mrs. Besant. Scores crowded up to the platform to shake hands with the speakers, and one woman walked around behind them for a time because she "wanted to feel their vibrations."

The next morning Annie Besant found herself splashed in big headlines across the front page of the *Tribune,* introducing a lengthy article which began:

Occultism and esoteric subjects held full sway last evening at the Hall of Washington. The hall was crowded with an audience eager and anxious to listen to the words that fell from the lips of the most prominent theosophist of the day . . . , Mrs. Annie Besant, on whom the mantle of Madame Blavatsky has fallen.

Though the reporter mentioned her emphasis on "the service of man," it was man's sevenfold nature, corresponding to the mystical seven aspects of the universe, that made the biggest impression and received the most attention. The response of the great audience, he wrote, was remarkable.

The Theosophical papers neglected to tell their readers that the next week the Christian Scientists managed to pack even more people into their meetings, particularly the one addressed by Judge J. S. Hanna of Boston. But the Rev. Joseph Cook, also of Boston, described by the *Tribune* as two hundred pounds of aggressive dogmatism, "who has come to be looked upon as, in a certain sense, the representative of orthodox Protestant Christianity of the stricter type," expressed some worry about the record attendance at these two upstart congresses and the apparently anti-Christian trend of the whole proceedings. Digging up the skeletons from Annie's past, he assured the world that he did not regard the size and enthusiasm of these meetings as "any very serious evidence of the abandonment of sound views on the part of the people at large. The thoroughly educated portion of the public seems to me to have little or no faith in theosophy." All of which may have somewhat consoled Dr. Barrow.

The name of Herbert Burrows appeared nowhere in connection with the Parliament of Religions, but Chicago citizens had occasion to know it nevertheless. Right underneath a long story about Mrs. Besant and Chakravarti on September 14 the *Tribune* ran a short note: "Herbert Burrows, the English Radical, who stirred so deeply the Labor Congress meetings by his eloquent words, is to speak on 'The Woman of the Future—Her Place in the Home and Nation'" under the auspices of the Woman's Club at the Art Palace. Three days later, readers were informed that Burrows had refused to meet a scheduled speaking engagement before several hundred Socialists because he had learned that local politics were to be introduced, whereupon a vote of censure had been passed and ordered sent to the "Social Democratic Federation of Labor in England." A week later he had apparently been forgiven, for he was reported as having given the first lecture in the new chapel of the Armour Institute, attacking prevalent wage systems, unemployment, etc. By this time he was identified as "a prominent social reform leader in the House of Commons"!

So far as the records go, Herbert Burrows and Annie Besant never met in Chicago. Mrs. Besant, after addressing many lodges in the United States and one in Toronto, sailed for England on September 20. She was accompanied by Professor Chakravarti, who in an interview had said that the most lasting impression the Parliament would leave behind was that "there is something to be learned of religion outside of the circle of the church, and that the Hindoos and the Buddhists are not quite the heathens that they have been represented by the American missionaries sent to India and Ceylon." As soon as the Theosophical party returned to England, the Blavatsky Lodge had the advantage of hearing both an

English and an Indian report on the Parliament. Mrs. Besant also put hers into print for the *Chronicle*.

Stories of Chakravarti's new ascendancy over her soon began to float to the surface. She had adopted him, and he had adopted her, for their mutual psychic development, said those on the inside. Some said that he had actually slept outside her hotel-room door in order to guard her from the intrusion of both human and occult adverse visitants. Others said this would have been too undignified for one whom she had taken for her new guru, but that Chakravarti had delegated others to perform this job. There was general agreement, however, that Annie Besant had joyfully come under a new influence, Brahmin rather than Buddhistic in nature, and that this would vitally affect her coming life.[4]

In the spring of the year Mrs. Besant had informed Olcott that in the fall, if her previous terms were met, she would pay her first visit to India, her true motherland. All the necessary money had not been raised, but enough had been sent her to meet her immediate traveling expenses. Chakravarti took ship in the middle of October. Mrs. Besant, detained by Theosophical business, left London on October 20 and dashed across France to catch the mail steamer "Kaiser-i-Hind" at Marseilles; the Countess Wachtmeister had used her title and influence to delay the vessel till her friend could get there. Again, the passengers, knowing that such a celebrity was aboard, demanded lectures—three of them this time: one in the Mediterranean, one in the Red Sea, and the last in the Indian Ocean, just before the boat reached Ceylon. This time they were not all on Theosophy; one was on "India, Her Past and Her Future."

At Colombo, the impatient Olcott had been waiting for her since October 30. Her lecture tour, from Colombo to Bombay, would take her through most of Ceylon and India, where she expected to learn a great deal about mysticism from the ancient sources. There were also certain highly disturbing problems in the Theosophical Society itself that she hoped to clear up, centering about William Q. Judge and his methods of achieving his ambition to become international president of the T.S. Having renounced politics on her conversion to Theosophy, she had no idea that she was eventually to have a political career that was for a time to make her one of the most notable and remarkable figures in the dramatic movement for Indian home-rule.

The primarily English phase of the strange lives of Annie Besant was over. The primarily Indian phase was about to begin.

[4] Kuhn, *Theosophy*, pp. 312–13; *The Theosophical Movement* (New York, 1925), p. 453. The latter book was actually written by a committee of the United Lodge of Theosophists, which by 1925 had broken completely away from the Theosophical Society.

Appendix

Appendix

Through a lucky chance and with the generous co-operation of H. G. Williams-Ashman of Chicago, I have unexpectedly been given access to a hitherto unsuspected collection of ten letters of Annie Besant to Mr. Williams-Ashman's grandfather, J. Williams Ashman, written between February 14 and August 3, 1889, a very critical period in her career. The letters run in length from a mere card to several pages, and are partly on personal and partly on London School Board stationery. They indicate a warm and suddenly developing friendship with a man whose name has never previously turned up in Mrs. Besant's saga. The association was initiated by him in February, though the occasion is not clear. Since, however, according to Mr. Williams-Ashman, his grandfather, though first having been trained as an engineer and then having become a clergyman in the Church of England, was interested in the occult and was acquainted with Mme. Blavatsky and her circle without ever leaving the church or embracing Theosophy, the contact may either have been suggested by someone in the group or come about through something he may have read in the papers. Or perhaps, as a reference in the second letter hints, Ashman was a follower of the American seer and mystic, Thomas Lake Harris, whom the *Pall Mall Gazette* was engaged in "exposing" and the *Contemporary Review* in defending (see p. 368).

The following excerpts from the most important passages in the letters reveal the warm, easy friendliness of Mrs. Besant's approach to people (even curiously rather humble at times, in view of her own prominence and his relative inconspicuousness), her rigorous work habits, and her willingness to learn from others. Allusions in the letters indicate that the Rev. Mr. Ashman (whose town address was the National Club, Whitehall Gardens) offered to give Mrs. Besant a course in psychic training, probably centering in telepathy, and that she undertook it, with more or less satisfactory results. The letters also reveal some of her early puzzlement with problems raised by H. P. B. and the Mahatmas, her continuing troubles with her matchgirls and with the School Board, her trip to the Socialist convention in Paris, and similar matters.

Feb. 14, 1889

DEAR SIR,

Thanks for your note. I am at 63 Fleet St every morning from 11 to 1, except on Tuesdays: and am generally there on Monday & Tuesday afternoons.

But could you come here to supper one evening? I am free Saturday, Tuesday, & Friday next (Feb. 16, 19 & 22).

I have *studied* nothing in "occult" science, only read anything that came in my way—two books of Sinnett's, some stray pamphlets. I have not been able to get anything. But I am quite ready to study carefully any works throwing light on the matter.

Thank you very much for giving me the possible chance of knowing more.

Sincerely

ANNIE BESANT

Feb. 17, 1889

DEAR MR. ASHMAN,

Your book arrived safely, & I will read it.

Mrs. [Thornton] Smith was with me last night, & I read out the sentence from your letter that you had an impulse to come here; & we agreed that if you had followed your intuitions we should have been very pleased to see you.

No, I have not heard of T. L. Harris. How should he know anything about me if he lives quite out of the world? But I am afraid I shall never know anything really about the "occult," as it seems that students have to go out of the world, & I have my work that I can't leave. While so many are suffering and in need of help, it does not seem to me right to please oneself by following knowledge only for personal gratification. Does what you know throw any light on what is called spiritualism? The results I get in that line puzzle me because I can't link them together by any rational explanation. . . .

March 13, 1889

. . . You do not quite approve of my East End work. Dear friend, how can I make you understand. I know the atmosphere is bad for me, but we have made it bad by leaving the poor alone & living better because they live worse. I hope you will not think I do not mean it, if I say to you that not in words, but in sober truth, I love the poor—these rough coarse people, who have paid their lives for our culture and refinement, & I feel that the devotion to them of the abilities cultivated at their cost is the mere bare debt that I owe, for my class, to them. I *love* & *reverence* YOUR *Christ* because he loved and served "the common people." I have no tie of love or friendship that I would not break to help them, & I will not even taste of your tree of knowledge if, to taste it, I must leave their service. To me, this is the supreme object in life. I would leave it for the moment if some years out of the world would make me stronger to serve them, but not merely to gain knowledge. . . .

March 22, 1889

. . . I am very much puzzled about Mme. B. I quite see that your view would explain her physical condition, which is the exact opposite of what is supposed to be the result of the occult training. Her life, instead of being prolonged & maintained at a high point of efficiency, is obviously wasting away. How is this consistent with the training she is supposed to have undergone? It seems to me that—for the moment accepting the Mahatma hypothesis—they have been working through her, not training her to work for herself, & so have exausted her vitality instead of strengthening & developing it. Another difficulty: the teaching of the Mahatmas, as viâ Sinnett, or as put on some points by Mme. B. the other night, is not fairly describable by your adjectives (I don't say that you applied them to that teaching); it is somewhat ascetic, in fact sometimes very ascetic, & it inculcates love of Humanity & service of others. Now what is Mme. B's *real* position. Does she hold the lofty principles, say, of Koot Hoomi? Holding them theoretically, & trained in them, has she practically repudiated them? If the latter, why should the Mahatmas employ an unworthy tool. And does it not seem rather cruel if they have used her, worn her out, & thrown her away? They remain strong and vigorous. If they trained her, why does she not share their higher vitality, instead of being exhausted? I am puzzled altogether. I can see that the "black" [Black Brotherhood?] might well wear out its practiser; but how did she, after & amid such tremendous advantages, *get on* such lines? The result is obvious, but the How? . . .

I was thinking very intently of you at our morning tryst yesterday; but I did not withdraw confidence; I was only puzzling my head about various questions, & so probably let my thought get cut up, losing its intensity &, presumably, its carrying power.

Now as to your question of the nearly 200 days. Will I do it? Yes, my *friend*, if you tell me that it will be useful, & if on talking it over we find it is possible to fit it into my other duties. I will take any amount of personal pains, or face any personal inconvenience, in following your directions. I do not yet feel that I should be justified in throwing up my present duties. I should like a quiet talk with you, & I will shew you exactly what are my fixed times & seasons. Then you will see if I am a possible person for your training. . . .

I am glad you used my first name in sending me your thought message. I don't like the formal address from people who care for me, & you must evidently come under that heading after giving me your valued pen! As to your prophecy about the thankless office to be hereafter performed by the seas [probably a reference to a proposed trip abroad by Mrs. Besant], I should be inclined to grumble, save for not wishing to contravene the instructions of a certain friend of mine, who bade me not to take up tomorrow's burden.

When do you next preach in London, & where? . . .

March 25. '89

You would look at me with very grave eyes if you were here, dear friend, for it is half an hour after midnight, & I must be up by five fortyfive. . . .

On Wednesday I find I can be free at 3.30 instead of 4.30, so if you are at liberty & want your pupil you can have her.

That queer pressure on the forehead as though some firm soft body were pressed against it was very noticeable to-day & it is so curiously "objective." What causes it?

Do you remember my saying to you that it was no effort to give up wine? Oddly enough the other evening at Mr. Bradlaugh's, I felt a perfectly over-powering desire to take some! . . . I felt much amused at the sudden wish.

I would like to have been at Sevenoaks, & to have gone for a ramble through that lovely country; but you would not have been left in peace to sit & meditate; you would have been dragged out. Let me remark in passing, that my eyes are not brown, unless you prefix greenish. I have a theory that eyes with green lights in them generally go with strong magnetism; they are so much more variable than the one-colored eyes. Mine have been described by the newspaper reporters as of all colors, often as black! . . .

You will be amused to hear that some journal is complaining (I was told of it, but have not seen it) that "Mrs. Besant sems to twist the London School Board round her little finger." I assured my informant that it was very good for the Board. Would that I may twist my tiresome matchgirls round my fingers to-morrow morning. Some 400 or 500 of them are out, & I must do all I can to get them back to work, heedless, headlong creatures. . . .

March 26.

[This postscript tells of her getting up at sunrise, walking across Primrose Hill in the dawn, reaching the factory at Bow, reconciling the manager and the "half-sullen half-yielding" girls, and then going on to spend two and three-quarters hours at a second factory to accomplish a similar but much harder task, because these girls had a real grievance. She then describes her troubles in trying fruit-lessly to get some wire brushes and rubber combs which Ashman had apparently required of her. Ending with an apology for writing such a long letter of "mere chat about nothing," she invites him to attend her "lecture at a club of very poor & very rough East Enders," and signs herself "Always affectionately your friend, Annie."]

March 28. 1889

. . . Yes, I had your kind little note from Eastwood, & was much struck with what you wrote, as I knew you could have no means of knowing that I was troubled. You certainly hit just on the truth, & the "strong but hurried appeal" was really made. It was quite a good test-case, for the news reached me just at noon.

. . . Does our Saturday tryst for tea hold good—raisins, brown bread, & milk? . . . You come here, do you not.

Goodnight, dear friend. I shall be very glad to see you. I am faithfully carrying out your instructions, & the cold water in the morning is odious. Nothing but a feeling that I must do what I am told would induce me to put my fingers into it! . . .

April 18. 89

[This is merely a card addressed to *Mrs.* Ashman, thanking her for an invita-tion to come at six on Monday. It is decorated with a presumably occult emblem of a cherub's face in the moon, surrounded with a constellation of stars.]

July 4, 1889

. . . I had seen the paper [probably the note in the *Sun* that she had not only joined the Theosophical Society but also been admitted into the Esoteric Section].

How are you? I am too much worried to be brilliantly well. Friday week I am off to Paris, to the Socialist Congress, & shall not be back till the 21st or 22nd. . . . It seems long since I have had any news of you. I think I am harder worked than ever! & there *is* such a row in addition [probably a reference to Bradlaugh's falling out with her in the pages of the *National Reformer* on the subject of Theosophy].

July 11. 89

. . . Do you see the *Freethinker?* There is a lot about me in it this week. I shall begin to wish myself in Thibet if this goes on! . . .

Aug. 3, 89

. . . Tomorrow I am going to lecture at the Hall of Science explaining why I became a Theosophist. There has been a perfect rain of paragraphs and articles on the subject, & I am doing a pamphlet as a general "apology" in the old sense of the word. . . .

The School Board had risen this week, so that is one burden laid aside for awhile, & I am going to busy myself with some articles to see if I can earn some money. What a nuisance it is that one must have money in order to live! If one could only subsist on air & camp out under an umbrella many problems might be more easily solved. . . . Or if one could find a cellar full of gold with a Kobold in it, as in the good old days! I don't *want* to *keep any of it,* but to *use* SUFFI-CIENT to *free myself* from *all my present business ties* & start clear, with only my very easily contented self to provide for. I wouldn't take a penny more than would do this, but these convenient Kobolds do not turn up now-a-days.

Let me know when you will be again visible to mortal eyes. Meanwhile,

always your faithful friend

ANNIE BESANT

Index

The following index is a combination of index and bibliography. It lists people, titles, and a few general topics, but no places. Each title, on its first occurrence, is fully described in a footnote, but thereafter abbreviated. References to listings in footnotes are set in italics.

415

PRINTED IN U.S.A.